Advance Praise for *Last Resort*

As a student of the assassination in Dallas for over thre[e] ... book is the first I've read that courageously addresses areas long neglected or avoided altogether, and above all to ask, finally, why didn't the US (re)invade Cuba before year end if it had been the most serious foreign policy conundrum right on our doorstep since Castro's revolution? It's a brilliant read, rising to the high standard set by his previous work.

– Leslie Sharp, Co-Author of *Coup in Dallas: The Decisive Investigation into Who Killed JFK*

In this new book by Walter Herbst, he asks a very interesting question and follows through with an answer. The depth of his research lends much credibility to this work. He names the names and the groups that were responsible for the assassination of President John F. Kennedy and spells out the reasons why. With over 1,650 footnotes and sound logic, Herbst unravels the decades long question – who was responsible for the death of our president.

–Jeffrey L. Meek, Renowned researcher and author of five JFK assassination publications, including his latest book of interviews, *The JFK Files: Pieces of the Assassination Puzzle, Volume II.*

Please don't overlook this book. It's crammed full of important and revealing information about the international connections to the events which led up to the political and financial conspiracy to assassinate U. S. President John F. Kennedy. Herbst has done a masterful job. It's lengthy and very detailed – but definitely worth your time to read.

–J. Gary Shaw, senior author with Brian K. Edwards of *Admitted Assassin*

Last Resort Beyond Last Resort dives deep into the question of why a second planned invasion of Cuba did not happen. The answer lies in West Berlin. Walter Herbst has brilliantly brought together all the players, allies, and enemies of President John F. Kennedy's assassination in one book. Men like Otto Skorzeny, Allen Dulles, Jean Rene Souetre, and James Angleton, to name a few. West Berlin was the key to JFK's foreign policy, along with Cuba, Indonesia, the Middle East, and Congo. Last Resort Beyond Last Resort dives deep into the reasons behind JFK's death. The information contained in this book will shock, stun, amaze, and anger the reader. Walter Herbst has meticulously pieced together all the players, all the policy's, all the reasons, all the circumstances that lead to JFK's assassination. This book is necessary for any researcher, either experienced or new to the case.

– Chris Gallop, JFK-The Continuing Inquiry, Researcher

Within the realm of Cold War rhetoric, Walter Herbst provides the reader with a 'real reason' and outcome as to WHY the United States never reinvaded CUBA in 1962. The tumultuous and disastrous years of President Kennedy's administration consumed with the difficulty of handling foreign policy and preventing WWIII opens the door for Walter's spectacular conclusion. Herbst demonstrates through his research a meticulous rendering of truthful and historical answers. These answers may not satisfy everyone. It does, however, open the gate for Walter's dazzling conclusion. This is an excellent book and a 'must read' for helping to resolving Cold War solutions.

– Casey J. Quinlan, Historian and JFK Assassination Researcher and Author

Author's Note

The recent release of JFK Assassination Files has revealed that CIA CI (Counterintelligence), led by James Angleton, looked to recruit Lee Harvey Oswald before his 1959 defection to Russia; that the CIA kept Oswald under surveillance until JFK was assassinated on November 22, 1963; that there was direct CIA CI involvement ™with Oswald in the period leading up to the assassination; that Oswald was never considered a security threat by the CIA; that the CIA was behind an attempted military takeover of the French government by the OAS; and that an attempted assassination of French President Charles de Gaulle by the OAS involved the CIA.

As you read *Last Resort Beyond Last Resort*, you, the reader, will learn that the information contained in this book is not only validated by the newly released files, but questions that the assassination files fail to address are answered herein. In short, the recently released information confirms that the JFK assassination plot presented in the pages of *Last Resort Beyond Last Resort* is close to what may have really happened.

–WH 3/31/25

LAST RESORT
BEYOND
LAST RESORT

THE JFK ASSASSINATION,
THE NEED TO PROTECT WEST BERLIN, AND WHY A SECOND INVASION OF CUBA NEVER HAPPENED

WALTER HERBST

LAST RESORT BEYOND LAST RESORT: THE JFK ASSASSINATION, THE NEED TO PROTECT WEST BERLIN, AND WHY A SECOND INVASION OF CUBA NEVER HAPPENED
Copyright © 2024/2025 Walter Herbst. All Rights Reserved.

Published by:
Trine Day LLC
PO Box 577
Walterville, OR 97489
1-800-556-2012
www.TrineDay.com
trineday@icloud.com

Library of Congress Control Number: 2025930613

Herbst, Walter. LAST RESORT BEYOND LAST RESORT—1st ed.
p. cm.

Epub (ISBN-13) 978-1-63424-506-7
Trade Paper (ISBN-13) 978-1-63424-505-0

1. Kennedy, John F. (John Fitzgerald), 1917-1963. Assassination. 2. Conspiracies History. United States. 3. Oswald, Lee Harvey . 4. Cuba Foreign relations United States. 5. United States History 1961-1969 . I. Herbst, Walter. II. Title.

FIRST EDITION
10 9 8 7 6 5 4 3 2 1

For more information: herbstbooks.com

Distribution to the Trade by:
Independent Publishers Group (IPG)
814 North Franklin Street
Chicago, Illinois 60610
312.337.0747
www.ipgbook.com

Our doubts are traitors and make us lose the good we oft might win by fearing to attempt.
— William Shakespeare, *Measure for Measure*

Death may beget life, but oppression can beget nothing other than itself.
–Charles Dickens, *A Tale of Two Cities*

To my wife Margaret, for always supporting me for the past forty-five years

ACKNOWLEDGEMENTS

A special thanks to my good friend Leslie Sharp, the coauthor of *Coup in Dallas*, whose help and willingness to share information with me has made this book possible.

I would also like to give a posthumous thanks to Hank Albarelli, Leslie's coauthor. Although I never had the pleasure of meeting Hank, his work and research paved the way.

Other JFK assassination writers and researchers have supported me, so I would also like to thank Gary Shaw, Casey Quinlan, Jeff Meek, and Alan Kent. I appreciate your input.

Some researchers are referenced many times in this book. Writers such as Dick Russell, John Newman, James Di Eugenio, Anthony Summers, Lamar Waldron, Ralph Ganis, John Newman, James Douglas, David Talbot, David Kaiser, Joan Mellen, and a host of others. Their work has been invaluable, and I owe them a debt of gratitude.

I would especially like to thank Kris Milligan, my publisher at Trine Day, as well as Bruce de Torres and Chana Gail Willis. I appreciate all your help in publishing and marketing this book.

I want to thank my family for always being my inspiration. My wife, Margaret; my son Michael and daughter-in-law Debra; and my daughter Diana and son-in-law Philip. Last but not least are my grandchildren Julia, Emily Ryan, Norah, and Colin. Their interest in the JFK assassination warms my heart, and I know they will keep the fire burning long after I am gone.

Contents

Acknowledgment vi

Acronyms ix

Introduction 1

1) Over Their Heads 21

2) The Defector Who Wasn't 36

3) The Pentagon Strikes Back 54

4) Nazis, Monarchists, French Fascists, and the CIA 75

5) Making a Killing in 1961 105

6) The Prodigal Son Returns 123

7) From White Russians With Love 132

8) The Pressure Mounts 144

9) Don't Dance With The Devil 165

10) Turning Point 179

11) You and Me Against the World 196

12) Birth of a Revolutionary 208

13) A Shot in the Dark 230

14) CIA and the Pentagon Flex Their Muscles 249

15) Enemies Within 267

16) Enemies On The Outside 284

17) Battle Lines Are Drawn 298

18) Into The Belly Of The Beast 315

19) The Summer of Discontent 333

20) Living Hard In The Big Easy 351

21) With Friends Like These Who Needs Enemies 369

22) Where's Oswald 386

23.) An Impostor In Mexico City 403

24) The Point Of No Return 429

25) By Any Means Possible 443

26) Countdown To Assassination 466

27) A November To Remember 488
28) Interlude 503
29) The Darkest Day – An American Tragedy 508
30) Nowhere To Run, Nowhere To Hide 536
31) Epilogue 552

Endnotes 581
Index 631

Anacronyms

ACLU .... American Civil Liberties Union
ACSI .... Assistant Chief of Staff (Intelligence)
AFA .... Air Force Association
AID ....Agency for International Development
ARA .... State Department's Bureau of Inter-American Affairs
AV .... Avanguardia Nazionale
AVG ....American Volunteer Group
BACC ....British – American – Canadian - Corporation, S.A.
BCRA .... Bureau Central de Renseignements et d'Action
CAP .... Civil Air Patrol
CCC ....Cuban Coordinating Committee
CHMAAG .... Chief, Military Assistance Advisory Group
CI ....Counterintelligence, CIA
CIA .... Central Intelligence Agency
CIC .... Counterintelligence Corp, U.S. Army
CINCPAC ....Commander-in-Chief, U.S. Navy, Pacific
CI/OA ....Chief of Counterintelligence/Operational Approvals
CI/R&A .... Counterintelligence Research and Analysis
CISC .... Committee for International Student Cooperation
CI/SIG .... Counterintelligence Senior Interagency Group
CFR .... Council on Foreign Relations
CINCLANT .... Commander in Chief of the Atlantic Command
CI/OA ....Chief of Counterintelligence/Operational Approvals
CORE ....Congress of Racial Equality
CPSU ....Communist Party Soviet Union
CPUSA ....Communist Party USA
CRC ....Cuban Revolutionary Council
DCI ....Director of Central Intelligence
DDCI ....Deputy Director of Central Intelligence
DDP .... Deputy Director of Plans. CIA
DGI .... Cuban Intelligence in the United States
DIA ....Defense Intelligence Agency
DOD .... Department of Defense
DRE ....Cuban Student Directorate
DST .... Directorate of Territorial Surveillance

EIN	Employee Identification Number, CIA
ELC	Ejercito Libertador de Cuba
ENI	Ente Nazionale Idrocarburi
FBI	Federal Bureau of Investigation
FBN	ederal Bureau of Narcotics
FLN	Front de Liberation Nationale
FOI	Field Operations Intelligence
FPCC	Fair Play for Cuba Committee
FRD	Cuban Revolutionary Front
G-2	U.S. Army Intelligence
HSCA	House Select Committee on Assassinations
ICBM	Intercontinental Ballistic Missile
ICDCC	International Committee for the Defense of Christian Culture
INCA	nformation Council of the Americas
INS	Immigration and Naturalization Service
IRC	International Rescue Committee
ISR	Interagency Source Register
JCS	Joint Chiefs of Staff
KGB	Soviet Intelligence Group
LAPD	Los Angeles Police Department
MAC	Movimento Anticommunista
MAC	Movement d'Action Civique..
MACV	Military Assistance Command, Vietnam0
MDC	Movimento Democratica Christiano
MI	Military Intelligence
MIRR	Insurrectional Movement for the Recovery of the Revolution
MIT	Massachusetts Institute of Technology
MK/NAOMI	CIA Mind Control Program
MK/ULTRA	CIA Drug Experimentation Program
MRP	People's Revolutionary Party
MRR	Movement of Revolutionary Recovery
MSI	Movimeneto Sociale Italiano
MVD	Ministry of Internal Affairs, Soviet Union
NAACP	National Association for the Advancement of Colored People
NANA	North American Newspaper Alliance
NATO	North Atlantic Treaty Organization
NCFE	National Committee for a Free Europe
NKVD	Soviet Domestic Law Enforcement Agency
NNGPM	Netherlands New Guinea Petroleum Company
NOPD	New Orleans Police Department
NORAD	North American Air Defense Command
NSA	National Security Agency

ANACRONYMS

NSAM	National Security Action Memoranda
NSC	National Security Council
NVA	North Vietnamese Army
NYPD	New York Police Department
OAS	Organisation Armee Secrete
OAS	Organization of American States
ODWU	Organization for Rebirth of the Ukraine
ON	Ordine Nuovo
ONI	Office of Naval Intelligence
ONUC	l'Organisation des Nations Unies au Congo
OPC	Office of Policy Coordination
OS	Office of Security, CIA
OSO	Office of Special Operations
OSS	Office of Strategic Services
PCB	Brazil's Communist Party
PCI	Italian Communist Party
PERMINDEX	Right-wing European CIA front company
POW	Prisoner of War
PPS	Policy Planning Staff
PRC	People's Republic of China
PSI	Italian Socialist Party
QJ/WIN	CIA assassin.
QKENCHANT	CIA program to recruit civilians.
RICO	Racketeer Influenced and Corrupt Organizations
RIS	Russian Intelligence Service
SAC	Special Agent in Charge, FBI
SAC	Strategic Air Command, Air Force
SACEUR	Supreme Allied Commander Europe
SAIMR	South African Institute for Maritime Research
SAS	Special Affairs Staff
SDECE	Service de Documentation Exterieure ey de Contre-Espionnage
SEATO	Southeast Asian Treaty Organization
SECDEF	Secretary of Defense
SGA	Special Group Augmented
SI	War Department's Secret Intelligence
SIG	Special Investigations Group, CIA
SIGINT	Signals Intelligence, NSA
SNFE	Second National Front of the Escambray
SNIE	Special National Intelligence Estimate
SOE	British Special Operations Executive
SOFINDUS	Sociedad Financiera Industrial
SRS	Security Research Staff, CIA

SSU	Strategic Services Unit
SWP	Socialist Workers Party
TFW	Task Force W (CIA, Cuban Operations)
TSBD	Texas School Book Depository
TSS	Technical Services Staff, CIA
U-2	CIA High-Altitude Spy Plane
UGEMA	Union Generale des Etudiants Musulmans Algeriens
UHO	Ukrainian Hetman Organization
UN	United Nations
UPI	United Press International
USIB	United States Intelligence Board
UWF	United World Federalists
WCC	World Commerce Corporation
WHD	Western Hemisphere Division
ZR/RIFLE	CIA Assassination Program

INTRODUCTION

*L*ast Resort Beyond Last Resort is a narrative about the JFK Presidency. It describes the tremendous pressure the President was under, as he faced overwhelming animosity and resistance from the CIA, the military, right-wing paramilitary groups, Cuban exiles, racists, and white supremacist organizations. It was this that set the stage for his assassination.

President Kennedy's foreign policy faced many challenges around the globe, including Cuba, Vietnam, Laos, the Middle East, Congo, Indonesia, and West Berlin. Foremost was Operation Mongoose and the war against Fidel Castro. Kennedy rarely saw eye to eye with the CIA and the U.S. military on how to deal with the Cuban struggle. However, we do know that West Berlin was intertwined with the Cuba affair, a little-known fact that has not gotten the attention it deserves until now.

Last Resort Beyond Last Resort delves deep into the importance of protecting West Berlin. It was especially true after the Missile Crisis when a second invasion of Cuba could have led to a takeover of West Berlin by the Soviets in retaliation. As Kennedy told Khrushchev when they met in Vienna in June 1961, "If we abandon West Berlin, it would mean the abandonment of Western Europe, which America had deemed essential to its security in two wars," and he was not about to do that. Still, Cuba remained a focal point of interest for both Kennedy brothers.

Early in 1963, JFK put his brother Bobby in charge of the AMWORLD/Omega Plan operation, which involved a second invasion of Cuba using the U.S. military to remove Castro. At the same time, maintaining control of the Cuban situation was the central issue for President Kennedy. As a result, he excluded violent right-wing Cuban exile groups from the coalition Bobby was putting together. The crackdown began almost immediately after the Missile Crisis was over, and it became clear the President was no longer an ally of the Cubans looking to remove Castro. Which was why, in the spring of 1963, an attorney from Chicago named Paulino Sierra Martinez created a coalition of various right-wing Cuban exile groups funded by organized crime and American businessmen who also wanted to see the Castro regime toppled. And the CIA remained part of this unholy Alliance that would result in JFK's assassination.

***

After forty-years of research, I have determined that one of the primary reasons President Kennedy was assassinated was to prevent the AM-WORLD operation from happening to protect West Berlin from Soviet intervention and keep the geopolitical status quo in Western Europe intact. It resulted in the U.S. military's focus changing from Cuba to Southeast Asia, which was the area the Joint Chiefs desperately wanted to engage the Communists on the battlefield.

Like many researchers, for years, I believed that a domestic coup d'etat assassinated President Kennedy to unleash a military that was chomping at the bit to flex its muscles against a Communist world that could not match America's firepower. The evidence seemed to point in that direction. Still, there was one thing I could never reconcile in my mind. Starting with Eisenhower, and while Kennedy was President, the Pentagon, a faction within the CIA, and the radical right were all adamant that Castro had to go by whatever means possible. So, if that were true, in the immediate aftermath of the assassination, why didn't the United States say Lee Harvey Oswald was working on behalf of Castro and invade Cuba? It would have been a logical claim to make, even if it were false, considering the available evidence at the time. The military was primed and ready. All they needed was approval from the White House, and they would have responded with a shock and awe operation the world had not seen since the Korean War. Instead, nothing happened, even though any justification the United States needed to invade Cuba with the U.S. military was handed to them on a silver platter with President Kennedy's assassination. The world would soon learn that the accused assassin, Lee Harvey Oswald, had defected to the Soviet Union, was considered a Communist, and was a vocal Castro supporter, even when he was in the Marines. A photograph supposedly taken of Oswald in the spring of 1963 showed him dressed all in black, holding his rifle, and wearing his holstered pistol. In his free hand, he held copies of the Communist Party USA's newspaper, *The Worker,* and the Socialist Workers Party's *The Militant.* He wrote his wife Marina a letter telling her what to do if he were "alive and taken prisoner" as if he were going behind enemy lines on a military operation. Shortly after that, he allegedly tried to shoot right-wing General Edwin Walker. He was a member of the pro-Castro Fair Play for Cuba Committee, corresponded regularly with them, the

Communist Party USA, and the Socialist Workers Party, and in the summer of 1963, he was arrested in New Orleans for handing out pro-Castro literature in public. Oswald appeared on a radio debate supporting Castro, and two months before the assassination, he tried to enter Cuba via Mexico City. While there, he visited the Soviet Embassy and met with a KGB assassin named Valery Kostikov.

It was a significant encounter because two days after the assassination, the CIA's Mexico City station learned that Kostikov had recently met in Mexico City with a Cuban assassin named Rolando Cubela. At the time of the JFK assassination, the CIA had also been meeting with Cubela for months, plotting to assassinate Fidel Castro. In fact, on the day of the assassination, the CIA's Desmond FitzGerald met Cubela in Paris to finalize the details of the Castro assassination plot."[1]

Even more alarming was that days after the assassination, Ruth Paine gave the FBI a letter written by Oswald referring to his meeting with Kostikov that implied Oswald was really a Soviet sleeper agent impersonating Oswald.[2] It was a frightening scenario for those looking to avoid a world war with Russia, especially when placed in context with the September 7th comment by Castro to Daniel Harker of the *Associated Press* in Brazil that "United States leaders would be in danger if they helped in any attempt to do away with the leaders of Cuba ... United States leaders should be mindful that if they are aiding terrorist plans to eliminate Cuban leaders, they themselves will not be safe."[3]

With all this damaging information, it was not hard to make a case that Cuba was involved with Oswald in the assassination. The following year, the U.S. would not have a problem staging the Gulf of Tonkin incident to justify sending military troops to Vietnam and starting a major war there, so why was there a reluctance to do something similar with Cuba after Kennedy's death, just ninety miles off the coast of Florida?

I understand that our government has a lot to be ashamed of from the way it conducted itself in the decades leading up to the Kennedy assassination. Anyone who has read my books, *It Did Not Start With JFK, Volumes 1 & 2*, can attest to that. I am also fully aware that believing a domestic coup d'etat removed President Kennedy is a plausible position to take. Many influential people at the time, in positions to do something about it, believed his foreign policy decisions and appeasement of communism placed the nation at risk. As a result, assassinating JFK was a viable option to curtail the spread of communism before President Kennedy had an opportunity to weaken America's position further, perhaps irrevocably.

Still, it gnawed at me that there must be another explanation, for Kennedy's assassination did not result in a government takeover by the military, and the conspirators seemingly ignored other less dramatic ways to remove JFK from office. His numerous sexual liaisons and his family's relationship with the Mafia were blackmailable offenses. If that had been made public in 1963, the American people would not have reelected him. His stance on civil rights would probably lose him the entire South, including Texas, and some of the North as well. The Mafia, who felt betrayed by the Kennedy brothers, would never help JFK get reelected as they had done in 1960. His so-called appeasement of communism labeled him a traitor in the eyes of many. It all meant there was a good chance he could lose the 1964 election.

I am not naïve by any stretch of the imagination, and I understand that the hatred Kennedy faced throughout his Presidency made him a prime target for assassination, as will be covered in this book. However, Cuba was such a critical issue as 1963 began. There was unfinished business to attend to, and I kept returning in my mind to the question I posed above – why didn't the United States invade Cuba after the assassination when it had the chance? Why kill a President and then not follow through on removing the Communist presence from the Western Hemisphere when the opportunity presented itself, which was what the powers that be always wanted to do? And I began to think that maybe the opposite was true, that the JFK conspirators perpetrated the assassination to ensure the United States did not invade Cuba to maintain the status quo.

In 1959, American mercenaries, working alongside Cuba's revolutionary army, planned an aerial and amphibious attack against Nicaragua. Prior to that, eighty-seven Cubans and Panamanians who had trained in Cuba landed at a remote beach in Panama. A month later, Cuban soldiers landed by plane in Nicaragua, followed by the capture of Havana-trained Nicaraguans trying to cross into Nicaragua from Honduras. Castro denied responsibility for all the above, and he probably was telling the truth. The purpose of these pinprick attacks was to provide President Eisenhower with a reason to invade Cuba under the pretext that our allies needed help staving off Castro's attempt to spread his revolution. It was one year after the coup in Iraq, and the CIA and the Pentagon were following the blueprint that was so successful there. But Eisenhower did not take the bait because he feared if he did so without plausible deniability, the Soviets might take over West Berlin and perhaps continue through Western Europe, and that would be a hundred times worse.[4]

Two years later, during the Bay of Pigs invasion, part of the operation was to stage an attack at Guantanamo Bay by anti-Castro Cuban exiles dressed as Castro's soldiers, but it never materialized. Once again, the purpose was to give President Kennedy the justification needed to engage the U.S. military to topple Castro. Since the attack on Guantanamo never occurred, Kennedy chose not to escalate for the same reason Eisenhower did. It would have made West Berlin vulnerable to attack.

Last Resort Beyond Last Resort investigates the Kennedy Presidency from start to finish and explains how Bobby Kennedy's planned second invasion of Cuba led to the JFK assassination. The stakes were high, and it is critical to understand that as early as 1961, the Joint Chiefs and the CIA's Director of Central Intelligence, Allen Dulles, had told JFK that the maximum nuclear weapon advantage the United States would ever have over the USSR would occur late in 1963. After that, the gap would begin to close. Considering that JFK had signed a nuclear test ban treaty with the Soviets on October 7, 1963, just six weeks before Dallas, there was reason for the militarists and hardline anti-Communists within the government to have pushed for a retaliatory invasion of Cuba when the opportunity presented itself after the JFK assassination.

We know that Secretary of State Dean Rusk signed off on a joint Defense-State Department contingency plan for the invasion of Cuba days after the assassination, which they agreed not to submit to President Johnson. Instead, Lieutenant Colonel Alexander Haig rushed the plan to Secretary of the Army Cyrus Vance and Secretary of Defense Robert McNamara for each man's approval. It died on the vine. Before the Rockefeller Commission in 1975, John McCone talked about what would have happened if they knew Castro was involved in the assassination. "The indignation of this country would have been so great that the Marines would have taken over Cuba," he said. So, the question remains – why wasn't anything done?[5]

Obviously, killing his brother was not part of Bobby's plan, but assassinating JFK would be a viable catalyst for those the Attorney General excluded from his Omega Plan/AMWORLD second invasion operation, such as right-wing Cuban exiles, American mercenaries, CIA operatives, Mafia figures, right-wing zealots, and retired members of the military, many of whom were aware the Kennedy assassination was going to happen. These groups did come together, huddled under Paulino Sierra's anti-Castro all-inclusive umbrella that united various right-wing Cuban exile groups with those that supported them to oppose Bobby Kennedy's operation. They were willing

5

to assassinate JFK to kickstart the second Cuban invasion because the Kennedy brothers had double-crossed them all. It also explains how they knew the assassination was going to happen before it did. Still, these were peripheral players in the assassination conspiracy, and they were not privy to the real reason the main conspirators intended to assassinate JFK. In short, they were pawns used to divert attention away from what was really happening because, despite what they expected, JFK's death did not lead to a second invasion of Cuba. In fact, the opposite happened, as America's focus soon switched to Vietnam.

So, I realized there must have been another reason why those behind the JFK assassination killed the President when they did, one month before Bobby Kennedy's second invasion of Cuba was supposed to happen, and did not remove Castro from the scene. After many years of research, I began to pursue an alternate theory that, considered in conjunction with what other have proposed involving Cuba, could provide the key to understanding what really happened in Dallas. *That the motive behind Kennedy's assassination was to sabotage Bobby's operation and prevent the second invasion of Cuba from occurring because it could have led to the fall of West Berlin, which brought with it potentially dire consequences.*

***

William Harvey, who headed the CIA's assassination program, not only called assassination the last resort beyond last resort, he said it was a sign of weakness. It is why I thought it was an appropriate title for this book. Harvey meant that assassination was acceptable only after every other option had been exhausted, which by the spring of 1963 was evidently the case regarding President Kennedy. For almost three years, he and his brother Bobby ignored the hardliners around them, even though many in the Pentagon and the CIA thought the fate of Western civilization hung in the balance. So, what was so egregious that warranted assassinating the President for the good of the country and the Western World?

Consider that many at the CIA and some at the Pentagon did not consider Cuba that significant of a pawn to risk going to war with the Soviet Union. True, Cuba was a potential spreader of communism in the Western Hemisphere, but it was an insignificant country the U.S. could control. The fact that Cuba has created little trouble for the United States over the last sixty-plus years is proof of that. Southeast Asia was a more critical area. Communism could spread quickly there, which could not be allowed to happen. That was where the United States needed to take a stand to contain the spread of communism, not in Cuba.

The second important point was West Berlin. During the second Kennedy/Nixon debate before the 1960 election, Kennedy predicted that the next president "is going to be confronted with a very serious question on our defense of Berlin, our commitment to Berlin. It's going to be a test of our nerve and will." During the third debate, Frank McGee of NBC News asked each candidate if they would be willing to take military action to defend Berlin. Kennedy responded that "we have a contractual right to be in Berlin coming out of the conversations at Potsdam and of World War II that has been reinforced by a number of other nations under NATO.... It is a commitment that we have to meet if we are going to protect the security of Western Europe, and therefore, on this question, I don't think there is not [sic] any doubt in the mind of any member of the community of West Berlin. I'm sure there isn't any doubt in the minds of the Russians. We will meet our commitments to maintain the freedom and independence of West Berlin."[6]

"The problem was the Kennedy brothers took what happened at the Bay of Pigs personally, which was why they desperately wanted to negotiate a deal with Castro at the end of 1962 to bring home the Cuban exiles who were being held prisoner. They thought they had a deal, until Castro demanded an additional $3 Million at the last moment on December 23, which forced Robert Kennedy to contact retired Army General Lucius Clay. Clay was the hero of West Berlin, solely responsible for orchestrating the Berlin Airlift, and President Kennedy had sent Clay to Berlin again after the Berlin Wall was erected in 1961. Despite that Clay had nothing to do with Cuba, he did have strong connections to big business and leaders in banking. So, he was able to secure the money, and another crisis was averted. Still, with the introduction of Clay, it further connected the affairs in Cuba with protecting West Berlin and the need to contain the spread of communism in both arenas."

The question then becomes, who wanted to prevent Bobby's second invasion of Cuba? To answer that, we must return to 1959, when a group of Cuban and American businessmen in Cuba, who had lost significant financial investments after Castro came to power, approached Allen Dulles about organizing a military uprising to remove the Cuban leader. Surprisingly, Dulles objected. "We're on good terms with Russia. Castro is their ally. We don't want trouble with Russia, and so we cannot back efforts against Castro," Dulles reportedly said, and he wasted little time in contacting the State Department. Philip Bonsal, the American Ambassador to Cuba, was notified, and Dulles knew he would warn the Cubans, which he did. "There is a conspiracy in your Army to betray you," Bonsal wrote, naming American mercenary William Morgan as the leader of the group, who was arrested and executed by firing squad.[7]

One reason Dulles sabotaged the operation was that he knew West Berlin was vulnerable if the U.S. was responsible for regime change in Cuba, and the tradeoff was not worth the risk. In addition to jeopardizing the safety of Western Europe, Dulles also knew some German companies he was connected to would suffer if the Soviets overran West Berlin, and other American and European businessmen shared his concern. Finally, if not done correctly, overthrowing Castro would have resulted in a left-wing government taking his place, which Dulles and the American and European right-wingers who supported him did not want. They wanted a Fascist government similar to what conditions were like under Batista. It was just as crucial as protecting West Berlin, perhaps more so, because Cuba was a building block in the international Fascist movement the JFK conspirators were trying to create.

Even though Allen Dulles was removed from the CIA after the Bay of Pigs, many at the Agency were still loyal to him, and he privately remained in the loop of what the CIA was up to. William Harvey had a connection to Germany when he headed the CIA's Berlin station from 1952 until 1960. After that, he took over Division D, the CIA's cryptological intelligence section of the Clandestine Services. By 1961, the CIA's assassination program, ZR/RIFLE, would become part of Division D under Harvey's direction. James Angleton, Tracy Barnes, Frank Wisner, and Henry Hecksher were all veterans of the war against Castro. Each man had strong ties to Germany from their OSS days in Europe during World War II and supported fascism in the war against communism. They considered West Berlin the gateway to Western Europe and would have wanted to protect it. These men, as well as Dulles, were strongly pro-German and had developed working relationships with European Monarchists, Fascists, and the right-wing anti-Communist stay-behind army groups the CIA had trained to protect Europe from communism.

Madrid was ground zero for Fascist and ex-Nazi groups who wanted to establish a new world order based on a "*Fascism without Hitler*" form of government. Ex-Waffen SS lieutenant colonel Otto Skorzeny headed the Nazi group in Madrid that remained loyal to fascism. He was close to Allen Dulles, and the others at the CIA mentioned above, who all shared his Fascist philosophy. From the day he arrived in Madrid in the early 1950s, there were reports that Skorzeny was forming a secret German army in exile of

INTRODCUTION

200,000 men. Recruits were to be based and trained in Spain to be used as a first line of defense against a Soviet attack against Western Europe. It was identical to the stay-behind armies the CIA had created, and it made perfect sense that these two groups worked together to contain the spread of communism.[8]

There was the well-connected Charles Willoughby, dubbed MacArthur's "Little Fascist," who worked with Skorzeny, Dulles, and Fascists in Germany and the United States. There was Texas oilman Jack Crichton, who headed a military intelligence group in Dallas at the time of the assassination. Crichton was well connected to the operations run out of Madrid and worked with Skorzeny on an oil venture in Spain in the 1950s. There are also many other individuals discussed in detail in this book, including some who looked to replace democracy in America, which they considered Socialist or Communist, with a more Fascist-like form of government. For now, understand that the groups and individuals mentioned above considered it acceptable to assassinate President Kennedy to advance their Fascist philosophy.

Equally important to the conspiracy was the OAS, the band of French military officers who had rebelled against France and Charles de Gaulle for granting independence to the one-time French colony Algeria. There was a French connection that aligned itself to the groups mentioned above long before 1963, so there was already an established working relationship. The Corsican-connected Jean Pierre Lafitte, along with Frenchmen Jean Souetre and Phillipe de Vosjoli, were very familiar to the Fascist right-wingers at the CIA, as well as the operatives in Madrid, and each played an essential role in the JFK assassination conspiracy.[9]

Jean Pierre Lafitte is a critical figure because of the datebook he left behind that provides a timeline for those involved in the assassination conspiracy. The datebook entries referenced in this book are from *Coup in Dallas*, which predominantly features Lafitte's datebook. For those entries where I required additional information or confirmation that what I was writing was correct, I received direction from Leslie Sharp, who coauthored *Coup in Dallas* with Hank Albarelli, to let me know if I was on the right track. Still, it is essential to clarify that the assumptions and conclusions I draw in this book related to Lafitte's datebook are based upon information provided to me by Leslie Sharp and may be subject to change once more information becomes available.[10]

***

Last Resort Beyond Last Resort explains that the JFK assassination was an international conspiracy consisting of CIA right-wingers, American Fascists, ex-Nazis who still clung to their ideology, French anti-Communists, and European Monarchists. The CIA believed they did not start wars but prevented them, and the moral aspect of the JFK assassination was rationalized by many within the Agency as the ends justifying the means. Wouldn't the world have been better off if they had killed Hitler before he had an opportunity to drag the world into World War II? Of course, the answer is yes, and it was this rationale that drove the proponents of assassination. These were men whose roots were deeply embedded in the 1950s, who shared the belief that democracy had God on its side in battling communism. That everyone was expendable in the war of good vs. evil. It included Presidents of the United States who, if misguided, could lead the country in the wrong direction with disastrous consequences. As Richard Bissell, the CIA's Deputy Director of Plans (DDP), stated in an interview, "Killing people is wrong, but it happens, and if someone had polished off Idi Amin, it would have saved a lot of people a lot of grief. But at the same time, it must be a decision in the hands of people you can trust and who will not take such a decision lightly."[11]

After reading this book, I trust the reader will accept that the Kennedy assassination was inevitable for a number of reasons. One was the total disrespect the upstart Kennedy brothers had for those who had much more experience than they in how the government operated. It applied to the CIA, the Joint Chiefs of Staff, members of Congress, and even members of JFK's staff. The Kennedys thought they knew best, and had no use for anyone who thought differently. Another reason was Bobby's backchannel meetings with Soviet representatives, many of whom were KGB, without letting the CIA and the Pentagon know what he and his brother were up to. It started before JFK was sworn in and continued throughout his Presidency, even during the Cuban Missile Crisis. However, President Kennedy's most serious mistake was that he looked to give peace a chance, which the Military-Industrial Complex believed was dangerous to the security of the United States. Still, they were willing to tolerate the Kennedy brothers until they played Russian Roulette with the second invasion of Cuba.

The Omega Plan/AMWORLD operation began early in 1963, and it involved the CIA on a limited basis. Cuban exile Manuel Artime, the military leader of the operation, was looking for a Latin country from which to launch his invasion of Cuba. As will be shown in this book, Artime was also still on the CIA's payroll, simultaneously working with Henry Hecksher,

INTRODCUTION

William Harvey, David Phillips, and James Angleton at the CIA. We know that Artime did not trust what Bobby was doing and gravitated towards the CIA and Paulino Sierra's right-wing Cuban exile consortium, joining the Batistaite Cuban exile groups and American mercenaries, their CIA handlers, Mafia figures, and European Fascists who found refuge there.

There were many layers to the assassination conspiracy, each with a different objective. How these layers came to be, as well as how Lee Harvey Oswald fit into the conspiracy and the role he played, is too involved to explain here. It is all covered within the pages of this narrative. For now, suffice it to say there were plenty of reasons for anti-Communist right-wingers at the CIA and European Monarchists and Fascists to have wanted JFK removed from power. In 1963 alone, JFK signed a nuclear test-ban treaty with the Soviets without Congressional approval, then went to the American people directly to pressure Congress into ratifying it. He signed a deal to sell wheat to Russia, which enabled them to feed their people and support the Soviet economy, a violation of George Kennan's Policy of Containment. He publicly spoke of coexistence with the Soviets in his American University speech, an unspeakable misstep. He began a pullout of troops from Vietnam and intended to institute a complete withdrawal during his second term. He knew about Russian missiles in Cuba months before October 1962 but waited until a month before the midterm elections for political reasons, putting the world in increased peril. He passed up the opportunity to invade Cuba during the Cuban Missile Crisis, even though this was what the hardliners around him advised him to do. He allowed the Soviets to remove missiles from Cuba after the Missile Crisis without verification while agreeing to remove U.S. missiles from Turkey and Italy and never to invade Cuba. He prevented right-wing Cuban exiles from engaging in sabotage raids against Cuba despite the fact that this was what the United States had trained them to do. He initiated talks to normalize relations with Castro's Cuba, even though he knew that appeasing Communists could not be tolerated. Finally, he attempted to normalize relations with President Sukarno of Indonesia, whom hardliners considered a Communist and wanted to remove from power.

There was a long precedence that looking to seek peaceful coexistence with the Soviet Union and Cuba, signing a test ban treaty, and engaging in arms reduction discussions with the Russians was a potentially dangerous road for President Kennedy to travel. In 1946, at the beginning of the Cold War, President Truman asked American diplomat George Kennan, who was serving in Moscow, to put his thoughts on paper regarding the future of

Soviet-American relations. Kennan wrote that "peaceful coexistence" was not possible because the Russians perceived themselves to be in a "deadly struggle for [the] total destruction of rival power." There was no ambiguity – if, given the opportunity, the Russians intended to destroy America.[12]

Kennan's warnings resonated throughout Washington and led to the Policy of Containment, which guided American foreign policy throughout the Cold War. The belief was the Soviets were economically unstable and would eventually succumb to internal unrest and self-destruct.

Then, at the beginning of March 1953, a little over a month after Dwight Eisenhower became President, the White House learned that Joseph Stalin was seriously ill. The radical right wanted to use the situation to foment unrest throughout Russian satellite countries, but others disagreed. The CIA's Frank Wisner thought it was too early. He said that if "the satellite peoples rose up in revolt now, the Red Army would crush them [and] the CIA needed time to organize its clandestine forces ... to exploit the situation." Allen Dulles agreed with Wisner, as did Eisenhower. The President released a statement the next day that said, "At this moment in history, when multitudes of Russians are anxiously concerned because of the illness of the Soviet ruler, the thoughts of America go out to all the people of the USSR."[13]

Stalin died on March 6. In his eulogy, the new Soviet premier, Georgi Malenkov, vowed to strive for "peaceful coexistence" with the West and suggested that the two superpowers talk to settle all outstanding security issues. Eisenhower concurred. "I am interested in the future," he said. "Both their government and ours have new men in them. The slate is clean. Now, let us begin talking to each other. And let us say what we have got to say so that every person on earth can understand it."[14]

The following month, Eisenhower extended an olive branch to the Soviet Union in a speech to the American Society of Newspaper Editors that shocked the radical right. "A nation's hope of lasting peace," he stated, "cannot be firmly based upon a race in armaments." He said, "The hunger for peace is in the hearts of all peoples – those of Russia and China no less than our own country."[15] However, two days later, his Secretary of State, John Foster Dulles, Allen's brother, speaking before the same Society of Newspaper Editors, set the record straight. Instead of promoting coexistence, he said the Russians "could never be trusted ... so long as vast power is possessed by men who accept no guidance from the moral law." It ended any opportunity to pursue peace.[16]

John Foster Dulles was a hardline member of the Military Industrial Complex. Instead of pursuing peaceful coexistence, he recommended telling the Chinese that if another country fell to communism, the U.S. would retaliate with measures of its choosing, an apparent reference to the employment of atomic bombs. He said another possibility was to incite subversion within the Soviet empire, especially in Eastern Europe. The goal was to "disturb the Kremlin; make it think more of holding what it has ... turn the Soviet bloc into a loose alliance, without aggressive capacities, far different from Stalin's monolith."[17]

It was called the "New Look" strategy, based on nuclear superiority and "massive retaliation." It frightened many around the world, which was why, on December 8, 1953, Eisenhower spoke at the United Nations and gave what came to be known as the "Atoms for Peace" speech. He said that "the miraculous inventiveness of man shall not be dedicated to his death, but consecrated to his life." He received a standing ovation, even from the Soviet delegation, but all hope for a thaw in the Cold War ended when John Foster Dulles spoke before the Council on Foreign Relations a month later. He warned the world that the U.S. would use nuclear weapons to stop Communist aggression wherever it occurred, and it would be unrestricted "massive retaliatory power ... by means and at places of our own choosing."[18]

Dulles's "Massive Retaliation" speech governed U.S. defense policy throughout Eisenhower's Presidency, and it had the full support of the military. As Joint Chiefs Chairman Admiral Arthur Radford put it, it was "high time" the administration publicly declared its willingness to use nuclear weapons. General Alfred M. Gruenther, the NATO Supreme Commander in 1954, said that "simply because atomic bombs do create casualties – and very heavy casualties against women and children – is no reason why we should become sentimental. ... The chore is to make war itself impossible."[19]

Unfortunately, JFK ignored all this and pursued his agenda of peaceful coexistence, which the militarists in the United States who opposed him considered naïve and dangerous. Throughout the Kennedy presidency, there was fear that the Pentagon might initiate a *Seven Days in May*-type military takeover. In fact, a potential military coup in the United States had been a concern since 1961, when the Senate Foreign Relations Committee investigated and determined a military revolt was possible. The committee cited "as an example of the ultimate danger" the recent uprising by army generals in France over policies in Algeria. "Military officers, French or American, have some common characteristics arising from their profession, and there are numerous military' fingers on the trigger' throughout the world." The committee called for an investigation into Lyman Lemnitzer, the Joint Chiefs, and their relationship to extreme right-wing groups.[20] Columnist

Marquis Childs warned that "in one country after another in recent years, the intervention of the military in politics has had disastrous consequences..." Drew Pearson echoed Childs, writing that "certain Pentagon brass hats were lining up with industrial right-wingers to foment a sort of neo-fascism despite the fact they were wearing Uncle Sam's uniform."[21]

During the Cuban Missile Crisis, Kennedy wrote to British Prime Minister Harold Macmillan that he believed Khrushchev put the missiles in Cuba "to increase his chances at Berlin, and we shall be ready to take a full role there as well as in the Caribbean." Despite the brave talk, JFK ignored the Joint Chief's call for military action in Cuba, which prompted General Curtis LeMay, the Air Force Chief of Staff, to comment, "If we don't do anything to Cuba, they're going to push on Berlin and push real hard because they've got us on the run." By this time, the military knew how much Berlin influenced JFK's decisions.

McMillan told the U.S. Ambassador to London, David Bruce, that Khrushchev wanted "to trade Cuba for Berlin ... might not this be the whole purpose of the exercise – to move forward one pawn in order to exchange it for another?" President Kennedy did worry that Khrushchev might take military action in Berlin. "That's really the choice we now have," he wrote. "If [Khrushchev] takes Berlin, then we will take Cuba."[22]

Despite all this, at the beginning of 1963, the Kennedy brothers engaged in third-party discussions to normalize relations with Castro while they were planning a second invasion of Cuba with a staged plot to make it appear Cuba was the aggressor. By June, JFK talked about peaceful coexistence with the Soviet Union during his American University speech.

None of it made sense. The Kennedys were sending mixed messages, which was irresponsible, considering the worries there were over a potential military coup.

***

Last Resort Beyond Last Resort is a narrative that takes the reader through a systematic year-by-year analysis of the Kennedy Presidency, the President's trials and tribulations, how the Kennedy brothers placed politics above what was best for the nation, the battles they fought with the CIA, the Pentagon, and the radical right, and the dangers JFK increasingly faced as his Presidency moved forward.

The book also covers in detail Lee Harvey Oswald's final years, from his time in the Soviet Union until his arrest for killing officer J.D. Tippit and President Kennedy. It follows Oswald's introduction and indoctrination into the assassination plot from Fort Worth to Dallas, to New Orleans, to

Mexico City, and back to Dallas and his date with destiny. No stone is left unturned, including Oswald's right-wing, anti-Communist new world order philosophy and how that brought him to the attention of right-wing paramilitary groups like the Minutemen, Alpha 66, the DRE, and European Nazis and Monarchists who share his view of a new world order, albeit from a different political perspective. The importance of an Oswald impostor is covered throughout the narrative, especially as it applied to Mexico City, where the assassination conspiracy came together and where Oswald may have tried to extricate himself from the plot but was unable to do so.

There is no doubt that Oswald was the designated patsy, even though the conspirators had doubts about Oswald up to the last minute. Unfortunately, he found out too late to save himself. As *Last Resort Beyond Last Resort* will show, the evidence proves Oswald did not shoot the President or Tippit. He was on his own, sitting in a movie theater in the Oak Cliff section of Dallas, waiting for a contact that would never arrive. Tippit's murder brought the police to Oak Cliff and led to Oswald's unexpected arrest, which was a necessary part of the plan. The possibility that Oswald might disclose what he knew aborted the second invasion of Cuba before it had a chance to get started.

I firmly believe that Lee Harvey Oswald was a willing participant in the plot to kill President Kennedy. However, unknown to him, he was the "indispensable tool" to use the words of Richard Case Nagell. By this, Nagell meant there were things Oswald knew about his Russian defection and the assassination conspiracy that U.S. intelligence needed to keep secret, such as Oswald's connection to the New Orleans radical right, the Mafia, and the role they played in the assassination conspiracy. The conspirators who sabotaged the operation knew Oswald's arrest would compel the U.S. Government to bury the truth, and radical right forces who thought the assassination would lead to an invasion of Cuba compelled Ruby to kill Oswald out of fear of what he might disclose if he talked. The details of what happened are covered in this book and provide closure to the JFK assassination, a crime that has remained unsolved for much too long.

It was almost the perfect crime, but the facts do not lie. When placed in their proper context alongside critical events as the Kennedy presidency progressed toward its tragic end, there is sufficient evidence to prove who was responsible for the assassination of JFK and why he had to die. I have no doubt the reader will not only be surprised as the facts in the narrative unfold but also feel a certain degree of sadness, as I did. Had Robert Kennedy not pursued his plan to overthrow Castro in December 1963 so vigorously, chances are the JFK assassination never would have occurred. So, in the final analysis, in a macabre sort of way, Bobby was responsible for his brother's death, and he knew it, which was why he was in a virtual catatonic state after he learned the facts of what transpired.

Robert Kennedy was unaware of the extent to which those who ran the CIA had become disillusioned by 1963. There were Agency leaders who felt the government had used them to instigate rebellions in Communist satellite countries throughout the Cold War but did not provide support once the rebellion began. It resulted in the slaughter of countless innocents who were expecting help the United States had promised to provide but had no intention of doing. Their intent was only to make the Kremlin look bad on the world stage because if America got directly involved, it may have led to nuclear war. After all, there were those like General Curtis LeMay who wanted to blow the Soviets into oblivion. However, cooler heads at the CIA knew that could not be allowed to happen. So, in the ever-present desire to win over the hearts and minds of oppressed people in third-world countries, the deaths that inevitably resulted were considered collateral damage in pursuit of the greater good, which was the containment of communism throughout the world.

The disillusionment of the CIA in Germany began in 1953 when East Germans revolted in the wake of Stalin's death, as many wanted to provide arms and ammunition to the rioters. It was not to be, as Washington told them to stand down and do nothing, even though radio broadcasts from the West had encouraged the people to revolt. The Soviets suppressed the rebellion, resulting in many needless deaths and injuries to rioters who expected American support.

In 1956, Khrushchev gave what came to be known as his deStalinization speech, which denounced what Stalin had done, and the Soviet Premier initiated a series of economic and political reforms. Sensing an opportunity, in June 1956, Polish workers revolted, but the Soviets quickly suppressed that, resulting in at least fifty-seven people killed and hundreds arrested.

In October 1956, a significant rebellion occurred in Hungary. By the time Russian tanks put an end to it, Hungarian casualties were 30,000 dead and 50,000 wounded. Frank Wisner arrived in Vienna on November 7, the day before Soviet tanks finished the job in Budapest. Future CIA Director William Colby recalled Wisner being "totally out of control" during the rebellion. "He kept saying, all these people are getting killed, and we weren't doing anything; we were ignoring it."[23] Wisner wanted to intervene in Hungary, for "this was exactly the end for which the Agency's paramilitary capability was designed [for]," but nothing happened. "Starkly," Colby observed, "we demonstrated that 'liberation' was not our policy when the chips were down in Eastern Europe as the price might have been World War III."[24] When Wisner traveled to Germany, he found Tracy Barnes on the verge of a nervous breakdown.[25]

Wisner and Barnes had good reason to be upset. The United States did not help the rebellion, even though they had led the rioters to believe they would. Three-quarters of Hungarian exiles who escaped said that Radio Free Europe broadcasts by the United States led them to believe America would help when the time came. It did not end with Hungary. In Romania and Czechoslovakia, thousands were rounded up and put in prison. [26]

President Eisenhower understood there was a disconnect between how the U.S. government could react to these rebellions and what the CIA expected the government to do. As a result, Eisenhower ordered General Lucien Truscott, the CIA's Special Consultant to the United States Commissioner in Frankfurt, Germany, to dismantle the liberation underground army in Europe before an international disaster happened. The stay-behind army concept, which consisted of exiles planted in satellite countries, became a thing of the past, at least officially. The Soviet satellite country insurgents and the CIA felt betrayed.[27]

Then, in 1961, there was the Bay of Pigs, and President Kennedy's failure to offer proper air support doomed the operation as Cuban exiles were left to die or be captured by Castro's troops on a beach in Cuba. Once again, the CIA felt betrayed, and many were livid over what Kennedy had failed to do.

The Kennedy brothers had shown zero inclination to engage the U.S. military in combat operations in the first three years of JFK's Presidency, and his peace initiatives during the summer of 1963 suggested nothing was going to change. Therefore, there was little confidence at the Pentagon and among the radical right that they would actually follow through with their second invasion of Cuba in December 1963. It was why a coalition of partners, specifically those who had come together under Sierra's group, conspired to assassinate JFK as the catalyst to justify an invasion of Cuba. However, as Richard Nagell said, the particulars of the operation changed at some point.

As the evidence will show, people at the CIA, like Dulles, Harvey, Angleton, Barnes, Wisner, and Hecksher, were tired of operations that led to the deaths of so many innocent people who thought they could count on the U.S. for support. They knew about the JFK assassination plot and understood that an invasion of Cuba that involved the U.S. military would once again lead to needless deaths that would make what they had experienced in the past pale in comparison. That was especially true if it led to a Soviet takeover of West Berlin, which would have escalated hostilities to a point not seen before. So, the CIA, who considered everyone expendable in the war against communism, had to do something to prevent that from happening, and the European Fascists and Monarchists they were working with agreed. To protect Western Europe and save the lives of countless innocent lives, perhaps reaching into the millions, Kennedy had to die. So, they sabotaged the assassination plot to ensure the invasion of Cuba would not come to pass, which prevented another round of slaughter from happening.

While researching this book, I asked myself a simple question that you, the reader, may want to ask yourself. Which is more believable? That a CIA/European Fascist/OAS cabal conspired to sabotage the original JFK assassination plot to prevent a second invasion of Cuba, or that the JFK assassination was a right-wing coup d'etat that was supposed to lead to an invasion of Cuba to remove Castro from power and communism from the Western Hemisphere?

If you believe it was the latter, what went wrong? A takeover of the U.S. government never happened; the U.S. military never invaded Cuba, Castro remained in place, and the American focus in the war against communism switched to Southeast Asia. In fact, over sixty years later, Cuba is still there, and Fidel Castro lived until 2016.

However, as far as the former option is concerned, the JFK assassination thwarted the Omega plan/AMWORLD operation, and the second invasion of Cuba never happened. Cuba and Castro proved to be irrelevant for decades. The Soviet Union never invaded West Berlin, and George Kennan's Policy of Containment theory proved to be correct when the Berlin Wall came down in 1989. To satisfy the war hawks at the Pentagon, the war against communism switched to Vietnam, but the carnage experienced there was nowhere near what it would have been had Bobby Kennedy not been prevented from invading Cuba in December 1963.

CHAPTER ONE

OVER THEIR HEADS

It was an inauspicious start. Less than one month after defeating Richard Nixon in the 1960 presidential election, John F. Kennedy asked his brother Robert to meet privately in New York City with Mikhail Menshikov, a KGB officer working undercover as a correspondent for the Russian newspaper *Investia*. The president-elect wanted Khrushchev to know he shared the Soviet Premier's desire for a face-to-face meeting to undo the damage caused by the U-2 spy plane fiasco the previous May. And he thought they could sign a test ban treaty in 1961.

Menshikov explained to Bobby that Khrushchev wanted peaceful coexistence between the two superpowers, but only if they agreed on a mutual nuclear disarmament program and solved the problem of a divided Berlin. Berlin was a critical pawn in the Cold War, but as time would tell, President Kennedy would embrace coexistence and stand idly by as East Germany constructed the Berlin Wall.[28]

The CIA and the FBI had good reason to keep tabs on the Kennedy brothers even before the 1960 election, and it remained that way throughout his Presidency. There was an arrogance about them that offended the Washington establishment, most notably J. Edgar Hoover and Allen Dulles. The sexual liaisons and Kennedy-family Mafia connections were part of it, but it ran deeper. Both brothers disrespected tradition and disregarded the conventional way of doing things in Washington. Perhaps it was growing up exceedingly wealthy and always getting what they wanted, with a rich and powerful father pulling the strings behind the scenes. Still, whatever the reason, they believed they were more capable of getting things done than those who had run the government before them. To the Kennedys, "The torch is passed to a new generation" meant destroying the old system and to hell with the old guard.

Khrushchev knew what he was dealing with. To impress the new President, he had *Pravda* and *Izvestia* run the full, uncensored text of Kennedy's inaugural address, stopped jamming Voice of America radio broadcasts, allowed 500 elderly Soviets to join their families in the United States, and created an Institute for American Studies. JFK responded by lifting a ban on Soviet crabmeat imports, resuming civilian aviation talks, and ending censorship of Soviet publications by the U.S. Post Office. Cold War hard-liners in the U.S. took exception. They rejected any attempt to normalize relations with the Soviets, whom they believed could not be trusted.[29]

Meanwhile, Khrushchev was receiving unflattering reports about the Kennedy brothers from Ambassador Menshikov and the Premier's son-in-law, Aleksei Adzhubei. The latter referred to them as "little boys in short pants." The former said JFK was "an inexperienced upstart" who would never be a good president. It concerned Khrushchev. If Kennedy were weak, financial interests and the Military-Industrial Complex would be able to control him. As Menshikov told *New York Times* correspondent Harrison Salisbury on December 15, 1960, the two leaders had to meet as soon as possible "before those [in the U.S.] who would like not to see [an] agreement have had a chance to act and prevent it."[30]

Khrushchev was concerned about what he called "militarists" in the United States. He had accused them of sabotaging the U-2 flight in May 1960, which killed a nuclear test ban treaty he and Eisenhower had planned, and he feared there could be more of the same ahead.

***

As Kai Bird described in *The Color of Truth,* it soon became clear to the Washington establishment that the President-elect:

> …was about to change all the rules. Prior to 1960, those recruited for assistant secretaryships … [had] an establishment education… practical experience as a corporate lawyer … or to have worked one's way up the bureaucratic ladder in the Foreign Service or some other government agency … John Kennedy would inaugurate a new era in which men with no experience other than found in the groves of the academy were elevated to power.[31]

Kennedy named McGeorge Bundy his national security advisor to "simplify the operations of the National Security Council." In truth, he looked to eliminate much of the NSC's bureaucracy created under Eisenhower. Kennedy and Bundy wanted to run the White House like Harvard, with Bundy as dean and Kennedy as president. According to Kai Byrd: "Within a month the NSC's staff was cut from seventy-one to forty-eight. In place of weighty policy papers…Bundy's staff would procure crisp and timely National Security Action Memoranda (NSAMs)." Advisors "would represent no bureaucratic constituency other than the president, and they would argue the merits ... based on substance. This was how intellectuals, not bureaucrats, would make foreign policy."[32]

The change was unprecedented. JFK also eliminated the Operations Coordinating Board and the Planning Board and replaced them with interagency task forces who, as described by Annie Jacobsen in *The Pentagon's Brain*, "were almost always chaired by men from his inner circle, Ivy League intellectuals on the White House staff or in the Pentagon." Secretary of Defense Robert McNamara attended Harvard Business School. His deputy, Roswell Gilpatric, graduated from Yale Law. Bobby Kennedy was a Harvard graduate. McGeorge Bundy went to Yale, as did Deputy National Security Adviser Walt Rostow and Deputy Assistant Secretary of Defense for International Security Affairs William Bundy (brother of McGeorge), who also attended Harvard Law School.[33]

Kennedy asked for a "shit list" of people he should fire at the State Department, which he thought needed a complete overhaul. He would control foreign policy from the White House, so he selected Dean Rusk as Secretary of State, who would take orders without complaint. [34]

Dean Acheson, the Secretary of State under Truman, was brought on as a special advisor. He considered the Kennedy people a "group of young men who regard themselves as intellectuals" but were "capable of less coherent thought than we have had since Coolidge." After Kennedy's assassination, he said JFK was "out of his depth" and given to "high-school thought."[35]

It was a dangerous game JFK was playing. According to an army officer detailed to the White House, Kennedy's national security staff was "an agglomeration of six to a dozen hearty individuals picking up balls and running with them ad libitum as the President or McGeorge Bundy directs." It was a "helter-skelter intellectual parlor game." General White of the Air Force was "profoundly apprehensive of the pipe-smoking, tree-full-of-owls-type of so-called defense intellectuals..." General Curtis LeMay called them "the most egotistical people I ever saw in my life ... they had no respect for the military [and thought] they were better than all the rest of us..."[36] Joint Chiefs Chairman General Lyman Lemnitzer echoed LeMay: The "civilian hierarchy was crippled not only by inexperience but also by arrogance arising from failure to recognize its own limitations.... The problem was simply that the civilians would not accept military judgments."[37]

It was worse than that. McNamara brought civilians to the Defense Department, who became known as the "Whiz Kids." *The New York Times* described them as "downy-faced lads who seek pretentiously to ladle the fog of war with mathematically precise measuring cups." The worst were the "cost-effectiveness and operations analysts," bean counters concerned with every penny. "Some ... had been children when the generals and admirals they were arguing against had already fought two wars. Backed by their charts and slide-rule figures ... [they] challenged military assumptions about proper weapons, proper organization, and proper procedure."[38]

One staff officer said, "McNamara's arrogance was astonishing. He gave General Lemnitzer very short shrift and treated him like a schoolboy. The general almost stood at attention when he came into the room. Everything was 'yes, sir' and 'no, sir.'"[39] The worst change for the JCS was what became known as JFK's "yo-yo form of government," which assigned tasks to specially appointed civilian groups rather than the military as was previously done.[40]

Chief of Naval Operations Admiral Arleigh Burke complained, "Nearly all of these people were ardent, enthusiastic people without any experience whatever in administering anything, including the president. He'd always been in Congress. He'd never had any sort of job that required any administration.... They didn't understand ordinary administrative procedures, the necessity for having [a] line of communication and channels of command."[41]

As this author described in *It Did Not Start With JFK*, America was at a crossroads as Kennedy's inauguration approached. There was fear of a possible military takeover as more and more senior officers thought communism had infiltrated American politics at the highest levels. And the election of the liberal, wealthy, Catholic Senator from Massachusetts did nothing to mitigate their concerns. According to one account, "The presence of a benign and popular General of the Army [Eisenhower] in the White House had a calming influence on people and kept the Rightists' audiences small. John F. Kennedy's election buttressed their worst fears." Within weeks of the inauguration, retired vice admiral Ralph Wilson complained in a speech: "It seems in this Administration that you can't talk about limited war or Cold War or the realities of the Russian Menace."[42]

There developed a hatred for the young president as his term progressed. He was considered a socialist, and it was not just the military who felt that way. Arthur Schlesinger recalled years later that Kennedy had so isolated himself that disdain for him spread to include members of his administration. According to Schlesinger, there were three branches of government, but "it became apparent that there was a fourth branch: the Presidency itself.... By 1961, the tension between permanent government and the presidential government was deep in our system."

"The permanent government soon developed its own cozy alliances with committees of Congress, its own ties to the press, its own national constituencies," Schlesinger continued. "Presidents come and go, but it went on forever. [It] was politically neutral; its essential commitment was to doing [sic] things as they had been done before.... The Bay of Pigs ... was a clear consequence of the surrender of presidential government to a permanent government."[43]

What Schlesinger called the permanent government we would call the Deep State today. They shared Douglas MacArthur's belief that their allegiance was to the Constitution and the people of the United States, not to temporary residents of the White House. It was the Military-Industrial Complex in action, which Eisenhower had warned the nation about. This group did not take kindly to change, especially from a young, inexperienced president whom the people had miraculously voted into the highest office in the land.

Allen Dulles had sabotaged Eisenhower by revealing details to Castro about an internal military coup planned in Cuba in 1959. The CIA destroyed a nuclear test ban treaty summit between Eisenhower and Khrushchev with the U-2 incident in 1960. There were other examples of sabotage as well. Dulles's CIA was not averse to working against a sitting president when it suited the Deep State's agenda.

***

It did not take long for the CIA and the Deep State to sabotage Kennedy. On November 15, 1960, just seven days after he defeated Nixon, a secret internal CIA memo, only released to the public in 2005, was prepared for Richard Bissell, who, along with Allen Dulles, was scheduled to meet with the President-elect three days later at his Palm Beach, Florida home. The memo pertained to the proposed plan to remove Castro from power and was very pessimistic regarding the operation's chance of success. The original guerilla concept of secretly infiltrating Cuban exile paramilitary types into Cuba, who would join with an already established underground to create a general uprising in conjunction with the assassination of Cuba's leaders, was abandoned because they knew an internal uprising was not going to happen. A new approach conceived the week after the election included a World War II-type amphibious landing of Cuban exiles who would establish a beachhead, declare a provisional government, and request American assistance, which was when the U.S. military would enter the fray. A note pertaining to this stated, "There will not be the internal unrest earlier believed possible, nor will the defenses permit the type [of] strike first planned. Our second concept (a 1,500-3,000 man force to secure a beach with an airstrip) is also now seen to be unachievable, except as a joint Agency/DOD action." In other words, the CIA needed direct intervention from the military to succeed.[44]

When Dulles and Bissell met with Kennedy on November 18th, they handed him a 300-page document describing the Cuban operation, but they did not disclose the details of the internal memo.[45] The intent was to keep this intel from Kennedy, for undoubtedly, he would have canceled the operation had they told him it was doomed to fail without the U.S. military getting involved.

The Eisenhower administration discussed Cuba for the last time on November 24th, and it is unknown if the CIA told Ike their existing plan would not work. Eisenhower had probably not forgotten that Allen Dulles had kept him in the dark about Castro being a Communist until December 1958, shortly before he would overthrow Batista. It angered Ike then, but apparently, he still trusted the CIA because he wanted the operation to continue.[46]

By December 8, the CIA presented a revised plan to the 5412 Committee, better known as the Special Group, whose responsibility was to sign off on sensitive covert operations. It called for preliminary air strikes against Cuban military targets from Nicaragua, followed by an amphibious landing of Cuban exiles that would result in an anti-Castro populace uprising. The plan, which would become the Bay of Pigs invasion, was approved, but the CIA remained aware that they needed the military's involvement to succeed, and Ike was also mindful of that. On his last day in office, he told JFK he had a "responsibility" to do "whatever is necessary" in the Cuban operation.[47]

On December 21, Dulles met again with the Special Group to discuss the concerns of American business leaders with strong ties to Cuba, such as Freeport Sulphur, Standard Oil, Texaco, and International Telephone & Telegraph. They wanted someone like Batista to replace Castro, a friend of American big business. Allen Dulles felt the same way. It did not bode well for John Kennedy.[48]

***

The Joint Chiefs disapproved of the CIA's proposed Cuban operation. They wanted an all-out World War II-type invasion that would eliminate communism from the Western Hemisphere for good. They intended to obliterate Cuba with air and sea power, overwhelm the island with a massive ground force, and take over the country until the United States found a suitable replacement for Castro. The Soviets could overrun West Berlin in response, but that did not concern them. They welcomed a military confrontation with their Communist adversaries as well.[49]

However, at a January 22 meeting, Secretary of State Dean Rusk "commented on the enormous implications of putting U.S. forces ashore in Cuba and said we should consider everything short of this..." He worried that invading Cuba might trigger "Soviet and Chi[nese] Com[munist] moves in other parts of the world," an apparent reference to West Berlin, which was what worried Kennedy the most. When Richard Nixon told Bobby Kennedy to create a catalyst for invading Cuba, Kennedy replied that an invasion risked going to war with Russia over Berlin, and his priority had to be world peace. The next world war, Kennedy believed, would begin with hostilities over Berlin.[50]

President Kennedy met with General Lemnitzer and the Joint Chiefs five days after his inauguration, and they reiterated that the CIA's proposed plan was doomed to fail without military support. "The hope is to get a government in exile, then put some troops ashore, and have guerilla groups start their activities. At that point, we would come in and support them." A concerned JFK wanted specifics, so he called another meeting three days later that included Dulles, Lemnitzer, and other national security people. He asked the military and the CIA to review their plans for a Cuban invasion, which the CIA already knew would not work without military intervention. "We can confidently assert that the Agency had no intelligence evidence," read a CIA report, "that the Cubans in significant numbers could or would join the invaders or that there was any kind of an effective and cohesive resistance movement under anybody's control..."[51]

The State Department and the Kennedy brothers insisted that the person to replace Castro had to be someone who initially supported Castro's revolution, which was a deal breaker for Dulles and his big-business cohorts. They anticipated an operation that would force JFK to introduce the U.S. military and install a right-wing government in Cuba. The belief was if that were to fail, left in its wake would be a maligned President, sabotaged by Dulles, who U.S. intelligence could manipulate, just as they had done to Eisenhower.

Weeks after the Bay of Pigs, Allen Dulles said on Meet the Press: "A popular uprising? That's a popular misconception. But no, I wouldn't say we expected a popular uprising. We were expecting something else to happen in Cuba ... something that didn't materialize."[52]

Meanwhile, Lemnitzer had secretly written a fifty-two-page handwritten summary of the Joint Chief of Staff's opinion of the Bay of Pigs operation, called "The Cuban Debacle," which was discovered after his death. He quoted an internal secret Joint Chiefs report stating, "In view of the rapid buildup of the Castro Government's military and militia capability, and the lack of predictable future mass discontent, the possible success of the Para-Military Plan appears very doubtful." Despite this, before the invasion, Lemnitzer submitted a recommendation to Secretary of Defense Robert McNamara that supported the invasion. "Evaluation of the current plan results in a favorable assessment ... of the likelihood of achieving initial military success," Lemnitzer wrote, and "could contribute to the eventual overthrow of the Castro regime."[53]

Based on Lemnitzer's report, McNamara endorsed the operation, but why did the Joint Chiefs mislead the new administration? Did they believe that Kennedy would succumb to pressure and bring the military into the engagement to save face when things went badly, or did they want to humiliate Robert McNamara and the Kennedy administration on the world stage?

***

There was more to the Bay of Pigs operation than JFK was aware of, which may have been the "something else" Allen Dulles referred to during his *Meet the Press* interview. Richard Bissell alluded to it when he and Dulles briefed President-elect Kennedy on the Cuban operation. Bissell said they were "contemplating some form of 'significant strike force to act as a catalyst' in ultimately provoking an anti-Castro uprising on the island."[54] Assassinating Castro was one option, and that was in the works, but there was also something else. On January 11, the CIA told Brigadier General David W. Gray, the Joint Chief's liaison to the CIA and the FBI, that the invasion included a staged attack at the U.S. military base at Guantanamo Bay, three hundred miles to the southeast. A decoy ship called the *Santa Ana* was to transport one hundred sixty Cuban exiles wearing Cuban revolutionary army uniforms who would fake an attack against the U.S. base. The thought was it would force Kennedy to retaliate with the U.S. military. However, they canceled this part of the operation when the Cuban exiles on board refused to take part out of fear that Castro's soldiers were waiting on the beach to ambush them. So, the CIA and the Joint Chiefs' trump card to force Kennedy to intervene militarily was gone.[55]

In his book *First Hand Knowledge*, ex-CIA agent Robert Morrow discussed an earlier staged attack against Guantanamo while Eisenhower was still President. "This diversionary force," Morrow wrote, "was slated to land thirty miles east of the U.S. naval base at Guantanamo.... The men who comprised the diversionary force were trained in New Orleans by Sergio Arcacha Smith. Smith was the associate of New Orleans' Mafia leader Carlos Marcello and ex-FBI man Guy Banister."[56]

On December 3, 1960, Cuban State Security arrested more than forty exiles from this diversionary force. At their trial, an alleged CIA agent and Anti-Communist League of the Caribbean Head of Action and Sabotage testified that the CIA was involved in the fake attack. The Eisenhower administration broke relations with Cuba a few days later, and on January 3, 1961, the U.S. Embassy in Havana closed its doors.[57]

The Anti-Communist League of the Caribbean was the group radical right-wingers Guy Banister and Maurice Gatlin in New Orleans were associated with. Less than three weeks later, on January 20, 1961, Banister's Friends of a Democratic Cuba tried to purchase trucks from the New Orleans Bolton Ford car dealership using the name "Oswald" while Lee Oswald was still in the Soviet Union. Oswald would work out of Banister's office in the summer of 1963.[58]

In *The Hidden History of the JFK Assassination*, Lamar Waldon explained that familiar CIA figures who would later become suspects in the JFK assassination were involved in the diversionary attack at Guantanamo:

> As a backup to the CIA-Mafia [Castro assassination] plots, he [Allen Dulles] had CIA officers such as [David Atlee] Phillips begin a new plan that recycled the failed "fake Guantanamo attack" from December. While the vast majority of the CIA's Cuban exiles were being trained at secret camps in Guatemala, a CIA memo "routed to David Atlee Phillips" says a secret exile training base was set up eight miles from New Orleans at the "Belle Chasse training camp," located "at the US Naval Ammunition Depot." JFK was told that the exiles being trained there were for a "diversionary landing" force that would stage a decoy attack on Cuba, far from the main exile force...[59]

Robert Morrow alleged that New Orleans crime boss Carlos Marcello and Sergio Arcacha Smith were involved in the Bay of Pigs operation and that Marcello financed right-wing Cuban exile Mario Garcia Kohly's underground in Cuba. According to Morrow, Kohly was "one of the most illustrious members of Cuba's investment banking elite ... and financial representative to the international community at large and major American energy-related industries in particular."

Kohly thrived under Batista. Tracy Barnes was his CIA case officer, and he had solid right-wing connections to people like William Pawley, an American businessman with close ties to Latin American dictators, including Batista. Kohly was interested in becoming president of Cuba once Castro was gone, which was how he met with Vice President Richard Nixon in 1959. Kohly claimed to have an underground army of 42,000 counter-revolutionaries in Cuba who wanted to overthrow Castro. However, after Nixon lost to Kennedy in the 1960 presidential election, Kohly realized he was too far to the right to be part of the Cuban exile government approved by the Kennedy brothers to replace Castro if the Bay of Pigs invasion was successful. Still, not to be denied, Kohly and members of his underground, along with a right-wing segment within the CIA, formed Operation 40, an assassination group that intended to murder the liberal Cuban exile government when they arrived in Cuba so they could install Kohly as Castro's replacement.

That never materialized, but Kohly's dream to replace Castro never ended. In 1963, a financially troubled Kohly would turn to Meyer Lansky and Santo Trafficante for help in exchange for Cuban casino rights if he became president.[60] Kohly and Trafficante had known each other for years, and their names appear in Jean Pierre Lafitte's datebook, which means each man may have played a minor role in the JFK assassination conspiracy.[61]

The CIA's Howard Hunt and Bernard Barker became involved in the Bay of Pigs invasion plans in early 1961. Hunt worked with exile leaders such as Tony Varona and Manuel Artime, whom the Kennedy brothers favored. Varona also worked on the CIA-Mafia Castro assassination plots that involved Trafficante, Sam Giancana, and Johnny Roselli, and Barker worked for Trafficante as well.[62]

It took until 2006 for confirmation of Howard Hunt's CIA work with Roselli to become known, when former CIA Agent Bayard Stockton wrote, "In March 1961 Roselli went to the Dominican Republic, accompanied by Howard Hunt of the CIA." In 2006, Stockton, who had left the CIA and was a *Newsweek* bureau chief, wrote *Flawed Patriot*, a book about William Harvey, where he confirmed that Hunt worked with Roselli. The book was reviewed and approved by the CIA.[63]

David Ferrie was sitting in a courtroom in New Orleans with Carlos Marcello when JFK was assassinated. In 1963, both men had a relationship with Guy Banister and were involved in Cuban exile activities centering around

Banister's office at 544 Camp Street. Ferrie was close to Lee Harvey Oswald at the time, and there is evidence that Oswald was known to Marcello. In 1961, Ferrie reportedly flew missions to Cuba before the Bay of Pigs on behalf of former Batista Congressman and Santo Trafficante associate Eladio del Valle, and considering his relationship with Banister and Arcacha, one can assume Ferrie was involved in the Bay of Pigs invasion in some capacity. At the time, he was a pilot for Eastern Airlines and took a vacation from April 16, the day before the operation, until April 30.[64] According to Victor Marchetti, a one-time Executive Assistant to the Deputy Director of the CIA, David Ferrie was a contract agent for the Agency.[65]

Let's consider what happened during late 1960 and early 1961. The CIA suspected that Santo Trafficante was a double agent working for Castro while he was simultaneously involved in CIA attempts to assassinate the Cuban leader. Carlos Marcello was financing right-winger Kohly's underground and was close to Richard Nixon, who had ties to organized crime. Marcello had contributed to Nixon's 1960 presidential campaign, and other mobsters likely did as well. They were all connected to ex-Cuban President Carlos Prio through left-leaning Tony Varona and mobster Norman Rothman, who had run guns to Castro.

In March 1961, with the invasion less than a month away, Richard Bissell, one of the more liberal members of the CIA, ordered the removal of Howard Hunt from the operation and replaced the Frente, the Cuban government in exile, with the Cuban Revolutionary Council. The CRC turned out to be more to the left than the Frente was. Many in the exile community accused its members of being Communists, such as Manuel Ray, Castro's former Minister of Public Works, and Tony Varona, who was Secretary of War. Manuel Artime, Howard Hunt's close friend who was too conservative for the Frente and the CRC, managed to survive the transition by being named "Delegate in the Invading Army." He was responsible for leading the invasion, but the CRC restricted his usefulness to the battlefield alone. It did not grant him a position in the new government once they overthrew Castro.[66]

Then things got ugly. On April 4, Carlos Marcello was kidnapped by U.S. Customs officials and flown to Guatemala. He was out of the country during the Bay of Pigs invasion and was a non-factor in what transpired.[67] On April 10, the notorious Rolando Masferrer, Batista's El Tigre, was apprehended and placed under guard at Jackson Memorial Hospital in Miami. Secretary of State Dean Rusk wrote Robert Kennedy that, "The continued presence at large of Rolando Masferrer … is prejudicial to our national interest …

[and] revoking this alien's parole, deporting him, or restricting his presence at large, would accordingly advance our foreign policy objectives." The Justice Department quietly released Masferrer after the Bay of Pigs was over.[68]

Bobby had Masferrer arrested because he was involved in a plan to invade Cuba from the Dominican Republic involving the Mafia, and Trafficante and Marcello had visited there not long before. Such an attack would have forced Castro to retaliate and justified a U.S. military retaliation after the Dominican Republic asked the United States to intervene. Recall that Roselli and Howard Hunt had met in the Dominican in March 1961, so this staged attack scenario does have merit.

Batista partially financed the Masferrer Dominican plot, putting up two million dollars of his own money. When Cuban police arrested four plot members, the operation ended. However, the United States still considered Masferrer a dangerous operative whom the Kennedys needed to have in custody until the Bay of Pigs operation was over. They wanted nothing to do with the ex-Batista henchman.[69]

William Pawley advised the CIA that Castro agents in Miami had offered a police officer $200,000 to help kidnap Masferrer, whom they intended to kill. In an interview with the FBI in 1960, Masferrer said Tony Varona was working for Castro and "was waging a private war against Cuban exiles." The importance of Varona, who would become one of Bobby Kennedy's boys in 1963, will become apparent as our narrative moves forward.[70]

Meanwhile, the U.S. military was ready if called upon. During the Bay of Pigs, one aircraft carrier and seven destroyers, with a combined five thousand sailors on board and two thousand Marines, stayed just beyond the horizon, waiting for authorization to engage. An additional twenty naval ships conducted routine training operations off Guantanamo.

Just days before the invasion, according to General Gray, several chiefs had doubts "about the absolute essentiality of air cover," which could not have been further from the truth. They told the President this, which was probably why, less than twenty-four hours before the D-2 airstrikes, Kennedy told Bissell to cut the number of planes to be employed, and Bissell reduced the number from sixteen to eight. Then, on the evening of April 16, the day before the scheduled amphibious landing of Cuban exile troops was to occur, Kennedy objected again. According to Secretary of State Dean Rusk, who was on the phone with JFK that night, the President was surprised "there were additional air strikes coming up" and said, "I'm not signed onto this."[71] So, that night, with Brigade 2056 just hours away from landing at the Bay of Pigs, Kennedy canceled the airstrikes when it was too late to call off the operation. At 2:00 A.M., just hours before the invasion commenced, General Lemnitzer was told of the change. "It was almost criminal," he said.[72]

On April 16, eight B-26 bombers with Cuban markings attacked Cuba but destroyed only five of Castro's three dozen combat planes, leaving the invasion force vulnerable to aerial attack. Castro's fighters sank two freighters loaded with ammunition and supplies.[73] At 5:00 A.M. on the morning of April 18, Rusk and Cabell phoned the President, asking for permission to introduce aircraft from the *USS Essex* to stabilize the situation. This time, Cabell spoke directly to President Kennedy, who said no. It doomed the operation.[74]

*****

During the Bay of Pigs invasion, Allen Dulles was giving a speech in San Juan, Puerto Rico. His absence from Washington was to distance himself from an operation that was bound to fail. Meanwhile, Khrushchev sent a threatening letter to Kennedy on April 18, the day after the invasion began. "Military armament and the world political situation are such at this time that any so-called 'little war' can touch off a chain reaction in all parts of the globe." He was referring to West Berlin. "There should be no mistake about our position: We will render the Cuban people and their government all necessary help to repel armed attack on Cuba."[75]

Kennedy did not know that Khrushchev feared the invasion had been staged by the CIA to sabotage the upcoming meeting between the two world leaders, just as they had done the year before with Eisenhower. He was probably right.[76]

On the domestic front, the fallout from the failed operation was immediate. The invasion "would have succeeded," wrote William Pawley, "had the Administration not made the terrible mistake of judgment in canceling the bomber strike on the Havana airport." Pawley told Eisenhower, "The hostile air was permitted to operate freely and succeeded in sinking our principal supply ship ... [and] [American] airplanes based on the carrier were over the attacking ships at the proper time but were recalled by the Admiral on what were said to be "orders from the White House."[77]

According to his wife, the CIA's Tracy Barnes was "sick at heart" with what transpired. "He was very bitter about how it happened – about the Kennedys." His brother said, "he thought he had been betrayed. He felt let down very seriously."[78] Many people at the CIA felt the same way.

President Kennedy was also affected. Supreme Court Justice William Douglas said, "This episode seared him. He had experienced the extreme power that these groups had, these various insidious influences of the CIA and the Pentagon on civilian policy, and I think it raised in his own mind the specter: Can Jack Kennedy, President of the United States, ever be strong enough to really rule these two powerful agencies? I think it had a profound effect ... it shook him up!"[79]

At a White House meeting arranged by Eisenhower, William Pawley lectured JFK that it was not too late to send Marines into Cuba. "I don't intend to spill one drop of American blood in connection with this matter," an angry JFK responded. Kennedy said American business had exploited the island, causing suffering that exceeded every other country in the Western Hemisphere, leaving no doubt where he stood.[80]

JFK formed the Cuban Study Group just days after the failed invasion to learn what went wrong. General Maxwell Taylor, forced out of the previous administration for criticizing Ike's emphasis on nuclear weapons, was called out of retirement to join Robert Kennedy, Allen Dulles, and Admiral Arleigh Burke to conduct a complete investigation. Privately, Kennedy told friends he wanted "to splinter the CIA into a thousand pieces and scatter it to the winds." "I made a mistake," JFK said, "in putting Bobby in the Justice Department ... Bobby should be in CIA..."[81]

The mandate for the Cuban Study Group is in the instructions Kennedy gave Taylor at the onset of the investigation, which was "to study our governmental practices and programs in the areas of military and paramilitary guerrilla and antiguerrilla [sic] activity which fell short of outright war with a view of strengthening our work in this area."[82]

Taylor submitted his report on June 13, and it blamed the CIA for the debacle, which suited the President just fine, for part of the commission's role was to deflect blame away from the White House. However, if Kennedy planned to destroy the CIA, Taylor wanted to wrest control of peacetime warfare operations away from the Agency and give that responsibility to the military. The report of the Cuban Study Group was primarily his work, and it stated, "We are in a life and death struggle," recognizing the inherent danger in allowing the CIA to run unchecked.

Counterinsurgency was how President Kennedy wanted to wage war in an era where a traditional confrontation could lead to nuclear war. Even limited conventional warfare was an option he would not entertain. At his first NSC meeting in February 1961, Kennedy told Robert McNamara to instruct the Pentagon to put more emphasis on counterinsurgency despite their objections.[83]

It was not in the military's character to consider anything but an all-out offensive, which is how they responded to the Bay of Pigs Commission.

According to Lemnitzer, the problem was decisions were made "without consulting or informing the JCS ... [they] then blamed the JCS because things went badly."[84]

The Bay of Pigs failure gave Maxwell Taylor a chance to shift unconventional warfare into the arms of the military, who knew Southeast Asia was where the next great showdown would be. In the meantime, respect for the young, inexperienced President was hard to find in the halls of Washington. Those who believed JFK threatened the security of the United States thought he had to be reined in, perhaps by resorting to sabotage again to embarrass him into submission. But the clock was ticking, and the time would come when sabotage would be considered inadequate.

The war against Castro was a mess in 1961. The Kennedy brothers wanted a left-wing Cuban exile government to replace Castro. At the same time, businessmen like Mario Garcia Kohly and William Pawley, and the right-wing ex-Batistaite Cuban exiles and American mercenaries they supported, wanted Cuba to return to what it was in the 1950s under Batista. The military was only interested in an all-out Normandy-type invasion, while the CIA wanted to maintain control with military support. And all the while, Khrushchev threatened to advance on West Berlin if the United States did not back off.

Chapter Two

The Defector Who Wasn't

Almost immediately after arriving in the Soviet Union on October 16, 1959, Lee Harvey Oswald told Rima Shirokova, the Intourist Guide assigned to keep an eye on him in Moscow, that he wanted to defect and become a Russian citizen. Five days later, the Soviet Union rejected his request, and he allegedly slit his wrist just before Rima arrived at his hotel room with those who were to escort him out of the country. It is the official story of what happened, but most likely untrue. Why would the Soviets release a Marine radar operator who had monitored U-2 flights and wanted to share classified information? It was probably a cover story to hide the fact that the Soviets had secreted him away to find out what he knew.

Oswald was placed in Botkin Hospital for a week, nursing his superficial wrist wound. Oleg Nechiporenko, an ex-KGB official who would meet Oswald in Mexico City in 1963, wrote in his book, *Passport to Assassination*, that "there was one other American in Ward no.7, who was often visited by his friend, an employee of the American Embassy. The latter used to ask Oswald if he had registered with the Embassy and what had happened to him, but Oswald said little. On one occasion, someone called from the Embassy and asked when he would be released."[85] If true, the American Embassy was already aware of Oswald's presence in Moscow before he visited them, and this must have concerned the Soviets. In a 1993 PBS Frontline documentary, a former hospital employee recalled that the KGB came to the hospital just before Oswald's discharge. They confiscated his medical records and whisked him away to "study him further."[86] On October 31, two weeks after his arrival, Oswald appeared at the American Embassy and announced his intention to defect.

The FBI responded by opening a security file on Oswald. They reported that "a stop was placed in the files of the Identification Division of the FBI on November 10, 1959, to alert us in the event... [that Oswald] returned under a different identity, and his fingerprints were received." On June 30, 1960, J. Edgar Hoover sent a memo alerting all FBI offices that "there is a possibility someone is using Oswald's birth certificate." By October, the FBI's "Legat, Paris" sent a memorandum to FBI headquarters in Washington that an investigation into Albert Schweitzer College, which was Oswald's intended destination, found that "there is no record of a person possibly identical with the subject [Oswald] who is registered for the [fall] courses beginning October 2." The wording used was intentionally cryptic and referred to a person identical to Oswald, which meant it was not necessarily him. The possibility of an Oswald impostor was a concern from the beginning.[87]

Colonel Philip J. Corso, a retired Army Intelligence officer working for the National Security Council under Eisenhower, told author Dick Russell he first discussed the possibility of an Oswald imposter with Assistant Director of the FBI William Sullivan, who was "a close friend of mine from my White House days." Sullivan told Corso that a phony defector named Oswald had gone to Russia as part of an operation run by Naval Intelligence. Then, while working on Senator Russell's investigation after the assassination, Corso was told by Robert Johnson, Deputy Director of the US Passport Division, that "We found out that there was a fake passport circulating also, which matched up with the birth certificate of a Lee Harvey Oswald who was in the Soviet Union..."[88]

The Oswald impostor concerns continued into 1961. On March 31, Edward J. Hickey, Deputy Chief of the Passport Office, in a letter to the Consular Section of the State Department, noted that there was "an impostor using Oswald's ID data and that no doubt the Soviets would love to get hold of his valid passport." By this time, the wheels were already in motion for Oswald's return to the U.S. The Embassy heeded Hickey's advice and agreed not to return Oswald's passport to him unless he appeared at the Embassy in person. Note that Hickey did not say someone might have been posing as Oswald. He definitively wrote that an impostor was using Oswald's ID data.

By July, Secretary of State Dean Rusk got involved as well. He wrote the Embassy in Moscow that "careful attention to the involved case of Mr. Oswald is appreciated. It is assumed that the person who has been in communication with the Embassy is the person who was issued a passport in the name of Lee Harvey Oswald."[8990]

The Oswald impostor scenario was a clever ruse perpetrated by U.S. intelligence to make it appear the Soviets had killed Oswald and a Russian impostor had taken his place. It was an operation that had nothing to do with the JFK assassination, at least not at the time of Oswald's defection. The real Oswald went to Russia and returned, apparently 2" shorter than the man who left, making it appear that a Russian "sleeper agent" had as-

37

sumed his identity. The Department of Defense ID card Oswald was issued when he left the Marines said his height was 5'-11", and he listed 5'-11" on both his passport and his Albert Schweitzer College application. However, the photos on the DOD ID card and his passport were of two different people, which added to the intrigue. We will discuss this further as we move forward.

Oswald left his passport at the U.S. embassy in Moscow and did not ask for it until he was ready to return home. Meanwhile, two reporters interviewed him. The first was Aline Mosby, who recorded his height as 5'-9". The second was the CIA-connected Priscilla Johnson, who wrote he was 5'-11".

After he returned to the United States, Oswald gave his height as 5'-9" on seven job applications and, on November 9, 1963, a driver's license application. On August 9, 1963, the police arrested him in New Orleans for handing out FPCC literature and measured him as 5'-9". The next day, FBI agent Quigley interviewed Oswald at the police station and also recorded his height as 5'-9", as did his autopsy report. The only time Oswald listed his height as 5'-11" was when he renewed his passport, which had to match the height on the original. So, the documented record showed that the Oswald who left the Marines and defected to the Soviet Union was 5'-11", and the man who returned was 5'-9". After the assassination, this did not go unnoticed by the FBI and CIA.

Eight days after Oswald's murder, the FBI went to Harris Hospital in Fort Worth to examine Oswald's early medical history. They learned he required surgery for acute mastoiditis of the left ear at age six, but there was no mention of the scars or bone removal in Oswald's post-mortem report. The CIA was also concerned, and on February 18, 1964, Richard Helms sent a memo to the FBI asking if there was any "evidence acceptable to the [Warren] Commission that he did, in fact, attempt suicide by cutting his wrist." Helms said they should exhume the body if necessary.

A week later, two Dallas FBI agents contacted C.J. Price, the Administrator at Parkland Memorial Hospital. Price said, "he failed to observe any scar on Oswald's wrist."[91] FBI agents Manning Clements and Tom Carter then spoke with autopsy doctor Earl Rose, who could not provide proof that the 5'-9" tall man he examined was Lee Harvey Oswald. A Warren Commission memo dated March 13, 1964, written by W. David Slawson two days after the FBI agents visited Dr. Rose, read: "The CIA is interested in the scar on Oswald's left wrist … the FBI is reluctant to exhume Oswald's body as requested by the CIA."

The bottom line is there appeared to be two Oswalds, and the FBI and the CIA could not explain how that was possible. As we will see, beginning in Mexico City in September 1963, up to the JFK assassination, there looked to be two Oswalds roaming around, and the authorities were puzzled by it all.

***

When Lee and Marina Oswald traveled to Moscow from Minsk in 1961 as a prelude to their return to the U.S., Lee looked up a person named in his address book whom he had first met when he arrived in 1959. After the assassination, FBI agents Heitman and Griffin asked Marina about him, and she said Oswald told her his name was Leo Setyaev, "a man who had helped him make some money ... by assisting him in a broadcast for Radio Moscow..."[92]

On June 24, 1960, HT/LINGUAL, the CIA's illegal mail opening program run by James Angleton, intercepted a letter addressed to Leo Setyaev from Charles John Pageenhardt. A May 1964 CIA report on the "Oswald" case referenced the letter. It said that Setyaev's name was in Oswald's address book and that Pagenhardt had "contemplated defecting to the USSR." And according to the same CIA document, "Setyaev and Pagenhardt are known to the FBI."[93]

Furthermore, in the summer of 1963, New Orleans police lieutenant Francis Martello interviewed Oswald after the police arrested him. Martello later told the Warren Commission that Oswald left a piece of paper for him to find. "This piece of paper, which was folded over twice and was about 2" x 3" in size, contained some English writing and some writing which appeared to me to be in a foreign language which I could not identify...." The paper had street addresses for relatives in Dallas and New Orleans on one side, but Russian writing on the back included the name "Leo Setyaev." Oswald had told Martello he wanted to speak to the FBI, and he knew the name Setyaev would be recognizable to them. It was a clue that he was working undercover in New Orleans, and he wanted the FBI to know that. Oswald did the same thing by stamping Guy Banister's address inside the pamphlet Crimes Against Cuba, which he gave to the FBI that same summer. It leads one to believe that Leo Setyaev was a U.S. intelligence asset told to contact Oswald when he arrived in Moscow.[94]

***

On January 7, 1960, the Soviets flew Oswald to Minsk, where he vanished from sight. Despite his mother's frantic effort to locate him, the FBI, the State Department, and U.S. intelligence could not confirm his whereabouts, and we depend on his diary to learn what his life there was like. The diary's validity is questionable since there are inconsistencies, and handwriting experts believe Oswald wrote it in one or two sessions at least one year later. However, we can still assume that the essential facts are accurate.

Arriving in Minsk, Oswald became attracted to an Intourist guide named Rosa, a pretty, twenty-three-year-old blonde. He was met by the mayor the following day and given a rent-free apartment. By Soviet standards, it was luxurious, with a private balcony overlooking the city. He was assigned work at a radio and television factory, where his salary, coupled with money he received from the Soviet government, earned him as much as the factory director.[95]

Rosa regularly tutored Oswald in Russian after work. "At night I take Rosa to theater, movie or operor [sic] almost every day," he wrote in his diary. I'm living very big and am very satisfied."[96] Meanwhile, according to what Eduard Shirkovsky, former KGB Chief of the Byelorussian Republic, told the newspaper *Investia* in August 1992, the KBG had conducted a detailed study of Oswald's personality and kept him under constant surveillance.[97] Perhaps that was why, by May Day, 1960, Oswald began to reconsider his decision to defect. His factory manager, Alexander Ziger, told him "to go back to the United States. It's the first voice of opposition I have heard...I feel inside, it's true!!" Later, he wrote, "As my Russian improves, I become increasingly conscious of just what sort of society I live in ... I am starting to reconsider my desire about staying."[98]

Around this time, the Soviets shot down the U-2 plane piloted by Francis Gary Powers. Oswald officially never left Minsk, but he wrote his brother Robert in February 1961 that Powers "seemed to be a nice, bright American-type fellow when I saw him in Moscow." In addition, two Intourist guides who had met Oswald when he first arrived told a writer for the *Saturday Review* that they had bought him a fur cap to get through the cold winter months, but "when they saw him again in Moscow several months later, he completely ignored them – didn't even speak to them."[99]

After the assassination, the *Miami Herald* reported that "the only possession of Lee Harvey Oswald not confiscated by government agents ... was an English, Russian dictionary in which numerous words were marked or copied, including a phrase meaning 'to hit or kill at a distance.'" "It hasn't been checked out for microdots or anything," said former sheriff's chief Deputy John Cullins. Marina gave Cullins the book and confirmed the handwriting and markings were Lee's. She had not noticed the handwritten practice words in the book until Cullins asked her to translate. Words like "radar" and "range," "eject," "razor," and "radar locator" are in Oswald's handwriting, and a definition of "range" is underlined and written in Russian as "to beat, hit kill at a definite distance."[100]

Did Oswald provide the Soviets with information related to the U-2? He may have hinted at this when he wrote, "After [the] death of Stalin and peace reaction, then anti-Stalin reaction. A peace movement leading up to the Paris conference. The U-2 incident and its aftermath." It may not have been a coincidence that Oswald's desire to return to the United States began after the Soviets shot down Powers' plane.[101]

In June, back in Minsk, Oswald fell in love with coworker Ella German and proposed marriage on New Year's Day 1961, but she rejected him because he was an American. A few days later, Oswald told the passport office in Minsk that he no longer wanted to become a Soviet citizen. Still, they extended his resident permit for another year.[102]

According to his friend Ernst Titovet, Oswald, who supported everything Russian in the Marines at El Toro, was now " proud of his service with the US Marines.... He would defend the American Army, American English, American girls, American food, and American ways – you name it."[103]

In mid-March, over two months after being rejected by Ella German and turning down an offer of Russian citizenship, Oswald "accidentally" met nineteen-year-old Marina Prusakova at a trade union dance. She recalled years later that he spoke Russian exceptionally well, which was unlikely unless he had received formal training in the Marines. It is also curious that Marina, who had been living with her uncle, a colonel in the MVD (Soviet Ministry of Internal Affairs) since 1959, had not heard about the only American who resided in Minsk.

A friend named Yuri Merezhinsky introduced them. Yuri's mother, Lydia Cherkasova, was a professor and biochemistry department chair at the State University of the Soviet Republic of Belarus. She headed the Laboratory of Radiation Research of the Science Academy. His father was also a professor, and both parents were members of the Communist Party. Cherkasova was important enough to accompany Khrushchev to the 15th General Assembly of the United Nations in New York City, the occasion when he banged the table with his shoe.

At the dance, Cherkasova gave a presentation on her trip to the United States, and Oswald helped Merezhinsky operate the slide projector. He was already briefed about Oswald, and the KGB may have instructed him to direct Oswald to the orchestra pit after the lecture, where he ran into

41

Marina. After they talked, Oswald went to a party at Cherkasova's home and walked Marina to her flat afterward, which was nearby. Cherkasova was very friendly to Lee, and he was a regular guest at her house. When Titovets interviewed her years later, she made no secret that she was in close contact with the KGB at the time.[104]

Titovets believes the KGB told Marina to contact Oswald because she had loose morals and was having sex with numerous men. After the Soviet Union collapsed, Titovets interviewed Yuri Merezhinsky about her. He "knew foreigners in Leningrad from where she had been deported for prostitution ... she would be with one guy, then with another one and another." "She had a pretty face and an empty head. Nothing else. She was mostly after men."[105]

Shortly after meeting Marina, Oswald was again admitted into a hospital, this time for an adenoid operation. Hospital records claim he stayed for a simple procedure from March 30 until April 11, a suspiciously long time. Marina allegedly visited him every day, and during one of her visits, Oswald proposed marriage. On April 30, they were married.[106]

Oswald proposed to three women in roughly three months and married Marina even though they hardly knew each other. In his book *KGB*, John Barron explained that it was common for the Soviets to arrange such marriages. He described the ordeal of an American named James Mintenbaugh, whom the Soviets had recruited to spy for them:

> "In Moscow the KGB settled Mintenbaugh in a pleasant third-floor apartment attended by an elderly housekeeper.... Initially his routine and training differed little from that of numberless other agents spirited to Moscow from throughout the world. Instructors came daily to indoctrinate him in the use of drops, microdots, invisible writing, photography, recognition signals, surveillance, and the Morse code.

"Midway through his third week in Moscow, Mintenbaugh ... [was asked] if he would be willing to marry and live with a female illegal, whom the KGB wished to station in the United States. Such professional marriages provide the female partner with the cover of a housewife and, by relieving her of the necessity of earning an income, make her almost entirely free for clandestine work. But there also are disadvantages. The normal tensions and conflicts that sometimes develop between a man and a woman have disrupted marital teams of illegals. There is also the danger that the man and woman will actually fall in love and become more concerned with the pursuit of their life together than with their secret duties. The KGB evidently reasoned that both risks could be averted by a marriage involving a homosexual husband."[107]

The CIA was concerned, and in the wake of the assassination, an internal memo written by an operative revealed that "at that time, I was becoming increasingly interested in watching develop a pattern that we had discovered in the course of our bio and research work: the number of Soviet women marrying foreigners, being permitted to leave the USSR, then eventually divorcing their spouses and settling down abroad without returning home. The [redacted] case was among the first of these, and we eventually turned up something like two dozen similar cases ... It was out of curiosity to learn if Oswald's wife would actually accompany him to our country, partly out of Oswald's own experience in the USSR, that we showed ... intelligence interest in the Harvey story."[108]

What worried the CIA were aspects of Marina's story that were difficult to accept. Regarding a vacation she claimed to have taken before meeting Oswald, a CIA memo reported, "It is almost impossible for her to have quit and gone on vacation so easily.... She would have been in trouble immediately..." In 1962, after Lee and Marina returned to the United States, the CIA intercepted a letter sent to Marina from a friend in Leningrad named Ella Soboleva. A check of the address revealed that Igor Sobolev, an agent of the First Chief Directorate, resided there. Also in 1962, the FBI intercepted a letter from Marina to the Soviet Embassy in Washington to advise them she had changed her address. It was a routine correspondence, were it not that Marina wrote the letter to Vitaley Gerasimov, who, according to CIA records, was "known to have participated in clandestine meetings in this country and to have made payments for intelligence information of value to the Soviets." Finally, Marina's birth certificate stated she was born in Severodvinsk, but the town wasn't called that until 1957.[109]

The questions surrounding Marina were troubling, but none more than a vacation she took at a government "Rest Home" in the fall of 1960, where she met a man named Lev Prizentsev, whose address was in Marina's address book after the assassination. The CIA checked the name and came up empty, but his address, "Kondrat'yevskiy Prospkt 63, Apt.7, Leningrad," was cause for concern. As the CIA noted afterward: "Robert E. Webster, who renounced his U.S. citizenship in 1959 when he defected to the U.S.S.R. and who returned to the U.S. as an alien under the Sov quota in May 1962, claimed to have resided in a three-room apartment at Kondrat'yevskiy Prospekt 63, Apt. 18, Leningrad, during his stay in the U.S.S.R."[110]

Webster was an American defector whose story paralleled Oswald's. That Marina would marry Oswald shortly after being interested in a man who allegedly lived in the same apartment building as the defector Webster was a coincidence that is difficult to accept.

The book *The Secret War* tells the story of Nora Murray, "a Russian woman who eventually married a diplomat she was to seduce. She had a room at the Hotel Metropole and was told to contact different diplomats. After Stalin's death, the use of these girls was abolished, although the secret police still kept lists of available women for this type of work."[111]

Was Marina directed to seek out both Webster and Oswald? After the assassination, an acquaintance claimed Marina said her husband had defected after working at an American exhibition in Moscow. Incredibly, that defector was Webster, not Oswald.[112]

Just two weeks before Oswald defected, Robert Webster did the same. A Quaker and former Navy man, Webster was in Moscow working on an exhibit with his employer, the Rand Development Corporation. He claimed his decision was for ideological reasons only, but others pointed to a waitress he had a relationship with. Webster asked permission to return to the United States within a year, which he did in 1962, a month before Oswald.

The Ford Foundation supplied the funding to create the Rand Corporation in 1948, and by 1959, it was a CIA think tank. Headquartered in California, its security was more sensitive than that of the Pentagon. When Webster appeared at the U.S. embassy in Moscow to announce his intention to defect, the company's president, Henry Rand, and a senior company official, George Bookbinder, accompanied him. Both men were World War II OSS veterans.[113]

Oswald and Webster supposedly did not know each other, but Oswald "asked about the fate of a young man named Webster" when he contacted the U.S. embassy regarding his return home. Interestingly, the Rand Corporation had long researched mind control and hypnosis techniques by the time Webster and Oswald defected. The CIA applied these practices to agents behind the Iron Curtain, and Oswald was probably involved in such a program while stationed at Atsugi Air Base in Japan (see *It Did Not Start With JFK, Volume Two*). In *The Man Who Knew Too Much*, Dick Russell explained Rand's interest in mind control:

> "In defensive applications, subjects can be specifically selected by a criterion of hypnotizability, and subsequently trained in accord with their anticipated military function.... Personnel entrusted with particularly sensitive material could be prepared against possible cap-

ture in many different ways: (a) by simple hypnotic suggestion, they could be 'immunized' against hypnotic interrogation and suggestion by the enemy; (b) with posthypnotic and autosuggestive training, appropriately timed amnesias could be induced; (c) posthypnotic depersonalization and related dissociative states could be built into the subjects so that if they fall into enemy hands, they would no longer function as rational, integrated individuals..."[114]

The specter of mind control drugs and hypnosis hovered over Oswald's defection. The military and intelligence communities were convinced mind control was a viable method of countering Soviet interrogation techniques, which could have been why they sent Oswald, Webster, and others to Russia.

***

There were other signs from the Soviet Union suggesting Oswald was sent there by U.S. intelligence. Ella German told journalist Peter Wronski in a 1991 interview that Oswald "said that he used to get some letters from his cousin. He received a package of books, he told me once. I said, 'Why not with things?' He said, 'No, the customs duty is very expensive here. And on books there is no customs duty.'"[115]

The cousin referred to was probably Marilyn Dorothea Murret. Murret worked with Harold Issacs, who specialized in the study of worldwide youth movements at the CIA-connected Center for International Studies at MIT. Isaacs was a Trotskyist and proponent of worldwide revolution, which would have interested the CIA's Cord Meyer. Still, he told the FBI he no longer adhered to such a radical philosophy by the time he began working at the MIT Center. Maybe so, but Oswald also considered himself a Trotskyite, so there likely was a connection here.

In 1970, a misfiled FBI document dated May 22, 1964, titled "MARILYN DOROTHEA MURRET," was inadvertently released. It did not contain a word about Murret. Instead, although related to the JFK assassination, it dealt exclusively with Harold Issacs. Another FBI document stated that "Murret was linked in some manner with the ... apparatus of Professor Harold Issacs."

At the time Oswald defected to the Soviet Union, Murret left the United States by steamer for Japan on an adventure of her own. She intended to work her way around the world working as a schoolteacher, which offered the perfect cover for a covert assignment. She returned to the United States in January 1963 after spending three and one-half years overseas, teaching in Japan and visiting Hawaii, Hong Kong, Australia, New Zealand, Singapore, Thailand, India, Iran, the Holy Land, and England. She was mysteriously detained for twelve hours in East Berlin but was eventually released.[116]

After the assassination, President Johnson ordered several agencies to investigate other defectors and a list of 137 names that included the "Ten Most Wanted" was compiled. Journalist Paul Scott said he saw the list, and Dorothy Murret's name was one of the top ten. Scott and fellow journalist Robert S. Allen wrote about it in their *Oakland Tribune* syndicated column on March 23, 1964. The Warren Commission ignored the column, and they never asked Murret about it when she testified before them. The FBI never questioned Murret about it either, but they were concerned enough to interview Scott and Allen to find out what they knew.[117]

We do not know if the allegation that Murret was a defector was accurate. However, in 1966, she planned to travel to Haiti and Santo Domingo for a "vacation." Frances G. Knight, director of the Passport Office in Washington, D.C., wrote to the CIA's Deputy Director of Plans asking for "any information of a security nature which may come to your attention concerning the individual (Murret) mentioned in the attached memoranda." Three years after the assassination, Murret was still a person of interest, which one would typically consider unusual. Perhaps it was because she was traveling to Haiti. As we will see, a lot was going on in Haiti in 1963 that had something to do with the JFK assassination.[118]

The books sent to Oswald by his cousin may have been a means of transmitting hidden messages. Found among Oswald's possessions after the assassination was a book written in Russian titled *Glaza Kotorye Sprashivayut*, from which someone had removed several letters on page 152. The National Security Agency examined the book and could not explain the reason for this. A possibility is that it was a coded message, which may have also applied to the books Oswald received from his cousin. On another occasion, Oswald gave his friend in Minsk a book but quickly pulled back the cover to razor out a dedication on the corner of the first page.[119]

In August 1961, three women, Rita Naman, Monica Kramer, and Marie Hyde, toured the Soviet Union by car. After the women returned to the U.S., the CIA asked if they could inspect the 150 photographs taken during their trip, and they made copies of five photos, which were placed in their "Graphic Register." After the assassination, investigators discovered that Oswald was in one of the photos standing next to a car in a public square in Minsk. The CIA maintained this was merely a coincidence, but the women said they encountered Oswald twice in two different cities. The odds of that happening and the CIA arbitrarily saving one photograph of Oswald long before the assassination were astronomical unless it was by design.[120]

Oswald's encounter with the three women occurred only one month after Secretary of State Dean Rusk wrote the Embassy in Moscow, stating, "It is assumed that the person who has been in communication with the Embassy is the person who was issued a passport in the name of Lee Harvey Oswald."[121] Author Anthony Summers contacted one of the women, Rita Naman. She explained that she and her friend, Monica Kramer, were in Moscow with their Intourist Guide when a young American they later discovered was Oswald approached them. They conversed through the car window, and Oswald prevented them from leaving. Finally, the Intourist guide became agitated and insisted they move along.

While still in Moscow, an older woman named Marie Hyde befriended Naman and Kramer. She had become separated from her tour group and asked if she could travel with them for the remainder of their trip. The three next traveled to Minsk, where a Soviet official accused them of being more than ordinary tourists. After an intense interrogation, they were allowed to leave, and they reencountered Oswald once again, 400 miles from where they had first met in Moscow.[122]

After the trio crossed the border into Poland, the same Soviet official they had encountered in Minsk questioned them again. Their car was "virtually taken apart." Hyde was separated from the other two and questioned privately by Polish officials, indicating they were more concerned with her.

It seems likely that Hyde was trying to establish contact with Oswald and purposely photographed him. By this time, Oswald had already written the Embassy in Moscow with a request to return to the United States. As described above, American authorities were trying to verify that it was the real Oswald who had contacted the Embassy. He had been living in Minsk for a long time in virtual obscurity, and the FBI and State Department were concerned that an impostor may have assumed his identity.

***

On January 21, 1961, less than one month before Oswald wrote to the Embassy in Moscow requesting to return to the U.S., his mother, Marguerite, traveled to Washington. She was concerned because she had not heard from her son in over a year. She suspected Lee was a government agent and demanded to see Secretary of State Dean Rusk. Two days later, right on cue, Oswald wrote to her from Minsk. On March 22, she received a letter from the State Department "informing me . . . that my son wishes to return to the United States." Five weeks after that, he married Marina. The timing of everything was quite suspicious.[123] A concerned Lee Oswald also began writing to his brother once again. In a

May 31, 1961, letter, he told Robert, "I can't say whether I will ever get back to the States or not if I can get the government to drop charges against me and get the Russians to let me out with my wife then maybe I'll be seeing you again...." He wrote Robert again on June 26: "I assume the government must have a few charges against me since my coming here like that is illegal. But I really don't know exactly what charges."[124]

In July, Lee and Marina traveled to Moscow because the State Department and the Passport Office wanted to ensure he was not an impostor before returning his passport. While there, Oswald again tries to contact Leo Setyaev, but it is unknown if he was successful.[125]

Oswald visited the U.S. Embassy, and on July 11, Richard Snyder wrote Washington that "Oswald indicated some anxiety as to whether, should he return to the United States, he would face possible lengthy imprisonment for his act of remaining in the Soviet Union... [Oswald] felt that in his own interest, he could not go back to the United States if it meant returning to a number of years in prison, and had delayed approaching the Soviet authorities ... until he 'had this end of the thing straightened out.'"[126] The State Department replied the same day but ignored Oswald's concerns: "It is assumed that there is no doubt that the person who has been in communication with the Embassy is the person who was issued a passport in the name of Lee Harvey Oswald."[127]

Unknown to Oswald, the Russians were reading his mail from Minsk and not forwarding everything he wrote to the American Embassy in Moscow. Oswald's letter of February 13 was the first the Embassy received from him. It stated, "Since I have not received a reply to my letter of December 1960, I am writing again asking that you consider my request for the return of my American passport." After the assassination, Marina told the FBI Oswald "had told her he had written the American Embassy letters about returning to the United States, and they had not answered the letters..."[128]

Snyder replied to Oswald on February 28, 1961: "We have received your letter concerning your desire to return to the United States. Your earlier letter of December 1960...does not appear to have been received at the Embassy." Oswald believed the U.S. embassy was ignoring him, but the Russians purposely did not forward the letter. So, they were aware of what he intended to do. Then, a couple of weeks later, Marina entered the picture. We must assume she married Oswald at the behest of the Soviets so she could get to the United States as possibly a sleeper agent. Still, the American plan was to make it appear the Russians had killed Oswald and replaced him with an impostor, so they played right into the hands of U.S. intelligence.

By January 1962, the wheels were in motion for Lee and Marina to return to the U.S. Oswald wrote two letters to the International Rescue Committee (IRC), asking "that it contact the American Embassy in Moscow in order to contribute financial assistance for his trip home." The IRC was initially known as the Emergency Rescue Committee during World War II when Allen Dulles had established it to help Nazis come to the United States and as a cover to place agents in Eastern Europe to gather intelligence.[129] The Warren Commission was sufficiently concerned that they contacted the IRC, and their Director sent a defensive letter to Warren Commission counsel Lee Rankin on May 1, 1964, explaining the organization was "strongly anti-communist." However, they did not explain how Oswald could have known about the IRC and what they did. He even knew their Park Avenue address in Manhattan. Oswald then wrote to his mother, urging her to contact the Red Cross in Vernon, Texas, so they could coordinate with the IRC to provide him with aid. Someone must have been telling the high school dropout from New Orleans and Fort Worth what to do.[130]

Another curious development was that the Office of Naval Intelligence reopened Oswald's file on March 19, 1962, because "Oswald might seek updating of his discharge in the near future." Three days later, right on cue, Oswald sent a letter from Minsk dated March 22, but postmarked March 21, to Rathvon M. Tompkins, Brigadier General, U.S.M.C., Assistant Director of Personnel, looking to have his discharge status changed back to desirable. The letter is too well written for Oswald to have done it alone. As an example, "I would like to point out in direct opposition to your information that I have never taken steps to renounce my U.S. citizenship. Also that the United States State Department had no charges or complaints against me what/so ever." The entire letter reads like this, as if it was written by a lawyer. Then it gets stranger still:

"I have not violated; Section 1544, Title 18, U.S. code, therefore you have no legal or even moral right, to reverse my honourable [sic] discharge from the U.S.M.C. of Sept. 11, 1960, into a undesirable discharge."[131]

The question is, how was Oswald aware of the code governing the misuse of passports? The code reads as follows:

> Whoever willfully and knowingly uses, or attempts to use, any passport issued or designed for the use of another; or
>
> Whoever willfully and knowingly uses or attempts to use any passport in violation of the conditions or restrictions therein con-

tained, or of the rules prescribed pursuant to the laws regulating the issuance of passports; or

Whoever willfully and knowingly furnishes, disposes of, or delivers a passport to any person, for use by another than the person for whose use it was originally issued and designed—

Shall be fined under this title, imprisoned not more than 25 years (if the offense was committed to facilitate an act of international terrorism (as defined in <u>section 2331 of this title</u>)), 20 years (if the offense was committed to facilitate a drug trafficking crime (as defined in <u>section 929(a) of this title</u>)), 10 years (in the case of the first or second such offense, if the offense was not committed to facilitate such an act of international terrorism or a drug trafficking crime), or 15 years (in the case of any other offense), or both.[132]

The code had nothing to do with whether or not Oswald renounced his citizenship. In fact, according to a 2023 Forbes Newsletter article, "Before 2010, U.S. citizens did not have to pay a fee to renounce, but in 2010, the government imposed a $450 renunciation fee. In 2015 the fee increased to $2,350, supposedly because it was more paperwork." It is a lengthy process to get your citizenship back, but Oswald would not have faced imprisonment if he did.[133] Which is curious because on July 11, 1961, Richard Snyder wrote the following about his interview with Oswald:

> Oswald indicated some anxiety as to whether, should he return to the United States, he would face possible length imprisonment for his act of remaining in the Soviet Union. Oswald was told informally that the Embasssy did not perceive, on the basis of information in its possession, on what grounds he might be subject to conviction leading to punishment of such severity as he apparently had in mind … [Oswald] simply felt that in his own interest he could not go back to the United States if it meant returning to a number of years in prison, and had delayed approaching the Soviet authorities concerning departing from the Soviet Union until he 'had this end of the thing straightened out.[134]

Section 1544, Title 18, U.S. code has to do with giving your passport to someone else to use, or using someone else's passport yourself, which takes us back to the Oswald impostor scenario. It seems Oswald was admitting a deception was part of his defection, he was aware of it, and he wanted a guarantee that he would not have to suffer the consequences of traveling to Russia under a falsified passport.

There were other hard-to-explain occurrences. Oswald allegedly met with Russian dissident and anti-Communist Boris Pasternak, whose hotel, meeting time, and room number were in Oswald's notebook. The CIA had helped with the publication of Pasternak's book, *Doctor Zhivago*, and he was a favorite of James Angleton's.[135]

Oswald was also in touch with other CIA-connected Russian dissidents. A name Kozlova was in his address book along with Vneshtory Bank, Bank of Foreign Trade Moscow Neglinnaya Ul. There were three Kozolva listings at the CIA, and the Agency claimed they did not know which one Oswald had contacted. However, a January 31, 1964, letter by M.D. Stevens described that:

> Olympiada KOSLOVA ... is the aunt of Nikolai Vasilievich Kozlov...who is currently employed as an agent by this Agency. CI/SIG has information on KOSLOV which makes reference to various female relatives of his by the name KOSLOVA. Olympiada KOSLOVA, a professor, is the Director of the Moscow Institute of Engineering and Economics. She is active politically, often travels abroad, and in November 1961 was scheduled to travel to Washington, DC, with a scientific group. It should be possible to obtain this woman's telephone number for comparison with that listed in OSWALD'S address book under the name KOSLOVA...[136]

M.D. Stevens was Marguerite D. Stevens, who in 1960 provided James Angleton's Counterintelligence Division with information on American defectors to the Soviet Union. She would later state she was instructed not to investigate seven defectors, one of whom was Lee Harvey Oswald. We can only assume that Oswald would not have been on the list of seven if he was a legitimate defector. Then, after the JFK assassination, Stevens investigated Koslova only because her name was in Oswald's notebook, and the CIA needed to disassociate themselves from Koslova, which Stevens did. She wrote: "Security Indices contain information on a number of women with the name KOSLOVA, none of whom can be identified as being the individual in question [in Oswald's notebook]; but any of whom might be."[137]

Then there was Mikailo Jelisavcic. Right before the onset of World War II, Jelisavcic was part of a special delegation sent to Moscow from Yugoslavia. He escaped during the war and came to the U.S., graduated from Columbia University in 1956, and became a U.S. citizen two years later. He then worked undercover for ten years as a businessman in Moscow as a CIA asset working for American Express (The CIA inadvertently declassified his espionage number years later). According to the FBI, he was the manager of American Express in Moscow at the time of Oswald's defection. It was a critical disclosure. The notation "Am EX" appeared in Oswald's notebook, along with the telephone number of the American Express office in Moscow and the name "Jelisavcic." Witten on the same page were "1-2 Dinner" and "Room 384." The telephone directory of the American Embassy in Moscow listed American Express Company Room 384, Hotel Metropol telephone 942000; manager Mr. Michael Jelisavcic. The number 9 and the letter K were interchangeable in the Moscow telephone system. Oswald's notebook listed K-42000.[138]

The letters "Am Ex" suspiciously appear six times in Oswald's address book. Consider that when he was arrested in New Orleans in August 1963 for a street altercation with anti-Castro Cubans, on the margin of the previously discussed note he handed to police lieutenant Francis Martello was the espionage number for Michael Jelisavcic. The number was classified at the time, so how did Oswald know what it was?[139]

Richard Case Nagell was an intelligence agent associated with Oswald, who, in September 1963, shot up a bank in El Paso, Texas. He wanted to be incarcerated and have an alibi when JFK was assassinated. In *On the Trail of the JFK Assassins*, Dick Russell explains:

> All [of] Nagell's actions in the bank were intended as a signal to someone waiting for him across the Mexican border in Juarez. When he asked teller Patsy Gordon for $100 in American Express traveler's checks, the specific reference was by design. At our last meeting, Nagell suggested that I examine his trial transcript and think about why the prosecution raised such an objection to his mention of American Express. And, in a letter he wrote Art Greenstein, Nagell indicated it was through American Express that he was supposed to receive payment for his intelligence work in 1962-63.[140]

On January 8, 1965, an internal FBI memo from J. Edgar Hoover to his Special Agent in Charge (SAC) in New York City, titled "Michael Jelisavcic, Espionage," instructed "you should closely question him concerning the circumstances surrounding his name and phone number being in the address book of Lee Harvey Oswald. The results of [the] interview concerning Lee Harvey Oswald should be set forth in a communication suitable for dissemination under the Lee Harvey Oswald caption."[141]

So, fourteen months after the assassination, the FBI in New York had an opportunity to interview Jelisavcic, and they wanted to learn about his relationship with Oswald. Even after the Warren Commission findings were released, the FBI was still uncertain about the legitimacy of the lone gunman theory.

Finally, on October 30, 1969, *The New York Times* reported:

> A US Travel Agent Expelled by Soviet Moscow: The manager of the
> American Express Company here said tonight that he has been or-
> dered to leave the Soviet Union 'as soon as possible.' He is Michael
> S. Jelisavcic, a United States citizen who was born in Yugoslavia and
> who has been in Moscow for nine years.... He said in an interview
> that the apparent reason for the expulsion order was his involvement
> of August 6 in an automobile accident...[142]

***

On June 2, 1962, after a prolonged struggle with American and Soviet authorities, Lee Oswald, Marina, and their infant daughter June left the Soviet Union. The facts suggest his defection was an illusion to make it look like the Soviets had killed Oswald and that an impostor had assumed his identity. Incredibly, the Director of the FBI, the Secretary of State, and the U.S. Passport Office were concerned if the Oswald who was returning was the same one who had defected. Past associates of Oswald's in New Orleans, such as Guy Banister and his group, Friends of a Democratic Cuba, would engage with Oswald again in the summer of 1963 and were using his name in the struggle against Cuba long before he returned to the U.S. Somehow, it doesn't add up, and the possibility that Oswald was an innocent, disenchanted defector is impossible to accept. Unknown to Oswald, less than sixteen months after his return to the United States, the JFK assassination would forever propel him into the history books. After his death, authorities would be puzzled by his apparent 2" loss in height and forged identification papers. However, those in the know at the CIA knew that a so-called "sleeper agent" was created who could take the fall for any crime – even the assassination of a President.

CHAPTER THREE

THE PENTAGON FIGHTS BACK

The 1960 election of a Roman Catholic, wealthy, liberal, desegregationist President from Massachusetts galvanized the radical right-wing movement. John Birch Society membership skyrocketed. The popularity of the violent right-wing Minutemen grew as their call for armed resistance against a Communist takeover of the U.S. government appealed to the Fascist element of society. Amazingly, considering World War II had ended only fifteen years before, the American Nazi Party flourished. Numerous groups arose after the Brown vs. Board of Education decision in 1954 that made racial segregation in schools unconstitutional, such as the National States Rights Party. They were hell-bent on maintaining a way of life they wanted to preserve.

Then there was the military. The U.S. government accused General Edwin Walker of indoctrinating the more than 10,000 Army troops he commanded in Augsburg, Germany, with a far-right anti-Communist ideology. He appeared on the cover of *Newsweek* under the headline: "THUNDER ON THE RIGHT: THE CONSERVATIVE, THE RADICALS, THE FANATIC FRINGE."[143] He gained national prominence in April 1961, when the American servicemen newspaper *Overseas Weekly* reported that in a speech, Walker called ex-President Truman, former First Lady Eleanor Roosevelt, and former Secretary of State Dean Acheson "definitely pink." He alleged that Edward R. Murrow, Eric Sevareid, and 60 percent of the American media were Communist-controlled. The article accused Walker of encouraging his men to read John Birch Society literature. On April 17, the same day as the Bay of Pigs invasion, Walker was relieved of command, which further fueled the military's animosity toward JFK.[144]

One Army captain told *The New York Times*, "I feel the general is being crucified. And I think the men feel the same way."[145] Echoing Douglas MacArthur, Walker lectured that "traditional civilian control of the military has been perverted and extended into a commissar-like system of control at all major echelons of command." It was a message his fellow soldiers found appealing. Even at the stately National War College in Washington, seminars would occasionally be reduced to "extreme right-wing, witch-hunting, mudslinging revivals" and "bigoted, one-sided presentations advocating that the danger to our security is internal only," according to a report prepared by Secretary of Defense Robert McNamara's staff.[146]

Conditions under Kennedy were so bad that the Senate Foreign Relations Committee investigated. Their report on right-wing extremism warned of "considerable danger" in the "education and propaganda activities of military personnel," with "a central theme that the primary, if not exclusive, danger to this country is internal Communist infiltration" and that the "nature of the Communist threat often is developed by equating social legislation with socialism, and the latter with Communism...Much of the administration's domestic legislative program ... would be characterized as steps toward Communism." They warned that a military revolt was possible and cited "as an example of the ultimate danger" the recent uprising by army generals in France over policies in Algeria. "Military officers, French or American, have some common characteristics arising from their profession, and there are numerous military 'fingers on the trigger' throughout the world." The committee called for an investigation into Lyman Lemnitzer, the Joint Chiefs, and their relationship to extreme right-wing groups. [147]

On July 20, 1961, at a National Security Council meeting attended by President Kennedy, his closest aides, the Joint Chiefs, Allen Dulles, and Secretary of State Dean Rusk, General Lemnitzer detailed a JCS proposal for an unprovoked first-strike nuclear attack against the Russians. He admitted Russian bombs would also kill millions of Americans, and there would be long-term consequences the planet would have to deal with, but this was the price they needed to pay to remove the Red Menace from the face of the earth. A disgusted Kennedy walked out of the meeting. "And we call ourselves the human race," he later told Rusk.[148]

According to Hanson Baldwin of the *New York Times*, that same month, Kennedy ordered FBI agents to "invade" the military commanders' Pentagon offices to find the source of a press leak about military contingency plans regarding Berlin, which the Chiefs considered "degrading." "The Kennedys used intimidation and pressure to force people into line," Baldwin wrote. "From my observation of many years in Washington dealing with many presidents, back to FDR, the Kennedys were ... the most ruthless of any of them."[149]

On July 21, the Senate Foreign Relations Committee released a memorandum detailing the threat posed by domestic right-wing militarism and "warned that right-wing propaganda activities ... may create important obstacles to President Kennedy's programs…. Running through all of them is a central theme that the primary, if not exclusive, danger to this country is internal Communist infiltration…"[150]

Meanwhile, two aides to left-wing Senator J. William Fulbright were concerned with the rise of the radical right in the Senator's home state of Arkansas, as military officers began uniting with far-right Christian groups in an anti-Communist crusade against liberal politicians. Once again, they compared it to the right-wing generals who were trying to overthrow the government in France and wondered if this could happen in the United States.[151]

Fulbright sent a memo on the rise of militarism to Defense Secretary McNamara, who issued a directive limiting military officers' ability to promote right-wing causes at public events. The radial right immediately denounced both men. South Carolina Senator Strom Thurmond said it was a "dastardly attempt to intimidate the commanders of the U.S. Armed Forces" and "constitutes a serious blow to the security of the United States." Fulbright did not care. "If the military is infected with the virus of right-wing radicalism, then the danger is worthy of attention," he told the Senate. "If by the process of the military educating the public, the fevers of both groups are raised, the danger is great indeed." He also raised the possibility of a military coup, again referencing "the revolt of the French generals as an example of the ultimate danger." Columnist Marquis Childs agreed, writing that "in one country after another in recent years, the intervention of the military in politics has had disastrous consequences…" Drew Pearson echoed Childs, writing that "certain Pentagon brass hats were lining up with industrial right-wingers to foment a sort of neo-fascism despite the fact they were wearing Uncle Sam's uniform."[152]

In response, Strom Thurmond urged the Senate Armed Services Committee to open hearings on the "muzzling of the military." In September, they called McNamara before the committee and hammered him on his censorship of military officers. "The military establishment is an instrument – not a shaper – of national policy," McNamara told them. It was a hostile exchange, and the 250 spectators in the room loudly booed Mc-Namara while Thurmond was cheered.

In late September, the onslaught continued. The Fourth U.S. Army sponsored a two-day propaganda show in San Antonio that drew thousands. Speakers like General A.C. Wedemeyer denounced the Kennedy administration for "appeasing" the Soviet Union and supporting the civil rights movement. Other anti-Kennedy seminars organized by the military occurred the following month, compelling McNamara to issue another ban against political agitation by the military.[153]

In October, Kennedy invited leading journalists from around the country to the White House. Among them was sixty-seven-year-old Ted Dealey, the publisher of *The Dallas Morning News,* whose father Dealey Plaza was named after. Not one to mince words, Dealey told JFK, "The general opinion of the grassroots thinking in this country is that you and your administration are weak sisters. ... We need a man on horseback to lead this nation – and many people in Texas and the Southwest think that you are riding Caroline's tricycle. ... We can annihilate Russia and should make that clear to the Soviet government. This means undoubtedly that they can simultaneously destroy us. But it is better to die than to submit to communism and slavery."[154]

It was an incredible display of disrespect for the office of the President, and John Kennedy had enough. On November 18, speaking in front of 2,500 Democrats assembled at the Hollywood Palladium, he fired back:

> There have always been those fringes of society who have sought to escape their own responsibility by finding a simple solution, an appealing slogan, or a convenient scapegoat ... convinced that the real danger comes from within. They look suspiciously at their neighbors and their leaders. They call for a "man on horseback" because they do not trust the people. They find treason in our finest churches, in our highest court, and even in the treatment of our water.
>
> They equate the Democratic party with the welfare state, the welfare state with socialism, and socialism with communism. They object, quite rightly, to politics intruding on the military, but they are very anxious for the military to engage in politics.[155]

Kennedy asked that America refuse to succumb to hysteria: Let "our patriotism be reflected in the creation of confidence rather than crusades of suspicion." He reached across the political aisle for support, and Eisenhower agreed to make a public show of solidarity by joining Kennedy when the president returned to Washington.[156]

Outside the Palladium, an estimated three thousand protesters shouted anti-Kennedy slogans and waved signs reading "Unmuzzle the Military," "Disarmament is Suicide," "Get the Reds Out of the State Department," and "Stamp Out Communism." Two days later, Congressman John Rousselot called his speech "another example of tough talk and carry a big pillow..."

It was 1961 America, just two years before the assassination of JFK. The military seemed ready to revolt, and they aligned themselves with radical right-wing business leaders, oilmen, industrialists, politicians, and racist hate groups who shared their views. The hatred would only intensify. In August 1963, just three months before the assassination, Kennedy asked White House counsel Myer Feldman to assess the continued rise of right-wing organizations. Feldman concluded that the radical right, which he described as a formidable force in American political life, was well funded by "70 foundations, 113 business firms and corporations, 25 electric light, gas and power companies, and 250 identifiable individuals" who saw "the Nation as imperiled on every front by a pro-Communist conspiracy" which was preparing the country for an imminent takeover. "The radical right wing," Feldman told Kennedy, "constitutes a formidable force in American life today."[157]

***

A month after JFK became President, Moscow warned that a peace treaty with East Germany was coming that would give the satellite nation control of access routes to West Berlin. President Kennedy asked former Secretary of State Dean Acheson to study the problem, and on April 3, Acheson advised there could be no Berlin "solution" without German reunification.[158]

Khrushchev and Kennedy agreed to meet in Vienna on June 3 and 4 to discuss Berlin and other issues facing the two world superpowers. Based on previous reports his advisers had given him on Kennedy's inexperience, Khrushchev was confident. On May 26, one week before the meeting, he told the Presidium he intended to conclude a peace treaty with East Germany that would force Western planes to land at East German airfields, and they would shoot down Allied planes trying to land in West Berlin. He assessed the balance in Central Europe as unfavorable to NATO and presumed that American and European public opinion would prevent the United States from resorting to force.

Meanwhile, reporters on both sides of the Atlantic were concerned the young President was not ready to take on Khrushchev so soon after the Bay of Pigs disaster. *The Wall Street Journal* said JFK projected the "strong impression ... of a faltering America desperately trying to regain leadership of the West in the Cold War." The Swiss daily *Neue Zurcher Zeitung* lamented that Kennedy had abandoned his prerequisite that the Kremlin must change its attitude before any such meeting occurs.[159]

Most telling was the unprecedented lecture Kennedy was given in writing on May 27 by the Joint Chiefs of Staff:

> In your conversations with Premier Khrushchev ... be assured that
> you speak from a position of decisive military superiority in any mat-

ter affecting the vital interests of the United States and our Allies...
It is the considered judgment of the Joint Chiefs of Staff that the military forces under your command ... can achieve decisive military victory in any all-out test of strength with the Sino-Soviet Bloc....
The military forces of the United States reaffirm their dedication to your command and wish you 'Godspeed' in your mission. [160]

The military had zero confidence in the new president, and Robert Kennedy's private meeting with a Soviet spy named Georgi Bolshakov did not help. The two men already knew each other, and on May 9, they met to discuss the upcoming summit. Over the next three years, they sometimes met twice per month. Nothing was in writing, and to make matters worse, JFK agreed they could meet without his chief foreign policy advisers present. It was too much responsibility to give to a young, inexperienced Attorney General, and if the Kennedy brothers thought they could do this discreetly, they were delusional.

They met again on May 12, and Bolshakov told Bobby what the Soviet Premier wanted him to hear. In other words, Khrushchev was playing the Kennedy brothers. A Moscow supervisor wrote regarding the meeting, "The situation when a member of the U.S. government meets with our man, and secretly, is without precedence." Not wanting to lose their advantage, Moscow sent directions to its embassy and intelligence operatives to keep the meetings secret from the U.S. press and the FBI. [161]

Before the summit, Kennedy visited Charles de Gaulle in Paris, who told JFK not to back down from Khrushchev's threats because if he had wanted to start a war, he would have done so already. "If you want peace," de Gaulle told Kennedy, "start with general disarmament negotiations." No one seemed to trust or have confidence in the young President. [162]

Throughout the Vienna summit, Khrushchev bullied Kennedy. JFK later complained that Khrushchev "went berserk, yelling, 'Miscalculation! Miscalculation! Miscalculation! All I ever hear from your people ... is that damned word, miscalculation!'" Khrushchev later described Kennedy as "very inexperienced, even immature. Compared to him, Eisenhower was a man of intelligence and vision." [163]

Khrushchev was unrelenting regarding East Germany. "No force in the world would prevent the USSR from signing a peace treaty," he said. He said that America would be responsible for any war fought over Berlin, and only a "madman, who ... should be put in a straitjacket" would even consider going to war over Germany. Kennedy responded that Khrushchev's threat to sign a peace treaty with East Germany and cut off access to West

Berlin upended the existing balance of power in Europe and would be the primary cause if war broke out, but Khrushchev brushed that aside. JFK asked Khrushchev to consider that there was a difference between signing a peace treaty and challenging America's rights of access to Berlin, but it had no impact. He blamed the U.S. for trying to humiliate the Soviet Union, and Moscow intended to counter any American aggression against East Germany with force.[164]

American officials were shocked when they read the transcripts of the Kennedy/Khrushchev discussions. Kennedy accepted that communism could remain in places like Poland and Czechoslovakia, where it already existed, a concession no previous American president had made. Worst of all, he put the word "West" before Berlin. No previous president had done that either. It was as if he conceded the city would remain divided. Considering the U.S. had a vast nuclear superiority over the Soviets, JFK should never have allowed Khrushchev to scold him like he did. From that point on, it emboldened Khrushchev to act more aggressively with bluster, convinced there would be little retaliation from such a weak president.[165]

When it was over, Kennedy asked the U.S. Ambassador to the Soviet Union, Llewellyn Thompson, with a dazed look, "Is it always like this?" A *New York Times* columnist wrote that Kennedy looked "very gloomy" and "had a hat over his eyes like a beaten man and breathed a great sigh." "Roughest day of my life," the President said. British Prime Minister Harold Macmillan said Kennedy was "completely overwhelmed by [Khrushchev's] ruthlessness and barbarity." Dean Rusk said he "wasn't prepared for the barbarity." Averell Harriman thought JFK was "shattered," while Lyndon Johnson enjoyed the moment, saying, "Khrushchev scared the poor little fellow dead."[166]

On June 14, the Joint Chiefs reviewed what happened with Dean Acheson, Admiral Dennison (Supreme Allied Commander, Atlantic), and General Norstad. Acheson feared the threat of U.S. nuclear power no longer restrained the Soviets from challenging the U.S. directly. The Joint Chiefs agreed and again began calling for a first strike against the Russians to counteract the weakness displayed by Kennedy.

As described by Walter S. Poole in *History of the Joint Chiefs of Staff The Joint Chiefs of Staff and National Policy Volume VIII 1961-1964:*

> The JCS on 21 June advised Secretary McNamara that there was "an urgent need to re-establish the credibility of the U.S. nuclear deterrent." Assuming a D-Day for Berlin of 31 December, they set out a sequence of actions. The more significant ones follow: Between July

and December, raise forces in Europe to full strength, declare a national emergency and initiate appropriate mobilization, resume U–2 flights over the USSR, and intervene, if necessary, in Cuba, Laos, and Vietnam. Between September and November, restart nuclear testing…The United States, in the Joint Chiefs' judgment, "clearly" could prevail if it struck first [with nuclear weapons]. If the Soviets did so, "the degree to which we are successful in prevailing depends on the timeliness of our response."[167]

It was a frightening proposal. Kennedy again turned to Dean Acheson to write a report on Berlin, which he believed would defuse what the Joint Chiefs wanted to do. He was mistaken; unknown to JFK, Acheson thought Kennedy was not qualified to be president. "Until this conflict of wills is resolved," Acheson reported, "an attempt to solve the Berlin issue by negotiation is worse than a waste of time and energy. It is dangerous…. At present, Khrushchev has demonstrated that he believes he will prevail because the United States and its allies will not do what is necessary to stop him."[168]

By the end of June 1961, stories in *Time* and *Newsweek* questioning Kennedy's determination to face down the Soviets in Germany angered him greatly. "Look at this shit. This shit has got to stop," he told Pierre Salinger. Nixon took advantage of the moment to say that "never in American history has a man talked so big and acted so little." Kennedy responded publicly on June 28 about the Soviet insistence on signing a peace treaty and "to make permanent the partition of Germany." "No one can fail to appreciate the gravity of this threat," he said. "It involved the peace and security of the Western world." However, privately, a bitter argument raged over what had become a full-blown crisis. On one side, Dean Acheson, the Joint Chiefs, Allen Dulles, and some State and Defense Department officials urged for an overt military buildup to intimidate Moscow. On the other, Dean Rusk, Adlai Stevenson, Chester Bowles, Averell Harriman, Arthur Schlesinger, and Ted Sorensen favored negotiations along with military preparations. During the first week of July, *Newsweek* added to Soviet-American tensions over Berlin by leaking a Pentagon national emergency memo that included the increase of American divisions in Germany and "some demonstration of U.S. intent to employ nuclear weapons." An undeterred Khrushchev responded that Moscow was ready for but horrified at the prospect of a nuclear war. "Why should two hundred million people die for two million Berliners?" In a July 25th speech, Kennedy clarified that the choice was "not merely between resistance and retreat, between atomic holocaust and surrender…We do not intend to abandon our duty to mankind to seek a peaceful solution." He understood Russia's concern "after a series of ravaging invasions," but he could not enter negotiations that threatened Berlin's freedom or Western treaty rights. "To sum it all up: we seek peace – but we shall not surrender."

France and Germany did not trust the young American President, and their opposition to negotiations made a Berlin settlement unlikely. Meanwhile, at home, Kennedy faced considerable pressure from right-wingers who were itching to fight a nuclear war.[169]

***

Laos was the most pressing issue in Southeast Asia when Kennedy took office. Eisenhower warned him the day before his inauguration that Laos was the "cork in the bottle. If Laos fell, then Thailand, the Philippines, and, of course, Chiang Kai-shek in Formosa [present-day Taiwan] would go."[170] He even said that unilateral intervention should be used as a last resort to prevent a Communist takeover. However, as Peter Dale Scott wrote, Eisenhower was unaware that the CIA and the Pentagon were purposely misleading him, and "the advice he was given was often either belated or deliberately misleading. For example, in December 1959, President Eisenhower was notified of Phoumi Nosavan's imminent right-wing coup in Laos. Although this coup had in fact been fomented by the CIA, Eisenhower was assured in a CIA memo that 'throughout this matter the U.S. has been making every effort to stand aside.'"

The truth was that the U.S. Ambassador, Horace Smith, opposed the CIA coup. It was Henry Hecksher, the CIA Station Chief in Laos, who worked behind Smith's back to put Phoumi Nosavan in power.[171]

In the early 1950s, the Viet Minh had nearly conquered Laos. The U.S. partnered with Thailand, which shared the view that Laos was the logical place where they should contain the spread of communism. At the time, *The New York Times* devoted three times more space to Laos than Vietnam. According to the *Pentagon Papers*, "Vietnam was a peripheral crisis...Even within Southeast Asia, [Vietnam] received far less of the administration's and the world's attention than did Laos."[172]

In August 1960, the Soviets helped Souvanna Phouma return to power, and the U.S. government ratified Souvanna's new government. However, the Pentagon and the CIA once again looked to oust Souvanna and reinstate Phoumi by orchestrating a military coup. By September, the CIA airline, Air America, was supplying Phoumi's rebel army. In December, Phoumi was back in power, while Souvanna-supporter Kong Le's neutralist army took shelter within the security of the Communist Pathet Lao, who were receiving significant support from the North Vietnamese government. All the while, Allen Dulles kept President Eisenhower in the dark about what was really happening.[173]

Kennedy learned shortly after taking office that the military wanted to intervene in Laos. In his first meeting with the Joint Chiefs, Walt Rostow, who had left the Center for International Studies at MIT and was now Kennedy's Southeast Asia specialist at the NSC, recommended introducing a token U.S. combat force there, which the Chiefs rejected. As Arthur Schlesinger recalled in *A Thousand Days*, the Joint Chiefs "recommendation was all or nothing: either go in on a large scale, with 60,000 soldiers, air cover and even nuclear weapons, or else stay out."[174]

In March 1961, JFK approved the Laos Task Force plan for the U.S.-backed forces of General Phoumi to drive the Pathet Lao army from the Plain of Jars, a crucial military position adjacent to Thailand. A false CIA intelligence report led JFK to believe that Phoumi's forces could take the position quickly, which was a lie. JFK was not told of a military intelligence report, which superseded the CIA report, that Phoumi would be unsuccessful. The attempt failed, and within two weeks, a somewhat overwhelmed JFK ordered a sizeable American combat force to be ready to ship to Laos as soon as he gave the go-ahead.[175]

Throughout the spring of 1961, the military remained ready. Battalions were strategically deployed, and naval ships headed for Southeast Asia. The plan was to thwart Chinese intervention by introducing 250,000 U.S. troops into South Vietnam, "followed by operations across North Vietnam into Laos to block Chinese intrusions." Were these forces overrun, the Joint Chiefs intended to use nuclear weapons to stop the Chinese. They only needed Kennedy's approval to proceed, something they would never receive.[176]

In April, while Kennedy faced tremendous pressure to intervene in Laos, the Bay of Pigs debacle occurred. It compelled the President to stay out of Laos, which would have developed into a major war. "Thank God the Bay of Pigs happened when it did," Kennedy said. "Otherwise, we'd be in Laos by now – and that would be a hundred times worse."[177]

Robert Kennedy agreed. "If it hadn't been for Cuba, we would have sent troops to Laos," he said. "We probably would have had them destroyed ... the Communists could send five men into Laos for every one that we sent in. That they could destroy the airports and therefore cut off our people after getting only a thousand or several thousand into Laos and that the only way really that we could win in Laos was [to] drop the atomic bomb [which would lead to] a major atomic war both with China and with Russia."[178]

A frustrated Admiral Burke, expressing the opinion of the JCS, asked: "If we do not fight in Laos, will we fight in Thailand where the situation will be the same sometime in the future as it is now in Laos? Will we fight in Vietnam? Where will we fight? Where do we hold? Where do we draw the line?"[179]

Immediately after the Bay of Pigs, the military tried to exploit a vulnerable JFK. Burke reiterated that losing Laos meant losing all of Southeast Asia. At an NSC meeting on April 29, General Decker said, "We cannot win a conventional war in Southeast Asia; if we go in, we should go in to win, and that means bombing Hanoi, China, and maybe even using nuclear weapons." General LeMay said if the Chinese intervened, "we should go to work on China itself." General Shoup suggested employing B–26s before they committed troops. Under Secretary of State Chester Bowles said that "we were going to have to fight the Chinese anyway," and it was "just a question of where, when, and how." In that case, General LeMay responded, "We should fight soon since the Chinese would have nuclear weapons within one or two years."

On May 1, McNamara presented a draft memorandum to the President that recommended sending U.S. troops into the Laotian panhandle. If North Vietnam and China intervened, they would use nuclear weapons to avoid defeat. McNamara and Deputy Secretary Gilpatric circulated a revised paper that advocated intervention unless they obtained a quick ceasefire. General Shoup believed massing forces in Thailand and South Vietnam was the best way to make that happen. General White said if the Communists did not accept a truce within 48 hours, aircraft should strike targets in Laos. If the Communists kept fighting, White proposed striking the Laotian Precipice. That would have ignited a conflict with China. However, he believed "that war with China is inevitable if we take decisive action in Southeast Asia, and I would seize the initiative." General Lemnitzer advised that only immediate military action could prevent losing most, if not all, of the remaining vital areas in Laos. A disgusted General White drafted a new paper stating the United States was incapable of waging a non-nuclear war against China. The other Chiefs agreed. They advised McNamara they could conduct a "full-scale non-nuclear war" in Laos and North Vietnam— but not against China. CINCPAC, they noted, already possessed enough nuclear power to destroy or neutralize a Chinese threat. It was clear that nuclear war with China was what the military wanted.

It was why the Pathet Lao opposition forces accepted a proposed ceasefire offer on May 3. However, the delay gave the North Vietnamese Army

(NVA) the time to conduct an offensive in southern Laos, capturing the crossroad village of Tchepone. In doing so, they gained the terrain necessary to extend the Ho Chi Minh Trail to the western side of the Annamite Mountains on the border between Laos and South Vietnam, which would have dire consequences in the future.

Diplomats now took center stage. On May 9, Kennedy advised U.S. negotiators that the goal should be "a neutral, independent, peaceful, sovereign, and socially and economically viable Laos." Averell Harriman led the American contingent in Geneva, which accused Communists of repeatedly violating the ceasefire, while JFK was accused of appeasement and allowing Laos to fall. Still, Kennedy held firm. They finally agreed on the composition of a coalition government on June 12, 1962. Kennedy's radical right-wing opponents feared this opened the door for a Communist takeover of Laos. At the same time, the U.S. lost an opportunity to take on China in a weakened military position. The frustration the military felt was a sign of things to come.

***

Vietnam became the next battleground in Southeast Asia between Kennedy and the military. On April 20, the day after the Bay of Pigs, JFK ordered a quick review of the Vietnam situation to determine what was needed to prevent Communist domination there.[180] By the end of the month, as it became clear JFK intended to do nothing in Laos, the Joint Chiefs told Kennedy to use air strikes against Hanoi to stop a North Vietnamese Communist offensive. Lemnitzer wanted to use nuclear weapons.[181]

To understand the struggle Kennedy faced, we must briefly turn our attention to Cuba. As mentioned in Chapter One, the Cuban Study Group, led by General Taylor, wanted to transfer peacetime operations away from the CIA to the military. Kennedy agreed, and in June 1961, he issued three National Security Action Memorandums, all based on Taylor's recommendations, to strengthen the role of the military and limit the power of the CIA. In NSAM #55, Kennedy called the Joint Chiefs "my principal adviser responsible for initiating advice to me ... I expect their advice to come to me direct and unfiltered," and "The Joint Chiefs of Staff have a responsibility for the defense of the nation in the Cold War similar to that which they have in conventional hostilities." The second, NSAM #56, "Evaluation of Paramilitary Requirements," requested an "inventory [of] the paramilitary assets we have in the United States armed forces." Finally, NSAM #57, "Responsibility for Paramilitary Operations," stated: "A paramilitary operation ... may be undertaken in support of an existing government friendly to the

United States or in support of a rebel group seeking to overthrow a government hostile to us."[182]

The President effectively transferred control of paramilitary operations away from the CIA to the military, even though the military was not a proponent of counterinsurgency and guerrilla warfare. The Joint Chiefs still wanted a nuclear confrontation with the Soviets or Chinese while the U.S. had an advantage. However, JFK also said more than that. He stated it was acceptable to support a rebel army that was looking to overthrow a government that was hostile to the United States, something Nixon had warned him during the presidential campaign could lead to World War III. There is no doubt that Allen Dulles and the CIA took notice of this last declaration.

Returning to Southeast Asia, in the latter part of April 1961, the Joint Chiefs gave Kennedy a report that included a Laos Annex, which assumed that Laos would fall to the Communists and recommended the introduction of U.S. combat troops into Vietnam. The person responsible for this was the CIA's Edward Lansdale, who sided with the Joint Chiefs and their desire to increase the American presence there.[183] Meanwhile, Lemnitzer cabled the Pentagon from East Asia on May 6, asking: "Does the U.S. intend to take the necessary military action now to defeat the Viet Cong threat or do we intend to quibble for weeks and months over details of general policy … while Vietnam slowly but surely goes down the drain of Communism as North Vietnam and a large portion of Laos have gone to date?"[184]

Four days later, the Joint Chiefs went on record that what was needed was an immediate intervention of American military personnel in Vietnam:

> President Diem [should] be encouraged to request that the United States fulfill its SEATO obligation, in view of the new threat now posed by the Laotian situation, by immediate deployment of appropriate U.S. forces to South Vietnam.
>
> Upon receipt of this request, suitable forces could be immediately deployed to South Vietnam in order to accomplish the above-mentioned purpose. Details of [the] size and composition of these forces must include the views of both CINCPAC [Commander-in-Chief of the Pacific] and CHMAAG [Chief, Military Assistance Advisory Group], which are not yet available.[185]

Throughout the summer, the military's attitude toward the President was condescending, as Kennedy faced continued pressure to intervene. Most advisors in his administration also believed intervention was necessary. On May 9, Kennedy sent Vice President Johnson to Vietnam to learn more. He returned with the recommendation that U.S. involvement there was inevitable. Johnson said the battle in South Vietnam must include a massive influx of U.S. combat troops or surrender the Pacific and establish defenses on our shores.[186]

By October, as the call for sending troops into Vietnam reached a fever pitch, Kennedy instructed General Taylor to go to Vietnam to get a first-hand look and to "bear in mind that the initial responsibility for the effective maintenance of the independence of South Vietnam rests with the people and the government of that country." Accompanying Taylor on the trip were the hawk Walt Rostow and the proponent of counterinsurgency, Edward Lansdale.

Kennedy trusted Taylor and expected him to submit a report to counter the military escalation the Joint Chiefs wanted. However, Taylor shocked Kennedy by describing the Vietnam situation as "the darkest since the early days of 1954. Vietcong strength had increased from an estimated 10,000 in January 1961 to 17,000 in October; they were clearly on the move in the delta, in the highlands, and along the plain on the north central coast." Diem and his generals "were watching with dismay the situation in neighboring Laos and the negotiations in Geneva, which convinced them that there would soon be a Communist-dominated government in Vientiane," the capital of Laos.[187]

Taylor proposed that JFK immediately dispatch 8,000 American combat troops into South Vietnam. "The last thing he [JFK] wanted," Taylor later said, "was to put in our ground forces. And I knew that. I had the same feeling he had on the subject. But all the way, starting with CINCPAC, the feeling was that we'd better get something into South Vietnam."[188]

Taylor also acknowledged the first eight thousand troops were just the beginning. "If the ultimate result sought is the closing of the frontiers and the clean-up of the insurgents within South Vietnam, there is no limit to our possible commitment (unless we attack the source in Hanoi)." Taylor's enthusiasm for additional troops was reiterated in a cable by Ambassador Frederick Nolting, who cited "conversations over past ten days with Vietnamese in various walks of life" showing a "virtually unanimous desire for introduction of U.S. forces into Viet-Nam."[189]

Taylor felt if the conflict in Vietnam continued to deteriorate, it would become increasingly difficult to "resist the pressure to reinforce." The problem was that Taylor incorrectly compared Vietnam to Korea, a war fought against a conventional army. As David Halberstam wrote in *The Best and the Brightest*, Taylor had "a complete misunderstanding of the nature of the war. It was arrogant and contemptuous toward a foe who had a distinguished and impressive record against a previous Western challenger. [Taylor saw] the limits of air power in Korea and now said that if things went wrong, air power would handle Hanoi any time we wanted. It assumed that the people and the government of South Vietnam were the same thing…"[190]

Kennedy rejected Taylor's recommendation. "I don't recall anyone who was strongly against [sending ground troops]," Taylor later said. "Except one man, and that was the President. The President just didn't want to be convinced that this was the right thing to do.… It was really the President's personal conviction that U.S. ground troops shouldn't go in."[191]

Taylor was wrong. JFK was not the only one who was against sending American troops to Vietnam. In October, after returning from an Asian trip, journalist Theodore White wrote Kennedy that" any investment of our troops in the paddies of the delta will, I believe, be useless – or worse. The presence of white American troops will feed the race hatred of the Vi-et-Namese." "The South Viet-Nam thing is a real bastard to solve – either we have to let the younger military officers knock off Diem in a coup and take our chances on a military regime … or else we have to give it up. To commit troops there is unwise-for the problem is political and doctrinal."[192]

That same month, JFK told *New York Times* columnist Arthur Krock that "United States troops should not be involved on the Asian mainland.… The United States can't interfere in civil disturbances, and it is hard to prove that this wasn't largely the situation in Vietnam." He told Schlesinger the same thing. Sending in troops "is like taking a drink. The effect wears off, and you have to take another." He believed that if the conflict in Vietnam "were ever converted into a white man's war, we would lose the way the French had lost a decade earlier."

George Ball told Kennedy committing American troops would be a tragic error, and he predicted that "within five years we'll have three hundred thousand men in the paddies and jungles and never find them again. That was the French experience," he reminded JFK. "Vietnam is the worst possible terrain both from a physical and political point of view." John Kenneth Galbraith, the U.S. Ambassador to India, agreed. He returned to the U.S. and warned Kennedy that the United States was in danger of becoming the new colonial force in Vietnam and destined to bleed as the French did. He advised that the U.S. should help forge a neutral coalition government in South Vietnam and leave. And above all, combat troops should not be considered.

Kennedy took what these men said to heart. He told Diem in a November 15, 1961, message that "the mission being undertaken by our forces

... are more suitable for white foreign troops than garrison duty or missions involving the seeking out of Viet Cong personnel submerged in the Viet-Nam population."[193]

On December 8, McNamara, his deputy Roswell Gilpatric, and the Joint Chiefs recommended in a memo to Kennedy that "we do commit the U.S. to the clear objective of preventing the fall of South Vietnam to Communism and that we support this commitment by the necessary military actions," including Taylor's proposed "U.S. force of the magnitude of an initial 8,000 men ... and expanding to as many as six divisions of ground forces, "or about 205,000 men."

Despite enormous pressure from all quarters, Kennedy refused to send combat troops into Vietnam. Instead, he increased the number of American advisers and military equipment, which was nowhere near what Taylor had requested. There were signs the pressure was getting to him, for on November 30, 1961, Kennedy approved the use of chemicals in Vietnam, violating the Geneve convention. The idea was to destroy the foliage the Viet Cong used as a protective cover, but untold innocents suffered horrific deaths as a result.[194]

***

In his speeches in August, Khrushchev threatened nuclear war if the United States continued to push the Soviet Union. On the night of August 1, the Berlin Wall went up, which cut off travel between the two sectors. With a potential crisis looming, Carl Kaysen, Deputy Special Assistant to the President for National Security Affairs, and Henry Rowen, one of Paul Nitze's (Assistant Secretary of Defense for International Security Affairs) deputies in the Pentagon, worked on a first-strike nuclear attack plan. They concluded that the U.S. had a 90 percent chance of destroying all Soviet strategic nuclear weapons before they could retaliate against American cities. The death toll would be unimaginable, but that did not matter. Victory over communism trumped everything.[195]

Other supporters of a first strike, like Senator Barry Goldwater, began attacking Kennedy. "Anytime diplomats begin talking of negotiations in a Soviet-created situation where there is nothing to negotiate," he said, "it is time for the defenders of freedom to become wary."[196]

David Bruce, a former ambassador to Germany, thought Kennedy's acceptance of the wall eroded West German morale. "I would consider it essential that we take, and make credible, the decision to engage, if necessary, in nuclear war rather than lose West Berlin, and consequently, West Germany."[197] General Lauris Norstad, the head of U.S. forces in Europe, said,

"If I had been commander, I would have taken a wire and flung a hook over and tied it to a tank and pulled it [the wall] down." Lemnitzer said the U.S. looked "hopeless, helpless, and harmless." Maxwell Taylor advised Kennedy that Khrushchev intended to use military force, and the President had better be prepared to do the same.[198]

Throughout August, Khrushchev applied psychological pressure in preparation for a treaty showdown. He invited foreign military attachés to observe Soviet army maneuvers and inspect nuclear-tipped battlefield missiles. At the end of the month, the Soviets announced their intention to break its self-imposed moratorium on nuclear testing. Two days later, the tests began anew.

This was why, on September 12, Kennedy ordered Secretary of State Rusk and his advisers to prepare negotiations to end the Berlin crisis. Tellingly, Dean Acheson, Lyndon Johnson, and the Pentagon were not part of these discussions. The divide between Kennedy and the militarists who wanted nuclear war grew wider.[199]

Kennedy used a speech at the United Nations to tell the world, "A peaceful agreement is possible which protects the freedom of West Berlin." He called for "general and complete disarmament" under international control because "every inhabitant of this planet must contemplate the day when this planet may no longer be habitable. In conjunction with this, the President sent only one additional army troop division to Europe instead of the six the Pentagon wanted to deploy. A military standoff was off the table.[200]

The West German paper *Bild-Zeitung* wondered if Kennedy suggested Moscow had the right "to split Germany or renounce reunification." West German Foreign Minister Heinrich von Brentano warned the country must "brace itself with all its strength against tendencies to get a Berlin settlement at West Germany's expense." West German Chancellor Konrad Adenauer arranged a trip to Washington to get Kennedy back on message before it was too late. In a television appearance that week, the famous French philosopher Raymond Aron warned, "What is at stake isn't just the fate of two million Berliners. It is the capability of the United States to convince Khrushchev that it has the tenacity not to give in to horse-trading." In the U.S., *New York Times* columnist James "Scotty" Reston wrote Kennedy "has talked like Churchill but acts like Chamberlain."[201]

As a group, the Western press did not believe Kennedy had what it took to start a nuclear war, and Khrushchev believed that to be true. Without question, Berlin was Kennedy's most significant concern. "He's imprisoned by Berlin, that's all he thinks about," cabinet members complained. It was the highest priority for almost everyone around the president because of "the need for re-establishing the credibility of the nuclear deterrent." Dean Acheson called for a formal proposition that the U.S. might have to resort to nuclear war. A failure to defend Western rights in Berlin, he argued, would destroy international confidence in the United States.[202]

Robert Kennedy once again established backchannel discussions with Soviet spy Georgi Bolshakov to prevent a nuclear war over the Berlin Wall. They met twice in mid-January 1962, which included a threatening note from Khrushchev to Kennedy via Bolshakov, where the Soviet Premier accused JFK of encroaching "on the interests of the USSR and its allies – socialist countries."[203] Then, in October 1961, Bobby met privately with Bolshakov again as U.S. and Soviet tanks stared each other down during the Checkpoint Charlie standoff. JFK and Khrushchev communicated through Bolshakov and RFK, with President Kennedy offering to go easy over Berlin if Khrushchev removed his tanks first. Bypassing the Joint Chiefs and the CIA once again served only to intensify their anger for the two brothers, who they thought were unqualified to handle such serious negotiations on their own.[204]

The Soviet threats continued, and on February 8, 1962, they flew L-2 military transports along the southern air corridor over Berlin as a warning of what they would do. The next day, the Soviet Air Force announced it was closing the northern air corridor. The following week, they closed the southern corridor for a limited time. Then, ten Soviet fighters buzzed six U.S. aircraft trying to fly in the southern corridor, which was "reserved" for Moscow and its allies.[205]

One cannot overstate the importance of keeping the Soviets out of West Berlin. It was where the West drew a line in the sand, and the feeling was if West Berlin fell to the Communists, all Western Europe could follow. What to do about West Berlin influenced every foreign policy decision President Kennedy made. If the United States wanted to become aggressive in any part of the world, was it worth chancing losing West Berlin? Kennedy did not think so, at least not until the very end of his life when he used West Berlin as a pawn to advance his political future. Regardless, the seed that was planted long ago in the minds of Kennedy's radical right opponents, that he was weak on communism and was willing to appease the Soviets instead of standing up to their military antics, was proving to be correct. The U.S. military would only tolerate such behavior for so long.

***

Indonesia was another battleground where President Kennedy received pushback from Allen Dulles. The story begins in 1935 when three Dutch geologists exploring Papua discovered the world's richest gold deposit. The men worked for the Netherlands New Guinea Petroleum Company (NNGPM), based in the Hague and controlled by the Rockefeller family, as was the mining company involved, Freeport Sulphur. At the time, Dulles was an attorney based in Paris, employed by Rockefeller's Standard Oil, and in 1935, he arranged controlling interest in NNGPM for the Rockefellers. And it was through the effort of Dulles and a select few that the Rockefellers and the Dutch government managed to keep the mine a secret. They exploited its riches, but after World War II, Indonesia became independent and threatened to throw the Dutch out. So, in the mid-1950s, Dulles implemented a strategy for regime change in Indonesia before they could learn about the massive gold deposit. The goal was to protect American business interests by having a military coup overthrow Indonesian President Sukarno, whom Dulles falsely claimed had turned Communist.

As early as 1953, Indonesian officers were trained in the United States, and by 1962, there were more than one thousand Indonesians studying operations, intelligence, and logistics, mainly at Fort Leavenworth Army base. The Indonesians were mostly army generals and were wined and dined by the US government. The intent was for them to become anti-Communists and oppose Sukarno.[206]

A 1958 attempted coup and assassination effort failed, but even after JFK became President, Dulles continued the charade that Sukarno was anti-American and insisted they remove him from power. However, JFK disagreed, having received favorable reports from others in Indonesia that Sukarno was someone the United States could work with. As a result, Kennedy reached out to Sukarno, looking to normalize relations, and offered a considerable aid and development package that would cement ties between Indonesia and the United States.

The U.S. would eventually pour more money into Indonesia than any Southeast Asian country other than Vietnam. After the Bay of Pigs, JFK was uninterested in pursuing another regime change of a foreign government. Especially one strongly endorsed by Allen Dulles, whom he no longer trusted. It was a critical time for Kennedy, as he simultaneously took on big business, the military, and the CIA in his search for a peaceful settlement. It would reach a head in 1965, two years after JFK's assassination, when a CIA-backed military coup removed Sukarno from power.[207]

***

By the fall of 1961, President Kennedy dealt with the military, the CIA, and the State Department as best he could, but he no longer had tolerance for advisers with whom he continued to butt heads. In what would later be called the "Thanksgiving Day Massacre," he decided to rid his administration of key personnel who disagreed with his policies. George Ball replaced Chester Bowles as Undersecretary of State, and Averell Harriman replaced Walter McConaughy as Assistant Secretary of State for Far Eastern Affairs. The result was the introduction of noninterventionists into the number two and three positions at the State Department.[208]

After JFK removed him, Bowles wrote privately about the Bay of Pigs: "The Cuban fiasco demonstrates how astray a man as brilliant and well-intentioned as Kennedy can go who lacks a basic moral reference point." He was not the only one during the Kennedy Presidency to question JFK's moral compass.[209]

The following day, there was a meeting at the White House of all the significant players directing American foreign policy, including General Taylor, Dulles and Lansdale from the CIA, McGeorge Bundy and Walt Rostow from NSC, Dean Rusk and U. Alexis Johnson from State, and Robert McNamara and General Lemnitzer from Defense. To all parties, Kennedy laid down the law. "When policy is decided on, people on the spot must support it or get out." It was clear Kennedy would not introduce combat troops into Laos or Vietnam, back a coup in Indonesia, or engage in a military confrontation over Berlin. It was also apparent he cared little for the opinions of those whose years of experience greatly outweighed his own. It was a frustrating time for those who believed the spread of communism threatened the United States.

The day after the meeting, Kennedy fired Allen Dulles and replaced him as CIA Director with John McCone, marking the end of the CIA's glory days. A conservative Republican, McCone had served President Truman as Undersecretary of the Air Force and President Eisenhower as Chairman of the Atomic Energy Commission. His role as DCI was sharply different from Dulles'. Where Dulles considered it his responsibility to interpret intelligence, Kennedy took that task upon himself, content to limit McCone's duties to managerial ones alone. Before long, the CIA fired General Charles Cabell, and Richard Helms replaced Bissell as the new CIA Deputy Director of Plans. Helms had stayed clear of the Bay of Pigs and frowned upon the recklessness displayed by Bissell. His appointment communicated what the President expected from the CIA in the future.[210]

Soon after taking over for Dulles, McCone went on a worldwide tour with the head of the CIA's Far East Division, Desmond Fitzgerald. According to Fletcher Prouty, before leaving, Fitzgerald met privately with key figures at the Pentagon to discuss what McCone should be allowed to see. Those who thought intervention in Vietnam was necessary were not about to give up so easily.[211]

In less than a year, President Kennedy had alienated the military, the CIA, big business, and key advisers in his administration. They thought his weakness under fire in Cuba led to failure at the Bay of Pigs. He responded by firing legendary figures at the CIA. Regarding Laos and Vietnam, the military called for combat troops and nuclear weapons, including a first strike against the Soviets and the Chinese, yet Kennedy resisted. It was increasingly clear to all that he had no intention of standing up to Communists militarily in Southeast Asia or anywhere else. For those of the right-wing who believed that Kennedy's reluctance to confront communism placed the nation in danger, it was a grave situation that needed to be corrected.

CHAPTER FOUR

NAZIS, MONARCHISTS, FRENCH FASCISTS, AND THE CIA

After World War II, Cairo, Santiago, Rome, Buenos Aires, Lisbon, and Madrid became havens for former Nazis and their World War II Fascist collaborators who were looking to escape Allied prosecution. These groups established an expatriate community in each city and became a transnational Fascist network. As described in *The Neofascist Network and Madrid, 1945-1953*, between the end of the war and the mid-1950s, these new and improved Nazis revised their wartime Fascist ideology to include "ultranationalism, visceral anti-communism, racism (mostly in the form of anti-Semitism), demands for a strong authoritarian state based on law and order, preference for charismatic leadership, a collective sense of crisis and national decline, a fascination with a glorious past, a rejection of the parliamentary process, a belief in European superiority, a defense of the values of tradition, [and] a justification of violence." Madrid quickly became their most essential urban city, mainly because Spain was in Europe, and the Franco regime was sympathetic towards fascism, which allowed them to conduct their business without fear of retaliation.[212]

Before the war, in 1936, businessman Johannes Bernhardt had been sent to Spain by the Nazis to supervise economic relations between Germany and the rebels headed by General Franco, which he did through the holding company SOFINDUS, of which Bernhardt was managing director. When the war ended, ex-SS member Bernhardt maintained contact with the highest echelons of the Franco regime and Spain's economic elites. He also established links with Allied authorities through Operation SAFEHAVEN, an Anglo-American program created to locate German assets and steer them into British or American humanitarian organizations.[213]

The Allies allowed Bernhardt to move freely within Spain and maintain control over a series of companies whose resources amounted to eighty million pesetas. Thus, he enjoyed the unique position of having essential contacts in Germany while under the protection of the highest echelons of the Franco regime. At the same time, he worked with the Allies and had substantial economic resources at his disposal. It allowed Bernhardt to develop a network in Spain that helped former Nazi members come to Madrid and, from there, make the necessary arrangements to secure their safety. According to the German Ambassador to Madrid in 1958, Karl-Hemrich Knappstein, there were around 3,000 nationals living in the Spanish capital. Many of those were well-situated financially and owned different businesses around the city.

Madrid was the center of a significant ratline that secretly helped former Nazis and Fascist collaborators escape from Europe to South America. Due to growing tensions between the United States and the Soviet Union, by the end of 1946, the governments in London, Paris, and Washington eased their efforts to prosecute war criminals, which was less important with the looming threat of communism on the horizon. Therefore, former Nazis and Fascists in hiding, which included Germans, French, Hungarians, Bulgarians, Italians, Romanians, Poles, Croats, Dutch, Austrians, Belgians, and others, felt more secure. They began to make their way to Madrid, which consolidated its position as the most important Nazi/Fascist hub throughout the world. As a result, some of the most prominent former Nazis settled there because it was a place they could become politically active again. One of those was Otto Skorzeny, an Austrian SS-Obersturmbannführer in the Waffen-SS, who had become a symbol of Fascist superiority throughout Europe due to his participation in different military operations during the Second World War, including the liberation of Mussolini from his prison of the Gran Sasso in 1943.[214]

Skorzeny was not averse to assassination. During the war, an American report about him explained: "The leader of a German group, who specializes in the kidnapping and assassination of higher personages, passed through our lines one or two days ago together with ... his men with the mission of killing General EISENHOWER. His name is SKORZENY ... SKORZENY and his men will be wearing American uniforms and have American identification papers, weapons, etc.... One of their rendezvous points is said to be the Café de la PAIS [sic] in Paris, where German stay behind agents and [their] collaborators will meet to furnish all the necessary information regarding General EISENHOWER'S whereabouts, security guard etc. These men are completely ruthless and are prepared to sacrifice their lives in order to carry out their mission."[215]

Skorzeny's exploits did not go unnoticed by the Allied forces. After the war, he was incarcerated for two years in a German prison and was tried as a war criminal. On the last day of his trial, Yeo-Thomas, a former British SOE

Commander, testified in Skorzeny's defense, and he was acquitted. Still, he remained in a detention camp until he received a letter from Yeo-Thomas telling him it was safe to escape. On July 25, 1948, as U.S. and British intelligence looked the other way, Skorzeny fled the camp and became a free man. He hid at a farm in Bavaria for eighteen months, which had been rented by Countess Ilse von Finckenstein, who was a family friend of Hjalmar Schacht, Hitler's former finance minister. Although not blood-related, she referred to him as an uncle.

Ilse was born in 1918 in Kiel, Germany. She spoke English, French, and Spanish fluently and was intelligent and sophisticated, and she and Otto eventually married. A CIA analyst observed that they formed a dangerous team: "He is extremely active, possessed of tremendous vitality, and willing to try almost anything... She is apparently a clever and intelligent woman who will not stop until she has reached the financial and social position which she believes is her due." Together, they were "capable of considerable mischief." After the war, the CIA suspected she was working for French intelligence. She is mentioned numerous times in Lafitte's datebook and was clearly an active and essential participant in the JFK assassination plot.

While in hiding, Otto was in contact with Reinhard Gehlen, the ex-Nazi intelligence officer who worked with pro-Nazi Eastern European groups during the war against the Russians. Gehlen recruited Skorzeny to become part of his organization.[216] On February 11, 1950, Skorzeny was secretly in Paris. He had fled to France because Gehlen had warned him about a Soviet attempt to kidnap him. "Gehlen was marvelous," Ilse recalled. "He and Otto respected each other very much..." Unfortunately, someone recognized him, and the French Communist newspaper *Ce Soir* dispatched a photographer and wrote a feature article that stated: "Skorzeny, No.1 killer of Hitler's personal guard ... is peacefully sipping a drink in a Champs Elysees café."[217]

Skorzeny arrived in Madrid in September 1950 as a fugitive from German justice. He would be de-nazified in absentia by the German courts in 1952 after they ruled he was not guilty of any war crimes or criminal acts. Undoubtedly, the Americans and the Brits had a hand in that, for they had bigger plans for him. Skorzeny saved enough money to open a small office in the heart of Madrid, where he conducted international trade and financial operations. On February 9, 1951, the U.S. Chief of the Madrid Permit Office, Hudson Smith, wrote in a report that Skorzeny "is ostentatiously here [in Madrid] undercover, but his presence is fairly common knowledge, and he has even given interviews to the press." In addition, the CIA explained that Skorzeny had already resumed his political activities. He developed a vast web of international contacts, including Johannes Bernhardt in Spain, Werner Naumann and Otto Remer in Germany, and Johann von Leers in Argentina. It was not by accident that Skorzeny managed to establish close contacts with the Allies through the Allied Commission for German Affairs in Spain, thus becoming an official CIA informant concerning possible Communist activities throughout the world. U.S. authorities even granted Skorzeny a Spanish passport for stateless persons under the name of Rolf Otto Skorzeny Steinbauer. After that, the CIA monitored Skorzeny's main activities and collected an extensive file on him.

In the 1950s, the Nazis and Fascists in Madrid set in motion a series of military initiatives to halt the potential spread of communism that threatened Western Europe. In conjunction with this, Skorzeny launched a plan to set up an army of German military men in Spain in the event of war with Russia. The purpose was to prepare for the defense of Western Europe, West Germany in particular, in the event of a Soviet attack. A Soviet invasion of Europe, Skorzeny argued, "would mean the inevitable collapse of European culture and, above all, the total destruction of European intelligence. Although Europe might again be liberated by an invasion, there would later be no men capable of bringing about reconstruction in the spirit of the West."[218]

To minimize the Soviet threat, Skorzeny proposed the formation of a German cadre in Spain, made up of active German forces, as well as the formation of European cadres, which would spring into action throughout Europe in case of war. Right-wing extremists and U.S. intelligence leaders, like Allen Dulles and William Donovan, supported the plan, who were simultaneously working on a stay-behind army concept of their own, of which Skorzeny was well aware. America was just as worried as the Europeans about Moscow advancing into West Germany, especially after the start of the Korean War in 1950.

Reinhard Gehlen shared the opinions of Skorzeny, Dulles, and Donovan that they needed stay-behind armies to contain the Red Army, and Germany should be armed and part of that network. According to Gehlen, "It is clear for the political leadership [in Moscow] that only the German Reich can offer military and political resistance to the Soviet claim in Europe. [The Reich] can be militarily valuable for the British and the Americans in keeping Bolshevik imperialism away from Europe."[219]

Skorzeny also feared that the worsening Korean War situation would lead to a third world war for which Western Europe was unprepared, with over two million Soviet troops in Eastern Europe. In the event of a Soviet invasion, NATO would be overwhelmed. For the past 18 months, reports had been coming in that Skorzeny was plotting a secret German army in exile of 200,000 men to disrupt a Soviet attack.

Major Robert Bieck, Assistant Air Attache at the U.S. Embassy in Madrid, was working for the CIA and became Skorzeny's confidant. In December 1951, he presented Skorzeny's stay-behind army plan to the CIA:

> 1. The formation of a basic German cadre in Spain, made up of Army, Air, and Naval personnel, which could at the same time be used as an organization to absorb the mass of German forces...
>
> 2. The formation of European cadres which would involve the thorough investigation of all European youth prepared to make the sacrifice. This model European organization could be used later in case of war to go into action throughout European territory.
>
> 2a. Later on, with the inclusion of Spanish commando units, I would propose the creation of special sharpshooter cadre within the Spanish Army.
>
> > 1. I should also like to propose, emphasizing that Proposal 1 requires previous American authorization and subsequent aid... that an organization be created for an orderly withdrawal from Germany. The seeds of such an organization already exist. It would have to be brought into play only in the case of catastrophe.[220]

Realizing that the Americans were concerned that Skorzeny and his Nazi collaborators were trying to create a new Nazi army, Skorzeny began describing his military force as "a patriotic Christian and Catholic force" preparing to roll back Communist evil. The idea gained traction in ultra-Catholic Spain, which was when Father Konrad Simonsen Mackey appeared to offer his support. Simonsen had personal access to the very highest echelons of the Vatican (including future pope Cardinal Montini) and the Francoist regime, including Franco himself. He had been chaplain to the Condor Legion in the Spanish Civil War, and since 1949 he had been establishing Vatican "ratlines" for Nazis escaping Europe. In 1951, Simonsen was organizing the Madrid chapter of the Verband Deutscher Soldaten veterans' group, whose founding members included Skorzeny.

The Vatican was supportive of Skorzeny because the Church was also worried about a Communist takeover of Western Europe, and for good reason. Germany was essentially defenseless in the 1950s, having no army of her own and only a token occupation force with which to face any attack.

As we will see, the Vatican was proactive and very involved with U.S. intelligence and international Fascists to curtail the spread of communism throughout the Cold War.[221]

Skorzeny also made contact in Germany with various nationalist groups and war veterans associations such as the Union of Sudeten Germans, the Union of Exiles, and the Brotherhood of Germans Union. All of them, Skorzeny explained, "fervently defended my own point of view and agreed with my comments, namely that something must be done to save the Germans."

Skorzeny ended up replacing Bernhardt as the main point of reference for German Nazis in Madrid. In the coming years, he would be one of the key figures within the Nazi/Fascist transnational network as well as the architect of the plot that assassinated President Kennedy. In the words of CIA officials, "Skorzeny is the most prominent figure in the international neo-Nazi-Fascist movement today, and perhaps is even a dominant force in it."[222]

***

William King Harvey joined the FBI in 1940 when the Bureau was busy hunting Nazi and Japanese spies in America. By 1945, with the war over and communism the new enemy, Harvey became one of three agents in the newly created Security Division, and his stock was on the rise due to his involvement in the Elizabeth Bentley case. Bentley had confessed to working with a Soviet spy ring that included Alger Hiss and other employees of the U.S. government. However, two years later, the FBI demoted Harvey for allegedly drinking on the job, prompting him to resign. He joined the CIA shortly after that.[223]

The newly formed CIA was the perfect place for Harvey, and according to Dennis Flinn, another FBI man who became deputy chief of operations at the CIA, Harvey was "the most highly trained, most professional man available for CI [Counterintelligence] work."[224] Harvey worked for James Angleton in a counterintelligence unit called Staff C, which was part of the CIA's Office of Special Operations (OSO). The two men, united by a common desire to eradicate communism, became close and worked together many times until Harvey left the CIA in 1968.[225]

Like Otto Skorzeny, future CIA Counterintelligence chief James Angleton was a key OSS operative interested in maintaining stay-behind units in Germany after the war. He had spent his childhood in Italy when his father Hugh moved the family there after purchasing the National Cash Register franchise in Milan. Hugh was an outspoken supporter of both Hitler and

Mussolini and had extensive contacts with elite aristocrats and business-people throughout Italy. These contacts would serve his son well, for James was transferred to Italy in November 1944, eventually becoming head of X-2 counterintelligence for all of Italy. He was not averse to dealing with Fascists if it served the interests of the U.S. in the war against communism.[226]

In the fall of 1949, William Harvey was present at a meeting in Washington that included CIA Director Walter Bedell Smith and two French intelligence officers named Roger Wybot and Pierre Bertaux. Both were prominent members of the Service d'Ordre, an anti-Communist network hidden within French intelligence that was at the forefront in the creation of anti-Communist stay-behind armies throughout Europe after the war. This privately-run French intelligence service was part of a larger organization called the Rassemblement du Peuple Francais (RPF). Wealthy industrialists secretly funded the group. The Service d'Ordre worked alongside American intelligence in this endeavor, which provides insight into what Harvey was doing during his early years at the CIA.

Wybot was the head of DST, the Directorate of Territorial Surveillance, which was responsible for foreign threats against France. During World War II, he organized the French intelligence service Bureau Central de Renseignements et d'Action (BCRA) and eventually led its counterintelligence section. He wound up in Italy at the end of the war, where he became close friends with James Angleton.

Bertaux was Director of the Surete Nationale, France's version of the FBI. During the war, he was a veteran leader of the French Resistance, where he worked with British SOE and American OSS operatives. More importantly, he was an authority on German culture and literature and had a high regard for the German people.[227]

As part of his plan to establish a German army to protect Europe, Otto Skorzeny developed a close working relationship with the Service d'Ordre du RPF for over a decade, which meant he was familiar to both Wybot and Bertaux, who attended the meeting with CIA Director Smith and Willaim Harvey, as mentioned above.[228]

Wybot and Bertaux were at the meeting to discuss ongoing anti-Communist projects in France, including the CIA's relationship with Paix et Liberté, a privately funded French intelligence group operating without government supervision. It would become "a large CIA front organization" highly financed by the Agency. Paix et Liberté participated in various American psychological campaigns, the mobilization of anti-Communist armies throughout Europe, anti-government coup plots, and, reportedly, assassinations of political figures. As early as 1949, there was a connection between American and French intelligence developing stay-behind émigré armies in Europe, and within a few years, Otto Skorzeny would be involved with them as well at the same time, and the relationship would continue up to and beyond the JFK assassination.[229]

A result of the meeting was the creation of a private American support group for Wybot and Bertaux called the American Friends of Paix et Liberté. A 1951 list of their board members included a Russian-born anti-Communist American journalist named Isaac Don Levine. In 1948, Levine was a central figure in Alger Hiss's case when he informed Assistant Secretary of State Adolf A. Berle, Jr. that magazine editor Whitaker Chambers had accused Hiss of being a Communist spy.

Levine remains a mysterious espionage figure. Immediately after the JFK assassination, he was given exclusive access to Marina Oswald, which prompted Allen Dulles to have Levine meet with the Warren Commission in a secret session. Levine claimed he was helping Marina translate her story on behalf of *Life* magazine. There was talk of Marina possibly having Russian intelligence connections, so her story was never published. Still, Levine's primary role may have been to ensure they controlled the narrative of what Marina disclosed.[230]

By the early 1950s, Skorzeny was working with the World Commerce Corporation, a private company founded by OSS chief Bill Donovan that collaborated with Allen Dulles to place former OSS and British MI6 officers in forty-seven countries to fight communism. It was a mercenary intelligence network that worked under the CIA's Office of Policy Coordination (OPC), run by Frank Wisner. OPC created the National Committee for a Free Europe (NCFE), which was a political front organization headed by Allen Dulles to serve as an umbrella under which Eastern European émigré groups could find refuge. Lieutenant Colonel Edward Lansdale joined OPC in 1949. Meanwhile, Wisner hired Isaac Don Levine to exploit Russian and Ukrainian émigrés populations that had inundated Germany and other Western European countries, and Skorzeny became part of this operation. Subsequently, with substantial CIA backing, Levine set up the American Committee for the Liberation of the Peoples of Russia, which was part of the OPC project with the cryptonym QKACTIVE.[231]

Rabid anti-Communists, both Angleton and Allen Dulles thought it was essential to protect ex-Nazis to rebuild Germany. Dulles was with the OSS in Switzerland during the war, attempting to negotiate a treaty with German officers who had become disillusioned with Hitler. He arrived in

Rome in October 1945, hoping to establish a new Italian resistance to the spread of communism, akin to what Gehlen had done during the war in Eastern Europe.[232]

As early as October 1951, Skorzeny began inviting sympathetic German right-wing politicians to Madrid to explain his political intentions. One visitor, known to the CIA as 'Carotid,' reported to his American contacts that Skorzeny hoped "to form a rightist coalition movement in Western Germany" and "lend his support to the international ultra-rightist movement." As we will see in the coming pages, there was a right-wing movement in the United States in 1963 that was part of an international Fascist organization that included Skorzeny and his Nazi group in Madrid. They would join forces to assassinate JFK.

Skorzeny aligned with the Sozialistische Reichspartei Deutschlands (SRP), Germany's most prominent post-war radical right-wing movement. Its deputy chairman was Otto-Ernst Remer, Skorzeny's old colleague who had been instrumental in upending the Valkerie coup that attempted to kill Hitler. The SRP's ideology was essentially National Socialism minus Adolf Hitler. Organizations like this intended to exploit their political clout by forging a new social contract with the Adenauer administration in West Germany to determine the future government and defense of Germany. Some, like Skorzeny's Nazi friend, Hans-Ulrich Rudel, thought this meant rejecting an alliance with the United States and the Western Allies. However, Skorzeny disagreed. He was willing to get in bed with the Americans in pursuit of his goal, which was "preventing German integration with the Western Powers ... with the ultimate objective of re-establishing an authoritarian German State." A CIA Covert Action Staff report in the spring of 1953 stated that Skorzeny is "believed to be in close contact with French and American intelligence officers or military attaches, to whom he reports every bit of information he receives on Fascist activities." Considering there was also a French involvement in the JFK assassination, it is telling that a working relationship between Skorzeny, the CIA, and the French went back as far as 1953.[233]

***

William Harvey was CIA station chief in Berlin during the heart of the Cold War, from 1952 to 1960. It was in Germany that he developed long-term relationships with many agency operatives who shared his passion for eradicating communism. Everything was acceptable in the war against the Red Menace, including working alongside ex-Nazi Reinhard Gehlen's stay-behind army network in Europe that the CIA ran as a first line of defense against communism. The network consisted mainly of ex-Nazis and ex-Eastern European Nazi collaborators from World War II, and they were all part of the Otto Skorzeny network to protect Europe.

The need to contain communism by any means possible led to a *"Fascism without Hitler"* mentality among right-wing adherents in postwar Europe as ex-Nazis collaborated with the CIA and European Fascists and Monarchists. They ran much of their anti-Communist activity out of Madrid. Many of those associated with this Fascist network are familiar names that repeatedly pop up while investigating the JFK assassination, including Otto Skorzeny, Lucien Conein, William Harvey, James Angleton, Charles Willoughby, Henry Hecksher, Tracy Barnes, Frank Wisner, Jack Crichton, William Pawley, Victor Oswald, Thomas Eli Davis, and others.[234]

West Berlin was located entirely within East Germany and, as a result, became ground zero in the covert war against the Soviet Union. Considering Harvey's counterintelligence experience, it was logical he was transferred there as the new CIA station chief in 1952. The CIA's William R. Corson said, "The edge Bill Harvey had over those folks was that he had been up against the enemy [while he worked at the FBI], and they hadn't. He understood the ruthlessness. To Harvey, the NKVD and, later, the KGB were criminals.... He was a cop, and he had a cop's view of counterespionage."[235]

Extremely anti-Communist and borderline Fascist, German-born Henry Hecksher, whose real name was Heinrich Detlev Heckscher, was one of Harvey's deputies in West Berlin. He would later be involved in the 1959 coup in Cuba that tried to overthrow Castro, which the CIA ran out of the Havana Embassy.[236] Ted Shackley also worked under Harvey in Berlin and served with him again as head of the CIA JM/WAVE station in Miami in the war against Castro while JFK was President. Shackley would sacrifice anything for the good of an operation. There was immediate chemistry between him and Harvey, and Harvey treated him like a younger brother.[237]

Camp King was an interrogation center utilized by the German Air Force during World War II, which the U.S. Army later used to detain Nazi prisoners such as Reinhard Gehlen and Otto Skorzeny. It also involved LSD experimentation and drug-induced interrogations of Nazi prisoners, and it was around this time that a relationship between men like Gehlen, Skorzeny, and U.S. intelligence began. Gehlen came to the attention of General Edwin Sebert, the highest-ranking U.S. Army intelligence officer in Europe, and Walter Bedell Smith, the Chief of Staff of the Supreme Allied Command and future CIA Director. Meanwhile, ex-OSS chief Bill Donovan and Allen Dulles knew about Gehlen and were equally interested in Skorzeny.

U.S. intelligence sent Gehlen and three assistants to Washington, D.C., for debriefing in August 1945. Allen Dulles had direct access to Gehlen, while Frank Wisner remained connected to WCC and ran OPC. Wisner also headed the coordination team. Gehlen furnished them with reports on Russian military strategy and capabilities obtained during World War II from four million Soviet prisoners of war. At least a half dozen of his first staff of fifty officers were former S.S. or S.D. men, including Hans Sommer, who had set seven Paris synagogues on fire in October 1941. Past atrocities did not concern U.S. intelligence or the military in the war against communism.

Gehlen modeled his stay-behind army network after Red Army General Andrey Vlasov, who defected to the Nazis during the war and created an anti-Communist army of German-held POWS, refugees, reassigned Nazis, and their Eastern European collaborators. They were ruthless and responsible for the mass extermination of Jews throughout Eastern Europe. These same ex-Nazis, now prisoners of war held by the U.S., became part of Gehlen's postwar stay-behind armies in Europe. In the event of a U.S. nuclear attack against the Soviets, they would provide covert resistance and encourage the local populace to overthrow Communist governments.[238]

Frank Wisner was also extremely anti-Communist. He was in Berlin just days after the Soviets took control of the city from the Nazis while American forces were still fifty miles away, and he was appalled by the Russian Red Army atrocities he witnessed, as rape and robbery happened on a massive scale. The experience, as well as that Wisner witnessed similar atrocities when the Red Army took control of Romania, forced him to focus on the Soviet Union and not the remnants of captured Nazis he no longer considered the enemy. Wisner fully expected the Russians to march west and take over Western Europe, and that had to be prevented. In May 1945, he and his deputy, Richard Helms, organized the Secret Intelligence unit of OSS Germany at OSS headquarters in Frankfurt, Germany. Their immediate supervisor and overall director of OSS operations was Allen Dulles.

In 1948, Wisner's stock was on the rise. In April of that year, he toured American-occupied zones in western Germany and Austria as the Deputy Assistant Secretary of State for Occupied Areas to see how the State Department could serve as a marshaling force between the United States and the Soviet Union. While there, he made a concerted effort to study how Germans had rallied so many non-Russian Soviets to their side during the war. He determined it was because they feared Russia, and he wanted to take advantage of that. There were hundreds of thousands of Soviet émigrés living in permanent exile throughout Western Europe, and they all opposed communism. Later that year, the CIA chose Wisner to head all Eastern European émigrés groups the Agency controlled, which certainly brought Wisner together with Gehlen and Skorzeny.[239]

In the U.S., part of Wisner's responsibility was to vet émigrés imported by the CIA, including those with questionable backgrounds. Wisner arranged to have these émigrés exempted from immigration laws, which had previously barred war criminals. "We knew what we were doing, "said Harry Rositzke, a Soviet expert at the CIA. "It was a visceral business of using any bastard as long as he was anti-Communist," a recurring theme. "Some of the people Frank brought in were terrible guys, but he didn't focus on it," said James Critchfield, a CIA officer who served as liaison to the Gehlen group. What these Nazis had done did not matter, for they were putting together a resistance army of unsavory characters void of government oversight.[240]

According to Vladimir Petrov, a leading Russian scholar in the U.S. and a one-time Vlasov Army adviser, these émigrés whom the Americans trained "were ready to go back [to Eastern Europe] at any time." America's leading anti-Soviet, George Kennan, noted that "their idea… was simply that the United States should, for their benefit, fight a war against the Russian people to achieve the final breakup of the traditional Russian state and the establishment of themselves as the regimes of the various 'liberated' territories."

"It became an article of faith that the USSR was going to fall apart at any time," noted Petrov. "Communists killed people to maintain their power, so the first chance [the people] had there would be a rebellion."[241] The United States formed anti-Communist governments in exile for each satellite country, which waited for the post-nuclear day of reckoning when resistance armies took control of Soviet puppet regimes. These émigré groups remained optimistic that they could be the catalyst that ignited hostilities, and many in the U.S. military and CIA supported them.

At the direction of Allen Dulles, Gehlen established a working relationship with the Unione Corse in Marseille, who helped him secretly send dozens of ex-Nazis to South America. In return, Gehlen's people helped arrange heroin shipments to North and South America for the Unione Corse. In 1951, Conein and Ted Shackley helped the CIA establish a base in Nuremberg, Germany. In later years, the Unione Corse would smuggle drugs into the U.S. for the Cuban-American organized crime syndicate. These groups were intertwined.[242]

Otto Skorzeny, arguably the most notorious ex-Nazi the Americans worked with, was in the middle of it all. As Dick Russell wrote in *The Man Who Knew Too Much*, "Skorzeny's name would be linked not only to CIA but also to Latin American death squads, global illegal arms deals, and assassination plots against de Gaulle and Castro."[243] Since 1951, Skorzeny was also a business partner with Victor Oswald in Madrid. Johannes Bernhardt had introduced them. Oswald was an arms dealer whose name reappeared in connection to the JFK assassination. He is mentioned here because it is essential to understand that this was the beginning of an international American and European Fascist collaboration that had the motive and wherewithal to assassinate JFK, but more about that later.[244]

In *Fugitives: A History of Nazi Mercenaries During the Cold War*, author Danny Orbach describes Skorzeny as follows:

> Otto Skorzeny was a shady figure. In the 1960s, he was suspected in various crimes: burning synagogues in Kristallnacht, killing "defeatist German soldiers," and even experimenting with a "poison gun" on prisoners... In the 1960s, there were judicial proceedings against Skorzeny in Austria, but nothing came out of it. He was described by Rafi Eitan, the Mossad spy chief in Europe, as "a soldier of the first grade." He kept in touch, through middlemen, with the highest circles in the US administration and the Republican Party, possibly including then-Vice President Richard Nixon.
>
> Skorzeny was an arms trafficker who dealt with various countries and insurgent groups. For that purpose, his company held branches in Cairo, Damascus, and Beirut. He smuggled WWII Mauser rifles and machine guns in large quantities to the Algerian FLN through Syria and Egypt.[245]

***

William Harvey's biggest coup while heading the Berlin station was the Berlin Tunnel, and he worked with Reinhard Gehlen's staff on the project. It meant Harvey must have been familiar with Camp King and the mind-altering drug experiments conducted there on ex-Nazi prisoners. Like Wisner, when he returned to Washington in 1959, Harvey would not forget his Nazi connections and what he had witnessed in Berlin because, within a year, he became head of ZRRIFLE, which included the CIA's assassination program.

Harvey wrote that the "purpose of ZR/RIFLE is to spot, develop and use foreign agent assets for Division D operations. Agents will be spotted in several areas, including the United States, but for operational security reasons [they] will probably not be used in their countries of residence. Present development activity is being conducted in the WE [Western Europe] and E.E. [Eastern Europe] areas, but it is anticipated that this will be extended to other division areas. The project will be operated against third-country installations and personnel."[246]

Europe was the area of focus for finding ZR/RIFLE operatives, which was why Harvey traveled there before officially taking over the program. A redacted document, written overseas and dated October 13, 1960, contained information that sheds light on who Harvey was interested in. There were references to "Corsicans" and "once selection is made, [redacted] to be eliminated." Perhaps the most critical person mentioned was Charles Siragusa of the Federal Bureau of Narcotics, who was a source for Corsican and Sicilian contacts. As described in *It Did Not Start With JFK, Volume One*, Siragusa was close to George Hunter White and Jean-Pierre Lafitte, who were involved in Mafia-connected mind-altering drug experiments for the CIA and had a history of involvement in assassination operations going back to their OSS days. The safehouse in New York City where they conducted their drug experiments was owned by Jean Jehan, a heroin trafficker and member of the Unione Corse.[247]

White and Lafitte had strong Mafia ties, and Lafitte used the alias Hidell, as did Lee Harvey Oswald. Siragusa also visited the mob-connected John Martino (who would admit to being involved in the JFK assassination plot) in a Cuban jail cell, where he was incarcerated with Santo Trafficante after Castro came to power. The year before, the CIA had approached Siragusa about contacting mobsters who could assassinate Fidel Castro, which eventually led to the CIA employing the services of John Roselli, Sam Giancana, and Santo Trafficante.[248]

After the JFK assassination, American mercenary Thomas Eli Davis was released from a Moroccan prison by QJ/WIN, one of Harvey's ZR/RIFLE assassins. Davis was also an FBN informant known to Charles Siragusa, George Hunter White, and Jean Pierre Lafitte. Davis had smuggled guns to Cuba with Jack Ruby, which connected ZR/RIFLE and William Harvey to the Mafia-connected thug who shot and killed Lee Harvey Oswald. Davis was detained in Tangiers because he carried a letter that referred to Victor Oswald (not Lee) in Madrid and the JFK assassination, which Davis was supposed to forward to attorney Thomas G. Proctor in New York. Proctor was associated with two important CIA assets in Mexico City, June Cobb and Warren Broglie, both prominent figures in the Lee Harvey Oswald saga.

During World War II, Victor Oswald was an intelligence operative for the OSS and the British. By the 1950s, he was a representative of the Chase National Bank in Spain and, in that capacity, worked for Warren Commission member John McCloy, the Chairman of Chase Manhattan Bank at the time. According to the author of *The Skorzeny Papers*, Major Ralph P. Gains, "Victor Oswald was also an original member of the SOE/OSS group that established the British-American-Canadian-Corporation (BACC) and the World Commerce Corporation (WCC)."[249] It connected Thomas Davis, through Thomas Proctor and Victor Oswald, to the Donovan/Dulles group that organized and funded the stay-behind guerilla armies in Europe after the war, which worked alongside Reinhard Gehlen and Otto Skorzeny.

At the time of the JFK assassination, Davis was recruiting an army to invade Haiti, which included assassination suspect Loren Hall, while Lee Oswald's friend George de Mohrenschildt was also in Haiti. If Davis were involved in the Donovan and Dulles WCC operation through Proctor and Victor Oswald, it would likely have connected his gunrunning partner Jack Ruby to this group also. De Mohrenschildt's presence in Haiti suggests there was a plan to assassinate Haitian President Papa Doc Duvalier and blame it on Castro to justify a U.S. invasion of Cuba. It is also possible that the army Davis was putting together to invade Haiti was to serve the same purpose as the staged attack against Guantanamo Bay, which used combatants dressed as Castro's soldiers, as described in Chapter One. The idea was for this to be a catalyst for a second invasion of Cuba at the end of 1963 as part of AMWORLD. However, as previously mentioned, the thesis behind our narrative is that the JFK assassination was to prevent this second invasion of Cuba from happening because it could have led to World War III. We will explore in more detail how all of this came together in the pages that follow.[250]

Lafitte, White, Siragusa, and Harvey were all involved with James Angleton, and they also had Corsican Mafia connections, like Paul Mondoloni, that put them in contact with the Mafia/ WCC/Corsican drug operation that funded the stay-behind armies, as described in *It Did Not Start With JFK, Volumes 1 & 2*. Harvey was linked to the Madrid right-wing group of ex-Nazis, Monarchists, and right-wing zealots from his Berlin days, so it was logical that when he became head of ZRRIFLE, he would approach them to help find European assassins.

Peter Wright was a former British counterintelligence officer with MI-5 who met with Angleton and Harvey in October 1961 at an out-of-the-way site in northern Virginia. "Would you hit him [Castro]?" Harvey asked

Wright. It was about a month before Harvey was assigned to assassinate Castro.[251] As Angleton recalled, "Bill came to me for help in obtaining phony backdated counterintelligence files to 'prove' that assassins had connections to the KGB, not the CIA, if their deeds ever became public. This material would be released to friendly newspaper reporters when necessary."[252]

Creating phony files to blame the Soviets was consistent with the CIA operation to make it appear that the Soviets had killed Lee Oswald in Russia and an undercover sleeper agent had taken his place. Two months before the assassination, a letter was written by Oswald falsely connecting him to a KGB assassin he met in Mexico City named Kostikov and that he had to leave Mexico unless he used his real name. Angleton was probably behind all this since he knew of Oswald from the time of his defection and worked with Harvey, creating fake bios long before Oswald became relevant. Making it appear Oswald was a pro-Castro Communist defector and possible Soviet impostor who killed JFK was part of the JFK assassination plot.

***

Hustler and casino operator Mike McLaney told Congressional investigators in 1978 that he had known Joseph Kennedy since the early 1950s. "I liked old man Joe Kennedy," McLaney said. "We used to golf together two or three times a week at the Palm Beach Country Club." McLaney also played golf with John Kennedy and met Bobby "many times," although, of all the Kennedys, Bobby was "the one I didn't like." At times, McLaney's longtime right-hand man, "Steve Reynolds" (pseudonym), was with him when they visited the Kennedys in Florida. "They were all there – Joe, Bobby, the President," said Reynolds. "It was when the Cuban thing really started to get going. Mike acted as a go-between for the White House and the Cuban exiles." They talked of "getting rid" of Castro. The Kennedys told McLaney they wanted Castro "taken out."[253]

On May 3, 1961, less than one month after the failed Bay of Pigs, the CIA's Sheffield Edwards told J. Edgar Hoover that the CIA had hired private detective Robert Maheu and mobsters Trafficante, Roselli, and Giancana to assassinate Castro. On May 21st, Hoover wrote a memo to Robert Kennedy advising him of the details. The FBI's liaison to the CIA, Sam Pappich, later said Bobby did not voice disapproval, but he "was concerned that this operation would become known, and [he] didn't want it to get out." If he wanted to, Bobby could have stopped the attempts to kill Castro, but he didn't. Between April 22 and May 30, he met with Allen Dulles at least twenty-one times. That the plots continued suggests he approved of them.[254]

On May 3, the same day Edwards briefed Hoover on the CIA/Mafia assassination plots, a cable was received in Washington from a Cuban agent code-named TEKLOK, which stated: "We are contacting all groups...to organize one united front with a coordinator. You name him or we elect him. Tell us. Will try to kill Fidel today..."[255] The following day, Jose Miro Cardona, President of the Cuban Revolutionary Council, met with JFK and received a formalized "pact which called for a new invasion" as the assassination attempts against Castro continued, endorsed by the Kennedy brothers. On June 4, the CIA's Deputy Director of Plans, Richard Helms, received the following: "Functionary Italian Embassy by the name of Moratori says ... he is in contact with Martin Elena and others and that you have plans for invasion within 30 days after killing Fidel, advise if we can confide in Moratori."[256]

In 1968, William Harvey told the FBI that "Robert Kennedy was knowledgeable of the operation which the CIA had devised with the collaboration of Roselli and his cohorts.... Kennedy is in an extremely vulnerable position if it were ever publicized that he condoned an operation which involved U.S. government utilization of hoodlum elements." Seven years later, testifying under oath before Congress, Harvey said: "I was completely convinced during this entire period that this operation had the full authority of every pertinent echelon of the CIA and had the full authority of the White House."[257]

***

In November 1961, as John McCone replaced Allen Dulles as CIA Director, JFK established the Special Group Augmented, designed to oversee the removal of Castro. General Taylor led the group, which included National Security Advisor McGeorge Bundy, CIA Director John McCone, Chairman of the JCS Lyman Lemnitzer, Deputy Defense Secretary Roswell Gilpatric, Undersecretary of State U. Alexis Johnson, and Robert Kennedy. By January 1962, they formed a more streamlined group – the Special Group (Counterinsurgency). It had only three members: Chairman General Taylor, Robert Kennedy, and U. Alexis Johnson. Between the two groups, these three men sometimes spent the entire day discussing Cuba and nothing else.

Robert Kennedy set the tone, declaring that "no time, money, effort, or manpower is to be spared" in getting rid of Castro. Unfortunately, Operation Mongoose was doomed to fail from the start, for the Cuban people had spent many years oppressed by Batista and found no advantage in revolting against Castro. A CIA Board of National Estimates concluded, "It is highly improbable that an extensive popular revolt could be fomented," which the Kennedys ignored since they no longer had faith in the Agency.[258]

The President established the ground rules for Cuba by claiming "the one thing that was off limits was [a] military invasion." As a result, the CIA concluded everything else was acceptable, including trying to create "internal dissension and resistance leading to eventual U.S. intervention," even though CIA estimates said internal resistance would not happen.[259]

Richard Helms reinstated the Mafia plots to kill Castro, but he did not tell the Kennedys or John McCone that he had done so. He brought in Harvey to take charge of the operation, who immediately contacted Roselli. Shortly after, Harvey and Ted Shackley delivered the mobster a U-Haul loaded with rifles, hand grenades, and explosives. Roselli then gave the weapons to Cuban exiles, mostly past supporters of Batista. It was right after Lawrence Houston and Sheffield Edwards assured Bobby that the CIA/Mafia assassination plots were over.[260]

Harvey cut Giancana and Trafficante out of the operation. He must have known that both men were playing the CIA, probably reporting directly to Castro, and had no intention of killing the Cuban leader, but Harvey knew Roselli could be trusted. Roselli posed as an army colonel with complete access to the CIA JM/WAVE station in Miami, where he met daily with David Morales.[261]

Task Force W was the CIA's name for their portion of the Cuban operation, and JM/WAVE in Miami became the largest CIA station in the world, with an annual budget exceeding $500 million. At the height of its activity, it controlled six hundred American agents and three thousand contract agents, with Ted Shackley as station chief.[262]

Shackley recruited thousands of Cuban nationalists from the émigré community, whom the CIA trained in sabotage and assassination. From these ranks would eventually spring violent right-wing Cuban exile groups like Alpha 66. They purchased waterfront homes in Key West, outfitted small boats with guns, and regularly conducted hit-and-run sabotage raids against Cuba. One problem they had was that CIA case officers did not understand Cuban culture, and counter-intelligence at the Miami station was almost nonexistent, which allowed Santo Trafficante's minions and Castro's intelligence agents to penetrate the base.[263]

William Harvey's first job was to restore the agent network in Cuba, which certainly put him in contact with Mario Garcia Kohly and Tracy Barnes. However, establishing an underground network of agents took time, which they did not have, considering the enormous pressure they were facing from the White House. So, simultaneous to this, Harvey applied ZR/RIFLE to Cuba, and for the first time, all CIA assassination operations came under the direction of one man.

Kohly was working with the CIA then. Marshall Diggs was the Washington attorney in whose office Kohly agreed to work with the CIA in March 1960. *Coup in Dallas* tells us that "Diggs was alleged to have been a CIA contract operative, and Mario Garcia Kohly, a known associate of Frank Austin, was a Cuban investment banker whom they considered to be the leader in exile."[264]

A CIA document released on January 1, 1976, contained the following February 18, 1963, report, written just weeks before the Diggs/Kohly quote mentioned above. "[Mitchell] WerBell and Arthur L. Smith," the report said, "were attempting to get Guatemala, Nicaragua, and El Salvador to recognize a de facto Cuban government in exile called 'United Organization for the Liberation of Cuba:' head of [the] organization was Mario Garcia Kohly (provisional president). WerBell reportedly offered $100,000 to Nic [Nicaraguan] Govt. Also associated with [the] group were Frank M. Austin, Marshall R. Diggs, Manuel Fuego (aka Firestone) and Col. John F. Kieffer…" The same CIA document contained a memo dated August 8, 1962, and mentions WerBell, Kohly, and Harvey together. "Relationship (with MW) terminated on friendly basis October 1959, KUBARK [CIA] opinion WerBell wished [to] use KUBARK funds to promote his personal interests.… Cable released by J.C. King, authenticated by William K. Harvey."[265]

Coup in Dallas also tells us that "the fundraising efforts fell under close FBI scrutiny, particularly a check in the amount of twelve million dollars which may or may not have come from a certain Texas oilman. It has been speculated that because Diggs was known to have direct access to oilman H. L. Hunt of Dallas, the check came from the archconservative known for funding private, clandestine operations. While the episode is intriguing, for this investigation we're led to hypothesize that the WerBell, Austin, Diggs, Kohly operation, whatever its purpose, was ancillary to the plot to assassinate the president."[266]

WerBell's name first appears in the January 11 datebook entry along with Lucien Conein, who was a longtime WerBell colleague. Conein had been an OSS Jedburg who parachuted into France during World War II to assist the Resistance, as was Tracy Barnes, and both worked for Harvey in Berlin. Meanwhile, WerBell lived in Costa Rica and worked with a "death squad" of drug trafficking Cuban exiles associated with Santo Trafficante.[267]

The datebook entry for the day before, January 10, contained only one word – "Harvey," suggesting a connection existed between the two entries. The next WerBell reference is on January 15 and reads, "Harvey called from DC. says Davis will come here with wife – who?" So, we have two Harvey references serving as bookends around the WerBell and Conein entry, with January 15 mentioning Thomas Eli Davis and his wife Carolyn traveling to New Orleans to see Lafitte. The next Harvey entry is January 18, "Harvey Here- Fl. Training." Even though the CIA had banished Harvey to Rome by this time, with the blessing of his good friend James Angleton, we know he continued meeting with Roselli in Miami every four to six weeks.

Meanwhile, in early 1963, Roselli was in Florida and, according to the entry above, was probably with Harvey, hooked up in Key Biscayne with Santo Trafficante associate John Martino. Lafitte's datebook mentions Trafficante on May 19 along with Paul Mondoloni and on August 13 with William Harvey. At the time, Bobby Kennedy was cracking down on the more violent Cuban exiles and the American mercenaries who supported them. As we will see, these groups turned to the Mafia and other private funding to work against Bobby, so Harvey's Florida visit likely had something to do with that.[268]

Smith was in the February 18 CIA report, the May 19 datebook entry with Mondoloni and Trafficante in Montreal, and was also mentioned in the January 24 datebook entry: "848 – Harvey-Soon White – Smith (Canada)." 848 may have been code for Henry D. Hecksher. If one assigns the corresponding number in the alphabet to each first letter in his name, it becomes 848. We will discuss the possibility of 848 being Hecksher in Chapter Twenty-Five.

Lafitte knew George Hunter White well, which explains why all datebook entries refer to him as George. So, the White in this entry is not him. This author believes a leading candidate was US Customs agent Ben White. In the early 1950s, White served in Mexico City and helped break up a Corsican heroin operation run by Antoine D'Agostino and Paul Mondoloni. Seeking to disrupt things before they could move narcotics through Texas, on April 8, 1960, White convinced the Mexican police to arrest Mondoloni. Still, the drug trafficker alluded authorities and wound up in Havana six weeks later. The FBN tracked him from Havana to Madrid and Marseilles, where they saw him with Lucien Rivard, Canada's reigning drug lord. The FBN had more luck working with Canadian officials, and they disrupted the drug operation there, but it continued to operate out of Mexico for years.

Paul Mondoloni was a member of the Corsican Mafia. He was a drug trafficker in the French Connection operation, which explains his inclusion with George White and Santo Trafficante. White and Lafitte had strong Mafia ties, so it is evident that the CIA was still working with organized crime in the spring of 1963, perhaps unrelated to the JFK assassination. In early March, Cuban police arrested one of Roselli's hit squads on a rooftop in Havana. So, all indications were that the CIA/Mafia attempt to assassinate Castro was still in place through Harvey and Roselli, funded by Mafia drug money, which the CIA was prone to take advantage of.

The March 26 Lafitte entry refers to "McWillie – Guns with Davis-Oswald." Considering the Thomas Davis/Victor Oswald connection, it is likely that the Oswald referred to here is Victor, not Lee. McWillie is Lewis McWillie, the Mafia operative whom Jack Ruby idolized. In 1959, McWillie was in Havana and summoned Ruby from Dallas to help extricate Santo Trafficante from a Cuban jail cell. John Martino was also in prison there and was visited by Charles Siragusa, per a notation in George Hunter White's notebook: "Siragusa re Martino Cuba." Siragusa also knew Thomas Davis, writing in a letter to George White that Davis was "a galloping clod whose testicles are larger than his home state of Texas, but who lacks the adjoining brains..." The McWillie entry referring to guns with Davis and Oswald ties everything together, considering that after the assassination, Ruby admitted that he was involved in gunrunning with Thomas Davis.[269] So, it is clear something was going on around March 1963 that involved the CIA and the Mafia, and it probably had nothing to do with the JFK assassination. That would come later.

***

In 1971, Jack Anderson of the *New York Times* wrote how the CIA dispatched "assassination and commando squads" to Cuba to kill Castro. They ran the operation out of "Zenith Technical Enterprises" (a CIA front company), and through "its doors passed some of the nation's most secret operators, such as John Roselli and Bill Harvey, 'Rip' Robertson and David Morales."[270] According to a June 2, 1961, CIA memorandum, Morales "arrived in Miami in October 1960 after spending two years at the Havana Station," where he worked with June Cobb, David Phillips, Pedro Diaz Lanz, Henry Hecksher, Frank Sturgis, and Bernard Baker trying to remove Castro.

In his 2007 book, *American Spy*, published just before his death, Howard Hunt wrote that William Harvey "posted Morales to the CIA's Miami station in 1961, where he became chief of Covert Operations for JM/WAVE...," and that "Morales and Harvey ... were hard-drinking, tough guys, possibly completely amoral." "Morales was rumored to be a cold-blooded killer, the go-to-guy in black ops situations when the government needed to have someone neutralized."[271]

Hunt's son, Saint John, released details of an alleged deathbed confession by his father that claimed Morales was part of a group that killed Kennedy. There was also an April 2007 article in *Rolling Stone* magazine by Erik Hedegaad that claimed Hunt, near death, "scribbled the initials 'LBJ'" on a piece of paper along with the names Cord Meyer and Bill Harvey and a line connecting Meyer's name to Morales, with a line from Morales to "French Gunman Grassy Knoll." None of this can be substantiated, but it is worth considering.[272]

Wayne Smith joined the State Department in 1957 and worked with Morales at the U.S. Embassy in Havana before Castro took over. He said, "Dave Morales did dirty work for the agency. If he were in the mob, he'd be called a hit man."[273] Author David Talbot wrote in *Brothers* that a relative told him Morales "was extremely loyal [to the Agency]. But I can see him being told to do something and do it. With no questions asked. One of Morales' jobs was to consort with the criminal element on behalf of the agency.... Morales might have been ordered to recruit 'those sleazy guys' and 'get them to wherever they were supposed to go' for the Dallas operation."[274]

Gaeton Fonzi worked for the HSCA in 1977. In his book, *The Last Investigation*, he described how Morales' career began as an enlisted man stationed in Munich during World War II, and he later joined the CIA. In 1954, he worked with David Phillips in the Guatemalan coup to overthrow Arbenz, as did Howard Hunt, Tracy Barnes, Johnny Roselli, Henry Hecksher, and William Pawley. Morales and Phillips worked together again in Cuba in 1959 in Havana and during the Bay of Pigs. A Marine officer who knew him in Vietnam said Morales was "a fairly heavy drinker when I met him. He was a 'macho' kind of guy, strongly opinionated, an enforcer type...I got the impression he was always able to control everyone who worked for him. I wouldn't want to cross him." Fonzi also learned that "Morales was a hitman for the CIA. He was a killer. He said it himself...he had killed people for the CIA in Vietnam, in Venezuela, in Uruguay, and other places..."[275]

According to Richard Mahoney, the author of *Sons and Brothers*, "Rosselli ... was the only person who could make the incendiary [Dave] M.[orales] laugh. They would drink until the sun came up, usually joined by Rip Robertson, the hard-bitten Texan and decorated veteran of World War II who was the favorite 'boom and bang' guy among the exiled Cubans....

Roselli was one of only two Americans authorized to go into Cuba on clandestine missions."[276]

By all accounts, Roselli, Morales, Robertson, Harvey, Barnes, and Hecksher had a lot in common. They all hated Fidel Castro. They were highly loyal and violently anti-Communist. And they accepted assassination as a necessary evil.

***

In 1967, in an apparent attempt at damage control, an allegedly shocked Richard Helms requested a CIA internal investigation into ZR/RIFLE and William Harvey. Quite revealing, the CIA's Inspector General report stated that Harvey:

> Personally handled the Castro operation and did not use any of the assets being developed in ZRRIFLE. He says that soon he came to think of the Castro operation and ZRRIFLE as being synonymous. The overall Executive Action [assassination] came to be treated in his mind as being synonymous with QJWIN, the agent working on the overall program. He says that when he wrote of ZRRIFLE/ QJWIN, the reference was to Executive Action Capability; when he used the cryptonym ZRRIFLE alone, he was referring to Castro.[277]

On January 25, 1962, William Harvey jotted down notes describing what he envisioned ZR/RIFLE to be. He referred to "The Magic Button," which may have been a reference to LSD, mind-altering drugs, and poisons used for assassination, all of which we know Harvey was interested in. He referenced "eye – Jim A – Contradestruct," which was James Angleton, implying the counterintelligence chief was involved with Harvey in assassination planning. The definition of contra is "opposite," and the opposite of destruct is to create, which suggests Angleton's responsibility was to create false identities for assassins as cover, as was already mentioned. It is also interesting that Harvey noted to "Never mention assassination," that it was a "last resort beyond last resort and a confession of weakness," and "No project on paper except for cover."

"Cover file – Create from RIS [Russian Intelligence Service – KGB] ... followed by "Note dangers of RIS counter-action & monitor if they are blamed." The illusion U.S. intelligence created that the Soviets had killed Oswald in Russia and replaced him with a "Sleeper Agent," along with the fabricated post-assassination evidence that showed the Oswald who died was 2" shorter than the one who was discharged from the Marines, fit nicely into this category and enabled the U.S. to blame the Soviets for the JFK assassination if they so desired. The point is the conspirators knew the United States would not blame the Soviets, at least not publicly, and they would have no choice but to cover up the story to prevent an international incident, especially since the Soviets were onto Oswald from the beginning when he defected. Oswald was the perfect pasty, and Harvey and Angleton knew this. Then there was the passage, "Cover: planning should include provision for blaming Sovs or Czechs in case of blow..." Oswald's setup as a Russian sleeper agent and assassination patsy met this criterion. [278]

Also, Harvey's report states, "Exclude organized criminals, e.g., Sicilians, criminals, those w/record of arrests, those w/ instability of purpose as criminals." His removal of Trafficante and Giancana from the Castro assassination plots coincided with this. The fact that he retained Roselli meant he did not consider him an organized crime figure but a CIA asset. Later, he wrote: "Corsicans recommended. Sicilians could lead to Mafia," reinforcing the need to avoid American Mafia figures. Operation Gladio, the CIA's program to place stay-behind armies in Europe, was financed by an illicit Corsican drug operation.

Then there was the reference to QJ/WIN, "who is under written contract as a principal agent, with the primary task of spotting agent candidates. QJ/WIN was first contacted in [nearly two lines redacted] in connection with an illegal narcotics operation into the United States. For a period of a year and a half, he was contacted sporadically by Luxembourg on behalf of the Bureau of Narcotics. Files of the Bureau reflect an excellent performance by QJ/WIN..."[279]

Douglas Valentine wrote in *The Strength of the Wolf* that in April 1959, QJ/WIN was approached by a French national and asked to join a narcotics ring. On April 29, Allen Dulles got involved and had "the nearest narcotics bureau officer" interrogate QJ/WIN and the Frenchman. QJ/WIN dispelled their concerns, for FBN files mention his "excellent" performance during the eighteen months leading up to November 1960. On that basis, Harvey decided to employ QJ/WIN as a principal agent in the ZR/RIFLE assassination program.[280]

Interestingly, QJ/WIN's story closely mirrors June Cobb's, who also worked for the FBN and CIA and had her loyalty questioned but eventually became a valuable CIA asset. She also associated with CIA assassins and possibly was involved with ZR/RIFLE.

***

In 1977, Texas researcher Mary Ferrell uncovered a CIA document dated April 1, 1964, regarding OAS assassin Jean Souetre, who was in Dallas on the day of the assassination. According to the document,

> Jean SOUETRE aka Michel ROUX aka Michael Mertz – On March 5, [redacted] the FBI advised that the French had [redacted] the Legal Attache in Paris and also the [redacted] had queried the Bureau in New York City concerning subject, stating that he had been expelled from the U.S. at Fort Worth or Dallas 18 hours after the assassination. He was in Fort Worth on the morning 22 November and in Dallas in the afternoon. The French believe that he was expelled to either Mexico or Canada.... Subject is believed to be identical with a Captain who is a deserter from the French Army and an activist in the OAS. The French are concerned because of de Gaulle's planned visit to Mexico. They would like to know the reason for expulsion from the U.S. and his destination. Bureau files are negative, and they are checking in Texas and with the INS (Immigration and Naturalization Service).[281]

In 1964, the FBI contacted Houston dentist Dr. Lawrence Alderson, who knew Souetre in France while he was in the military. Souetre had reached out to Alderson in January 1963, hence the FBI's interest in him, which means they must have been tracking Alderson and kept an eye on the mail he sent and received. The FBI "felt that Jean knew who, or he himself had, assassinated Kennedy," Alderson said. In an interview with author Dick Russell, he added: "They told me that Souetre was in Dallas that day and was flown out that afternoon by a private pilot. As far as they were concerned, in a government plane. But there was no record whatsoever of the plane being there. They said Jean was a very questionable character, a freelance soldier of fortune. They had known he was in the United States and had traced him as far as Dallas the day before the assassination."[282]

An investigator for the HSCA uncovered that Souetre "was connected with people involved in murders or political assassinations in Europe. He most definitely traveled in the same circles as OAS-connected killers. The agency admits that its own handlers of WIN and ROGUE were afraid of them, that they were not following CIA directives and were off on assassination plots of their own. The CIA was trying to keep them on a leash.... So, Jean Souetre is not the kind of guy you like to see was arrested and deported from Texas that day."[283]

According to a released CIA file, Souetre was an OAS captain who "was alleged to have been involved in an assassination attempt against de Gaulle."

A May 1963 memo by Richard Helms said Souetre had approached the CIA, but the "U.S. had absolutely no intention of working with any person or group against the duly constituted government of France." From what we know about the CIA's support of the Algerian military revolt, this last statement is absurd. It was written in another typescript from the rest of the memo, so someone likely added it later to conceal an involvement with Jean Souetre.[284]

Assuming Dr. Alderson understood correctly what the FBI agents had told him, what he said is quite revealing. Jean Souetre was a known OAS assassin. The FBI was aware of that, which was why they were tracking him during his stay in the U.S. Since they also knew he was in Fort Worth on the morning of November 22 and in Dallas that afternoon, doesn't that suggest that they likely did not let Souetre out of their sight that day? It makes sense that was the case, considering the agents knew JFK was in town and they were aware of what Souetre was capable of. And unless the FBI agents were incompetent, they kept a watchful eye on Souetre the entire day of the assassination. It explains why the November 19 Lafitte date-book entry reads: "Souetre to go overt. With Jack C." It leads us to believe that Souetre was probably supposed to be one of the shooters, but he knew the FBI was watching him. So, he came out of hiding and pulled himself off the project so as not to jeopardize the operation. As a result, the FBI knew he was not one of the shooters since they never lost sight of him, and their close surveillance of Souetre explains how they knew a private pilot flew him out of Dallas that afternoon in a government plane. It clarifies a lot of things. Such as, why was it so crucial for J. Edgar Hoover to conclude so quickly that Oswald was the lone gunman when so many people thought shots had come from two separate locations? What was the harm in saying Oswald had an accomplice? The answer is that Hoover knew Souetre being in Dallas could not have been a coincidence. It was a major international conspiracy, which meant they had to get Souetre out of Dallas as fast as possible before anyone knew he was there. And the desperate need to cover up the crime began.

The CIA document discovered by Mary Ferrell says that Michael Mertz was an alias Souetre used. We know that three people with the same name, John Mertz, Irma Rio Mertz, and Sara Mertz, all flew from Houston to Mexico City on the day of the assassination. Was it just a coincidence that Souetre used the name Mertz, or was there a connection here?[285]

According to the Pulitzer Prize-winning book *The Heroin Trail*, Michael Mertz was a leader in the French Resistance during World War II. After the war, he was a captain in the French Secret Service in Germany, Turkey, and Morocco. By the late 1950s, he became one of France's leading heroin smugglers into the United States and Canada. In April 1961, Mertz returned to duty posing as an OAS sympathizer. In an act that resembled Oswald's alleged pro-Castro demonstration in New Orleans in the summer of 1963, the police arrested Mertz for publicly distributing pro-OAS literature. He wound up in an internment camp where he uncovered a plot to assassinate de Gaulle. Mertz saved de Gaulle's life and became virtually untouchable. Between 1961 and 1969, Mertz and his associates exported two tons of heroin to North America, and U.S. officials cited ties between Mertz and Santo Trafficante, but authorities did nothing.[286]

One of Mertz's contacts was Christian David, a small-time crook recruited by French intelligence in their battle against the OAS. As described in *The Great Heroin Coup*, "David has been a pimp, robber, hired assassin for French intelligence, hatchet man in Algiers torture chambers, arms trader, spy, narcotics trafficker and lover of beautiful women. He knew the truth about the Ben Barka affair that shook France in 1965, the French intelligence power struggle with SDECE, collaboration of SDECE with the Corsican Mafia, and of secret CIA operations with Latin America.[287]

In 1988, author Steve J. Rivele learned from David the names of three French gangsters he claimed had killed Kennedy. When Rivele contacted the U.S. government about David, they put him in touch with Lucien Conein, the shadowy figure who was an honorary member of the Unione Course, the Corsican crime syndicate that was involved in the mass movement of hundreds of ex-Nazis from war-torn-Europe to South America. They were all committed to fighting communism, even the Corsicans. CIA notes regarding ZR/RIFLE state: "QJ/WIN was first contacted in [redacted], in conjunction with an illegal narcotics operation into the United States. For a period of a year and a half, he was contacted sporadically by CIS Lucien Conein on behalf of the Bureau of Narcotics."[288]

According to the CIA, Conein's first contact with QJ/WIN was on behalf of the FBN, around when Sheffield Edwards, the CIA's security officer for Project Artichoke, was working with the FBN's liaison to the CIA, Charles Siragusa, who also was an ex-military intelligence officer during World War II. Edwards wanted Siragusa to put him in contact with organized crime figures to assassinate foreign leaders. Lucien Conein, also known as Black Luigi, often bragged about his connection to the Corsican Mafia and the Unione Course, who were heavily involved in the Indochina drug trade. Conein had a relationship with William Harvey, QJ/WIN, and

Tracy Barnes. Recall it was Harvey who wrote "Corsicans recommended" as candidates for political assassins.[289]

In Indochina, one group that Conein almost certainly knew of was the secretive Field Operations Intelligence (FOI), to which Richard Case Nagell belonged. "During my service with the FOI in the Republic of Korea and during my service with the FOI … in Japan," Nagell said, "the FOI sponsored, financed, supported, or otherwise participated in assassinations, kidnappings, blackmailings [sic] and a host of other illicit practices…"[290]

We know of a connection between FOI and the defection of American service members behind the Iron Curtain, which applied to Oswald. Nagell also stated that the Berlin Tunnel was an FOI operation, which placed William Harvey, Tracy Barnes, and everyone else in the Berlin station in direct contact with FOI. It means Oswald's defection may have been an FOI/CIA operation and that Harvey, Barnes, Hecksher, and Conein were aware of Oswald as early as 1959 when he defected.

In this author's opinion, Souetre was in Dallas on November 22, 1963, not Mertz. Consider that an FBI Memorandum sent to Hoover dated April 8, 1963, stated that "Houston is requested to identify the ALDERSONS, and when this information is forthcoming, the Bureau is requested to advise what, if any, information may be furnished to this source."[291] The FBI would only be interested in Alderson because of his connection to Souetre, which meant Souetre was on the Bureau's radar more than seven months before the assassination. In addition, someone was deported from Dallas two days after the assassination, and the FBI questioned Alderson about that. The FBI would only have done so if Souetre was the one deported. If they had thought it was Mertz, they would not have questioned Alderson after the fact because he did not have a relationship with Mertz. Since Mertz was considered a hero for saving de Gaulle's life, why was France worried about de Gaulle's safety in Mexico City if it were Mertz who was secretly flown there on November 22 from Fort Worth? Therefore, it had to be Souetre who was in Dallas.

***

From the moment Operation Mongoose began, Bobby Kennedy was the unofficial head of the war against Castro, even though he had no previous experience running a complex covert operation. He wrote that his plan was "to stir things up on the island with espionage, sabotage, general disorder, run & operated by Cubans themselves with every group but Batistaites & Communists. Do not know if we will be successful in overthrowing Castro but we have nothing to lose…"[292]

Though well-intentioned, Bobby's main problem was that people much more qualified than him didn't believe Cuba was that critical to devote so much energy to. Sam Halpern, the CIA executive assistant to William Harvey, recalled, "Everyone at CIA was surprised at the Kennedy's obsession with Fidel.... They thought it was a waste of time. We all knew he [Fidel] couldn't hurt us. Most of us at CIA initially liked Kennedy, but why go after this little guy? One thing is for sure: Kennedy wasn't doing it out of national security concerns. It was a personal thing. The Kennedy family felt personally hurt by the Bay of Pigs and sought revenge. Papa Joe taught his sons well: 'Don't get mad, get even.'"[293]

Those in charge tried to convince the Kennedy brothers early on that overthrowing Castro was not going to be a walk in the park. On January 22, 1961, two days after JFK became President, Secretary of State Dean Rusk led a meeting where Bobby Kennedy was present. Thomas Mann, the Assistant Secretary of State for Inter-American Affairs, said, "It seemed clear there was little hope now" in getting rid of Castro. He cited Cuba's ties to the Sino-Soviet bloc and the Cuban militia as two reasons to walk away. JCS Chairman Lyman Lemnitzer followed and said Cuba was an armed camp. The Revolutionary Army had 32,000 soldiers, the Revolutionary National Police had 9,000, and the Militia had over 200,000. They had received more than 30,000 tons of arms and equipment over the past five or six months. The message was clear. The only way to succeed was a full-fledged attack that included all branches of the U.S. military, which JFK said was not an option, and Dean Rusk agreed with that. He thought "there were enormous implications of putting U.S. forces ashore in Cuba ... we might be confronted by serious uprisings all over Latin America..."[294]

Bobby Kennedy heard what was said, and he should have told his brother to walk away. Maybe he did. Either way, the Kennedy brothers had no one to blame but themselves for the Bay of Pigs disaster and what was to follow.

Richard Helms considered Bobby's militaristic approach no "more than pinpricks" against Castro, and he quickly tired of him "hammering us for results." He later complained that under Bobby's "relentless" reign, I was "getting my ass beaten. You should have enjoyed the experience of Bobby Kennedy rampant on your back." The young upstart had only "a slight idea what was involved in organizing a secret intelligence operation," Helms said.[295]

Five days before JFK won the election, at a meeting of the Special Group without Allen Dulles, Deputy Secretary of Defense James Douglas, Under Secretary of State Livingston Merchant, and National Security Adviser Gordon Gray concluded that the covert operations proposed by the CIA would not work. Gray thought, "We will never be able to 'clean up' the situation without the use of overt U.S. military force." Gray favored "a simulated attack on Guantanamo" to justify using the military. Merchant responded that "if Castro's support were such that an uprising was out of the question, then an open invasion by the U.S. would be met by a hostile population, and we would be plunged into a situation like [the French] in Algeria."[296]

So, even before JFK became President, the consensus was that Fidel Castro was insignificant and trying to remove him from power was not worth the effort and was doomed to fail.

However, as David Martin wrote in *Wilderness of Mirrors*, "Sometimes, the Attorney General would take things into his own hands. ... He sent Lansdale down to Miami in a futile effort to form a cohesive government-in-exile and kept the trip a secret from the CIA. ... The Attorney General frequently dealt directly with some of the Cuban exiles who were supposed to be Harvey's agents. They would troop in and out of the Justice Department, bearing firsthand reports of CIA ineptitudes." "For Harvey, it was all too much amateurish meddling," Martin continued, and he "began suggesting that some of the Attorney General's actions bordered on the traitorous."[297]

Tom Parrott, Allen Dulles's assistant, said: "Everyone was fed up with Bobby. He was a dreadful little guy. I didn't see any saving grace in him ... he would come into meetings with his necktie down and his shirt unbuttoned when everyone else was formally dressed. He was always picking, picking. Bobby affected everyone. No one wanted to deal with him if they didn't have to. ... He was abrasive."[298]

The bottom line was that patience with the thirty-six-year-old, whose only claim to fame was that his brother was President, was wearing thin with people you dared not cross, especially William Harvey. They would tolerate him for a while until they perceived that his actions threatened the security of the United States and placed Western Europe in danger.

On one occasion in 1961, Lyndon Johnson told his top aide Walter Jenkins, "Bobby Kennedy has turned the damn CIA over into some Murder Incorporated." In 1962, Johnson predicted, "someone is going to try and get even."[299]

The CIA, ex-Nazis, Monarchists, and French assassins could no longer tolerate the Kennedy brothers. They had worked together since the early 1950s, protecting Europe from a Soviet attack. Once they concluded that President Kennedy placed Europe in jeopardy, specifically West Berlin, they considered it their duty to remove him from office before it was too late.

CHAPTER FIVE

MAKING A KILLING IN 1961

The CIA's effort to kill Castro using the Mafia was a disaster, but the results were much better when they attempted murder on their own. With the establishment of the Soviet's Department 13 assassination unit in the 1950s, it was inevitable that American intelligence would follow suit. Cuba and Batista had taught the U.S. a valuable lesson in dealing with third-world leaders who ruled with an iron hand, for supporting such a figure could lead to a Communist government when the people determined they had been oppressed long enough. For the CIA, it was better to institute a change before circumstances got to that point.

One of the more notorious Latin American dictators of the era was General Rafael Leonidas Trujillo, who ruled the Dominican Republic for thirty-one years with an iron hand. A ruthless and sadistic torturer, he used the military to maintain power, giving his officers and soldiers authority to terrorize the people to keep them in line. Despite this, the United States supported Trujillo, or at least tolerated him. They gave the Dominican Republic $5 million in aid in the fifteen years before his death in 1961. In 1962-63, his successors received $70 million, a sign that Trujillo's murder was to improve the American position in Latin America.[300]

By the late 1950s, domestic opposition to Trujillo grew, especially among those who considered Castro's revolution a blueprint for what they could accomplish in their country. Trujillo responded with increased oppression, and criticism came swiftly from his Latin neighbors. It was especially true of Venezuelan President Romulo Betancourt, an outspoken critic of the Dominican dictator, for whom Trujillo had great contempt. Betancourt plotted to overthrow him by conspiring with Dominicans who wanted a change, while Trujillo backed numerous plots by Venezuelan exiles to remove Betancourt. The Venezuelan government complained to the Organization of American States (OAS), which so incensed Trujillo that he had Betancourt's car bombed. It increased the opposition to Trujillo worldwide, and the OAS voted unanimously to sever diplomatic relations with his government and impose economic sanctions on the Dominican Republic. The actions, though warranted, only made matters worse. On

November 25, 1960, when three sisters, Patria, María Teresa, and Minerva Mirabal, were brutally murdered by Trujillo's henchmen, it was the last straw for the United States.[301]

As early as February 10, 1960, Allen Dulles hinted at a Special Group meeting that the Trujillo regime "might be coming to an end." Eisenhower's position was that to keep the Organization of American States happy, the U.S. needed to get rid of Trujillo simultaneously with the removal of Castro; otherwise, they would face criticism throughout Latin America.[302]

At a March 30 Special Group meeting, Dulles mentioned "certain confidential aspects" pertaining to the Dominican Republic, which may have been a reference to assassination. He also brought up a contingency plan to seal off the land entrance from Haiti into the Dominican Republic. The plan was for Haiti to invite the U.S. to send troops into their country to prevent a general uprising following Trujillo's demise from spilling over into Haiti. There was also concern that a leftist government might take control of the Dominican Republic with Trujillo dead and invite Castro's followers into their country. So, the U.S. wanted to control the narrative after Trujillo was gone. It was the exact blueprint they had for Cuba. Eliminate Castro and establish a provisional government that would ask the U.S. military to come in and keep peace.[303]

In May, William Pawley and Florida Senator George Smathers, known as "The Senator From Latin America," met with Eisenhower to ask for a chance to convince Trujillo to hold free elections. Eisenhower was initially willing; however, by June, he instructed the State Department to form a provisional government to replace Trujillo so "we could then move in with troops on their request if [the] need should arise."[304]

On August 20, the OAS broke off diplomatic relations with Trujillo. The U.S. supported the action and left a skeleton crew at the U.S. Embassy in Ciudad Trujillo, which led Trujillo to believe "an assassination plot was being hatched."[305] The attempt to remove Trujillo began when U.S. operatives contacted anti-Trujillo dissidents to set things in motion. By December, the U.S. sent guns to generals looking to orchestrate a coup, but things slowed after Kennedy took office. It wasn't that JFK favored Trujillo. He despised him but thought it unwise to overthrow his regime without knowing who his replacement would be. "If Trujillo goes, he goes, but why are we pushing that," he asked. As far as killing him was concerned, the "U.S. as a matter of general policy cannot condone assassination." Maybe so, but Trujillo's days were numbered.[306]

106

Despite the objections of JFK, with the help of the CIA, Trujillo was assassinated on May 30, 1961. Two carloads of killers fired twenty-seven shots into the dictator's body. The operation was supposed to occur six weeks prior, during the Bay of Pigs invasion, to appease the OAS, but Castro was still standing, so they decided to take out Trujillo on their own.

The murder weapons were supplied by the CIA, with funds passed from a shell company to the Jacob Merrill Kaplan Fund, then onto the Institute of International Labor Research, and finally into the hands of Juan Bosch and his co-conspirators. Meanwhile, the infamous Cord Meyer, responsible for the CIA's control of international student groups, used Bosch and his revolutionaries to rally Latin American nations against Castro.[307]

Colonel William Bishop of the CIA, who had served under General MacArthur during World War II, claimed to be part of the CIA hit squad, Operation 40, that was involved in the Trujillo assassination. He told author Dick Russell: "Both the CIA and the Pentagon wanted Trujillo dead, and it's more effective to kill one man than it is to lose a thousand with an all-out invasion. I made the hit on Trujillo.... It was a professional challenge for me.... You don't allow yourself to become emotionally or psychologically involved..."[308]

Justifying the killing of one man to save thousands was a CIA mantra and a philosophy that one could apply to the JFK assassination. Some thought Kennedy's policies would lead to a major nuclear war, and those in a position to do something about it considered the murder of a President acceptable to prevent that from happening.

The CIA's role in Trujillo's killing is referenced in a 1973 CIA internal investigation into the murder, which disclosed "quite extensive Agency involvement with the plotters." The CIA described its role in "changing" the government "as a 'success' in that it assisted in moving the Dominican Republic from a totalitarian dictatorship to a Western-style democracy."[309]

Juan Bosch, the head of the Dominican opposition to Trujillo in exile and a recipient of CIA funding, was elected president in 1962. On September 25, 1963, less than two months before the JFK assassination, Bosch was overthrown by a military coup. He survived, but the radical right in the United States finally had what they wanted in charge of the Dominican Republic – a right-wing military government. Duane Luther, the president of Texaco in the Dominican Republic, was accused of supporting Bosch's opponent and bringing in weapons to overthrow him. It was a sign of the change planned for Cuba by the end of 1963 if it was allowed to happen.[310]

***

In 1960, the United Nations was only fourteen years old as European decolonization created a dramatic shift in the balance of power. Afro-Asian bloc countries now accounted for forty-seven U.N. members out of one hundred, and the West could no longer rely on automatic majorities in the General Assembly. Sixteen African nations joined the U.N. in 1960 alone, as Africa made up one-quarter of the U.N.'s membership.[311] Of those sixteen, the Belgian Congo was the largest and most prosperous, but Belgium granted them independence without preparing the people for self-government. As a result, Congo's civil service, army, and economy remained in Belgium's control, as they quietly privatized much of Congo's industry and transferred the headquarters of Congolese companies to Belgium. The plan was for Belgium to reap the benefits of having a colony without the responsibilities that went along with it.[312]

There was good reason for Belgium and the West to want to maintain control of Congo's affairs. During World War II, the most critical uranium ore source was the Shinkolobwe mine in the Congolese province of Katanga, owned by the Belgian mining company Union Miniere du Haut Katanga. The United States controlled access to the mine, which benefited some of America's largest chemical and engineering firms, such as Bechtel, Dupont, Ratheon, Eastman Kodak, and Union Carbide. The OSS maintained a presence in the Congo, and their mission was to keep uranium out of the hands of the enemy. By 1958, Congolese uranium ore had become less important, but the U.S. worried about the Soviets acquiring it from the Shinkolobwe mine stockpile. In addition, by 1959, 9 percent of the world's copper, 49 percent of cobalt (54 percent in 1960), 69 percent of industrial diamonds, and 6.5 percent of tin came from the Congo. It was a strategically important country, and many high-profile Americans profited greatly from the available minerals.[313]

Christian Herter, Eisenhower's Secretary of State from 1959 to 1961, had family ties to Mobil Oil with direct investments in the Congo; C. Douglas Dillon, the Undersecretary of State, had family ties to Dillon, Read, and Company, which managed the Belgian Congo's bond issues; Thomas Gates, the Defense Secretary, was linked to Drexel and Co. and to Morgan Guaranty Trust, which arranged for two $20 million loans to the Belgian Congo. As always, satisfying big business interests motivated politicians who were in a position to direct American foreign policy.

William Armistead Moale Burden, Jr. became the American ambassador to Belgium and the Belgian Congo in September 1959. He was heir to the Vanderbilt fortune and a significant contributor to the Republican Party, with an impressive resume. At various times, he was director of Lockheed Aircraft Corporation, the CBS television network, Hanover Bank, Allied Chemical, and American Metal Climax, a mining company with extensive holdings in central Africa connected to the Belgian Congo. He was also director of the Fairfield Foundation. This CIA front company financed the Congress for Cultural Freedom, and Burden referred to Allen Dulles as a lifelong friend (as did Harold Hochschild, Climax's Chairman of the Board). Burden and Hochschild were both trustees of the African-American Institute, as were Dana Creel, who later headed the Rockefeller Brothers Fund, and Alan Pifer, who led the Carnegie Corporation. The United States had a vested interest in ensuring that raw minerals in the Congo did not fall into Soviet hands. Allen Dulles always went where the money was.[314]

***

Katanga, the wealthiest province in the Congo, seceded from its newly formed mother country on July 11, 1960, and Belgian mining companies, in collaboration with Western governments, supported the move. The impact was disastrous, for the Congo could not sustain itself economically without Katanga's wealth and resources. The day before, Belgium sent troops to the Congo, claiming they wanted to protect private citizens. Desperate, Patrice Lumumba, the independent Congo's first prime minister, turned to the U.N. to help remove the troops and keep Katanga part of the country.[315]

Ignored by the UN, on July 17, Lumumba called for the Soviets to intervene. It prompted Burden to cable the State Department that the "objective of our political and diplomatic action must therefore be to destroy [the] Lumumba government." Shortly after that, the first United Nations troops arrived in the Congo's capital city of Leopoldville, and ONUC (l'Organisation des Nations Unies au Congo) became a reality. Except in Katanga, an ONUC force of 3,500 men was spread throughout the country, but things were about to go from bad to worse. [316]

The Belgians were still in Katanga when, on August 9, Albert Kalonji, the province leader of South Kasai, declared independence, creating another crisis. South Kasai was the center of the Congo's diamond wealth, and Kalonji had a similar relationship with Forminiere, a Belgian diamond company, that Moise Tshombe, the President of Katanga, had with Union Miniere. Both men relied heavily on white mercenaries to stay in power.[317]

As mentioned by Major Ralph P. Ganis in the *Skorzeny Papers, Evidence for the Plot to Kill JFK*, "Skorzeny would have been closely following the Katanga developments from Madrid, due to his various business connections in Africa, and the effect of the crisis on his private intelligence network."

Skorzeny's interest in the Congo actually began in 1943 during World War II when his group was involved in a mission to sabotage oil wells. They also knew about uranium, and his team was to receive support from "a small group of missionary fathers and [a] few disaffected Belgian colonist" Fascists, but nothing materialized. During the 1950s, "Skorzeny's mercenary contacts in the Congo included his paramilitary trainers. Contract negotiations were underway by Skorzeny with Major Guy Weber, Tshombe's senior military adviser and new military chief of staff, to provide military support to the new nation."

In addition to Weber, Jean-Francois Thiriart was the driving force behind an organization called the Comité d'Action et de Défense des Belges d'Afrique (CADBA). Belgian Monarchists created the organization soon after Katanga seceded and hired former French soldiers dismissed from service after the 1958 putsch in Algeria against President de Gaulle. It was all about preserving French and Belgian colonialism. There is also evidence that Skorzeny may have sold surplus aircraft to Tshombe. Clearly, the pro-European Monarchist Skorzeny had a vested interest in Congo remaining a Belgian colony.[318]

Meanwhile, Lumumba began to lose faith in the U.N.'s ability to hold a democratic Congo together. On August 15, he asked the Soviet Union for military assistance, and just over a week later, Soviet technicians and equipment arrived. They eventually sent planes, weapons, and military advisers to support their African ally.[319]

Lumumba's relationship with the Soviet Union became clear on August 5, when he received a letter from Nikita Khrushchev promising that "the Soviet Union is prepared to give ... the Republic of Congo comprehensive support and assistance.... We know that the imperialists are mounting every possible intrigue against your young government... In their arsenal of subversive action is not only sabotage and economic diversion but ... plots and terrorist acts of every kind ..." Khrushchev assured Lumumba the Soviets wanted a united Congo and considered Katanga's separation a Western conspiracy.[320]

The U.S. government was appalled. It was still smarting from the 1959 Castro revolution and was determined to prevent the Soviet Union from staking a claim in the heart of Africa. A concerned Ike told his foreign policy team on August 1 that "the Communists ... have succeeded to the extent that students in many cases are now saying that the Communists are thinking of the common man while the United States is dedicated to supporting outmoded regimes."[321]

As early as August 1959, nearly a year before Congo's independence, the CIA sent Larry Devlin there as its Chief of Station. His cover was agricultural attaché at the American Embassy. Devlin recognized that this vast region in the center of Africa was a strategic linchpin in the Cold War and quickly identified Lumumba as an enemy. Allen Dulles agreed, calling Lumumba "Castro or worse." When he heard about the arrival of Soviet assistance in Leopoldville, Dulles sent an urgent telegram to Devlin: "The removal [of Lumumba] must be an urgent and prime objective ... this should be a high priority of our covert action."

At a January 14, 1960, NSC meeting, Eisenhower said he wanted "access to such military rights and facilities and strategic resources as may be required in our national security interests." Allen Dulles concurred, and they decided to back military strong men in Africa to control the uneducated population, which was the CIA's blueprint for nation-building.

Meanwhile, on March 1, 1960, a plan to assassinate Lumumba was proposed by Belgian Count Harold d'Aspremont Lynden, assistant private secretary to the prime minister and a nephew of the grand marshal of the royal court. American ambassador Burden agreed, writing, "Lumumba ... was the Communist-inspired leader ... working if not directly for the Russians, very closely with them." "Lumumba was such a damn nuisance," he declared, "it was perfectly obvious that the way to get rid of him was through political assassination."

On August 17, Devlin cabled CIA headquarters warning of a Communist plan to take over the Congo, for which there was no evidence, and that Lumumba was "anti-white." At an NSC meeting the next day, Undersecretary of State Dillon said Lumumba was serving the Soviets, and Allen Dulles agreed. Furthermore, Dulles, whose decisions were always based upon what was best for American big business, argued it was "important to preserve Katanga as a separate viable asset." Eisenhower agreed and said the U.N. needed to recognize Katanga and eliminate Lumumba. On August 19, the CIA told Leopoldville to proceed with Lumumba's removal.[322]

Minutes of the Special Group on August 25, 1960, suggest that Eisenhower approved Lumumba's assassination, as did those of the NSC on September 21: "It was finally agreed that planning for the Congo would not necessarily rule out 'consideration' of any particular kind of activity which might contribute to getting rid of Lumumba." Allen Dulles warned that "Lumumba was not yet disposed of and remained a grave danger as long as he was not disposed of."[323] Dulles next traveled to Brussels to tell Burden that the United States intended to back Colonel Joseph Mobutu, second in

111

command of the Congolese army. According to the Church Committee, Devlin said: "The coup of Mobutu ... was arranged and supported, and indeed, managed, by the Central Intelligence Agency."[324]

On September 5, just eleven days after the NSC discussed "getting rid of Lumumba," the CIA instructed Larry Devlin to tell Congo President Joseph Kasa-Vubu to dismiss Lumumba and six other ministers of his democratically elected government. Then, on September 14, once again directed by the CIA, Kasa-Vubu dissolved Parliament. That evening, Mobutu proclaimed in a radio address that he was taking military control. Richard Bissell sent Devlin a coded cable to assassinate Lumumba five days later.[325]

It was not just the United States that wanted Lumumba dead. England did as well. "I see only two possible solutions to the problem," wrote Howard Smith of the Foreign Office in September 1960. "The first is the simple one of ensuring Lumumba's removal from the scene by killing him."[326]

In November 1960, the month JFK was elected, a U.S. naval task force visited various countries along the west coast of Africa, which included preparation for amphibious landings on beachheads. They stayed for months in the Gulf of Guinea, within striking distance of the Congo, and landed at Matadi, the Atlantic port of the Congo.[327] Meanwhile, Lumumba was arrested and imprisoned, but his supporters remained a menace, so Belgium introduced a few hundred additional European recruits to maintain control. They were "Belgium paratroopers, former members of German SS and former Italian fascist soldiers," perhaps part of Skorzeny's network.[328] President-elect John Kennedy opposed the introduction of such troops, which created concern among right-wingers that, as President, he would call for freeing all political prisoners, including Lumumba. Eisenhower strongly opposed such a move for fear it would return Lumumba to a position of power. Belgium was especially interested because they knew that in 1957, Kennedy had called for Algeria's independence when France was engaged in a war with Algerian rebels.[329]

The first sign of trouble occurred on December 12, 1960, when a group of American senators, accompanied by Edward Kennedy, met with President Nkrumah of Ghana and called for the release of political prisoners. Then, Dean Rusk, Chester Bowles, and Averill Harriman, all destined to play prominent roles in the Kennedy Presidency, told the U.N. Special Representative to the Congo, Rajeshwar Dayal, "that the new administration would take a firm position ... with regard to the problem presented by Belgium and Belgian technicians." Therefore, it was not a coincidence that Lumumba was murdered on January 17, 1961, just three days before Kennedy's inauguration.[330]

In the 1970s, the Church Committee blamed Allen Dulles for Lumumba's assassination. On September 24, 1960, he sent a telegram to Leopoldville, stating: "We wish [to] give every possible support in eliminating Lumumba from any possibility [of] resuming governmental position." The following exchange took place during the Church Committee hearings in the 1970s:

> Hedgeman: "It is my recollection that he [Dulles] advised me, or my instructions were, to eliminate Lumumba."
>
> Church Committee: "By eliminate, do you mean assassinate?"
>
> Hedgeman: "Yes."[331]

The Church Committee concluded that Hedgeman "clearly had prior knowledge of the plan" to transfer Lumumba to where it was "probable that he would be killed ... and the place was known as the 'slaughterhouse.'"[332]

***

Sidney Gottlieb of the CIA's Technical Services Division was at the center of the plot to kill Lumumba. The intent was to poison Lumumba's food, but Gottlieb explained anything was acceptable provided it could "not be traced back...either to an American or the United States government." Plausible deniability had to be maintained.[333] A mandate to comply with these instructions brought QJ/WIN to the Belgian Congo. As Richard Helms said of him, "If you need somebody to carry out [a] murder, I guess you had a man who might be prepared to carry it out."[334]

A Senate Intelligence Report described QJ/WIN as a "foreign citizen with a criminal background, recruited in Europe... capable of doing anything." Regarding the mission, "he was not told precisely what we want him to do.... [and] it was thought best to withhold our true, specific requirements pending the final decision to use [him]."[335]

In *White Malice, the CIA and the Covert Recolonization of Africa*, author Susan Williams identifies QJ/WIN as Jose Moise Czeschlak, a forty-seven-year-old Luxembourg citizen of Basque origin who went by the name of Jose Marie Andre Mankel. Mankel was given the cryptonym QJ/WIN/I, with QJ the designation for Luxembourg. Not surprisingly, one of the first CIA files related to Mankel was headed "ZRRIFLE" and included a dispatch sent to William Harvey on November 1, 1960.

113

According to Williams, Mankel was a professional criminal involved in "East/West nickel smuggling" and "the clandestine shipment of atomic devices from Poland to the U.S.," as well as the smuggling of large amounts of opium from China to America. "He had previously worked for French, Luxembourgian, Belgian, and West German intelligence." For the Congo assignment, Mankel solicited the help of two French contacts – Jacques Santelli and Edmond Perroud – "who agree to undertake [an] unspecified job." Meanwhile, Williams wrote that the "allocation of funds to the CIA to persuade lawmakers in the Congo to support a Mobutu government – as approved by NSC Special Group – had failed utterly." The Special Group then "authorized the CIA to provide arms, ammunition, sabotage materials, and training to Mobutu's military."[336]

Arnold Silver, the CIA's chief of the Luxembourg station in 1960, recruited QJ/WIN, and Silver fits in well with Harvey and some of the other characters who are central figures in our narrative. As John Newman wrote in *Countdown to Darkness*, "Silver received his B.A. in German Language and Literature from Tufts University (magna cum laude) in 1941, and his M.A. in German Philology from Harvard in 1942. In WWII, he enlisted in the Army and served as a prisoner-of-war interrogator, first in the 66th Infantry Division and later in the 7707th European Intelligence Center. At the 7707th, he interrogated Nazis such as Otto Skorzeny and Walter Schellenberg. Silver joined the CIA in December 1948 and rose quickly to become a very senior Agency officer in charge of counterespionage in Western Europe. He took over as chief of the Operations Branch in Staff D in June 1960, just before William Harvey became the chief."[337]

***

Silver also interrogated Otto Skozeny while incarcerated in Germany after World War II. After Skorzeny's trial, Silver thought he was rightfully acquitted because Silver disingenuously said that Skorzeny was not a Nazi but a patriotic German. Still, in 1956 the State Department declared Skorzeny persona non grata, even as a tourist, due to "a large amount of unconfirmed reports of intelligence peddling, sale of Spanish arms to Egypt, formation of neo-Nazi groups and planning a coup d'etat in Germany," although the CIA, having interrogated him in Madrid, recommended he be granted a tourist visa. The Agency dared to suggest that "it strains the imagination that Subject has designs which are prejudicial to the United States." However, the State Department denied Skorzeny's visa, perhaps for good reason. There was a rumor that in 1958, Skorzeny was to kill Fidel Castro on behalf of Batista. Skorzeny's Austrian passport had a visa for Cuba that was unstamped, so he backed out for some unknown reason. There was also an allegation that Skorzeny was assisting Moise Tshombe's 1961 secession from the Congo by training some 30 Katangan rebels in Spain.[338]

It was not just the United States that did not want Skorzeny in their country. In 1959, he was in Italy, which resulted in a high-profile deportation by Italian authorities, who thought he was hatching a coup d'etat. By the early 1960s, Skorzeny was the man to turn to if you had an assassination or a government overthrow on your agenda.[339]

There was another agent sent to Leopoldville, code-named WI/Rogue, whose resume was even more notorious than QJ/WIN's. A "forger and former bank robber" and "soldier of fortune," he was "essentially stateless." He was given "plastic surgery and a toupee" by the CIA and trained in "demolition, small arms, and medical immunization." According to a dispatch sent to Leopoldville, "he is indeed aware of the precepts of right and wrong, but if he is given an assignment which may be morally wrong in the eyes of the world, but necessary because his case officer ordered him to carry it out, then it is right, and he will dutifully undertake appropriate action for its execution without pangs of conscience. In a word, he can rationalize all actions."[340]

WI/Rogue proved to be trouble for his CIA associates. Victor Hedgman, who worked closely with him, testified: "I had difficulty controlling him.... He seemed to act on his own without seeking guidance or authority... I found he was rather an unguided missile...the kind of man that could get you in trouble before you knew you were in trouble."[341]

Susan Williams wrote that WI/ROGUE's real name was David Tzitzichvili, a "stateless man of forty-two who was born in Georgia, USSR. He served in the French Foreign Legion and volunteered in 1942 for work in Germany, where he spent time in German prisons and concentration camps after being arrested for forgery. He spoke French, Georgian, German, and English." A connection to the Skorzeny group is a definite possibility.[342]

WI/ROGUE's freewheeling approach led him "to recruit QJ/WIN for an execution squad, " supposedly unauthorized by his superiors, who did not follow through for fear it might compromise the CIA's relationship with him. It was around this time that Richard Bissell was establishing an assassination squad, which he called "Executive Action." It would become ZR/RIFLE, and per William Harvey, it required "most professional, proven operationally competent, ruthless, stable, C.E. [counterespionage] – experienced ops officers."[343]

Then, there was Mario Garcia Kohly's Operation 40 group. As described by Frank Sturgis, their job "was to train people to infiltrate a foreign country … plus there was also a group formed in which was the assassination section … [that] would … assassinate … members of the military in the foreign country, members of the political parties of the foreign country … and if necessary some of your own members, who were suspected of being foreign agents." It sounded a lot like QJ/WIN and WI/ROGUE.[344]

The bottom line is that by the time John Kennedy became President, assassination was an accepted weapon in the CIA's arsenal. The question was, how far would they go with it?

***

After Lumumba's assassination on January 17, 1961, the unrest in the Congo worsened. There were street protests in Lagos, New Dehli, New York, London, Paris, Vienna, Warsaw, Moscow, Damascus, and Shanghai. In Belgrade, a mob stormed the Belgian embassy. In Cairo, protesters tore down a portrait of King Baudoin inside the Belgian Embassy there, replaced it with one of Lumumba, and then set the building on fire. A large crowd invaded the U.S. embassy in Accra, Ghana. On February 20, 1961, in retaliation, the Congo executed six Lumumba supporters, and the next day, fifteen political prisoners were shot and killed in Stanleyville.[345]

All this violence prompted the U.N. Security Council to authorize the U.N. peacekeeping army to do whatever was necessary to prevent civil war, including "the use of force." By the end of February, fifteen thousand U.N. troops, representing eighteen countries, fifteen from Asia and Africa alone, were rushed to the Congo. Meanwhile, French soldiers of fortune began arriving in January, and many had a "fanatical personal hatred for [UN Secretary General] Dag Hammarskjold, whom they believed had undermined the French Empire in North Africa." Many were former members of the OAS, and according to Larry Devlin, after fighting in Algiers, some were offered a pardon by the French government if they would fight for Tshombe in Katanga against a united Congo. "They were very bad stuff," said Brian Urquhart, who joined ONUC in late 1961. "They had been in Dien Bien Phu, Algeria and God knows where else … and were fanatical all-white, anti-black, right-wing officers."[346]

In the fall of 1961, a private psychological warfare group called *The Committee for Aid to Katanga Freedom Fighters* aligned with right-wing elements within the U.S. government in support of an independent Katanga. According to Ganis, Skorzeny was linked to the committee "from all available evidence in the Skorzeny papers … his principal contact to the group was one of his main business partners, Clifford Forster … [who was involved with the] Paix et Liberté.… Significantly, a member of the Katanga committee was [a] Dallas, Texas oil executive and U.S. Army Reserve intelligence officer, Colonel Jack Crichton. Crichton also knew Skorzeny from the Delta oil drilling project in Spain, beginning in 1953 and continuing through 1963."[347]

While this was happening, Hammarskjold visited South Africa, where large crowds of blacks and whites who appreciated his opposition to white minority rule greeted him. He told the Prime Minister apartheid was morally unacceptable, and three months later, the U.N. General Assembly passed Resolution 1598, condemning the racial policies of South Africa.

On September 11, 1961, the UN issued five warrants for the arrest of Katanga's President Tshombe and four other government leaders.[348] Tensions were high. There was an atmosphere of war in Katanga as Tshombe's troops, backed by Western governments and multinational corporations, went against U.N. troops supported by Prime Minister Adoula's government.

Rhodesia announced on September 13 that they were moving troops to Ndola to support Katanga, which the white-only Rhodesian Parliament enthusiastically approved. Their Prime Minister, Roy Welensky, accused the U.N. troops of doing things "only equaled by the Nazis and some of the other gentlemen from behind the Iron Curtain." He was horrified by "the language used by India's Nehru. It's identical with the stuff that was used by Hitler before he liberated Austria and Czechoslovakia."[349]

Rhodesia acted as it did because India's ONUC leadership led to an eight-day military engagement between ONUC and Katangese forces, resulting in thirteen U.N. troops and two hundred Katangese civilians and mercenaries killed. Britain, France, and Belgium responded with a vengeance, and when the U.K. threatened to withdraw its support for UNOC unless the fighting stopped, Hammarskjold ignored them.[350]

Meanwhile, President Kennedy and Secretary Dean Rusk were furious because the U.N. initiated hostilities without consulting the U.S., which, in return, angered Hammarskjold, who considered it an attack on the integrity of the U.N.[351] Despite the tension, Hammarskjold resolved to rectify the situation. He asked the British government to arrange for him to meet Tshombe in Ndola to negotiate a ceasefire.

***

While things were heating up in the Congo, in August 1961, John McCloy, Kennedy's chief disarmament advisor, told the President that achieving total disarmament was remote "until we have a means of settling international disputes." It did not stop the State Department from creating Bulletin 7277, titled "The United States Program for General and Complete Disarmament in a Peaceful World." The bulletin called for disbanding all national armed forces, eliminating national arsenals of all armaments, including weapons of mass destruction, and an effective means of enforcement by the U.N. to ensure compliance. Kennedy approved Bulletin 7277 on September 25. At home and abroad, the radical right accused him of intending to disarm the U.S. as part of a one-world United Nations initiative.[352]

**

On the evening of September 17, 1961, a plane carrying Dag Hammarskjold and an entourage of fifteen took off from Leopoldville, the Congo capital, headed for Ndola, a town in the British colony of Northern Rhodesia. Just after midnight, the DC-6B aircraft *Albertina* crashed near the Ndola airport, close to the Congo border. Only one of the sixteen passengers was found alive – Harold Julien, chief of security, who died six days later.

As described by Susan Williams in her book *Who Killed Hammarskjold? The U.N., The Cold War And White Supremacy In Africa*, there were immediate questions about the crash. "Why did the airport manager close down the airport," Williams asked. "Why did it take until four hours after daybreak to start a search, even though local residents, policemen, and soldiers reported seeing a great flash of light in the sky shortly after midnight?" "Why was the missing aircraft not found for a full fifteen hours, even though it was just eight miles away from the airport where it had been expected to land." "What about the second plane that had been seen to follow the Secretary-General's aircraft?" "Why did the survivor refer to an explosion before the crash?" "Why did Hammarskjold have no burns when other victims were so badly charred?"[353]

In 2005, eighty-seven-year-old retired Norwegian Major General Bjorn Egge, who had been the U.N.'s head of military information in the Congo in 1961, stated he saw Hammarskjold's body in a mortuary. "He was not burnt as were the others...but had a round hole [like a bullet hole] in his forehead. On photos taken of the body, however, this hole had been removed.... Similarly, the autopsy report had been removed from the case papers..."[354]

Two security guards also had bullet holes in their bodies. A Rhodesian inquiry concluded an explosion of cartridge cases during the fire caused this, which many doubted to be true. Major C.F. Westrell, a Swedish explosives expert, stated, "Ammunition for rifles, heavy machine guns, and pistols cannot, when heated by fire, eject bullets with sufficient force for the bullets to get into a human body." Arne Svensson, chief of the technical department for the police in Stockholm, agreed with Westrell's assessment.

As far as eyewitnesses, a European Police Officer in Mufulira described a flash in the sky towards Ndola at half past midnight. Drillers in a camp east of Mokambo heard an explosion in the direction of the Ndola road. A Rhodesia Light Infantryman also saw a flash in the sky, as did a man named D.E. Peover. The Ishik Lake Pump Works municipal security guard said he saw an aircraft flying over Ndola sometime after midnight. Its navigation light appeared to go out, and within a minute of clearing the airport vicinity, he saw a flash.[355]

Like his body, Hammarskjold's briefcase was not burned and was intact a short distance away. All the officers leading the investigation were white, even though the majority living in the Federation of Rhodesia and Nyasaland were black.

Timothy Jiranda Kankasa saw two aircraft in the sky. "I was out on a road in Twapia town when I heard a noise which sounded unusual ... like two airplanes. The bigger one was low. The smaller one not low." He saw a flash of light twice, which "seemed to come from the small aircraft and go to the big aircraft." David Simango also saw two planes flying close together. There was a flash; then, one plane went down. Dickson Buleni saw a large aircraft with a small plane flying above it. He saw "fire" coming from the small plane to the roof of the larger plane, heard an explosion, and then the big plane crashed. The small plane circled once, then flew off to the west. Journalist James McKenzie Laurie heard a second aircraft over Ndola airport sounding like a DC-3.[356]

Nurse Angela McGrath reported that the lone survivor, Julien, said that "all the others were trapped. We were on the runway when Mr. Hammarskjold said go back, then there was an explosion." If true, Hammarskjold survived the crash, and evidence supports this.

Margaret Ngulube recalled that "Twapia residents were not allowed to rush to the scene," and it was not until morning that several people went to the crash site. "We found bodies mutilated ... only Hammarskjold's body and that of his other counterpart were intact, but the rest were cut into pieces." Timothy Kankasa confirmed this, but it was omitted from the Rhodesian final report. "All the black witnesses were supposed to be unreliable," Kankasa later said. "And the white witnesses, those who gave evidence... that there was nothing fishy, that it was pure accident, were reliable. But some of the people who gave evidence were nowhere near the site of the crash."[357]

Despite an official report that foul play was not involved, it is clear Hammarskjold was murdered. Congo Prime Minister Adoula, who had met with Hammarskjold in Leopoldville hours before, said Hammarskjold had "fallen victim to the shameless intrigues of the great financial Powers of the West." The world believed the white rulers of the Central African Federation were responsible. There was a call from Leopoldville for war against the Federation, followed by similar outcries from nations led by people of color. Britain, who had been critical of the UN Congo mission and had backed Katanga's secession, was also accused of being involved. The African population in and around Ndola were "furious" when they heard the news of the crash and wept tears of anguish.

Meanwhile, whites in central Africa were happy to learn Hammarskjold was dead. When he arrived in Ndola, the Swedish Consul from Leopoldville found "gaiety" among whites and "raw flaming hate" against the U.N. Sture Linner, the Officer-in-Charge of ONUC, was shocked: "Their attitude and badly hidden scorn of what had happened ... were so terrible that I can't help believing that there were British, Belgian, and French interests behind what happened. In Leopoldville, he was appalled when he received invitations from Belgian parties celebrating the passing of Hammarskjold.[358]

It was clear to many that the responsibility for Hammarskjold's murder lay with Fascist Europeans who wanted colonialism to remain throughout Africa. As previously stated, there were "Belgium paratroopers, former members of German SS, and former Italian Fascist soldiers sent to Rhodesia to support Katanga." France sent French soldiers who were former members of the OAS who had fought in Algiers. Mixed up in the toxic soup of right-wing Fascist mercenaries were the CIA and radical-right businessmen from America. These groups from both sides of the pond were vehemently anti-Communist and supported European colonialism, which was rapidly slipping away. Third-world independence meant the loss of vast resources of strategic minerals and oil that could eventually fall into the hands of the Soviets, who threatened Europe's very existence. Anyone who supported self-determination for third-world countries was an enemy of this Fascist European/American alliance and had to be dealt with. The most vocal supporter of third-world self-determination was the leader of the free world, President John F. Kennedy, which made him an enemy of Fascists and Monarchists throughout Europe.

***

When JFK became President in January 1961, he made it clear that he backed the African nationalist movement and supported the U.N. against Belgian interference in the Congo.

His Assistant Secretary of State for Africa, George "Soapy" Mennen Williams, explained: "What we want for Africa is what Africans want for themselves." White settlers in the Rhodesian Federation were infuriated by this. Still, JFK backed Williams, saying: "The statement of 'Africa for the Africans' does not seem to be very unreasonable. [Williams] made it clear that he was talking about all those who felt that they were Africans, whatever their color might be, whatever their race might be. I do not know who else Africa should be for."[359]

At the same time, powerful interests in the U.S. were sympathetic to Tshombe and Katanga's right to separate from the Congo. Senator Thomas Dodd of Connecticut, who had substantial investments in Katanga, warned Congress that U.N. meddling in Congolese affairs would result in a Communist takeover of the country. Allen Dulles felt the same way and wrote on August 31 that African radicals "tend to be more strenuous in trying to impose authoritarian discipline and revolutionary zeal. For them, freedom requires the elimination of all special ties to the West as the only guarantee against "neo-colonialism." He was concerned it was "bound to attract Cold War competition."

On September 25, in honor of Dag Hammarskjold, John Kennedy spoke at the U.N. and voiced the same anticolonial sentiments that the deceased Secretary-General would have said. He talked about "the exploitation and subjugation of the weak by the powerful, of the many by the few, of the governed who have given no consent to be governed, whatever their continent, their class, or their color."[360]

One thing was undeniable – Allen Dulles opposed John Kennedy and African nationalism, which brings us to August 1998 and the release by Archbishop Desmond Tutu of eight documents discovered by chance in a folder from the National Intelligence Agency. The documents pertained to Operation Celeste, which involved a plan to assassinate Hammarskjold and included Allen Dulles's name. Bearing the letterhead of the South African Institute for Maritime Research (SAIMR), the documents contained the following: "UNO [United Nations Organization] is becoming troublesome, and it is felt that Hammarskjold should be removed. Allen Dulles agrees and has promised full cooperation from his people." The documents contained information provided by Dulles, including the type of plane the Secretary-General used and the date he would arrive.[361]

According to the 1970s Church Commission, when Leopoldville contemplated assassinating Lumumba, Dulles wrote, "We wish [to] give every possible support." The wording was similar to Dulles's promise of providing "full cooperation of his people" for the assassination of Hammarskjold, which the documents state was carried out by SAIMR using European mercenaries. There is no doubt Dulles was referring to assassination in his Operation Celeste transmittal. Author Susan Williams believes that. She confirmed that SAIMR was involved in covert action operations for many years and had the means to take down Hammarskjold's plane.

One month after the JFK assassination, ex-President Harry Truman wrote an op-ed for the *Washington Post*: "There is something about the way the CIA has been functioning that is casting a shadow over our historic position, and I feel that we need to correct it." Undoubtedly, he was thinking about JFK's murder. Interestingly, just two days after Hammarskjold's death, Truman told *New York Times* reporters, "Dag Hammarskjold was on the point of getting something done when they killed him. Notice I said, 'When they killed him.'"[362]

Truman knew who was responsible. He believed the CIA was involved in Hammarskjold's death and Allen Dulles was the puppet master pulling the strings. It was a harbinger of things to come.

***

On June 18, 1961, the French revolutionary army OAS bombed a Strasbourg to Paris train, resulting in 28 fatalities and over 100 injured. The bombing targeted an express which derailed while traveling at high speed. Investigators determined that an explosive device went off when the train passed over it.[363]

On October 17, in what became known as the Paris Massacre of 1961, under orders from the head of the Parisian police, Maurice Papon, the National Police attacked a demonstration of 30,000 pro-National Liberation Front (FLN) Algerians. The actual death toll is unknown, but historians estimate that between 200 and 300 Algerians died from beatings by police and mass drownings as police threw demonstrators into the Seine River.[364]

No doubt, Papon did not support Algerian independence and was undoubtedly pro-OAS, as were Allen Dulles and the CIA. Two years before the JFK assassination, the advancement of a Fascist, Monarchist, Nazism without Hitler, right-wing movement to protect and defend Europe made anyone and everyone expendable who opposed them.

CHAPTER SIX

THE PRODIGAL SON RETURNS

The assassination of John F. Kennedy was slightly more than seventeen months away when Lee Harvey Oswald, accompanied by his wife Marina and four-month-old daughter June, left the Soviet Union for the United States. The couple had been married in April 1961, and according to Marina, Lee began to consider returning to America about one month after that. Their trip started innocently enough. They traveled to Moscow and signed a promissory note at the U.S. Embassy for a State Department loan of $435.71, which would be needed to finance their trip home. They then left Moscow by train on June 1, 1962, bound for Amsterdam, where they stayed at a private residence the embassy in Moscow had recommended. Marina described it as a "private apartment," a "boardinghouse." She later said their hosts spoke English, which suggests U.S. intelligence interrogated them during their stay, as would be expected.

The official record shows they spent one night in Holland, which later confused Marina during questioning by the HSCA. She recalled staying three nights in Holland, and it is improbable she was wrong about such a thing. It leads one to believe that the official record is untrue, which is understandable since the CIA would have wanted to debrief Oswald while he was there. Still, the Warren Commission was puzzled. As Chief Council Lee Rankin said at an executive session of the Commission, "It is unexplained why they happened to go there and stay, and got a place to live, some little apartment, and what they were doing in the interim...."[365]

There was also an inconsistency in the train ride from Moscow to Amsterdam. They reportedly entered the West through Helmstedt, a major checkpoint on the East German border. Soviet customs officials stamped Marina's passport there, yet Lee's suspiciously was not. How could this be if they traveled together? A possible explanation is that the passport Oswald took to the Soviet Union listed his accurate height as 5'-9" with his actual photograph, which he would have needed for the Soviets to allow him into the country. However, the purpose of his defection was to make it appear he was 5'-11" when he left the United States, and that a 5'-9" tall Russian sleeper agent returned in his place. Therefore, to legitimize the ruse U.S.

intelligence wanted to create, it made perfect sense that they gave Oswald a new passport after he crossed the border out of East Germany. A passport that listed his height as 5'-11" but did not have the Helmstedt stamp.[366]

Oswald may have also visited West Berlin for one night. His notebook contained the cost of fares out of Russia, and travel from Minsk to Berlin by train was the least expensive. The notebook also listed the name of the German Embassy, its address, and a person's name – Miss Kaisenheim. There is even a rudimentary map of Berlin, with an address, phone number, and a dot indicating where he was to meet someone.[367]

There is no proof that Oswald went to Berlin. Still, ex-CIA agent Robert Morrow claimed in his book, *First Hand Knowledge*, that in 1961, he was on assignment in Europe and met a man named Hamilton, who had just returned from Minsk while Oswald was living there. Hamilton gave Morrow a package and instructed him to "tell [Tracy] Barnes that this is the information he wanted from Harvey."

As mentioned in Chapter Four, there was a relationship between Tracy Barnes and William Harvey going back to the Berlin Tunnel, dug by Gehlen's group of ex-Nazis and White Russians. Richard Nagell claimed the Berlin Tunnel was a Field Operations Intelligence (FOI) operation, and there was a link between the CIA, the military's Counterintelligence Corps (CIC), and FOI in West Germany. According to Sanche De Gramont in *The Secret War*, "The CIC's main task is finding Communist agents in U.S. military installations ... who come to West Berlin as refugees. Agents thus found are turned over to the CIA for possible use as double agents. Army Intelligence in West Germany also had an operational espionage group, the mysterious Field Operations Intelligence (FOI)..."[368]

Let's consider a possible connection between Military Intelligence, Oswald, and the White Russian spy network. It would confirm that Lee Oswald's defection was part of a right-wing anti-Soviet operation and that his eventual placement into a White Russian community in Texas after his return was anything but accidental. U.S. intelligence may have sent him to Fort Worth to weed out potential Soviet sleeper agents among the White Russians.

FOI might have been just a footnote in the Oswald saga were it not that Richard Nagell claimed to have been part of this underground intelligence group. During the 1950s, FOI was a most specialized and revered branch of Military Intelligence (MI). It was part of the Army, believed to have been created by General MacArthur's "Little Fascist," General Charles Willoughby, during the occupation of Japan. It became part of CIA special (military) operations, "in effect a covert extension of CIA policy and activity designed to conceal the true nature of CIA objectives." According to Nagell, he was with FOI in the Far East until he became disenchanted with their illegal activities, which included assassinations. In 1957, while Oswald was at Atsugi Marine Base, Nagell was transferred from FOI to Army Counterintelligence in Tokyo, where he worked for the CIA. It was here that Nagell first encountered Oswald, seen loitering outside the Soviet Embassy in Tokyo, after which Oswald entered the embassy and spoke with Soviet Colonel Nikolai G. Eroshkin, believed to be a military intelligence officer (see *It Did Not Start With JFK Volume 2*).[369]

Returning to Morrow's story about his encounter with Hamilton, if true, then Barnes was aware of Oswald and the purpose of his mission to the Soviet Union, which supports Nagell's other claim that Barnes was familiar with FOI, as well as Morrow's assertion that the Harvey referred to by Hamilton was William Harvey and not Oswald.[370] It means both Barnes and Harvey were aware of Oswald as early as 1961. After the assassination, a CIA memo described how the Agency was interested in the activities of Marina Oswald before she left the Soviet Union. It concluded, "It was out of curiosity to learn if Oswald's wife would actually accompany him to our country, partly out of Oswald's own experience in the USSR, that we showed [redacted] intelligence in the Harvey story."[371]

The odd thing about the memo is that the writer referred to "the Harvey story" after using Oswald's name twice in the same sentence. From this, we can deduce that the Harvey referred to was not Lee Harvey Oswald but likely William Harvey, which supports Morrow's story. As previously mentioned, Angleton wrote fake bios of assassins and other operatives for Harvey, which would have been necessary for Oswald's false defection operation. It confirms that Harvey was warning the CIA to be aware of Oswald and his wife, who were about to return to the United States, and further shows that crucial figures like Barnes, Harvey, and Angleton knew of Lee Oswald and his phony defection to the Soviet Union long before 1963. When the time came to find a JFK assassination patsy, they did not have far to look.

***

The mystery surrounding Oswald's return from Russia did not end with his European stay. In an interview given to the Secret Service shortly after the assassination, Marina claimed they "arrived in New York by air... stayed in some hotel in New York City for one day and then went by train to Texas." This conflicts with the official story that they traveled to America by ship and arrived in Hoboken, New Jersey, on board the S.S. Maasdam on June 13, 1962. Tickets, documents, and Marina's later testimony support this. Unfortunately, the Secret Service never had an opportunity to ask Marina about the discrepancy because within a week of Kennedy's death, President Johnson designated the FBI solely responsible for the investigation, and the Secret Service turned over its files to them. What Marina told the Secret Service was ignored by the Warren Commission because, as their chief counsel noted on February 28, 1964, "Marina has repeatedly lied ... on matters which are of vital concern."

Marina only spoke Russian and was coached on how to respond to the Warren Commission by the CIA-connected Isaac Don Levine of *Life* magazine. Prior to that, Jack Crichton of the 488th Military Intelligence Detachment, mentioned in Chapter Four in connection to Otto Skorzeny, had asked White Russian Ilya Mamantov immediately after the assassination to act as Marina's translator. We do not know if what Marina said was translated accurately. What we do know is there should not have been so much confusion about Marina's answers that warranted a consistent response.[372]

There is also the story of their mysterious missing baggage. On the day they left New York, one of the officials assigned to assist them noticed they had only five pieces of luggage, two less than when they arrived. Upon being questioned, Oswald said he had sent two bags ahead by rail, but the mystery deepened when they landed in Texas. Oswald's brother Robert recalled they had only two bags when they exited the plane – the disappearance of the other five remains unexplained.

It was also suspicious that the Oswalds flew through Atlanta on their way to Texas, even though there were direct flights from New York. Oswald's address book contained an Atlanta entry for Natasha Davidson, whose son Alexi was the doctor at the American Embassy in Moscow. Davidson examined Marina before their departure, and he suggested they look up his mother upon their return. Whether the Oswalds did this is unknown, but five months after they departed Moscow, the Russians accused Dr. Davidson of conspiring with Colonel Oleg Penkovsky to spy against the Soviet Union. Penkovsky was a senior GRU official with the Intelligence Directorate of the General Staff and a defector in place for the West since April 1961, supplying the CIA and British MI5 with military intelligence about the Soviets that was unparalleled, including data on Soviet missiles that proved to be beneficial during the Cuban Missile Crisis. Around the time of the Crisis, Penkovsky was arrested and charged with treason. He admitted spying for the U.S., and the Soviets executed him in May 1963.

Davidson, who acknowledged being a courier for Penkovsky, was asked to leave the Soviet Union.[373]

***

Spas T. Raikin, whom the Warren Commission described as "a representative of the Traveler's Aid Society," met Oswald at the dock in Hoboken when he arrived in the U.S. Raiken was also secretary-general of the American Friends of the Anti-Bolshevik Bloc of Nations (ABN) – an international, fanatically anti-Communist, pro-Fascist, and pro-Nazi organization whose origins dated back to World War II. The "Little Fascist," Charles Willoughby, who was familiar with Skorzeny's Madrid group, was closely associated with them. They were Ukrainian nationalists who longed for the end of communism and the tsar's return. Hitler considered them a dependable ally battling the Soviets. Strongly anti-Semitic and racist, they supported Hitler, recognizing that a German victory was the only hope for the recovery of their homeland.[374]

According to CIA documents, Raikin was a CIA asset hired on August 22, 1957. It began a fifteen-year relationship with the Agency.[375] The CIA's background information on Raikin is limited. On May 6, 1951, he and two others deserted their Trudovaks (Bulgarian Labor Corps) military unit "and made their way to Plovdiv [Bulgaria] and then to Greece." According to a November 1957 FBI report: "The reason for [Raikin's] desertion was to join an alleged illegal group working in the mountains south of Plovdiv ... [they] wandered around ... and entered Greece on June 19, 1951." Raikin was brought to Athens to work for LKB and GASP/10, two elite, ultra-secret CIA interrogation teams. It occurred while Operation Gladio and the Gehlen stay-behind armies were interrogating Iron Curtain exiles to determine what life was like there. The operation also included George Fischer from the Russian Research Center and Harold Isaacs from the MIT Center for International Studies. As described in Chapter Two of *It Did Not Start With JFK, Volume 2*, these groups, Priscilla Johnson, Cord Meyer, and probably Oswald's cousin Dorothy Murret, played a role in Oswald's defection to the Soviet Union. It explains why Raikin was assigned to greet Oswald when he returned to America.[376]

Raikin later told Dick Russell, "Oswald tried to avoid me on the ship. He was being paged and asked to come to the purser's office, but apparently, he was hiding from me. I finally found him with his Russian wife and baby out on the pier, where the baggage was...."[377]

Perhaps that was true, but we should also consider that Oswald's notebook contained the passage "SPAS (SPASEEBA)," followed by the Russian word for thank you, separated by one line. So, maybe Oswald was not so unhappy to meet Spas Raikin after all.[378]

Raikin spent about an hour with Oswald before taking him and his family to the Manhattan Traveler's Aid Office. There, they met Cleary F'N Pierre, a Haitian professor who took the Oswalds to various welfare offices looking for money to get them to Texas. When Lee's brother Robert offered to pay for the journey, F'N Pierre drove them to Penn Station, believing they were to return to Texas by rail. However, as we know, this was not the case.

In *Legend*, Edward Jay Epstein speculated that "Oswald took a train to Washington, D.C., that evening. A psychologist, code-named Cato, who was on assignment for the CIA, claimed to have interviewed a Russian defector at the Roger Smith Hotel who resembled Oswald. Oswald could then have returned in time to visit the Welfare Department the following morning."[379] It could explain why Marina claimed they had left New York by rail.

***

On June 14, 1962, the plane carrying Lee Harvey Oswald and his family touched down at Love Field in Dallas, Texas, the same airport John Kennedy would arrive at the day of his assassination. Lee's brother, Robert, and his wife, Vada, were waiting for them. Essentially penniless and without work, Lee had already accepted Robert's offer to move in with his family until he could find a job. Although generous, the modest two-bedroom home was too small to accommodate two families comfortably, and the diversity of their backgrounds exacerbated the inherent tension. Nevertheless, it offered a temporary solution until Lee could find a job.[380]

Nothing was remotely abnormal regarding Oswald's conduct or associations in the initial weeks following his return. He visited the Texas Employment Commission, where FBI informant Robert Adams worked, looking to secure a job as a Russian translator, and they sent him to Peter Gregory, a petroleum engineer of Russian origin who lived in the area. After their first meeting, Gregory was impressed and furnished Oswald with a letter stating he was "capable of being an interpreter and perhaps a translator."[381]

Gregory was Oswald's initial contact with the White Russian community in the Dallas area, a group that would be very influential in his life in the coming months. Interestingly, the alleged Marxist defector and his one-time Communist party member wife somehow fell into the lap of an ultra-right, anti-Soviet Fascist group. As described by Dick Russell, "Most of these émigrés had arrived since 1949 under the auspices of the Tolstoy Foundation, which carefully screened applicants to exclude those of 'left-wing' views. The Warren Commission would learn that the Tolstoy Foundation received "as much as $400,000 a year subsidy from the U.S. government." Why was it that these right-wing people were interested in the Oswalds?[382]

America's involvement with Eastern European and Russian refugees began almost immediately after World War II and led to the establishment of the East European Fund. The new organization relied on the Ford Foundation for financial support, but it also coordinated its activities with other refugee support groups that received secret CIA funding. The intent was to collect intelligence on the USSR and its satellite countries.[383]

In many cases, the CIA did not even bother to change the names of groups that had served the Nazis. The North Caucasian National Committee, the Georgian Government in Exile, and the Belorussian Central Rada are some examples. Frank Wisner, the head of the CIA's Office of Policy Coordination (OPC), whose name appears in Lafitte's datebook on May 26 and June 20 along with Angleton, French intelligence operative Philippe Vosjoli, and Otto Skorzeny, worked with the State Department's George Kennan to establish the American Committee for the Liberation of the Peoples of Russia (AMCOMLIB). Using its considerable financial resources, much of it private, the OPC induced the various émigré groups, including ex-Nazi groups, to unite into a single anti-Communist organization.[384]

The CIA was not authorized to work within the United States. However, it was acceptable if they worked through émigré political organizations that still had a connection to the old country, such as the Committee for a Free Latvia, the Committee for a Free Albania, and other private exile organizations. Thousands of Waffen S.S. veterans and ex-Nazi collaborators were among the people from central and eastern Europe who entered the United States legally during the 1950s. It resulted in a revival of extremist right-wing political movements inside émigré communities after they came to America.[385]

As early as 1950, the CIA financed selective émigré groups through private cutout foundations and overt government programs. Primary recipients included the International Rescue Committee (IRC), the National Catholic Welfare Conference, the United Lithuanian Relief Fund of America, and other similar ethnic and religious-based charities. The CIA went to considerable lengths to portray the leaders of these groups as legitimate representatives when for the most part, they were former Nazi collaborators.[386]

The term White Russian originally referred to partisans of the old Tsarist regime and followers of anti-Bolshevik generals who were active during the Russian Civil War. By the 1920s, it included all Russian émigrés who had left their homeland following the Russian Revolution. Later, it included émigré's children who, for the most part, embraced fascism.[387]

In *The Russian Fascists*, author John J. Stephan detailed how this group had managed to spread its philosophy around the world:

> Being immigrants or the offspring of immigrants, they lived in Russian conclaves scattered around the world.... During their twenty-odd years, this strange band brewed a quixotic crusade to take over the Soviet Union and build a fascist Russia that would surpass Mussolini's Italy and Hitler's Germany.... They courted young exiles, cultivating their agonized patriotism and their half-hostile fascination with the way Mussolini and Hitler crushed domestic Communists and seemingly breathed vitality into Italy and Germany. They collaborated with anyone who would cater to their illusions: Chinese warlords, Japanese generals, Nazi satraps.... In 1941, the climactic year of their movement, Russian fascists feverishly prepared to 'inherit' their motherland from the Third Reich's conquering legions.[388]

In the United States, the White Russians' desire to wrest their homeland from the Soviets was intense, especially with the Organization for Rebirth of the Ukraine (ODWU) and the Ukrainian Hetman Organization (UHO). Their leaders were former members of the White Guard, a terrorist tsarist organization responsible for acts of violence and murder in Poland and the Balkans. By the late 1930s, terrorist leaders of the ODWU arrived in the U.S., accompanied by leaders of the German Army who specialized in espionage. The German-American Bund contributed financially to the UHO and the German Library of Information furnished propaganda material.[389]

American White Russians were also closely linked to the America First Committee, which steadfastly believed the United States should avoid the European war and maintain a supportive, peaceful relationship with the Third Reich. Its leadership consisted of prominent American businessmen, and its popularity was widespread. It eventually had five million members nationwide, with two hundred-fifty chapters. Their philosophy was a combination of protecting their financial interests and a desire to eliminate Jews and Communists, which they considered the same. They were a Fascist organization that supported the Third Reich in the battle against the true enemy of all humanity, the Soviet Union.

***

In 1956, after the CIA failed to assist the Hungarian Revolution's attempt to throw off the chains of Soviet oppression, William Harvey was assigned the task of closing the CIA's European immigrant operations so the slaughter that had happened in Hungary would not happen again. It left many White Russian groups without financial support. They then turned to the private sector, where men like H.L. Hunt were willing to give them what they needed to continue the fight against communism. He reportedly gave the Tolstoy Foundation substantial money so they could continue their war against the Soviet Union.[390]

The definition of fascism is "a popular mass movement in which large masses of the 'common people' have become imbued with a highly emotional, indeed often fanatical, zeal for a cause. These mass movements, which are, in an important sense, revolutionary movements, are above all what distinguishes fascism from ordinary conservatism.... A second important feature is the role played by privileged elite groups, groups with a 'vested interest' in their position. While from some points of view the combination of these two elements in the same movement is paradoxical ... it is of the very essence of the phenomenon and perhaps more than anything else throws light on the social forces at work."[391]

The White Russians were Fascists, as were the American anti-Communist groups who supported their anti-Communist fight with private funding. Texas oilmen and industry titans still clung to the idea of a new world order, and they were Fascists in every sense of the word. They supported Skorzeny's ex-Nazi Fascist group in Madrid, right-wing ex-American generals, European Monarchists, and anyone who opposed colonialism and supported the American way of life they wanted to preserve. Anyone who disagreed with them, including Presidents, was considered a Communist. Somehow, Oswald and his Russian-born wife found themselves in a White Russian community that embraced these people. More importantly, for the remainder of his life, Oswald was surrounded by White Russians and American Fascists wherever he went. That was not a coincidence, especially when George de Mohrenschildt entered his life.

CHAPTER SEVEN

FROM WHITE RUSSIANS WITH LOVE

In compliance with J. Edgar Hoover's memo written while Lee Oswald was still in the Soviet Union, on June 26, 1962, FBI Agent John W. Fain met with the returned defector at the FBI office in Fort Worth. "You should be alert for the subject's return," Hoover instructed, "and immediately upon his arrival, you should thoroughly interview him to determine whether he was recruited by Soviet Intelligence or made any deals with Soviets in order to obtain permission to return to the United States."[392]

Fain had been trying to establish contact with Oswald when he burst into the FBI office unannounced and said, "Here I am; what do you want to talk to me about?" "Oswald exhibited an impatient and arrogant attitude," Fain's report stated. "He denied that he went to Russia because of his lack of sympathy for the institutions of the United States or because of an admiration for the Russian system."[393]

Oswald assured Agent Fain he had not been in touch with Soviet intelligence since his return, but Fain asked him to take a polygraph test nonetheless. The memo from Hoover explicitly stated this was the proper course of action. "If any doubt exists as to subject's truthfulness ... you should consider requesting his consent to a polygraph examination."[394] Oswald refused, prompting Fain to keep his file open so he could interview him again. Meanwhile, the FBI sent a report of the interview to the INS, the Office of Naval Intelligence, and the State Department, but they considered this a domestic matter, so they did not alert the CIA.[395]

In early July, Oswald moved out of his brother's house and into his mother's apartment ten blocks away, which occurred soon after the FBI showed an interest in him. Avoiding the FBI was important to Lee Oswald. By the middle of July, Oswald landed a job at Leslie Welding Company as an assembler of doors and windows. It was monotonous work, but he earned enough to move into a small two-room duplex on Mercedes Street in Fort Worth on August 10. Five days earlier, Oswald had subscribed to *The Worker*, the newspaper of the Communist Party U.S.A. Next, he wrote to the Socialist Workers Party. The FBI considered both subversive organizations. The SWP responded to Oswald's inquiry on

August 23, and three days later, Oswald wrote back, requesting material on Leon Trotsky.[396]

Oswald's sudden interest in subversive literature was odd since he knew the FBI was watching him. Was he aware that informants within the post office would report what he received from the CPUSA and the SWP to the FBI? Did he want them to believe he was a potential Soviet spy? Did the FBI instruct him to purposely draw attention to himself as part of some domestic operation that remains unknown to us? Recall that his defection to the Soviet Union was an illusion created by U.S. intelligence to make it appear he had died in Russia and an impostor had taken his place. Was he laying the groundwork to work undercover as an infiltrator of leftist groups to weed out subversives in the U.S. on behalf of the FBI or another agency?

We know that Oswald hated the American capitalist system because of the inequality of wealth and class structure he was exposed to during his youth. It was why Marxism appealed to him. We also know he had an equal dislike for the Soviet Union and its distorted brand of communism. Anna Meller, a White Russian émigré who befriended the Oswalds in the summer of 1962, recalled he "was not really for anything." He was "all anti, anti-the Soviet Union, anti-the United States, anti-society in general and anti-us."[397]

Another White Russian friend, Alexandra Taylor, had a similar recollection. Oswald "disliked Russia very much. He didn't agree with communism, and he didn't agree with capitalism. He believed in the perfect government, free of want and need, and free of taxation, free of discrimination, free of any police force, the right to be able to do exactly as he pleased, exactly when he pleased, exactly where he pleased, just total and complete freedom in everything. He believed in no government whatsoever...." Oswald's writings support this: "The Soviets have committed crimes unsurpassed even by their early day capitalist counterparts, the imprisonment of their own peoples, with the mass extermination so typical of Stalin, and the individual suppression and regimentation under kruschev [sic]."[398]

The CPUSA and SWP were rivals, and it was unusual for someone to be a proponent of both groups. Oswald soon rejected the CPUSA, and his condemnation of them was as strong as it was for the Soviet Union. "The Communist Party of the United States has betrayed itself," he wrote. "[It] has turned itself into the traditional lever of a foreign power to overthrow the government of the United States not in the name of freedom or high ideals, but in servile conformity to the wishes of the Soviet Union and in the anticipation of Soviet Russia's complete domination of the American continent."[399] It was a powerful statement, and one wonders if Oswald had help writing it. We should not rule this out, considering the lack of spelling mistakes that usually typified his writings.[400]

It was the Socialist Party that attracted Lee Oswald's attention. He professed to be a Marxist but not a Marxist-Leninist. The purity of Marxism and its true revolutionary spirit interested him. During his New Orleans radio debate in August 1963, when asked about his political philosophy, Oswald proclaimed, "I am a Marxist." In Dallas, George de Mohrenschildt asked Oswald if he was a member of the Communist Party. Once again, "I am a Marxist," was his reply.[401]

Shortly after contacting the Socialist Workers Party, Oswald became interested in Leon Trotsky, who was assassinated in Mexico in 1940 by supporters of Joseph Stalin. Trotsky turned against Stalin and went into exile in 1929 because, like Oswald, he supported the purer form of Marxism and worldwide revolution. The fifty-four-page pamphlet the SWP sent Oswald described "the Stalinist degeneration [that] welled out of Moscow and began corrupting young Communist parties everywhere." The SWP was interested in revolution only to "save us from capitalist barbarism and open up a new world for humanity." This rejection of Soviet communism and American capitalism and the promotion of worldwide revolution was what Oswald was looking for in political philosophy, so the next day, he ordered *The Teachings of Leon Trotsky* from the Socialist Workers Party.[402]

On August 16, as Oswald corresponded with Communist and Socialist groups, FBI agents Fain and Brown appeared at his Mercedes Street home for a second interview, which took place in the agent's car parked in the street in front of Oswald's home. Fain was not pleased. "When we asked him again why he went to the Soviet Union … he still declined to answer.… He said he considered it nobody's business.… He said, 'I went, and I came back. It was something I did.…' He seemed to be a little bit derisive of our questions." Fain also wanted to know the names of Marina's relatives in the Soviet Union, but Oswald refused to say because he "feared some harm might come to them if he did so."[403]

According to Fain's report, "Oswald agreed to report to the FBI any information concerning contacts or attempted contacts by Soviets under suspicious circumstances." This satisfied Fain, who later reported that Oswald "had settled down. He had got a job with Leslie Machine Shop, and he wasn't so tense. He seemed to talk more freely with us…"[404]

Surprisingly, Fain gave Oswald's file a closed status, even though he had been evasive in answering questions, and they had learned nothing new since their first interview. The FBI sent their report to the CIA, which they previously had ignored. Maybe Oswald's correspondence with subversive groups was the reason. In addition, Oswald's routine letters to the Soviet embassy were to the attention of Vitaly A. Gerasimov, whom a CIA report said was "known to have participated in clandestine meetings in this country and to have made payments for intelligence information of value to the Soviets."[405]

The fact that a returned Russian defector with a Russian wife had his case file closed by the FBI so abruptly has led to speculation that Oswald may have become an FBI informant. It raises the question, did Oswald begin corresponding with subversive groups after initially meeting Fain at the FBI's request? Oswald desperately needed money, so this was possible. Using undercover informants was a common FBI practice to smoke out subversives locally who might try to contact someone like Oswald. Were they using him to gather information on the White Russian community? Perhaps. We know Oswald was suspicious of the FBI and anticipated their scrutiny before settling in Texas. Why would he have subversive literature sent to his home, which would have drawn them to him unless the FBI was involved?

An FBI report written the following year described how, in September 1962, "Dallas confidential informant T-1 advised that Lee H. Oswald...was a subscriber to *The Worker*, an East Coast communist paper."[406] Also, an FBI source in New York, someone working undercover within the SWP, sent photographs that included Oswald's subscription to Dallas, which is how the FBI learned of Oswald's interest in this group. On October 17, New York gave Oswald's name and address to the Dallas office and alerted them that he was corresponding with the SWP.[407] It should have prompted renewed interest in Oswald, but it did not. Their reaction was to close their file on him that same month when agent Fain retired. It was a sign of extreme incompetence, or they had a working arrangement with Oswald. It is also suspicious that following the closure of his file, Oswald's contact with subversive organizations increased dramatically.

In *Oswald and the CIA*, author John Newman described how, on October 27, Oswald notified the Washington Book Store, from whom he had previously ordered Russian magazines, of his change of address to PO Box 2915, Dallas, Texas. Three days later, he applied for membership in the SWP. Perhaps suspicious of the returned defector's motives, the SWP dismissed him on November 5, responding that "as there is no Dallas chapter, there can be no memberships in this area." On November 10, Oswald sent a self-addressed envelope to *New York Labor News,* and they responded three days later. On December 6, he sent examples of his photographic work (he had a new job by that time) to the SWP, and they responded on December 9. He also sent samples of his photographic work to the Hall-Davis Defense Committee, a Communist front in New York. They replied on December 13. On December 15, Oswald subscribed to the *Militant.* On December 19, Louis Weinstock of the *Worker* wrote to Oswald. On January 1, 1963, Oswald contacted *Pioneer Press* for speeches by Castro, his first interest in Cuban affairs since returning to the U.S. For all correspondence, Oswald used his new PO Box.[408]

The FBI was aware of all this correspondence, so why didn't it result in more aggressive surveillance of Oswald and his wife and more interviews. On the contrary, the FBI continued to ignore him, so they must have supported what Oswald was doing.

Meanwhile, Oswald and his wife became more involved with the White Russian émigré community, who claimed to be sympathetic to the young family living on the brink of poverty. Many felt obligated to help Marina and supplied her with clothes and other essentials. Oswald was another story, for they disagreed with his political views, which differed drastically from theirs, but tolerated him for Marina's sake.[409]

On August 5, 1963, a Dallas newspaper article described how Military Intelligence from the Army, Navy, and Air Force, along with the FBI and local police, were uniting to combat "subversives seeking to harm the nation's security." They planned to penetrate various groups with undercover agents who "actually joined these groups to get names, addresses, past activities, and future plans, or have established networks of informants to accomplish the same result...."[410] It would not be a stretch to believe that they used Lee Oswald in such a way.

***

George De Mohrenschildt arrived in the United States in 1938 as Jerzy Sergius von Mohrenschildt. Born in 1911 in Mozyr, Russia, his lineage was a mixture of Russian, Polish, Swedish, German, and Hungarian, and he claimed Swedish Queen Christina was one of his ancestors. His father, who served the tsar as Marshal of Nobility in Minsk, was arrested for openly opposing the 1917 Russian Revolution. He was eventually released and secured a position in the new government until the Bolsheviks arrested him again. He, his wife, and George were sent to Siberia. Meanwhile, George's brother Dmitry had troubles of his own. He was already in prison and sentenced to be shot.

George's father became ill, and doctors convinced prison authorities that he should recuperate at home, which allowed them to escape to Poland. However, his mother died from typhoid, and the fact that the Communists were responsible did not go unnoticed by eleven-year-old George.[411]

George spent the first summer on Long Island with his brother, who managed to avoid his death sentence as part of a prisoner exchange. Here, he rubbed noses with the White Russian nobility who had survived the revolution. The upper class of America was also well represented, and George managed to ingratiate himself in their affairs, including the mother of Jacqueline Kennedy, Janet Lee Bouvier.[412]

George's involvement in the world of espionage began in 1941, working for French counterintelligence in New York. He made two trips across the United States on their behalf to establish an agent network that provided information related to oil exports to Europe. Still, it is doubtful his loyalties lay with the Allies during the war. He later told his wife Jeanne that he was "playing a double game while working for the French."

Like many White Russians, De Mohrenschildt was a supporter of Nazi Germany. In 1941 he made a propaganda film with a distant cousin named Baron Konstantin Von Maydell, who was an agent of Abwehr, the intelligence arm of Nazi Germany. After the U.S. entered the war, Maydell was arrested as a "dangerous alien" and placed in an internment camp. De Mohrenschildt escaped unscathed, even though he corresponded with Germany through Saburo Matsukata, the son of a former Prime Minister of Japan, who coordinated German and Japanese intelligence in the United States. A woman in Washington D.C. suspected of being a Nazi agent had George listed in her address book, and British intelligence claimed he was working against the Allies.[413]

George next went south of the border at a time when Axis nations began funneling money into Mexico, fast becoming the center of German intelligence in the Western Hemisphere. The FBI detained him at Port Aransas, Texas, for sketching a strategic Texas Coast Guard installation, and a search of his private papers revealed two identities. The first said he was "of Swedish origin, born April 17, 1911." The second was that he was a "Greek Catholic."

De Mohreschildt eventually made it to Mexico, only to be expelled nine months later. In 1942, he applied for a job with the Office of Strategic Services (OSS), but a CIA document written after the war noted that he "appears to be a dubious character. In 1942 he was considered a Nazi sympathizer and possible intelligence agent; he spent a good deal of time in Mexico, where he was suspected of possible subversive activities; and at the University of Texas, where he enrolled in 1944, he was said to have Communist tendencies."[414]

The FBI and Military Intelligence kept a close eye on George as the war progressed, but it is hard to believe the Communist tendencies he displayed in 1944 were genuine. A Russian aristocrat who had lived under the tsar and whose family had fled to escape the wrath of the Bolsheviks would not feel that way. Nor would someone who just two years prior had been accused of supporting Nazi Germany. Most likely, he was still "playing a double game," as he called it, for as late as 1958, a CIA file noted "that he was a member of the Communist Party; and that after the war he was sympathetic toward Communism and the U.S.S.R."[415]

By 1952, de Mohrenschildt was in Dallas, married for a third time to oil heiress Winifred Sharples. The marriage lasted only four years, but he maintained an interest in the oil business long after that. In 1957, he traveled to Yugoslavia on behalf of the International Cooperation Administration, allegedly looking to develop oil resources there. It may have also involved the CIA, for he twice tried to reach the private island of Marshal Tito by boat, only to be fired upon by security guards. He again claimed innocence, suggesting he only intended to do some harmless sketching. Upon return to the United States, J. Walton Moore of the CIA debriefed him, and a CIA file forwarded to the Warren Commission revealed that "the CIA representative obtained foreign intelligence which was promptly disseminated to other federal agencies...."[416]

Undercover as a philatelist, George visited Ghana, Togoland, and Dahomey the following year. He was gathering intelligence on the region's oil potential for a Swedish outfit centered in New York. He eventually returned to the United States through Poland and married his fourth wife, Jeanne LeGon, who had also caught the intelligence community's attention. Born in Harbin, China, her given name was Evgenia Fomenko, the daughter of a White Russian who was the director of the Chinese Far Eastern Railway. If George blamed Communists for the death of his mother, Jeanne could sympathize because it was Communists who had killed her father.

In the summer of 1960, George and Jeanne were off on an 11,000-mile walking trip along the Indian trails leading from Mexico to South America. They disappeared for almost a year, resurfacing in April 1961 in Guatemala within a few miles of where the CIA trained Cuban exiles for the Bay of Pigs invasion. After leaving Guatemala, they continued through Panama and Haiti, where they stayed for two months. They then returned to Dallas, where they met Lee Harvey Oswald several months later.

In *The Quiet Americans: Four CIA Spies at the Dawn of the – Cold War*, author Scott Anderson wrote that during World War II, "the need for intelligence from deeper inside Germany led the Seventh Army OSS unit to send some of their agents across on 'tourist missions…' who would then go on a 'walking tour' along a prearranged route. Told to take meticulous note of any installations they passed of military interest, the tourist spies then relayed their findings to high-flying communications planes…" It seems that George and Jeanne de Mohrenschildt were engaged in something similar.[417]

What de Mohrenschildt saw in Oswald was a mystery to all who knew them. Among his associates were leaders in the oil industry, such as H.L. Hunt and Clint Murchison. Other friends included associates of Lyndon Johnson, such as George and Herman Brown and Jean De Menil of Schlumberger Wells Services Company, not to mention a most intriguing entry found in his notebook: "Bush, George H.W. (Poppy) 1412 W. Ohio also Zapata Petroleum Midland."[418]

Future President of the United States, George Herbert Walker Bush, was in the oil business in the 1950s, so a relationship with de Mohrenschildt was not out of the question. Along with an associate, Bush started Zapata Petroleum Corp. in 1953. He eventually sold his interest in the company and founded Zapata Off Shore Co. He served as its Chief Executive Officer from 1956 to 1964 and moved from Midland, Texas, to Houston. That the CIA's secret code name for the Bay of Pigs invasion was "Operation Zapata" may not have been a coincidence. According to Colonel Fletcher Prouty, Bush personally secured vessels for the invasion and renamed them "Barbara" and "Houston."[419]

***

In addition to the William Harvey report mentioned in the previous chapter, there is evidence the CIA kept tabs on Oswald. As one CIA officer wrote: "We were particularly interested in the [redacted] Oswald might provide on the Minsk factory in which he had been employed, on certain sections of the city itself, and of course we sought the usual [redacted] that might help develop personality dossiers..."[420]

Another CIA officer claimed that in the summer of 1962, he "reviewed a contact report from representatives of a CIA field office who had interviewed a former Marine who had worked at the Minsk radio plant following his defection to the U.S.S.R." As the same CIA officer wrote: "I remember that Oswald's unusual behavior in the USSR had struck me from the moment I read the first [redacted] dispatch on him, and I told my subordinates something amounting to 'Don't push too hard to get the information we need, because this individual looks odd.'"[421]

The most plausible account of how de Mohrenschildt and Oswald met was given by George to author Edward Jay Epstein in May 1977, just hours before he allegedly committed suicide. He said J. Walton Moore of the CIA's Domestic Contact Division approached him in Dallas late in 1961, while Oswald was still in the Soviet Union, regarding an ex-Marine who worked in an electronics factory in Minsk and asked George to check him out when he returned to the U.S.[422]

The Domestic Operations Division, under Tracy Barnes, was only a couple of months away from officially being formed. Moore's Domestic Contacts Division would fall under its supervision. As already discussed, there is strong evidence that Barnes was aware of Oswald while he was still in the Soviet Union. It is interesting that J. Walton Moore, under Tracy Barnes' direction, was the one who instructed de Mohrenschildt to approach Oswald in Fort Worth.

Before the HSCA, Moore admitted he "had 'periodic' contact with de Mohrenschildt for 'debriefing' purposes over the years...." Jeanne de Mohrenschildt said he "seemed to be aware of Oswald. He knew who we were talking about..."[423] Moore and de Mohrenschildt dined together with their wives on several occasions. Moore's parents had been missionaries in China, so he got along well with Jeanne and enjoyed listening to her reminisce about her life there.[424]

By the time George met Lee Oswald in the summer of 1962, he had already spent the better part of his twenty-four years in the United States involved in the world of intelligence. It was the only common denominator that brought the product of nobility to the doorstep of the disenchanted ex-Marine. In addition to dominating him, George tried to separate Lee from Marina and the rest of the White Russian community, leading to unexplained absences and secretive behavior that would characterize the remainder of Oswald's young adult life.

One of the first people de Mohrenschildt took to meet Lee and Marina in the summer of 1962 was Colonel Lawrence Orlov, who also knew CIA agent J. Walton Moore. The Warren Commission never called Orlov to testify, which may have been because he had intelligence connections, and there is no record of what this secretive man was doing between 1948 and 1961. Orlov's obituary stated that he belonged to the Unitarian Church, which may have been why George brought Orlov to meet Lee. At that point, Unitarians had played a role in Oswald's life, from his time in the Marines at El Toro Station in California, his relationship with Kerry Thornley, and the Unitarian Church in Los Angeles that played a role in his defection to the Soviet Union (see *It Did Not Start With JFK, Volume Two*). Orlov's name also appears in Lafitte's datebook on October 27 with William Harvey. It suggests that the de Mohrenschildt/Orlov visit to Oswald's home was not an innocent encounter.[425]

The amount of time the de Mohrenschildts spent with Lee and Marina was excessive, so they must have had an ulterior motive for doing so. Samuel Ballen told the Warren Commission, "George and his wife were visiting my home two or three or four times a wee.... And I know that quite frequently they came to our house at 9:00 or so in the evening, and they would have just come from the Oswalds trying to cheer them up...."[426]

The word in the White Russian community was that Lee and Marina were having marital troubles. There were accounts that Oswald beat his wife. Marina testified that "immediately after coming to the United States, Lee changed. I did not know him as such a man in Russia." He "was very irritable ... very unrestrained and explosive..."[427] On October 1, George attempted to separate Lee from Marina for the first time when he, Jeanne, and Marina appeared at the door of Admiral and Mrs. Burton, acquaintances whom the de Mohrenschildts had met earlier that summer. George asked Mrs. Burton to allow Marina to temporarily move in with her, saying Lee had abandoned her and her baby. The plan backfired when Lee arrived unannounced at Burton's door while they were there.[428]

On October 7, there was a gathering at the Oswald's apartment. George was there with his daughter and son-in-law, Alexandra and Gary Taylor, Russian émigrés George Bouhe, Anna Meller, Lyola Hall, and Lee's mother, Marguerite. Oswald shocked everyone when he said Leslie Welding had fired him, which was untrue. According to Gary Taylor, George directed Oswald's next move by suggesting it would be easier to find work in Dallas. Anna Meller had a friend who worked at the Texas Employment Commission and offered to help.

Meanwhile, the group decided that until Oswald found a job, Marina could stay with the Taylors. There were those in attendance, including Gary Taylor, who believed de Mohrenschildt already knew about Oswald's potential job prospects and that he may have been financing him. The evidence seems to support this.[429]

When Oswald returned from the Soviet Union, he owed the State Department $435 and his brother Robert $200. Around October, when Oswald left Leslie Welding, he paid his brother what he owed him. Oswald continued to pay the State Department loan in $10 increments until he could pay the remaining $396 in less than seven weeks. His income during this period was $490 (he had found another job), and after deducting $68 for rent, only $4 per week remained for him to provide for his family. It suggests someone was providing Oswald with financing.[430]

That evening, Marina and her baby left to stay with the Taylors. The following day, Lee worked all day at Leslie, then quit without saying anything. That night, he boarded a bus to Dallas. And as Gary Taylor observed, de Mohrenschildt was likely telling him what to do.

With the help of the Texas Employment Commission, Oswald found work in Dallas at Jaggars-Chiles-Stovall. He began work on October 12, four days before the Cuban Missile Crisis began. This graphics-arts company prepared advertisements for newspapers, magazines, and other periodicals. The pay was $1.35 per hour, close to what he made at Leslie Welding. However, it involved photography, which interested Oswald much more than the monotony of his previous job. On the surface, it all seemed innocent enough, but Jaggars-Chiles-Stovall also handled classified contracts for the U.S. Army Map Service and set type for the names of places shown on maps of Cuba taken by U-2 spy planes. Somehow, a newly returned defector from the Soviet Union became involved in sensitive work. Fellow worker Dennis Ofstein told the Warren Commission that on one occasion, he helped Oswald enlarge a photo he had taken in Russia that showed "some military headquarters and that the guards stationed there were armed with weapons and ammunition…"[431]

After the assassination, the word "microdots" was discovered in Oswald's address book beside his JCS listing. Microdots were photographs and messages reduced to the size of a pinhead that could be placed undetected under a postage stamp. Also found in Oswald's home by the Dallas police was expensive equipment that could be considered the tools of a spy, including a tiny Minox "spy camera," three other cameras, two binoculars, a 15-power telescope, a compass, and a pedometer. There was no rational explanation for how Oswald could afford them.[432]

In 1978, a Freedom of Information Act lawsuit resulted in the release of twenty-five photographs developed from film confiscated with Oswald's other possessions. Most photos depicted civilian sites in Europe, but three showed military scenes from Asia or Latin America, including a barbed-wire encampment. One image appeared to be taken from a boat, depicting a tanker anchored at sea in a mountainous area. Oswald did not take these pictures, but George de Mohrenschildt turned up in places like this.

Oswald arrived in Dallas on October 8, but where he stayed is unknown until October 15, when he registered at the local YMCA. He stayed there a few nights, but on October 21, he again disappeared. He resurfaced on November 3 when he rented an apartment at 604 Elsbeth Street. Where Oswald was living for almost three weeks cannot be accounted for. Marina and daughter June joined him on November 4, but Lee left around 10:00 P.M. and spent the night at the YMCA, claiming he had paid for the room, so he might as well use it. The next evening, their landlady told Lee she had received a phone call from George, a man with a foreign accent. He immediately phoned de Mohrenschildt. Later that evening, Marina called Anna Meller, claiming she had a fight with Lee and needed a place to stay. So, after only one night together, Oswald and Marina were separated again. Marina stayed with Anna Meller for a few days, then shifted to the home of Katya and Declan Ford. The Oswalds remained apart until November 18, so for another two weeks, Lee Oswald was again free to do as he pleased.[433] Meanwhile, de Mohrenschildt told everyone in the White Russian community that the differences between Oswald and his wife were irreconcilable. To some, it was a long time coming. Dorothy Gravitas had been warning others about him, claiming "the town where Oswald lived in Russia had the KGB Academy, and that it took exactly two years to graduate [from] it." It was how long Oswald had spent in Russia.

Gravitas' son-in-law was Ilya Mamantov, the geologist for Sun Oil Company who would serve as Marina's interpreter after the assassination. That request came from Jack Crichton, a former Military Intelligence officer and the president of Nafco Oil & Gas, Inc. Also present at the initial questioning of Marina was Unitarian Ruth Paine, who would become a mentor to Marina as de Mohrenschildt was to Lee. Dorothy Gravitas had been acting as Paine's tutor in her attempt to learn the Russian language. It was a highly suspicious group.[434]

Around Christmas, Katya Ford did not invite the Oswalds to a party at her house. It did not stop de Mohrenschildt from arriving late with the two uninvited guests. From that point on, the White Russians stayed away from the young couple whom they could no longer tolerate.[435]

What Oswald was up to when he first moved to Dallas is unknown. Still, his mysterious absences after arriving there indicate he was involved in something predetermined before he left Fort Worth. And George de Mohrenschildt was an integral part of the whole affair.

143

CHAPTER EIGHT

THE PRESSURE MOUNTS

Change was in the wind as the calendar turned to 1962, and the hatred directed at the Kennedy brothers continued to escalate. The previous November, JFK replaced Allen Dulles with John McCone and accepted the resignation of General Edwin Walker. Richard Bissell and Charles Cabell submitted their resignations early in 1962, and JFK reduced the CIA's budget to try to reel the Agency in.[436] In February, Defense Secretary McNamara told the Senate Foreign Relations Committee that the U.S. had "a clear military superiority for major nuclear conflict." A month later, JFK discarded the doctrine "that the United States would never strike first with the nuclear weapon …" He told columnist Stewart Alsop, "In some circumstances, we might have to take the initiative."[437]

He sounded like a President who was unsure of himself and uncertain of what he wanted to do. He was now open to launching a nuclear first strike against Russia but was unwilling to involve the military during the Bay of Pigs invasion. It did not make sense.

1962 was a pivotal year for Kennedy, with mid-term elections coming. He continued to buck the establishment as he tried to control the military, the CIA, big business, Texas oilmen, anti-Castro Cuban exiles, and the radical right. Cuba remained the most pressing of many issues he and Bobby had to deal with successfully if he wanted to get reelected.

CUBA

Operation Mongoose began on November 3, 1961, with Robert Kennedy, Maxwell Taylor, and Brigadier General Edward Lansdale in charge. The latter was a military man but was on loan to the CIA. William Harvey headed the massive CIA portion of the operation. National Security Advisor McGeorge Bundy, who chaired the Special Group Augmented (SGA), disapproved of the attention given to Cuba by the Kennedys.[438] He felt introducing a personal vendetta into foreign policy decisions was destined for disaster. Like many, he did not think Cuba was that important.

Meanwhile, the Joint Chiefs began developing ideas to justify a second invasion of Cuba. They knew an internal revolt was not feasible, so the overthrow of Castro "will require a decision by the United States to develop a Cuban 'provocation' as justification for positive U.S. military action."[439] It's something for the reader to remember, for creating a provocation to justify a second invasion of Cuba involving the military would remain a necessity until the end of 1963 and lead directly to JFK's assassination.

On March 13, JCS chairman Lemnitzer submitted Operation Northwoods to Secretary McNamara with a laundry list of options. Much of it had to do with creating an incident at Guantanamo, such as the ever-popular dressing up of anti-Castro Cuban exiles in Cuban army uniforms, launching explosives at the American base at Guantanamo, general sabotage against Guantanamo, etc. However, other suggestions were downright frightening, such as to "develop a Communist Cuban terror campaign in Miami … [and] other Florida cities and even in Washington," assassinating Cuban immigrants in America, "sinking a boatload of Cubans en route to Florida (actual or simulated), or fabricating the shooting down of a U.S. Air Force fighter plane," and blaming it on Castro.[440]

Of course, Lemnitzer believed "that the responsibility for both overt and covert military operations [should] be assigned [to] the Joint Chiefs of Staff." It did not matter, for Kennedy blocked each suggestion. In a private meeting with Bundy and Secretary of State Dean Rusk, he voiced his displeasure with the military brass. "I just see an awful lot of fellows [diplomatic advisers] … who don't seem to have cojones…. The Defense Department looks as if that's all they got. They haven't any brains…. And I know that you get all this sort of virility over at the Pentagon, and you get a lot of [Admiral] Arleigh Burke: admirable, nice figure, without any brains."[441]

Then JFK did a complete reversal, saying he was not against a massive military invasion of Cuba if conditions were right and warranted such action. Per the President's instructions, on February 2, the Pentagon ordered Admiral Robert L. Dennison, the Commander in Chief of U.S. Forces in the Atlantic (CINCLANT), to expedite the lead time to initiate two contingency plans already in place. Kennedy wanted to be ready for a rapid all-out strike if that became necessary, but confusion reigned as the President still preferred to control Castro peacefully. He suggested they look to create partnerships with major American and multinational corporations to work with U.S. intelligence in Latin America. He approached David Rockefeller in May at a meeting of the Harvard Board of Overseers about getting substantial private U.S. investment into the region. Rockefeller said a financial guarantee against political instability was required, resulting in the creation of the Business Group for Latin America, a CIA front established to funnel private funds to secret operations that Robert Kennedy thought important. The group's mandate was to provide cover for corporations, bribe crooked politicians, and conduct other unsavory political activities in Latin America.[442]

In the end, Kennedy's wavering weakened the overall effectiveness of the Cuban operation. Richard Helms told CIA director McCone that, because of the disparity between the Kennedy brothers' unreasonable impatience to remove Castro and the limitation on political risks they were willing to entertain, Mongoose would consist more of planning than action for some time.[443]

The CIA continued to press the Kennedys that they could not do it alone if they wanted Castro removed quickly. An internal CIA memorandum, dated April 6, 1962, recommended the "creation of an office in the DD/P to be known as Paramilitary and Air Support Operations, under the direction of an Assistant DD/P, to develop the capability for covert and paramilitary and air support operations," that was to be headed by someone "drawn from military service and be a senior Colonel or a Brigadier General with wartime paramilitary experience."[444] William Harvey agreed. In April, he wrote McCone that "the decision to use the military force must be made now."[445]

As early as June 1961, George Ball had asked during a Cuban Task Force meeting what it would take to invade Cuba – "A half-million men? One million men?" He also questioned what the United States would do if the Soviets seized West Berlin in response. West Berlin was a critical pawn, and JFK knew he could not allow the Soviets to take it.

Ball also brought up the civilian deaths that would result, as had happened in the 1920s when the U.S. invaded Haiti. Bobby Kennedy knew little about this and Latin American history in general or what was involved in a combined airborne and amphibious assault. The Attorney General was way over his head and had too much responsibility.[446]

The bottom line is the CIA was no closer to overthrowing Castro in the summer of 1962 than in 1961, as Castro enjoyed strong support from twenty percent of the Cuban people, and the rest were too afraid to oppose him. The best they could expect was appreciable civil unrest in 1963, but they would soon conclude even that was unlikely. If the United States were to remove Castro within the timetable set by the administration, a dramatic catalyst was required so the military could be involved. The Kennedy brothers were delusional if they thought they could do it any other way.[447]

***

146

The Cuban operation remained dysfunctional as the CIA coped with restrictions placed on it by the Special Group. Harvey called it "stultifying." As a result, the CIA did not begin placing agents inside Cuba until August 1962, which resulted in an exchange that killed ten Russians and Cubans.[448] In the U.S., there were numerous exile groups and their American mercenary supporters whom the government had to deal with. Many of these groups were unhappy with the Kennedy brothers. Miro Cardona of the CRC traveled to Washington early in 1962 to talk with Robert Kennedy. He returned disappointed because the administration was still leaning in a liberal, anti-Batista direction and putting its trust in leftist Manuel Ray, who publicly announced the formation of the group JURE in July. The situation was unacceptable for the Cuban exiles who had once supported Batista, and the chasm between the Kennedys and the boots on the ground, right-wing Cuban exiles, continued to grow. As a result, exile groups such as Orlando Bosch's MIRR and right-wing American mercenaries like Gerry Patrick Hemming, Frank Sturgis, and Alexander Rorke began to operate independently of U.S. government oversight.[449]

By April, Hemming joined forces with a mixed Cuban and American band, including Larry Laborde and a former Castro revolutionary named Tony Cuesta, who wanted to purchase a boat to run operations against the Cuban mainland. According to an FBI Airtel dated July 2, 1962, Laborde was an "American form [sic] New Orleans, LA, was employed by Alberto Fernandez Hechevarria when Fernandez bought boat known as 'Tejana III.' In late 1960, Fernandez had asked … Czarnikow-Rionada Co, NYC, and the King Ranch of Kingsville, TX, to help purchase the boat."[450] The inclusion of the 1960 reference to Czarnikow-Rionada and King Ranch is significant and will be discussed in more detail later in this chapter.

In conjunction with this, Hemming and a friend named Howard Davis visited New Orleans in late June and met with Frank Bartes and Luis Rabel, the leader of the New Orleans branch of the CRC. An FBI and CIA informant, Bartes was an important figure who would have contact with Lee Harvey Oswald the following year in New Orleans. He informed the CIA's New Orleans office that Hemming, Davis, and Rabel intended to work outside CIA supervision because the U.S. was not doing anything about Castro.

Two press stories emerged in the *New Orleans States* and the *Miami Herald* that New Orleans Cubans had been supplying "Jerry Patrick" Hemming with military equipment since February. In the spring, "Patrick" was offered a large tract of land, including an airstrip, on the north shore of Lake

Pontchartrain, just north of New Orleans, for a training camp. The articles also mentioned Hemming's link to Frank Sturgis. They speculated that ex-Cuban President Carlos Prio was bankrolling him, but the anonymous donor may also have been mobster Mike McLaney. Either way, Hemming returned to Miami and developed alliances with Sam Benton and the notorious ex-Batista henchman Rolando Masferrer, known as El Tigre, who provided arms and men for the training camp. By the fall, he was training about ten Americans and ten Cubans. It began an independent movement within the exile community as they searched for funding and support outside the U.S. government to fight Castro.[451]

The FBI knew that Prio, who was involved in trafficking arms with mobsters before Castro came to power, had approached Jimmy Hoffa for financial help. Hoffa's Puerto Rico Teamster lieutenant Frank Chavez confirmed this to FBI agents on March 1, but Hoffa refused to see Prio.[452] The FBI also learned that Sturgis claimed he would be Prio's military coordinator. A year later, an informant told the FBI that Hoffa had offered Prio fifty men to infiltrate Cuba as guerillas, which Prio denied. Prio also gave Gerry Hemming money in mid-1963 and discussed forming a new training camp with him.

Hoffa and his Teamsters hated the Kennedys, especially Bobby. After JFK's assassination, Chavez wrote the Attorney General that he was raising money to put flowers on Oswald's grave. Leopoldo Ramos Ducos, the organizer for Teamster Local 901 in Puerto Rico, told the FBI on November 27, 1963, that he heard Chavez "mention the name of one Jack Ruby as someone connected with the Teamsters Union." The previous day, a Justice Department memo noted "a connection between Rubenstein [Jack Ruby] and Frank Chavez and [mobster] Tony Provenzano."[453] So, even though Hoffa had earlier rejected an alliance with Carlos Prio, it didn't mean there wasn't a connection between Hoffa, the Mafia, and other Cuban exile groups in desperate need of money.

Colonel William Bishop, a CIA contract agent who claimed to be involved in the Trujillo assassination, also played an active role in the Cuban exile war against Castro. In *The Man Who Knew Too Much*, Dick Russell wrote that Bishop told him, "Hoffa gave [Rolando] Masferrer $50,000.... Expense money. To partially set up the assassination team [to kill JFK]." According to Bishop, "They [the Mafia] wanted the pressure off because Bobby Kennedy was after organized crime ... they wanted the pressure taken off Jimmy Hoffa.... So, when organized crime, through Trafficante in Tampa, eventually provided the money for carrying out the assassination, the Cubans fell right into it." Bishop called Masferrer "...the key bagman... for Alpha 66. Primarily the funding came through the Syndicate because of Masferrer's connections with those people back in Cuba. He had ties with Santo Trafficante, Jr., and other criminal elements..."[454]

Alpha 66 was one of the more violent Cuban exile groups, and a connection between them and the Mafia was logical if Masferrer was the go-between due to his relationship with Mafia figures like Trafficante while Batista was in power.

Cuban exile Antonio Veciana, who had served under Batista while secretly assisting Castro, founded Alpha 66. He declined a position in the new government when he realized Castro was a Communist, and he and a small group of counterrevolutionary friends began plans to overthrow him.[455] It was in mid-1960 that an American named Maurice Bishop (not to be confused with William Bishop) contacted Veciana to work against Castro. Veciana described the mysterious Bishop as six feet two inches tall, with dark hair, blue eyes with sunspots below them, and a high forehead. He was in his early forties, spoke French, and carried a false Belgian passport. He was involved with US intelligence but would not reveal who he was working for. Bishop's people trained Veciana in propaganda, psychological warfare, sabotage, and explosives. Veciana began attending meetings with others to coordinate their efforts. One of those was Frank Sturgis. "At that time," Veciana stated, "I remember Bishop saying to me about Fiorini that he wasn't just another soldier; he was more than that."[456]

Veciana later adamantly admitted that the mysterious Maurice Bishop was David Atlee Phillips, who was involved in the 1959 failed coup attempt against Castro run out of the US Consulate in Havana that involved Frank Sturgis, David Morales, June Cobb, Paul Bethel, Henry Hecksher, and Bernard Barker.

Eloy Gutierrez Menoyo, the leader of the Second Front of the Escambray in 1959, was also involved in an attempt to overthrow Castro. After the Cuban Missile Crisis, it was logical that the two groups joined to form Second Front/Alpha 66. Commandos L, headed by Tony Cuesta, was an offshoot of Alpha 66. The MIRR was Dr. Orlando Bosch's group and worked closely with Alpha 66 and Operation 40.[457]

To provide some context, we should return briefly to 1959, for a lot was happening in Havana that year, which gives clarity to our narrative. As described in Chapter One, Allen Dulles sabotaged the 1959 coup by Captain William Morgan and Eloy Gutierrez Menoyo, which destroyed an internal military uprising within Castro's revolutionary army to overthrow him. The story begins with an FBI report dated May 1, 1959, that "Carlos Prio ... and the Dominican Republic are supplying ... arms and equipment" to the coup plotters. The Bureau had learned about the coup from lobbyist Irving Davidson, who had worked with Jimmy Hoffa the previous year selling guns to Castro. He was also involved with Carlos Marcello, Clint Murchison, and Bobby Baker in Haiti.[458] Davidson set up a meeting with FBI assistant director August Belmont on behalf of Cuban millionaire banker and sugar magnate Julio Lobo, whose conservative exiles, the Crusade of Revolutionaries Against Communism (CRAC), also had designs on getting rid of Castro. Davidson advised the FBI that unless CRAC received backing from the United States, they would join Eloy Gutierrez Menoyo's group and become part of the invasion force from the Dominican Republic.[459]

Recapping from Chapter One, long-time CIA asset and Knight of Malta Jack Malone worked for George and Ronny Braga through Czarnikow-Rionada, and they merged with Texas rancher Robert Kleberg. George Braga and Kleberg knew Allen Dulles well, Malone was good friends with David Phillips, and Kleberg and Phillips were on a first-name basis. Kleberg also knew Alberto Fernandez and Gustavo de los Reyes. They all became part of the William Morgan/ Gutierrez counterrevolution. The person who brought the cattlemen into the fold in 1959 was David Phillips, who was introduced to de los Reyes by Malone.[460]

The importance here is that the same group of CIA operatives working out of the American embassy in Havana, American businessmen with interests in Cuba, and Cuban exiles involved in the 1959 coup resurfaced in 1962 in conjunction with the Second Front of the Escambray/ Alpha 66 alliance, which worked independently and outside the constraints of the Kennedy brothers, for whom they felt nothing but contempt. Their alliance would grow stronger in 1963 as the consensus in the Cuban exile community was that they needed something dramatic to remove Castro from power.

In addition, Robert Morrow wrote that Eladio del Valle was a liaison between Rolando Masferrer and the Cuban exile community. As previously mentioned, del Valle was a close associate of Trafficante from their days in Cuba and close to David Ferrie, who worked with mob boss Carlos Marcello throughout the fateful year of 1963. As we know, del Valle was part of the New Orleans group, which included Sergio Arcacha Smith and Guy Banister. Morrow also claimed that del Valle was Mario Kohly's right-hand man in Miami and Kohly's CIA case officer was Tracy Barnes.[461]

***

According to John Newman, as described in his book *Into The Storm*, on December 7, 1960, Antonio Veciana entered the U.S. Embassy in Havana to speak with CIA Station Chief James Noel, looking to obtain visas to get family members of his team out of Cuba. He told Noel about a plot to assassinate Castro and his top associates. Noel was aware that Veciana had previously spoken to a State Department "political officer" who had made other "wild-eyed" proposals. Noel assessed that Veciana was "sincere but a little wild," so he turned him down. At the time, Veciana worked for sugar magnate Julio Lobo, so we can assume that Veciana was working with the Kleberg/ Czarnikow-Rionada/Lobo group. It included Rolando Masferrer, Eladio del Valle, and the Mafia, and they were working with Eloy Gutierrez to either invade Cuba from the Dominican Republic or assassinate Fidel Castro.

Operation Patty was the first attempt to assassinate Fidel and Raul Castro after the Bay of Pigs fiasco. It was to occur on July 26, 1961, a Cuban holiday, in conjunction with a faked attack against Guantanamo Bay that included the shooting and killing of Americans and Cubans. The belief was this would lead to a U.S. military invasion of Cuba. The operation was the brainchild of ONI (Office of Naval Intelligence) and not the CIA.

At the time, Veciana was working with the People's Revolutionary Party (MRP) on sabotage raids financed by the CIA, and the Agency wanted complete control of their operations. On December 29, 1961, the CIA JM/WAVE station requested approval to use Veciana as an MRP sabotage asset, which CIA Headquarters granted on January 30, 1962. However, by the spring, the relationship between the CIA and Veciana had soured because Veciana was not the type of operative the Kennedy brothers approved of. Shortly after that, Veciana settled in Puerto Rico and created Alpha-66.

Meanwhile, JCS Chairman Lyman Lemnitzer and U.S. Air Force Brigadier General and Assistant to the Secretary of Defense Edward Lansdale could not convince the Kennedy brothers to invade Cuba a second time. Not to be deterred, Lansdale showed an interest in Alpha 66 at a time when Veciana told the CIA he would work with them as long as there were no strings attached to what he could do. It was something the CIA could not accept, so they ended their relationship with Veciana and Alpha 66. The result was that Lansdale brought Alpha 66 under the direct control of U.S. Army Intelligence and Lansdale's Office of Special Operations in the Pentagon.

On August 8, 1962, an FBI report from San Juan, Puerto Rico, stated that Veciana told an informant that the U.S. had no intention of liberating

Cuba and Alpha 66 would have to force JFK's hand by killing the Russian Ambassador to Cuba, blowing up the Esso Oil Refinery in the Regla section of Havana, destroying the power plant in the Tallapiedra suburb of Havana, sinking a Russian ship in Havana Harbor, and killing a high-ranking Cuban official.

By September, because of the looming Missile Crisis, the U.S. Government looked to contain the paramilitary actions of Cuban exiles. Still, Alpha 66 continued to move forward, and William Harvey was aware of it. Harvey relayed the message that if an operation slated for September 10 were successful, Julio Lobo would commit $250,000 for future Alpha 66 endeavors. The operation began at 2:50 A.M. at the small town of Ponce when an Alpha 66 launch fired more than sixty rounds at a British freighter and a Cuban ship. There were no casualties, but President Kennedy was immediately concerned, and the CIA told its offices in Panama and Puerto Rico to "report all information on Alpha 66 plans and activities." Harvey, who by now knew that Alpha 66 was working with the Army, instructed San Juan and Panama City to contact their local Army representatives to monitor what Alpha 66 was doing.

Meanwhile, Veciana's representative, a U.S. citizen named Jordan James Pfuntner, reported to the Army that Alpha 66 intended to continue conducting raids against Cuba, land agents on the island, and provide intelligence information in exchange for funds, equipment, and arms.

By mid-November 1962, the CIA agreed to an Army request to transfer formal Interagency Source Register (ISR) control of Veciana to the Army. The record of the meeting was written by U.S. Army Colonel Jeff W. Boucher, Chief of the Army's ACSI Collection Division, in a memorandum to General Lansdale and declassified on October 7, 1997. It was a critical turning point in the war against Castro and would have disastrous consequences related to the plot to assassinate President Kennedy. Lansdale was head of the Office of Special Operations, a Department of Defense group serving directly under Secretary McNamara, along with the Joint Chiefs. He was also the chief of operations for Operation Mongoose and was subservient to Robert Kennedy. By the end of the Missile Crisis, Lansdale was already siding with Lemnitzer over Kennedy regarding the necessity of going to war with Cuba. Alpha 66 would play a significant role in what they intended to do about that.[462]

***

A group affiliated with Alpha 66 was the Student Revolutionary Directorate (DRE), which had also looked to overthrow Batista. In early 1960,

Castro appointed one of its leaders, Rolando Cubela, to head the Federation of University Students. After Castro declared he was a Communist, he instructed Cubela to get rid of those who opposed him, which drove into hiding any students who were against the turn to communism. After student leaders Alberto Muller and Manuel Salvat Roque reached the U.S. in June 1960, the CIA helped them set up the DRE in September with Muller as leader and Salvat as propaganda chief. During the next six months, while Antonio Veciana was looking to assassinate Castro, the DRE arranged attacks on radio stations and other sabotage raids. However, as was the case with Veciana, the CIA treated the DRE as a propaganda operation and provided them with a monthly stipend of $44,000. It forced them to become a rogue group that purchased arms on their own and started an independent training camp in the Florida Everglades.[463]

By the spring of 1962, the DRE was upset with the U.S. Government's failure to remove Castro, and they left the Cuban Revolutionary Council in protest. By this time, the DRE had 5,000 members in the U.S. and throughout Latin America.

By late summer 1962, the CIA was frustrated with the DRE, as the Cuban exile group skimmed money from their monthly stipend to build a war chest. On August 24, two DRE vessels shelled the Sierra Maestra Hotel in Havana, where numerous Soviets and Czechs resided, and the Blanquita Theater, where Castro was to speak. DRE leader Fernandez Rocha appeared on Miami television to take credit for the attack. Another member discussed it on *Meet the Press*, which prompted William Harvey to tell Richard Helms that he could not control the DRE. The JMWAVE station was concerned that a DRE attack on a Soviet ship might trigger a full-scale war, and there were calls within the Agency to terminate the CIA's support.[464] Preventing a conventional war with the Soviet Union remained a consistent objective for the CIA, for their mandate was to fight covertly so that a World War II-type engagement would not be necessary.

However, as JFK assassination researcher and one-time editor of the *Washington Post*, Jefferson Morley, wrote, "In Miami the DRE-in-Exile quickly attracted the support of independent CIA covert operations officers such as David Phillips and Howard Hunt."[465] Recall that Phillips was close to Kleberg and Malone and their group, which was looking to overthrow Castro, which also included Alpha 66 and its affiliates. As a result, the DRE continued their terrorist ways, planting bombs that disrupted a campus speech by Castro and using napalm to burn down El Encanto, Havana's largest department store.[466]

Phillips respected the DRE, who he said was the one Cuban exile group that could keep a secret. Meanwhile, in the summer of 1962, Robert Kennedy pressured William Harvey to build a resistance movement inside Cuba. Harvey hated RFK's meddling in Cuban affairs. As a result, Harvey and Helms began to rely on the DRE, which prompted their leader, Luis Fernandez Rocha, to secretly enter Cuba to reassure his increasingly isolated supporters that help was on the way. However, frustration continued to build. When Bobby Kennedy voiced dissatisfaction to Helms over the lack of progress in overthrowing Castro, the deputy CIA director angrily asked what the goal was "since the Cubans with whom we have to work were seeking a reason for risking their lives." He said the DRE was "willing to commit their people only on operations which they regarded as sensible," which meant actions that "would contribute to the liberation of their country, another way of saying that the United States, perhaps in conjunction with other Latin countries, would bail them out militarily." It was also what the CIA wanted.[467]

As the DRE continued harassing Cuba on their own, President Kennedy voiced his displeasure. "The refugees are naturally trying to build up their story to get us to invade," he complained. "Such refugee statements...could make the problem almost unmanageable." In response, Helms moved to bolster Agency control by placing a new case officer, George Joannides, in charge of the DRE in late November 1962, a month after the Missile Crisis. We will revisit him moving forward when we cover 1963 and Lee Harvey Oswald's attempt to infiltrate the DRE in New Orleans. [468]

During the Missile Crisis, a leading DRE member complained at a press interview that the CIA refused to help them and confiscated their arms. "Now we have to work in an underground way," another member said. "The prices of things are high, and we have to deal with anybody we can, the Mafia and all. They don't say they are the Mafia, but you ought to see their faces." It was a threat born out of necessity, and just like the Second Front/ Alpha 66/MIRR collaboration previously mentioned, the DRE was willing to work with the Mafia to regain control of Cuba. It is probable that they had all joined forces by this time and were working together.

According to the CIA's William Crozier, the DRE had "a flagrant disregard for the recent months of patient efforts ... during which time CIA has been the sole and generous supporter of a consistently intractable [DRE]." When Crozier complained about this, he learned the DRE had begun negotiating with Texas oilmen and business titans for financial help. They threatened to pursue this avenue if the CIA did not loosen its reign on them. So, with financial backing from Texas oilmen, businessmen like Robert Kleberg's group and William Pawley, and the likes of Carlos Prio, Santo Trafficante, Carlos Marcello, and perhaps Jimmy Hoffa providing arms, and help from CIA renegade operatives and American mercenaries, the pieces began to fall into place. The independent DRE became part of a group operating outside U.S. government control that was willing to resort to extreme violence to achieve its goals, even assassination.[469]

They would eventually turn their propensity for violence away from Castro and toward JFK as they became increasingly disenchanted with the young President. They had the means, motive, and connections to do so unless an outside group was willing to stop them.

***

In 1960, while Antonio Veciana was still in Cuba, Maurice Bishop suggested he contact Colonel Samuel G. Kail at the American Embassy in Havana. Kail was the US Army attaché at the embassy from June 3, 1958, until it closed on January 4, 1961, and he worked with those involved in the 1959 failed coup attempt to remove Castro. In February 1962, he was transferred to Miami and became responsible for debriefing newly arrived Cuban refugees.[470]

At the time, Dorothy Matlack was the Army's assistant director of the Office of the Domestic Exploitation Section, Army Chief of Staff for Intelligence, and their chief liaison to the CIA with a "Top Secret" clearance. Fletcher Prouty, who was then the Pentagon's logistics liaison with the CIA within the Office of Special Operations, said she was "one of Lansdale's special 'black' intelligence associates in the Pentagon," which meant she must have had an involvement with Alpha 66. In the spring of 1963, Kail, who was also assigned to work with the CIA, insisted that Matlack meet with George de Mohrenschildt and Haitian banker Clemard Charles in Washington, D.C., before the two departed on their mysterious trip to Haiti, which we will cover in more detail in a subsequent chapter. Matlack and Kail were close to Frank Brandsetter, an undercover Army Intelligence agent who managed the Havana Hilton when Castro ousted Batista. Brandstetter knew David Phillips and George de Mohrenschildt, which explains the inclusion of Kail and Matlack in the Washington meeting regarding Haiti.[471]

Matlack was a fascinating figure. In 1956, she was in charge when 30,000 escaped Hungarian refugees were interrogated and debriefed at Camp Kilmer in New Jersey. The U.S. Army website states that Matlack "played an instrumental role in establishing Department of Defense procedures for debriefing defectors, escapees, and refugees of intelligence interest."[472] Based on Matlack's expertise, it stands to reason that she would have interrogated Cuban exiles who had fled Castro, which potentially applied to both Alpha 66 and the DRE. It explains her connection to Kail, Brandstetter, and the group operating out of the U.S. Embassy in Havana in 1959.

Gerry Patrick Hemming, the American mercenary close to Frank Sturgis, said he was approached in Havana in 1959 by Colonel Kail, Sturgis' contact inside the U.S. Embassy. As CIA's Justin Gleichauf described, "My deputy, Col. Samuel G. Kail, former Army attaché in Havana ... handled military administrative matters. The arrangement worked well; we never had a case of dissension between military and civilian personnel or rivalry among services..." Kail also worked with Brandstetter, who was David Morales' connection to mobsters in Cuba. He knew David Phillips, June Cobb, and Henry Hecksher.

Meanwhile, Morales knew John Martino. As we know, Martino worked for Santo Trafficante, and his name was in George Hunter White's address book and Jean Lafitte's notes concerning his trips to Florida and Cuba. Martino was also one of the many aliases Lafitte used, and Lafitte visited Martino in prison in Havana, as did Charles Siragusa of the FBN, who had Mafia connections. And like Morales, years later, John Martino would claim to have been involved in the assassination of JFK. [473]

Future Watergate burglar Bernard Barker was part of Batista's police force before Castro came to power. He was smuggled out of Cuba later that year and landed in Tampa, working with anti-Castro Cuban exiles. Fellow Watergate burglar Howard Hunt was his CIA case officer.[474]

Morales worked with Barker while he was in Havana, and Barker was a "support agent" for "Woodrow C. Olien" (real name James Noel), who was the CIA station chief in Havana.[475]

This group operated outside the Special Group's control and favored a right-wing replacement for Castro, and they were willing to go rogue. They also would not have been pleased with the limited role the CIA was given in Operation AMWORLD, which was the second invasion of Cuba planned for December 1963, especially if the U.S. military was working with ex-CIA-supported groups like Alpha 66. It was an essential piece to the assassination puzzle, which we will revisit later, for many of the names that came together in the war against Castro mentioned here are also included in Lafitte's datebook as having taken part in JFK's assassination.

***

After the CIA ended the Mafia plots to kill Castro, they retained the services of Johnny Roselli. At first, William Harvey was unsure of Roselli, and according to the mob and CIA-connected Washington D.C. cop Joe Shimon, Harvey kept Roselli in seclusion for six weeks to determine if he could work for the CIA while maintaining a close connection to leading Mafia figures. As it turned out, Harvey and Roselli were cut from the same cloth and developed a close relationship.[476]

How close were Harvey and Roselli? Ted Shackley later explained that Harvey would visit the JM/WAVE station in Miami to see Roselli. Others recalled that Johnny "frequented JM/WAVE ... sometimes attending the staff briefings ... or heading off with Dave M[orales] for drinking bouts." Morales worked with Roselli's team of Cubans to keep things under control and professional, and the two kept Harvey informed of their operation's progress. In May 1962, Johnny reported that lethal pills and guns had arrived in Cuba to kill Castro, and a month later, they had dispatched a three-person team there. Still, Harvey knew that assassinating Castro would not be enough to retake the island, and U.S. military intervention was necessary.[477]

By August, Harvey's frustrations boiled over when Edward Lansdale circulated a memorandum to Special Group members mentioning Harvey and the "liquidation of leaders." The head of ZR/RIFLE lambasted Frank Hand, Lansdale's deputy, for referencing assassination on paper. The next day, Harvey complained to Richard Helms because Robert McNamara also mentioned an assassination option in Dean Rusk's office on August 10. The military was acting irresponsibly, but more likely, they were trying to remove the CIA from the military-led operation against Castro. Still, Harvey's complaints were mainly about Robert Kennedy. Dean Acheson concurred, calling Bobby an "inexperienced fool" behind his back. As a result, the disconnect between the White House and CIA personnel responsible for carrying out Cuban affairs continued to grow. Their frustration was almost at a breaking point as Bobby Kennedy organized his left-wing Cuban government in exile, while the military seemingly gravitated towards the more violent Cuban exile groups, Mafia characters, and American mercenaries that worked with them. The CIA recognized the inherent danger in allowing the amateurish operations promoted by the Kennedy brothers to move forward while allowing the military's recklessness to orchestrate a second invasion of Cuba without regard for the international ramifications it would cause. One thing was sure – it was not in the CIA's DNA to sit idly by and allow this to happen.[478]

VIETNAM

On January 13, 1962, the Joint Chiefs sent McNamara a memo urging President Kennedy to introduce combat troops into Vietnam by April.[479] On January 22, Maxwell Taylor, who had moved from the White House to the Pentagon, also sent a memo to McNamara stating, "A loss of South Vietnam to the Communists will presage an early erosion of the remainder of our position in that subcontinent." Taylor's memo was from the Pentagon's Special Assistant for Counterinsurgency and Special Activity, who worked with the CIA and had become a regular conduit for CIA operations.[480]

Vietnam was where the military and the CIA wanted to take a stand against communism, but JFK ignored them. In April, Lieutenant Colonel William Corson was brought from Laos to Washington to brief the President on conditions there. Corson later said, "Kennedy had already lost faith in the CIA. Crisis after crisis was hitting him ... he asked me to brief him on what the Agency was doing in Vietnam. He asked because he no longer trusted what he was hearing from the military or up the river at Langley. He caught them in lies."[481]

On April 4, U.S. Ambassador to India, John Kenneth Galbraith, proposed that the United States explore disengagement from North Vietnam and consider mutual withdrawal from the growing war in the South. He intended to use Soviet or Indian diplomats "to ascertain whether Hanoi can or will call off the Viet Cong activity in return for phased American withdrawal ... and talk about reunification after some period of tranquility." The military and the CIA objected, but Kennedy found the idea intriguing. Two days later, he told his newly appointed Assistant Secretary of State, Averell Harriman, to instruct Galbraith to pursue the matter, but Harriman sabotaged the President instead. He sent a telegram to Galbraith that "changed the mutual de-escalation approach into a threat of US escalation of the war if the North Vietnamese refused to accept US terms," which Harriman knew the North Vietnamese would never agree to. Kennedy, who remained in the dark about this, kept the pressure on. He told Harriman and the State Department's Michael Forrestal, "He wished us to be prepared to seize upon any favorable moment to reduce our involvement [in Vietnam], recognizing that the moment might yet be some time away."[482]

In May, McNamara was misled by General Harkins when he visited Vietnam, who made it appear the war was going well. The military doctored maps showing Communist locations, and McNamara returned saying they could achieve victory by staying the course. The military still wanted to escalate and thought by creating the illusion that things were going well, the President would relent and send combat troops to the region.[483]

But Kennedy would not give in. As he moved steadily toward a settlement in Laos with Khrushchev, he instructed McNamara to initiate a plan to withdraw U.S. military advisers from Vietnam. Following a Secretary of Defense (SECDEF) conference on the war in Saigon on May 8, McNamara told JCS chairman General Lyman Lemnitzer, Admiral Harry Felt, General Paul Harkins, Ambassador Frederick Nolting, and the Defense Intelligence Agency's top expert on Vietnam, civilian analyst George Allen, that: "It is not the job of the US to assume responsibility for the war but to develop the South Vietnamese capability to do so." He asked them when the South Vietnamese would be ready to conduct military operations alone.[484]

McNamara was echoing the President's position. As early as 1952, during a radio address, Congressman John F. Kennedy was clear on what should be done in Vietnam. "For the U.S. to have aligned itself with the desperate efforts of a French regime to hang on to the remnants of empire," he said, "without exacting political reform was a terrible mistake. The task is rather to build a strong native non-Communist sentiment within these areas and [to] rely on that as a spearhead of defense."[485]

When McNamara asked when the South Vietnamese would be ready, "Harkins's chin nearly hit the table," recalled George Allen. He told McNamara they "had scarcely thought about that." They were too busy with plans to expand their efforts in Vietnam "to think about how it might be dismantled." McNamara ordered Harkins, as the commander of MACV (Military Assistance Command, Vietnam), "to devise a plan for turning full responsibility over to South Vietnam and reducing the size of our military command, and to submit this plan at the next conference."[486]

It was a shocking development for the Joint Chiefs. Not engaging in Laos was terrible enough, but pulling out of Vietnam was unthinkable, and they would not give in without a fight. So, Harkins ignored McNamara's directive, but on July 23, McNamara repeated the order and called for a "conservative" three-year timeline for the end of US military assistance in Vietnam. Three days later, the JCS formally directed the Commander in Chief of the Pacific to "develop a capability" for South Vietnamese forces to operate "without the need for continued US special military assistance" by the end of 1965.

Still, the lies continued. Throughout 1962, Kennedy received cables from Ambassador Nolting and General Harkins that the counterinsurgency strategy of gathering South Vietnamese peasants in "strategic hamlets"

159

was succeeding. Nolting even told visiting Senate Majority Leader Mike Mansfield in Vietnam, "We can see the light at the end of the tunnel." However, after returning to Washington, Mansfield sent Kennedy a confidential report that disclosed the truth as he saw it: "Seven years and billions of dollars later…we are at the beginning of the beginning," he wrote. The only alternative was "a truly massive commitment of American military personnel and other resources – in short going to war fully ourselves against the guerillas – and the establishment of some sort of neo-colonial rule in South Vietnam."[487]

Kennedy invited Mansfield to Palm Beach over the 1962 Christmas holidays to discuss Vietnam further. Regarding Mansfield's report, an angry Kennedy said: "This is not what my advisors are telling me!" Mansfield told him he was courting disaster unless he stopped increasing the number of advisers and began withdrawing the ones already there.

At the end of December, JFK sent the NSC's Michael Forrestal and the State Department's Director of Intelligence and Research, Roger Hilsman, to Vietnam to assess the situation further. Their "eyes only" report for Kennedy described it as "fragile." Meanwhile, the Joint Chiefs wrote McNamara that if the Diem government could not bring the Vietcong under control, there was "no alternative to the introduction of US military combat forces."[488]

JFK had had enough. He asked Averell Harriman to be ready "to seize upon any favorable moment to reduce our involvement." He told Deputy Secretary of Defense Roswell Gilpatric at the end of 1962 that he believed the US had been "sucked into Vietnam little by little." There was no doubt where JFK stood.[489]

Kennedy ordered McNamara to begin planning a US military exit from Vietnam. According to Gilpatric, JFK "made clear to McNamara and me that he wanted to not only hold the level of U.S. military presence in Vietnam down, but he wanted to reverse the flow." McNamara then drew up a three-year plan for the reduction of U.S. forces in Vietnam. Military planners told him "advisers" could leave by 1965, but McNamara extended the date to 1968. The plan was to phase out all U.S. military involvement.[490]

According to the Pentagon Papers, JFK was worried about a Communist takeover of West Berlin if the United States were to escalate the fighting in Vietnam, the same concern he had with expanding hostilities in Cuba. He knew it could start World War III, and he was determined to prevent that from happening. On the other hand, the Joint Chiefs seemed to welcome the opportunity.[491]

There were nearly ten times as many Americans killed or wounded in action in Vietnam in 1962 as in 1961, which closely paralleled the tenfold build-up in American forces to 11,000 men by the end of 1962.[492] Still, Harkins continued to ignore McNamara, whose memo on October 8, 1962 stated: "General Harkins did not have time to present his plan for phasing out US personnel in Viet-Nam within 3 years."[493] Kennedy knew what Harkins and the rest of the military were doing was treasonous. On December 18, he issued National Security Action Memorandum Number 217, forbidding "high-ranking military and civilian personnel" from going to South Vietnam without State Department clearance. It infuriated the Joint Chiefs. Who did JFK think he was to tell them how to conduct a military situation? Clearly, if they were to "provide for the common defense" and "promote the general Welfare," as stated in the preamble to the Constitution, which they interpreted as their mandate, JFK could not be allowed to serve a second term.[494]

INDONESIA

Since the 1950s, Allen Dulles had wanted regime change in Indonesia, but instead, President Kennedy looked to improve relations with President Sukarno and end Dutch colonialism there. In February 1962, the U.S. signed a $92.7 million food aid agreement with Jakarta as a first step toward Papuan independence, which followed a military clash between Holland and Indonesia. Holland was adamant it wanted to maintain control, so Robert Kennedy traveled to the Hague, where he spoke so rudely about Holland's intentions with former Dutch Foreign Minister and NATO Secretary General Joseph Luns that he approached JFK about the encounter. An unmoved President Kennedy told Luns it would be a disaster if "Indonesia goes to war" over the dispute, for "from the strategic point of view, we believe that West New Guinea as such is of little consequence, since ... the additional territory does not alter the strategic position."[495]

What JFK did not know, and Allen Dulles and the Dutch did, was that Papua was one of the richest areas in the world, with an abundance of oil, gold, copper, and other minerals. Dulles intended to impede Indonesian access to the vast natural resources there by any means possible, which threatened JFK's plan for a peaceful resolution.

On March 20, talks were held thirty miles outside Washington between Indonesian Adam Malik (who in 1965 would be involved in President Sukarno's overthrow) and Herman van Roijen of the Netherlands. American Ellsworth Bunker suspiciously served as mediator, for Allen Dulles had known the Bunker family for over thirty years. Despite this, the outcome was never in doubt, and on May 1, 1963, the Duth gave Indonesia control of the region. However, the transfer date was changed on the lease for access to the gold deposits until after the Dutch had ceded control, and as a result, American mining giant Freeport Sulphur, which was part of Freeport Texas Company, gained access to the site, which was what Dulles wanted. All that was left for Dulles to do was to prevent Kennedy from improving relations with Indonesia. It meant orchestrating a military coup to remove the so-called Communist Sukarno from power to satisfy the greedy appetite of the American corporations he supported. The coup would not occur until 1965, and throughout the remainder of Kennedy's first term, Dulles knew he had to keep JFK in the dark about the importance of West New Guinea and its abundance of raw minerals.[496]

THE STEEL CRISIS

Concerned with rising steel prices and potential inflation, President Kennedy brokered a contract on April 6, 1962, in which the United Steel Workers union accepted a modest settlement from U.S. Steel, which agreed not to raise steel prices. However, four days later, U.S. Steel chairman Roger Blough issued a press release stating that the next day, they "will raise the price of the company's steel products by an average of about 3.5 percent..." Bethlehem Steel raised its prices the following day, and four more companies did the same.[497]

McNamara told JFK the price increase would cost them one billion dollars. A livid Kennedy ordered the government to give steel contracts to smaller companies that had kept prices the same. At the same time, Robert Kennedy convened a federal grand jury to investigate potential price fixing. In an April 11 press conference, JFK said, "The American people will find it hard, as I do, to accept a situation in which a tiny handful of steel executives whose pursuit of private power and profit exceeds their sense of public responsibility can show such utter contempt for the interests of 185 million Americans." Four days later, the steel executives succumbed to the pressure and kept steel prices the same.[498]

While JFK felt betrayed, Henry Luce's *Fortune* magazine considered Blough a capitalist hero for defying the President's authority. It was also not a coincidence that Blough served with Allen Dulles at the Council on Foreign Relations and the Lafayette Fellowship Foundation, which was part of the Ford Foundation.[499]

In a *Fortune* magazine editorial, an outraged Henry Luce added a sinister postscript to the story, warning JFK to "beware the Ides of April." JFK never heeded the warning. Based on Bobby Kennedy's earlier Grand Jury probe, in October 1963, just weeks before JFK's assassination, the Justice Department filed price-fixing charges against U.S. Steel and other steel companies. Kennedy would have been wise to pay more attention to the hatred that had begun to engulf him by that time, especially when one considers the relationship U.S. Steel had had with the Eisenhower administration.[500]

On April 1, 1960, while Eisenhower was President, there was a strategy meeting to discuss the pending Cuban operation. Allen Dulles, J.C. King, Jake Esterline, William Pawley, Nixon's military aide Colonel Cushman, and Walter Donnelly, the vice president of U.S. Steel were in attendance. Donnelly was a former diplomat who was close to Nixon, and he was at the meeting because of Dulles' closeness to U.S. Steel Chairman Roger Blough. So, with U.S. Steel's involvement in high-level discussions regarding the removal of Castro under Eisenhower, it is not surprising that Blough believed he could ignore President Kennedy in 1962 and get away with raising prices. The Chairman of U.S. Steel was used to getting what he wanted.[501]

France and An Assassination Attempt Against Charles de Gaulle

The official Algerian cease-fire between France and the Front de Liberation Nationale (FLN) became effective on March 19, 1962. In June, the Evian Accords led to a second referendum overwhelmingly approving Algerian independence on July 5. A little over a month later, on August 22, another assassination attempt against Charles de Gaulle occurred.

Traveling in his car with his wife and son-in-law, de Gaulle entered a "kill zone," an avenue lined with vehicles loaded with sharpshooters armed with submachine guns, grenades, and Molotov cocktails. Somehow, they shot only two tires and the rear window as de Gaulle's car skidded out of control and almost collided with an oncoming vehicle. One bullet did pass between de Gaulle and his wife and narrowly missed their son-in-law sitting in front.

Arrested was Lieutenant-Colonel Jean Marie Bastien-Thiry, a 35-year-old air force engineer. He claimed at his trial that the intent was to kidnap De Gaulle. He may have been a patsy set up to take the fall, for there was also a Hungarian trio of sharpshooters who wanted to assassinate the French President. The press would report that the attempt on de Gaulle's life included an extremist military group and a secret deep state organization manipulated by NATO.[502]

***

The warning signs were there for President Kennedy in 1962. Right-wing assassination against left-wing leaders was in the air, but he underestimated the danger he faced and that there were those at home who wanted him removed from power for the good of the country. He was violating the policy of containment that defined U.S. foreign policy since the end of World War II; he violated the Constitution by placing the nation in danger, as his opponents perceived it, and he marginalized the CIA in pursuit of his agenda. The CIA mantra that the world would have been better off if someone had killed Hitler before he had the opportunity to start World War II applies here, for there were those who believed President Kennedy was leading the world toward the next world war. They would use this logic as justification for assassinating him.

CHAPTER NINE

DON'T DANCE WITH THE DEVIL

The relationship between the Kennedy family and organized crime began with the start of Prohibition on January 29, 1919. Joe Kennedy saw it as an opportunity to make money. In time, he became the largest distributor of Scotch in the country, ordering liquor from overseas distillers and supplying it to the Mafia. One of the principal figures he worked with was New York Mafia bigwig Frank Costello, who boasted about their relationship during the 1920s. There were also reports that Joe serviced Al Capone's crime empire in Chicago. It would eventually make the senior Kennedy extremely wealthy. [503]

Joe was never averse to making money illegally. While U.S. ambassador to England during World War II, he shorted Czechoslovakian securities knowing the country was about to be overrun by Hitler's Nazi troops and made a $500,000 profit.[504]

Kennedy wanted one of his sons to become President and attempted to control everything in their lives to ensure that happened. In 1941 JFK's affair with a suspected Nazi spy named Inga Arvad put that in jeopardy. The FBI bugged Arvad's apartment and tapped her phones, picking up sounds of the two in bed together. It prompted J. Edgar Hoover to call Joe to tell him what his son was up to. John Kennedy immediately told Inga they were through, and the Navy transferred him from Washington to the South Pacific.[505]

It was the start of a close relationship between the senior Kennedy and the FBI Director. In 1953, the agent in charge of Boston, J.J. Kelly, told Hoover that Joe Kennedy praised him "personally and the bureau generally." When a newspaper column criticized Hoover, Joe said the writer did it to please the "Jews, Negroes, and the Communist element behind the civil liberties outfit, as well as the NAACP." Hoover wrote Joe a thank you in return.[506]

As the 1960 election approached, Joe Kennedy spared no expense to get John elected. New York congressman Eugene Keough said Joe knew "instinctively who the important people were, who the bosses were behind the scenes. From 1958, he was in contact with them constantly by phone, presenting Jack's case…"[507]

The one problem the Kennedys faced was Bobby's war against organized crime. While serving on the McClellan Committees during the 1950s, Bobby developed a vendetta against Carlos Marcello, Sam Giancana, and Teamster boss Jimmy Hoffa. Still, Joe was not worried. Lee Server wrote in *Handsome Johnny, The Life and Death of Johnny Rosselli: Gentleman Gangster, Hollywood Producer, C.I.A. Assassin*, that Joe approached Frank Sinatra, whom he knew from his days working in Hollywood, and asked him to contact Giancana on his behalf. "I believe in this man [JFK]," Sinatra told Giancana during a game of golf in Florida. "I think he's going to make us a good president. With your help, I think we can work this out." It led to the infamous meeting at Felix Young's restaurant in New York during the 1960 campaign. "I took the reservation, and it was as though every gangster chief in the United States was there," recalled hostess Edna Donovan. "There was John Roselli, Carlos Marcello from New Orleans, the two brothers from Dallas, the top men from Buffalo, California, and Colorado. They were all the top people, not soldiers. I was amazed Joe Kennedy would take the risk."[508]

Others were also in attendance, like Sam Giancana and Mario Brod, the attorney who was CIA counterintelligence chief James Angleton's liaison to the Mafia. That the Agency wanted a seat at this table was quite telling. Giancana told Joe that the mob was concerned about what Bobby might do if his brother became President. Joe said he would owe them if they helped Jack, and he would keep Bobby under control. Brod recalled Joe saying, "It's Jack who's running for president, not Bobby." "This is business, not politics."[509]

After Joe Kennedy left, according to Brod, Roselli said, "It was Kennedy who came to them, and this was significant." Meanwhile, Giancana returned to Chicago, and the consensus was that the Chicago mob liked having the President of the United States indebted to them. They decided to help JFK get elected, but unknown to them, the FBI was bugging their conversations.[510]

***

The same month as the dinner at Felix Young's restaurant, presidential hopeful John Kennedy was in Las Vegas visiting his sister Pat, the wife of actor Peter Lawford. Frank Sinatra introduced him to an attractive brunette named Judith Campbell. Sinatra had been introduced to Campbell by Johnny Roselli, who had known her since she was seventeen. The two were close. She was in the Hollywood/Malibu circuit, somewhere between a "party girl and a trophy-wife-to-be." By 1959, she was seeing Frank Sinatra, which was how Campbell got to know JFK. It was a setup – the Mafia told Sinatra to introduce Campbell to the presidential candidate, whose weakness for beautiful young women was well known to them.[511]

Within a month, JFK and Campbell met again at the Plaza Hotel in New York City, and there were other meetings at various places across the country. The relationship lasted roughly two years and involved about seventy phone calls to and from the White House while Kennedy was President. It was a potentially dangerous situation, for Judith was also seeing Sam Giancana at the same time while he was involved in the CIA/Mafia plots to kill Castro. Sinatra had brought them together in March 1960, shortly after her affair with Kennedy began. Based on what she said years later, Judith was not romantically involved with Giancana. It was her closeness to JFK that interested him.[512]

In April 1960, Campbell visited Giancana after stopping in Washington to spend time with Kennedy. She claimed she delivered a payoff to the mobster for his help in the upcoming election. On other occasions, they met immediately before or after Judith met with JFK, which continued after Kennedy became President. In August 1961, she had lunch at the White House with JFK and met with Giancana at the Mayflower Hotel that evening.[513] The implication was she was reporting to Giancana, and the Mafia may have considered blackmailing the President. Robert Kennedy was the Attorney General, and despite the assurances Joe had given the Mafia, he was clamping down hard on organized crime. Giancana told a group of FBI men at O'Hare Airport in July 1961, "I know all about the Kennedys ... and one of these days ... I am going to tell all." On another occasion, an FBI wiretap picked up Giancana saying to Roselli that he expected that "one of these days, the guy [JFK] will do me a favor." Roselli replied, "If I ever got a speeding ticket, not one of these fuckers would know me." "You told that right, buddy," Giancana responded.[514]

As told by Seymour M. Hersh in his book, *The Dark Side Of Camelot*, Campbell alleged that she became pregnant with Kennedy's baby and had it aborted, and it was Giancana to whom she turned for emotional support. If true, John Kennedy had leaped from the frying pan into the fire, for Giancana had a soft spot in his heart for damsels in distress.

White House telephone records show that Campbell called JFK on November 7 and 15, 1961. On both days, she also received a call from John Roselli, which meant she was also reporting to him.[515] Was this further proof they were looking to blackmail Kennedy? Perhaps, but there may have been another explanation. Were Giancana and Roselli using Campbell as a conduit to inform the President of the CIA/Mafia assassination plots to kill Castro? Or was JFK using mobsters to keep tabs on the CIA? From Giancana, Roselli, and Trafficante's point of view, a relationship with the President meant they should have been immune from prosecution, the efforts of his brother Bobby notwithstanding. It also explained Giancana's introduction into the assassination group, considering his relationship with Campbell was a pipeline to the White House. From Kennedy's perspective, using Giancana through Campbell was the only way to learn what the CIA was up to. Years later, Judith Campbell Exner said, "I feel like I was set up to be the courier. I was a perfect choice because I could come and go without notice, and if noticed, no one would have believed it anyway."[516]

Even after FBI agents questioned her, Kennedy told her not to worry. "They won't do anything to you. And don't worry about Sam. You know he works for us." It was a logical reaction by the President, for the mob had cultivated a favorable relationship with his family for quite some time.[517] However, by December, Giancana and Roselli had tired of Robert Kennedy's antics. Bobby pushed for legislation to strike at the mob's revenue sources and lowered the restrictions on using wiretaps; he increased protection for witnesses involving the Mafia; he instituted an immunity statute for grand jury witnesses that said if they used the Fifth Amendment against self-incrimination, they faced a contempt of court charge. Finally, he instituted the RICO Act (Racketeer Influenced and Corrupt Organizations), which said those who did not participate in a crime but ordered it could also be convicted.[518]

The Mafia blamed Frank Sinatra for not controlling Bobby. An FBI wiretap picked up Roselli complaining to Giancana: "I said, Frankie, can I ask one question? He says Johnny, I took Sam's name, wrote it down, and told Bobby Kennedy, this is my buddy; this is what I want you to know, Bob." A few days later, the topic again turned to Frank Sinatra. "He's got it in his head that they're going to be faithful to him," Roselli said. Giancana replied: " In other words, then, the donation that was made." "That's what I was talking about," Roselli interrupted.[519]

Early in 1962, Giancana spoke with John D'Arco, a Chicago First Ward politician. The FBI recorded D'Arco saying, "I heard that the President, when he is in California, is with Sinatra all the time." "He can't get change of a quarter," Giancana replied. "Well, they got the whip, and they're in office, and that's it... So, they're going to knock us guys out of the box and make us defenseless."[520] Something had to give.

***

J. Edgar Hoover knew about the Mafia/CIA connection and approached Richard Bissell with the following information: "During recent conversations with several friends, Giancana stated that Fidel Castro was to be done away with very shortly... Moreover, he allegedly indicated that he had already met with the assassins-to-be on three occasions...Giancana claimed that everything had been perfected for the killing of Castro and that the 'assassin' had arranged with a girl... to drop a 'pill' in some drink of Castro's."[521]

The FBI's wiretap recordings of conversations between Giancana and Roselli enabled Hoover to piece together the Giancana-Campbell-Kennedy puzzle. Their surveillance of Campbell and wiretaps of her apartment provided irrefutable proof that the Kennedy/Campbell affair continued after Kennedy was elected. Then, after discovering that Campbell had made two phone calls to JFK's secretary Evelyn Lincoln on February 27, 1962, Hoover discretely sent a memo to Robert Kennedy stating: "The relationship between Campbell and Mrs. Lincoln or the purpose of these calls is not known."[522]

Considering everything the FBI director knew, it appears Hoover exercised tact by allowing the Attorney General to inform his brother that the FBI was aware of his affair with Campbell. It soon became apparent that Bobby had no intention of confronting JFK on such a sensitive topic. As a result, on March 22, 1962, Hoover met with the President at the White House to set things straight. White House records show a call to Judith Campbell shortly after Hoover departed, but according to Seymour Hirsh, the relationship did not end. "The president was angered, [Judith Campbell] Exner told me," Hirsh wrote, "over the fact that Hoover would have the audacity to come into his office and confront him with this information. He called him an S.O.B. and said, 'He tried to use, you know, this information as leverage.' [Kennedy's] attitude was 'the gall of the man to try to intimidate him.' He was absolutely livid." The President, Exner added, "was well aware that Hoover knew every move that he made, and he did not care. That's the reckless side of Jack – that he would allow himself to be in that position."[523]

Hoover also told Kennedy he knew about Campbell's relationship with Giancana and Roselli and the CIA/Mafia plots to kill Castro. The next day, he sent a memo to the CIA's Sheffield Edwards, asking if the Agency "would or would not object to the initiation of criminal prosecutions" of those involved. As Hoover subsequently said, the CIA was afraid it "would lead to exposure of most sensitive information relating to the abortive Cuban invasion in April 1961 and would result in most damaging embarrassment to the U.S. Government."[524]

Hoover's meeting forced Kennedy to break with Sinatra. In late March, he canceled a scheduled West Coast visit to Sinatra's home and stayed with Bing Crosby instead. Shortly after that, the Justice Department investigated the relationship between Sinatra and organized crime. When completed, it totaled nineteen pages in length.

There was another story told under oath by Joe Shimon, the shady Washington D.C. police detective. As Lee Server wrote in *Handsome Johnny*:

> "Hoover had come to Bobby Kennedy in March with some of the latest audio from Giancana's bugged telephones. Hoover played the selected tape, and they listened to Giancana and Sinatra in private conversation. The gangster demanding the singer get them relief from the government... Sinatra, the dialogue made clear, was having an affair with the President's sister, Pat Kennedy Lawford (Peter's wife). He was fucking the sister, Sinatra told Giancana, to get her to use her influence on the brothers. Sinatra made it sound like quite a sacrifice. He vowed he would "*sleep with this goddamn bitch until I get something going.*

"The tapes were played to Bobby," said Shimon, "And overnight you saw Sinatra out. No more White House. No nothing. Shut him *off*." (Italics from original)[525]

By now, the mob realized they were wrong to help JFK get elected. A Giancana henchman named Johnny Formosa thought it would be a good idea to show Kennedy that they meant business by "knocking out a couple of those guys," referring to Sinatra, Dean Martin, and Peter Lawford. "No," Giancana said, "I got other plans..."[526]

***

The Mafia notwithstanding, no one hated the Kennedys more than Teamster boss Jimmy Hoffa. "Bobby Kennedy is just another lawyer now," he told a Nashville interviewer just two days after JFK's death. At the time, Hoffa was busy preparing his defense for jury tampering related to a trial from the previous year that ended in a hung jury. There was no rest for Hoffa as the Attorney General's "Get Hoffa Squad" was determined to put him behind bars. The Justice Department utilized all available assets and relentlessly tried to destroy him, including around-the-clock surveillance, electronic eavesdropping, and the bugging of phone lines. Hoffa was not one to give up quickly, and years later, he claimed to have "seamy" material pertaining to the Kennedys. He never disclosed what that was, but some believe it had to do with the relationship each brother had with Marilyn Monroe.[527]

On August 20, 1962, shortly after Monroe's death, an FBI electronic bug picked up the following conversation between three leading Mafia figures: "They [the Kennedys] will go for every name...it's big enough to cause a scandal against them. Would he like to see a headline about Marilyn Monroe come out... He has been in there plenty of times. It's been a hard affair – and this [redacted] said she used to be in all the time with him – do you think it's a secret?"[528]

Marilyn also hinted at her relationship with the Kennedys. She told her psychiatrist right before she died that she had recently had sexual relations with "extremely important men in government... at the highest level." There was an FBI transcript of a conversation where Meyer Lansky told his wife he knew Bobby was "running around with a well-known woman." In a spring 1962 FBI wiretap, a member of the Genovese family said, "I want the President indicted because I know he was whacking all those broads. Sinatra brought them out. I'd like to hit Kennedy. I would gladly go to the penitentiary for the rest of my life, believe me."[529]

It was Sinatra who brought Marilyn Monroe into contact with West Coast mobsters. Reportedly, one was Johnny Roselli, who had a habit of taking advantage of Hollywood's wealthiest stars. "I met Roselli with Marilyn a couple of times," recalled actress Jeanne Carmen, a friend of Marilyn's who also dated Roselli.[530] Roselli knew of the Giancana/Campbell/JFK relationship and understood the value of using Marilyn to blackmail the Kennedys.

Hoffa allegedly began wiretapping Marilyn's home around mid-1961 and had recordings of her in bed with each of the Kennedy brothers, and the FBI may have been aware of it. John H. Davis wrote in *Mafia Kingfish* that "former FBI Assistant Director Courtney Evans, who had functioned as liaison between Kennedy and FBI Director Hoover, told British journalist Anthony Summers that he and Hoover were aware that Sam Giancana and Jimmy Hoffa were possibly attempting to blackmail the Kennedys over their relationship with Marilyn Monroe and other women."[531]

Kennedy's brother-in-law Peter Lawford claimed he listened to the tapes. "You could apparently hear the voices of Marilyn and JFK as well as Marilyn and RFK, in addition to Marilyn Monroe and Dr. Ralph Greenson [Marilyn's psychiatrist]. In each case, you could hear the muted sounds of bedsprings and the cries of ecstasy."[532]

The plan to use the Monroe tapes to blackmail JFK backfired with the untimely death of the actress on August 4, 1962. Although ruled a suicide, she was probably accidentally murdered to protect the President from another embarrassing situation.

On May 19, 1962, Marilyn sang her sultry rendition of Happy Birthday to JFK at Madison Square Garden in New York City. Five days later, Hoover requested a personal interview with the President "on an urgent matter of national security," and the next day, White House switchboard operators were told not to accept any more calls from Marilyn. Hoover knew of her relationships with Kennedy, Sinatra, Giancana, and Roselli, which mirrored Judith Campbell's, and he undoubtedly warned JFK he risked being blackmailed by the Mafia.[533]

On June 25, Marilyn placed a call from Los Angeles to the Justice Department in an unsuccessful attempt to reach Bobby. Around the same time, a tearful and angry Marilyn called her old flame Robert Slatzer. They met, and she showed him a little red book, which she called "her diary," plus a bundle of handwritten notes on U.S. Justice Department stationery. After her death, the coroner's assistant, Lionel Grandison, saw the diary. Out of curiosity, he flicked through the pages and saw references to the Kennedys and the words "Cuba" and "Mafia." The notebook disappeared after the LAPD took possession of it, and within twelve hours, her phone records with Bell Telephone Company were gone.[534]

The Cal-Neva Lodge at Lake Tahoe, Nevada, was a favorite hangout for mobsters and Hollywood celebrities. There was a ban prohibiting Sam Giancana from staying there, but that did not stop him. On the weekend of July 27, Marilyn stayed as a guest of Sinatra in one of the hideaway bungalows he reserved for special guests. She flew there with Peter Lawford and his wife Pat, the Kennedy sister with whom Sinatra was sleeping. About three hours after they arrived, the Lawfords saw Giancana in the Cal-Neva lobby, which upset Pat. "That's it. We have to go," she said, loud enough for Giancana to hear. Marilyn was in the lobby as well. As Lawford tried to smooth things over with Giancana, Pat took Marilyn to the apparent safety of her room.[535]

What happened next is hazy, but several published accounts claim Marilyn abused pills and had sex with Giancana while under the influence. FBI wiretaps picked up Roselli talking to Giancana, and FBI agent William Roemer claimed Marilyn "engaged in an orgy. From the conversation I overheard, it appeared she may have had sex with both Sinatra and Giancana."[536]

On August 3, the day before Marilyn's death, columnist Dorothy Kilgallen, who always seemed to know things before anyone else did, wrote that Marilyn has "proved [to be] vastly alluring to a handsome gentleman who is a bigger name than Joe DiMaggio in his heyday."

Two days later, a somewhat startled Kilgallen wrote: "Why was Marilyn's door locked that night, when she didn't usually lock it? If she was just trying to get to sleep and took the overdose of pills accidentally, why was the light on? Usually, people sleep better in the dark." "Why did the first doctor [to arrive on the scene] have to call the second doctor before calling the police? Any doctor, even a psychiatrist, knows a dead person when he sees one...Why the big time gap in such a small town? [Housekeeper] Mrs. Murray gets worried at about 3 A.M. and it's almost 6 A.M. before the police get to the scene." [537]

Peter Lawford told author C. David Heymann, "Marilyn realized the [JFK] affair was over but couldn't accept it. She began writing these rather pathetic letters to Jack and continued calling. She threatened to go to the press. He finally sent Bobby Kennedy out to California to cool her off... that evening they became lovers and spent the night in our guest bedroom. Almost immediately, the affair got very heavy, and they began seeing a lot of each other. Now Marilyn was calling the Department of Justice instead of the White House... Marilyn announced that she was in love with Bobby and that he had promised to marry her." She threatened to call a press conference and make public her sexual liaisons with both Kennedy brothers. It prompted Bobby to contact Dr. Greenson because Marilyn threatened to destroy his career as well. It was clear that this was not going to end well. [538]

As told in *The Murder of Marilyn Monroe*, Peter Lawford suffered from deep guilt and recalled that on the afternoon of Marilyn's death, he and Bobby arrived at her home. "They argued back and forth for maybe ten minutes," Lawford said. When Marilyn became hysterical and threatened to call a press conference, "Bobby became livid. Marilyn presently lost it, screaming obscenities and flailing wildly away at Bobby with her fists." They called Dr. Greenson, and he was at Marilyn's home within the hour. Marilyn's publicist, Pat Newcomb, said she "was at her [Marilyn's] house that afternoon until three, and that's when Greenson came and told me to leave." In a 1985 documentary, *Say Goodbye to the President*, housekeeper Eunice Murray also said Bobby was at Marilyn's house that afternoon and was visibly upset. [539]

Robert Kennedy testified in a sworn deposition to Captain Edward Michael Davis of the LAPD that he was at Marilyn's home that afternoon (Four women playing cards next door saw him enter and leave on at least two occasions). According to a confidential source, "Bobby said in his deposition that he and Peter Lawford went to Marilyn's house... There was a violent argument, and Marilyn was grabbed by Bobby and thrown to the floor... Then she was given an injection of pentobarbital in her armpit, which settled her down....."[540]

Eunice Murray's son-in-law, Norman Jeffries, also saw Bobby and Peter Lawford that afternoon, and that night, while he and Eunice were watching television, "between 9:30 and 10:00 P.M.," Bobby and two men dressed in suits ordered him and Eunice out of the house. They were veteran LAPD partners Archie Case and James Ahern, members of Chief William Parker's notorious Gangster Squad, which allegedly performed illegal activities for the LAPD.[541]

According to Anthony Summers, Marilyn was on the phone with her friend Jose Bolanos after 9:30 P.M. when she mentioned "something that will one day shock the whole world." Then, there was a crash. While Bolanos waited, Marilyn went to investigate the noise coming from the guest cottage, where she found Bobby, Case, and Ahern rifling through her file cabinets.

Professional wiretapper Bernie Spindel and detective Fred Otash claimed that what happened next was recorded on tape. Bobby ordered Case and Ahern to inject Marilyn with a relaxant. In his memoirs, Deputy Coroner's Aide Lionel Grandison confirmed in writing that he learned that Bobby had instructed them to "give her something to calm her down."[542]

Eunice and Jeffries found Marilyn around 10:30 p.m. after Bobby, Case, and Ahern had left. "I thought she was dead," Jeffries said. Eunice called an ambulance and Dr. Greenson. Schaefer Ambulance attendant James Hall, Eunice, and Jeffries all claimed Marilyn was alive when Greenson got there. He "pulled out a loaded hypodermic syringe and injected the fluid into her heart." After trying heart massage, Greenson told Hall, "I'm releasing you. She's dead."[543]

Bobby did not kill Marilyn, but his presence there was troubling, which he later tried to hide. In 1970, biographer Patte Barham interviewed Peter Lawford's mother, Lady May Lawford, who said that "a dark helicopter, like the one that the Kennedy boys used, had been parked on the beach [by Lawford's house]. And I knew that neighbors saw Bobby dashing in and out on Saturday." Lawford's next-door neighbor, Ward Wood, recalled, "It was Bobby all right. He was in khakis and a white shirt open at the neck." Reporter Joe Hyams' friend, William Woodfield, learned about a flight log entry for August from a pilot for Conners Helicopter Service in Santa Monica. "The time in the log was sometime after midnight," Woodfield remembered. "I think between midnight and two in the morning. It showed clearly that a helicopter had picked up Robert Kennedy at the Santa Monica Beach." James Zonlick was a pilot for Hal Conner's helicopter service. He recalled, "Hal had picked Robert Kennedy at the beach house and left him at Los Angeles International Airport...."

Meanwhile, reporters grew suspicious of the secrecy surrounding Marilyn's death. The *New York Herald Tribune's* Joe Hyams recalled, "A source at the telephone company came back and said the Secret Service has already been here and taken our records..... That's the first time in my memory as a reporter that they ever, ever stepped in that fast to start a hush." On August 8, columnist Florabel Muir wrote in the *New York Daily News* that her sources said, "Strange 'pressures' are being put on Los Angeles police investigating the death of Marilyn Monroe." Muir wrote that Lawford's mother told her: 'The night that Marilyn died, I called Peter out at the Santa Monica beach house....In the background, I thought I heard that awful Boston accent of Bobby Kennedy." "I knew that Marilyn was seeing Jack Kennedy," Lawford's mother said. "I also knew that Marilyn was seeing Bobby Kennedy. They often used Pat and Peter's beach house... Peter had a part in the cover-up."[544]

On July 8, 1964, Hoover wrote Bobby regarding the soon-to-be-released book, *The Strange Death of Marilyn Monroe*. "His book will make reference to your alleged friendship with the late Miss Marilyn Monroe," Hoover wrote. "He will indicate in his book that you and Miss Monroe were intimate and that you were in Miss Monroe's home at the time of her death." "He said she was murdered," Hoover's teenage neighbor Anthony Calomaris told Anthony Summers decades later. "That it wasn't a suicide, that the Kennedys were involved."

After Marilyn's death, the Kennedys gave her publicist Pat Newcomb a job in Washington and sent her to Europe so the American press could not talk to her. The Kennedy family knew how to keep things quiet.

***

If the Mafia were using Marilyn Monroe to blackmail JFK and believed the Kennedy brothers' attempt to silence her led to her death, their reaction would have been to strike back in kind. Perhaps that was why, the month after Marilyn died, Santo Trafficante, Carlos Marcello, and Jimmy Hoffa all said they wanted the President killed.

In September 1962, private investigator Edward Becker met with Carlos Marcello at the mobster's three-thousand-acre estate outside New Orleans. When Becker mentioned how terrible it was that Bobby was leaning so hard on Marcello, he jumped to his feet in a rage and quoted an old Sicilian oath: "Livarsi na pietra di la scarpa!." Take the stone out of my shoe. "Don't worry about that Bobby son of a bitch! He's going to be taken care of," Marcello said. "If you want to kill a dog, you cut off its head, not its tail." The implication was clear – the way to stop Bobby was to get rid of his brother.[545]

Louisiana Teamster official Edward Partin had known Jimmy Hoffa since 1957. He became an FBI informant in August 1962 when Hoffa seriously began planning to kill the Attorney General. "What I think should be done," Hoffa said, "if I can get hold of these plastic bombs, is to get somebody to throw one in his house, and the place'll [sic] burn after it blows up…"[546] On another occasion, Hoffa suggested "the possible use of a lone gunman equipped with a rifle with a telescopic sight…. without any identifiable connection to the Teamsters organization…"[547]

Federal investigator Hawk Daniels, who later became a Louisiana judge, listened in while Partin spoke to Hoffa on the phone and was sufficiently alarmed to notify the Justice Department. "Hoffa fully intended to carry the threats out,' Daniels said. "It was a question of how and when, not a question of whether he had doubts…of eliminating at least Mr. Bobby Kennedy and possibly his brother also."[548]

In September 1962, Santo Trafficante met in a Miami hotel with Jose Aleman Jr., for whom he had arranged a $1.5 million loan from the Teamsters. When Hoffa's name came up, Trafficante lamented, "Have you seen how his brother is hitting Hoffa, a man who is not a millionaire, a friend of the blue-collar? He doesn't know that this kind of encounter is very delicate… Mark my word, this man Kennedy is in trouble, and he will get what is coming to him." When Aleman told Trafficante that Kennedy was sure to be reelected based on his enormous popularity, Trafficante replied, "No, Jose, he is going to be hit…."[549]

Aleman reported the conversation to Miami FBI agents George Davis and Paul Scranton, who kept tabs on Cuban exiles. Both men later admitted meeting Aleman on numerous occasions. As far as Trafficante's allegation that the Mafia was planning JFK's assassination, Scranton declined to answer. "I wouldn't want to do anything to embarrass the Bureau," he said.[550]

Former Trafficante and Hoffa attorney Frank Ragano confirmed there were discussions to kill the President. In early 1963, Hoffa instructed him to travel to New Orleans to tell Marcello and Trafficante he wanted Kennedy killed, which he did. "They made me think they already had such a thing in mind," he said.[551]

***

In 1979, Richard Case Nagell, who claimed to know what Lee Harvey Oswald was up to throughout 1963, wrote to the chairman of the HSCA, Congressman Louis Stokes, regarding the possible involvement of organized crime in the JFK assassination. Nagell suspected the committee's final report "will conclude that the murder may have been 'arranged' by members of organized crime and their associates, namely, by James Hoffa, Carlos Marcello or Santos Trafficante, et al." "I doubt," Nagel continued, "that there is any person alive today, at least not in the United States, who knows more about Lee Oswald's associates, activities and frame of mind during the months of July, August and September 1963 (the period when certain well-laid plans were formulated) than I do, and I state for the record that none of the aforenamed individuals or their alleged associates (including Jack Ruby, Charles Murret and Nofio Pecora) influenced or bore even the slightest responsibility for the later actions of Mr. Oswald."[552]

It is this author's opinion that Nagell was generally truthful. At times, his writing is cryptic, which is not surprising considering his intelligence background. He told Stokes that organized crime had nothing to do with Oswald, but he did not say the Mafia was not involved in the assassination plot. They had a motive and the means, and their inclusion in the conspiracy in a supporting role makes sense, but Oswald was not their responsibility. And what about Nagell's statement that there were people outside the United States who knew more about Oswald's actions in the summer of 1963 than he did? Was he alluding to Otto Skorzeny, Jean Pierre Lafitte, Charles Willoughby, and the right-wing Fascist group operating out of Madrid? He may have been.

It is disturbing that the FBI was aware of Mafia threats against the Kennedy brothers and did nothing to stop it. There were the Marcello, Hoffa, and Trafficante threats and FBI wiretap recordings with mobsters threatening the Kennedys. They knew about the Judith Campbell affair that included Giancana and JFK, the CIA/Mafia assassination plots, the murder of Marilyn Monroe, and the attempt to blackmail the Kennedys. Still, they failed to investigate the assassination properly and ignored the Mafia entirely. It was likely why, as Curt Gentry wrote in *J. Edgar Hoover: The Man and the Secrets*, an ex-Bureau deputy director told him that the FBI "destroyed in the hours after Kennedy was assassinated... dozens, perhaps even over a hundred documents relating to threats on the life of the President."[553]

Did J. Edgar Hoover have an agenda that was almost as sinister as those plotting the assassination? Was he irresponsible for ignoring critical facts? Probably so. Hoover may not have been part of the conspiracy, but he knew what was going down, and the Kennedy brothers were two men he despised. He considered them an embarrassment, naïve, and a threat to national security. So, he chose to keep quiet and let the chips fall where they may because they brought the assassination upon themselves with their recklessness. As Hoover said in a speech twelve days after the assassination, "The public should have more adequate guarantees for the immediate removal of those who prove by their unjustifiable actions that they cannot be entrusted with the important responsibilities of their office…"[554]

CHAPTER TEN

TURNING POINT

With the secret war against Fidel Castro failing, and knowing he was perceived to be a timid Commander-in-Chief, on February 7, 1962, President Kennedy told the Pentagon to be ready to launch a rapid, deadly strike against Castro if necessary. Their plan involved an assault by two Army paratrooper divisions from Fort Campbell, Kentucky, and Fort Bragg, North Carolina; two Marine Corps divisions would follow with an amphibious landing supported by the Navy; and naval air assets and air force tactical units would provide air cover.[555]

The next day, the Soviet Presidium approved a $133 million military aid package for Cuba. The head of the KGB added a postscript on February 21. "Military specialists in the USA had revised an operational plan against Cuba," he warned, "which, according to the information, is supported by President Kennedy." There was a leak within the JFK hierarchy, and the KGB knew about the top-secret revised plan for a second invasion that JFK had approved only two weeks before.[556]

The Soviets were concerned, and for good reason. Between the fall of 1961 and the spring of 1962, the number of American ICBMs went from thirty to seventy-five, and based on publicly available documents, by the end of the year, the U.S. arsenal, with the addition of the first Minuteman missiles, would grow to more than two hundred. Deployment of the Minuteman system, the most significant strategic threat to the Soviets, was due to begin in the fall, and there was talk of deploying a thousand. On April 20, 1962, the first eighteen of fifty-four U.S. Titan missiles, a first-generation ICBM, were deployed in Colorado, while forty-five intermediate-range Jupiter missiles were sent to Italy and Turkey and pointed at Moscow.

Khrushchev could not come close to matching this level of firepower, so he asked his Minister of Defense, Rodion Malinovsky, if they could put nuclear missiles in Cuba. Malinovsky thought it was a good idea but politically dangerous. Regardless, Khrushchev presented his plan to the Presidium for approval and said, "This will be an offensive policy" designed to take the pressure off Russia as well as to deter U.S. aggression against Cuba.[557]

On April 12, the Presidium confirmed the delivery to Cuba of four SA-2 antiaircraft launchers and two technical support divisions, including 180 missiles, as well as the Sopka cruise missile system, which they had previously refused to send. To confirm how serious they were, the Soviets sent General N.I. Gusev, along with a 650-man contingent of Soviet soldiers, to protect and train the Cubans in using these advanced weapons systems.[558]

The CIA's Warren Frank later recalled that in May, "the National Intelligence Estimate said 'it was most improbable' that the Russians would bring missiles into Cuba." "We were told, 'HQ doesn't want any reports from Cuban sources...everyone had to toe the party line.... [they] skewed their reports to fit headquarters' position...People signed off on reports knowing they weren't true." According to Shackley: "The trapezoid [launching site] had been identified by human sources. But the Kennedys only believed in photos. That's all they wanted, even though we had the intelligence they demanded. Then came the U-2 photos."[559]

Serge Mikoyan, the son of Deputy Premier Anastas Mikoyan, recalled, "In the spring of 1962, we in Moscow were absolutely convinced that a second Bay of Pigs was at hand...but this time with all the American military might, not only with proxy troops."[560]

On May 27, Khrushchev told a Soviet delegation on their way to Cuba, "An attack on Cuba is being prepared, and the only way to save Cuba is to put missiles there...there is no other path than one which could equalize the security of the United States. And this logically could be done only by our nuclear missiles, our long-range missiles. So, try and explain it to Fidel."[561]

With the President's blessing, in early June, Robert Kennedy met "secretly" again with Georgi Bolshakov at his home in Virginia. Bolshakov asked Bobby if there were people within the government who were interested in starting a war. "In the government, no," he replied, "[b]ut among the generals in the Pentagon...there are such people." He reassured Bolshakov that the President "had decisively rejected any attempt by zealous advocates of a clash between the United States and the Soviet Union to force [him]...to accept their point of view." Khrushchev, who did not trust American militarists, was troubled by this. And if U.S. intelligence had bugged RFK's home, which they likely did, they would have considered the disclosure treasonous.[562]

Based on their history, Khrushchev believed the young, inexperienced American President could be intimidated. On July 5, he sent JFK a threatening letter, demanding an immediate fifty percent cut in Allied forces in West

Berlin, to be replaced with troops from the Warsaw Pact and small NATO countries like Denmark. Khrushchev wanted to deflect attention away from Cuba by raising the stakes in Berlin, which he knew was a hot-button topic for the West.[563]

Soviet missiles began arriving in Cuba in mid-July, and according to CIA Director John McCone's notes, Bobby asked the SGA to consider "the feasibility of provoking an action against Guantanamo which would permit us to retaliate, or [of] involving a third country in some way." It was reminiscent of the JCS Operation Northwoods proposal and a precursor to what Bobby intended to do in December 1963 to initiate a second invasion of Cuba with the military.[564]

As early as July 20, 1961, at a meeting of the National Security Council, Thomas Francis Hickey, Staff Director of the NSC's Net Evaluation Subcommittee, with JCS Chairman Lyman Lemnitzer and Allen Dulles present, briefed President Kennedy on plans for "a surprise attack [against the USSR] in late 1963, preceded by a period of heightened tensions." The consensus was that the end of 1963 was the point when the United States would have the optimum advantage over the Soviets in nuclear firepower. After that, the Soviets would start closing the gap.[565]

On July 24, the NSA reported there were "at least four, and possibly five … Soviet passenger ships en route [to] Cuba with a possible 3,335 passengers on board." Admiral Robert Lee Dennison, who headed the Atlantic fleet, recalled, "There were large numbers of Soviet-bloc military personnel prior to August, and then there was a buildup during August and September when nine passenger ships arrived in Cuba with a totality of 20,000 passengers." The NSA also noticed that ships leaving Russia destined for the Far East and Africa went to Cuba instead. The vessels had far less cargo than their manifests called for, leaving a great deal of room for weapons and military supplies to be transported undetected.[566]

On July 26, Khrushchev met with Ambassador Llewelyn Thompson and warned he "could not wait indefinitely" for a German peace treaty and seemed "deeply troubled."[567] Khrushchev was planting the seed that if Kennedy attempted to prevent what he intended to do in Cuba, he would retaliate by taking West Berlin.

***

The stress level ratcheted up a notch in August. On the 17th, an operator on the USS Oxford heard the electronic call of Soviet radar codenamed Whiff, which meant there were Russian antiaircraft weapons in Cuba. At the NSA, Sigint experts learned "there was evidence of offensive missiles."

Before long, the number of intercepts increased, and the Russian language they heard spoken indicated the Soviets controlled military matters in Cuba. Three times, American aircraft flew along the Cuban coast searching for signals coming from where surface-to-air missile sites were under construction.[568]

In mid-August, CIA aerial photographs showed Soviet ships riding unusually high in the water, which meant the large crates on their decks carried lightweight cargo. A Cuban refugee described a long truck convoy he encountered before dawn on August 5: "After about every third truck, there was a long flatbed pulled by a tractor-like vehicle. On each vehicle, there was a round object as tall as a palm tree and covered by a tarpaulin." The State Department and military intelligence assumed they were defensive missiles.[569] However, CIA director John McCone thought they were ground-to-ground offensive missiles capable of reaching the U.S. McCone said it only made sense "if Moscow intended to use them to shield a base for ballistic missiles aimed at the United States." On August 10, McCone sent a memo to JFK predicting that the USSR was preparing to introduce ballistic missiles into Cuba.[570]

As the evidence of offensive nuclear missiles in Cuba became increasingly undeniable, JFK insisted that this secret intelligence remain quiet. As a result, the NSA limited who had access to information and placed restrictions on intercepts that revealed there were offensive weapons in Cuba. So, as early as August, the President was aware of the increased danger these missiles posed to the U.S., but he did nothing. Was he motivated by fear of a confrontation in Cuba, a Soviet takeover of West Berlin, or was there another reason behind this gross act of negligence?[571]

On August 21, National Security Advisor McGeorge Bundy told McCone that any U.S. actions against Cuba must remain covert because "overt actions would involve serious consequences all over the world...," which was a reference to West Berlin. Two days after that, McCone convinced JFK to consider the development of options "to provoke a full-scale revolt against Castro that might require US intervention to succeed." The plan would include "the instantaneous commitment of sufficient [US] armed forces to occupy the country [Cuba], destroy the regime, free the people, and establish in Cuba a peaceful country..."[572]

Bolshakov met with JFK in late August and said the President looked "tired and a bit worried." Kennedy did not confront him about the missiles or threaten nuclear retaliation, but Bobby begged Bolshakov to work with his brother. "God damn it, Georgi, doesn't Premier Khrushchev realize the

President's position? Doesn't the Premier know that the President has enemies as well as friends … my brother really means what he says about American-Soviet relations. But every step he takes to meet Premiere Khrushchev halfway costs him a lot of effort. If the Premier just took the trouble to be, for a moment at least, in the President's shoes, he would understand him." It was another embarrassing display by Bobby.[573]

Bolshakov arrived in Russia several days later and met with a "suntanned and smiling" Khrushchev. The Premier was "anxious about Cuba" and asked if "the United States would go to the length of an armed confrontation" with Castro. Bolshakov emphasized the President was under heavy pressure from "reactionary forces" eager to crush the Cuban leader. When told of RFK's comments, a perplexed Khrushchev responded, "They can't mean it. Is he the President, or isn't he? If he is a strong President, he has no one to fear. He has full powers of government, and his brother is the Attorney General in the bargain."[574]

Khrushchev had a point. Could the Kennedy brothers have been so naïve to think the Soviet leader would help JFK deal with his domestic opponents who were itching to use whatever force was necessary to prevent the Soviets from installing missiles in Cuba? Did they fully understand the magnitude of the crisis facing them?

Philippe de Vosjoli was a French intelligence operative whose allegiance leaned more towards America. His name appears twice in the Lafitte datebook – on May 20, with Carolyn Davis and Thomas Proctor, and on May 26, in D.C. with Frank Wisner, James Angleton, and L.O., who could have either been Oswald or Lawrence Orlov, but was likely the latter.[575] In the summer of 1962, the CIA asked de Vosjoli to travel to Cuba to confirm whether or not the Soviets had installed offensive nuclear weapons. "What I have learned," he later wrote, "I passed on to Paris and shared with the American intelligence authorities." He provided McCone with photographs of offensive missiles and antiaircraft rockets. He also gave New York Senator Kenneth Keating photos showing Soviet nuclear war material in Cuba (the CIA had previously briefed Keating about Cuba before they reported to JFK). On August 31, on the floor of the Senate, Keating revealed intelligence on Soviet offensive missiles in Cuba, which even JFK was unaware of, including that the Soviets had 1,200 troops stationed there. "Those CIA bastards!" Kennedy fumed, according to journalist Sander Vanocur. "I'm going to get those bastards if it's the last thing I ever do." But what choice did the CIA have with a President who negotiated with the Soviets behind their back?[576]

On September 4, Kennedy invited eight leading Democrats and seven Republicans from Congress to a meeting about Cuba. Flanked by Dean Rusk and Robert McNamara, he downplayed what the CIA and the Pentagon knew, saying the Soviets were building up Cuba's defensive capability and nothing more. He lied to leading members of Congress so he would not have to act decisively, at least not yet.[577]

On September 19, 1962, the United States Intelligence Board (USIB) approved a secret Special National Intelligence Estimate (SNIE-85-3-62) stating that "intelligence indicates the ongoing deployment of Soviet nuclear missiles in Cuba."[578] Shortly after that, Ernesto Betancourt, the Assistant Administrator of the Economic Branch of the Organization of American States, met with Bobby Kennedy. Betancourt was soliciting help for the Ejercito Libertador de Cuba (ELC), a group that was planning an uprising in Santiago Province later that month. The ELC consisted of former soldiers from Batista's Regular Constitutional Army, as well as Castro's Rebel Army.

Robert Kennedy spoke with Deputy Director of Central Intelligence (DDCI) General Marshall S. Carter, who contacted Task Force W chief Willliam Harvey. Harvey had Task Force W Special Agent Charles Ford meet with Bobby, who advised Ford that just like Antonio Veciana, "Betancourt wants to work outside the framework of the U.S. Government and, in particular, does not want to work with the CIA. Ford met with Betancourt, who used the alias "Don Barton," which was an alias once used by David Phillips. Nothing came of the encounter because the CIA did not believe the ELC had 15,000 people in Cuba who were ready to revolt, and "a higher authority" shot down the operation.[579]

At a news conference on September 4, Press Seretary Pierre Salinger read a presidential statement: "Information has reached this Government in the last four days from a variety of sources which established without a doubt that the Soviets have provided the Cuban government with a number of antiaircraft defense missiles."[580] The statement was to deceive the American people, as JFK's speechwriter Ted Sorensen explained years later: "If we had known that the Soviets were putting forty missiles in Cuba, we ... [would] have drawn the line at one hundred and said with great fanfare that we would absolutely not tolerate the presence of more than one hundred missiles in Cuba. McGeorge Bundy said, "We did it because of the requirement of domestic politics, not because we seriously believed that the Soviets would do anything as crazy from our standpoint as placement of Soviet nuclear weapons in Cuba."[581]

In other words, Kennedy lied to the American people and placed the country in mortal danger to score political points in advance of the upcoming midterm elections, which were pivotal. A good showing by the Democrats was imperative if the progressive policies of the New Frontier were to continue. Kennedy emphasized how important it was at a press conference, stating, "If we can win five seats or ten seats, it would change the whole opinion in the House and the Senate." He traveled more miles campaigning in 1962 than Eisenhower did in 1954 and 1958 combined. "The question really is," he said, "can we interest enough people to understand how important the congressional election of 1962 is?" It seems Kennedy knew about the missiles in August but purposely waited until October to maximize the favorable impact it would have for Democrats in the midterms.[582]

Clare Boothe Luce also claimed to have advanced knowledge of Soviet offensive missiles in Cuba, and she contacted the Kennedy administration earlier in the year to make them aware of it. Failing to arouse interest, she then turned to Senator Keating. Based on what Luce told him, Keating publicly stated there was "100 percent reliable" evidence that missile sites were under construction.[583]

Luce received her information from the Cuban Student Directorate (DRE), the Cuban exile group she was close to. The DRE had a well-established underground in Cuba, which explains how they knew missile sites were under construction. Robert Morrow also claimed it was the underground in Cuba that discovered the missiles. He received his information from Tracy Barnes, who said it was Mario Kohly's underground that warned the CIA. Considering that both Kohly's people and the DRE located the missiles at about the same time, the two groups were probably working together.

The greatest fear the military had during the Cold War was that a politician would set in motion a nuclear confrontation with the Soviets. Politicians started wars, they believed, not the military, and it was up to the military to clean up the mess. It meant Kennedy had crossed the line separating political miscalculation from outright disregard for the people he served.

***

In September, Khrushchev told U.S. Secretary of the Interior Stewart Udall that the German situation was "no longer tolerable." Based on the backchannel information he received from Bolshakov, Khrushchev crudely said Kennedy didn't have the "courage [to] help him solve the problem. We will give him a choice – go to war or sign a peace treaty... Do you need Berlin? Like hell, you need it... It's been a long time since you could spank us like a little boy. Now we can swat your ass." Khrushchev knew Udall would tell Kennedy what he said, and his objective remained to intimidate JFK and take his attention away from Cuba.[584]

On September 4, the Russian Ambassador to the United States, Anatoly Dobrynin, told a "highly agitated" RFK that there "would be no ground-to-ground or offensive weapons placed in Cuba" since "Khrushchev would do nothing to disrupt the relationship of our two countries during this period prior to the election." Two days later, Dobrynin read Sorensen a personal message from Khrushchev to Kennedy: "Nothing will be undertaken before the American Congressional elections that could complicate the international situation or aggravate tensions in the relations between our two countries." The Kennedys knew they were being lied to, yet they continued to do nothing about it.[585]

Khrushchev did not trust the Pentagon and realized the Soviet Union might have to defend Cuba. His generals gave him a list of battlefield nuclear weapons that could be positioned quickly and were powerful enough to deter any attempt by U.S. forces to establish a beachhead. On September 7, he sent these weapons to Cuba. The next day, the Ministry of Defense drafted an order permitting the Soviet commander in Cuba, General Issa Pliyev, to use these nuclear weapons should communications with Moscow be cut off, but Khrushchev never sent it.[586]

Kennedy was aware that potential danger was on the horizon, which was why he asked Congress to call 150,000 reserve troops to active duty on September 11. The Soviets continued to lie, responding that "arms currently being sent to Cuba were solely for defensive purposes" and that an American attack on Cuba would bring retaliatory action against Berlin.[587]

Also on September 11, Hans Kroll, the West German ambassador to the Soviet Union, advised the U.S. Embassy in Moscow that he had met with Khrushchev and that a significant Berlin crisis was in the offing. His warning somehow fell into the lap of Vice President Johnson's military aide, Colonel Howard Burris, who wrote: "Khrushchev has come to the conclusion that Western leaders [i.e., the Kennedy brothers] have proven themselves so anxious to avoid conflict that they will accept the [Berlin] treaty and accommodate themselves to it." A frustrated Burris, seemingly writing on behalf of the Joint Chiefs, concluded his report with the Kennedys in mind: "It is impossible to negotiate politely with the Soviets on an issue like Berlin. The Russians traditionally, and especially the Communists more recently, understand and respond only to recognized strength and willingness to apply it..."[588]

Also in September, Wisconsin Republican Senator Alexander Wiley called publicly for a blockade of Cuba. It was further evidence that it was well-known the Soviets were installing missile sites in Cuba. "It's an act of war," Kennedy replied. He was afraid that a blockade would result in Moscow cutting off access to West Berlin in retaliation. For JFK, seemingly all decisions were made based on what would happen in Berlin.[589]

On September 28, Khrushchev sent a letter to Kennedy proposing a new basis for a test ban treaty and the need to discuss Berlin. He suggested they meet in early November after the U.S. elections were over. It was a smokescreen designed to draw attention away from Cuba, but the White House knew too much at this point. On September 15, U.S. listening devices revealed for the first time that Russian SA-2 missiles were operational and capable of shooting down any aircraft at a moment's notice.[590]

The day before, Kennedy had discussed with McNamara and the Joint Chiefs a detailed plan for an attack against Cuba. That evening, Admiral Dennison ordered his fleet to "take all feasible measures necessary…to execute [an air strike] by October 20." U.S. Army commanders prepared for a full-scale invasion. It sounded like JFK planned to invade Cuba just weeks before the midterm elections, which would have catapulted the Democratic Party into control of both Houses. He scrapped the idea the next day after learning that SA-2 missiles were operational and getting Americans killed invading Cuba would not serve him well politically. Politics was always the driving force for the Kennedy brothers, regardless of the consequences. [591]

***

On October 3, Georgi Bolshakov contacted Bobby Kennedy to reiterate that "the weapons that the USSR is sending to Cuba will only be of a defensive character." On October 8, Cuban President Osvaldo Dorticos declared at the UN that Cuba could be "the starting point of a new World War." "We are…well equipped to defend ourselves," he revealed, with "weapons we wish we did not need and that we do not want to use." Raul Castro said Cuba's people "are invincible. We will repel, crush, and annihilate any attempt to set foot in our country."[592]

At an October 4 SGA meeting, just twelve days before the Cuban Missile Crisis began, Robert Kennedy told the group that his brother was "concerned about progress on the Mongoose program and feels that more priority should be given to trying to mount sabotage operations." RFK wanted "massive" Mongoose activity unleashed, which, considering all the Kennedy brothers knew about offensive missiles in Cuba by this time, was irresponsible.[593]

It is interesting that on the same day that the Kennedys were looking to increase Mongoose sabotage operations, the CIA canceled Antonio Veciana and Alpha-66 for use as an MRP sabotage asset. On October 8, Alpha-66, which was now clearly working for General Lansdale and the U.S. Army and not the CIA, conducted a raid on a Soviet ship at La Isabella in Puerto Rico along with Eloy Gutierrez Menoyo's SNFE.[594]

On October 10, Senator Keating announced from the Senate floor that independent sources had told him the construction of launch sites for intermediate-range ballistic offensive missiles was underway. An angry JFK claimed he was purposely left in the dark and was convinced someone in the Defense Department was Keating's source. Clare Boothe Luce later told CIA director William Colby that "it was me who fed the missile stuff to Keating."[595]

On the 14th, Kennedy agreed to a U-2 flight over Cuba to prove the Republican Senator was wrong. However, photos showed that four medium and two intermediate-range installations with twenty-one crated bombers carrying nuclear weapons capable of reaching Washington were in Cuba.[596] That same day, Bobby told the SGA to "considerably" expand sabotage operations and ordered them "to develop new and imaginative approaches… of getting rid of the Castro regime." Bobby had to know that by this point, it would take more than sabotage operations to get the missiles removed.[597]

Two days later, on the day the Missile Crisis began, McNamara said at a meeting that the Joint Chiefs warned the balance of power would substantially change if missiles were allowed to remain in Cuba. JFK disagreed, but General Taylor contradicted him, saying the missiles "can become a very, a rather important adjunct and reinforcement to the strike capability of the Soviet Union." Kennedy countered that "it doesn't make any difference if you get blown up by an ICBM flying from the Soviet Union or one that was ninety miles away. Geography doesn't mean that much." He then said something astounding: "Last month, I should have said…we don't care. But when we said we're not going to [allow missiles in Cuba] and then they go ahead and do it, and then we do nothing, then…"[598]

So, at this point, Kennedy's only concern was that he had made a public statement that the U.S. would not tolerate missiles in Cuba, and backtracking from it would be political suicide. He was boxed in and seemingly not up to the task that lay before him: "What difference does it make," he said. "They've got enough to blow us up now anyway… after all, this is a political struggle as much as military."[599] In what way were missiles in Cuba a political struggle? Kennedy was more concerned about losing the midterms than the security of the nation.

What would happen to Berlin also concerned JFK. Dean Rusk said that "Berlin is very much involved in this." Moscow may be hoping to "bargain Berlin and Cuba against each other," he said., or use a U.S. attack on Cuba as an excuse to act against Berlin. Adlai Stevenson predicted an attack against Cuba could bring reprisals against Turkey or Berlin and "would risk starting a nuclear war..." McGeorge Bundy thought they should do nothing because any action would bring a reprisal against Berlin, which would "divide the NATO alliance."[600]

By October 18, Kennedy and his inner circle had reduced their options to a military attack or a blockade of Cuba, and the Joint Chiefs were not part of these discussions. It was not until the morning of the 19th that JFK asked them to join a meeting, and that was for forty-five minutes only.[601]

Kennedy needed the Joint Chiefs to support him because domestic dissent might encourage Moscow to defy the blockade or strike at Berlin in the belief that the president would lack national support for a military response. He candidly discussed his concerns with the Chiefs and explained that an attack on Cuba would probably provoke Khrushchev to take Berlin. Meanwhile, America's allies would complain that "we let Berlin go because we didn't have the guts to endure a situation in Cuba," while the Berlin crisis would likely touch off a nuclear war. However, by this time, the Joint Chiefs had zero respect for the President and did not care what he had to say.[602]

Air Force Chief of Staff Curtis LeMay said, "We don't have any choice except direct military action," and he predicted there would be no Soviet response to an airstrike in Cuba. He called Kennedy's blockade idea "almost as bad as the appeasement at Munich." Marine Corps Commander David Shoup and Maxwell Taylor agreed. "I do not see that, as long as the Soviet Union is supporting Cuba, that there is any solution to the Cuban problem except a military solution," Admiral George Anderson lectured the young President. Army Chief of Staff Earle Wheeler called for "the full gamut of military action."[603]

Then, LeMay doubled down. "If we leave them [the missiles] there," he said, the Soviets would have a "blackmail threat against not only us but the other South American countries." He said foreign countries would consider Kennedy's administration cowardly, and "I'm sure a lot of our own citizens would feel that way too," knowing the President had played politics with national security. An astonished Ted Sorensen recalled that what "LeMay said is almost out of *Seven Days in May*. Telling Kennedy this is like Munich, this is too soft, and the American people will think so too!"

Kennedy and McNamara left the Cabinet room as the secret taping system recorded the Chiefs privately attacking the President. Shoup said: "If somebody could keep them from doing the goddamn thing piecemeal. That's our problem. You go in there and friggin' around with missiles. You're screwed...Either do this son of a bitch and do it right and quit friggin' around."[604] The military wanted a large air strike with eight hundred individual sorties to take out the missiles. Dean Acheson, Maxwell Taylor, John McCone, Paul Nitze, and Douglas Dillon agreed. Acheson: "Here they [the missiles] were in the hands of a madman [Castro] whose actions would be perfectly irresponsible..."[605]

On October 22, the NSA reported that at least five Soviet missile regiments would soon become operational in Cuba, with eight missile launchers and sixteen missiles each. That same day, Strategic Air Command (SAC) "quietly and gradually" initiated a partial airborne alert and dispersed bombers to air bases around the country. The Navy began evacuating dependents from the American base at Guantanamo. That night, President Kennedy went on television to explain the crisis facing the nation and that he was placing a blockade around Cuba to prevent Russian vessels from reaching the island. [606]

At 10:00 A.M. the next day, SAC went to DEFCON 2, one level below general war. They put all American long-range missiles and bombers on alert. For the first time, planes loaded with atomic bombs, fueled by aerial tankers, stayed airborne around the clock over Greenland and northern Canada, waiting for the signal to unleash their fury over predetermined Soviet targets. The SAC commander, General Thomas Power, took it upon himself to send uncoded messages so the Russians were aware of what was occurring.[607]

At the request of the Pentagon, William Harvey dispatched six three-person teams to Cuba. The military wanted the CIA in the country to support the invasion.[608] The *New York Daily News* later tracked down "intelligence sources" who confirmed that one of the teams was "an execution squad [sent] to ambush Castro near Santiago de Cuba as he drove to a memorial service...snipers hid along trees and bushes lining the road [and] machine guns and rifles sprayed the second jeep with bullets, killing the driver and his passenger, who was Castro's lookalike bodyguard."[609]

Harvey had sent the teams into Cuba even though Robert Kennedy ordered the CIA to cease all operations until things calmed down. Harvey gave the weak excuse that he believed the order only applied to active operations, not infiltrating agents in anticipation of an operation. The CIA would send him to Italy soon after that.

The military and their supporters wanted war, and they looked to goad the Soviet Union into initiating hostilities. Curtis LeMay's Air Force launched an ICBM from Vandenberg Air Force Base. It was an unarmed test missile destined for the Marshall Islands, but the Soviets had no way of knowing that. Considering the heightened tensions, we can assume LeMay hoped the Soviets would respond in kind. Three days before, a test missile at Vandenberg was outfitted with a nuclear warhead, changing it to full alert status. By October 30, they had armed nine Vandenberg "test" missiles. Meanwhile, SAC bombers deliberately flew past their customary turnaround points toward the Soviet Union. Had the Soviets retaliated, there is little doubt the Pentagon would have responded with a massive counterattack.[610]

As the waiting game continued and the military pushed for an all-out invasion, there was concern within the administration as to how the Navy would react if Soviet vessels ran the blockade. McNamara wanted to know if each American ship had a Russian-speaking officer on board. Admiral Anderson's reply to his boss was insulting: "Now, Mr. Secretary, if you and your deputy will go back to your offices, the Navy will run the blockade."[611]

***

During the Missile Crisis, with the approval of his brother, Bobby once again engaged in backchannel discussions at the Soviet Embassy without letting anyone know. Ambassador Dobrynin reported to Moscow that he "looked exhausted. One could see from his eyes that he had not slept for days…" "The president is in a grave situation," Robert Kennedy said, "and he does not know how to get out of it…we are under pressure from our military to use force against Cuba…Even though the president himself is very much against starting a war over Cuba, an irreversible chain of events could occur against his will…the president is not sure that the military will not overthrow him and seize power. The American army could get out of control."[612]

If true, it was a disgraceful display by Robert Kennedy. Khrushchev would later write that Bobby "was almost crying. I haven't seen my children for days now, and the president hasn't seen his either…I don't know how much longer we can hold out against our generals." Did the Kennedys really think that Khrushchev, who had fought at Stalingrad, would be moved because they had not seen their children for a week?[613]

According to Khrushchev's son Sergei: "The president was calling for help: that was how father interpreted Robert Kennedy's talk with our ambassador…The temperature in the Washington boiler had apparently reached a dangerous point and was about to explode." Khrushchev confirmed what Sergei said: "For some time, we had felt there was a danger that the president would lose control of his military, and now he was admitting this to us himself." "We could sense from the tone of the message that tension in the United States was indeed reaching a critical point." Moscow feared a military coup might overthrow Kennedy, and they had good reason to believe that.[614]

***

On October 26, the largest concentration of American military force since the Korean War came together in the southeastern United States. The Joint Chiefs were pushing for airstrikes and an amphibious invasion, and it appeared to be just a matter of time before they got what they wanted. Then came a turn of events that changed everything. On that morning, an intelligence report given to Khrushchev said the invasion plan against Cuba was complete and "the attack could begin at any moment." But it was false. A Russian émigré bartender at the National Press Club reported a conversation between two American journalists he had overheard, and both the Soviet Embassy and the KGB investigated and believed the story was credible.[615]

The next day, a U-2 spy plane was shot down over Cuba, exacerbating tensions. The military saw this as an opportunity, but Kennedy held firm. A panicked Khrushchev sent JFK a lengthy emotional letter that did not include the nuclear threats that characterized his previous ones. War would be a "calamity for all peoples. You can be calm in this regard, that we are of sound mind and understand perfectly well that if we attack you, you will respond the same way. But you too will receive the same that you hurl against us…We are willing to remove from Cuba the means [weapons] you regard as offensive…" The Missile Crisis appeared to be over, but was it?[616]

The deal Kennedy struck with Khruschev called for the removal of missiles from Cuba in exchange for the United States agreeing never to invade Cuba again, contingent upon UN inspectors verifying the removal of all missiles. However, Castro refused to let UN inspectors into Cuba, so Kennedy had to take Khrushchev's word that all the missiles were gone, which raised other concerns. "Do we tell them," Kennedy told Harold Macmillan, the Prime Minister of the United Kingdom, "If they don't remove the missiles, that we are going to invade Cuba? He will then say that if we invade

Cuba there's going to be a general nuclear assault, and he would, in any case, grab Berlin. Or do we just let the nuclear work go on, figuring he won't ever dare fire them, and when he tries to grab Berlin, we then go into Cuba?" Then there was the option of keeping the missiles in Turkey. If they did that, Kennedy believed "we are either going to have to invade or have a massive strike on Cuba which may lose Berlin." Once again, it was always about Berlin. Kennedy decided to ignore these critical questions and assume Khrushchev was telling him the truth. At a news conference on November 20, he announced that "all *known* offensive missile sites in Cuba have been dismantled" (author's italics). The keyword was known, which indicated JFK had no idea if the Russians had removed all the sites. He had no choice but to live with the consequences, at least until he decided to invade Cuba, which by the beginning of 1963 would be on the table again, scheduled to take place in December of that year.[617]

***

On October 30, President Kennedy ordered all sabotage activity against Cuba to come to a halt. He instructed the CIA to do everything possible to control the Cuban exile groups for the next several days while negotiations continued. President Kennedy then addressed Alpha-66 directly, who he incorrectly thought was still working with the CIA. First, he instructed the CIA to stop all Alpha 66 actions. When the DCI informed JFK that the CIA no longer had control over Alpha 66, the President told McCone to order the Cuban exile group to stand down. He then suspended all approved sabotage, infiltration, and guerilla activity. That same day, McCone told Lansdale that JFK decided to "hold back Operation Mongoose" until he finalized negotiations with Khrushchev, and he specifically mentioned Alpha 66.[618]

Despite what the President mandated, on November 1, an expanded gathering of Pentagon ACSI and DOD officers met to consider what to do about Alpha 66 operations. Regarding whether the Pentagon should share its support of Alpha 66 with the CIA, Lansdale quickly turned that down, confirming that he and Veciana wanted to work independently of the Agency. The decision was made, despite JFK's suspension of covert activity, for the Army to visit an offshore island with Veciana, one and one-half days out from Miami by boat, to inspect where the training of Cuban exiles was taking place.

The Joint Chiefs were not ready to give up and sent a memo to the President: "The JCS interpret the Khrushchev statement, in conjunction with the buildup, to be efforts to delay direct action by the United States while preparing the ground for diplomatic blackmail." They still wanted to launch an air strike against Cuba the next day, followed by an invasion of Cuba seven days later, unless there was "irrefutable evidence" that the Soviets had dismantled the missiles. What did they mean by diplomatic blackmail? The JCS believed Khrushchev knew something about JFK that they could use as leverage against him.[619]

"We have been had," Admiral Anderson yelled at JFK when he next met with the Joint Chiefs. LeMay pounded the table with his fist and said, "It's the greatest defeat in our history, Mr. President...We should invade today!" "We had a chance to throw the Communists out of Cuba." McNamara looked at Kennedy and saw that "he was absolutely shocked. He was stuttering in reply."[620]

Defense analyst Daniel Ellsberg recalled, "There was virtually a coup atmosphere in Pentagon circles. Not that I had the fear that there was about to be a coup – I just thought it was a mood of hatred and rage. The atmosphere was poisonous, poisonous."[621] Kennedy told Schlesinger, "The military are [sic] mad. They wanted to do this [invade Cuba]. It's lucky for us that we have Mac over there." He told Ben Bradlee: "The first advice I'm going to give my successor is to watch the generals and to avoid feeling that just because they were military men, their opinions on military matters were worth a damn."[622]

Many politicians felt the same as the military. Nixon thought Kennedy had "enabled the United States to pull defeat out of the jaws of victory." Democratic Senator Daniel Patrick Moynihan called the Missile Crisis a "defeat...When anybody puts missiles into a situation like that, he should expect to have a lot of trouble with the United States...and all that happened was the agreement: 'O.K., you can have your man [Castro] down there permanently.'"[623]

Considering the failed attempts at removing Castro over the past year and a half, an agreement never to invade Cuba was an admission that Castro was there to stay. For the military, if the President did not have the strength to engage the Soviets 90 miles off the coast of Florida to remove nuclear missiles pointed at the United States, what chance was there for him to call on the military halfway around the world? And when the Soviets created a disturbance somewhere else, what would it take for JFK to stand up to them? The military and the CIA feared that if Kennedy's Presidency was allowed to run its course, it might be too late to correct the damage he could potentially inflict by his reluctance to take a firm stand.

One month after the Missile Crisis, the Joint Chiefs continued to push for a buildup of U.S. strategic forces. On November 20, they sent a memorandum to McNamara stating: "The Joint Chiefs of Staff consider that a first-strike capability is both feasible and desirable..."[624] They would remain relentless for the remainder of Kennedy's presidency.

***

The Cuban Missile Crisis exacerbated the tension between the military, the CIA, and the President. Many thought he was too weak to handle the responsibilities of his office. Worst of all, he took the world to the brink of nuclear war for political reasons, an unforgivable offense.

The military considered the loss of innocent lives collateral damage in the war against communism. A confrontation with the Soviets was inevitable, and backing down allowed them to challenge America's resolve somewhere else in the world. Kennedy was troubled by this doomsday philosophy and considered coexistence the only viable option if the world was going to make it into the twenty-first century. Douglas MacArthur warned in the mid-1950s of a "dangerous concept that the members of our armed forces owe primary allegiance or loyalty to those who temporarily exercise the authority of the Executive Branch of the Government rather than to the country and to the Constitution which they are sworn to defend...."[625]

It was a philosophy military leaders identified with. Who was to "provide for the common defense" and to "promote the general welfare," as the preamble to the Constitution called for? For the military, it was not the President. His temporary residence at 1600 Pennsylvania Avenue did not entitle him to redirect America's focus away from her values and ideals. It was their responsibility, which they took seriously. Undoubtedly, the issue of how to remove President John F. Kennedy from office by force was already discussed in the wake of the crisis.

CHAPTER 11

YOU AND ME AGAINST THE WORLD

Long before President Kennedy played politics with the Missile Crisis that almost resulted in a military coup, animosity had grown exponentially for the two upstart brothers who repeatedly took on the Washington establishment.

On February 1, 1962, an article on the front page of the *New York Times* began: "President Kennedy called today for a Congressional investigation of the war-emergency stockpiling program. He said it was overgrown and a 'potential source of excessive and unconscionable profits.'" JFK was "'astonished' to find the cost was $7,700,000, much greater than the $3.4 million required. He called for a Congressional investigation, which the *New York Times* called a "significant" step. The newspaper pointed an accusatory finger at Eisenhower, for this excess had occurred under his watch. Stockpiling war materials was part of the ever-expanding military-industrial complex, and Kennedy wanted to curtail the profits big business was making from this practice. It widened the rift between JFK and the companies involved in the war machine, many of whom were from Texas.[626]

Also, on February 1, Robert Kennedy and his wife left on what the *New York Times* dubbed a "One-Month Goodwill Trip Around The World." It shocked those who considered the young Attorney General naïve and unqualified to represent the United States on the world stage. The couple spent one week each in Japan and Indonesia, with shorter visits to Hong Kong, Iran, Italy, West Germany, the Netherlands, and other countries.

The *Times* article irritated RFK's detractors, referring to him as "the second most powerful man in Government... Far more than any previous Attorney General, he is involved in affairs outside the problems of law enforcement – foreign policy, intelligence, even the farm program..." The writer also mentioned that "he and Mrs. Kennedy entertained... Aleksei I. Adzhubei at lunch yesterday. It will be no great surprise if the now disavowed approach made to him to visit the Soviet Union leads eventually to such a visit." The article concluded with the question, "Will he run for President himself someday?"[627] JFK had only been President for one year, and the CIA, the Joint Chiefs, Texas oilmen, big business, organized crime, and the radical right had all tired of Bobby's youthful arrogance and close relationship with high-level Soviets in Washington. Their worst nightmare was JFK being reelected, followed by eight years of a Bobby presidency, and then brother Ted. It could not be allowed to happen.

***

In March 1962, an event occurred that would have enormous ramifications for President Kennedy in the future. In France, a ceasefire led to Algerian independence. The following month, a *New York Times* article on April 22 explained that OAS leader Raoul Salan was "captured in Algiers as the head of the Secret Army Organization, [and] was indicted by civilian authorities yesterday for crimes against the security of the state." Salan had left his exile home in Madrid and had taken control of the OAS rebel army in Algeria. As described in *Coup In Dallas*, he was "preferred as the next leader of France and Algeria by powerful Texas oilmen," who were aware of the large amount of untapped underground oil in Algeria and the surrounding area. According to the *New York Times*, "a death sentence in absentia was imposed upon Salan for his part in the [French general's coup the previous year], but under French law, he must be tried again."[628]

On April 27, "it was announced in Algiers that Lt. Pierre Guillaume, OAS Chief in the South Zone of Algeria, had [also] been arrested. And 'sources' reported that he had been replaced by ex-Captain [Jean] Souetre... In August, a large number of OAS groups and individuals in exile merged into the Armee Nationale Secrete, which had representatives in Canada, New Orleans, and Latin America..." They joined forces with like-minded groups who wanted to remove left-leaning Communists from power in the U.S., France, and around the world. The die was cast.[629]

As previously mentioned, on the day of the Kennedy assassination, Souetre was in Dallas. So, it was not a coincidence that on the day after Souetre took over for Guillaume, a *New York Times* April 28, 1962 article titled, "*Terrorists Shoot Up French Police Station*," described how "terrorists attacked a police station and a newspaper office in this town of Etampes, near Paris... Both buildings were severely damaged... Authorities said the attackers were apparently members of the rightist Secret Army Organization [OAS] waging an underground campaign to keep Algeria French."[630] In the same issue, there was another article headlined "HOLLYWOOD, Calif., April 27 (UPI) – A small bomb exploded harmlessly in front of the French consulate here tonight. It followed a recent anonymous threat that the building would be blown up if the French Algerian leader, Raoul Salan, was arrested, as has been done." The violence of the OAS had spread to the United States.[631]

President Kennedy was on record since his Senate days of supporting Algerian independence. He should have paid more attention to the Algerian resistance movement against France. The OAS was made up of assassins for hire and were not only staunch anti-Communists but Fascists. When they brought their war to the United States and joined forces with right-wingers at the CIA, Cuban exiles, and American mercenaries fighting a similar battle against Fidel Castro, it did not bode well for JFK.

***

The building of the TFX aircraft was a massive $6.5 billion project that began during the Eisenhower administration. Selecting a bidder was an important decision, but Ike elected to allow incoming President Kennedy to make the selection. All senior members of the military involved assumed Kennedy would award the contract to Boeing Aircraft. Still, as described by Colonel Fletcher Prouty in *JFK*: "McNamara scheduled a meeting for November 24, 1962, to announce the decision. He [Kennedy] ignored the vote of the Source Selection Board and all its senior military members and selected the General Dynamics design."[632]

The military, still reeling over the decision not to invade Cuba the month before, was now incensed. Curtis LeMay later testified that no one from the original Air Force-Navy evaluation teams or the final Air Force-Navy board had recommended General Dynamics, and he "was surprised that the decision was made without consultation..."[633]

Unknown to LeMay, Kennedy had a reason for selecting a bidder that was unrelated to who most deserved the award. The story begins on August 7, 1962, just three days after Marilyn Monroe's death, when, during a routine FBI surveillance of the home of JFK's mistress, Judith Campbell, agents witnessed two men break into her Los Angeles apartment. Could it have been just a coincidence that the FBI was staking out Campbell's home just days after Monroe was killed under questionable circumstances, possibly by Bobby's henchman? Maybe not. The FBI traced the getaway car to an I.B. Hale of Fort Worth, Texas, and they learned Hale's two sons were the culprits who had broken into Campbell's home. Hale headed security for General Dynamics, so the defense contractor must have been aware of the JFK/Campbell/ Giancana affair and what truly happened to Marilyn Monroe, and may have been using that to possibly blackmail the President into awarding the contract to his employer.[634] If this was true, the award to General Dynamics came less than four months after Marilyn Monroe's suspicious murder and a month after he played politics during the Missile Crisis. For those who despised JFK, it may have been the last straw. For almost two years, he ignored the military's request to intervene in Vietnam, Laos, and Cuba, and Khrushchev bullied him in Berlin. With the Missile Crisis, he placed the nation in danger for selfish reasons, which he did again with the TFX decision. Add that he had used the Mafia to get elected and keep him informed of the CIA/Mafia plots, all while Bobby was aggressively trying to destroy the mobsters. There is no doubt that he was considered a traitor by many.

It is worth noting that on the day Kennedy died, Don Reynolds, a close associate of Bobby Baker, testified before the Senate Rules Committee on Capitol Hill. Reynolds said he had witnessed Baker give a $100,000 payoff to Lyndon Johnson for his role in securing the TFX contract for General Dynamics. His testimony ended when they learned Kennedy was dead.[635]

On October 24, 1962, *before the administration awarded TFX the contract*, reporter Seth Kantor wrote in the *Fort Worth Press* that: "General Dynamics of Fort Worth will get the multibillion-dollar defense contract to build the supersonic TFX Air Force and Navy fighter plane, the *Fort Worth Press* learned today from top Government sources."[636] General Dynamics was a client of Bobby Baker's, and he had bribed members of Congress to grant a $7 billion contract to General Dynamics.[637]

In the summer of 1962, Baker opened the Carousel Club in Ocean City, Maryland. The beautiful women who worked there provided sexual favors to the members of Congress and their wealthy supporters who frequented the club. One of those was Ellen Rometsch, who was close to Baker's secretary and mistress, Carole Tyler. Rometsch may have been used to sway Congressmen into voting for General Dynamics. She also may have been an East German spy, and less than a year later, she was having an affair with President Kennedy, which was why Bobby Kennedy deported her to East Germany on August 28, 1963. We will discuss this in more detail in the following pages.

***

When Lyndon Johnson made his decision to run alongside John Kennedy, there was talk that Texas oilmen wouldn't support the ticket because they disliked the liberal northern candidate. The oil industry was a $50 billion business, even more significant than the steel, automotive, and chemical industries combined. As a result, Johnson's old Texas friend Sam Rayburn, the Speaker of the House, approached the oil industry giants with a choice. They could not be Democrats 364 days a year and then vote Republican in the Presidential election. If they did, the tax advantages of the oil depletion allowance, which enriched oilmen like Clint Murchison, H.L. Hunt, David Harold Boyd, and the emerging Bush dynasty, might be repealed. Politics aside, there was no question about who the oilmen supported.[638]

However, things did not go as planned, for on October 16, 1962, JFK pushed a bill through Congress that cost the oil industry 15 to 30 percent of their foreign investment returns by removing the distinction between repatriated oil profits and profits reinvested overseas. Then, on January 17, 1963, JFK called for a general tax cut financed by eliminating the Oil Depletion Allowance, which had saved the oil industry $280 million in taxes annually.[639] It was another transfer of wealth from the haves to the have-nots, which elites considered unconstitutional. JFK justified his actions by claiming that "no one industry should be permitted to obtain an undue tax advantage over all others." So, the oil industry found itself being lectured to by a bootlegger's son. These men, who made up a large portion of the prestigious Suite 8F Group, were not used to being disrespected this way. Along with other like-minded Texans, they were furious with the liberal President from the north – and this was one group Kennedy should never have alienated.[640]

***

Civil rights dominated headlines as 1962 moved forward. Southern right-wing Fascists accused the President of being a Communist and blamed him for the erosion of the Southern way of life they continued to cling to. By 1962, the movement was well organized and included many from the military who felt something dramatic was needed to turn the tide before it was too late. That moment came in September 1962, when a twenty-nine-year-old African American Korean War veteran named James Meredith became the first black student to enroll at the University of Mississippi. The school administrators and Mississippi governor Ross Barnett, who spoke of the "Zionist" influence in the NAACP and the Congress of Racial Equality when he was elected, were hell-bent on keeping him out. The case went all the way to the Supreme Court, which ruled Meredith could not be denied entrance to the school based on race. Barnett refused to back down and surrounded the school with the state police to physically stop Meredith from registering.[641]

From Dallas, radical right-wing Fascist General Edwin Walker told a nationwide radio audience, "Now is the time to be heard. Ten thousand strong, from every state in the union. Rally to the cause of freedom, the battle cry of the republic … It's now or never."[642] A crowd of twenty-five hundred demonstrators, many armed with weapons, assembled on September 27 to forcibly prevent Meredith from enrolling. Crosses burned, and students at a pep rally shouted, "Hotty, toddy, we want a body." The governor told JFK on the phone that he could not guarantee Meredith's safety. In response, Kennedy federalized Mississippi's National Guard and ordered five hundred U.S. Marshals to go to the school. As tensions mounted, Walker flew by private plane to Mississippi, and other armed men from across the South joined him there.[643]

On September 30, heavily armed U.S. Marshals arrived on campus accompanied by James Meredith. By evening, the crowd, some waving Confederate flags, chanted, "Go to hell, JFK," and "Yankee, Go Home." Eventually, the mob got out of control. Protesters threw rocks, bricks, and bottles at the marshals, and when the marshals responded with tear gas, some in the crowd fired their guns at them. Walker pointed toward the marshals and shouted, "Go get 'em boys...charge!" Soon, parts of the campus were in flames, and marshals fell to the ground, some shot and gravely wounded. The mob overtook a fire engine, hooked a high-pressure hose to a hydrant, and blasted the marshals. A bulldozer drove full speed toward the federal agents, who fired a hail of bullets and stopped the dozer just thirty feet away. Cars were overturned and set on fire. Journalists were chased and beaten. One reporter was killed, shot in the back at close range.

Two people died, and many marshals were injured, twenty-seven by gunfire. The school looked like a war zone. Kennedy ordered fifteen thousand federal troops to the school, which was the most significant military force used to quell an insurrection since the Civil War. Confederate flags flew at half-mast, and hundreds of jeering civilians hurled bottles at army trucks as they made their way down the streets, but their presence was enough to stem the riot.

U.S. Marshals escorted Meredith into the administration building, where he was officially enrolled, but the theatrics were not over. Bobby Kennedy had Walker arrested for rebellion, insurrection, and seditious conspiracy against the U.S. government, all federal crimes. Dr. Charles E. Smith, the medical director and chief psychiatrist of the Federal Bureau of Prisons, submitted a report to a federal judge in Mississippi, who committed Walker to a federal psychiatric prison for evaluation in Springfield, Missouri. Walker's attorney, Robert Morris, said his client was "the United States' first political prisoner. One would think we're in Havana or Budapest, the way General Walker has been treated." Thousands of angry telegrams and letters sent to the White House demanded Walker's release, while hundreds protested outside the prison. In six days, the government released Walker.[644]

The James Meredith incident galvanized the segregationist radical right. Southern racists hated JFK for trying to destroy their way of life, and many believed Communists funded the civil rights movement to foment insurrection in the United States.

The incarceration of General Walker, whom many believed to be a patriot defending the principles of the Constitution, only made things worse. It incensed the military, who viewed it as another attempt by the Kennedy brothers to appease communism and silence them. A month later, they would be saying the same thing after the Cuban Missile Crisis.

***

Cuba remained a question mark after the Missile Crisis was over. There was still a chance the Pentagon would get the invasion they wanted because Soviet Il-28 bombers were still there. In response, the Navy sent an American carrier task force to the region. Exiting the Panama Canal on November 8, they headed to Puerto Rico as a second brigade shuttled between northern Florida and South Carolina, waiting for orders to invade.[645]

Things settled down on November 20 when JFK announced the Soviets agreed to withdraw the Il-28s within thirty days, but the Pentagon still wanted their pound of flesh. Kennedy assured them that military action would be possible in the next few years if they pulled off a successful invasion with minimum destruction. At a Christmas meeting with the Joint Chiefs in Palm Beach, Kennedy again said he was determined to remove Castro. "Although we feel that the present Cuban situation is dormant," Kennedy reiterated, "we must assume that someday we may have to go into Cuba." Based on how Kennedy had treated the Pentagon, it was condescending, and it was doubtful that any member of the military brass believed what he said.[646]

***

Kennedy appeared confused, but he was confident he needed to defuse the aggressiveness being applied against Cuba by Cuban exiles operating from American shores. The October cessation of all CIA-sponsored sabotage operations against Cuba remained in effect, and Kennedy terminated Operation Mongoose in the early part of 1963. The SGA, which had overseen the war against Cuba, was replaced by an interagency Cuban Coordinating Committee, and a Standing Committee on Cuba became part of the National Security Council. In a move that certainly widened the chasm between JFK and the military and intelligence communities, JFK chose Robert Kennedy to be in overall charge of the new Cuban effort.[647]

In consideration of the non-invasion pledge, William Harvey wrote that CIA-controlled paramilitary and guerilla operations would now be "unacceptable as a matter of policy." Harvey anticipated that a "higher authority [RFK]" would continue to pressure the CIA, even though the U.S. could not overthrow Castro without the military. "In view of these factors," he wrote, "unlimited support of Cuban exiles and exile groups with no real control or objective purpose in the hope that these groups will be able to shake the Castro regime will, although unrealistic, become increasingly attractive at various levels in the US government." He would be proven correct. Military intervention was off the table, even though it was the only prerequisite for success.

With the new Kennedy policy in mind, Harvey said the proper course was to "induce a split in the Cuban regime and maintain the capability of capitalizing immediately through clandestine means...on any significant [internal] uprising... The effectiveness of assets aimed at actually splitting the regime, i.e., a palace revolt, will, of course, depend, to an extent, on the willingness of the United States Government to support them, and...any such effort might fail" without American military support. Harvey knew what was needed, but within a month, he and Task Force W would be gone for sending CIA operatives into Cuba against the direct order of Robert Kennedy.[648]

How to remove Castro remained the primary objective for the CIA and the Joint Chiefs as 1962 neared its end, but for the Kennedy brothers, how to return the 1,100 Bay of Pigs prisoners held in Cuba was their primary concern. They agreed to pay a ransom of $53 million to Castro in pharmaceuticals and food. On January 1, 1963, a rally at the Orange Bowl in Miami honored the recently returned Cuban veterans. The crowd was charged with excitement as the President said he still supported their effort to rid Cuba of Castro, but it was a promise he could not keep. Handed the banner the Cubans had carried during the invasion and caught in the euphoria of the moment, an excited President raised the flag in his arms for all to see. He then proclaimed, "I can assure you that this flag will be returned to this brigade in a free Havana."[649]

It was a day fraught with patriotic fervor, but not everyone shared in the excitement, as most Cuban exiles questioned Kennedy's commitment to their cause. Pepe San Roman, the Cuban exile leader during the Bay of Pigs, now "hated the United States... Every day, it became worse, and then I was getting madder and madder, and I wanted to get a rifle and come and fight against the US...And they knew before they sent us... that they were not going to go ahead with it."[650]

Days later, JFK told reporters that he would not support another rebel invasion or impose a new regime upon Cuba unless Castro committed an act of aggression. Control of the Cuban problem was now the central issue. Kennedy could not trust the military, and the CIA posed an even more significant threat, for the President could never be sure what they were up to. The Kennedy policy was now to curb Cuban exile activity. As a result, the same government that trained Cubans in terrorist tactics now threatened to arrest them if they applied these skills against Castro. The crackdown began almost immediately after the Missile Crisis was over, and it became clear the President was no longer an ally. Gerry Patrick Hemming's group Interpen and Sturgis's IAB were two groups targeted from the beginning. On December 4, federal agents arrested Hemming and three other members at their training base at No Name Key, Florida, as they were about to depart on a mission against Cuba. It was a clear signal that times had changed.[651]

Dr. Orlando Bosch headed the Insurrectional Movement for the Recovery of the Revolution (MIRR). The CIA had trained them in the mountains of Cuba, and Sturgis's boat runs supplied them in the days prior to the Bay of Pigs. Early in 1963, the CIA reduced one of Bosch's operations to a single, five-person crew, which so angered him that he published a pamphlet entitled *The Tragedy of Cuba*, which detailed Kennedy's betrayal of the exile cause. Shortly after that, feeling abandoned by the government that had previously encouraged them, the MIRR joined forces with the IAB.

In March 1963, members of the MIRR-IAB collaboration, including Frank Sturgis and Alexander Rorke, took off for Cuba on Rorke's cabin cruiser, the *Violin Three*. Also on board was Jerry Buchanan, the brother of James, who would be instrumental in spreading propaganda in the wake of the assassination that tried to connect Oswald to Castro. However, someone informed the FBI, who notified British authorities in the Bahamas, where authorities impounded the vessel when it stopped to refuel.[652]

It wasn't that JFK did not want to prepare for a possible invasion of Cuba. As he told the National Security Council on January 22, he wanted contingency plans in place in the event the Soviets advanced on West Berlin. However, his mandate was that any invasion force would have to be restricted to Cubans who had opposed Batista and fled the island after Castro came to power, not the more violent groups that had created trouble for him during the months leading up to the Cuban Missile Crisis.[653]

204

The DRE was one such troublesome group. As 1963 began, the DRE was obtaining arms and ammunition from the Mafia while being financed by William Pawley and Clare Boothe Luce. They told the CIA they were negotiating with big money interests in Texas and were prepared to go rogue in their war against Castro. On December 13, in total defiance of the U.S., DRE Secretary General Luis Fernandez Rocha stated: "Should the end of the crisis tend to prolong the agony of our people, Cubans will never renounce the right to fight, by every means possible, those who have seized our national sovereignty."[654]

In late November 1962, Richard Helms installed a new CIA case officer in charge of the DRE named George Joannides, whose name is in Lafitte's datebook. His job was to try and keep them under control.[655]

Eloy Gutierrez Menoyo, who was involved in the 1959 coup attempt to oust Castro (see Chapter Eight), had a history of working with the Mafia in Cuba. Now, Carlos Prio, who was close to Santo Trafficante and well-connected to the Mafia, tried to get Guitierrez to work with him. A CIA document in the National Archives states that on November 21, 1962, "the CIA received a report that Santos Trafficante Jr. had given Eloy [Gutierrez] Menoyo $250,000 worth of arms, which he had not yet paid for." As a result, the "informant reported that the Mafia planned to have Eloy Menoyo killed somewhere outside the US."[656] The bottom line was that right-wing Cuban exiles, abandoned by the Kennedy administration, were forced to turn to the Mafia and other sources for help if they were ever to regain their homeland.

***

The crackdown against Cuban exiles did not go unnoticed by the Soviets, who became convinced President Kennedy was among the least likely in his administration to take aggressive action against Cuba. As described by authors Aleksandr Fursenko and Timothy Naftali in *One Hell of a Gamble, Khrushchev, Castro, and Kennedy, 1958-1964*:

> One KGB source described a White House under siege from congressmen and governors to take action. These hard-liners equated the Castro problem with the state of Kennedy's chances for reelection in 1964. The fault line in the administration debate over a military solution to the Castro problem ran between a pro-interventionist group led by McGeorge Bundy, most of the Pentagon, and a minority in the State Department, and the critics of the military option, most notably Adlai Stevenson, Arthur Schlesinger Jr., and the chairman of the JCS, Maxwell Taylor. The opponents of an invasion explained that

it would take at least twenty thousand men and a long time. On the issue of this scheme, Kennedy leaned to the side of the opponents of using force.[657]

There were still Cuban exiles favorable to the Kennedy administration. With Robert Kennedy now in charge of the war against Castro, Manuel Artime became one of his leading conduits to the exile community. By March, Bobby told exile leader Enrique Ruiz Williams that the U.S. would help him find a new base outside the country to train a Cuban exile army. That same month, Artime was in Nicaragua looking to do the same thing. As far as the Kennedy brothers were concerned, gone were the radical, violent groups like Alpha 66, and in were leftists like Manuel Ray and his group JURE. By early February, they were receiving significant support from leftist Caribbean governments in addition to the U.S. Ray told a CIA informant in early January that he wanted to infiltrate the Cuban militia to arrange the "assassination [of the] Cuban government hierarchy."

The CIA continued to work with groups and individuals whom Robert Kennedy approved, which included Artime, whose case officer was Howard Hunt. In *Strength of the Wolf,* Douglas Valentine explained: "Hunt certainly knew that Artime was using drug money to finance his operations in Miami, as did Hunt's bosses, Angleton, Helms, and Barnes. As the CIA's domestic operations chief, Barnes was well-placed to protect Cuban drug distributors. He was in charge of domestic operations involving anti-Castro Cubans and the Mafia; he controlled sixty-four branch offices across America; and, in conjunction with Angleton's counterintelligence staff, he worked with police forces to provide security for CIA safehouses, including those in Dallas, Texas."[658]

Angleton, Helms, Hunt, and Barnes were all ardent CIA right-wingers, and other than Helms, all are listed in the Lafitte datebook as having been part of the JFK assassination conspiracy. There are also datebook references alluding to drug money to finance operations, which sounds very much like Operation Gladio and the stay-behind armies installed in Europe after World War II. The August 29 entry reads: "Call George [Hunter White] for shipment of LSD for New Orleans & Dallas. – Texas laws?" So, despite Artime's close connection to Robert Kennedy, this group, consisting of Cuban exiles supported by the Mafia and CIA officers and operatives opposed to Bobby, may have been organizing an effort to remove Castro without Bobby's approval.

There was a great deal of chatter within the exile community as those on the "outs" talked about redirecting their anger toward President Kennedy. Manuel Artime set up a meeting with Bobby to warn him about the threats made against his brother.[659] However, JFK remained blind to the danger he faced. Right-wing zealots at the Pentagon and CIA, international anti-Communists, Texas oilmen, industry leaders, Mafia crime bosses, Southern segregationists, OAS militants, Madrid Fascists, European Monarchists, and Cuban exiles all wanted Kennedy dead.

CHAPTER TWELVE

BIRTH OF A REVOLUTIONARY

As 1963 began, and the clock ticked closer to Dealey Plaza, Lee Harvey Oswald acted like a revolutionary in pursuit of a cause. He was isolated from the White Russian community in Fort Worth, which left him free to conduct his affairs undetected. His political philosophy remained unchanged – an interest in Marxism while rejecting Soviet communism and American capitalism. A fellow employee at Jaggars-Chiles-Stovall, Dennis Ofstein, told the Warren Commission Oswald said the only Russians who had money "were Communist Party officials or high ranking members in the party, and I asked him at one time if he were a Communist and he said, 'No.'" [660]

Virginia Hale of the Texas Employment Commission helped Oswald look for a job after he arrived in Dallas. When she learned that Marina spoke only Russian, she gave Oswald's phone number to a friend named Max Clark, whose wife Gali was Russian. It sounds innocent enough; however, Virginia's husband was I.B. Hale, who, as described in the previous chapter, was head of security at General Dynamics and whose two sons broke into the home of Judith Campbell. In addition, Max Clark had a CIA security clearance, was an industrial security supervisor for General Dynamics, and was George de Mohrenschildt's lawyer. Hence, chances are George told Oswald to contact Virginia Hale, knowing it would lead him to Gali Clark, who came from an extremely wealthy family that had lost everything to the Bolsheviks. Her sister was Princess Sherbatoff, and her cousin, Alexis Scherbatow, worked for the Tolstoy Foundation. She was a virulent anti-Communist but was not considered important enough to be called to testify by the Warren Commission. Maybe there was a connection between Oswald, de Mohrenschildt, the Clarks, and the Hales that had something to do with the covert activities Oswald was about to embark upon. This unlikely connection is, at the very least, suspicious. [661]

As we will see, Gali and other individuals Oswald encountered early in 1963 mysteriously reappear in Lafitte's datebook less than a month before the assassination, even though there was no known contact between them for almost a year. We will discuss this at the appropriate time. For now, it tells us these people probably had a role in directing Oswald as 1963 began.

In January, Oswald read a variety of material related to Marxism and political activism. From Pioneer Publishers, he ordered three political writings – *The Coming American Revolution, The End of the Comintern,* and *Manifesto of the Fourth International.* The first book was related to anarchism, communism, Marxism, and socialism. The second was about Trotskyism and the end of traditional Bolshevism. The third pertained to Leon Trotsky, whose declared goal was the overthrow of global capitalism and the establishment of worldwide socialism via international revolution.[662]

From de Mohrenschildt, who was still a driving force in his life, Oswald borrowed two books by George Orwell – *1984* and *Animal Farm.* The former dealt with the danger of allowing a government to control every aspect of the lives of its constituents. The latter was a parody of the Soviet Union and showed that the Russian Revolution, though successful, was poisoned by those who had abandoned its original ideals.[663]

Perhaps the best explanation for the impact de Mohrenschildt had on Oswald came from his ex-son-in-law, Gary Taylor, who told the Warren Commission: "The only thing that occurred to me was … if there was any assistance or plotters in the assassination, then it was, in my opinion, most probably the de Mohrenschildts."[664]

The FBI's handling of Oswald's case continued to be odd. They had closed his file in October 1962, and Agent James Hosty was now responsible for keeping track of him. Hosty planned to interview Marina in six months, which was March 1963. In the interim, Oswald received issues through the mail of the Socialist Workers Party's *The Militant* on January 24 and March 24 and the Communist Party USA's *Daily Worker* around March 27. On February 20, he wrote to the CPUSA and, on March 24, to the SWP. Three days later, the SWP wrote back to him via his Dallas PO Box 2915. The Dallas Post Office was on the lookout for Oswald receiving provocative material, and the CPUSA, SWP, and other left-wing groups were also having their mail inspected by post office informants. Their job was to alert the FBI if they came across anything suspicious, and they were very vigilant about doing that. So, they must have told the FBI about Oswald on multiple occasions. Yet, Hosty remained uninterested and left Oswald and Marina alone. Hosty was negligent, or the FBI had an ulterior motive for ignoring them. Oswald may have already been an FBI informant looking to infiltrate subversive groups on their behalf.[665]

209

Jerry Brooks was a thirty-eight-year-old right-wing extremist who spied on Communists for the radically violent right-wing group, the Minutemen. He also spied on the Minutemen for the FBI and the Treasury Department. Could Oswald have been doing something similar? It would explain why the FBI allowed him to receive leftist literature and why Hosty, who dealt exclusively with right-wing extremist groups in the Dallas area, was assigned to his case. As Hosty described in his book *Assignment Oswald*, "Right-wingers dominated my caseload in the four-person counterintelligence squad in the Dallas office. I spent much of my time tracking the movements and actions of both Klan members and members of [General] Walker's radical militia group, known as the Minutemen...the Minutemen had been arming themselves with an impressive array of weapons."[666]

Meanwhile, George de Mohrenschildt was unaware that throughout 1963, the CIA and the 902nd Military Intelligence Group (nicknamed "90 Deuce"), a highly secretive organization, were monitoring him.[667] On February 12, 1964, Warren Commission counsel Lee Rankin asked the FBI for a "full-scale background intelligence type report of the de Mohrenschildts. Hoover replied six days later that the FBI had conducted an investigation "concerning George de Mohrenschildt based on his alleged pro-German sympathies and activities... In the past, FBI field offices that had looked into George as a matter of national security were as follows: New York, Albany, Newark, Cincinnati, El Paso, Dallas, Philadelphia, San Diego, Miami, Phoenix, Denver, San Francisco, Los Angeles, Washington, D.C., Houston, and New Orleans." They even asked the CIA if George worked for them, to which Richard Helms replied: "George de Mohrenschildt is not and has not been an employee of CIA, nor is he a contract employee of CIA." Then Helms defensively added that he "may possibly be a contact of that Agency."[668]

In *Our Man in Haiti*, Joan Mellen wrote that in the "two weeks before the Warren Commission released its report, the U.S. government destroyed de Mohrenschildt's federal employment file – which would have linked de Mohrenschildt with the CIA dating from 1957, at least."[669]

***

While the FBI ignored Oswald, de Mohrenschildt subjected his young protégé to a right-wing, pro-Nazi indoctrination. He left Oswald a copy of *Mein Kampf*, which Oswald had already read in the Marines, and asked him to reread it. After the assassination, the CIA found the following notation on the last page of Marina's "Notes on Poetry" notebook: "Shil'kgruber, Adol.f (G.)." Schickelgruber was Adolf Hilter's real surname, which his father had changed when he was thirty-nine years old. Why the Russian Marina knew this and wrote it in her notebook is hard to understand.[670]

In late February 1963, the Oswalds attended a couple of social gatherings that had serious overtones for them moving forward. It begins with the strange story of Everett Glover, who told the Warren Commission he met Jeanne de Mohrenschildt, George's wife, quite often at an ice skating rink between 1956 and 1959. According to Glover's Warren Commission testimony, "The name she wanted to be called was 'Jon,' the French J-e-a-n-n-e." For some reason, the wife of George de Mohrenschildt wanted people to believe she was French. Whether or not this had something to do with a possible French connection to the JFK assassination cannot be proven, but it is worth considering. [671]

Eugenia (Jeanne) Fomenko was born in Harbin, China, on May 5, 1914. Her parents were both born in Russia, and her father was the director of the Chinese Eastern Railroad until he resigned in 1925. In 1932, she married Valentin Bogoiavlensky, and they later moved to Shanghai, became a successful dance team, and changed their names to Robert and Jeanne LeGon. In 1938, they emigrated to the United States. Her father remained in China, and according to her testimony before the Warren Commission, he was doing secret work for the U.S. government. Jeanne later heard from another family member that Communists had killed her father in 1941. In 1956, she met George de Mohrenschildt, and when her husband Robert LeGon learned of their relationship, he wrote a letter to the FBI accusing her of being a "Communist spy." It resulted in the FBI investigating her political activities.[672]

Everett Glover met George when he showed up with Jeanne at the skating rink. He lost touch with them until 1962, when Glover's friend, Sam Ballen, asked him to play doubles tennis with another couple. Glover agreed, and against all odds of probability, the other couple turned out to be George and Jeanne. The four played tennis often after that, and the relationship grew, which led to the de Mohrenschildts inviting Glover to a dinner party at their home. It was there that Glover met Marina Oswald. She was alone, and Glover met her two or three more times with the de Mohrenschildts after that, each time without Lee. Then, sometime in February, he and Lee finally met at another de Mohrenschildt affair. Another party followed, attended by Lee, Marina, Glover, and Glover's mysterious roommate, Volkmar Schmidt.[673]

Schmidt had been in the United States for about one and a half years and worked at the Magnolia Laboratory of Standard Oil. He was a Fascist and

211

did not attempt to hide it. De Mohrenschildt called him "Messer Schmidt," a reference to the Nazi World War II fighter plane.

One would have expected the Marxist Oswald to have little interest in conversing with the German Fascist, but that was not the case. The two engaged in a private political discussion for over three hours in another room, and George did not join in, even though politics was something he did not shy away from. Schmidt later said he was impressed by Oswald's "burning dedication" to what he referred to as "political truth." At the same time, Oswald explained why he was a Marxist who rejected the political systems of the United States and the Soviet Union. According to Schmidt, Oswald reacted violently when the discussion shifted to Kennedy's foreign policy, especially as it applied to Cuba. He called the Bay of Pigs and the Cuban Missile Crisis examples of American "imperialism" and "intervention" and that America's policy towards Cuba was setting the stage for a nuclear holocaust.

Recognizing the futility of arguing with Oswald, Schmidt changed the subject to the right-wing zealot, General Walker. He employed a technique he had learned studying with Dr. Wilhelm Kuetemeyer, a professor of psychosomatic medicine and religious philosophy at the University of Heidelberg in Germany, which was to agree with Oswald so he would solicit his opinions more freely. Schmidt compared Walker to Hitler and blamed him for the University of Mississippi uprising, which Oswald agreed with. According to Schmidt, Oswald became highly excited and said the United States was moving toward fascism.[674]

De Mohrenschildt likely arranged the meeting so Schmidt and Oswald could talk, probably to determine if Oswald was a suitable candidate for a pending operation, considering it was de Mohrenschildt who had him relocate to Dallas. Considering Oswald's history of drug experimentation, hypnosis, and mind manipulation while in the Marines in preparation for his defection, Volkmar Schmidt's presence at the party must have been in connection to something along those lines. Schmidt's interest in Oswald was probably the start of a new round of mental indoctrination into another operation, possibly the attempt on General Walker's life, which could be considered a dress rehearsal for the JFK assassination.

Glover and Schmidt, who worked together at Magnolia Research Laboratories, decided to throw another party and share the costs. They invited Lee and Marina, but Schmidt inexplicably left for Germany on business and never saw Oswald again.[675]

There was also a mystery surrounding Glover and Schmidt. Like Gali Clark, their names appear in Lafitte's datebook a month before the JFK assassination, after a prolonged absence. Glover's was an interesting entry because his name and phone number were also in Oswald's notebook with the notation, "Georges [sic] friend." It is innocent enough, but on the same page is the address "Norman, OK., 1318 ½ Garfield." It suggests Oswald had a connection to Norman, which is revealing since Thomas Eli Davis, Loran Hall, and CIA asset June Cobb, all of whom were probably Oswald associates, also had connections to Norman. We know the CIA conducted mind-altering drug experimentation in Norman as part of the MK/ULTRA program, which may explain Oswald's recent encounter with Volmar Schmidt. At the same time, Oswald, Davis, Hall, and Cobb may have been part of a mind control program run out of Norman.[676] The question is, what did Glover have to do with this?

Cobb claimed to have attended the University of Oklahoma but only took one or two classes. She claimed she was "politely suspended" after her sophomore year. As John Newman writes in *Where Angels Tread Lightly*, she was "involved in university organizations connected with politics, acting, media, French language and the Civil Air Patrol – all at the same time...she had worked on the staff of the campus radio station, WMAD." Did Cobb attend school only to provide cover for covert work she was engaged in, such as mind-altering drug experimentation? Maybe so, because Newman writes that she "did not attend university classes in Oklahoma or Mexico City, in spite of registering at both schools." It is reminiscent of Oswald applying to Albert Schweitzer College before defecting to Russia and never attending classes there either. Also, like Oswald, June did not need money even though she never had a good-paying job. As she told her CIA interviewer in 1960, "I have some generous friends who know I don't work for money and say June, do you have any money? I say no. And they say, well here, take this, you must be broke, take this money...Well, anyway, this is what my friends – are the type who pay hospital bills for me and give me tickets if I want to go to Mexico or whatever, you know." And just like Oswald, she spent extended periods in hospitals. "The pattern of Cobb's very short jobs and very long hospitalizations is remarkable," Newman noted.[677]

Recently released CIA documents reveal that William Harvey, through Jane Pierson, June Cobb's case officer, was kept informed about what June Cobb was up to while in Havana, New York City, and Mexico City throughout the early 1960s. It is unclear if Cobb was part of ZR/RIFLE, the assassination program, or if it just pertained to Task Force W. However, we learn from the documents that the CIA paid for Cobb's hospitalization while she was in Mexico City and was very interested in Cobb's testimony before Congress, so it does reveal a connection between Harvey and Cobb, even if it was only through Pierson. Considering the parallel paths traveled by Oswald and Cobb, this clarifies things and opens up a myriad of possibilities, especially if Cobb were part of Harvey's assassination team.[678]

Dr. Louis West was an Air Force doctor in the 1950s involved in MKULTRA experiments conducted at Norman. He was also the doctor who performed a psychiatric evaluation on Jack Ruby during his trial for killing Oswald. West found Ruby insane. His connection to Norman is significant, considering that Thomas Eli Davis and Loran Hall both briefly lived in Norman. Davis ran guns with Jack Ruby, was CIA-connected, and, in 1963, tried to organize a paramilitary force to invade Haiti. From July 16 to October 1, 1958, he received psychiatric treatment at Detroit, Michigan's Lafayette Clinic. At the time, the CIA conducted MKULTRA mind-control experiments there, and Dr. West visited the facility.[679]

Loran Hall was involved with Thomas Davis in organizing mercenaries for an operation in Haiti. In March 1959, he was in Cuba involved in an attack against Nicaragua that never materialized, and Castro's people arrested Hall on suspicion of being an American agent. It means the attack was an American operation. The Cubans arrested a man named Wilson-Hudson as well, an important character we will revisit later. For now, considering all the chatter about launching an attack against Guantanamo or the Dominican Republic and making it look like a pro-Castro operation to justify an attack against Cuba by the U.S. military, it is likely this was what was happening in 1963 with the attack against Nicaragua. While in prison, Hall served time with Mafia boss Santo Trafficante. Three months later, he was released and returned to the United States.[680]

Oswald returned to Dallas from his mysterious Mexico City trip on October 3, 1963. Three days later, the Lafitte datebook entry reads: "Oswald – Issue (!) with Caretaker," indicating there was a problem with Oswald. Shortly after that, the October 16 and 24 entries mention Volkmar, Glover, and OK.[681] Based on the above, the OK must stand for Oklahoma, and the timing suggests Volkmar and Glover were needed again because there was trouble with Oswald that required their input. If true, the services they were providing a month before the assassination were a continuation of what they had done earlier in 1963, which had something to do with mind control and Norman, Oklahoma.

***

Returning to Glover's second party, he went forward with it even though Volkmar Schmidt was not going to attend. In addition to the Oswalds, he invited George and Jeanne de Mohrenschildt, fellow Magnolia Research employee Norman Fredricksen and his wife Elke, and Magnolia employee Betty McDonald. Michael Paine did not attend, but Glover was also friends with Ruth Paine, so he invited her. As he told the Warren Commission, "I became acquainted with Ruth Paine either through the Unitarian Church here in Dallas or through a singing group…from the Unitarian Church…"[682]

Glover's connection to the Unitarian Church adds to the mystery because of the church's history with Oswald. We know that it was through the Unitarian Church in Los Angeles that Oswald learned about Albert Schweitzer College, which he applied to and was supposed to attend as part of his Soviet Union defection deception. He was brought to the church by a regular attendee, fellow Marine Kerry Thornley, whom Oswald already knew from New Orleans in the mid-1950s and would soon meet again in the same city in the summer of 1963. George de Mohrenschildt's friend, Colonel Orlov, whom George introduced to Oswald in Fort Worth in 1962, was a Unitarian. The Unitarian Church had CIA connections and was involved with anti-Communist European *émigrés* and freedom fighters in Europe since World War II, which included White Russians like the people in Fort Worth. One can't help but ponder a possible connection to Otto Skorzeny, Reinhard Gehlen, Allen Dulles, Frank Wisner, James Angleton, and William Harvey as well.

It was not a coincidence that various Unitarians "babysat" Lee Oswald from the time he was in the Marines. Now it was Marina's turn, for Ruth Paine, a fellow Unitarian, became her babysitter, and the two only became acquainted because of the party thrown by Everett Glover. One must assume the real reason for the party that night was to introduce these two women so that Lee Harvey Oswald would be free to come and go as he pleased.

Raised a Quaker, Ruth Paine became interested in US-Soviet relations during her college years. She later became an active member of the Young Friends Committee of North America, where she was the primary liaison between its East-West Contact Service and the State Department, arranging cultural exchanges between Americans and Soviets engaged in the arts. It was what was happening at the Russian Research Center and MIT Center for International Studies, the groups that may have played a role in Oswald's defection. There was also a strong possibility that Ruth Paine had intelligence connections, and authorities were clearly concerned about her, Michael Paine, and the Unitarian Church. According to researcher Mary Ferrell, government agencies visited Unitarian Church parishes across the country after the assassination, trying to uncover information about the mysterious couple and what involvement the church may have had in Oswald's life.[683]

Ruth Paine may have had a connection to George de Mohrenschildt. Although each claimed they first met at Glover's party, George knew William Avery Hyde, Ruth's father, from the time he spent in Haiti while George was there.[684] After the assassination, the CIA was interested in why the alleged anti-Communist Hyde shared the political views of six-time Socialist Party presidential candidate Norman Thomas. The answer was that being a Socialist and an anti-Communist at the same time was not that unusual. Michael and Ruth Paine, the CIA's Cord Meyer, Priscilla Johnson, Harold Isaacs, Lee Harvey Oswald, and a host of others all fell into that category. Thomas was also a proponent of eugenics, which appealed to many right-wing Socialist/Marxists. He wrote: "If we are not to be overwhelmed by the 'rising tide of color,' we must breed against the world."[685]

Hyde's support of Thomas mirrored Michael and Ruth Paine's strange connection to Nancy and Frederick Osborn, Jr., whom they gave as character references after the assassination when asked by the FBI. The Osborns were elitist right-wingers who should not have had an interest in the leftist Paines. Henry Fairfield Osborn, the uncle of Frederick Osborn Jr.'s father, was president of the Second International Congress of Eugenics. By 1937, he passed this responsibility on to Frederick Henry Osborn, Sr. The Pioneer Fund, established by him, was "a group of wealthy Northeastern conservatives" who were well known for their support of southern segregationists.[686] It implies that the Unitarians Michael and Ruth Paine were not as far left as they wanted everyone to believe.

Ruth's parents, William Avery and Carol Hyde, were also Unitarians. William worked for the Agency for International Development (AID), a CIA offshoot, as did Ruth's brother-in-law, John Hoke. Ruth's sister Silvia, the wife of John Hoke, worked for the CIA. Meanwhile, Michael Paine's father, George Lyman Paine, was a Marxist who lived in California. His mother, Ruth Forbes Paine Young, was close friends with Mary Bancroft, who amazingly was Allen Dulles's mistress while Dulles was with the OSS in Europe during World War II. Shortly after the war, Ruth Forbes Paine joined the World Federalist Movement, like Cord Meyer and Priscila Johnson, and founded the International Peace Academy.[687]

In 1968, Marina Oswald testified before a grand jury in New Orleans. A juror asked Marina if she stayed in contact with Ruth Paine. Marina replied, "No, I like her and appreciate what she did. I was advised by [the] Secret Service not to be connected with her." Marina said the reason the SS advised her to stay away from Ruth was because "she was sympathizing with the CIA." Marina was then asked, "In other words, you were left with the distinct impression that she was in some way connected with the CIA?" To which she responded, "Yes."[688]

Michael Paine was an intellectual who studied at Harvard and Swarthmore and worked for Bell Helicopter. Like de Mohrenschildt, there was no reason for him to be interested in Oswald until we consider that he was an avid Trotskyite, and his father was one of the leaders of the Trotskyite movement in the United States.

There was also the mysterious phone conversation between Michael Paine's office and his home shortly after the assassination, which was likely between Paine and his wife and remained classified until 1976. Taken from an FBI wiretap, the document stated that a "Confidential Informant 'had' advised that the male voice was heard to comment that he felt sure that LEE HARVEY OSWALD had killed the President but did not feel OSWALD was responsible, and further stated, 'We both know who is responsible.'"[689]

There may have been a reason why Glover hastily called the social gathering so that Ruth and Marina could meet. Just days before, Marina had written to the Soviet embassy in Washington D.C., asking to return to the Soviet Union.[690] Marina said Lee forced her to write this letter. As she told the Warren Commission, "Lee would say that it would be better for me to go to Russia. I did not know why...."[691] Ruth offered Marina the option to move in with her. Marina declined, at least for the time being, for she had to ascertain if Oswald would approve.[692]

***

On Sundays in the spring of 1963, Michael Paine ate lunch at Luby's near Southern Methodist University and held "conversations or debates" with SMU students. According to the FBI, he would argue for "peaceful coexistence" in Eastern Europe and support of Castro.[693] Paine later recalled that Oswald believed violent revolution was inevitable in the United States, and he received revolutionary instructions "by reading between the lines of *The Militant.*" So, why did Paine show an interest in Oswald, who opposed the peaceful coexistence he promoted?

Despite his Marxist tendencies, for the remainder of his life, Oswald traveled in right-wing circles with people who supported a revolution that he and the radical right both perceived to be imminent. Volkmar Schmidt said Oswald was excited about the rise of fascism in the United States. The name of the secretary of the American Nazi Party was in Oswald's address book after the assassination, as was the name and telephone number of General Walker. They were unusual entries for a Marxist to carry around.[694]

Near the end of his life, de Mohrenschildt claimed he introduced Oswald to the right-wing operations of Dallas oilman H.L. Hunt. John Currington, Hunt's chief staff assistant during this period, confirmed they were aware of Oswald, telling author Dick Russell he "had run across Oswald before the assassination. He was sort of known in certain circles as being an extremist, very vocal about certain issues..." Currington and Hunt would not have been interested in Oswald were the extremism he referred to been leftist.[695]

We know Hunt was an avid supporter of Cuban exiles and right-wing groups, many of whom would become associated with Oswald in the months leading up to the assassination. Hunt had his finger on the pulse of the right-wing in Dallas; he supported General Walker and the John Birch Society and was a member of the Minutemen, who shared Oswald's doomsday philosophy.

Extremely violent, the Minutemen advocated arming militia groups nationwide in preparation for a final war between the United States and the Soviet Union, which they saw as inevitable. California Governor Pat Brown was troubled by the group, and he told an audience he would not tolerate "any move toward anarchy...We hear reports that there are twenty-three guerrilla bands with 2400 among their number in California who wish to be their own civil defenders, carry their own arms, and choose their own hiding places in the event of nuclear war...."[696]

Rich Lauchi, a one-time Minutemen member and arms dealer, said they were preparing for "THE DAY." "And I say this – I say that what the individual is doing today in this country is the greatest deterrent to Communism...I'm telling you, this is an armed camp! There's millions...of weapons put away for THE DAY, and I'm not talking about hunting guns and so forth...."[697]

Minutemen leader Robert DePugh described the coming revolution as a "revolt" that would be instigated by "mass indignation rallies and a complete stoppage of everything against the government policy. Then, anything could happen. Maybe federal troops would move into some areas to force the people to do something against their wishes."[698]

The Minutemen believed people needed to take control of the government, which Communists ran, and revolution was the only means of removing them from power. According to DePugh, "the Communists already have such complete control over the American news media and political processes that it is impossible to change our own government's policies by the customary means of politics and public opinion... that a life-and-death conflict is raging right now between the forces of freedom and advocates of world slavery... that if the American people expect to be saved from slavery, they are going to have to do so themselves... the Minutemen are the most experienced, most dedicated and best-disciplined organization that is involved in this fight...."[699]

Lee Harvey Oswald shared the Minutemen's belief that revolution was inevitable. He was dissatisfied with the American form of government, despised the Soviet brand of Communism that enslaved its people, and considered it incumbent upon the people to correct the situation. The question is, could Oswald have become involved with a right-wing revolutionary group such as the Minutemen and still maintain ideological loyalties to the Marxist doctrine that he professed? The answer is a definitive yes!

In New Orleans in the summer of 1963, Oswald became involved with Guy Banister, a notorious member of the Minutemen. When Oswald was spotted on the street handing out Fair Play For Cuba literature by one of Banister's supporters, Banister replied, "Don't worry about him. He's a nervous fellow; he's confused. He's with us; he's associated with this office."[700]

The first mention of a possible link between Oswald and the Minutemen occurred in January 1964, two months after the assassination. In a speech before a group in Anaheim, California, Attorney General Stanley Mosk told his audience:

> I know Lee Harvey Oswald was on the Far Left, and these groups are generally on the Far Right. But we know Oswald had rejected our system...We know he pursued political causes with fanaticism and without regard for democratic processes. He was a political agitator who was alienated from our society and our political order.
>
> It is this alienation which is most disturbing in the attitudes of so-called Minutemen...They feel that our system has failed. They feel that our two major political parties are shams – simply a choice between two evils. They feel our processes have been totally perverted and are of no use. They admitted looking forward to a time of armed conflict with an enemy they only vaguely identify.[701]

U.S. Representative Henry B. Gonzalez was a Texas Democrat who rode in the motorcade. After the assassination, he made a special request to Earl Warren to determine if the Minutemen were involved with Oswald. Shortly after that, the *New York Post* reported that the Commission was investigating a possible Oswald- Minutemen link.[702]

There are underlying references to a group like the Minutemen in Oswald's writings that suggest an association with the group may have existed. In the spring of 1963, he wrote: "It is readily foreseeable that a coming economic, political or military crisis... will bring about the final destruction of the capitalist system..." "We do not have any interest in directly assuming the head of Government in the event of such an all-finising [sic] crisis... we are merely interested in opposing foreign intervention [Soviet communism] ..." He wanted to establish a "separate, democratic, pure communist society...one with union-communes [sic], democratic socializing and without regard to the twisting apart of Marxist Communism by other powers." Oswald's philosophy was there were "two world systems, one twisted beyond recognition (communism)... the other decadent and dying (capitalism). A truly democratic system would combine the better qualities of the two upon an American foundation."[703]

Oswald went on to note that patience was preferred to "loud and useless manifestation's [sic] of protest...these preferred tactics now may prove to be too limited in the near future. They should not be confused with slowness, indesision [sic], or fear; only the intellectually fearless could even be remotely attracted too [sic] our doctrine, and yet this doctrine requires the utmost restraint, a state of being in itself majustic [sic] in power."[704]

Perhaps Oswald's most interesting comment was: "There are organizations already formed in the United States, who have declared they shall become effective only after the military debacle of the United States. Organizations such as the *minute men* [sic] ...There will also be small armed communist and probably fascist groups. There will also be anarchist and religious groups at work." (Author's Italics)[705]

It is an understatement to say that Oswald mentioning the Minutemen by name is an important point. There is no doubt that their revolutionary beliefs would have appealed to him. It is also not too presumptuous to assume that the JFK assassination was the type of crisis Oswald believed could initiate the final conflict he and the Minutemen foresaw as inevitable. Therefore, it is probable that Oswald was a willing participant in the death of JFK, even though he may have unknowingly allowed himself to become the fall guy for the assassination.

Frank Ellsworth was an agent with the Treasury Department's Alcohol, Tobacco, and Firearms Division in Dallas in 1963. Testifying before the Warren Commission, Ellsworth stated, "An organization known as the Minutemen is the right-wing group in Dallas most likely to have been associated with any effort to assassinate the President. The Minutemen are closely tied to General Walker and H.L. Hunt."[706]

Extremist groups like the Minutemen worked closely with the more violent Cuban exiles. There were gunrunning duties to perform and various unsavory services to provide that brought these groups together. If Oswald became involved with the Minutemen after moving to Dallas from Fort Worth, it was only a matter of time before he met with radical Cuban exiles. Although Oswald had once supported the Cuban revolution, he would have rejected Castro after he became a Communist, as did many past Cuban supporters. They also opposed the American imperialism that subjugated Cuba for many years and despised the American government for abandoning them in their attempt to regain control of their homeland. They were revolutionaries in the truest sense of the word, for all they wanted was the liberation of their country from communism and the return of a government that served the best interest of the people, which would have appealed to Oswald and his belief in Marxist worldwide revolution.

***

As George de Mohrenschildt continued his right-wing indoctrination of Oswald, stories about OAS assassination plots in France appeared in the newspapers. On February 16, the *Washington Post* reported that in Paris, "police said today that they had foiled a plot apparently organized by military officers to kill President Charles de Gaulle by shooting him from a rooftop with a rifle equipped with telescopic sights. At least five persons and possibly seven were arrested in the plot...."[707] According to the *New York Times*, "The plot to kill the President apparently was extremely simple. An assassin, equipped with a high-caliber rifle fitted with telescopic sights, was to station himself in a window overlooking the cobblestone courtyard where General de Gaulle was to inspect the students."[708]

Just twelve days later, the *New York Times* reported: "A band of nine right-wing terrorists whose reported aim was to kill Premier George Pompidou has been rounded up by the police. According to informed sources the Government is now in possession of documents indicating that the terrorist movement has its back against the wall and is now preparing a last desperate campaign. Consequently, guards have been reinforced around key buildings and around members of the Government...."[709]

***

On March 2, Lee and Marina Oswald moved from their apartment on Elsbeth Street to 214 West Neely Street. The apartments were roughly a block apart, making a move hard to explain, except that it occurred around the time the FBI's interest in the Oswalds began anew. So it was that on March 10, Agent Hosty visited the Elsbeth Street apartment to find the Oswalds had relocated. The apartment manager, Mrs. Tobias, told Hosty that Oswald "drank to excess and beat his wife on numerous occasions. They had numerous complaints from the other tenants due to Oswald's drinking and beating his wife."[710]

As a result of Hosty's failure to locate Marina, the FBI reopened Oswald's case on March 26. The reason given was that Oswald subscribed to the *Worker*, which does not make sense since they knew this in October and closed his file anyway. Maybe what changed was that Hosty learned Lee was abusing Marina, but he still waited forty-five to sixty days before revisiting them, and by that time, Oswald had left Dallas for New Orleans. It was as if Hosty was going through the motions and purposely avoiding the Oswalds so Lee could go about his business.[711]

There is also the possibility that Hosty's renewed interest in Oswald was related to his work investigating right-wing groups. As he confirmed to Mary La Fontaine in *Oswald Talked*, during this time, he was interested in "the investigation of mostly right-wing subversives, like the Minutemen," the group that keeps coming up in discussions about Oswald.[712]

Did the Minutemen have anything to do with Oswald's change of address? Consider that the Minutemen publication *On Target* counseled readers to blend into the surroundings, remain "anonymous," and avoid being called a "fear monger [or] racist." Revolutionary upheaval could arrive at any time, so it was important not to bind yourself to one area. As they suggested, "You can leave a rented house faster than one you own." *On Target* told readers to find a job that did not require too much responsibility. Live frugally because to do so "might mean the difference between life and death."[713]

On Target's message described Lee Oswald's life perfectly. In early March, he received a letter from his brother Robert, who asked for Lee's new address because he was moving to Arkansas. Lee provided only his post office box number, writing that "I shall always have it." Lee Oswald had been on the move and planned to be on the move again.[714]

On March 12, Oswald allegedly used the alias A. Hidell to order the infamous Mannlicher-Carcano Italian Carbine rifle. The Warren Commission stated he ordered the gun through an ad in *American Rifleman* on March 12, 1963, included a $21.45 money order to Klein's Sporting Goods in Chicago, and instructed them to send the rifle to his Dallas P.O. box. Prior to that he had ordered a pistol from Seaport Traders Inc., in Los Angeles. It happened right after Oswald moved to Neely Street, and as described by J. Harry Jones, Jr. in *The Minutemen*, members "continued their target practice, either secretly or openly at established target ranges where the members naturally would not identify themselves as Minutemen. Some obviously devoted considerable time to acquiring various weapons and hiding them."[715]

Where Oswald obtained the money to pay for these weapons is hard to understand, for he could not afford to buy them. He allegedly purchased the money order to pay for the rifle on the morning of March 12. It reminds us of John Newman's question regarding June Cobb and how she paid for things without having a good-paying job. We know the CIA was taking care of June, and maybe the same applied to Oswald.

The Post Office did not open until 8:00 A.M. the morning Oswald allegedly picked up his rifle, yet his time sheet at work showed he punched in at that time. The time sheet included a notation that "time shown hereon must agree with clock register," which suggests it was hard to misrepresent what time your workday began. It meant Oswald likely had an accomplice who obtained the money order, and Hidell was not an Oswald alias but a different person.[716]

As John Armstrong noted in *Harvey and Lee*, we know the rifle coupon was mailed to Klein's at about 10 A.M. on March 12 because of the time stamp on the envelope. However, the FBI and Warren Commission stated that the money order was deposited by Klein's at the First National Bank of Chicago the following day. It meant that the envelope had traveled 700 miles from Dallas to the Chicago post office and delivered to Klein's. Klein's then processed the purchase order and deposited the money order in the bank the same day. Anyone old enough to have been alive at that time knows this was improbable.

Upon receipt of Oswald's order, Klein's microfilmed the mailing envelope and the order coupon but not the $21.45 money order. In addition, the extra bank deposit slip provided by the bank reads February 15, 1963, not March 13, which means it was not Oswald's. And the money order deposited by Klein's had none of the usual endorsements that First National Bank of Chicago vice president Robert Wilmouth said it should have had, such as stamps for the First National Bank of Chicago, the Federal Reserve

Bank of Chicago, or the Federal Postal Money Order Center in Kansas City. Not surprisingly, Wilmouth did not testify before the Warren Commission.

Things get stranger still. A copy of the February issue of *American Rifleman*, which Oswald allegedly used to buy the rifle, does not appear in the Warren Report. Instead, they included a copy of Klein's ad from November 1963, which appeared in *Field and Stream*. The February ad that the Warren Commission said Oswald used to order the rifle was for a 36" long Carcano weighing 5.5 pounds., while the November ad included in the Commission's report was for a 40" long Carcano weighing 7 pounds. Not surprisingly, the rifle allegedly taken from the Book Depository, which the Commission said Oswald used to kill JFK, was 40.2" long, matching the November ad.[717]

On March 15, just three days after Hidell ordered the rifle, *On Target* had this to say:

> See the old man at the corner where you buy your paper? He may have a silencer-equipped pistol under his coat. That extra fountain pen in the pocket of the insurance salesman that calls on you might be a cyanide gas gun. What about your milkman? Arsenic works slow but sure. Your auto mechanic may stay up nights studying booby traps.
>
> These patriots are not going to let you take their freedom away from them. They have learned the silent knife, the strangler's cord, the target rifle that hits sparrows at 200 yards. Only their leaders restrain them.
>
> Traitors beware! Even now the cross hairs are on the back of your necks.[718]

While Oswald was busy purchasing firearms, Marina continued corresponding with the Soviet Embassy. On March 8, she received a response to her February 17 request to return to the Soviet Union. She needed to file an application form, which would take five to six months to process. As a result, there was little chance she would be gone before Oswald had an opportunity to put whatever he was up to in motion. Marina took her time responding, mailing the embassy the information they requested on March 17.

***

It was at this time that Richard Case Nagell appeared on the scene. He was "investigating activities of anti-Castro organizations and their personnel" [and] "conducted inquiries relative to 'dissident' members of several

Cuban refugee groups based in the United States; I [Nagell] checked out an alleged connection between a Miami resident named Eladio Del Valle and New Orleans CIA informant Sergio Arcacha-Smith; I investigated an associate of the now deceased right-wing extremist David W. Ferrie of New Orleans... I conducted a surveillance on a man, said to have been an ex-CIA employee, observed talking to [exile] leader Manuel Artime and former Cuban senator/racketeer Rolando Masferrer."[719]

In conjunction with this, Nagell said he also traveled to Dallas to investigate Lee and Marina Oswald. Immediately after the assassination, a Military Intelligence file on Nagell reported that "in April 1963, SUBJECT [Nagell] conducted an inquiry concerning the marital status of Marina Oswald and her reported desire to return to the USSR." An FBI report written January 2, 1964, said Nagell advised them that "he had been acquainted with MARINA, LEE HARVEY OSWALD's wife, and pointed out that OSWALD was having marital difficulties with MARINA."[720]

In September 1963, Nagell was arrested for firing a gun harmlessly into the ceiling of a bank in El Paso. He did not intend to rob the bank, but he was looking to extricate himself from involvement in JFK's assassination. In 1991, Harrison Edward Livingstone interviewed Marina Oswald for his book *High Treason 2*. They discussed if Oswald was JFK's assassin or a patsy set up to take the blame. Then, for seemingly no apparent reason, Marina said to Livingstone, "I wasn't married to an angel. I could be married to a thief, *but he didn't rob that bank at that time*."[721] [emphasis added]

We know Oswald never robbed a bank. There was only one person Marina had in mind, and that was Richard Nagell. It means a relationship had developed between Nagell and Marina during his investigation into the couple that was more involved than either dared admit. Nagell later stated that Oswald "had problems with his wife. She was going to divorce him and go back to Russia. That's something not generally known...." Nagell was right. The question is, how did he know?[722]

The FBI was sufficiently concerned about a possible relationship between Nagell and Marina that they questioned her about it shortly after the assassination. An FBI report kept secret until the Secret Service released it in the mid-1970s said that an interview took place on January 18, 1964: "10:00 A.M.-SA Jamison arrived and interviewed Mrs. Marina Oswald re Richard Case Nagell.12:00 noon-SA Jamison departed."[723] It is unlikely the FBI would have spent two hours talking to Marina about Nagell if she did not have something of substance to offer. And why keep it hidden from the public if it was just routine?

225

Nagell claimed he investigated a Cuban exile group that was plotting to assassinate JFK. They were considering Oswald, but the group had not yet brought him into the assassination plot, which was why Nagell was also looking into him. So, at the time that Oswald moved to Dallas and received right-wing indoctrination from George de Mohrenschildt and may have become involved with the Minutemen, Ruth Paine offered Marina the opportunity to move in with her, and Oswald switched addresses to make it harder for the FBI to locate them. Meanwhile, a Cuban exile group contemplated bringing Oswald into a plot to assassinate JFK.

Nagell admitted using the alias Hidell while working for American intelligence in Japan. It was the same name used to order Oswald's revolver and pistol, which happened when Nagell appeared on the scene. Oswald's Post Office box had two people authorized to pick up mail in addition to himself – A.J. Hidell and Marina. If it was Oswald, he used an alias to obscure his identity when he ordered the weapons, but he linked the alias to himself by listing the name Hidell on his Post Office box application. It does not make sense and adds to the possibility that Hidell was another person, most likely Richard Case Nagell. And why would Oswald write the name Hidell in his address book if it was a name he was using? Was he afraid he was going to forget his alias? Likely not. The logical answer is that Nagell was Hidell.[724]

***

On March 31, around when Nagell was investigating the Oswalds, Marina photographed Lee in the backyard of their home. He was dressed entirely in black, and his revolver was in its holster on his hip. The rifle, later identified as the assassination weapon, was held in his right hand. In his left hand, he grasped two newspapers – the Communist Party U.S.A.'s *The Worker* and the Socialist Workers Party's *The Militant*. *The Worker* contained an article accusing General Walker of trying to become an American Fuhrer. The photos were arguably the most damning evidence against Oswald after the assassination. Since then, they have come under intense scrutiny.

The photos were discovered by the Dallas police among Oswald's possessions in Ruth Paine's garage the day after the assassination. Marina initially claimed to have taken one photo but revised her testimony before the Warren Commission in June 1964. "I had even forgotten that I had taken two photographs," she testified. Marina used Oswald's hand-held Imperial Reflex camera, handing it back to him between shots so he could advance the film. One would think she would have remembered taking more than one photo if she had to hand the camera to Oswald between shots.[725]

Marina's testimony received additional scrutiny in 1976 when a Senate Intelligence Committee discovered a third unpublished photo in the possession of the widow of former Dallas policeman Roscoe White. During their attempt to recreate the backyard photos to prove they were authentic, a Dallas policeman adopted a pose of Oswald for comparison purposes. The pose was identical to Oswald's, as shown in the missing photo held by Roscoe White. There can be no confusion, for it was completely different from the two submitted to the Warren Commission.[726]

White was also a Marine, and in 1957, he and Oswald took the USS *Bexar* to Japan and served there at the same time. In November, they were both at Subic Bay in the Philippines and were later involved in a secret invasion off the coast of Indonesia. Oswald left the Marines in 1959, and in the fall of 1962, he moved to Dallas. White obtained a hardship discharge from the Marines and moved to Dallas as well.

Assassination witness Beverly Oliver knew Roscoe White. He was married to her friend Geneva, who worked for Jack Ruby as a hostess at the Carousel Club, and Roscoe would pick her up after work. She claimed she saw Roscoe on the grassy knoll immediately after the shooting. "He was wearing part of his policeman's uniform but not all of it," she reported. "He was wearing his shirt, his badge, his trousers, but he was not wearing a hat, nor was he carrying a gun."

Roscoe White died in 1971 at the age of thirty-six from burns suffered during an explosion. His son claims his father's military footlocker contained a handwritten diary in which he admitted shooting JFK and some never-before-seen photos of Oswald. Later the diary was missing.[727]

Much of Roscoe White's story is circumstantial and cannot be substantiated. However, he did have a third Oswald backyard photo in his possession; his Marine career mirrored Oswald's; his wife worked for Jack Ruby; and he joined the Dallas police force around the time of the assassination. Maybe it was all coincidence, but considering how many Dallas police officers were members of the KKK and other right-wing groups, like the Minutemen, maybe it is not so farfetched to think Roscoe White had a connection with Oswald and was one of the shooters.

Attempting to determine if the backyard photos are authentic is beyond the scope of this book. There are many sources available for readers to investigate this angle further. Still, there are a few points worth mentioning.

The importance of the third Roscoe White photo was that Marina never alluded to it, which makes one wonder if she took any pictures at all. The police sequestered Marina after the assassination. At the request of Dallas oilman/military intelligence officer Jack Crichton, an anti-Communist White Russian émigré who worked for the Sun Oil Company named Ilya Mamantov acted as her translator. Because there is no record of what they said to each other, it is possible that what Marina said in Russian was not translated correctly. Did Mamantov say Marina said she took the backyard photos, but maybe she never did? If that were true, it means someone other than Marina photographed Oswald and helped portray him as a revolutionary.[728]

FBI agent James W. Bookhout's report after the assassination said: "Oswald stated that he would not discuss the photograph without [the] advice of an attorney. He stated that the head of the individual in the photograph could be his but that it was entirely possible that the Police Department had superimposed this part of the photograph over the body of someone else."[729]

Captain Fritz had a similar recollection. He testified that Oswald said: "That is not a picture of me: it is my face, but my face has been superimposed – the rest of the picture is not me at all, I've never seen it before... That small picture is a reduction of the large picture that someone I don't know has made... someone took a picture of my face and faked that photograph."[730]

Why would Oswald claim the photo shown to him was a forgery if that were not so? He had photographic experience and knew that experts could easily prove or disprove that the pictures were genuine or doctored. To understand their importance, one must place the photos in their proper context. There was the opportune arrival of Nagell in the lives of the Oswalds and the purchase of the rifle and pistol. There was an attempt to have Marina leave the country. There was Oswald's likely association with the Minutemen, the Volkmar Schmidt incident, Oswald's involvement with George de Mohrenschildt, and Ruth Paine's attempt to separate Marina from Lee. There were address changes to stay ahead of the FBI, and it was also around the end of March that Oswald put down on paper his revolutionary philosophy that mirrored the radical right. At the same time, it appears he associated with the Minutemen, who claimed they needed a catalyst to jump-start their revolution.

Meanwhile, Oswald was involved in something in the spring of 1963 that required him to look like a Communist revolutionary. He was holding the *Worker* and *The Militant* in the photos, and Oswald received "revolutionary direction" from *The Militant*, as he told Michael Paine. However, the *Communist Party USA* issued *The Worker*, and Oswald was not a Communist.

He wrote: "The Communist Party of the United States…has turned itself into the traditional lever of a foreign power to overthrow the Government of the United States…in anticipation of Soviet Russia's complete domination of the American continent…"[731] Whatever operation Oswald was involved in, it appears he was to play the role of Communist patsy who would take the fall for something big. It was a test run for the JFK assassination.

***

In early April, although he worked a great deal of overtime in the preceding weeks, Oswald was fired from Jaggars-Chiles-Stovall. On an October 1963 job application for a different company, there is a handwritten notation: "Bob Stovall [of Jaggars] does not recommend this man. He was released because of his record as a troublemaker – Has communistic tendencies."[732]

Oswald had worked at JCS for six months without offending anyone. Perhaps the FBI had inquired about him, or Oswald created an incident to ensure he lost his job. Either way, his last day at Jaggars-Chiles-Stovall was April 6. After that, he was free to come and go as he pleased. He had only about seven-and-one-half months left to live.

Chapter Thirteen

A Shot in the Dark

Anger permeated throughout the South during the short presidency of John F. Kennedy, and nowhere was it more pronounced than in the city of Dallas. He was a northeast Catholic liberal elite born with a silver spoon in his mouth and no regard for the Southern segregated way of life most Texans wanted to preserve. Texas oilmen, titans of industry, retired and current military officers, political leaders, law enforcement members, paramilitary groups, and others all shared a desire to stop the rising tide of northern intervention. Their discontent mainly had to do with race and the perceived rise of domestic communism, which they considered to be interconnected. Hidden from view was their involvement in abhorrent organizations that secretly bound them together – the KKK, the Minutemen, the John Birch Society, the White Citizens' Council, the Dixie Klan, and other similar anti-Communist, race hate groups.

The John Birch Society regularly called for the impeachment of Supreme Court Chief Justice Earl Warren, claiming he "voted 92 percent of the time in favor of Communists and subversives." Their mailings spewed hatred: "The DESEGREGATION DECISION…aids and abets the plans of the Communist Conspiracy to (A): create tension between Negroes and Whites; (B): to transform the South into a BLACK SOVIET REPUBLIC; (C): to legalize and encourage intermarriage between Negroes and Whites and thus mongrelize the American White Race!"[733]

On February 17, 1963, a J. Edgar Hoover essay appeared in the *Sunday Visitor,* decrying the rise of materialism over spirituality and morality. By then, he had spent the better part of two years concentrating on the multiple affairs of President Kennedy, some having a Mafia connection, and Hoover was probably thinking of JFK and Bobby when he put pen to paper. Hoover wrote.

> Today, subtle forces seek to…substitute adulation of the material for worship of the spiritual…They know that the human creature who is without…moral scruples…can, with great ease be led into the arid desert of communism… [which] outlaws morality…Absolute principles of right and wrong are thrown into the discard…Our Nation

[now] faced an enemy which sought to attack it by secularizing its citizens in order to stultify their will to stand against encroaching communism.... *It is visible in instance after instance of the sellout of honor and integrity to a vicious, totalitarian enemy.* Today... religion and morality are the stoutest weapons against the enemy.[734] [Author's italics]

Hoover's speech was similar to what he had told the American Legion in Las Vegas on October 9 the previous year, two months after the death of Marilyn Monroe. "Self-indulgence – the principle of pleasure before duty – is practiced across the length and breadth of the land....There is a quest for status at the expense of morality.... There is a pattern of flight from responsibility... A soft approach toward the menace of communism can lead only to national disaster. Our Nation's efforts to deal effectively with this menace are not enhanced by those... of the extreme left who endeavor to minimize the real danger of communism...."[735]

The Kennedy brothers were two who minimized the danger of communism. Bobby told an NBC radio program on September 2, 1962: "The Communist Party, I don't believe, has any political following in the United States.... It's...a disservice to say that there is a Communist under every bush or behind every tree. Or when the State Department or the Government does something with which you disagree to indicate it must be run by a bunch of Communists." The year before, he said the CPUSA's "membership consists largely of FBI agents."[736] There was some truth to that. Hoover had instituted a massive infiltration of subversive groups so the FBI could take credit for marginalizing Communist organizations that posed no threat at all. At least, that is what the Attorney General believed. Not everyone agreed with him.

There was Dr. Fred C. Schwarz, the head of the Christian Anti-Communist Crusade, who said when Communists "deny the foundation of civilization, our Christian heritage; when they deny God... they destroy the very foundations on which our individual value is built...A few years back, the American Communist party would openly acknowledge that having conquered this land, they would need to put to death one-third of the American people...it is the fulfillment of Marxism-Leninism...."[737]

There were the Minutemen, who anxiously awaited the coming of the final Armageddon against the Communists: "The UN is one of their ways... the UN would declare an act of overt aggression and would come in and occupy us. They'd do away with our Constitution and put in new laws... Kennedy has more power than any other President has ever had. If he wants to do anything, he just issues an executive order. Even if it's against the will of the people."[738]

Reverend Billy James Hargis founded the Christian Crusade. He believed "our greatest threat is not internal communism... the greatest threat to freedom... is the powerfully entrenched Liberal Establishment [which] is a sinister brotherhood that reaches into the fields of education, politics, religion, labor, and management...to abolish the free enterprise system and bring about a world government of socialist nations...the Liberal Establishment works feverishly to enslave us all."[739]

Hargis added the *Foreign Intelligence Digest* as a supplement to his *Weekly Crusader Newsletter* in the latter part of 1961, with a plan to bring all right-wing groups together under one umbrella. "My goal is of a coalition of effort...There are more than 2,000 right-wing organizations...Well, too often, they've gone off in 2,000 different directions...My plan calls for getting the leaders of the major conservative groups to meet quarterly in Washington with conservative congressmen. There, they can formulate a united plan of action on how to rally support for conservative legislation and candidates."[740]

On March 21, 1962, Hargis's dream came true with the formation of the Anti-Communist Liaison, which brought together one hundred delegates from seventy-five right-wing groups in Washington D.C. A leading figure was retired Brigadier General Bonner Fellers, a member of MacArthur's staff in World War II and his military secretary during the first year of Japanese occupation. Another was Colonel William P. Gale, who served under MacArthur as an organizer of American guerrilla forces in the Philippines. He served over three years in Japan with the American Caesar. After that, Gale organized a paramilitary unit named the Rangers, whose goal was to "build an underground network for the conduct of guerrilla warfare....Under Col. Gale's leadership, some of the recruitment effort has been directed toward former military servicemen to serve as an organizational nucleus."[741]

This guerrilla force, made up of former military men, looked to organize a revolutionary movement based on MacArthur's belief that the military owed its allegiance to the Constitution and the American people. They believed John Kennedy's government was unprepared to meet the challenges of the modern era, so their duty was to create a civilian guerilla force to combat that. It was the first sign that the military and the radical right civilian populace were willing to come together for a common cause, which was to keep America free from communism and remove the President by whatever means necessary. One of those involved was Texas billionaire H.L. Hunt, the number one financier of right-wing causes in the early 1960s. Hunt's *Life Line* radio broadcast, which filled the airwaves with anti-Communist rhetoric, cost him $2,000,000 annually. He directed much of his frustration at the Kennedy brothers, for whom he had nothing but contempt, and he threatened to shoot "those traitors out of government."[742]

***

On January 15, 1963, FBI informant William Somersett, who was close to various radical right-wing groups, reported that the Council for State-hood met in Florida to plan the mass assassination of a large number of individuals. Ex-military officers General Pedro del Valle, Major Archibald Roberts, Generals Clyde Watts, and General Edwin Walker were in attendance. They were part of the military underground that intended to take over the U.S. government by establishing zones throughout the United States where they would carry out assassinations. According to Miami FBI documents, "The Dixie Klan ... an offshoot of the hardcore membership of the KKK, John Birch Society, White Citizens' Council, and other groups is pushing hard for assassinations."[743]

Del Valle had also served under MacArthur. He was involved with the John Birch Society, Citizens' Council, National States' Rights Party, Congress of Freedom, and the American Nazi Party. He had previously written to JBS leader Robert Welch that, "The time has come for action. Treason sits enthroned in the seats of Power, and treason will soon land us in the Red One Worlder's Paradise unless we take steps to prevent it ...." He urged for the creation of an armed resistance force. On another occasion, del Valle wrote the National States' Rights Party: "When a free people find their elected servants following a destructive course of action regarding the Constitution, the people must take effective action to restore same by taking the matter into their own hands and forcing the traitors out of power."[744]

On March 12, 1963, del Valle wrote to Mary Davidson, the founder of the Council for Statehood, telling her that for years, he had lobbied Congress to impeach federal officials who had violated their oaths of office. He conceded the legal approach was too slow and the "enemy" was moving too fast, writing: "Perhaps your approach may produce the needed action, and as far as I am able, I will lend a hand." It was a reference to the discussions about assassination held in January, and he concluded the letter as follows: "State sovereignty can only be rescued by the states themselves. If the state governments are also in the grip of the terror induced by the Invisible Government, then there is nothing left but violence and bloodshed. And that, of course, will be our lot whether we resist or whether we surrender without a fight. The advantage of the former lies in the satisfaction men feel when they know they are on the side of Christ against the anti-Christ which is, whatever his disguise, our ever-present enemy."[745]

There was also similar correspondence between del Valle, Walker, and four former generals who had served under MacArthur in World War II – Willoughby, Stratemeyer, Wedemeyer, and Fellers. Meanwhile, on January 21 and 22, the FBI noted that Walker met with American mercenary and Cuban exile supporter Gerry Patrick Hemming. On February 3, Hemming wrote, "Spent some time with General Edwin Walker...[It] appears he plans to involve his element in the Cuban fight. Contacted money people in Dallas to finance lectures and travel for the leaders of the raider groups, i.e., Alpha 66, D.R.E., Cardenas Raiders, and Major Vidalis Raiders." By this time, Alpha 66 was working with the military, and the DRE had gone rogue. Hemming also stated his group was financing DRE lectures in Denver, and they hoped to take their anti-Castro message to Texas and California. It was around the time Richard Case Nagell was investigating anti-Castro Cuban groups and learned there were preliminary talks about assassinating President Kennedy, which would eventually lead him to Oswald's doorstep. It makes one believe Oswald was already involved with these people in the early months of 1963.[746]

Authorities were aware that the anti-Communist far-right had taken a more violent turn. During April 4-6, 1963, the anti-Semitic and racist Congress of Freedom, formed in 1952, held its annual convention in New Orleans. Detective Lochart F. Gracey, Jr., who had informant William Somersett placed inside the convention, reported they discussed "the overthrow of the present government of the United States" and that the plan included the establishment "of criminal activity to assassinate particular persons...." In addition, "high-ranking members of the Armed Forces... secretly belonged to the organization."[747]

According to Somersett, "As sure as we are sitting here...there will be some people killed this time next year, and it will be in high places.... Whenever the high command gives the orders to kill people, that's when it's going to happen." He continued, "This is supposed to be headed and directed by military men from the top," and he mentioned that General del Valle was heavily involved.[748]

One recipient of Gracey's report was Charles Sapp of the Miami Police Intelligence Unit, who was already aware that the right-wing and Cuban exiles had grown impatient with the President. In April, Sapp advised his superiors: "Since President Kennedy made the news releases that the US government would stop all raiding parties going against the Castro government, the Cuban people feel that the US government has turned against them... Violence hitherto directed toward Castro's Cuba will now be directed toward various governmental agencies in the US."[749]

As described in *General Walker and the Murder of President Kennedy*, author Jeffrey H. Caufield discovered a document in the FBI files on Mary Davidson's Council for Statehood that stated Guy Banister also attended the Congress of Freedom convention. As did the ultra-right racist Joseph Milteer, who in October 1963 would be taped saying they would kill Kennedy from a tall building with a high-powered rifle. Milteer tape-recorded the Congress of Freedom festivities, which included Banister standing and taking a bow, an indication of how highly the attendees of this anti-Communist, racist gathering thought of him. Oswald would leave Dallas for New Orleans in April 1963, where he would work out of Banister's office. Oswald was already involved with radical right-wing groups in Dallas, which was how the future accused assassin of JFK showed up at Banister's doorstep.[750]

In April and June, George Harding, Jr., a member of a group led by Colonel Gale and Dr. Wesley A. Swift, told the FBI they planned to assassinate three hundred high-level public officials in government and industry. The group would assign eight men to each of those targeted for assassination, and the killings were all to be carried out at the same time. Swift was a minister from southern California known for his white supremacist views. He was connected to the Ku Klux Klan and militant Christian groups in The International Underground, which received much of its funding from Reverend Billy James Hargis. Joseph Milteer was also part of the underground, and after the JFK assassination, he wrote: "Notice to all Christians. The Zionist Jews killed Christ 2,000 years ago, and on November 22, 1963, they killed President Kennedy. You Jews killed the president. We're going to kill you. – The International Underground."[751]

In January 1964, the FBI learned that Colonel Gale was the founder of the Army of the American Kingdom of Evangelists, or AWAKE, which included an "Inner Den" made up of the most militant and violent members of his Christian Knights of the Invisible Empire. Gale's group aligned itself with General del Valle's Defenders of the American Constitution, Inc. Gale was also close to General Walker's former aide-de-camp, retired Major Archibald Roberts, who had served with Walker in Germany. Roberts was the military liaison to Mary Davidson's Council for Statehood that was planning assassinations, as described above. The Miami FBI learned

235

that Roberts was at the January 15 meeting of the Council for Statehood and was "the person that set up the military underground for this national organization. ROBERTS is reportedly a close friend of General EDWIN WALKER."[752]

These men, all disciples of General MacArthur, were serious about forcibly changing the government and, in true MacArthur fashion, believed they were constitutionally justified in doing so. And no one felt stronger about this than General del Valle. On July 2, he wrote to Wickliffe "Wick" Vernard, a leader of the Constitution Party, stating he had been in touch with a worldwide Christian movement headquartered in Madrid, Spain, "whose objectives are in accord with yours," which meant they favored assassinating the traitors who ran the government. As we have already discussed, there was a right-wing group operating out of Madrid that included Victor Oswald, Thomas Proctor, ex-Nazis like Otto Skorzeny, Charles Willoughby, Jack Crichton, William Pawley, and others. They aligned themselves with Texas oilmen, leaders of industry, and right-wing groups in Dallas, and this undoubtedly was the same group del Valle was instructing Vernard to contact. No wonder they referred to themselves as an International Underground that intended to wage worldwide war against communism.[753]

On June 10, the FBI interviewed Gerald L. Beasley, Jr., M.D., a member of the John Birch Society from Duncan, Oklahoma, regarding a salesman for a Houston pharmaceutical company named Charles Elkins. Elkins's job was to make contacts in the area on behalf of the Minuteman to find dependable recruits. They obtain weapons through the military, including rifles, grenades, and explosives. Elkins said the local groups were actually "assassination squads," confirming what the FBI had learned from other sources.[754]

Things were on the move. The radical right was contemplating a violent government takeover, and retired members of the U.S. military were at the center of it all. After the JFK assassination, the FBI sent documents related to Gale's plot to the Warren Commission, which chose to ignore it. Unearthing the truth was never their objective.

***

By the spring of 1963, General Walker had become a symbol of the anti-Communist, radical right-wing movement. Still, there was a divide among insiders as to how vital the embattled military leader was to their cause. In 1962, despite pleas from far-right radicals not to bring unnecessary exposure to the grassroots movement they were trying to create, Walker ran for governor. It was a disaster. When he spoke in Dallas before the Daughters of the American Revolution in January 1962, those in attendance were shocked by his performance. As reported by Bill Minutaglio and Steven L. Davis in *Dallas 1963*, "he is trembling, quivering, clearly on the verge of tears. Through misty eyes, he looks down at his prepared speech and then at the audience."[755]

H.L. Hunt endorsed Walker and financed his campaign, but he began to question his decision. Some voters were offended when they received violently anti-Jewish and anti-African American literature in the mail. They were unaware that Walker's business partner, Robert Surrey, was also secretly active within the upper echelon of the American Nazi Party. Then, in April, a large crowd filled the Caucus Room of the Old Senate Office Building in Washington to listen to Walker speak before a Senate Committee investigating charges that the Kennedy administration was trying to silence high-ranking military officers like him. "I am a Christian martyr, personally victimized by the international Communist conspiracy," Walker said, and "The Kennedy administration is filled with communists."[756]

He sounded deranged, and the hearings turned into a circus. When Walker admitted he had not read any of the books he said were Communist-inspired, William F. Buckley Jr., editor of the *National Review*, said he should be "consigned to history's ashcan." Ted Dealey, the right-wing publisher of the *Dallas Morning News*, was shocked. His paper had promoted Walker, and now he conceded he had to go.[757]

Meanwhile, the Minutemen locked horns with the John Birch Society in the spring of 1963. According to JBS leader Robert Welch, Minutemen leader Robert DePugh "had made the most continuous and determined effort to bring about [the] extensive collaboration of the Minutemen with the John Birch Society." However, it soon became apparent that the JBS was much too passive to satisfy them. As DePugh described it, "They [the JBS] don't have the courage to stick their necks out too far."[758]

The Minutemen, who operated in the shadows and remained anonymous, also believed Walker had become a liability with his flamboyant public style. It is not out of the question that they hatched a plan to use a "Communist" assassin to shoot Walker and instigate a riot among extremist groups anxious for revenge. Such logic was consistent with Minutemen philosophy.

Charles Willoughby was active in right-wing circles in Dallas at the time. Walker met with him during his 1963 travels with Hargis but claimed he did not know him well, which suited Willoughby just fine. Willoughby was an intelligence professional, and his International Committee for the Defense of Christian Culture preferred to conduct business quietly. He was more suited to align himself with the previously mentioned Nazi group operating out of Madrid involving Otto Skorzeny than the likes of General Edwin Walker.[759]

***

On February 14, 1963, Walker announced he was joining right-wing evangelist Billy James Hargis on a cross-country speaking tour to alert the nation to the dangers of communism. "Operation Midnight Ride" was to begin in Miami on February 27 and finish in Los Angeles on April 3. Walker was attempting to remain relevant.[760]

Around the same time, on March 11, a reader named L.H., believed to be Oswald, sent a long letter to *The Militant* under the heading NEWS AND VIEWS FROM DALLAS. The letter described Dallas as a city where poor renters live at the mercy of exploitative landlords, and he congratulated the paper as "the most informative radical publication in America." It was a sign that Oswald still stayed true to his Marxist beliefs while being indoctrinated with right-wing Nazi propaganda by the likes of Volkmar Schmidt and George de Mohrenschildt. Oswald was about to become part of an attempt on General Walker's life, whom *The Militant* called an American Fuhrer. He then started a campaign to make it appear he was a supporter of Castro.[761]

In the middle of all this militant behavior, Oswald ordered his pistol on January 28 and his rifle on March 12. At the beginning of April, just days prior to when someone fired a shot at Walker in his home, Oswald drafted a letter to his wife, whose attempt to return to Russia was unsuccessful. He left her detailed instructions in anticipation of a separation he expected to occur shortly. It was written in Russian and found among Oswald's possessions after the assassination. The letter read as follows:

> 1. Here is the key to the post office box which is located in the main post office downtown on Ervay Street, the street where there is a drugstore where you always used to stand. The post office is four blocks from the drugstore on the same street. There you will find our mailbox. I paid for the mailbox last month so you needn't worry about it.

> 2. Send information about what has happened to me to the Embassy and also send newspaper clippings (if there's anything about me in the papers). I think the Embassy will come quickly to your aid once they know everything.

> 3. I paid our rent on the 2nd so don't worry about it.

4. I have also paid for water and gas.

5. There may be some money from work. They will send it to our post office box. Go to the bank and they will cash it.

6. You can either throw out my clothing or give it away. Do not keep it. As for my personal papers (both military papers and papers from the factory), I prefer that you keep them.

7. Certain of my papers are in the small blue valise.

8. My address book is on the table in my study if you need it.

9. We have friends here and the Red Cross also will help you.

10. I left you as much as I could, $60 on the second of the month, and you and Junie can live for 2 months on $10 a week.

11. If I am alive and taken prisoner, the city jail is at the end of the bridge we always used to cross when we went to town (the beginning of town after the bridge)."[762]

Supporters of the Warren Commission considered this proof that Oswald tried to kill Walker by himself. However, the tone suggests he was part of a larger plot. As critic Sylvia Meagher wrote, Oswald was involved in a "project other than the attack on General Walker – one that involved risk of arrest or death...."[763] It seems Walker's death was supposed to be a catalyst for something bigger, such as a right-wing retaliatory riot that would ensue after Walker was dead, with the Communist Oswald blamed as the assassin. It makes sense since Oswald and the right-wing Fascists he collaborated with all wanted to instigate a hostile event to trigger a revolution, albeit perhaps for different reasons.

The letter provides insight into what was happening in Oswald's life in April 1963. As an example, he allegedly was a horrible husband who drank excessively and beat his wife. Yet, items 1, 3, 4, 5, and 10 sound like a concerned spouse who cared for Marina.

Item 1: Oswald gave Marina the key to his post office box. It was a sign he did not expect to return.

Item 2: Oswald assumed that what he was involved in would be covered in newspapers, so he told Marina to send clippings about him to the Soviet Embassy in Washington D.C. Now, if Oswald were a lone gunman who shot at Walker, we must assume he expected to get away, so the newspapers would be unaware of what he had done, meaning there would not have been any clippings to give to the Embassy. So, whatever Oswald was up to, it involved multiple people and was a more extensive operation than just shooting at Walker. Still, he was unsure if he would be worthy of mention in the paper, even if he were apprehended. Oswald also wrote that the Russian Embassy in Washington would rush to help her. Considering that Oswald had earlier forced Marina to write to the Embassy saying she wanted to return to Russia, the help he referred to was likely in regard to this. The reason Oswald wanted her out of the country beforehand was so he could focus on his revolutionary pursuits without Marina being in harm's way.

Item 6: Oswald began by telling Marina to get rid of his clothing, another indication he would never return, but why did he tell her to keep his military and personal papers? He supposedly despised the U.S. military, had defected to Russia, promised to provide military secrets to them, and complained about his dishonorable discharge. The only plausible explanation was that his military papers contained information related to his defection that would have proved he was involved in an intelligence mission. He wanted authorities to know about that, or maybe it would have been helpful in his defense were he apprehended and forced to stand trial.

Item 7: It may provide a clue to Item 6. Lee specifically told Marina that some of his papers were in a blue valise, separate from the others. Remember that Marina did not speak English well and did not know what these papers contained, yet Lee went out of his way to point them out to her. He attached importance to these papers because they were in a location Marina was unaware of. It confirmed that what we surmised under Item 6 was correct – there was something important about his military papers that Marina needed to protect.

Item 8: Oswald referred Marina to his address book. Why? The book contained the names and addresses of American neo-Nazis and right-wingers who allegedly would be angry if Oswald killed Walker. Still, his next thought immediately after that, listed in Item 9, is to tell her they had friends in Dallas who could help her if needed, whose contact information she could only find in his address book. It further indicates that Oswald was part of a group and was not acting alone. Oswald's message to Marina was she could rely on his right-wing friends if she needed help.

Item 11: This is the most telling of all. If the police apprehended Oswald for killing Walker, the logical thing for him to have said was, "If I am arrested." Not, "If I am alive and taken prisoner." No one who had committed a crime on his own, even murder, would have written it that way. It sounded more like a spy going behind enemy lines on a secret mission than a sniper attack by a lone gunman. That is unless you were involved in a paramilitary operation designed to instigate a right-wing revolution. Then, "If I am alive and taken prisoner" made perfect sense.[764]

FBI agent James Hosty investigated right-wing extremist groups in Dallas, and it was also his responsibility to keep tabs on Oswald throughout 1963, which confirmed where the FBI believed Oswald's true allegiance lay. According to what Hosty wrote in *Assignment Oswald*, the Minutemen were suspects in the shooting attempt on Walker right from the beginning.

"The police had no suspect in the Walker case... [they] asked me if I had any ideas on possible suspects. I had an informant who was a member of Walker's Minutemen who told me that the Minutemen were upset with Walker... Through Walker's blunders there, he had caused himself and one of his aides to be arrested [at the University of Mississippi]. When arrested, the aide had in his possession confidential documents revealing the strength of the Minutemen. My informant told me that because of all this, there was now talk among the Minutemen of replacing Walker as their leader. After I relayed all this information to the police, the police concentrated on Walker's own followers as suspects."[765]

Consider the following newspaper interview of Minutemen leader Robert DePugh in April 1963, when the attempt on General Walker's life took place. "The thing that is really a little terrifying about it," DePugh said, "is that we could very easily be sitting on the edge of a bloodbath in this country. If something happened to spark this thing off ... [If] I was killed by a Communist, our organization would take immediate reprisal against the other side, and in turn, they would take reprisal against the ones of us that they know, and it could spread like wildfire to the point where it would just be mass murder on both sides. That could happen- it could happen very easily...."[766]

The killing of Walker was to initiate a right-wing retaliation, which would have led to the revolution the Minutemen and Oswald desperately longed for. They needed a Communist to blame the shooting on, which explains Oswald's involvement. The man who subscribed to Marxist and other left-wing literature and posed for backyard photos holding *The Militant* and *The Worker* was a willing participant. Based on his writings, initiating a right-wing revolution was something Oswald would have eagerly embraced.

***

Walker protégé Robert Surrey was fascinated by the racial purity espoused by the American Nazi Party and studied the beliefs of their founder George Lincoln Rockwell. Surrey had a secret name inside the Nazi Party – Max Amman, in honor of one of Hitler's favorite publishers and allies.

Surrey and Walker were co-owners of American Eagle Publishing, the company that releases Walker's books and pamphlets, which was why Surrey chose that alias.[767]

General Pedro del Valle corresponded with Rockwell in 1963, which should not come as a surprise.[768] And we know Oswald's notebook contained the location of Nazi headquarters and the notations, "Nat. Sec. Dan Burros" and "Lincoln Rockwell, Arlington, Virginia. American Nazi Party." Rockwell was publicly known as George Lincoln Rockwell, but his friends knew him as Lincoln Rockwell. Oswald's entry of Lincoln Rockwell suggests a familiarity with him only his close friends had, which means a connection between Surrey and Oswald, considering their mutual involvement with neo-Nazis, was possible.[769]

Hosty reportedly played cards regularly with Robert Surrey, and Robert DePugh of the Minutemen told author Michael Caufield that Rockwell was "a 100% FBI informant."[770] After the assassination, Rockwell advised the FBI on March 7, 1964, that he was aware that ex-military officers Crommelin, Gale, and del Valle planned to overthrow the government. Just five days after the assassination, Rockwell wrote a letter on American Nazi Party stationery to J. Edgar Hoover that stated, "We believe in the Constitution and government by law. We also believe that these things are under deadly attack by world Communism … Inevitably, however, such an extreme political movement [such as the American Nazi Party] attracts irresponsible and lunatic elements, who are not welcome, but who force themselves upon the movement and are very hard to get rid of. The assassination of the president was, I believe, the work of such a 'nut' over on the other side from us … Such bloody and violent events tend to generate further violence and bloodshed by deranged and violent people. For this reason, I have made a list of persons […] whom I believe might conceivably be involved in further incidents …"[771]

Rockwell then provided Hoover with twenty-seven names of his stormtroopers he felt were capable of such violence. Was his letter an admission that Oswald was one of his men? During a press interview, Rockwell said, "The president brought it on himself, the way he has been pillorying the white race. The people of the South hated that man with a passion, and I don't blame them." When the FBI asked Rockwell why his name appeared in Oswald's address book, he said he had no idea, but he added: "I believe Kennedy was shot by a right-winger… American Nazis are going to have a hard time for a while. I wouldn't be a bit surprised to be picked up on it."[772]

***

On April 8, Robert Surrey "saw two men around the house [Walker's] peeking in windows." He identified their car as a dark-colored new Ford sedan without license plates. He followed the vehicle as it drove away, but when it doubled back, he thought he was spotted, and he abandoned his pursuit. The next day, he told Walker about the incident, who notified the Dallas police.[773]

Around the same time, Walker's aide, Max Claunch, noticed another mysterious car driving around the general's home. It was a 1957 Chevy, driven by a dark-complected man.[774]

On the night of April 10, a shot was fired at Walker at approximately 9:30 P.M. and barely missed him while he sat at his desk. According to the *New York Times* account of the incident: "The police said that a slight movement by Mr. Walker...presumably saved his life...The bullet, from a 30.06 rifle, was fired from an alley behind the Walker home...."[775]

A fourteen-year-old boy named Walter Coleman was standing in the doorway of a nearby home when he heard the shot. Peering over a fence, he saw three men. He then saw two of them speed away down an alley in a white or beige older-model Ford. (Dick Russell pointed out in *The Man Who Knew Too Much* that Richard Case Nagell drove a 1957 yellow and cream-colored Ford Fairlane). Coleman stated a man in the Ford looked back at him. Floodlights from a nearby church kept the area well-lit. He described the man as white, nineteen or twenty years old, about 5'-10" tall, and weighing about 130 pounds. He had dark, bushy hair and a thin face with a large nose and was "real skinny."

Coleman also noticed a 1958 black and white Chevrolet, likely the same car Max Claunch had seen days before. The car was in the church parking lot adjacent to Walker's home. A third suspect was bent over the back seat, placing something onto the floor of the car. Coleman described him as a white male, about 6'-1" and 200 pounds. After the assassination, Coleman said none of the three men he saw resembled Oswald.[776]

Police found photos of the rear of Walker's house among Oswald's possessions after the assassination. One depicted a 1957 Chevrolet parked outside Walker's home, possibly the same one Coleman had seen. The photo, included among the exhibits of the Warren Commission, had a hole where the license plate should have been, making it impossible to trace the vehicle. The Dallas policemen who discovered the photo said the hole was there when they found it and "surmised that Oswald had evidently taken the license plate number out of the photograph to keep anyone from identifying the owner of the automobile." It was strange, for why would Oswald want to

243

protect someone whom Walker associated with? However, Marina said the license plate number was visible in the photo when the FBI showed it to her after the assassination. For once, she was telling the truth.

In 1969, Dallas police chief Jesse Curry wrote a book about his experiences on the day of the JFK assassination. Among the photos included in the book was the one with the car and the missing license plate. However, his photo was an unmutilated copy with the license plate intact. Unfortunately, it was impossible to read the number, but this did not diminish the significance of the discovery. Obviously, someone within the Dallas police department tampered with the evidence and removed the license number to protect the owner of the vehicle.

The Dallas police sought a 1957 Chevy on the day of the assassination. According to a police transcript, with Oswald already in custody, the car was last seen near the murder of Officer Tippit. A trace of the license plate number showed that a Dallas man owned the car, but he claimed he had sold the vehicle prior to the assassination. The implication was that the Chevy the police were looking for had stolen plates.[777]

It is compelling to consider that the 1957 Chevy sought by police on the day of the assassination and the one seen driving around Walker's home were the same car. Interestingly, there was someone frequently seen in Walker's company who drove such a car: a Cuban exile named Filipe Vidal Santiago, who was a member of Alpha 66. By this time, Alpha 66 was working with the military, not the CIA.[778]

The evidence that Oswald was the shooter is shoddy at best. There was the 30.06 bullet reportedly found, which became a smaller 6.5 mm after the arrest of Oswald, to match his rifle. Even Walker, after he had seen the bullet at the Assassination Committee hearings, said it was not the same one recovered from his house on the night of the shooting. That bullet, he said, was so severely damaged it was almost impossible to recognize.[779] On February 17, 1979, Walker wrote a letter to Attorney General Griffin Bell, in which he called the bullet "a ridiculous substitute." He was sure of his facts: "I saw the hunk of lead, picked up by a policeman in my house, and I took it from him, and I inspected it carefully. There is no mistake. There has been a substitution for the bullet fired by Oswald and taken out of my house."[780]

While none of the evidence completely exonerates Oswald (Oswald was probably involved in the Walker shooting), he did not act alone. According to Marina, he rushed home on the night of April 10 and claimed he had just shot at General Walker. "If someone had killed Hitler in time, many lives would have been saved," Oswald told her. It was the same rationale the CIA used to justify its most despicable deeds.[781]

As previously stated, Oswald's behavior prior to the Walker shooting indicated he was involved in something bigger than trying to kill an ex-military general whom the radical right no longer had any use for. Consider that four days later, on Easter Sunday, neo-Nazis swept through the city during the night and vandalized the homes of several prominent Jews with a custom-printed decal that was blood red with a black swastika. Under the swastika were the words: "WE ARE BACK." It was a reference to the return of the Nazis. The next night, the vandals struck again. This time, they plastered Jewish-owned businesses in downtown Dallas with swastikas. Was this connected to the Walker shooting? No one knows, but it was the type of thing a young man who warned his wife, "if I am alive and taken prisoner," might have found himself involved in.[782]

***

In October 1962, Larry Schmidt, who had served two tours of duty in West Germany, was discharged and came to Dallas straight from Munich even though he was not a native Texan. He was an ardent supporter of the radical right and had already mapped out plans while in West Germany for an organization called CUSA, *Conservatism-USA*. As *Look* magazine later described it, Schmidt "had trained a small, disciplined band of soldier-conspirators to follow him stateside and do, he hoped, 'whatever is necessary to accomplish our goal.'" That goal was to contact right-wing groups across the U.S. and to meld them into CUSA, with the grand design of taking control of American politics. Schmidt planned to gain financial support from wealthy right-wingers such as the Hunt family. On November 2, 1962, he wrote, "Arrangements are being made for me to meet the heads of the Dallas John Birch, General Walker, and H.L. Hunt...." On January 4, 1963: "I want big men ... if I have a dozen such men, I can conquer the world. I will go down in the history books as a great and noble man or a tyrant." And by February 2: "Friday night I attended a gathering of the top conservatives in Dallas. The meeting was at the home of Dr. Robert Morris, President of the Defenders of American Liberty...." (Morris was Walker's lawyer against the Kennedy administration's charges pertaining to the Mississippi "insurrection.")

Schmidt aligned his group with the Young Americans for Freedom [YAF], which had 50,000 members. One of their leading board members was Charles Willoughby, and according to a former acquaintance of Larrie

Schmidt's, Willoughby had worked with Schmidt to expose General Walker's radical right-wing activities in Germany.

Not long after Schmidt arrived in Dallas, Walker hired his brother Bob as his chauffeur, but according to *Look* magazine, Schmidt's real purpose was "to spy on him." The CUSA had infiltrated Walker's inner circle.[783] The American Nazi, Robert Surrey, was the one who brought the Schmidt brothers to Walker. Bob Schmidt joined Walker in January-February 1963, running errands in Walker's station wagon, picking up people, etc. Larrie just hung around and made a nuisance of himself.[784]

On December 29, 1977, *Dallas Morning News* reporter Earl Golz wrote to Walker: "A friend of Larry [sic] Schmidt's recently told me that Larry and his brother, who he said was then associated with you, had accompanied Oswald in the brother's car to the scene of the [Walker] shooting. What he didn't say was if they made the trip before, during, or after the Walker shooting. Larry Schmidt supposedly has protected himself since that time by placing written accounts of this story in safe deposit boxes around the country."[785]

***

Among Oswald's possessions found after the assassination was a 1962 envelope with the return address of the Fair Play for Cuba Committee in New York. Sent to Oswald's Mercedes Street address, it meant he received it in early October 1962 at the latest. From that point on, there was no known contact between Oswald and the FPCC until April 16, 1963, six days after the Walker shooting. On that day, Oswald wrote to V.T. Lee, the chairman of the FPCC in New York, stating: "I stood yesterday for the first time in my life with a placard around my neck passing out fair play for Cuba pamphlets ect [sic]...I was cursed as well as praised by some. My home-made placard said HANDS OFF CUBA! and VIVA FIDEL! I now ask for 40 to 50 more of the fine, basic pamphlets."[786]

Oswald had lost his job on April 6, and three days before he left for New Orleans, the FBI in New York intercepted Oswald's letter to the FPCC. The letter was airmailed and postmarked on April 18, and it is unlikely Oswald was capable of paying the extra postage an airmail letter required. The next day, the FPCC's New York office sent Oswald the pamphlets he requested. Oswald's correspondence soon resulted in the New York FBI reporting to Dallas what Oswald was doing. The fact that Oswald gave the FPCC his Dallas address suggests that, as late as April 16, when he sent the letter, he had not planned to leave Dallas, even though it was only eight days before he departed. So, that had to have been a spur-of-the-moment decision, most likely per the instruction of George de Mohrenschildt or the Minutemen. On the other hand, maybe it was a deception so the FBI would think he had never left Dallas.

On April 21, Dallas confidential informant "T-2" reported the letter where Oswald said he passed out FPCC literature with a placard around his neck. Two Dallas policemen later recalled a man standing on Main Street wearing a pro-Castro sign, handing out literature.

The pamphlet Oswald requested was *Crime Against Cuba* by Corliss Lamont. Perhaps not by accident, Richard Nagell also had a copy of *Crime Against Cuba* in his trunk when the police arrested him at the bank in El Paso on September 20, 1963, as well as a tiny Minolta 16-millimeter camera and a complete film-developing kit. Apparently, Lee Oswald wasn't the only one interested in photography.

Nagell later commented, "Mr. Oswald had no significant connection with the Fair Play For Cuba Committee."[787] On another occasion, Nagell said he could not agree "Oswald himself was penetrating anything. His involvement with the Fair Play For Cuba Committee in New Orleans was something entirely different. There was no chapter of the committee that he was associated with, not in reality. It was a ploy."[788]

Why did Nagell write "Oswald himself" and not just Oswald? Was an Oswald impersonator penetrating the FPCC? Was it others Oswald associated with who were doing this? It seems odd.

If Oswald's New Orleans FPCC endeavor was a charade, portraying himself as an FPCC supporter in Dallas was also. Considering how soon this came after the shooting attempt on Walker, the two events were related, as was the anti-Semitic activity previously described.

On April 13, three days after the Walker shooting, de Mohrenschildt and his wife appeared unannounced late in the evening at Oswald's front door. According to Marina, the first thing George said to Lee was, "How come you missed?" The question shocked both Lee and Marina.[789]

***

The strange relationship between Oswald and George de Mohrenschildt ended abruptly. On April 19, five days before Oswald left for New Orleans, George and his wife left Dallas for Washington, D.C. According to de Mohrenschildt, his sudden departure involved an oil contract with the government of Haiti. Whatever his role was regarding Oswald, we can assume he had completed what he had set out to do.

Oswald left Dallas for New Orleans on April 24, leaving Marina and daughter June behind to live with the always accommodating Ruth Paine.

By that time, the Marxist revolutionary was deeply involved with mercenaries from the far-right. The evidence will show he was used and manipulated by them to cast himself publicly as a supporter of Castro. Unknown to Oswald, he had already gotten in way over his head, and he was rapidly approaching the point of no return.

CHAPTER FOURTEEN

CIA AND THE PENTAGON
FLEX THEIR MUSCLES

Things remained contentious in the wake of the Cuban Missile Crisis. Kennedy said, "We have an awful lot of megatonnage to put on the Soviets sufficient to deter them from ever using nuclear weapons…You can't use them as a first weapon yourself; they are only good for deterring…if we fail to deter them and they attack us, then it's just – just destroy them…we just drop it on their cities and destroy them and ruin the Russians. I don't see quite why we're building as many as we're building."[790]

Despite what JFK said, the Pentagon still wanted enough weapons to launch a first strike against the Soviets. They estimated that through the end of 1963, with the few bombs they had, a Russian retaliation would kill ten to twenty million people in the U.S. "Now it's still not good with ten million people lost," Taylor said, "but nonetheless we don't think we should give up that possibility." McNamara agreed. "If we don't buy them [the missiles], then two claims will be made which we can't rebut…," he said. "One, that we're changing the basic military strategy of this country to exclude procurement of weapons necessary to destroy the nuclear capability of the Soviet Union…The second charge is [that] the Soviets have more megatonnage and more warheads than we do."[791]

In the end, Kennedy approved the military budget without any cuts. Still not forgotten was that two months prior, the Joint Chiefs wanted to launch an attack on Cuba during the Missile Crisis, and Kennedy turned them down.

On January 1, 1963, Army General Lyman Lemnitzer began his tenure as Supreme Allied Commander of all NATO forces in Europe. JFK had unceremoniously exiled the right-wing zealot because the general was a war hawk who disrespected the President and had proposed Operation Northwoods, so he had to go. Sending him into the heart of Europe where like-minded rabid anti-Communist Gladio armies and ex-Nazi militarists operated may not have been the wisest decision.[792]

On January 14, in his third State of the Union address, Kennedy tried to appear tough on communism. "We are not lulled by the momentary calm of the sea or the somewhat clearer skies above," he said. "We know the turbulence that lies below and the storms beyond the horizon this year..."[793] Privately, the President told his advisers that Khrushchev "was more forthcoming about Berlin than he's ever been... I completely agree that he's a liar and Castro is impossible... he's under attack from the Chinese [and] there's a major collision going on here and what result it will bring... I don't know." It sounded like a President who wanted to trust Khrushchev.[794]

The next day, Khrushchev said Berlin could not be the cause of the crisis in 1963, so he took his Berlin ultimatum off the table. With détente on the horizon, on February 8, Kennedy told his key arms control advisers the time was right to offer further concessions in test ban treaty negotiations. He admitted the Russians would try to cheat. Still, he believed the benefit far outweighed the danger if Moscow supported a comprehensive worldwide nuclear test ban, which would delay Chinese atomic missile development.[795]

There was opposition to any test ban treaty because the Soviet economy was weak. In a February 27 speech, Khrushchev blamed it on the cost of keeping up with the U.S. in the Cold War, which was the whole point of George Kennan's policy of containment. The belief was the Soviet economy would implode, which was why Eisenhower regularly increased military spending. He knew the Soviets did not have the resources to keep up. Yet, Kennedy was willing to sign a treaty even though he believed he could not trust the Soviets. It was foolhardy and politically motivated, but to those who distrusted the Soviets, it was nothing short of treason.[796]

There were sixty-seven Democrats and thirty-three Republicans in the Senate, but the thirty-three Republicans joined with twenty-two southern Democrats to create a majority who opposed Kennedy. In the House, there were 258 Democrats and 176 Republicans, with southerners controlling the most important committees.[797]

The ire of southern Democrats ratcheted up a notch on April 17, when the U.S. Civil Rights Commission recommended that JFK cut off funding to Mississippi because of their racist policies. The following day, Mississippi's State Sovereignty Commission discussed allocating funds to carry out Governor Barnett's anti-Kennedy free elector plan designed to thwart Kennedy's reelection.[798]

On June 4, the President continued to disrupt the status quo when he issued Executive Order 11,110, which took back the Federal Reserve's right to issue currency and gave the U.S. Treasury the power "to issue silver certificates against any silver bullion, silver, or standard silver dollars in the Treasury." As Fletcher Prouty wrote, "Kennedy challenged the 'government of money' by challenging the two most successful vehicles that have ever been used to drive up debt – war and the creation of money by a privately owned central bank. His efforts to have all troops out of Vietnam by 1965 and Executive Order 11,110 would have severely cut into the profits and control of the New York banking establishment."[799]

Around the same time, the Soviet military withdrew additional troops from Cuba, as they had agreed to do. Recent KGB reports portrayed Kennedy as being pressured by the military and the radical right to resume efforts to overthrow Castro, so they were concerned.[800] Meanwhile, reports from various sources suggested a "deep crisis was underway in the USSR" because of pressure from China. "I am becoming increasingly concerned," Llewellyn Thompson wrote Dean Rusk in the first days of April, "that the Soviets may be tempted to shoot down one of our many flights along the periphery of the Soviet Union." On April 3, Soviet Ambassador Dobrynin requested a private meeting with Robert Kennedy. That afternoon, he handed him a twenty-five-page message from Khrushchev wrapped secretly in a newspaper. "It was full of poison," Bobby later confided to his brother. It was a tough reiteration of Khrushchev's standard arguments against U.S. positions on the test ban, Berlin, and Cuba. "It was as if a person had come down from Mars and written this," Kennedy said. It appeared that JFK underestimated that his Soviet counterpart also had a right-wing military to contend with.[801]

In April, the cease-fire in Laos that Kennedy and Khrushchev had agreed to collapsed when a pro-Pathet Lao faction attacked the armed forces of the Souvanna government. The White House was unsure if the Soviets controlled the Pathet Lao, but they had no doubt the North Vietnamese and their Laotian ally had launched the offensive. Unsure how to react, JFK asked the Pentagon to provide military options, including the reintroduction of U.S. Marines into Thailand, launching an attack against the North Vietnamese, or even applying pressure on Cuba to get the Kremlin's attention. At an April 24 press conference, Kennedy told reporters: "If Laos fell into Communist hands, it would increase the danger along the northern frontiers of Thailand. It would put additional pressure on Cambodia [and] South Vietnam, which in itself would put additional pressure on Malaya..."[802]

In June, Kennedy's NSC confirmed that "the root of the problem in Southeast Asia is the aggressive effort...to establish Communist control in Laos and South Vietnam as a stepping stone to control all Southeast Asia." Privately, Kennedy worried that Laos was too essential to do nothing, but he did not want to introduce U.S. ground troops there.[803] He asked Harriman to speak with Khrushchev about this, whom he believed still influenced Soviet world policy. However, this unexpected turn of events only exacerbated the belief of his right-wing opposition that Kennedy was over his head and incapable of handling the pressures inherent to his job.[804]

Laos was not the only nation around the world where internal unrest was forcing Kennedy to make tough decisions at a time when all he wanted to do was focus on détente.

***

Unhappy with President Duvalier, in January 1963, Kennedy stopped shipments of war material to Haiti and suspended a highway loan. Still, he allowed construction of a new jet airport in Port-au-Prince to continue since it might be needed "to meet a United States military requirement." At the time, the CIA was "involved in discussions with an exile group who wanted to overthrow Duvalier," William Colby would later testify to the Church Committee. They were considering "a couple of efforts to send people into Haiti...a paramilitary operation...sort of like the Bay of Pigs, that kind of invasion." Was this going to be another staged attack to make it appear Castro was responsible?

Having cut off most aid and encouraged contact between the U.S. military attaché and dissident officers, the administration had been hoping to provoke a coup since the previous October.[805] However, Kennedy refused to consent to the CIA's request to assassinate Duvalier. Despite this, the CIA and military intelligence planned to remove the Haitian leader on their own, and it was this that brought Haitian banker Clemard Charles to their attention. U.S. intelligence placed him under surveillance, and as early as August 1962, the 902nd Military Intelligence Group, "90 Deuce," asked the FBI to check on Charles' business activities in Miami. Looking to ingratiate himself with U.S. government officials and the CIA, Charles aligned himself with George de Mohrenschildt. It confirmed that de Mohrenschildt was part of U.S. intelligence, for why else would Charles have approached him, and how did he know to do that in the first place? Charles made his intentions clear. For the good of his country, he wanted the CIA to overthrow Duvalier and install him as President.[806]

Even though he was still in Dallas, keeping a watchful eye on Oswald, de Mohrenschildt took an avid interest in Clemard Charles. On April 17, he wrote to Vice President Lyndon Johnson, requesting an appointment "to talk to you about an important strategic country" and to introduce him to "a Haitian businessman and banker, president of the only private bank in Haiti, Mr. Clemard Joseph Charles." Meanwhile, on April 26, assassins in Haiti fired upon Duvalier's limousine while he was traveling with his children. All escaped unharmed.

As described in Chapter Eight, in the coming months, Charles and de Mohrenschildt had a series of meetings in Washington with Army Intelligence's chief liaison with the CIA, Dorothy Matlack, and other intelligence operatives to allegedly discuss business ventures de Mohrenschildt and Charles were about to embark upon in Haiti. However, there must have been more to it since it involved the Army and the CIA, and the assassination of Papa Doc was the logical topic of discussion. Long-time CIA asset Colonel Sam Kail was involved. He was close to Alpha 66 and part of the 1959 attempted coup to oust Castro that the CIA ran out of the U.S. Embassy in Havana. Matlack and Kail were close to undercover Army Intelligence agent Frank Brandsetter, who managed the Havana Hilton when Castro ousted Batista. He knew David Phillips and George de Mohrenschildt, which explains the inclusion of the military's Kail and Matlack in the Washington meeting.[807]

On May 7, Charles, de Mohrenschildt, and George's wife Jeanne had a meeting with Matlack and Tony Czajkowski, who worked under Tracy Barnes. Czajkowski's impression was that George dominated Charles, who wanted the U.S. to send Marines to Haiti to support Haitian army officers. They also wanted Matlack to set up a meeting with U.S. government officials, and Charles requested an appointment with Edmund Wise of AID about a loan. Another of Matlack's AID contacts was CIA-connected William Avery Hyde, Ruth Paine's father.[808]

As described by Joan Mellen in *Our Man in Haiti*, there was a great deal of CIA interest in the mysterious George de Mohrenschildt: "On May 9th, CIA's Frank Stone receives a response to his April 26th request for traces on de Mohrenschildt from the CIA operations component. There is considerable information in the de Mohrenschildt file, with many records residing in the Western Hemisphere office in Mexico City... There are FBI files dating from 1941 to 1948."[809]

"On May 15, 1963," Mellen continued, "in New York, Thomas J. Devine and Frank Stone conferred once more... The documents make clear that de

Mohrenschildt is the subject of their meeting. Stone reports to Devine that the CIA has now completed an exhaustive trace on de Mohrenschildt, coming up with 'a large amount of derogatory information regarding the USA.' They know that in 1945, de Mohrenschildt had told the FBI that 'Communism was best for Europe,' if not for the US. They know de Mohrenschildt is not a Communist and that he worked for CIA in Yugoslavia and Hungary."[810]

On May 21, de Mohrenschildt let his CIA contacts know he had obtained "some Texas financial backing" for his Haitian operations, which may have involved oilmen like Clint Murchison, whose Haitian business ventures with Bobby Baker had gotten him in trouble.

According to David Kaiser, the author of *The Road to Dallas*, "The expedited check on de Mohrenschildt was done by Gale Allen, a case officer in the CIA's Domestic Operations Division, run by Tracy Barnes. In 2004, Allen confirmed he had been working in Domestic Operations, whose tasks included the establishment of U.S. companies abroad that could serve as fronts. He claimed to have no recollection of de Mohrenschildt and was quite sure that he [Allen] was not involved in anything having to do with Haiti at that time." So, Allen believed the check was done on someone's behalf who had plans for de Mohrenschildt.[811]

Meanwhile, not everyone in the U.S. wanted Duvalier removed from power. Clint Murchison and arms dealer and Washington lobbyist Irv Davidson remained close to the Haitian leader. It was through Davidson that Carlos Marcello did business with Murchison, who was involved in the meatpacking operation with Bobby Baker, who was close to LBJ, whom de Mohrenschildt tried to set up a meeting with. Clearly, the same names that were prominent in Cuban affairs also popped up regularly in what was happening in Haiti, and for a good reason, for the events unfolding in both countries were connected. We will revisit this later.

***

For years, the CIA attempted to remove Abd al-Karim Kassem from power in Iraq because he was too close to the Iraqi Communist Party. In 1958, Allen Dulles appeared before the U.S. Senate to explain that an "intelligence failure" allowed Kassem to come to power in the first place. CIA backed the Iraqi Ba'ath Party to overthrow Kassem, and in 1959, the Agency solicited the services of a young Iraqi Ba'athist named Saddam Hussein to assassinate him. The attempt failed, and Hussein took refuge in Cairo, where the CIA continued to support him.[812]

A successful CIA-backed coup occurred in February 1963, resulting in Kassem's death by an Iraqi firing squad. James Critchfield, the CIA chief of the Near East division, called it a textbook CIA operation: "We really had the t's crossed," and a Ba'ath leader also acknowledged, "We came to power on a CIA train." However, there were reports that Communists had penetrated the CIA, so by March, the Ba'athists arrested about ten thousand Iraqis and executed an estimated five thousand. The Soviet Union charged the U.S. with enabling a bloodbath, but in the war against communism, anything was acceptable. It was why a senior U.S. official later commented, "We were frankly glad to be rid of them [suspected Communists]." It turned out the CIA-funded U.S. National Students Association supplied the student names of suspected Communists. Such an effort would have involved Cord Meyer, who was responsible for managing student movements around the world at the CIA. It apparently never occurred to the students that the information they provided would result in mass murder.[813]

Reports from Iraq reached Moscow within ten days that the new regime was violently anti-Communist, and the Kremlin was powerless to do anything. They were also troubled that Egypt, which they considered an ally, said nothing while the bloodbath in Iraq continued. On February 23, Iraq accused "some socialist states" of attempting to provoke the Kurdish tribes in northern Iraq to overthrow the regime. The next day, Iraqis arrested the first secretary of the Iraqi Communist Party, Husain Ahmad ar-Radi, and two other top leaders. They killed a fourth leader who resisted. Ordinarily, Khrushchev responded to significant events in the third world by lashing out at the U.S. This time, he passively accepted what had occurred. However, it did not go unnoticed at the Kremlin how different the American involvement in Iraq was to the détente President Kennedy was simultaneously promoting.[814]

The Russians knew JFK would never have approved of mass murder, so they concluded that the CIA initiated this on their own. Khrushchev was already worried that the U.S. military and the CIA had taken matters into their own hands by sabotaging the Francis Gary Powers U-2 flight in 1960, and they had questions regarding the Cuban Missile Crisis the previous October. Kennedy should have been equally concerned. If the CIA and the Pentagon could so heinously allow the murder of thousands of innocents because they suspected their leaders were Communists, they would have no problem assassinating a U.S. President whom they accused of the same.[815]

***

Cold War concerns about another potential Communist country in Latin America compelled President Kennedy to approve a CIA covert operation to rig the 1964 national elections in British Guyana, then a British colony pushing for independence. U.S. intelligence concluded that Prime Minister Cheddi Jagan, a presidential candidate, was a Communist. As early as mid-1962, JFK told British Prime Minister Harold McMillan that "we simply cannot afford to see another Castro-type regime established in this Hemisphere."[816]

When Kennedy and McMillan met on June 30, 1963, at Birch Grove, England, Kennedy warned that a Communist Guyana "would create irresistible pressures in the United States to strike militarily against Cuba," even though he had agreed not to do so as part of the Missile Crisis settlement. Undoubtedly, Kennedy felt he had to do something with the 1964 election looming on the horizon.[817]

On April 15, Cord Meyer briefed JFK's Foreign Intelligence Advisory Board about Guyana. He proposed a CIA-supported general labor strike by the Trade Union Council in response to a labor bill Jagan introduced that would have given his government power over the unions. The strike continued for eighty days and was the longest in Guyanese history. British journalists later uncovered that the CIA had furnished strike pay for workers, distress funds, travel expenses for leaders, plus money for propaganda and a daily fifteen-minute radio broadcast.[818]

The war to oust Jagan and his Communist administration was inevitable, but it did not occur under Kennedy. It would have to wait until Lyndon Johnson was President.

***

By the early 1960s, the Italian Communist Party once again gained popularity, and with a membership of 1,350,000, it was the largest in the free world. They received between $40 and $50 million annually from the Soviet Union, which concerned the anti-Communist opposition in the U.S. and Europe. The fear was that if Italy became Communist, so might France and a host of other countries. Despite this, the Vatican, under Pope John XXIII, ignored what was happening and called for a rapprochement between Catholicism and Communism. To make matters worse, the pope held a private audience with Khrushchev and developed a genuine affection for the Soviet leader.[819]

On election day in April 1963, the Communists gained twenty-five percent of the votes in Italy while all other parties lost seats. In response, Prime Minister Aldo Morro named Socialists to cabinet posts, which angered

Communists who also wanted key government positions but were left out in the cold. In May, the large union of construction workers, directed by the PCI (the Italian Communist Party), held a demonstration in Rome. An alarmed CIA utilized the services of local Gladio underground armies who, disguised as police, dispersed the rally, leaving more than two hundred demonstrators injured.[820]

What followed was a collaboration of right-wing Christian Democrats, top political managers, high-ranking military officials (Italian military intelligence leader General de Lorenzo planned a silent coup in close cooperation with CIA secret warfare expert Vernon Walters), newly arrived CIA Rome station chief William Harvey, and Colonel Renzo Rocca, director of the Gladio units within the military secret service. Four thousand undercover agents were recruited to work with Rocca and his Gladio army, including members of the Mafia, Italian street gangs, and neoFascist organizations such as Movimeneto Sociale Italiano (MSI – the Italian Social Movement); Ordine Nuovo (New Order); and Avanguardia Nazionale (AVthe National Vanguard). The coup was to include the assassination of Prime Minister Aldo Morro and the installation of Christian Democrat Cesare Merzagora as Italy's new president. It was called off at the last minute when they reached a compromise.[821]

Pope John passed away on June 3, and Pope Paul VI replaced him, who was an ardent supporter of Catholic Gladio. The former Cardinal Montini had worked with the OSS during World War II and had received millions in black funds from the CIA. He was also the son of the founder of Italy's Christian Democratic Party, with whom the Mafia was allied.

William Harvey's main job was to help General de Lorenzo subvert the government of leftist Prime Minister Aldo Moro. So, although Harvey allegedly was banished from Washington to Italy because of his confrontation with Bobby Kennedy, he may have been sent there to wage war against the Communist uprising. In September 1962, General Lyman Lemnitzer was also sent to Europe to head NATO, possibly to control the spread of communism in Europe. As we will discuss, Harvey's relationship with Johnny Roselli was far from over. The one-time head of CIA assassinations was still involved in what the CIA and Mafia were doing in the U.S. just five months before the assassination of JFK.[822]

One of Pope Paul's first acts was to anoint Licio Gelli as Knight in the Order of St. Silvester, one of Catholicism's highest awards, despite that Gelli was an atheist who never performed an act of service for the Church. Gelli had been a critical liaison officer to the German SS under Goering

257

and had worked closely with William Colby and Allen Dulles during the war. It was Colby who provided an entrance to the Vatican for Gelli, where he set up ratlines for ex-Nazis to escape to South America. He was involved with Permindex, the CIA front organization, and served as the CIA's liaison to General de Lorenzo, mentioned above. With the appointment of de Lorenzo came a directive from Harvey to initiate Operation Demagnetize, which authorized him to use political, psychological, and paramilitary tactics to diminish the Italian Communist Party. It raised the so-called "strategy of tension" to a new level, which had begun on October 27, 1962, with the assassination of Enrico Mattei, the founder of Italy's most significant oil concern, ENI (Ente Nazionale Idrocarburi). Gelli later told BBC correspondent Allan Francovich that tactics conducted by Gladio units were in accordance with US Army Field Manual 30-31B, which promoted violent attacks against innocents that would be blamed on radical left-wing groups so allied governments justifiably could respond in kind. It was reminiscent of what the military had proposed for Operation Northwoods.[823]

JFK visited Rome in the summer of 1963. On July 1, he met with Italian President Antonio Segni at the Quirinale Palace. During his toast, JFK remarked that "war is not inevitable and that an effective end to the arms race would offer greater security than its indefinite continuation." It was not what the right-wing and the Holy See in Italy wanted to hear, for since the mid-1950s, their country had been dealing with l'apertura a sinitra -"the opening to the left," which was the union of the Socialist Party with the ruling Christian Democrats. Years ago, future CIA Director William Colby supported this. At the same time, U.S. Ambassador Clare Boothe Luce and James Angleton would not collaborate with Socialists or anyone else in Italy who wasn't part of the radical right. Now, Luce had not changed her opinion. As early as February, she had sent a letter to President Kennedy stating: "Italy's pro-West government has one foot on the Moscow banana peel for seventeen years." If the "pro-Communist Socialists" were brought into power, "the Italian Communist Party will negotiate Italy's future with the USSR." Angleton was so furious he called Arthur Schlesinger a Communist.[824]

In the spring of 1963, Henry and Clare Boothe Luce actively supported the cause of the anti-Castro Cuban exiles so intensely that they were summoned to the White House by JFK, who wanted them to curtail their fanatical activity. The meeting had no effect, for they continued to ignore the President. According to reports, an Italian Fascist friend had convinced

Henry Luce that the best way to topple Castro was to keep the fires burning in the press, which he did incessantly.[825]

The reference to an Italian Fascist friend is interesting, considering Gelli's involvement with Permindex. As ambassador to Italy under Eisenhower, Clare Boothe Luce was very familiar with Italian politics and the Fascist movement there. So blatant was the disregard for JFK's directives regarding Italy in 1963 that when Arthur Schlesinger had visited the country in January, he felt compelled to cable Kennedy: "Lest you think you run the United States Government, the matter is still under debate." According to Schlesinger, in Italy, "it was evident that, if those in State [Department] who wanted to block apertura (opening to the left) had their way, they might well bring into power a right-wing government with fascist support...."[826]

Shortly after JFK flew home from Italy, Dino John Pionzio, the CIA's leading operative in Italy at the time, met with Moro's administrative secretary, Sereno Freato, who would soon become Italy's prime minister. Pionzio, a Skull and Bones member at Yale and a zealous right-wing anti-Communist, was opposed to the Christian Democratic Party's lean to the left. When he asked Freato what Moro had discussed with JFK, Freato said they agreed that apertura should go forward, which the radical right would not let happen, regardless of the cost.[827]

In November 1963, Moro formed a coalition government with the Socialists, and Kennedy once again turned his back on the anti-Communist radical right-wing movement. It was another nail in the coffin. JFK had not just become a liability to the Fascist movement in the U.S.; he threatened their agenda worldwide, especially in Europe. It was clear that assassination was the only way to stop him, which, as will be shown, was already in the works.

Moro would be luckier than Kennedy. He would live until 1978, when his opponents unceremoniously kidnapped him, threw him into the trunk of a car, and shot him ten times. Forces associated with Gladio were responsible.

***

Indonesia wanted West Guinea to be granted independence from the Netherlands. The region's abundance of natural resources made it a vital pawn in the struggle between the United States and the Soviet Union. Meanwhile, President Sukarno remained a problem, as almost everyone other than President Kennedy thought he was a Communist. The situation worsened in the spring of 1963 when Sukarno told Caltex and Stanvac, two American oil companies operating in Indonesia, that he wanted to acquire their refining and distribution facilities. With their contracts running out, the companies threatened to leave, and as of June 15, their oil tankers no longer stopped in Jakarta. Since Indonesia could not produce or refine oil, the Kennedy administration worried this would invite economic chaos, and the Chinese would likely rush in and draw Indonesia into the Communist bloc. Things settled after Averell Harriman intervened and JFK became involved. Still, the situation in Indonesia remained an issue of concern for those who felt Sukarno was a threat to American security.[828]

Meanwhile, the United States strong-armed the Dutch to cede control of West Guinea to Indonesia on May 1. JFK, who understood the lucrative prospects for U.S. investment throughout the archipelago, was unaware that the most significant potential was in the territory of Western New Guinea. Allen Dulles understood the importance of the region but kept this hidden from the young president because he feared Kennedy would award those mineral rights to Sukarno.[829]

As 1963 progressed, relations became seriously strained in September with the burning of the British Embassy in Jakarta. Kennedy's aid package to Indonesia, already under fire from his opponents, now faced criticism from British officials who "told the White House with increasing frequency that UK and US interests regarding Indonesia were beginning fundamentally to diverge." Numerous U.S. Republican Congressmen agreed, and they demanded that Indonesia not be a recipient of U.S. aid. Left no alternative, Kennedy planned to visit Indonesia early in 1964, where he was well-liked by the Indonesian people and Sukarno. It was also crucial for another reason. Kennedy wanted to secure relations with Indonesia before beginning troop removals in Vietnam.[830]

According to Mike Forrestal, JFK stated that "Indonesia is a nation of 100 million with perhaps more resources than any other nation in Asia... It doesn't make any sense for the U.S. to go out of our way to permanently alienate this large group of people sitting on these resources unless there is some very, very persuasive reason."[831]

Those like Allen Dulles and the Joint Chiefs, who opposed Kennedy, had no answer for his charisma and how that would advance his Indonesian agenda after he visited there. If allowed to happen, the alleged Communist Sukarno would remain in power, and the Indonesian army would be on the outside looking in, which the radical right did not want. With Sukarno in control, U.S. business access to the abundance of Indonesian raw minerals would be limited, which was unacceptable to American businesses and their radical right supporters. JFK was at odds with the U.S. military, the

CIA, industry titans, and the extreme right over Indonesia. They all wanted to stop him, and by the spring of 1963, it was becoming increasingly clear there was only one way to accomplish this.

It is telling that after the JFK assassination, America curtailed aid to Indonesia, and LBJ took a hard line toward Sukarno. The Indonesian leader even believed that the JFK assassination happened because he wanted to visit his country in February. In the next few months, all aid to Sukarno ended. The United States poured money into Indonesia's armed forces, and American military advisers worked with the high command of the Indonesian Army. Sukarno became anti-American and turned to the Soviet Union. In March 1965, the U.S. government approved a secret CIA plan to bring about a military coup, which occurred on September 30 of that year.[832]

***

On September 8, 1961, Jango Goulart became President of Brazil. He was considered a leftist and potential Communist, and it did not take long for the Kennedy White House to take notice. Jango visited Washington in early 1962 but failed to receive any financial aid or trade concessions. On the contrary, on July 30, 1962, Kennedy met with American Brazilian Ambassador Abraham Lincoln Gordon. They agreed it was prudent to unseat Goulart, and the U.S. allocated millions of dollars to prepare the groundwork for a military coup. Gordon said, "I think one of our important jobs is to strengthen the spine of the [Brazilian] military. To make it clear, discreetly, that we are not necessarily hostile to any kind of military action whatsoever if it's clear that the military action is" – "Against the left," Kennedy finished. Gordon: "He's giving the damn country to the" – "Communists," added Kennedy. The President was for self-determination, but he was also an anti-Communist when it applied to the Western Hemisphere.

Soon, CIA money began pouring into Brazil. They initiated a "counterinsurgency" assessment, authored by General William H Draper Jr., who concluded that "every effort should be made" to provide US training for the Brazilian Army. The US maintained its largest service missions in Brazil, and Brazilian officers received extra appointments to train at Fort Leavenworth's command school alongside the soldiers from Indonesia. One of Brazil's far-right groups, Movimento Anticommunista (MAC), covered Rio de Janeiro in graffiti, with slogans like "Death to the traitors," "Let us shoot, fellow Brazilians, Moscow's secular forces," and "War to the death for the PCB," the country's illegal Communist Party. They received funding from the CIA and carried out several bombings, as well as shooting up the National Student Union.

In late November, just days after the Kennedy assassination, Jango attended the country's annual celebration of the defeat of the fabled Intentona Comunista on the Red Beach in Rio de Janeiro, which angered many of the country's committed conservatives. In March 1964, with the help of the U.S. military, a military coup overthrew Goulart.

***

Ecuador's Vice President Carlos Julio Arosemena Monroyvice became president in 1961 when the populist, pro-working class president Jose Veleasco Ibarra was ousted. The CIA had infiltrated the government and set up news agencies and radio stations to discredit Ibarra. They recruited Ecuadorians to bomb right-wing agencies and churches and then claimed the left perpetrated these violent acts. Just like in Italy, this conduct was in accordance with US Army Field Manual 30-31B. Meanwhile, CIA agents worked with right-wing groups and recruited Ecuadorian military officers to orchestrate a coup, which was how Arosemana became president. As has been shown multiple times, right-wing terrorism blamed on a Communist was the favored method of removing a left-leaning leader in 1963. [833]

But Arosemana was also a problem. He ignored the CIA and recognized Fidel Castro's Cuban government. After only four months, soldiers led by Colonel Ayrelio Naranjo forced Arosemana to sever ties with Cuba, and he dismissed his Socialist Minister of Labor. In July, the Ecuadorian army surrounded the presidential palace, and Arosemana surrendered. The new military regime outlawed the Communist Party, suspended civil liberties, and canceled the 1964 elections. It was the way the CIA dealt with Communist leaders in the Western Hemisphere.[834]

***

At the beginning of 1963, President Kennedy questioned the progress of the war in Vietnam, so he sent Michael Forrestal and Roger Hilman there to determine what was really happening. Their report, submitted to JFK on January 25, described the overly enthusiastic optimism at the U.S. Embassy and among American military leaders about the long-term prospects, which the two visitors could not understand. "Things are not going nearly so well as the people here in Saigon, both military and civilian, think they are," they reported. "At the rate it is now going, the war will last longer [and] cost more in terms of both lives and money than we anticipated…"[835]

It was not a pretty picture. As Forrestal told columnist Joseph Kraft in a series of off-the-record interviews in 1964, "Both our army and the Vietnamese Army tended to want to fight the Viet Cong by whatever mechanical means they had at their disposal (artillery, airpower, napalm) and without much attention paid to the populace." American pilots were flying "unofficial" combat missions. "They bombed the hell out of the villages... certainly without the Americans checking on what kind of villages these were." The Viet Cong knew in advance when the planes would arrive, so "of course, we and the Vietnamese ended up bombing peasants." He reported to McGeorge Bundy that Admiral Felt "defended it on the grounds that the enemy is the enemy, and if you have to kill a few innocent people to get him, better kill innocent people."[836]

On February 1, after Kennedy met with General Wheeler, Dean Rusk, Robert McNamara, Maxwell Taylor, Averell Harriman, and John McCone to hear Wheeler's report on Vietnam, Forrestal apologized to Kennedy for the "complete waste of your time." The rosy picture Wheeler provided was worthless, and JFK knew it. He had described a situation that had changed from near desperation not long ago to a likely near-term victory, and America had only to stay the course to be successful.[837]

In February 1962, with the appointment of General Paul D. Harkins as Vietnam commander, a dramatic change occurred in how the military reported the war's progress. From that time until JFK's assassination, their requests for an increased military presence in Vietnam ceased. Harkins began reporting on "a spirit of optimism and growing confidence within Vietnamese and U.S. military and civilian circles," which was not valid. It was to deceive JFK to ensure America maintained a presence in Vietnam. In addition, JCS Chairman General Lemnitzer told Harkins that "the apparent growing strength of the VC [Viet Cong] makes it look like we are losing." Such thinking did not coincide with the military's reporting, so in addition to lying about the morale of American and South Vietnamese troops, from that day forward, they lied about the superior strength of the enemy for the sole purpose of deceiving the President.[838]

Sam Dowling, an officer under MACV Intelligence Chief Colonel James Winterbottom, reported that the enemy had over 40,000 men. Harkins objected, saying, "We can't tell McNamara that there's that many [Viet Cong] in the country." So, Dowling cut the size down to 20,000-25,000. "I remember General Harkins saying he would not buy a figure that high," Dowling recalled, "so, we went back and... I think we got something in the neighborhood of 17,500, and that's the figure he would allow us to publish."[839]

General Taylor was aware of the deception, as were the Joint Chiefs. As described by David Halberstam in *The Best and the Brightest*, Harkins was selected by Taylor "not because Harkins was the ablest general around, but because... he was Taylor's man and Taylor could control him."[840] Considering that the plan to deceive the President began soon after Harkins took charge in Vietnam, we can assume Taylor told him to do it. It was another example of the treason that permeated the military and was consistent with their philosophy that they were to protect the nation from a President whom they perceived was ill-equipped to lead.

In *JFK and Vietnam,* John Newman described the extent of the deception:

> The Secretary of Defense was purposely misled on nearly all of the crucial aspects of the war: the size of the enemy; the number and quality of enemy operations versus the number and quality of friendly operations; the territory controlled by the enemy versus the territory controlled by friendly forces; the number of desertions from South Vietnam's armed forces; the success of the placement of U.S. intelligence advisors; and the problems of the Self Defense Corps. The maps, statistics, and briefings he was given led him to remark at a press conference... that "every quantitative measurement... shows that we are winning the war...."[841]

Kennedy understood what the military was doing, and he made his intentions clear to Senator Mike Mansfield, a leading opponent of his Vietnam policy. According to Kennedy's aide Kenneth O'Donnell, JFK told Mansfield he agreed there was a "need for a complete military withdrawal from Vietnam. 'But I can't do it until 1965 – after I'm reelected.' [That] if he announced a withdrawal of American military personnel from Vietnam before the 1964 election, there would be a wild conservative outcry against returning him to the Presidency for a second term." After Mansfield left, Kennedy told O'Donnell: "In 1965, I'll become one of the most unpopular Presidents in history. I'll be damned everywhere as a Communist appeaser. But I don't care. If I tried to pull out completely now from Vietnam, we would have another Joe McCarthy scare on our hands, but I can do it after I'm reelected. So, we had better make damned sure I am reelected."[842]

It did not take long after that for discussions about reducing America's involvement in Vietnam to begin. Per Kennedy's instructions, in May 1963, Robert McNamara told the military they "should have a plan for phasing out.... 1,000 or so personnel late this year if the situation allows." Then, at the May 6 SECDEF Conference in Honolulu, the Pacific Command presented their plan for the requested troop withdrawal, which McNamara rejected because the timeline was too slow.[843] Three days later, a Joint Chiefs directive said they should develop "a plan for the withdrawal of about 1,000

U.S. troops before the end of the year [if] the counter-insurgency campaign would warrant such a move...."[844] The removal of troops was conditional, but it was clear that total withdrawal from Vietnam was inevitable.

As described in *The Pentagon Papers*, other things were happening in Vietnam that supported American withdrawal unless a dramatic change occurred. On May 8, in the central Vietnamese city of Hue, Government troops fired into a crowd of Buddhists displaying religious banners in defiance of a Government decree. Nine were dead, and 14 were injured, crushed by armored vehicles. The Diem government blamed it on a Vietcong provocateur, while the Buddhists demanded the government admit their guilt and compensate the injured families. Diem refused, which resulted in mass Buddhist demonstrations and monk immolations. Madam Nhu, President Diem's sister-in-law, typified the indifference their administration showed to the Buddhist plight when she called the fiery monk suicides "barbecues."[845]

Diem met American outrage with disdain. On May 12, a *Washington Post* front-page article headlined "Viet-Nam Wants 50% of GIs Out" described that "South Viet-Nam would like to see half of the 12,000 to 13,000 American military personnel stationed here leave the country." At a May 22 press conference, JFK responded, "We would withdraw the troops...any time the Government of South Viet-Nam would suggest it...if requested to, we will do it immediately."

Roger Hilsman was the State Department's primary officer responsible for Vietnam. As he later said in an interview: "[Kennedy] began to instruct me...to negotiate the neutralization of Vietnam...He did not make it public, of course, but he had certainly communicated it to me as I say, in four-letter words, good earthy Anglo-Saxon four-letter words, and every time that I failed to do something he felt endangered this position, he let me know in very clear language."[846]

Events began to spiral out of control as Kennedy's advisers conducted business without his approval. In *Secret History of the CIA*, Joseph J. Trento wrote that "by 1963... [Averell] Harriman was running Vietnam without consulting the president or the attorney general."[847] On June 12, Dean Rusk instructed Acting Ambassador William Trueheart to give Diem an ultimatum that JFK had not authorized him to do. Rusk then talked Kennedy into appointing Republican Henry Cabot Lodge as the new Ambassador to Vietnam, even though he was the wrong person for the job. In January, the Pentagon briefed him for a month on Vietnam and counterinsurgency.

Lodge was a CIA/Pentagon man, the opposite of whom Kennedy would need to implement his withdrawal strategy.[848]

The U.S. Embassy tried to prod Diem into meeting the Buddhist demands, but he would not listen. By early July, the CIA learned of two "rapidly developing coup plots," and it was clear Diem's days were numbered. There were consequences for not listening to the CIA, the Pentagon, and the Deep State, which was why JFK's days were numbered as well.[849]

266

CHAPTER FIFTEEN

ENEMIES WITHIN

Cuba remained the number one issue facing the Kennedy administration as 1963 began. The question was, what exactly did the President want to do? At an April 12 press conference, he said: "There will not, under any conditions, be an intervention in Cuba by United States armed forces, and the government will do everything it possibly can... to make sure that there are no Americans involved in any actions inside Cuba... The basic issue in Cuba is not one between the United States and Cuba; it is between the Cubans themselves."[850] He would have the same thing to say about removing American troops from Vietnam.

Normalizing relations with the U.S. interested Castro. After Lisa Howard of ABC News interviewed him, she concluded he was "looking for a way to reach a rapprochement...."[851]

Meanwhile, the Soviets learned from State Department sources that Kennedy might deal with Cuba more aggressively. Assistant Secretary of State Edwin Martin was on record saying, "Castro would be out by July." The State Department's Venezuela desk officer told a KGB source that Venezuela had joined with Guatemala to "urgently demand that the U.S. accept decisive measures against Cuba." However, Khrushchev continued to trust JFK and believed that potential aggression would come from radical militarists within his government.[852]

Still, there was concern in Moscow that Kennedy's Cuban policy might become more hawkish. Cuban subversion throughout Latin America worried JFK, especially in Venezuela, and public patience over the continued presence of the Soviet Union in Cuba was wearing thin. On March 15, even though Mongoose was over, the Special Group (Augmented) initiated a "subtle sabotage program," which led to increased pressure from the Kennedy brothers to solve the Cuban problem. It prompted the CIA to warn that a massive popular uprising inside Cuba remained "unrealistic." And if an uprising did happen, they would face the dilemma of the U.S. intervening militarily or standing by helplessly as a Hungarian-type bloodbath occurred under their noses, like what happened in 1956. "[T]he only potential effective course of action," the CIA suggested, was to "establish channels of communication to disaffected and potentially dissident non-Communist elements in the power centers of the regime." In other words, find someone within the Cuban military who was willing to orchestrate a coup.[853]

Robert Kennedy continued to reassure Soviet representatives that his brother would not break his word and that the United States would not intervene in Cuba. Khrushchev believed he could trust Kennedy. "This [Missile Crisis] commitment will bind Kennedy; it will bind the government of the United States. Two years remain before the next presidential elections. Everyone is now saying that Kennedy will be reelected. This means that for the next six years, the president of the U.S. will be bound by public pledges not to invade Cuba."[854]

***

There is no doubt that JFK was willing to normalize relations with Cuba in the spring of 1963 if the opportunity presented itself, but others were not so eager. As Sterling Cottrell of the State Department told McGeorge Bundy in January, the military remained in favor of "increasing degrees of political, economic, psychological and military pressures" to bring about "the overthrow of the Castro-Communist regime." Despite Kennedy's agreement never to invade Cuba, the military steadfastly maintained that the country "should be in a position to respond with open military support... up to the full range of military forces." The last option, of course, referred to the potential use of nuclear weapons.[855]

Among the military's proposals was to create a war between Cuba and one of its Latin neighbors, which would give the Joint Chiefs an excuse to enter the fray on the side of Cuba's adversary. The plan, as always, was to instigate "a contrived 'Cuban' attack on an OAS member... and the attacked state could be urged to 'take measures of self-defense and request assistance from the US and OAS... for collective action against Cuba."[856]

In May, Assistant Secretary of Defense Paul H. Nitze proposed that a Cuban "attack on a United States reconnaissance aircraft could be exploited." It was Operation Northwood all over again. The U.S. sent reconnaissance planes at low altitudes, expecting the Cubans to shoot one down. About a month later, a low-level flight across Cuba produced only a protest.[857] Instigating a scenario that forced Castro to attack a neighbor or create an illusion that one had occurred was given sincere consideration before the Bay of Pigs. Then, it was a fake attack against Guantanamo, which remained an option in 1963. Now also included were potential staged attacks against Haiti, Nicaragua, Venezuela, or the Dominican Republic. It would define America's military policy towards Castro up until the JFK assassination.

***

The NSC Standing Group formed a Cuban Coordinating Committee (CCC) to manage issues related to Cuba. As Vice President Johnson's military adviser told him, they needed to decide "whether an invasion of Cuba...is to be supported, or whether, in a lesser sense, serious provocations or incidents should be a part of that basic policy."[858]

Joseph Califano, Special Assistant to Secretary of the Army Cyrus R. Vance, was on the phone with Bobby Kennedy almost daily regarding which Cubans they should recruit for a second invasion if that was the direction they wanted to go. Two experienced Lieutenant Colonels assisted him – James Patchall for covert operations and Alexander Haig to manage the new brigade if that became a reality. In early 1963, the program took in two hundred exiles per week, and 2,600 Cubans completed U.S. military training. By this time, Alpha-66 and SNFE were working with the military. Undoubtedly, other exile groups were as well. The military was in charge now, and they had Bobby Kennedy's support. Meanwhile, the CIA was looking in from outside.[859]

The CCC's primary purpose was the coordination and promotion of anti-Castro aggression that would culminate in a coup by late 1963 or early 1964, which would have a positive effect on JFK's reelection. The operation was called the Omega Plan, or AMWORLD, and the intent was to create a catalyst that would justify the U.S. military's involvement in removing Castro from power. According to Haig, "Bobby Kennedy was running it – hour by hour...We were conducting two raids a week at the height of that program against mainland Cuba. People were being killed, sugar mills were being blown up, bridges were demolished. We were using fast boats and mother ships, and the United States Army was supporting and training these forces....." Haig said, "Bobby was the President. He was the President! Let me repeat, as a reasonably close observer, HE WAS THE PRESIDENT!"[860]

Just five weeks after the Missile Crisis, the Joint Chiefs wrote a memo to the president stating, "Our ultimate objective remains the replacement of the Castro regime." One month later, the Coordinator for Cuban Affairs wrote that the NSC should support "the developments within Cuba that offer the possibility of replacing the Cuban government." He was pushing for an internal uprising, even though most informed people knew this was not possible.[861]

President Kennedy was involved, and on April 29, he wrote McNamara, asking, "Are we keeping our Cuban contingency plan up to date?" Expecting Cuban resistance to be stronger than anticipated, Kennedy wondered if "we should strengthen our contingency plans on this operation." One week later, McNamara responded: "I wish to assure you that our contingency plans for an invasion of Cuba... are being maintained up to date," and the " planned employment" of U.S. forces and more aircraft were added to the plan. Through these measures, "the weight of our early attacks will be increased, and the probability of their success will be enhanced."[862]

Most alarming was the lack of concern that this could lead to war with the Soviet Union: "U.S. planning should include plans...for the possible neutralization or elimination of Soviet forces in Cuba."[863]

Bobby Kennedy supervised this potential coup operation, which was still contingent upon instigating an internal uprising in Cuba, and only the most trusted Kennedy allies were aware of the plan. They even kept it secret from Secretary of State Dean Rusk, who years later claimed he only learned of it after the assassination.

The CIA was responsible for finding a disenchanted military officer within Castro's army who would be willing to initiate a coup. AM/TRUNK was the CIA's codename, and while the military oversaw large-scale logistical planning, the CIA was responsible for the highly sensitive "Unconventional Warfare" aspects of the plan. The Church Committee learned in the 1970s that "the CIA also sponsored a separate operation to 'penetrate the Cuban military to encourage either defections or an attempt to produce information from dissidents, or perhaps even to forming a group which would then be capable of replacing the then present government in Cuba.'"[864]

***

With the crackdown against the more radical Cuban exile groups continuing, Jose Miro Cardona, the President of the Cuban Revolutionary Council, accused President Kennedy of switching to a policy of "peaceful coexistence" with Cuba. He flew to Washington to plead his case with the Attorney General, but Bobby ignored him. Cardona resigned from the CRC in protest, accusing the Kennedys of "breaking promises and agreements" with the exiles. JFK exacerbated the situation by canceling all government subsidies to the CRC. The rift between the exiles and John Kennedy was approaching the point of no return.[865]

Arthur Schlesinger Jr. advised the President in writing that he should restrain his comments regarding Miro, who "has not told all he knows, and if driven into a corner, could do us a lot more damage...If goaded, Miro could give a hopelessly squalid picture of our covert dealings with the exiles."[866]

In March, a conference held at the Miami field office of the FBI included representatives from various agencies, including Customs, Coast Guard, Navy, State, CIA, Border Patrol, INS, FBI, and Justice. The point was to emphasize that they should work together to curtail raids into Cuba by the more violent Cuban exile groups.[867]

It was around this time that Desmond FitzGerald replaced William Harvey to head Task Force W. FitzGerald had been CIA's chief of Far Eastern Operations when Oswald was in Japan and was a logical choice as Harvey's replacement. He had served on the Army G-2 staff of General Joseph Stilwell during World War II as the liaison officer to the Nationalist Chinese Sixth Army. FitzGerald worked for the CIA in East Asia during the Korean War, eventually becoming station chief in both the Philippines and Japan. More importantly, he was a Harvard graduate who shared the Kennedy's Boston-Irish heritage. He was the opposite of Harvey, which must have pleased the Kennedy brothers.[868]

FitzGerald joined the likes of Ted Shackley, who wanted Cuban exiles and American mercenaries who violated the nonaggression policy toward Cuba prosecuted.[869] However, distancing the United States from right-wing Cuban exiles was easier said than done. Private sources funded groups that insisted on continuing the secret war against Cuba regardless of what Kennedy had agreed to.[870]

The Free Cuba Committee announced its formation on April 10 in Washington, and its members included Arleigh Burke, retired chief of naval operations, John Fisher, president of the conservative American Security Council, and Clare Boothe Luce. In its inaugural press conference, they talked about the need to eliminate Castro and were willing to fight him without help from the U.S. government, if necessary. In July, the State Department learned that the committee planned to seize an island off the Cuban coast to force Castro to retaliate, which would compel JFK to intervene with military troops.[871] According to Antonio Veciana, the operation included Alpha-66, and Texas oilman H.L. Hunt funded these operations.[872]

Compared to the other Cuban exile groups, Alpha 66 was better organized and much more violent, and they continued their sabotage raids working with the U.S. military, who did not trust Bobby Kennedy's commitment to overthrow Castro by force. They turned their back on the CIA as well. It was a direct violation of JFK's directive to crackdown on independent sabotage activity and a sign right-wing exile groups were prepared to defy President Kennedy.

Alpha 66 was not the only group singled out by the U.S. government. Six American pilots, including Frank Sturgis, were told to discontinue raids against Cuba.[873] The Justice Department indicted Rolando Masferrer, prompting the President to comment on April 12 that he was not the type of person the United States wanted in power in Cuba.[874] The pressure was on, which only intensified the resolve of the more violent exile groups to continue the struggle against Castro. They realized they were too far-right to be part of a future U.S.-approved Cuban government in exile and would have to pursue an agenda separate from the Cuban exile group Bobby Kennedy was working with. Before long, they would redirect their anger at the President.

Alpha 66 began directing attacks against Russian ships in the hope of increasing tensions between the Soviet Union and the United States. Later that month, Commandos L, an offshoot of Alpha 66 and equally ferocious, sank a Russian freighter, which prompted a stern reply from the Soviets. Pravda called the CIA "bandits hiding behind the skirts of Cuban malcontents who had deserted their country to embrace capitalism." Since Alpha 66 was working with the U.S. Army, there was no doubt that the military was trying to provoke Castro to retaliate so that President Kennedy would allow the U.S. military to enter the fray.[875]

Sturgis had been involved with Sam Kail in the 1959 coup to remove Castro that the CIA ran out of the U.S. Embassy in Havana. During that operation, Kail worked closely with Frank Brandsetter, an undercover Army Intelligence agent acting as a hotel manager. At the time, Brandsetter was close to David Phillips and knew June Cobb, who worked with Phillips in Mexico City in the summer of 1963 while Oswald visited there. Phillips was the one who suggested that Antonio Veciana contact Kail at the Havana Embassy, where he was the U.S. Army attaché. In February 1962, the Army transferred Kail to Miami, where he was in charge of a unit that debriefed newly arrived Cuban refugees. It was when he met Dorothy Matlack. He reported directly to the Chief of Army Intelligence in Washington.[876]

As described in *Coup in Dallas*, Jean Pierre Lafitte met with Kail on November 6, sixteen days before the assassination. The authors also reference a page from Lafitte's financial ledger, which mentions Charles Willoughby, Conrad Hilton, a board member of General Dynamics behind the TFX scandal, ad man Rosser Reeves, a wealthy financier of right-wing causes, and Charles Spofford, a Brigadier General who served NATO during the early 1950s.[877]

The inclusion of Conrad Hilton by Lafitte may surprise some readers, but rest assured he belongs in the discussion. As early as 1951, Hilton was a member of the Committee to Proclaim Liberty, whose goal was the advancement of conservatism. Other members were Herbert Hoover, Douglas MacArthur, Henry Luce, and leaders of significant businesses, such as US Steel, Republic Steel, Gulf Oil, Hughes Aircraft, United Airlines, Chrysler, Kraft Foods, Marshall Field, Jones & Laughlin Steel, Eastern Airlines, and General Motors.[878]

CIA assassin and JFK assassination suspect David Morales operated out of the Havana embassy in 1959 when the attempted coup to remove Castro took place. He had access to the Mafia-run casinos through Frank Brandstetter, who managed the Havana Hilton hotel at the time. Morales often met with Brandstetter and associated with June Cobb while she was working as Castro's public relations aide. Brandstetter and Kail were long-time friends with U.S. Army Intelligence officer Colonel George Lumpkin, who, in 1963, was deputy chief of police in Dallas at the time of the assassination.

Morales also worked closely with Bernard Barker, whom the FBI hired to work undercover in Cuba after Castro came to power while he continued to function as a CIA asset. On June 21, 1972, Morales was questioned about Barker by the CIA's Chris Hopkins, who was in the Latin American division. Morales said Barker was recruited in Havana in 1959 as a "support agent" by "Woodrow C. Olien," aka James A. Noel. Morales added, "The Agency exfiltrated [Barker] to Tampa in 1959 and put him in touch with the FRD in Miami. He had a job in the FRD recruiting candidates for the [Bay of Pigs] invasion. He worked with CARDONA on propaganda. Howard Hunt became [Barker's] case officer on CIA matters at JM/WAVE Station."[879]

Hecksher, Morales, and Tracy Barnes worked with William Harvey in Germany. Frank Brandsetter led an interrogation team at Camp King near the end of the war in Germany while Skorzeny was there and must have known Harvey during this period. Harvey was responsible for assassinations, or as he called it, Last Resort Beyond Last Resort. Harvey and Morales worked with Johnny Roselli, while Brandsetter had access to Mafia leaders from his days in Havana. "Here I am helping the government, helping the country," said Roselli, "and that little sonofabitch [Bobby] is breaking my balls. Let the little bastard do what he wants. There isn't anything he can do to me...I got important friends in important places in Washington that'll cut his water off."[880] All these men resented Bobby Kennedy and the private war he was waging against Castro without them. Counterintelligence chief James Angleton was one of their leaders, as was Allen Dulles, who was close to big business heads who wanted Kennedy removed from power. This group would have been willing to assassinate JFK to prevent Bobby from invading Cuba because they did not trust him. Eventually, they would conclude that killing the President was a necessary evil to prevent losing West Berlin to the Soviets, which would have led to World War III.

***

As right-wing Cuban exile groups continued their sabotage attacks on Cuba in the spring of 1963 without government approval, the potential for disaster did not escape President Kennedy. There were still 17,000 Soviet troops in Cuba, along with five hundred antiaircraft missiles. As a result, Kennedy responded to the Commandos L sinking of the Russian vessel by saying that such attacks "may bring counteraction. I think that when these issues of war and peace hang in the balance, the US government and authorities should... have a position of some control on the matter."[881]

Despite what the President wanted, how much control his administration had was debatable. On March 30, both the State and Justice Departments announced they were taking "every step necessary to ensure that such raids are not launched, manned, or equipped from U.S. territory."[882]

In a private April 15th meeting with JFK, CIA Director McCone told him to either "establish relations with Castro" or "overthrow him." Surprisingly, JFK "suggested that both options were simultaneously being pursued" – a dual strategy that was still in place at the time of his assassination. McCone followed with a memo saying that "a military coup in Cuba [was] the United States' only hope" to get rid of Castro. Two days before, McNamara told an NSC subcommittee "that Castro must be overthrown, preferably by provoking an internal revolt that would allow the United States to intervene."[883]

By April, the President was looking to curtail right-wing Cuban exiles, while an element within the CIA and the private sector were still supporting these groups. McGeorge Bundy and others were calling for the "...gradual development of some form of accommodation with Castro," while the Joint Chiefs were planning an amphibious invasion of Cuba supported by an internal Cuban uprising. Others, like John McCone, wanted to instigate a military coup within Cuba. When James Donovan and John Nolan traveled to Cuba to wrap up the Bay of Pigs prisoner exchange, they came away with the impression that Castro supported Bundy's call to normalize relations. Robert Kennedy, who spearheaded the operation to take over Cuba, now asked the question, "Can we do business with this fellow?"[884]

***

Not to be confused with the Maurice Bishop previously mentioned, William Bishop was heavily involved in training anti-Castro Cuban exiles in the early 1960s at a Florida camp called No Name Key. Bishop had been a "Military Intelligence Aide" on the General Staff of General MacArthur's Army Intelligence team during the Korean War era, which meant he would have served under the Fascist Charles Willoughby. An FBI file confirmed "Colonel BILL BISHOP" had "been the military leader and instructor of the group at No Name Key," and another FBI document listed "William Bishop" as an associate of Rolando Masferrer in anti-Castro activities and an attempted 1967 invasion of Haiti.[885]

During an interview, Bishop showed author Dick Russell his old notecards, which included Robert Morrow's name and address, a listing for "MASFERRER, ROLANDO (TIGER LEADER)," and phone numbers for other prominent exiles such as Carlos Prio, Antonio Varona, Mario Garcia Kohly, and David Ferrie associate Eladio del Valle. He also told Russell that Richard Nagell was involved with Alpha 66 and that he (Bishop) was in New Orleans in the summer of 1963 to obtain funds from Rolando Masferrer's Mafia contacts for Alpha 66. "We had a coup d'etat on November 22, 1963," Bishop said. It made sense since Alpha 66 was working for the military at that time and confirmed that the Mafia was financing Alpha 66.[886]

A classified document released from the National Archives on March 25, 2010, pertained in part to "Col. William C. Bishop, U.S. Army CIC [Counterintelligence Corp]." The document states that Bishop "claims to have been assigned to the Trade Mart speech site as Presidential protection until he left his post (upon hearing that the President had been shot) to go to Parkland Hospital."[887] Considering Bishop's CIA, Military Intelligence, and Cuban exile connections and that he claimed he was involved in the assassination of Trujillo, it is troubling that he was at the Trade Mart allegedly to protect the President on the day of the JFK assassination. Bishop was part of a group of ex-Batista supporters, such as Masferrer, right-wing Cuban exiles like Alpha 66, and the Mafia. They hated JFK, and that Bishop was part of a team to protect JFK does not seem feasible. It is more believable that Bishop was part of a backup team to kill JFK at the Trade Mart in case the assassins in Dealey Plaza aborted the operation. It is also possible that the JFK assassination was to happen at the Trade Mart, which would have served as a catalyst to initiate the Omega Plan and the second invasion of Cuba. However, a second group may have killed JFK in Dealey Plaza before he got to the Trade Mart to prevent the Omega Plan from happening.

For those who looked at the worldwide big picture, like Allen Dulles, James Angleton, and Otto Skorzeny's group in Madrid, who feared that the invasion of Cuba would result in the Soviet takeover of West Berlin, they would have done anything to prevent that from happening, even killing Kennedy as a last resort. We will discuss this further in the following chapter.

Richard Nagell would later state that while in Miami in January 1963, "I conducted surveillance on a man, said to have been an ex-CIA employee, observed talking to [exile] leader Manuel Artime and former Cuban senator/racketeer Rolando Masferrer." He said Artime was not involved in the JFK assassination, but he "may have been in meetings with certain people." He claimed that another CIA man, whom he knew as "Bob," was also involved. Nagell was with Bob in Japan when he met Lee Oswald for the first time. That was when he followed Oswald to the Soviet Embassy in Tokyo related to the Colonel Eroshkin incident. Nagell would run into Bob again in Mexico City in September 1962, and Oswald would mysteriously show up there the following year. For the next year, Bob, who reported to Desmond FitzGerald, became Nagell's CIA point of contact.[888]

Dick Russell believes "Bob" was Henry Hecksher, who was involved with June Cobb, David Atlee Phillips, Frank Sturgis, David Morales, Bernard Barker, and others in the 1959 coup in Havana previously mentioned. The success of that effort was contingent upon an internal military uprising within Castro's revolutionary army led by William Morgan and Eloy Gutierrez Menoyo, a scenario being pursued by some again in 1963.[889]

Hecksher was the senior political officer for the CIA's AMWORLD project, which was part of the Omega Plan. In Mexico City, the only officer designated for involvement in AMWORLD was David Atlee Phillips, aka Maurice Bishop. And as Russell wrote, "Hecksher and Phillips, it turns out, went way back." As described in Chapter Eight, Hecksher, with his German background and connection to Harvey, Barnes, Morales, Phillips, and Hunt, fits in well with the group that might have wanted to stop the Omega Plan.[890]

There was something about this group of anti-Communist CIA malcontents, who had a history with Lee Harvey Oswald and were in a position to set him up as the assassination patsy. They considered the containment of communism their primary objective. They didn't consider Castro's Cuba a significant threat and would have been willing to assassinate Kennedy to protect Western Europe and transfer the war against communism to Southeast Asia.

***

It was not a secret that the Mafia hated the Kennedy brothers. Frank Ragano was the attorney for Santo Trafficante and Jimmy Hoffa in 1963. In March, Hoffa told him that if something happened to JFK, Lyndon Johnson would get rid of Bobby. "He hates him as much as I do," he said. "Don't forget, I've given a hell of a lot of money to Lyndon in the past." Jimmy then ordered Ragano to go to New Orleans to meet with Marcello and Trafficante. It was when Carlos told him, "Someone ought to kill that son-of-a-bitch. That fucking Bobby Kennedy is making life miserable for me and my friends. Someone ought to kill all those goddamn Kennedys." Later, Trafficante told Ragano: "Bobby Kennedy is stepping on too many toes. You wait and see. Somebody is going to kill those sons of bitches. It's just a matter of time."[891]

On May 9, the government indicted Hoffa for jury tampering. Another indictment followed in June for taking $25 million in fraudulent loans from the pension fund.[892]

On June 25, J. Edgar Hoover informed Bobby Kennedy that Sam Giancana had stopped in Miami the previous month on his return from the Dominican Republic. He attended the meeting that launched the Eddie Bayo-William Pawley raid against Cuba, which also involved John Martino and representatives from *Life* magazine who wanted to run a story on a Cuban exile raid against the Cuban mainland. Desmond FitzGerald approved the operation, even though the Kennedy administration said any operations involving the mob, private mercenaries, and Cuban exiles not directly under their control were off-limits. It was a defiant gesture to show the Kennedys they intended to continue their war against Castro.[893]

In July, Jimmy Hoffa and Frank Ragano met with Bobby Kennedy at the Justice Department to discuss the evidence against Hoffa. After keeping them waiting for forty-five minutes, Bobby walked in with his dog. Hoffa almost choked him to death, and had to be pried off. On July 23, before leaving Washington, Hoffa told Ragano: "The time has come for your friend [Trafficante] and Carlos to get rid of him, kill that son-of-a-bitch, John Kennedy." Hoffa continued, "Be sure to tell them what I said. No more fucking around. We're running out of time – something has to be done." The next day, Ragano relayed the message to Marcello and Trafficante. Their reaction indicated it was already in the works.[894]

***

In the spring of 1963, David Phillips' young friends at the DRE also felt betrayed by the Kennedy brothers. In an open letter that received wide distribution in southern Florida, DRE leaders declared they intended to keep striking at Cuban government targets, regardless of the new U.S. policy. The Cubans and the Soviet Union accused the United States of condoning piracy on the high seas, exactly what JFK wanted to avoid. Bobby Kennedy responded by ordering the INS to confine the most militant exiles to metropolitan Miami.[895]

Kennedy's Cuban policies have "always culminated in abandonment, treachery, and broken promises," DRE leader Luis Fernandez Rocha, one of the targeted militants, told the *New York Times*. "The United States has effected a blockade to stop the attacks against the Communist regime in Cuba and are, thus, strengthening the Communist position," he stated. The CIA's Miami station chief, Ted Shackley, had heard enough and tried to cut off Agency funding for the DRE, but Richard Helms overruled him. Helms admired the DRE style, even though they engaged in unauthorized attacks on Castro. The DRE remained on the CIA payroll.[896]

***

It was on April 15, 1963, that an attorney from Chicago named Paulino Sierra Martinez, a one-time aide to a Cuban senator under Batista, met with Allen Dulles and retired Army General Lucius Clay. Clay was a senior partner with Lehman Brothers, the Wall Street investment firm, and a member of the board of directors at General Motors and other major companies, so he represented big monied interests along with Dulles. The following month, Sierra approached various exile groups as the representative of a coalition of American businessmen who wanted to see the Castro regime toppled. United Fruit, Esso, Standard Oil, DuPont, and U.S. Steel were some of the names Sierra said were interested in supporting the exiles, and they were willing to put up $30 million if the exiles would unite under a provisional government with Carlos Prio as President and Sierra as Secretary-General. Sierra also claimed to have the support of many high-ranking Army and Navy officers who could procure arms and establish training bases for troops in a foreign country.[897]

Sierra was not a flash in the pan. Prior to the revolution, he had worked in Batista's foreign ministry, so there was ample reason for Dulles and Clay to have met with him, especially since Sierra had brought together members of the Mafia, Texas oilmen, wealthy business people, cattle ranchers, American mercenaries, and right-wing Cuban exiles groups, all of whom had a strong motive for wanting JFK removed.[898]

Also involved with Sierra was William Trull, an American entertainer from Dallas who frequently performed for Cuban audiences. He was also on good terms with numerous wealthy Texans, including the powerful and well-connected Kleberg family, whose Cuban ranch Castro confiscated in 1959. As described in Chapter Eight, Kleberg's King Ranch and Czarnikow-Rionda merged into a single Cuban company, *Compania Ganadera Becerra,* with Jack Malone as president. Gustavo de los Reyes was the owner of the ranch closest to *Becerra,* a sugar plantation called *La Caridad.* Kleberg also knew Alberto Fernandez, a thirty-four-year-old Cuban who owned five cattle ranches on the island. By the summer of 1959, David Phillips brought this group into the William Morgan/Gutierrez coup attempt that involved the U.S. Embassy in Havana.

So, considering how the names of interested parties hell-bent on getting rid of Castro remained the same four years later, an alliance between Sierra, the Kleberg family, and their business associates was within the realm of possibility. As far as wealthy Texans offering financial assistance, Trull claimed Sierra made light of it, bragging that "representatives of the Las Vegas and Cleveland gambling interests" had offered him up to $14 million in exchange for a 50 percent interest when gambling was reinstituted in Cuba.[899]

It was not the only reference to organized crime. During many meetings with the exiles in Miami, Sierra repeatedly said it was organized crime providing the financing. In May, a headline in the *Miami News* about Sierra and the exiles read "Gamblers Pop Out Of Exile Grab Bag," and a CIA report pertaining to Sierra referred to "gamblers from the West" financing him.[900]

In *The Hidden History of the JFK Assassination,* author Lemar Waldron wrote that "Marcello, Trafficante, and Rosselli...used mob money to fund a phony Cuban exile group, the JGCE (Junta of the Government of Cuba in Exile), run by Paulino Sierra. CIA agent Bernard Barker, also working for Trafficante, helped spread the word about the new group. The mob bosses wanted Sierra's group to get [Enrique] Williams's – and the Kennedy's – blessing, in which case it would be used as a cover for the plot to kill JFK."[901]

On May 10, 1963, an AP article appeared in the *New York Times* and other papers, which reported: "A new all-out drive to unify Cuban refugees into a single, powerful organization to topple the Fidel Castro regime was disclosed today by exile sources. The plan calls for [the] formation of a junta in exile to mount a three-pronged thrust consisting of sabotage, infiltration, and ultimate invasion. The exile sources said the plan had been discussed with Cuban leaders by US Central Intelligence agents. Seeking to put together the junta was Enrique Ruiz Williams, a Bay of Pigs invasion veteran and friend of US Attorney General Robert F. Kennedy....[Tony]

Varona, former Premier [of Cuba], said he had told Mr. Ruiz Williams he would cooperate in plans to unify exiles.[902]

This junta was Bobby Kennedy's group and was not the one Sierra was putting together. Kennedy did not want anything to do with Sierra's violent right-wing Cuban exiles who had once supported Batista and now conducted sabotage raids in violation of the mandate set forth by President Kennedy. Enrique Williams was Bobby's man, and he wanted Williams and people like him to be a part of the subsequent invasion of Cuba and run the Cuban government when the time came. And Bobby made it clear he did not want Cubans coming to him directly asking for money. They had to go through Williams, which allowed Bobby to act independently of the CIA. It was Williams who would decide which Cuban exile groups could join with them. As reported by *Newsweek* editor Evan Thomas: "Increasingly through 1963, RFK relied on Williams, organizing and motivating the others to keep the pressure on Castro." Hayes Johnson wrote in the *Washington Post* that of all of "the Cuban leaders of the Bay of Pigs invasion," Williams "was the closest such person to the administration" in 1963.[903]

The question is, was it possible that Enrique Williams, the mob-connected Tony Varona, and Manuel Artime considered an alliance with Sierra's group because they did not have confidence in Bobby Kennedy's ability to overthrow Castro? Carlos Prio had a long, well-established relationship with Varona, who was John Roselli's contact in the Castro assassination plots, so it is not out of the question. Obviously, Bobby Kennedy would not have welcomed Sierra's coalition, which included violent exile groups like November 30, the Second Front of the Escambray, Alpha 66, MIRR, and Commandos L. But it does not mean the Cubans he was working with would have rejected them.

On May 18, an FBI report titled *Unity Efforts* stated that Alpha 66, Second National Front of Escambray (SNFE), People's Revolutionary Movement (MRP), November 30 Revolutionary Movement, and the Anti-Communist Front of Liberation had joined forces after "signing a pact for joint action." Their singular purpose was "to facilitate the raising of funds, make propaganda, infiltrate men inside Cuba, and carry out guerrilla warfare within Cuba." The importance of the coalition was that Alpha 66 was already working with the Pentagon, which meant the other groups in the alliance were now doing so as well.[904]

Rolando Masferrer headed November 30. The group was close to Gerry Patrick Hemming's Interpen and shunned the CRC because it leaned too far to the left. As previously mentioned, Colonel Bishop described Masferrer as "the key bagman... for Alpha 66. Primarily, the funding came through the Syndicate...He had ties with Santos Trafficante Jr. and other criminal elements.... He also had different ties with Jimmy Hoffa...."[905]

The Second Front was led by Eloy Gutierrez Menoyo, who had managed to survive the 1959 attempted coup to oust Castro, sabotaged by Allen Dulles. He also helped Antonio Veciana put Alpha 66 together. The two groups merged during the Missile Crisis and formed Second Front/Alpha 66. Commandos L, headed by Tony Cuesta, was an offshoot of Alpha 66. The MIRR was Dr. Orlando Bosch's group, which was close to Alpha 66 and Operation 40. As can be seen, Alpha 66 was the common denominator that brought all these groups together.

Enrique Molina and Victor Paneque of the MDC had established a Louisiana training camp. In July, they traveled to Nicaragua, and Somoza offered them a base. When the CIA learned about this, it dropped its connection with the MDC in August, but reports in the fall suggested Carlos Prio was financing them. Also in July, Evelio Duque of the Cuban Anti-Communist Army had fallen out with the CIA and planned to land forces on the Keys north of Cuba to provoke a conflict with Castro.

In September, Prio and Varona visited Somoza in Nicaragua, a sign there was a connection between Sierra's group and Bobby Kennedy's Cubans. They wanted to get involved in Somoza's plan to topple Castro with American backing. Meanwhile, sources reported that Sierra was working with mobsters and American mercenaries for Cuban Freedom, based in Los Angeles, which was the same group Loran Hall was working with that summer, which probably meant Thoms Eli Davis was aligned with this group as well.

In October, the CIA reported that Sierra had a boat stored at the home of Manuel Aguilar, who was a close associate of Loran Hall. At the time, Hall and Thomas Davis were planning a possible invasion of Haiti that they would blame on Castro, which may have been a ruse to justify an invasion of Cuba by the U.S. military. On October 29, the boat was loaded onto a trailer headed for the Florida Keys, "accompanied by another automobile and a station wagon," according to the Customs Office, who was monitoring the boat and found in one car two Cubans, arms, ammunition, explosives, and supplies. Loran Hall drove the other car. The weapons and supplies were those he had obtained in California and brought from Dallas a week or two earlier.[906]

Interpen was also involved with Sierra's group. When Sierra purchased a shipment of guns from the Minutemen's Rich Lauchi, an Interpen instructor picked them up. Colonel Bishop, who claimed to have been a CIA case officer for Alpha 66, was the exile instructor at No Name Key, which was the home of Interpen. And because of Sierra, the opposition to Bobby Kennedy's group was well organized.[907]

***

Throughout 1963, Sierra's coalition of Cuban exiles, American mercenaries, CIA operatives, Mafia figures, Texas oilmen, and titans of business gained momentum, while the United States policy towards Cuba was mired in confusion and headed in two directions. On June 3, the Special Group considered it worthwhile to investigate "various possibilities of establishing channels of communication to Castro," which both Kennedy brothers thought was worth pursuing. Then, on June 19, the same Special Group seemingly reversed itself by approving a sabotage program against Cuba, which violated the Missile Crisis agreement. Back in April, McGeorge Bundy stated at an SGA meeting that sabotage raids were unnecessary, and the SGA "had decided... that such activity is not worth the effort expended on it." Why, then, did the SGA approve sabotage raids two months later?[908]

According to Bradley Ayers, an ex-Army captain assigned to the CIA, after the June 19 decision by the Special Group, the CIA told the Miami station to "increase the effectiveness and frequency of hit-and-run raids by exile commando groups." In addition, General Krulak, the JCS counterinsurgency specialist, told Ayers that the exile operations were mainly "planned and conducted under the supervision of the CIA... from bases in southern Florida."[909]

The decision to escalate came from the Special Group, and Robert Kennedy ensured that the President was aware of this. Although seemingly a contradiction to JFK's desire to pursue coexistence with the Soviets and Cuba, they increased the sabotage raids because they "could lead to significant defections and other byproducts of unrest." It was a last desperate attempt to create an internal uprising in Cuba by an administration whose experts no longer thought such an effort was possible. Not to mention, the groups huddled under Sierra's umbrella were separately working with the military on sabotage raids in violation of what the President wanted. Now, JFK wanted to reinitiate sabotage raids to advance the leftist group he and Bobby were organizing. The JCS, the CIA, and Sierra's group had tired of this waffling, and undoubtedly Enrique Williams, Tony Varona, and Manuel Artime did not appreciate this either.

Robert Kennedy had sent his brother a telegram in March following an NSC meeting. "John McCone spoke... about revolt amongst the military [in Cuba]," RFK reported. "He described the possibilities in optimistic terms... What can and should we do to increase the likelihood of this kind of action?... Do we have evidence of any breach amongst the top Cuban leaders?"[910]

Unknown to Bobby, a Cuban leader who wanted to overthrow Castro was about to enter the arena. They should have ignored him and stuck to their plan because they were alienating all other Cubans who maintained they needed a significant event to be a catalyst to involve the U.S. military to overthrow Castro.

CHAPTER SIXTEEN

ENEMIES ON THE OUTSIDE

Because the Fascist dictator Francisco Franco was in control of Spain during the Cold War, Madrid became the worldwide center of radical right-wing, Fascist activity. SOFINDUS, a Spanish corporation that was a cover for Nazi intelligence during World War II, remained in place after the war and attracted many high-profile Nazis, such as Otto Skorzeny, Hjalmar Schacht, and Reinhard Gehlen. Charles Willoughby, MacArthur's "Little Fascist," associated with them as well. Another key figure was Madrid businessman Victor Oswald, who was also connected to SOFINDUS and was an original member of the World Commerce Corporation.

Richard Coudenhove-Kalergi wrote in *Crusade for Pan-Europe: Autobiography of a Man and a Movement,* that Hjalmar Schacht was one of the forces behind the Pan-European movement to create a central Nazi European society. "His vivid mind was fascinated by the prospect of a European currency and federal banking system, and hopeful of the idea of equality among the competing European nations on the African continent. When the German branch of the Pan-European Union held its first meeting in the assembly hall of the Reichstag, it was Schacht who was the principal orator in favor of Pan-Europe…"

Kalergi wrote in 1948 that "Europe required not only material but also moral assistance, not only dollars but also unity; that without some form of European Union, American dollars would be squandered, since money alone can prevent neither a third world war nor the total destruction of Europe which would follow such a war. America… had a vital interest in European integration … For, once European governments realize that America's readiness to continue with Marshall Aid depends on their own readiness to unify, the pace of unification will be considerably accelerated."[911]

It was a clear message, as early as 1948, that Europeans recognized there mere survival was in jeopardy if they did not protect themselves from the Soviet Red Menace. According to a State Department report, during 1947 and 1948, there was continued growth "in Spain of a secret international Nazi-Fascist movement. Information conveyed through a reliable source in Brussels advised that the movement was to be called 'The New Socialist Europe..."' There were three Nazi leaders behind this, including "Otto Skorzeny."

Betrand Russell wrote *On the End of Nation-States,* published in *The Bulletin of Atomic Scientists,* that "there is only one way in which great wars can be permanently prevented, and that is the establishment of an international government...There is one other method by which in theory the peace of the world could be secured, and that is the supremacy of one nation of one closely allied group of nations... America at this moment, if it were bellicose and imperialistic could compel the rest of the world to disarm, and establish a worldwide monopoly of American armed forces...in a few years the opportunity will be gone. In the near future a world war, however terrible, would probably end in American victory without the destruction of civilization in the Western Hemisphere. An American victory would no doubt lead to a world government under the hegemony of the United States, a result which for my part I should welcome with enthusiasm."[912]

The New Socialist Europe organization "envisaged the destruction of the democratic system in the world and the installation of strong and authoritarian governments..." With reference to the USSR, the report continued, "the organization would combat the anti-Communists, their object being to allow the Communist parties a freer hand, the more to discredit themselves in the eyes of the democratic governments." The post-WWII Nazi plan was "to press their adversaries until they would destroy each other, and thus to profit, in the long run, from the disorder so created, in order to impose their new system."[913]

As described in Chapter Twelve, Oswald referenced the Minutemen in his writings. Oswald's political philosophy, which he put on paper in the spring of 1963, was similar to what the New Socialist Europe Nazis believed in. "It is readily foreseeable that a coming economic, political or military crisis...will bring about the final destruction of the capitalist system...we are merely interested in opposing foreign intervention...," Oswald wrote. He wanted to establish a "separate, democratic, pure communist society... one with union-communes, democratic socializing and without regard to the twisting apart of Marxist Communism by other powers." Oswald's philosophy was there were "two world systems, one twisted beyond recognition (communism)... the other decadent and dying (capitalism). A truly democratic system would combine the better qualities of the two upon an American foundation."[914]

The State Department report also mentioned that Nazi SS officer "Walter SCHELLENBERG was associated with SKORZENY's operations in

Madrid in 1951," and there was a "German intelligence network...headed by a General Otto WIEDEMAYER."[915] Schellenberg was part of the group that had tried to overthrow Hitler near the end of the war. It was called Operation Sunshine, and Allen Dulles, who was the CIA's lead negotiator with the Nazis and was trying to make that happen, knew him. Dulles' Vatican contacts told him that SS chief Heinrich Himmler and Walter Schellenberg were interested in discussing a separate peace with the United States. Austrian Prince Max von Hohenlohe had already met Allen Dulles in 1916 when Dulles was in Austria, and the two met again in Bern to discuss the Hitler situation. Prince Max was surprised to learn that Dulles believed a strong Germany was necessary as the first line of defense against the Soviets after the war. Dulles always considered the Soviet Union the true enemy of the United States.[916] Dulles allegedly told Prince Max that a "Greater Germany" and a "Danubian Confederation" would provide a bulwark against Bolshevism.[917] As a result, there was good reason for Dulles and Nazis like Otto Skorzeny to collaborate, for they shared the same goals and a desire to preserve European civilization.

After the war, these ex-Nazis proposed a "Europe-wide social movement, sponsored principally by former German officers who would band together to combat Communism and work for a powerful, independent, unified Europe, of which Germany would be the hub...by systematic infiltration into other groups and institutions." By 1953, they formed a "secret society pledged to overthrow democracy in Germany... Seven prominent former Nazis were arrested on charges of conspiracy to overthrow the West German Federal Republic..." It was called the Gauleiter Circle, and Skorzeny in Spain and his good friend, Nazi Hans-Ulrich Rudel, were undoubtedly part of this group.[918]

Hans-Ulrich Rudel was a decorated Nazi pilot who surrendered in 1945 and emigrated to Argentina. Unrepentant, he helped fugitives escape to Latin America and the Middle East. According to historian Peter Hammerschmidt, based on files of the German Federal Intelligence Service and CIA, he was in close contact with former SS and Nazi Party members. Rudel returned to West Germany in 1953 and became a leading member of the Neo-Nazi nationalist political party. In his political speeches, he claimed to be speaking on behalf of most former German soldiers of World War II, and he heavily criticized the Western Allies for not having supported Germany in its war against the Soviet Union.[919]

The State Department report stated that Rudel "is convinced that Russia has what it takes politically and militarily and that the US, which he mistrusts completely, has no potentialities. He believes that America is interested only in profiting from Germany...Rudel is primarily interested in the reconstitution of an independent Germany with its own army separate from a Western Army...this can be accomplished by German action with international Fascist support...he admires the USSR for its efficient totalitarian organization...he despises the US and will resist...its proposals for a democratic alliance of Western European countries.... Rudel's position and that of his associates in neo-Nazi circles fosters the policies of the USSR whether their cooperation is deliberate or unwitting."[920]

Skorzeny and Rudel worked together during this period. Skorzeny may not have shared Rudel's anti-American views, but he did support a more Fascist America. It was why, as time went on, these ex-Nazis from Madrid collaborated with their American counterparts who supported their Fascist approach in protecting West Berlin and Germany in the war against communism as a first line of defense for Western Europe. There is ample evidence that they joined forces to assassinate JFK.

A July 22, 1953, State Department document, titled German Nationalist and Neo-Nazi Activities in Argentina, declassified in 1980, is applicable to our discussion here. It stated:

> Preparations for the future resurgence of Nazism was made before the defeat of the German armies was certain. In Portugal, Gestapo agent Erich SCHROEDER made plans as early as 1943 for a post-war "Black Organization to be directed against Western powers. In Germany, plans for an "International Waffen-SS," composed of Nazi veterans scattered throughout the world, presumably were outlined before the last days of the war....*Otto SKORZENY,* with Gauleiters KAUFMAN, KREBS, and LAUTERBACH, was involved in the first of these manifestations in Germany. There, they formed a group called the 'Neue Ordnung' (New Order), a predecessor of the Bruderschaft." (Author's Italics).[921]

As described in Chapter Four, Otto Skorzeny was "linked not only to CIA but also to Latin American death squads, global illegal arms deals, and assassination plots against de Gaulle and Castro" and was the architect behind the JFK assassination.[922]

***

In 1948, Secretary of State George Marshall asked the right-wing businessman and political activist William Pawley to accompany him to a UN General Assembly meeting in Paris. Shortly after they arrived, Pawley left for

Madrid to discuss the possibility of the U.S. building airbases in Spain. He met with Franco on September 11, and the Spanish dictator approved the airbases in exchange for the repeal of a UN resolution that had called him "an enemy of world peace." However, Truman's surprise victory over Thomas Dewey in the 1948 election delayed the signing of a treaty with Spain.[923]

By 1950, Dwight Eisenhower was appointed Supreme Allied Commander, Europe (SACEUR) by President Truman. Eisenhower and Pawley were close, and the future President wanted Pawley appointed ambassador to Spain, which did not happen. However, in February 1951, Pawley became special assistant to Secretary of State Dean Acheson, which led to another trip to Madrid shrouded in mystery. After a third visit, Pawley submitted a report to U.S. Embassies in London, Paris, and Madrid, stating that "Franco does not object to the use of Spanish troops in Western Europe.... Franco is willing to make available to US air, naval and other bases ... and he would have no objection to Spain's ultimate integration into NATO...." Eventually, due mainly to Pawley's efforts, the U.S. military "acquired the Air Force bases at Torrejon, Zaragosa, and Moron; the Navy complex at Rota; and the pipeline across Spain from Seville to Madrid and Zaragosa."[924]

At the same time as Pawley, General Charles Willoughby was also in Madrid to discuss potential U.S. military bases with Franco. For three months, Franco lavished Willoughby with government limousines, and he was in constant contact with Franco's ministers. Spain under Franco was, in Willoughby's words, "a cradle of supermen."[925] Like with Pawley, the public did not know why he was there. The *Portland Oregonian* reported that "he will confer with Spanish military men."[926]

Willoughby was a racist, anti-Semite Fascist whose heroes were Franco and Mussolini. In 1939, he wrote about the Italian Fascist leader: "Historical judgment, freed from the emotional haze of the moment, will credit Mussolini with wiping out a memory of defeat by re-establishing the traditional military supremacy of the white race." Willoughby did not share the admiration Nazis like Rudel had for the Soviet Union. He believed the West should liquidate Communists, Russians, and Eastern Europeans who represented "the historical continuity of 'Mongoloid-Pan Slavism'" which threatened Western society.[927]

Willoughby had a longtime relationship with both William Donovan and Allen Dulles. Before World War I, he chased Pancho Villa in Mexico with Donovan. And in the mid-1950s, he and Dulles maintained a back-and-forth correspondence, with Willoughby offering his services to the CIA, writing on one occasion, "I have an exceptional entrée in Spain." Dulles rejected Willoughby's request, at least publicly, but the two maintained a behind-the-scenes professional relationship. Willoughby had proposed the development of a "youth movement" between young American and German servicemen within Germany. "The new generation has less to remember – and to resent," he wrote. "I do not want to stand alone (though the Germans will take it up), and I suggest that you examine it from the viewpoint of a 'discreet' penetration and the 'making of friends.'"

Dulles was interested and responded, "I trust we may soon get together for a personal account of your conversation with the German gentlemen. I have also had two very interesting meetings with them..." One of the two was General Hans Speidel, chief of staff for Rommel during World War II. Since the ex-Nazi was not a Communist, working with him was acceptable, no matter what dastardly deeds he had perpetrated in the past.

The discussion between Willoughby and Dulles must have pertained to the stay-behind armies Dulles had established with Donovan, which also interested Skorzeny and was in full swing at the time they spoke. The German "youth movement" could have been helpful to that operation, and Willoughby most likely did get involved with this, based on the path he would follow during the ensuing years. He eventually became a member of the radical right-wing Committee of Correspondence for the Anti-Communist Liaison. Bonner Fellers, the retired Brigadier General and ex-MacArthur military secretary in Japan was also involved with this group. Fellers advocated a rollback of communism, but he was not a CIA supporter, calling the organization "a group of Marxist-Socialist Pro-Communists." It did not preclude his dealing with Donovan and Dulles, for their private army operated outside the CIA. Fellers became a military attaché in Spain after Franco came to power. With his right-wing credentials and background, it is plausible that Fellers was also involved with Willoughby, Skorzeny, and the group operating in Madrid.[928]

By this time, Skorzeny was already in Spain promoting his stay-behind army idea, which coincided with what Dulles and Willoughby were discussing. In addition, many leading German businessmen, such as Hjalmar Schacht, whose name is in Lafitte's datebook, established themselves there. The Francoist elite still admired German military culture, which was why over 10,000 Germans relocated to Spain, many of whom were ex-Nazis who enjoyed living in a Fascist country.

Willi Messerschmitt was a German aircraft engineer and manufacturer who spent two years in prison after the war for using slave labor. He settled in Madrid, and he and Skorzeny plotted "the physical transplanting of German industry to Spain." In 1951, when the Portuguese government thwarted a meeting between Skorzeny and Rudel in Lisbon because they were concerned about two high-profile Nazis being in their country, Skorzeny complained to his "friend," Spanish foreign minister Ramon Serrano Suner, who read the Portuguese ambassador in Madrid the riot act. The meeting went ahead at a cocktail reception organized by the Spanish embassy in Lisbon.

Skorzeny planned to act as an honest broker between the Spanish and the Americans. At the same time, the discussions between the two countries about American military bases in Spain were happening, and there must have been a connection to that and what Skorzeny was up to. He claimed the Spanish were too proud and would not join NATO, but in September 1953, the two countries signed the Pact of Madrid, which enabled the US to build air and naval air bases in Spain in return for economic and military aid.[929]

Franco and his generals profited from the pact of Madrid. Spain ended its precarious isolation and received billions of dollars of American military and economic aid in return for the right to construct and run the bases. More importantly, it solidified the relationship between Skorzeny and the American players involved, like William Pawley, Charles Willoughby, and Allen Dulles. In addition to that, it appears that there were active and retired U.S. military officers with a radical right-wing ideology who became part of the international Fascist organization that would continue to grow in the coming years. It is no surprise that these men found each other when the time came to remove President Kennedy from office.

***

The Clint Murchison and Jack Crichton group from Texas also appeared in Madrid at the same time as Pawley and Willoughby. Crichton was there for the Delta oil drilling project in Spain, which is how he also got to know Otto Skorzeny. Or, should I say, it was how Skorzeny got to know Crichton.

Crichton was a former OSS intelligence officer in Europe during World War II. After the war, he was an associate of oilman Harold Byrd, the owner of the Texas School Book Depository. Crichton was president of Nafco Oil and Gas, and he and Byrd were directors of Dorchester Gas Producing. According to author Russ Baker in *Family of Secrets,* Clint Murchison was a director of one of Crichton's companies. Crichton also served as President of the Dallas Petroleum Engineers Club. In July 1963, he became director of the board of the H.L. Hunt Foundation, so he was part of the "Big Oil" network in Dallas and was well-connected. In addition, Crichton's diary revealed "his unit's participation" and "concealed involvement" during Kennedy's trip to Dallas. It is just conjecture, but it would be logical to assume that William Bishop, who claimed to be assigned to the Texas Trade Mart while working for military intelligence, may have been associated with Crichton and his 488th Military Intelligence group. We know Frank Brandsetter was in Dallas the day before the assassination, reportedly conducting a similar service for Army Intelligence. According to *Coup in Dallas*, Brandsetter was "an anointed member of Crichton's 488th," and Crichton was involved in something significant in Dallas in the days leading up to the assassination since Lafitte's datebook mentions him.

Crichton had maintained a relationship with U.S. intelligence from his time with the OSS up to and including the Kennedy assassination. In August 1953, he joined Empire Trust Company and eventually became vice president. Empire had a worldwide network of associates that was a private version of the CIA, which could also describe Donovan and Dulles' WCC organization.[930] By 1956, he organized the 488th Military Intelligence Detachment, a U.S. Army Intelligence unit operating out of Dallas, and during an interview, Crichton said, "There were about a hundred men in the unit, and about forty or fifty of them were from the Dallas Police Department."[931]

According to an ex-Cuban intelligence officer under Fidel Castro, Fabian Escalante, the CIA's "Tracy Barnes... called a meeting on January 18, 1960" to discuss a possible invasion of Cuba to get rid of Fidel Castro. Invited to the meeting, said Escalante, was an "important group of businessmen headed by George Bush [Sr.] and Jack Crichton, both Texas oilmen, to gather the necessary funds for Operation 40."[932]

If true, over three years before Kennedy's assassination, Crichton was at the heart of U.S. intelligence when the CIA was trying to kill Castro. Also noteworthy is that in 1963, Tracy Barnes was head of CIA's Domestic Contacts Division. It was a local Dallas agent from this division who asked George de Mohrenschildt to contact Oswald when he returned to Texas from the Soviet Union. The reference to Operation 40 is equally significant, for it was the CIA group responsible for assassination during the Bay of Pigs invasion.

The relationship between Crichton and George H.W. Bush is also a matter of record, and we can assume that if Tracy Barnes included a group of businessmen in 1960 to discuss getting rid of Castro, he would have also done so in 1963. In the 1964 election, George Bush and Jack Crichton stumped together; the former ran for the U.S. Senate, the latter for Texas Governor. Crichton would later state that they "spoke from the same podiums."[933]

As previously discussed, after the assassination, Crichton asked Ilya Mamantov to act as Marina's interpreter. George de Mohrenschildt called Mamantov the one "excessive rightist" among the Russian émigré community. They effectively silenced Marina. To be given that responsibility speaks volumes about Crichton's connection to U.S. intelligence and local law enforcement. Isaac Don Levine also coached Marina around the same time on behalf of *Life* magazine, which one must assume connected him to Crichton and Mamantov. Frank Wisner hired Levine to develop a secret program to export Russian and Eastern European émigrés into Germany. Levine was also a board member of the American Friends of Paix et Liberte, associated with Service d'Ordre du RPF, which worked with the WCC and further connected Levine to the Donovan/Dulles stay-behind armies and Otto Skorzeny.[934]

There was a French connection to what was happening in Madrid. Bill Donovan instituted a plan under the cover of WCC to form private paramilitary resistance groups made up of former American, British, Canadian, and French operatives, which partnered with the Service d'Ordre du RPF. This privately-run French intelligence service was part of a larger organization called the Rassemblement du Peuple Francais (RPF). Wealthy industrialists secretly funded the RPF. They had a non-Communist vision to maintain French colonial rule throughout the third world. It operated independently, with the French government unaware of its existence. So, two intelligence organizations- the WCC and the Service d'Ordre- worked together as they waged war against communism. Meanwhile, the WCC and their elitist supporters were working with Otto Skorzeny's Nazi organization, so it is safe to assume the French who opposed de Gaulle and favored European colonialism and fascism were doing so as well.[935]

***

Around 1952, Otto Skorzeny was involved in a Spanish oil venture. As Major Ralph P. Ganis writes in *The Skorzeny Papers*, "Hjalmar Schacht was handling financial aspects of the venture and was on hand to greet the visiting Dallas oil executives, including Jack Crichton, when they arrived." Skorzeny knew Schacht well through his wife Ilse, and had met Schacht at Camp King shortly before the CIA helped Skorzeny escape. Schacht was released only two months after Skorzeny and eventually became head of a banking house in Dusseldorf. It was Allen Dulles who worked behind the scenes to arrange for Schacht's not-guilty verdict at Nuremberg, and at some point, Schacht became an agent for Dulles.[936]

Schacht was "a major financial backer of Skorzeny's many business ventures." The Schacht-Skorzeny financial network would remain active until well into the 1960s," and numerous assassination suspects had a relationship with these men and what was transpiring in Madrid.[937]

Also, in the eventful year of 1952, according to German author and political scientist Matthias Kuntzel, "the Mossadegh government [in Iran] chose as their economic adviser none other than Hitler's former finance minister, Hjalmar Schacht...who [years before] had been dispatched to Tehran in 1936 at Hitler's behest. In the same year [1952], Mossadegh sent his economic expert Ali Amini to Bonn with the task of recruiting hundreds of German oilmen to replace the British experts after the planned nationalization of the Iranian oil industry [that he envisioned would take place]."[938]

Lucien Conein, who we discussed in Chapter Four, spent time at Skorzeny's Madrid training camp in 1954, where OAS assassin Jean Souetre was Skorzeny's chief trainer.[939]

Victor Oswald was a Madrid businessman connected to SOFINDUS, the WCC, the Donovan/ Dulles stay-behind armies in Europe, Otto Skorzeny, Thomas Eli Davis, Jean Pierre Lafitte, and the Nazi group operating out of Madrid. It was an international Fascist group that involved big business interests, CIA right-wingers and assassination operatives, ex-Nazis, European Monarchists, and American far-right Fascists, who worked together for over a decade before JFK's murder. And Schacht felt right at home with ex-SOFINDUS Nazis and their Fascist collaborators from the West. "Liberty is not synonymous with laziness," Schacht wrote in his diary. "Freedom is not given away: it must be earned daily...Whoever desires better housing, clothing, and food must work for it. That's God's law...The idea of a welfare state as a kind of public benefactor under official leadership is an assumption leading directly to totalitarian communism, but which has nothing whatever in common with the sense of responsibility to the individual."[940]

As for Skorzeny, a CIA officer in the Madrid embassy, who knew Skorzeny socially, wrote in 1960 that: "He is a proud and rather vain individual who loves to talk about his wartime experiences...In discussions, it is evident that he is rather anti-Semitic and violently anti-Communist..." Former British Army officer H.M.S. "Dusty Miller," discussing the war with Skorzeny over dinner, mentioned Hitler's invasion of the Soviet Union. Surely, he mentioned naively, the Germans would have had a much easier campaign had they befriended the people they conquered. "At that, there was silence," Miller recalled. Then Skorzeny said, 'It's not possible to make friends with them... because they are sub-humans.'"[941]

Men like Skorzeny and Schacht still embraced Nazi ideology and would have done anything to protect their beloved homeland from the Communist horde from Russia.

***

In April 1963, the United States quietly dismantled Jupiter missiles deployed in Italy and Turkey in compliance with the agreement Bobby Kennedy made with Soviet Ambassador Anatoly Dobrynin at the time of the Cuban Missile Crisis. They agreed that in exchange for the Soviet withdrawal of missiles from Cuba, the United States would never invade Cuba again. They agreed to remove the Jupiter missiles from Turkey in "four or five months." The missiles in Italy were not part of the agreement; however, the Kennedy brothers decided to include them as well so that it would not appear that the removal of Turkish missiles was an even swap for the Russian removal of missiles from Cuba. Both Italy and Turkey were not pleased with what transpired. Each country considered the missiles symbols of a U.S. security commitment. Turkish Defense Minister İlhami Sancar worried it would have an adverse impact on his country's "confidence" in the U.S. At the same time, Italian Defense Minister Giulio Andreotti thought it represented a "graphic step backward" for Italy's role in nuclear deterrence.[942]

On December 21, 1962, JFK and Britain's Harold Macmillan met in the Bahamas to settle what was called the Skybolt Crisis. The U.S. had previously agreed to supply Britain with Skybolt missiles in return for a ballistic missile submarine base near Glasgow, Scotland. However, Macmillan rejected Kennedy's offer because he wanted the U.S. to supply Britain with Polaris missiles instead, which were more technologically advanced than Skybolt. Kennedy only wanted Polaris available as part of a multilateral force within NATO.

The Nassau Agreement they agreed to became the basis of the Polaris Sales Agreement, which allowed the mounting of British nuclear warheads on Polaris missiles in times of "supreme peril." The treaty was signed between Britain and the U.S. on April 6, 1963, the same month the U.S. removed missiles from Turkey and Italy. JFK offered De Gaulle the same deal, but he refused. De Gaulle did not trust the Americans to defend Europe with nuclear weapons because he believed JFK would let Western Europe fall under Communist control rather than risk a Soviet nuclear attack on American cities. De Gaulle considered Germany a more reliable ally. Germany's Adenauer agreed. He also did not think Kennedy was strong enough to stand up to the Soviets and feared he would ultimately recognize East Germany and resist German unification. Back in February, Germany and France signed a mutual defense pact that stated they jointly would rely less on NATO and the United States to protect themselves. Adenauer had resented Kennedy ever since he made a public declaration to the Russians that made him question JFK's determination to protect Germany. "If Germany developed an atomic capability of its own," Kennedy said. "If it developed many missiles or a strong national army that threatened war, then I would understand your concern, and I would share it."[943]

April 1963 was a critical month in the JFK assassination saga. Missiles were removed from Italy and Turkey, weakening Europe's defense network. De Gaulle and Adenauer did not trust President Kennedy, and they were not the only ones who felt that way. It was around April that the collaboration between Otto Skorzeny and his Nazi group in Madrid, the OAS French revolutionary officers, European Monarchists, the CIA, and others began to plot to remove JFK from office. They all distrusted President Kennedy's ability to protect Europe for the same reasons as de Gaulle and Adenauer. To make matters worse, the Kennedy brothers were moving forward with another attack against Cuba in December 1963 that would have potentially resulted in World War III. In the collective mind of those who realized they waited too long to recognize the threat that Hitler posed to the security of the world, they had no choice – President Kennedy had to go.

***

Coup in Dallas tells us that on April 30, 1963, Lafitte's datebook reads: "Walker & Souetre in New Orleans/arms (Davis? – where?) Then, on May 9, Lafitte writes: "Souetre and Davis in April here [Hotel] – Shaw Where? Davis is Thomas Eli Davis, and Shaw refers to Clay Shaw, whom Jim Garrison tried in a court of law for complicity in the JFK assassination. As we know, Shaw was part of the anti-Castro movement in New Orleans and aligned with Permindex. This Italian company provided funding for the OAS French Generals fighting de Gaulle and other European anti-Communist operations. Davis ran guns with Jack Ruby and knew Lafitte. There is evidence he was in New Orleans in the summer of 1963, which we will address in the appropriate chapter. For now, consider that Oswald arrived in New Orleans on April 24 after the Walker shooting incident. Six days later, Walker and OAS assassin Jean Souetre came to New Orleans, and Lafitte wondered where Davis was, suggesting he was supposed to be in New Orleans as well. Then, on May 10, the day after a Lafitte May 9th entry that reads, "Souetre and Davis in April here [Hotel] – Shaw Where?", Reily Coffee Company hired Oswald. Reily also had a connection to the anti-Castro movement in New Orleans. As will be shown, Davis stayed at the LaSalle Hotel in New Orleans in August and may have also stayed there in May.

Interestingly, Lafitte's entry for May 10 reads: "T. says tail LO [Oswald] – no direct contact – calls No. Report to Angleton." The logical conclusion one can draw from this is that Oswald passed a test in Dallas, which must have been the Walker shooting attempt. They were to stay away from Oswald but kept an eye on him to see how he would react, which was the day after Lafitte's entry says that Thomas Davis arrived in New Orleans, where Oswald was. He was already the prime candidate to be the assassination patsy, and chances are it was Davis who was tailing Oswald.

On September 17, a week before Oswald leaves New Orleans for Mexico City, Lafitte writes, "Willoughby, Shaw?" So, it appears something was happening between Willoughby, Davis, and Shaw that began in May, continued at least until September, and had something to do with tracking Oswald.[944]

Clay Shaw's intelligence connections throughout the Cold War are well known. In the mid-1950s, he was involved in international spying on behalf of the CIA. In 1955, he traveled to Czechoslovakia as "a CIA observer." The following year, he was in Spain and Italy, also on the Agency's behalf. It was around that time, when various Fascist groups descended on Madrid, that Shaw purchased an apartment in the Spanish capital.[945]

***

The French connection to the Fascist international network is indisputable. Philippe de Vosjoli had served with French intelligence during World War II and, in 1951, became de Gaulle's liaison with the CIA's counterintelligence. It put him in touch with James Angleton, whom he had known since the early post-war years. The two men bonded, and before long, de Vosjoli was reporting to Angleton at the CIA as often as he was reporting to his superiors in France.

De Vosjoli approved of the OAS resistance during the Algerian war for independence, which meant he supported Algerian Governor General Jacques Soustelle, who was willing to assassinate de Gaulle if it kept Algeria a French colony. On December 7, 1960, de Vosjoli hosted a luncheon in Washington, D.C., in honor of Soustelle. Many CIA dignitaries were in attendance, including Richard Bissell and Richard Helms, which infuriated de Gaulle. On April 29, 1961, James Reston wrote in the *New York Times* that the CIA "was involved in an embarrassing liaison with the anti-Gaullist officers..." *Time* magazine reported in its May 12 issue that Maurice Challe, another OAS leader, had been "encouraged by the CIA."

CIA financed OAS through its front companies, which included Permindex and the Centro Mondiale Comerciale, which involved Clay Shaw and his New Orleans associates, like Banister and Maurice Gatlin, who were familiar with Lee Harvey Oswald. And because President Kennedy had been a strong supporter of Algerian independence since his Senate days, it was one more reason to make him an enemy of the old guard in Europe. [946]

Permindex and Shaw served to tie things together and explained why the New Orleans group played a subordinate role to the lead Fascist group in Madrid in the assassination. As previously described, Souetre and Davis were working on a weapons deal with Clay Shaw that must have been for the OAS. We know Souetre met with Davis in New Orleans again in April, this time with Clay Shaw, regarding the arms deal they had previously discussed. Shaw's involvement is not unexpected, considering Permindex's close relationship with the OAS in France, which connects him to de Vosjoli.[947]

Frank Brandsetter was friends with Jack Crichton and David Phillips, and also knew Phillipe de Vosjoli. During the war, he led an interrogation team in Germany while the U.S. Army had Skorzeny and Gehlen incarcerated there. Brandsetter was close to George de Mohrenschildt, Sam Kail, and Dorothy Matlack. Clearly, there was sufficient opportunity and justification for American, German, and French operatives to come together long before the JFK assassination.

In *The Skorzeny Papers*, Major Ralph P. Gains writes that Victor Oswald was an original member of the SOE/OSS group that established BACC and the WCC. It connected Thomas Davis, through Thomas Proctor and Victor Oswald, to the Madrid Fascist group. In 1963, Davis was recruiting an army with Loran Hall to invade Haiti while running guns with Jack Ruby. After the JFK assassination, Davis was released from custody in Morocco by QJ/WIN, a CIA assassin who worked for William Harvey as part of the CIA's ZR/RIFLE, which further connected Davis and the Madrid group to the CIA.[948]

There was ample justification for the U.S. military to have invaded Cuba after the JFK assassination. Still, nothing happened. West Berlin and Europe remained safe, and the United States and the Soviet Union averted a nuclear holocaust. The ex-Nazi, French, and American international network of anti-Communist Fascists chose to sacrifice an American President so the Fascist eutopia they envisioned for Europe and the U.S. remained a reality.

CHAPTER SEVENTEEN

BATTLE LINES ARE DRAWN

Despite talking about normalizing relations with Castro, Jack and Bobby Kennedy still wanted to get rid of him. Violent sabotage raids by militant anti-Castro groups were an option, but for the most part, were out of the question. At a February 1963 press conference, President Kennedy said one way to eliminate communism in Cuba was through an internal revolt.[949] However, the CIA was on record that Castro was too popular for that to happen, and they were appalled that the Kennedy brothers were still considering this. It was a repudiation of the CIA's own 1963 National Intelligence Estimate on Cuba, which said that Castro was secure in power and had sufficient popularity to repel all challenges against him. Even worse, since JFK terminated Mongoose and the CIA's Cuban exile sabotage raids, Bobby Kennedy had taken matters into his own hands with a new group of Cuban exiles that leaned to the left. It made Richard Helms livid.[950]

Bobby assembled a group of Cuban exiles who the administration believed would be more appealing to the people of Cuba than the right-wing exiles favored by the CIA. It included men like Enrique Ruiz (Harry) Williams, a former Havana bus driver and union leader who had been imprisoned during the Bay of Pigs invasion and recently released. He and Bobby became close. There was Manolo Ray, a moderate leftist who had served briefly in Castro's government. And Howard Hunt's friend Manuel Artime, who gained Bobby's confidence with his substantial following among the armed Cuban exile soldiers. Bobby's plan was for Ray and Williams to take the political lead in Miami and Washington while Artime organized the exile military force in Nicaragua. The plan was to launch an invasion from a Latin American country in conjunction with an internal military revolt within Cuba. If Castro attempted to suppress the internal challenge from rebellious officers forcibly, the U.S. considered itself justified to intervene militarily to allow the people of Cuba to decide what was best for their country. Another possibility was a staged attack against Guantanamo or another Latin American country allied with the United States.[951]

The plan was essentially an admission by Bobby Kennedy that to remove Castro from power, the U.S. military had to be involved. It was why an internal military coup in Cuba was essential. It would have allowed the Cuban government in exile to enter Cuba and establish itself as Castro's replacement. Once that happened, Castro was bound to retaliate, and the government in exile would have asked the United States for help. Somehow, Bobby Kennedy convinced himself that this was probable cause for the U.S. military to enter Cuba and get rid of Castro, and the Soviets would sit idly by and do nothing. But then, did he really care? The intent was to get his brother reelected, and he needed Castro gone to guarantee that would happen.

In January 1963, New York Republican Governor Nelson Rockefeller, a 1964 presidential hopeful, accused Kennedy of withholding facts before the Missile Crisis blockade (which was true) and doing it again regarding the "Cuban war-making build-up. This, as the first, probably is just a starter," Rockefeller said. Two weeks later, Rockefeller continued, "Increasingly it is clear that Kennedy did negotiate with the Russians about Cuba; did get a half agreement to withdraw some troops; did impliedly at least accept a Russian force of greater or less strength in Cuba – in a word, was jockeyed into the position of agreeing to merit a Russian force in Cuba. This will raise hell as it increasingly comes out." He told Texas Congressmen that "there has been a sharp change of policy of which the public has not been advised." The message was that President Kennedy was soft on communism. A concerned Rockefeller said he found the suspension of raids against Cuba "very hard to understand. I hope it is not an arrangement to appease Khrushchev."[952]

Nelson Rockefeller was a formidable opponent and a leading Republican challenger in the early months of 1963. He was the only Republican who could win the large Northern industrial cities, as well as the conservatives from the West and Southwest. White Southerners found him more appealing than JFK. According to Roswell Gilpatric, who knew the Rockefeller brothers, "JFK regarded Nelson Rockefeller as his probable opposition in 1964. He had both a fascination and a fear of Rockefeller" because he was a liberal Republican whose wealth and prestige were more formidable than the Kennedys.[953] It was why John Kennedy supported what his brother was doing. He knew Cuba would be a weakness for him unless they did something about Castro. On February 28, JFK met with the Joint Chiefs and asked them how long it would take to put American troops in

Cuba. The projected eighteen days was too long, he thought, and he wanted it shortened.[954]

Desmond FitzGerald was the one man at the CIA who gave the impression, perhaps disingenuously, that he supported Bobby's plan, even though he had sent a memo to John McCone saying a revolt by the Cuban people was unrealistic. What FitzGerald wanted was to squeeze the Cuban economy while simultaneously trying to put together a military coup. If McCone agreed, then FitzGerald would look to identify dissidents in the Cuban military and other high-level officials in the Castro government who could lead a revolt. He was adamant that the U.S. military would have to get involved.[955]

On March 14, Bobby sent JFK a memo suggesting they pursue a combined program to stop Cuban subversion abroad and to appeal to Cuban military leaders within Cuba to overthrow Castro. "I would not like it said a year from now that we could have had this internal breakup in Cuba, but we just did not set the stage for it," wrote Bobby.[956]

As we will see, before long, the CIA embraced the idea of an internal military coup, probably because it was the only way they could stay relevant in the war against Castro. For despite his alleged close relationship with the Kennedys, as David Talbot described in *Brothers*, FitzGerald "raged against the way the President's brother was micromanaging Cuba policy and running his own secret game with the exile leaders he favored....The more affiliated Artime became with Bobby, the less the CIA trusted him." According to declassified CIA files, FitzGerald ordered surveillance placed on Artime in July 1963.[957]

***

After being released by Castro with the other Bay of Pigs prisoners, Manuel Artime, Pepe and Roberto San Roman, and Harry Williams met with the President at the Kennedy compound in West Palm Beach, Florida. Angelo Kennedy (no relation), a close aide to Artime, recalled: "I remember Artime leaving Kennedy's office with a broad grin...he gave me a huge hug, saying, 'We got it! We got everything!'"[958]

According to Artime, Bobby told him to negotiate a deal to train an invasion force outside the U.S., and the money would flow. Soon, Artime negotiated agreements with Guatemala, Monkey Point in Nicaragua, and on the property of Colonel Vico Jimenez in Costa Rica to train for the upcoming invasion. Bobby made good on his promised financial support. The CIA estimated the total given to Artime was $4,933,293.00, but the exiles said it was closer to $9 million. Money was sent from Canada to banks in Switzerland, then to Costa Rican and Nicaraguan front companies. Most exile training took place in Central America, as well as the CIA's 'Farm" in Camp Perry, Virginia.[959]

While Bobby Kennedy was developing a cadre of Cuban exiles who would one day head a liberal government in Cuba, the right-wing, ex-Batista Cuban exiles wanted to know where they fit in. A group in Miami wrote a letter to Bobby explaining that the other Brigade members were "seething with indignation."[960] It got them nowhere, which was why they eventually turned to Paulino Sierra's group for help.

Meanwhile, the CIA was not happy with their subordinate role and that the Attorney General was funding training camps in Latin America without keeping them involved. According to Army Intelligence documents released in 1998, Miami CIA Station Chief Ted Shackley "has not been given responsibility for the autonomous operations springing from Central America, and he is personally skeptical about these operations. Shackley is a very knowledgeable and professional individual." Professionalism was essential to the CIA, and when it came to covert operations, Robert Kennedy was an amateur. Tom Clines, the liaison between Artime and the JM/WAVE station, recalled that Shackley "hated the idea that the Cubans had gotten to the Kennedys and convinced them that they could operate on their own." Cuba Project Executive Officer Sam Halpern said, "It was insanity. If the exiles didn't like what their case officers told them, they'd just pick up the phone and call Bobby. Nobody knew who was running the thing." More importantly, Shackley recalled: "We didn't see any evidence that the military revolt would be successful. There was no proof of large numbers of Cuban officers interested."[961]

***

The CIA's plan to instigate a military revolt within Cuba was called AMTRUNK. A contact within Cuba told Tad Szulc of the *New York Times* that some Cuban military officers were dissatisfied with the current state of affairs. He approached Bobby Kennedy, who then took Szulc to meet with JFK. By all indications, the CIA as a group never supported the plan. By April 5, Shackley concluded the CIA should terminate AMTRUNK "at the earliest possible moment:" CIA Headquarters cabled JMWAVE five days later that they agreed because "CIA could not be certain that hostile elements were unaware of the plan."[962]

In *Robert Kennedy and His Times*, Arthur Schlesinger commented on the CIA's concerns:

"The CIA wished to organize Castro's overthrow from outside Cuba, as against the White House, the Attorney General's office and State who wished to support an anti-Castro movement inside Cuba. The CIA's idea was to fight a war; the others hoped to promote a revolution. Any successful anti-Castro movement inside Cuba would have to draw on disenchanted Castroites and aim to rescue the revolution from the Communists. This approach, stigmatized as Fidelismo sin Fidel, was opposed by businessmen, both Cuban and American, who dreamed of the restoration of nationalized properties. But the CIA alternative was probably dictated less by business interests than by the agency's preference for operations it could completely control – especially strong in this case because of the Cuban reputation for total inability to keep anything secret."[963]

After the Bay of Pigs, President Kennedy took responsibility for paramilitary operations away from the CIA and gave it to the military, which was why responsibility for AMTRUNK, an interagency operation, was given to the Department of the Army under Cyrus Vance and his aides Joseph Califano and Alexander Haig. The CIA was not pleased.[964]

Sam Halpern, who served as Richard Helms's long-time executive assistant, had nothing but contempt for the Kennedys thirty-five years later. He told an interviewer: "You're dealing with two guys in the White House who made a botch of things at the Bay of Pigs and haven't a clue what it means to run clandestine operations or covert operations or whatever you want to call them. They've got their fingers all over the place trying to make amends, and the more they try to make amends, the worse it gets. Kennedy wouldn't listen. They believe in keeping on doing all this, busy-ness, busy-ness, busy-ness."

Halpern was referencing the minutes of a meeting of the NSC in May, where McGeorge Bundy said the time had come to consider that Castro might be here to stay. McNamara thought they should "buy off Castro" by ending the American embargo of the Cuban economy in exchange for Castro breaking ties to the Soviet Union. The CIA's FitzGerald did not mention anything about an internal military revolt in Cuba. Instead, he listed all the covert operations they could launch if they were allowed to do so. Bobby Kennedy entered as FitzGerald was speaking and chimed in: "The U.S. must do something even though we do not believe our actions would bring him down." In other words, for political reasons, with the 1964 presidential election on the horizon and JFK's reelection in jeopardy, the American people had to believe the Kennedys were committed to doing something about Cuba. Bundy responded, "We can give an impression [of] busy-ness in Cuba, and we can make life difficult for Castro." Halpern did not look at Cuba through a political lens. "I'll tell you one thing," he said, "I didn't know that word 'busy-ness.' Des never mentioned it [FitzGerald]...and it was a good thing he didn't because you might have had a *Seven Days in May* at that point." "If that word 'busy-ness' had gotten out to the military forces...and everybody else in the U.S. government that was knocking their balls off trying to do this nonsense [the pinprick raids against Cuba], there might have been a revolt of some kind," he said. "I might have led it."[965]

Still, publicly, the CIA continued to support a military revolt from within. At a Special Group meeting on April 25 attended by President Kennedy, McCone recommended an internal military coup as the best source of action. FitzGerald added they knew of several high-level Cuban officials who were unhappy with Castro.[966]

The military agreed, or at least pretended to. On May 10, Maxwell Taylor sent Secretary of the Army Cyrus Vance a study explaining that the best course of action was for the U.S. to exploit any revolution that showed a reasonable promise of success. The best scenario was for the U.S. to encourage disaffected leaders in the Cuban government to turn against Castro. They would inevitably have to ask the United States for help, and at that time, the military could apply full strength to an invasion that would succeed. So, just six months before the JFK assassination, both the Joint Chiefs and the CIA agreed that a U.S.-initiated internal military revolt within Cuba, followed by a U.S. military intervention, was the best course of action to get rid of Castro, even though there wasn't evidence that an internal military revolt was possible.[967]

At a May 28 NSC meeting, Bundy opined there was no certainty they would be able to get rid of Castro. McCone altered his position once again, saying the plan should be to increase economic hardship in Cuba, continue sabotage raids, and maybe the Cuban military would overthrow the Communists and restore relations with the U.S. But maybes did not sit well with those trying to develop a viable solution to eliminate Castro.[968]

McNamara did not think the sabotage McCone called for would be successful. Instead, he liked the idea of provoking Castro to provide an excuse for the United States to invade Cuba. An attack against Guantanamo, as an example, but the Kennedys wanted something that would not lead to World War III and, at the same time, give JFK a political shot in the arm. Sabotage raids against Cuba would provide that. So, the Kennedys did an about-face and pressured FitzGerald to develop a sabotage program. On June 8, FitzGerald presented a paper to the Standing Group that made it

303

clear that U.S. military intervention or any effort to provoke a confrontation with the Cubans was not acceptable. He called for maximum pressure without the use of U.S. military forces. It contradicted what he had said on April 25, that military intervention might be necessary.[969]

Then, on June 19, FitzGerald reversed his position again. He said sabotage was not acceptable because it made it impossible to maintain plausible deniability. Someone would be captured and talk.[970] It seemed the CIA just wanted to remain part of the operation and was willing to say anything to ensure that was the case. Meanwhile, in an apparent attempt to sabotage the Kennedy brothers, the CIA advised Army Intelligence that Manuel Artime was in Nicaragua and Costa Rica looking for a country from where he could launch an attack against Cuba – without input from the CIA or the Joint Chiefs.[971]

What Artime was doing was not secret. On July 24, the *Washington Post* quoted him as saying: "We are leaving the United States to establish a base in Central America." "In much less than one year, we'll be fighting inside Cuba." The article also said he was seeking help from Costa Rica, Panama, Venezuela, and Columbia.[972]

The State Department and Dean Rusk remained unconvinced and wanted to know what the prospects were for reconciliation with Castro. If the U.S. invaded Cuba, a potential movement by the Soviets against West Berlin was what worried Rusk. As John McCone wrote: "I have the impression that Secretary Rusk…seems to feel that there is some opportunity for a rapprochement with Castro." Despite this, by July 25, a memo distributed by the State Department's Intelligence and Research Special Studies Group proposed that reputable leaders be organized under the banner "Authentic July 26 Movement" to engage in sabotage and guerilla warfare against Castro. Of course, State was referring to the leftist anti-Batista exiles working with Robert Kennedy.[973]

Five days after the *Washington Post* quoted Manuel Artime bragging about how he was looking for a Latin American country to launch an invasion against Cuba, the Department of Defense completed a four-month study that concluded Cuba was not a military threat to the Western Hemisphere, that Cuba had been isolated from free-world trade, and needed the Soviet Bloc to survive; that covert action was "too low to have an impact;" that the U.S. did not make any noticeable advancements in an attempt to develop opposition groups inside Cuba; that countersubversion efforts in Latin America were working and limited Castro's ability to expand his revolution; that diplomacy had proved to be unsuccessful in eliminating the presence of the Soviet military in Cuba; and finally, that change was unexpected.

The study recommended the following courses of action, called "Tracks," going forward: Track 1: Maintain current economic sanctions and diplomacy; Track 2: Track 1 plus contingency planning that would allow for a quick response to new developments, turning small events into a crisis that the U.S. might resolved to their advantage; Track 3: The U.S. would take affirmative action, one of which might be a "covertly-assisted rebellion," Track 4: Reach an accommodation with Castro.[974]

There appeared to be something for everyone, except the option to train an exile army in a Latin American country to invade Cuba, which was the one option Robert Kennedy was pursuing. It was not surprising since Bobby's primary motivation was to impact the 1964 election positively. Still, an invasion run by an amateur without the inclusion of the military or the CIA remained a matter of concern. On August 9, FitzGerald wrote McGeorge Bundy about Luis Somoza, the ex-president of Nicaragua, and Artime's dealings with him. According to FitzGerald, Somoza wanted to initiate an uprising in Cuba, which he thought would force the United States to get involved militarily. Or, if Castro decided to retaliate militarily against Nicaragua, the U.S. would come to its aid, triggering a military confrontation with Cuba. Somoza claimed that "leading United States Government officials" had assured him this was the case, which likely was a reference to Robert Kennedy, to whom Artime was reporting.[975]

On August 13, an obviously concerned FitzGerald wrote a memo titled "US Courses of Action in the Event of a Military Revolt in Cuba" to Califano at the Pentagon. The National Archives has a record that the memo did exist, but it is now conveniently missing. Based on the title, we can surmise that FitzGerald told the Defense Department to be prepared to react to a military coup in Cuba, should one occur.

Two days later, FitzGerald met with JFK, Bundy, and others at the White House. It was not an ordinary Standing Group or Special Group meeting. John McCone, Richard Helms, William Colby, and Bruce Cheever from the CIA were present. It was the most men from the CIA to attend a meeting up to that time. The White House recording system taped the conference. It can be listened to at the John F. Kennedy Presidential Library in Boston, with the following caveat: "Eighteen minutes are deleted as secret." What were they possibly discussing that had to remain hidden? Well, Colby was involved in Vietnam at the time, and discussions about forcibly overthrowing Diem had already begun, so it is safe to assume that a potential coup in

Cuba was also on the agenda. And it warranted the erasure of eighteen minutes of tape to keep forever secret what they intended to do. Was assassination still an option? We can only guess, but considering the assassination of Diem occurred on November 2, the group probably discussed this being applicable to Cuba as well.[976]

***

Years later, Richard Helms told the Church Committee that JFK wanted to instigate a revolt inside Cuba. "Activity against Cuba picked up sometime in that subsequent year [1963]....," he testified. "[JFK] mentioned the desire to have the military or some force inside and rise up against Castro, some internal revolt." According to Helms, that was why the CIA began recruiting high-level agents in Cuba, which coincided with FitzGerald contacting the U.S. Army to get them involved. The CIA was looking to put together biographies of the significant Cuban commanders that the Army had, and they were more than happy to furnish that to the Agency in late July.[977]

In the first five months of 1963, three drafts of a "Plan for a Coup in Cuba" were investigated on a purely hypothetical basis. However, starting in the critical month of May and over the next four months, ten additional drafts were approved by the CIA and the State Department. The program remained secretive – only about a dozen people knew these were not just contingency plans but actual plans designed to be part of the overall attempt to get rid of Castro. How secret was this? They remained classified for over three decades.[978]

According to the plan, the objective was to find a leader in Cuba who had "some power base in the Cuban army," and in conjunction with this, the U.S. would "seek the cooperation of selected Cuban exile leaders." The latter, of course, would be the left-leaning Cuban exiles who were working with Bobby Kennedy unless the CIA and the Joint Chiefs did something to change that, such as removing from office the man who gave Bobby all his unbridled power.

The intent was to stage an internal "palace coup in Cuba [that would] neutralize the top echelon of Cuban leadership." And it was important that "the revolt appear genuine and not open to the charge of being a facade for a forcible U.S. overthrow of Castro [so] a well-planned and successful 'rescue' of a revolt could be made politically acceptable" to U.S. allies and the Soviets under the right conditions. In other words, maintaining plausible deniability was a must. Then, after Castro's death, President Kennedy would "warn Soviets not to intervene." The leaders of the coup "would have announced via radio and other means the … establishment of a Provisional Government. They would have appealed to the U.S. for recognition and support, particularly for air cover and a naval blockade, ostensibly to make certain that the Soviets do not intervene but actually, by prearrangement, to immobilize the Cuban Air Force and Navy." That was necessary because "twelve to thirteen thousand military personnel of all kinds remain [in Cuba]." After "completion of such initial air attacks as may be necessary, provision will be made for the rapid, incremental introduction of balanced forces, to include full-scale invasion."[979]

The goal for the Kennedys remained a free and democratic Cuba run by Cuban exiles who had opposed Batista. So, in the plan proposed, "the OAS will send representatives to the island to assist the Provisional Government in preparing for and conduct [sic] of free elections." The "Provisional Government" would include the Cuban-American exile troops and the leaders of four exile groups, who would secure bases outside the U.S. prior to the coup. The four exile leaders were Manuel Artime, the liberal Manola Ray (JURE), and Eloy Menoyo (SNFE), who had tried to overthrow Castro in 1959 with William Morgan and was now working for the U.S. Army along with Alpha 66. How Menoyo wound up being a part of this group is hard to understand, other than he was a military asset, as was Artime. Tony Varona, who was still working with the Mafia but also had leftist leanings, was included as well.[980]

It is hard to imagine that the same CIA who sabotaged the 1959 coup out of fear that the Soviets would march into West Berlin would favor such a plan. If successful, it could have led to World War III, which the U.S. military wanted, but no one else did, which was why, within months, CIA memos voiced their displeasure with the operation. One memo noted that Manola Ray's "JURE was currently sponsoring a plan to assassinate Fidel Castro and other high-ranking Cuban government officials as part of an operation designed to incite an internal rebellion in Cuba." Which meant assassination was still going on but without the CIA's involvement. The same memo continued, "This plan involves an internal uprising with the report of certain Cuban military figures … among the key figures in the plot are [sic] Juan Almeida." At that point, no one at State knew about Almeida, and Dean Rusk would only be told about him after JFK's death, even though he would quickly become the central figure in the Omega Plan.[981]

***

Two declassified memos, first published in 2006, reveal that more than two months prior to the Bay of Pigs invasion, the CIA was aware that Commander Juan Almeida, the head of Cuba's army, "was disgusted with the communistic situation" in Cuba and wanted to defect. His name surfaced again in mid-May 1963 when the Cuban Commander learned from an *Associated Press* article that the CIA was backing "a new all-out drive to...topple the Fidel Castro regime." The article also stated that "the plan calls for a junta in exile [with a goal of] ultimate invasion [and] seeking to put together the junta was Enrique Ruiz-Williams, a Bay of Pigs veteran and friend of US Attorney Robert F. Kennedy." Almeida knew Williams. They had first met in Cuba in the early 1950s when Almeida and Castro's revolutionaries were still fighting in the mountains.[982]

Almeida reached out to Williams and asked him to call a number that was safe from wiretaps. When they talked, Almeida told Williams that Castro was a dictator and that he wanted to stage an internal coup to topple him if he had assurances that JFK would back him. Almeida was never properly vetted, which did not stop negotiations from happening, with Williams acting as a go-between for Bobby and Almeida. At the same time, Bobby kept President Kennedy up to date as things progressed. Bobby's official phone logs at the National Archives show that on May 13, at 5:50 P.M., he took a call from President Kennedy. Fifteen minutes later, the Attorney General spoke with Williams, and Bobby told the Cuban exile that JFK had accepted Almeida's offer to orchestrate a coup from within.[983]

On May 29, just over two weeks after the Kennedys approved of Almeida, a memo from Joint Chiefs Chairman Maxwell Taylor said it was "a matter of priority" to examine the possibility "of an invasion of Cuba at a time controlled by the United States in order to overthrow the Castro government." The memo included "a proposed date for the invasion."

There was also a 1963 report that confirmed the Almeida plan was in the works. Sent to the CIA Director, it contained information from Bernard Barker about an "operation including Juan Almeida" that was to "overthrow" Fidel, who would be replaced by a new Cuban government to "be recognized immediately" by the Kennedy administration. A second CIA dispatch discussed a plan for "an internal uprising" in Cuba by "Cuban military figures, who are conspiring against Fidel Castro. Among the key figures in the plot [is] Juan Almeida."[984]

Meanwhile, as the military was busy formulating coup plans once they knew Almeida was on board, JFK and Bobby further restricted the CIA to a supporting role. Their primary function was to provide secret support to the exile leaders working with Bobby and to get additional U.S. intelligence assets into Cuba prior to the coup. CIA's JM/WAVE Miami station, which had been so instrumental in waging a war against Castro the previous year, now became irrelevant. They were too close to the right-wing Cuban exiles and American mercenaries who supported them to play a pivotal role in the new operation. Only John McCone, Richard Helms, and a handful of leaders at the CIA knew about Almeida and the plan to overthrow Fidel.[985]

However, the CIA still had to be involved to a certain extent, for if the exiles assassinated Castro, Almeida could not be held responsible for his death. If he were, the Cuban people were sure to rebel against the new Cuban exile regime that would take control of the government. In *The Hidden History of the JFK Assassination*, author Lamar Waldron wrote, "Williams told me someone else would 'take the fall' for Fidel's death. Williams said he had no involvement in finding the 'fall guy' that Robert Kennedy was handling with the CIA." Evidence taken from CIA memos and coup plan files indicates that a Russian sympathizer would be the one blamed for the crime. It was the same role Lee Harvey Oswald would play in the JFK assassination, and one wonders if he was initially the one to take the fall for killing Castro, which could explain why he wanted to enter Cuba via Mexico City in September 1963. Blaming a Communist defector to the Soviet Union like Oswald guaranteed Khrushchev could not use Castro's assassination as an excuse to take West Berlin. When that failed to materialize, those at the CIA who were trying to thwart the Robert Kennedy/Almeida plan concluded that the best way to do that was by turning their attention toward JFK and assassinating him, with Oswald's role becoming the patsy for JFK's assassination.[986]

***

Bobby Kennedy had William Harvey removed from all CIA Cuban operations after the Missile Crisis. However, with the blessing of James Angleton, he still met with his friend Johnny Roselli in Miami every four to six weeks. At other times, Roselli visited Harvey in Washington.[987] They remained close throughout 1963, and according to CIA files, "on February 18, 1963, Harvey and Roselli had drinks together in Los Angeles…[and] they agreed to put the assassination plotting on hold but leave the bounty on Castro of $150,000 where it was…but there is evidence that Harvey's collaboration with Roselli continued… A hotel receipt indicated that Harvey had paid the bill of a 'Mr. John A.' Walston' at a Miami hotel. Roselli's CIA alias was variously 'John A Ralston' or 'John Ralston….'" The CIA admitted that "on June 20, Roselli flew into Dulles airport in Washington and was picked up there by Bill Harvey…"

Meanwhile, in early 1963, Roselli hooked up in Key Biscayne with Santo Trafficante associate John Martino. Then, in early March, the Cubans picked up one of Roselli's hit squads in Havana, so the CIA/Mafia attempts to assassinate Castro were still in place.[988]

According to investigator Dr. Michael L. Kurtz, John Martino worked with Guy Banister and Carlos Marcello in the summer of 1963. He quoted the former Superintendent of the New Orleans Police Department saying that Martino "met with Marcello himself at the Town and Country Motel." FBI files also show that Martino knew the Kennedys intended to use Almeida in a military revolt within Cuba and that "President Kennedy was engaged in a plot to overthrow the Castro regime by preparing another invasion attempt against Cuba." Then, according to an FBI file not revealed until 1998, Martino told a small-time newspaper two months after the assassination that "Kennedy was embarked on a plan to get rid of Castro. There was to be another invasion and uprising in Cuba."[989]

Others with connections to New Orleans knew about the second invasion plan as well. An FBI report written just weeks after JFK's assassination said Jack Ruby stated, "the United States Government was sponsoring an invasion of Cuba." Another FBI memo later revealed that a close associate of David Ferrie told the Bureau about Ferrie's "dealings with the late Attorney General Robert Kennedy [and] plans for a Cuban second invasion." A friend of Banister wrote in the summer of 1963 that there was secret "Kennedy Administration planning" where Castro "would be the fall guy in a complete reorganization for the regime which will [then] be free of Soviet influence." Banister wrote that following Castro's removal, "a new government [would be] set up with such men as ... Manola Ray..." How did these men in New Orleans, who were close to Lee Oswald, know so much about an operation that was supposed to be secret? And how did these far-right wingers and Mafia figures know about a plan that involved Robert Kennedy and left-leaning Cuban exiles? The answer must be that the Cubans working with Bobby Kennedy told them, which means they were working together behind Bobby's back.[990]

Enrique Williams told author Lemar Waldron that Howard Hunt was one of two prominent CIA officers assigned to assist Williams. Kennedy's aides, former FBI agent William Turner, and *Vanity Fair* magazine all confirmed this to be the case. Bernard Barker was Hunt's assistant in 1963 with Williams while still maintaining a close relationship with the Mafia and CIA operatives like Morales, Hecksher, and Phillips. As Waldron wrote in *The Hidden History of the JFK Assassination*, Barker's declassified CIA re-

310

ports from the summer and fall of 1963 show him linked to the mob and the coup. He wrote "about a meeting between Manuel Artime and Tony Varona to discuss unity and noting Artime's meeting with Trafficante 'bagman' Frank Fiorini [Sturgis] in Dallas to buy an airplane." Another report mentions "Eloy Menoyo's plan to overthrow Fidel and the operation of Manolo Ray." He reported on the "efforts of Sam Benton, another private detective working for Carlos Marcello, to recruit an American mercenary as part of the CIA-Mafia plots to kill Fidel. The mercenary backed out when he learned that an associate of Johnny Roselli was involved in the plot."[991]

We know that Menoyo's Second National Front of the Escambray had joined forces with Alpha 66 and was working with the U.S. Army by this time and was also part of Paulino Sierra's group that received financing from the Mafia. Sam Papich was the FBI's liaison to the CIA. He was told by Harvey, "They [CIA] couldn't tell those Mafia types to go to hell. They were in bed with 'em…" There was "a very pregnant possibility… of this government being blackmailed either by Cubans for political purposes or by figures in organized crime for their own self-protection or aggrandizement."[992] The CIA was probably working with Sierra's group to prevent Bobby Kennedy's attempt to install a left-wing government in Cuba a reality.

Joe Shimon was a mysterious Washington D.C. detective who was a liaison between the CIA and the mob. Years later, he told his daughter Toni that a cabal of wealthy industrialists and influential people were responsible for the JFK assassination. They brought in a group of CIA-backed Cubans and several high-level disgruntled American intelligence agents who felt JFK had betrayed them. This group would have been operating independently from Bobby's group.[993]

"Angleton ran everything, controlled everything in the CIA," Shimon said. He also told his daughter he was close to Bill Harvey. As Peter Janney wrote in *Mary's Mosaic*, "Toni remembered a lot of strange people coming to her father's house during the early 1960s. Shimon confided that he was the CIA's principal liaison to the Mafia. When they started working on Castro's assassination, they held meetings in Shimon's house. People like Roselli, Giancana, Trafficante, Bill Harvey, and sometimes Angleton. "My father loved Bill Harvey," said Toni. "He was also close friends with Jim Angleton and, of course, Sam and Johnny."

"Bobby Kennedy was a mean son of a bitch," said Shimon, obviously remembering how the former attorney general had tried to implicate him in a wiretapping scandal. "No one I knew liked him. He was mean and nasty and thought it was him who should be president."[994]

Richard Helms would testify that he saw no difference between the Cuban exile effort and hiring the Mafia to assassinate Castro. Helms also believed that having mobsters shoot Fidel and having him replaced by a right-wing dictator was preferable to an internal coup that would lead to a coalition government, free elections, and democracy.[995] So, Helms continued the CIA/Mafia assassination plots in the summer of 1963 using David Morales and Roselli, but he did not tell McCone. We know Morales and Roselli were close, so this is entirely credible.[996]

Army officer Bradley Ayers helped the CIA train Cuban exiles in 1963. He said: "I further state with certainty that 'Dave' [Morales] controlled John Roselli," and he was unaware "that John Roselli was, in fact, a Mafia functionary, but I did know that he was involved in the planning and execution of the assassination [attempts] of Fidel Castro." "Morales held sway with Ted Shackley," the Miami station chief, Ayers said, "and dominated the entire operation agenda at the Station." He added that "from time to time, a man called 'Colonel' John Roselli, who worked out of CIA headquarters in Washington, used [an exile] team for raids and other clandestine operations. Roselli...was one of the few Americans authorized to actually go on commando missions into Cuba." Regarding the relationship between the CIA and Bobby Kennedy's second invasion operation, "people treated us with detachment and suspicion, regarding us as intruders in their secret," he said.[997]

David Morales was the Chief of Operations at JM/WAVE, and Roselli was "using an action group [of Cuban exiles] that, obviously, came under [his] supervision." Morales also worked closely with David Phillips at the Mexico City station. Morales took many trips to Mexico City in 1963, presumably to see Phillips.[998]

Winston Scott, who had been good friends with William Harvey for years, was the head of the CIA station in Mexico City, and he delegated all responsibilities related to AMWORLD to David Phillips. At the same time, Scott increased his anti-Castro operations. He hired four more secretaries to transcribe the mass of surveillance information the station was receiving. In May, Scott told headquarters that they had tapped six phone lines in the Cuban Embassy, five in the Soviet Embassy, and two in the Czech Embassy. He passed along eighty-seven pages of transcripts of conversations of people in the Cuban embassy. In late September, Lee Harvey Oswald would pay a visit to the Cuban and Soviet Embassies, trying to gain entrance to Cuba, and would be photographed and recorded.[999]

Winston Scott died in Mexico City in 1971 at the age of sixty-two of an apparent heart attack. Richard Helms late told congressional investigators that he "may" have authorized James Angleton to travel to Mexico City because Scott had written an unpublished memoir that allegedly refuted the CIA and Warren Commission claims about what the Mexico City station knew about Oswald and his Cuban contacts. "There may have been some concern that maybe Scott had something in his safe that might affect the Agency's work," Helms casually told investigators. Shortly after that, James Angleton flew to Mexico City and removed all incriminating evidence that could have embarrassed the Agency.[1000]

***

In summation, in the spring of 1963, the Kennedy brothers considered normalizing relations with Fidel Castro while planning for a second invasion of Cuba. With no experience whatsoever, Robert Kennedy ran the operation and hand-selected left-leaning Cuban exiles to manage the invasion and become the next Cuban government after they removed Castro. The key was to create an internal revolt within the Cuban military that would lead to a coup, even though the consensus was that an internal revolt would not happen. Once completed, the U.S. military would become involved in maintaining order in Cuba. At best, the CIA played a minor supportive role in the operation.

Meanwhile, Paulino Sierra was organizing various pro-Batista right-wing Cuban exile groups and American mercenary types in opposition to the leftist groups Robert Kennedy had assembled. The Mafia, oilmen, and industry leaders supplied the financing for this group, which had their hands tied by the Kennedy brothers, who refused to let them launch raids against the Cuban mainland. SNFE/Alpha 66 was working with them, as well as with the U.S. Army, although a relationship with specific individuals at the CIA still existed.

CIA secretly kept William Harvey involved in their operation along with John Roselli and other Mafia leaders, and the CIA continued the assassination plots against Castro. This group was supportive of the Paulino Sierra collection of Cuban exiles, and the CIA was a driving force behind this alliance. CIA operatives from the 1959 Havana coup attempt to oust Castro were frustrated by their exclusion from Bobby Kennedy's war against Castro, and these operatives were the ones who supported Sierra's group; people like David Morales, David Atlee Phillips, Howard Hunt, Henry Hecksher, Frank Sturgis, and Bernard Barker. Recall that during the Bay of Pigs, Operation 40 was going to murder the Cuban government in exile after they arrived in Cuba. The same fate may have awaited Enrique Williams and his compadres had they been successful. That is unless Enrique Williams was working with the CIA and right-wing Cuban exiles without Bobby knowing. If there is one thing we know about the CIA at that time, it is that they did not like to relinquish control, and they did not intend to do that here.

An operation designed to remove Castro from power may have included assassination, with Oswald traveling to Cuba to become the designated patsy. When that failed to materialize, the target became JFK. The Kennedy brother's objective was to get JFK reelected President by any means possible, even if it meant orchestrating a military takeover of Cuba that could lead to the Soviet occupation of West Berlin and the onset of World War III. That could not be allowed to happen. So, at some point, the anger of those who opposed the Kennedys and were not part of the Omega Plan was redirected away from Castro and toward John F. Kennedy to stop them before they created an international incident they would all regret.

Chapter Eighteen

Into the Belly of the Beast

Lee Harvey Oswald arrived in New Orleans by bus on April 25, 1963, a city that was a hotbed of anti-Communist, anti-Castro, and racist activity. As previously mentioned, Oswald had written about "the minute men [sic]" and "small armed communist and probably fascist groups." The Minutemen and fascism were flourishing in New Orleans. Before long, Oswald would enter the world of prominent Minutemen, such as ex-FBI man Guy Banister, whose office was called the Cuban Grand Central Station. Banister was well known for using informants to infiltrate Communist groups, which would define Oswald in the coming months and explain why the FBI focused on him in the summer of 1963.

On July 15, 1963, a *New York Post* article alleged that the "debilitated CPUSA is kept alive by the work which FBI undercover agents do for it in the course of maintaining their 'masquerade'... Hoover [should] be required to explain his use of public funds to strengthen a subversive body that he claims to oppose." Two days later, JFK held a press conference and said there was no evidence that civil rights leaders were Communists.[1001]

When he first arrived in New Orleans. Oswald moved in with his aunt and uncle, Lillian and Dutz Murret. As the HSCA reported, Dutz was "in the 1940s and 1950s and possibly until his death in 1964 an associate of significant organized crime figures affiliated with the Marcello organization. The committee established that Oswald was familiar with his uncle's underworld activities and had discussed them with his wife, Marina, in 1963."[1002]

According to FBI informant Joe Hauser, Carlos Marcello said he and some of his men did know Oswald: "I used to know his fuckin' family. His uncle, he work[ed] for me. Dat kid work for me, too." Marcello said Oswald had worked as a runner for his gambling network, the same one that involved Oswald's uncle. If true, it may have occurred in the mid-1950s when Oswald previously lived in New Orleans with his mother.[1003]

Oswald next visited the Louisiana Department of Labor employment office, and the interviewer wrote on his application that he was "Neat. Suit. Tie. Polite."[1004] On May 9, he found a job at William B. Reily Company as an oiler of coffee-making machinery. It was mundane work and not worthy of mention were it not that Reily was located just off Canal Street, on the 600 block of Magazine Street, less than a block away from Guy Banister's office. Owner William Reily was a significant financial supporter of the anti-Castro movement, including the Free Cuba Committee. As Jim Garrison wrote, "You would have to be practically a stranger to the city not to know that William Reily... had actively supported the anti-Castro movement for years."[1005] So once again, the Marxist Oswald found himself in the heart of right-wing America, and there is no indication he objected to the arrangement.

Recall that also on May 9, Lafitte's datebook entry reads, "Souetre and Davis in April here [Hotel] – Shaw Where?," and the entry for the next day reads: "T. says tail LO [Oswald] – no direct contact – calls No. Report to Angleton." The Lafitte group, under the direction of James Angleton, was keeping an eye on Oswald.[1006]

On his job application, Oswald listed two references: Sgt. Robert Hidell and Lt. J. Evans. Hidell was the name Oswald used in Dallas to purchase the mail-order rifle and the known alias of Richard Nagell and Jean Pierre Lafitte. Before long, the name Hidell would reappear in New Orleans related to Oswald's involvement with the Fair Play for Cuba Committee, and at the time of his arrest after the assassination, Oswald's wallet contained a fake military ID card with Hidell's name on it. So, his use of the name as a reference has significance. The same did not apply to the name Evans. Myrtle and Julian Evans had once rented an apartment to Oswald's mother, and they now helped him find a home at 4907 Magazine Street.[1007]

Later that day, Oswald telephoned his wife in Dallas and told her to join him in New Orleans since he had a job and a new apartment. "Papa loves us," Marina happily told Ruth Paine. Two days later, driven by Paine, Marina arrived in New Orleans. They gathered Oswald's belongings from the Murrets and settled into their new apartment with their daughter, June. A new life was about to begin for the struggling couple. On the surface, there was nothing unusual or mysterious going on, except that nothing was ever typical about Lee Harvey Oswald.

***

It is indisputable that Lee Oswald was in contact with both David Ferrie and Guy Banister in the summer of 1963. As I describe in *It Did Not Start With JFK*, the evidence suggests he originally crossed paths with both of them when he previously lived in New Orleans as a teenager in the mid-1950s. In addition, a New Orleans FBI report dated January 26, 1963, stated that "Gerard F. Tujague, owner of Gerard F. Tujague, Inc. Forwarding

Co....[was] a member and officer (vice president) of Friends of Democratic Cuba, a Cuban exile group (FDC) in New Orleans." Banister was associated with this group in 1961 when they attempted to purchase trucks using Oswald's name while he was still in the Soviet Union. [1008] According to the House Select Committee on Assassinations, "Tujague ... had employed Oswald as a messenger from November 1955 to January 1956....," so there was a previous Banister connection to Oswald that the FBI was aware of prior to the assassination.[1009]

Delphine Roberts was Guy Banister's secretary in the summer of 1963. They were romantically involved, which may explain why she knew as much as she did. According to Roberts, that summer, "Oswald introduced himself by name and said he was seeking an application form [to work for Banister] ... I gained the impression that he and Guy Banister already knew each other. After Oswald [had] filled out the application form, Guy Banister called him into the office. The door was closed, and a lengthy conversation took place. The young man left. I presumed then, and now am certain, that the reason for Oswald being there was that he was required to act undercover."[1010]

Oswald worked out of the Newman Building, which housed Banister's office. "Oswald came back a number of times," Roberts said. "He seemed to be on familiar terms with Banister and with the office ... he had the use of an office on the second floor, above the main office where we worked ... several times, Mr. Banister brought me upstairs, and in the office above I saw various writings stuck up on the wall pertaining to Cuba. There were various leaflets up there pertaining to Fair Play for Cuba. They were pro-Castro leaflets. Banister just didn't say anything about them one way or the other. But on several occasions, when some people who had been upstairs would bring some of that material down into the office, Banister was very incensed about it...."[1011]

Delphine's daughter also used the office upstairs to do photographic work. She told author Anthony Summers that she saw Oswald occasionally. Ross Banister told the HSCA that his brother "had mentioned seeing Oswald hand out Fair Play for Cuba literature on one occasion." He confirmed "Guy's interest in the assassination and Oswald."[1012] Ivan E. Nitschke, who had served in the FBI with Banister and also worked at 544 Camp Street, told the HSCA in a deposition that "Banister had some of these handbills [FPCC] in his office or made reference to them..." Allen Campbell, an ex-Marine who worked in Banister's office, recalled that Roberts told Banister she had seen Oswald outside. "Don't worry about him," Banister said.

317

"He's a nervous fellow, he's confused. He's with us; he's associated with the office."[1013]

Michael Kurtz was a professor of history at Southwestern University in Hammond, Louisiana. In 1980, he published an article in *Louisiana History* titled *"Lee Harvey Oswald in New Orleans: A Reappraisal."* Citing a "confidential source," he wrote that twice people had seen Ferrie and Oswald conversing at Mancuso's restaurant.

Jack Martin also worked out of Banister's office. He told Jim Garrison that Oswald had "offices" in Banister's building. He had spotted Ferrie "once or twice, maybe" with Oswald at Banister's office. Once, Ferrie walked in wearing "an army-type fatigue suit and sunglasses," accompanied by three or four young men, one of whom was named "Lee." "He used to be with me in the CAP when he was a little kid," Ferrie said of Oswald. "Oswald is a friend of mine."[1014]

Thomas Beckham said he and Oswald became "good buddies." He saw Oswald and Banister together at both the Newman Building office and a local cafeteria. He told the HSCA: "I can't understand this Russia thing because he was always 100% American, he seemed like." Oswald told him communism was Jewish because "Karl Marx was a Jew."[1015]

Beckham saw Oswald at Thompson's restaurant, as well as at Banister's office, where he heard Oswald call Banister "the chief." He recalled Lee had nothing good to say about Governor Connally, who, as Secretary of the Navy, refused to overturn Oswald's dishonorable discharge from the Marines. "I hate that son of a bitch," Oswald said. Both Gerry Patrick Hemming and Richard Case Nagell thought Connally was a target in Dallas.[1016]

Consuela Martin was a witness uncovered by Kurtz. Her office was next to Banister's, and "she saw Oswald in Banister's office at least half a dozen times in the late spring and summer of 1963....on every one of these occasions, Oswald and Banister were together." She also claimed Oswald asked her to type documents in Spanish.[1017]

William Gaudet admitted he worked for the CIA from 1947 through 1969. He published the *Latin American Report,* and his office was in Clay Shaw's International Trade Mart. The two men knew each other well. After one of Shaw's trips to South America, he wrote a letter of introduction for Gaudet, who was about to embark on an adventure to Lima, Peru.[1018] Three days after Ruby killed Oswald, the New Orleans FBI learned that in the summer of 1959, Ruby had purchased paintings while passing through their city. Ruby had been in New Orleans that August, stopping there on his way to Havana, so the story is credible.[1019] Amazingly, it was Gaudet who had telephoned the FBI about this, and there was no way his encounter with Ruby was an accident. Gaudet's focus was the Cuban exile community, so we can assume Ruby was already an important enough part of the New Orleans anti-Castro operation in the summer of 1959 for Gaudet to remember him and phone the FBI four years later. As previously described, Thomas Davis was in New Orleans regarding an OAS gun deal in the spring of 1963, and Davis and Ruby ran guns together, so Gaudet seeing Ruby in New Orleans in 1959 supports the idea that Ruby was not a stranger to the Cuban activity surrounding Banister's office.

"I do know that I saw him [Oswald] one time with a former FBI agent by the name of Guy Banister," Gaudet told Anthony Summers. "What Guy's role in all of this was... I really don't know. I did see Oswald discussing various things with Banister at the time, and I think Banister knew a whole lot of what was going on. I suppose you are looking into Ferrie. He was with Oswald... Another vital person is Sergio Arcacha Smith. I know he knew Oswald and knows more about the Kennedy affair than he ever admitted." Those who worked for Banister told Summers that Gaudet was a frequent visitor to Banister's office in the summer of 1963.

Gaudet was vague when describing how well Oswald knew Banister and Sergio Arcacha Smith. Yet, when it came to David Ferrie, his explanation was strikingly different. "Ferrie was with Oswald," he stated categorically. The implication was that Ferrie and Oswald worked closely together.[1020]

David Lewis worked for Guy Banister. On December 15, 1966, he told the Garrison investigation that he had seen Oswald in late summer 1963 with Sergio Arcacha Smith in Mancuso's restaurant and "three or four times in the neighborhood of Lafayette and Camp Streets and Banister's office in the Newman Building." During a follow-up interview in 1967, Lewis's wife reminded him they had also seen Ferrie and Oswald together at Mancuso's.[1021]

Sergio Arcacha Smith had fled Cuba to escape Castro. He settled in New Orleans and was a member of the Cuban Revolutionary Council. Still, his Batista ties were not in line with the type of government the Kennedys wanted in power once the Bay of Pigs invasion toppled Castro. He moved to Dallas in the early part of 1963, banished from the CRC for misappropriation of funds, around the same time that Oswald met Volkmar Schmidt and became involved with right-wing extremists there. Recall also that Arcacha was one of the Cubans investigated by Richard Nagell prior to his inquiry into Lee and Marina Oswald in the spring of 1963. Paul Rothermel, the former security chief for H.L. Hunt, said Arcacha was a frequent visitor to the Hunt offices during that time, and "Sergio and General Walker were pretty good friends."[1022]

The suspicious connections of Arcacha are seemingly endless. After the Bay of Pigs, he and Ferrie established the Cuban Democratic Liberation Front. According to an April 1961 FBI report, when Arcacha needed funding for his anti-Castro activities, Carlos Marcello offered him a "substantial donation" in exchange for gambling rights once the Cubans overthrew Castro. David Ferrie was likely the man Marcello used to pass money to Arcacha. According to Cuban exile Carlos Quiroga, "Ferrie lent [Arcacha] money when he needed it for his family. He had $100 bills around all the time...."[1023]

Exactly how Ferrie and Marcello came together is unclear, but Marcello's New Orleans attorney, G. Wray Gill, once represented Ferrie in a dispute with Eastern Airlines. There is also evidence that Ferrie worked for Carlos Marcello as early as the spring of 1961. According to a border patrol report, he was probably the pilot who secretly flew Marcello back from Guatemala in June of that year after Robert Kennedy forcibly deported the New Orleans mob boss just prior to the Bay of Pigs.[1024]

There is sufficient evidence to support a Marcello – Ferrie – Arcacha link. CIA records also indicate that Arcacha "maintained extensive relations with the FBI.... Two of his regular FBI contacts were [redacted] and ... Guy Banister." Does this mean Banister kept the Bureau informed about what was going on in the anti-Castro Cuban exile community, which included Carlos Marcello?[1025] Banister did receive direct calls from J. Edgar Hoover. Mary Brengel, who worked for Banister, and former partner Joseph Ostre both recalled Hoover telephoning him. Her job consisted primarily of clipping articles about racial problems throughout the country and articles on communism. She noted Banister was "a fanatic on these two subjects." [1026]

It was Banister's suggestion that led Sergio Arcacha Smith to 544 Camp Street, which was not long before the CRC began leasing an office directly across the hall from him. With Banister and Arcacha working together, 544 Camp Street became a hotbed of anti-Castro activity. Together, these two ardent supporters of the far-right formed the Crusade to Free Cuba and the Friends of a Democratic Cuba, both designed to raise money and support for the Cuban exile cause.[1027]

In the early 1960s, there were groups raising funds for anti-Castro operations that had similar sounding names – the Committee to Free Cuba, Cuban Freedom Committee, Citizens for a Free Cuba, Free Cuba Committee, and the Crusade to Free Cuba, to name a few. The CIA used them to funnel money and arms to the exiles and to raise money from private sources. According to the authors of *Coup D'Etat in America*, the Citizens Committee for a Free Cuba, the Cuban Freedom Committee, and the Free Cuba Committee were really one organization.[1028]

The Free Cuba Committee was the group District Attorney Henry Wade said Lee Oswald belonged to during a press conference in Dallas on the night of the assassination. Jack Ruby corrected him that Oswald belonged to the Fair Play for Cuba Committee. We also know the Freedom for Cuba Party was associated with the Alpha 66 house on Harlandale Street in Dallas that, as we will see, was frequented by Oswald, Cuban exiles, and probably Jack Ruby. Eladio del Valle worked with Mario Garcia Kohly (whose name is in Lafitte's datebook), David Ferrie, and Santo Trafficante and was a leading figure in the Free Cuba Committee. So was Thomas Davis associate Loran Hall. Hall was a member of Gerry Patrick Hemming's Interpen, aligned with Frank Sturgis's Anti-Communist Brigade. Guy Banister belonged to the Friends of Democratic Cuba. It was these intertwined groups that linked Lee Oswald and Jack Ruby to assassination suspects in both Dallas and New Orleans.

There was also an allegation by Richard Nagell that Tracy Barnes headed the Movement to Free Cuba. As the case officer for Mario Kohly, Barnes had to have known Eladio del Valle and David Ferrie. At the time of the assassination, Barnes headed the Domestic Contacts Division, with Howard Hunt as his right-hand man. In his book *Undercover*," Hunt described how a Washington-based public relations firm named Mullen & Co. had "established and managed a Free Cuba Committee for the CIA." Hunt undoubtedly had a hand in the creation of fund-raising groups such as this, considering it was he who had established the Cuban Revolutionary Council in the first place. It was how he developed a relationship with Sergio Arcacha Smith.[1029]

Paul Bethel founded the Citizens Committee to Free Cuba. An ardent right-winger, in 1969, Bethel wrote *The Losers*, which portrayed John Kennedy, members of his Cabinet, Robert Kennedy, and Martin Luther King as Communists. His background was in the military, but his connections were strictly to the intelligence community. He was in Germany when William Harvey was CIA station chief; he was a press officer in Tokyo when Lee Harvey Oswald was at Atsugi; and in 1959, he worked at the U.S. Embassy in Havana and knew June Cobb, David Atlee Phillips, David Morales, Frank Sturgis, Henry Hecksher, and others. More importantly, Bethel was close to two exile groups in particular – the DRE and Alpha 66.[1030]

321

There were also familiar names who were members of the Citizens Committee to Free Cuba, most notably Clare Boothe Luce, William Pawley, and retired Admiral Arleigh Burke. Luce was also linked to the DRE, while Pawley was associated with Alpha 66. Another was Nathaniel Weyl, who collaborated with Frank Sturgis immediately after the assassination to portray Oswald as a Castro sympathizer. Wehl had ties to John Martino, Santo Trafficante, and John Roselli. Years later, Martino confided to a friend that it was the "anti-Castro people who put Oswald together."[1031]

Regarding Ferrie, Delphine Roberts said, "he used the private office behind Banister's...doing private work...connected with the CIA rather than the FBI...." She also said Ferrie "had to act the part, of being what many people would call wishy-washy, one side and then the opposite side. It was important for him to be that way because he was acting like a counterspy. He knew both sides."[1032]

His detractors called David Ferrie many things, but wishy-washy about communism or Castro was not one of them. Roberts suggested that Ferrie posed as a Castro supporter while Oswald was doing the same thing as they both worked out of Banister's office.

Roberts thought Ferrie was CIA, and there is evidence to support her claim. Victor Marchetti, the former Executive Assistant to the Deputy Director of the CIA, stated that "Ferrie had been a contract agent to the Agency in the early sixties...in some of the Cuban activities." He was told by his boss, Richard Helms, "that David Ferrie was a CIA agent" in the fall of 1963.[1033]

Michael Kurtz interviewed Hunter Leake, the Deputy Chief of the New Orleans CIA station, in 1963. Leake told Kurtz, "Oswald indeed performed chores for the CIA during his five months in New Orleans during the spring and summer of 1963." In fact, "Leake personally paid Oswald various sums of cash for his services." When Kurtz interviewed Helms about this and other assertions, "Helms neither confirmed nor denied Leake's story."

Leake admitted that while Oswald was in New Orleans, he worked with Ferrie and Banister, both of whom had intelligence ties. And two years before that, "Ferrie performed a series of tasks for the CIA: supplying weapons and ammunition to Anti-Castro guerilla fighters in Cuba; [and] training Cuban units for the 1961 Bay of Pigs invasion..." Banister "served as a key CIA liaison with many anti-Castro Cuban refugees in southern Louisiana....," while Leake "provided Banister with substantial sums of cash, and... [he] would use the money to purchase needed supplies and to pay the salaries of the men working in certain anti-Castro operations."[1034]

Kurtz also identified "Hamilton Johnson, a geologist who later served on the faculty of Tulane University... [as one who] observed Guy Banister, David Ferrie, various anti-Castro Cubans, and agents of both the CIA and FBI" at the Schlumberger facility in Houma, Louisiana, sixty miles from New Orleans. Schlumberger supplied oil drilling equipment, but according to Johnson, "it was an open secret among company employees that the federal government was using the large facility for intelligence activities" and to store weapons for the war against Castro. Johnson told Kurtz that "on at least two occasions in the summer of 1963, Lee Harvey Oswald accompanied Banister and Ferrie to Houma...Cubans told him that they were using the weapons for 'training exercises for another invasion of Cuba.'" Kurtz wrote that "Hunter Leake...confirmed that Banister, Ferrie, and even Oswald visited the camp from time to time."[1035]

Vernon Gerdes told Jim Garrison's investigators that he worked for Banister between 1960 and 1963. He said Ferrie frequented the office and was involved in right-wing activities. There were large quantities of ammunition in a back room, with the name "Schlumberger" printed on the boxes, but Banister said it was safe because officials at Schlumberger knew about it. Gerdes quit working for Banister when he hired an ex-FBI agent named Ivan Nitschke, who had worked with Banister in Chicago. Nitschke said Banister became "interested in Oswald" in the summer of 1963, and he saw pro-Castro placards in Banister's office. [1036]

***

In 1967, Jim Garrison uncovered an alleged munitions burglary at Schlumberger in Houma, Louisiana, prior to the Bay of Pigs. It involved a CIA operative named Gordon Novel. A close friend of Banister's had seen wooden crates marked "Schlumberger" around the office. "Five or six of the boxes were open" with weapons inside, he said. Banister told him, "The stuff would just be there overnight, that somebody was supposed to pick it up. He said a bunch of fellows connected with the Cuban deal asked to leave it there overnight."[1037]

Garrison attempted to subpoena Novel, but he had sold his New Orleans bar and fled the state. Meanwhile, the *New Orleans States-Item* reported that Novel had admitted to friends he worked for the CIA, and he said: "The munitions burglary was no burglary at all – but a war material pickup made at the direction of his C.I.A. contact." Novel also admitted that Arcacha and Ferrie were involved, as well as Cubans he did not know. A letter in Novel's handwriting was discovered in his apartment after he left, which referred to Garrison's investigation and the "actions of individuals connected with DOUBLE-CHEK CORPORATION in Miami in [the] first-quarter of 1961." Double-Chek was a CIA front created prior to the Bay of Pigs, and Novel implied that Arcacha, Ferrie, and Banister were associated with it.[1038] "Our... activity of that period," the letter continued, "involves individuals... about to be indicted as conspirators in Mr. Garrison's investigation." "Mr. Garrison... is unaware of Double-Chek's involvement in this matter but has strong suspicions. I have been questioned extensively by [the] local FBI recently as to whether or not I was involved with Double-Chek's parent-holding corporation [CIA]... Bureau unaware of Double-Chek's association in this matter...."[1039]

It was not Double-Chek's involvement in the Bay of Pigs that interested Garrison, but the connection of Ferrie, Arcacha, and Banister to the JFK assassination. Therefore, we can deduce that Novel was suggesting that Double-Chek, i.e., the CIA, was involved in Kennedy's murder. The letter ended: "Our attorneys and others are in possession of complete sealed files containing all information concerning this matter. In the event of our sudden departure, either accidental or otherwise, they are instructed to... release same for public scrutiny..."[1040]

Hugh Ward was a pilot and private investigator who worked with Banister. Vernon Gerdes alleged that Ferrie and Ward ran guns to Miami. Delphine Roberts confirmed that Ward sent guns to Cuba to fight Castro. Nitschke recalled that the Minutemen's Rich Lauchli was involved with an anti-Castro training camp north of New Orleans. Minutemen member Jerry Brooks reported that Banister, Ward, and attorney Maurice Gatlin, a Banister associate, were all Minutemen.[1041]

Gatlin was general counsel for the Anti-Communist League (ACL) of the Caribbean, which was part of an international right-wing clique. Jim Garrison uncovered in 1962 that Gatlin secretly sent $100,000 to the OAS in France that was plotting to assassinate Charles de Gaulle, which confirmed that the right-wing connection between Dallas and New Orleans extended internationally. As previously discussed, there was a connection between Otto Skorzeny's Fascist organization in Madrid and the group in New Orleans through Clay Shaw and Permindex, who were simultaneously working with the OAS rebellious army in Algeria and France. Gatlin told Brooks, "I have pretty good connections. Stick with me – I'll give you a license to kill." Gatlin also claimed that one of his functions was to serve as a "transporter," moving people in and out of the country and delivering money abroad. According to Brooks, "He showed me his passport... filled with the stamps of airports all over the world."[1042]

Ronnie Caire, Sergio Arcacha Smith's public relations director, told a similar story. He said that Friends of a Democratic Cuba, the group formed by Arcacha and Banister, was actually "an undercover operation in conjunction with the CIA and FBI which involved the shipment and transportation of individuals and supplies in and out of Cuba."[1043]

As Richard Belzer and David Wayne wrote in their book *Hit List*, Gatlin also served as legal counsel for the Minutemen, and he and Ward died under suspicious circumstances. The plane Ward was flying crashed on May 23, 1964, just before the Warren Commission concluded its hearings. New Orleans Mayor DeLesseps Morrison was on board and died as well. Gatlin would die that same year after falling from the sixth-floor window of a hotel in Panama.[1044] The official cause of death was a heart attack. However, foul play was a possibility, considering that the 1952 CIA Assassination Manual stated: "The most efficient accident, in simple assassination, is a fall of 75 feet or more onto a hard surface. Elevator shafts, stairwells, unscreened windows, and bridges will serve."[1045]

The specter of the Minutemen hovered over the characters who frequented Guy Banister's Camp Street office, which included Lee Harvey Oswald, who was involved with the Minutemen in Dallas, which explains how he wound up at Banister's office.

***

Oswald officially moved to New Orleans on April 24, 1963. However, he may have already been there in February when the police arrested a man alleged to be him. The man told an INS agent he was a Cuban exile. Unfortunately, the agent left New Orleans on April 1 and could not later recall the details of Oswald's arrest. Still, there may be confirmation supporting that Oswald was in New Orleans before April.[1046]

Shortly after the assassination, the FBI in Savannah, Georgia, was contacted by a Darian businessman who claimed that, while in New Orleans earlier that year, he had witnessed the suspicious behavior of a man who resembled Oswald at a place connected to the Carlos Marcello crime family. At the time, the public was unaware of a possible Marcello link to the assassination, so it was unlikely Sumner would make that connection unless it was true.

The businessman's name was Sumner, an inadvertent disclosure by the FBI, who typically kept such information hidden to protect the identity of an informant. The FBI found him to be a respected member of his community with no apparent ties to organized crime. He claimed he had witnessed Oswald receive money at the Town & Country Motel from a man he believed to be the restaurant owner. The FBI in New Orleans questioned the restaurant manager, Joseph Poretto, and the motel manager, Anthony Marcello. Both denied any connection to Oswald.

On November 27, the New Orleans FBI notified Bureau offices in Dallas and Savannah "that both Poretto and Marcello had criminal records and that Joseph [sic] Marcello was the brother of New Orleans crime boss Carlos Marcello." The reference to Joseph instead of Anthony was a careless mistake, but a reason for concern was evident. Recall that the FBI was already aware that Carlos Marcello had threatened the life of the President in September 1962. The FBI report went on to state that Carlos Marcello had a financial interest in the Town & Country, that it was "a known hangout for the hoodlum element," and that Poretto and the Marcello brothers were "known hoodlums of the New Orleans Division."

On November 29, the Savannah FBI office notified New Orleans, Dallas, and Washington that Sumner had expanded his original testimony. "Sometime between February fifteen and March fifteen," the report stated, he had traveled to New Orleans on business with an associate named Ernest Insalmo. While dining at the Town & Country restaurant, Sumner "observed a young couple enter [the] dining room and sit at a table about two tables from where he and Insalmo were sitting. This man greatly resembled photo of Lee Harvey Oswald...[The] restaurant owner joined [the] couple at [the] table, and [Sumner] observed [the] owner remove [a] wad of bills from his pocket which he passed under [the] table to [a] man sitting at the table. A few minutes later the couple left without ordering any food or drinks." Later that night, Sumner, Insalmo, and a couple of others were joined in the cocktail lounge by the restaurant owner. According to Sumner, "this was the only occasion he met restaurant owner and he knows nothing of his background, associates, or racial or extremist views or activities. [Sumner] states [the] individual he believed identical with Oswald was dressed in [a] blue suit and dark tie. His woman companion was [a] white female, age twenty-two dash twenty-six, blonde hair, flashy dresser...."[1047]

What makes this story so compelling is that the FBI was concerned with the owner's potential "racial or extremist views or activities." Considering the known mob connections of the Marcello family, which the FBI referenced in their original report, one would have expected the agents to have asked Sumner about that. Instead, they were concerned with his potential extremist views in the context of a potential connection to Lee Oswald, which leads us to deduce that the FBI suspected there was right-wing involvement in the JFK assassination.[1048]

As John H. Davis wrote in his biography of Marcello, *Mafia Kingfish*, "Carlos was an avid racist and bigot who vigorously opposed the civil rights movement of the sixties... also known to be an enthusiastic supporter of the Ku Klux Klan." So, the FBI was right to ask about Marcello's right-wing extremist views, considering that James Hosty investigated Oswald in connection with that in Dallas.[1049]

The FBI's conclusion of the incident was brief and to the point. Sumner had seen a man who resembled Oswald accept money under the table from the restaurant owner. Still, he knew "nothing of his [the owner's] background, associates, racial or extremist views or activities." Clearly, the FBI thought the radical right was responsible for JFK's death, despite what Director Hoover was stating publicly.[1050]

Two days after Sumner, an ex-Marine named Eugene DeLaparra, who had worked in a Marcello-backed bar and restaurant in New Orleans in the spring of 1963, reached out to the FBI's Philadelphia office. He said that he had overheard the bar's owner, Ben Tregle, tell some friends: "There is a price on the President's head and other members of the Kennedy family. Somebody will kill Kennedy when he comes south." The FBI learned that "Vincent Marcella [sic], New Orleans racketeer reported to travel to Dallas on many occasions, was one of Tragel's [sic] principal financial backers."[1051]

According to the FBI's report, Ben Tregle "stated that he recalls November 22, 1963, and all during that day he was around his place of business... Tregle said he has never known anyone frequenting Tregel's [sic] Bar called 'the Professor.'" Now, there was no mention of "the Professor" in the original story told by DeLaparra. Yet, the interviewing agents were sufficiently concerned to ask Tregle about him, and for good reason. The only person in New Orleans nicknamed the Professor at the time of the assassination was David Ferrie.

The FBI report stated that "Tregle... believes in segregation...[but] he can never recall at any time making any comments which could be construed as a threat on his part to kill the President of the United States or anyone else... he could not recall ever saying that the President of the United States would be shot if he [visited] the Southern area of the country."[1052]

Once again, the FBI's questioning focused on a possible right-wing militant connection to the assassination, not an organized crime connection, even though DeLaparra never mentioned anything political in his statement. But their interest in David Ferrie was appropriate, considering he was already an assassination suspect by then and was close to Carlos Marcello, which was why, after Ferrie's mysterious death in 1967, DeLaparra contacted the FBI again to expand on his original story. He said he had worked at Tregle's Bar in June 1963 and that around June 22, he noticed that "Tony Marcella [sic] came into the premises to service the pinball machine. Dela Parra [sic] advised [that] Tony Marcella is the brother of Vincent Marcella, who owns motels in New Orleans." The FBI report continued:

> Vincent Marcella [sic] has another brother, who is a part-time gambler in New Orleans. Del Parra [sic] advised that on this particular date, Tony Marcella stated to Ben Traegel [sic] and three or four others at the bar that "the word is out to get the Kennedy family..." Ben Traegel came to Dela Parra in the back room of the bar and repeated the statement. Ben Traegel was laughing and added they are only paying one hundred thousand dollars... Dela Parra reported the info to the New Orleans office and immediately subsequent to the death of President Kennedy, Dela Parra advised that he furnished the info again to the Philadelphia office of the FBI. Dela Parra advised that after reading about the death of David W. Ferrie in New Orleans yesterday, he wanted to pass on info to the effect that Ferrie was the personal pilot for Vincent Marcella... Vincent used to take several trips by plane to Dallas. Dela Parra added that Ben Traegel knew Lee Harvey Oswald very well."[1053]

In DeLaparra's expanded story, he claimed he told the New Orleans FBI office about Ben Tregle's comments immediately after he made them. Still, the FBI apparently did nothing about it and covered it up. It is disconcerting because their questioning once again indicated they suspected a right-wing conspiracy in the JFK assassination. As previously discussed, there was a Minutemen connection between Guy Banister's office and the international radical right-wing, Fascist, anti-Communist movement, which explains the FBI's questioning along these lines. However, why didn't the FBI pursue this connection, as well as the connection between Banister's office and Carlos Marcello? They knew of Oswald's relationship with Banister and 544 Camp Street, as well as Banister's relationship with Marcello, so did they purposely bury this story? It appears they did.

Perhaps more importantly, did the FBI know Oswald was sent to New Orleans by his right-wing handlers in Dallas after the Walker shooting to start a fictitious FPCC chapter and infiltrate the Cuban exile community as an informant? It would have been done under Banister's tutelage, furthering the pro-Castro persona the Oswald patsy needed to have. It is possible. The Lafitte April 7 datebook entry states: "Walker – Lee and pictures – Planned soon- Can He Do It Won't." It appears to confirm the Walker shooting was a test to see if Oswald was a candidate the conspirators could manipulate, and the FBI knew it. Recall that the May 10 entry reads: "T. say tail LO – no direct contact – calls No. Report to Angleton + not here…" So, while Oswald was in New Orleans, the conspirators were watching him to see if he was qualified to be the designated patsy, and from what we know, the person following Oswald and those he associated with was William Gaudet. And not surprisingly, Gaudet's name appears in the Lafitte datebook as well: "September 22 – Mexico City Gaudet."[1054]

If J. Edgar Hoover knew an assassination attempt was going to happen in the South and he received reports that it might involve the Mafia, his failure to investigate organized crime properly for years would have left him open to intense criticism after the fact. It was probably why, in July 1963, Hoover sent an internal directive to FBI offices in the key cities of New Orleans, Dallas, and Miami, telling them to start providing meaningful reports on the Mafia because "certain offices took the position that Cosa Nostra did not exist in their respective territories, only to learn…that this organization…is in fact in existence in the area and has been for many years." Why the sudden interest? Did Hoover want to be on record before the assassination to prove the FBI had not ignored the potential danger posed by organized crime?

The FBI director was under pressure. It makes one wonder if Oswald was playing a double game, creating a false FPCC chapter for the radical right while simultaneously reporting to the FBI about groups like the Minutemen and the Mafia. It was what Minutemen Jerry Brooks had done, as described in Chapter Twelve.

***

In *Oswald and the CIA*, John Newman described how the FBI secretly monitored Oswald's movements. "A confidential source advised our New York Office on June 26, 1963, that one Lee H. Oswald, Post Office Box 30061, New Orleans, Louisiana, had directed a letter to 'The Worker,' New York City. Our New Orleans Office checked this post office box and determined it was rented to L.H. Oswald on June 3, 1963, residence 657 French Street, New Orleans." It was an incorrect address, and further inquiries showed Oswald resided at 4905 Magazine Street, New Orleans. That address was verified on August 5 by his landlady, Mrs. Jesse James Garner. On the same date, the FBI verified his employment at William B. Reily Coffee Company, 640 Magazine Street, New Orleans.

As Newman wrote, "On July 1 New York sent Dallas an Oswald letter with a Dallas PO address; on July 5 New York sent New Orleans the letter to *The Worker* with the New Orleans Post Office box address; and on July 8 New Orleans and New York learned of Oswald's Magazine Street residence and said nothing about it to the Dallas office." Then, a July 17 New Orleans memo to Dallas stated: "Since New Orleans has received no information subsequent to [the] referenced [July 5] letter, Dallas is requested to advise New Orleans of the status of Dallas case captioned above. New Orleans is instituting inquiries to determine [the] residence address of [the] holder of P.O. Box 30061, New Orleans, Louisiana." [1055]

James Hosty wrote a memo to his boss, Gordon Shanklin, on May 28 explaining he had attempted to interview Marina and Lee Oswald at their 214 Neely Street, Dallas home and found "they had moved from their residence…and left no forwarding address…." The problem with this is that Oswald left a forwarding address. Warren Commission Exhibit 793 is a change-of-address card Oswald sent to the Dallas Post Office after he arrived in New Orleans. The card was stamped "May 14, 1963," the day the post office received it. So, Hosty knew two weeks before he wrote the above letter to Shanklin that Oswald was in New Orleans. In addition, within hours of the assassination, the Dallas FBI advised the New Orleans FBI office that on May 14, the Dallas PO had received notice that mail for "Mr. Lee H. Oswald to be forwarded to four nine zero seven Magazine, New Orleans, La…" [1056] So, on May 28, why did Hosty act like he didn't know where Oswald had gone when he knew he was in New Orleans?

There was also Oswald's May 17 change-of-address card to the Soviet Embassy in Washington and a June 4 letter the Embassy sent to Marina at Magazine Street that FBI informants would have flagged. Meanwhile, Lafitte's May 23 datebook entry reveals: "Ask T about Oswald? Magazine?" So, Lafitte knew in May that Oswald was in New Orleans, living on Magazine Street, but the FBI in New Orleans maintained they only learned on June 26 that Oswald had moved there, which was an outright lie. So, either the FBI was incompetent, or they purposely denied knowing that Oswald had moved from Dallas to New Orleans in May. A possible explanation is the FBI wanted to keep hidden that Oswald was working for them.

***

Oswald's presence in New Orleans may have been part of a joint FBI/INS operation. A New Orleans patrolman remembered arresting Ferrie and Oswald together at the lakefront and taking them into custody. According to what Joan Mellen wrote in *A Farewell to Justice*, "At Customs, Oswald's handler was a man named David Smith. His employment with Customs was so sensitive that the HSCA interview with bar owner and FBI informant Orestes Pena was sealed for twenty-five years. As an FBI informant, Pena reported to [FBI agent] Warren de Brueys beginning in 1959 or 1960. Pena placed Oswald with Customs officials on a regular basis. So explosive were Pena's revelations about Oswald's relationships with Customs officers that Pena's files were systematically destroyed by the FBI in a multicity effort that stretched across Europe. A document survives, a teletype dated January 14, 1976: "Rome file regarding 'Orestes Pena: IS-Cuba' Destroyed."

The fact that clandestine activity in New Orleans had something to do with Rome and the destruction of files returns us to the Clay Shaw/Permindex connection to the Nazi Madrid group run by Otto Skorzeny. It proves that the idea that an international Fascist conspiracy with a New Orleans connection, where Lafitte resided, was responsible for JFK's assassination has merit.

INS brought Cubans who arrived illegally to the U.S. at the Port of New Orleans to Pena, whose role was to provide room and board and help them find jobs. According to Mellen, Pena reported that "Oswald would meet at a Greek restaurant on Decatur and Iberville with 'other federal agents from the Customs House Building,' which housed FBI, ONI, CIA and Immigration. At least ten or twelve times, Pena testified, he observed Oswald having breakfast with his Customs handlers. He had seen his own handler, De Brueys, at the same Greek restaurant when Oswald was there with federal agents. 'I believe they knew each other very, very well.'"

"Pena also observed Oswald, de Brueys, David Smith, and Wendall Roache of INS leave the restaurant together and head for the Customs House building," Mellen continued. In his testimony, Warren de Brueys acknowledged knowing Border Patrol agent Smith and the Church Committee knew Smith "was involved in CIA operations in the New Orleans area in the early 1960s." Roache also knew de Brueys. "I knew him," Roache said. An investigator for the INS in New Orleans, Theophanis E. Pappelis, swore under oath before the Church Committee that de Brueys "had a working relationship with the New Orleans INS office."[1057]

After the JFK assassination, INS transferred David Smith to Uruguay and Wendall Roache to Puerto Rico. When the Church Committee contacted Roache in 1975, he said, "I've been waiting twelve years to talk to someone about this." He told the committee David Ferrie and his Cuban associates were under surveillance at the Newman Building, and INS inspectors saw Oswald repeatedly going in and out of the office of Ferrie's group through a side entrance to Guy Banister's office.[1058]

331

According to a May 1967 CIA document, Sergio Arcacha Smith also worked for the FBI, CIA, and Customs, and his FBI case officer was Warren de Brueys. We also know Oswald had a relationship with Cuban customs house broker Juan Valdes, who was a suspect in the strange 1964 murder of Mary Sherman right before the Warren Commission came to New Orleans.

There was something suspicious going on – the FBI, CIA, and INS were all keeping tabs on Oswald in New Orleans in the summer of 1963, and he appeared to be working for them. However, their interest had nothing to do with the JFK assassination at that time, but things were about to get hotter as Oswald became more deeply involved with Banister and Ferrie.

CHAPTER NINETEEN

THE SUMMER OF DISCONTENT

In New Orleans in the summer of 1963, Lee Harvey Oswald attempted to infiltrate Communist groups and portray himself as a supporter of Fidel Castro. He did so under the watchful eye of Guy Banister, David Ferrie, and William Gaudet while working out of Banister's office building, and the entire effort was a scam. Lafitte's datebook tells us the Walker shooting was a test and that the conspirators were watching Oswald because he was a candidate to become the designated assassination patsy. So, what happened in New Orleans must have been related to this. We know Banister hired students to infiltrate groups at Tulane University and other colleges as early as 1961. William A.R. Martin, a Tulane Law student, befriended Cubans and other foreign students "ferreting out subversive activities in the State of Louisiana." George Higganbotham was given false credentials from Banister to infiltrate Communist groups. Tommy Baumler told Garrison that Banister used him to penetrate "liberal elements on college campuses and elsewhere in order to determine where the Communists were." Banister associates Hubert Badeaux, Ed Butler, and Willie Rainach did the same thing because it was an integral part of their effort to defeat communism and the civil rights movement, which they believed to be the same.[1059] The question is, was Banister aware of the JFK assassination plot, or was he unaware that he was used to create a pro-Castro persona that was a prerequisite for the assassination patsy?

On December 17, 1962, approximately six months prior to Oswald's move to New Orleans, the supervisor of Tampa's Police Intelligence unit replied to his New Orleans counterpart, P.J. Trosclair, regarding Trosclair's December 3 letter to him about the FPCC. "This unit has not received any information with reference to the New Orleans area," wrote Sergeant J.S. De la Llama. "However, the Fair Play for Cuba Committee is very active in the Tampa area...." Why, more than six months prior to Oswald's establishment of the first FPCC chapter in New Orleans, was the city's Police Intelligence supervisor so interested in this pro-Castro group? According to an August 12, 1963, interoffice memo written after Oswald was arrested for the Bringuier altercation, "Oswald...had talked to Major Trosclair about getting a permit for F.P.C.C., and the Major advised him to consult an attorney." It must have happened during Oswald's earlier trips to New Orleans in February when he was arrested and believed to be a Cuban alien.[1060]

Once he moved into his own home, it did not take Lee Oswald long to write to the FPCC. On May 26, he wrote to the New York headquarters requesting "formal membership in your organization... I have been thinking about renting a small office at my own expense for the purpose of forming an F.P.C.C. branch here in New Orleans." He asked that they grant him a charter, and "could you give me some advice... I am not saying this project would be a roaring success, but I am willing to try."[1061]

The letter is significant because it lacked Oswald's usual abundance of misspelled words caused by a condition called dyslexia. It suggests Oswald either had assistance writing the letter or someone else wrote it. Either way, he was not acting alone.[1062]

That same day, Oswald withdrew *Portrait of a Revolutionary: Mao Tse Tung* from the library. It was an insight into what was on his mind at that time. However, although the Cuban revolution supposedly consumed his attention over the next few months, none of the 27 books Oswald read during this period dealt with Cuba.[1063]

On May 29, the national director of the FPCC, Vincent Lee, responded to Oswald's letter of the 26th:

> You must realize that you will come under tremendous pressures [sic] with any attempt to do FPCC work in that area...Even most of our big city Chapters have been forced to abandon the idea of operating an office in public...it is easier to operate semi-privately out of a home and maintain a P.O. Box for all mailings and public notices...We do have a serious and often violent opposition...I definitely would not recommend an office, at least not one that will be identifyable [sic] to the lunatic fringe in your community... [1064]

Later that day, Oswald visited Jones Printing Company at 422 Girod Street, across from where he worked. He ordered 1000 handbills using the name Osborne instead of the Hidell alias he allegedly used in Dallas when ordering his rifle. On June 3, Oswald visited Mailers Service Company and ordered 500 printed copies of an application form for the FPCC. Once again, he used the name Osborne. Oswald took Vincent Lee's advice and opened PO Box # 30061 at Lafayette Square Station, located on the first floor of the Federal Building. As he had done in Dallas, the people designated to receive mail other than himself were Marina Oswald and A.J. Hidell.

His decision to use the Hidell alias in lieu of Osborne was odd since he used the name Osborne earlier that day. Perhaps Hidell was not an Oswald alias but a different person. We know Richard Case Nagell and Jean Pierre Lafitte both used the Hidell alias, and Lafitte resided in New Orleans at the time. Either man could have been working with Oswald. If true, it is also possible that Osborne was not an Oswald alias but an accomplice.

As described in *It Did Not Start With JFK*, Kerry Thornley was a suspicious radical right-wing character who had known Oswald in the Marines. He introduced Oswald to the pro-Castro left-wing Unitarian Church in Los Angeles, which was where he received an application to Albert Schweitzer College and how his Russian defection adventure began. Thornley had also known Oswald in New Orleans in the mid-1950s when they were both teenagers and again in 1963 when Oswald attempted to portray himself as a Castro supporter. Not surprisingly, Thornley knew Guy Banister, stating he "accidentally" ran into him in 1961, and they discussed the book Thornley was writing on Oswald, who was in the Soviet Union at the time. Equally suspicious was Thornley's claim that when he met David Ferrie in 1962, it was also "accidental." Thomas Beckham, a regular at Banister's office, told the HSCA that Thornley was part of Banister's cell, along with Oswald, which makes sense, for Thornley may have had something to do with the handbills Oswald just had printed.

After the assassination, the FBI showed a photo of Oswald to the employees at Jones Printing, and none recognized him as the person who had picked up the handbills. However, assassination researcher Harold Weisberg took a standard police mug shot identification book, with a picture of Thornley included, to Jones Printing, and the employees picked out Kerry Thornley's photo immediately. So, it is probable that Thornley picked up the handbills and used the name Osborne.[1065]

Also, on June 1, Oswald withdrew two books from the library: *The Berlin Wall* and *The Huey Long Murder Case*. The right-wing blamed JFK for the erection of the Berlin Wall, and was a symbol of the danger West Berlin faced. A right-wing assassin allegedly killed Huey Long to put an end to Long's far-left politics. It was a sign that the manipulation of Oswald's psyche had already begun.[1066]

As described in Chapter Fifteen, Dick Russell claimed Henry Hecksher was Richard Nagell's CIA handler "Bob" in the summer of 1963. Considering the timing, if Hecksher was "Bob," his introduction into the assassination plot must have had something to do with Oswald's move to New Orleans and the opening of Oswald's FPCC chapter. If true, it suggests a personal involvement between Nagell and Oswald, which means A.J. Hidell was not an Oswald alias but Nagell himself. It confirms what Oswald claimed was the truth, that Hidell was the FPCC chapter president whom he talked to on occasion. [1067]

On June 4, someone, likely Thornley, picked up the handbills at Jones Printing. They read, "HANDS OFF CUBA! Join the Fair Play for Cuba Committee…New Orleans Charter… Everyone Welcome!" Shortly after that, Oswald wrote an undated letter to Vincent Lee of the FPCC no later than June 15 because the next day, he handed out FPCC leaflets at the dock in New Orleans and referred to that in a letter at the end of July.

Referring to the handbills in the undated letter, Oswald wrote, "I see from the circular I had jumped the gun on that charter business but I don't think its [sic] too important, you may think the circular is too provocative, but I want it too [sic] attract attention, even if its [sic] the attention of the lunatic fringe...." He also mentioned he had opened PO Box 30061, as Vincent Lee suggested. Still, he added, "against your advice, I have decided to take an office from the very beginning…I will keep you posted, even if the office stays open for only 1 month more people will find out about the F.P.C.C. than if there had never been any office at all, don't you agree?"[1068]

The fact that Oswald wrote he had "decided to take an office from the beginning" has led some to believe the letter was written in early August after he became involved at 544 Camp St. However, the letter did not state that he had already rented an office but that he intended to do so despite Vincent Lee's objections. It was an important distinction.

The letter was again comparatively well written. The only mistakes were the improper use of the words "too" and "its," which were caused by human error, not dyslexia. Then there was Oswald's statement, "I see from the circular that I had jumped the gun on the charter business," which is odd. It was as if Oswald first learned what was on the handbills after he saw the printed copy. And if he genuinely intended to open a charter FPCC branch, he didn't need the handbills to remind him of that, which was why he was so apologetic in his response to Lee. It appears someone else wrote the handbills, for Oswald was unaware of what was going on.

On June 10, Oswald's FPCC campaign began in earnest when he sent one of his handbills and application cards to the *Worker*. He wrote, "It would be very nice to have your literature among the 'Fair Play' leaflets (like the one enclosed) and pamphlets in my office." Two days later, he instructed *The Militant* to use his PO Box 30061.[1069]

336

On June 16, Oswald distributed FPCC leaflets on the dock at the port of New Orleans to civilians and sailors from the aircraft carrier USS Wasp, which was docked from June 13 to June 20. Harbor patrolman Girod Ray approached the man, whom he identified as Oswald after the assassination, and Oswald only departed after Ray threatened to arrest him. He corroborated Ray's account in a letter to Vincent Lee, writing that he "managed to picket the fleet when it came in, and I was surprised at the number of officers who were interested in our literature."[1070]

The incident at the dock did not go unnoticed. Four days after the assassination, U.S. Army Major Robert H. Erdrich of the 112th Intelligence Corps Group notified the FBI that they had found pro-Castro handbills "laying on the grounds of the Port of Embarkation, New Orleans." It was during the last week of May or the first week of June. The handbill was stamped, "FPCC – A.J. Hidell P.O. Box 30016 New Orleans, Louisiana."[1071]

On July 14, 1964, the Office of Naval Intelligence (ONI) received a request from Mr. Morrissey of the FBI, asking if they could substantiate a report about Oswald's activities during June 1963 in New Orleans. What made the FBI think ONI knew what Oswald was doing unless they were aware of a continued relationship between them?

Major Erdrich also reported that around the same time, one of his agents "picked up a handbill of the Fair Play for Cuba Committee, which was attached to a wall on the campus of Tulane University." The stamp on this handbill was identical to the others and bore the name A.J. Hidell and P.O. Box 30016. A student at Tulane named Harold Gordon Alderman also contacted the FBI after the assassination regarding an FPCC handbill. A supporter of the FPCC himself, Alderman kept the handbill tacked to a wall in his apartment. Only after learning that Oswald had used the Hidell alias that was on the handbill did Alderman contact the FBI.

Patrolman Ray wrote a report on June 16 titled "Distribution of Propaganda Literature." It was later found in the Church Committee files with two attachments – a handbill and a flyer under the headline, "The Truth About Cuba Is In Cuba!" The Church Committee handbill had "A J Hidell P.O. Box 30016" stamped on it, while the FBI said the Army handbill bore the stamp "FPCC – A.J. Hidell P.O. Box 30016." Ray said the leaflets he saw were white and yellow, while Erdrich said they were faded green. Were there two people handing out different handbills, or was Oswald handing out two different colored handbills at separate locations? If he was, where did he get the money to pay for them?[1072]

Then, there was Martin Samuel Abelow, who was on the dock when Oswald handed out the leaflets. On June 21, he submitted one of the fliers he received to the security office of the NASA Houston Manned Spacecraft Center, where he worked. Lloyd W. Blankenbaker, director of security at NASA, sent the Warren Commission a copy of the Abelow handbill. The stamp read "FPCC-A J Hidell P.O. Box 30016." It was the same as the Wasp handbill.[1073]

A letter dated June 29, 1963, was received at FBI headquarters on July 8. It read: "Attached hereto please find a panflet [sic] given to me by a young American that was at Canal Street with a big advise [sic] 'HAND OFF CUBA...'"[1074] It was different from the other two!

On July 11, Oswald checked *Russia Under Khrushchev* out of the library. In the coming weeks, he would also read *Ape and Essence*, by Aldous Huxley, a satire on the large-scale warmongering in the 20th century that painted a pessimistic view of the potential for mutually assured destruction; *Brave New World*, also by Aldous Huxley, about a frightening vision of a future society; and spy novels by Ian Fleming, including *Goldfinger, Thunderball, Moonraker,* and *From Russia With Love*.[1075] It was Kerry Thornley who got Oswald interested in Aldous Huxley at El Toro Marine Base before Oswald's defection, so it may have been Thornley who initiated Oswald's interest in Huxley again. Regardless, Oswald was reading books about James Bond, worldwide destruction, and a frightening future while someone was directing him to act as a Castro supporter.

Oswald made a concerted effort at the end of May/beginning of June to distribute pro-Castro leaflets at various places around New Orleans. Most likely, it was done by Oswald alone, although it could have involved others, like Kerry Thornley. However, as John Newman pointed out in *Oswald and the CIA*, there was a problem, for if Oswald legitimately wanted to create a branch of the FPCC in New Orleans, why did he make it impossible for anyone to contact him? Not only did the handbill and application form bear the alias Hidell instead of Oswald's real name, but PO Box 30016, which he stamped on the handbills, was incorrect. His P.O. Box number was actually 30061. It is hard to believe this was an inadvertent mistake by Oswald since the only time he falsified his PO Box was on the FPCC literature he distributed. He did so on various handbills of different colors.

Oswald ceased to pursue affairs related to Cuba for almost two months after the Wasp incident. What happened to the revolutionary who was allegedly consumed by Castro's Cuba? His public interest in Cuba came to a dead halt. The only rational explanation is that Oswald wanted to create the illusion that he was an ardent supporter of Fidel Castro, probably for the benefit of others he was trying to impress. It was all a scam.

It is telling that eight days after distributing handbills on the dock, Lee Oswald applied for a passport, listing "England, France, Holland, USSR, France, Findland [sic], Poland" as the countries he planned to visit. It was an ambitious itinerary for anyone, let alone someone who had very little money. Considering the timing, it must have had something to do with the pro-Castro charade Oswald had created for himself. There were also rumors that around this time, Jack Ruby had gone to Havana. It is compelling to consider that this may have also been Oswald's intended destination, considering he would try to get to Cuba in September. If so, it must have had something to do with whatever Ruby was up to. In any event, Oswald received his passport the following day at a time when it usually took two weeks. The fact that the returned defector's name did not appear on a watch list raises additional questions.[1076]

***

While Oswald was involved with the FPCC and applying for a passport, Marina renewed her effort to return to the Soviet Union. Recall that in Dallas, Oswald wanted Marina to leave the U.S. in the period leading up to the attack on General Walker. Now, it started again. Lee Oswald was up to something and was protecting his wife and child by trying to have them leave the country. On June 4, Marina received a letter from the Soviet embassy in Washington, asking her to explain why she wanted to leave the U.S. She responded almost a month later, not sounding so desperate. She wrote that "things are improving due to the fact that my husband expresses a sincere wish to return together with me to the USSR." Unknown to her, Lee mailed a separate letter along with hers. "Please rush the entrance visa for the return of Soviet citizen Marina N. Oswald... As for my return entrance visa please consider it separtably [sic]."[1077]

Ruth Paine had other ideas. On July 14, she wrote to Marina, suggesting that she move in with her in Dallas. "I want to learn Russian very much, but how can I? It is very difficult to study at home with children and I have little practice... I would consider that it would cost me little to buy groceries (food, soap, etc.) and pay for the doctor and hospital in return for acquiring the knowledge of the Russian language and to get help with my mistakes in speech and letters."[1078]

In summation, during Oswald's first two months in New Orleans, he corresponded with the FPCC using his real name and post office box. The spelling suggests someone else wrote the letters. He had help from someone using the name Osborne when he had handbills and application forms printed, which pertained to a local FPCC chapter that did not exist. He used the name Hidell when distributing the handbills, which was either an alias or someone else, and he falsified his PO Box, making it impossible for anyone to contact him. During this apparent interest in Cuba, Oswald read many books, but none about Cuba, and after the single Wasp incident, he lost complete interest in Cuba for almost two months. Eight days later, he applied for a passport, perhaps for travel to Cuba. Meanwhile, he was desperately trying to rid himself of his family so he could be free to pursue his covert interests.

In June 1963, June Cobb, who had previously infiltrated the FPCC, was a CIA asset working under the watchful eye of Willliam Harvey in some capacity, was reapproved for her new role "as an informant" for CIA's Western Hemisphere Division in Mexico. The previous October, a CIA security memo to the CI/OA (Chief of Counterintelligence/Operational Approvals) had warned, "It is recommended that no contact [with Cobb] beyond assessment be permitted at this time, in view of the … Subject's controversial background, the office will not conduct any additional investigation on the Subject until the available note-worthy and derogatory information has been reviewed thoroughly." The warning was likely a smokescreen, for by June 17, CI/OA certified the use of Cobb to Security, but "only for the proposed assignment." In Mexico, she would be working under David Atlee Phillips, and Oswald would make at least two visits south of the border while she was there. One is inclined to believe Cobb's new assignment had something to do with Oswald's New Orleans activity. The Chief of Counterintelligence, James Angleton, must have known what was going on, primarily since his name is found numerous times in Lafitte's datebook as being an essential part of the assassination plot.[1079]

***

Throughout July, Oswald's interest in Cuba and the FPCC was nonexistent, and what he was doing during this period is, for the most part, unknown. He was unhappy with his job at Reily, and his coworkers remembered him being lazy and irresponsible. He took extended breaks and spent hours at the Crescent City garage next door with garage manager Adrian Alba, who was an avid gun collector. He and Oswald passed the time discussing firearms. As Alba later described it, Oswald wanted to know "how many guns had I ever ordered, and how long did it take to get them, and where had I ordered guns from."[1080]

340

After the assassination, Alba disclosed that the garage maintained a carpool for Secret Service and FBI agents visiting from out of town. On one occasion, he gave a man he believed to be an FBI agent a green Studebaker, and the next day, Alba noticed the same car stop in front of Reily Company. "Lee Oswald went across the sidewalk," Alba said. "He bent down as if to look in the window and was handed what appeared to be a good-sized envelope, a white envelope. He turned and bent as if to hold the envelope to his abdomen, and I think he put it under his shirt. Oswald then went back into the building, and the car drove off." Alba also witnessed a meeting between Oswald and the same agent a few days later.[1081]

Reily fired Oswald on July 19. Before leaving, which left him without any known means of income until October, Oswald visited Adrian Alba one last time. "I have found my pot of gold at the end of the rainbow," he said. Oswald did not elaborate on what that meant. [1082]

***

Jim Garrison's investigation uncovered that a man named Dante Marachini, who began working at Reily the same day Oswald did, visited David Ferrie at his home on numerous occasions. His address was 1309 Dauphine Street, next door to Clay Shaw's home. Garrison learned that James Lewallen, who was also living at 1309 Dauphine Street, had once shared an apartment with David Ferrie. It adds to the possibility that Ferrie, Shaw, and Oswald knew each other.[1083]

Clay Shaw was part of an Army counterintelligence group during World War II. After the war, he played a prominent role in creating the International Trade Mart in New Orleans. CIA asset William Gaudet kept an office there. The people who ran the Trade Mart had CIA connections and were involved with white supremacy groups like the Knights of the White Camellia, the Knights of the White Christians, and the Robert E. Lee Patriots.[1084] Shaw was recruited by the CIA, and by 1952, he enjoyed the highest of six CIA security clearance categories. According to Joan Mellen, he coordinated CIA activities and initiated "relationships with ... non-Agency persons or institutions ..." through Project QKENCHANT. A "Secret" CIA file uncovered years later said that in August 1960, the CIA was interested in Guy Banister. Since Shaw was the CIA QKENCHANT recruiter in New Orleans, he would have been the one to reach out to Banister.[1085]

In 1958, Shaw became affiliated with PERMINDEX, the right-wing anti-Communist organization in Europe allegedly founded to promote worldwide trade. It was a CIA front, as was Centro Mondiale Commerciale, PERMINDEX's sister company, and the CIA used both to launder money

LAST RESORT BEYOND LAST RESORT

through the Vatican Bank for illegal covert espionage operations. The intent was to put money in the hands of European political parties and right-wing organizations the Agency approved of, including the OAS. As an example, in tracing the money used to finance the July 1961 de Gaulle assassination plots, French Intelligence discovered that about $200,000 in secret funds were sent to Permindex accounts in the Banque de la Credit Internationale.[1086]

In 1962, Italy expelled Centro Mondiale Commerciale and Permindex for engaging in subversive intelligence activity. According to the Italian newspaper *Paesa Sera*, the Centro was "the point of contact for a number of persons... whose common denominator is anti-Communism so strong that it would swallow up all those in the world who have fought for decent relations between East and West, including Kennedy."[1087]

The Board of Directors of Centro read like a Who's Who of Fascism. There was Italian prince Gutierrez di Spadaforo, who was a former Mussolini undersecretary and related through his daughter-in-law to Hjalmar Schacht; Giuseppe Zigiotti, president of the Fascist National Association for Militia Arms; Carlo d'Amelio, a lawyer and administrator for the House of Savoy whose interests included dealings with King Farouk of Egypt; Frank Wisner's contact Ferenc Nagy, a supporter of European Fascist movements and a former premier of Hungary who headed an anti-Communist party. By 1963, Nagy had an office in Dallas, and his benefactor was Clint Murchison, who was also an early investor in Otto Skorzeny's oil scheme in Spain. There was also White Russian Paul Raigorodsky, the friend of George de Mohrenschildt, who had befriended Lee Oswald, and Jean de Mil, who married into the Schlumberger family.[1088]

There was also an association with the World Commerce Corporation, which Bill Donovan and Allen Dulles established after World War II to fight communism throughout Europe. It would eventually become a CIA operation. The WCC created 275 front companies under the Permindex umbrella.[1089]

Clay Shaw's address book contained the names of several European Fascists, including Herman Bochelman (who admired the Nazi Waffen-SS) and John DeCourcy (imprisoned in England for Fascist sedition).[1090] Through his connection to Banister's office, he knew Maurice Gatlin, who provided financing to the OAS, David Ferrie, and Banister. There was Jean Pierre Lafitte, who shared the Hidell alias with Oswald and Richard Nagell, and Jack Martin, who also worked out of Banister's office and was another alias Lafitte used. Not to mention the Schlumberger connection, which

342

shipped arms around the world, and the ex-Nazi Otto Skorzeny, who was involved in Fascist operations worldwide and is mentioned extensively in Lafitte's datebook. The connection between Skorzeny's Madrid Nazi operation and the anti-Communist groups in New Orleans is undeniable.

There is sufficient proof that Clay Shaw frequented Guy Banister's office, and on numerous occasions, people saw him with Oswald. Thomas Beckham told the HSCA that Oswald associated with "a group of ex-CIA members who plotted, [and] carried out the assassination," and then framed him. He did not elaborate on this, but he said Ferrie, Shaw, and Sergio Arcacha Smith were there with Oswald.[1091]

Beckham was accompanied to the Grand Jury proceeding at Shaw's trial by A. Roswell Thompson, the leader of the New Orleans National States' Rights Party and the KKK, and was the subject of an FBI "Racial Matters" investigation. Beckham told the HSCA that Thompson knew Jack Ruby, and he had seen Ruby in New Orleans on two occasions in 1962 and 1963. He also claimed he saw Ruby with Shaw.[1092]

Garrison interviewed Mrs. Esther Stein, who had worked at Shaw's house and saw Oswald there. A painter named George Clark saw Oswald playing cards with another man at Shaw's house. The two said they were "friends of the owner." Kerry Thornley admitted to meeting Shaw and talking to him twice. Vernon Bundy was shooting heroin when he witnessed Shaw hand Oswald an envelope of cash at the Lake Pontchartrain sea wall. His testimony was credible despite his drug addiction.[1093]

Permindex was not the only Shaw link to the far right. Garrison learned that Shaw was at the San Francisco World Trade Center on the day of the assassination. The day before, he visited a virus laboratory with extremely right-wing, anti-Semitic people who openly used the term "dirty Jews." Workers there often talked about a "super race" theory and Nazism, which makes one think of Skorzeny, Rudel and the Madrid Nazis. Another source said Shaw was involved with a shipment of weapons from the West Coast.[1094]

CIA agent Robert Morrow described Shaw as the brains behind a group of fanatical Minutemen and anti-Castro Cubans training paramilitary teams around Lake Pontchartrain, which traced back to Banister's office, Ferrie, Oswald, Arcacha, Jack Martin, and Jack Ruby.[1095]

According to author James DiEugenio, International House, which had a connection to the International Trade Mart, was founded by the Rockefeller Foundation. Both David and William Rockefeller III served as trustees. John McCloy, the former president of the World Bank, was chairman of the board in the 1950s and 1960s. These men were proponents of global trade and opposed John Kennedy's view of self-determination for third-world nations.[1096] It further confirmed there was an international connection to world fascism that ran through New Orleans at a high level.

***

After ignoring Cuba for two months, Lee Oswald's interest began anew on July 24, the same day he applied for a passport and five days after Reily fired him. He contacted Cuban exile Arnesto Rodriguez that day, who was one of the controllers of funds for the Crusade to Free Cuba Committee, the group established by Guy Banister and Sergio Arcacha Smith. As Rodriguez told the FBI, the committee was founded "primarily to raise funds with which to buy arms and supplies for use by the CRC."[1097]

A CIA file from Mexico City, written shortly after the assassination and declassified in 1976, reported: "Maria Rodriguez de Lopez said her son-in-law ARNESTO was well acquainted with OSWALD; runs Spanish Language School, is anti-Castro and 'has a taped conversation with Oswald.'" Questioned by authorities, Rodriguez confessed that Oswald did seek him out "concerning a Spanish-language course." He also disclosed to a Dallas reporter that Oswald had offered his services to train anti-Castro Cubans in guerrilla techniques.[1098]

According to Sam Newman, the owner of the building at the corner of Camp and Lafayette streets where Guy Banister's office was located, sometime in July or August, he had rented an office to an olive-skinned man in his thirties for $30. The man told Newman that "he worked as an electrician by day [Rodriguez's father was an electrician] and desired to teach Spanish by night." A week later, the man returned, stating he could not generate enough interest to rent the office, and told Newman to keep the deposit money.[1099]

Further proof of a connection between Oswald and the Crusade to Free Cuba Committee came from advertising man Ronnie Caire, who knew Sergio Arcacha Smith. After the assassination, he "seemed to recall" a visit from Oswald, who had been "applying for a job."[1100]

Also, on July 24, an FBI informant reported that "approximately ten Cuban refugees arrived in New Orleans from Miami... for the purpose of attending a training camp some two hours from New Orleans, after which they were to be transferred to a training camp in Guatemala." The FBI later learned the camp was located near Lake Pontchartrain and run by Laureano Batista, a leader of the Movimento Democratica Christiano (MDC). A CIA report written during the Garrison investigation stated the "camp was... about 15 miles from New Orleans... [and] belonged to some American millionaires who were defraying expenses for maintenance of men in training and providing equipment. Approx 30 men were in training there ... "[1101]

The camp was established in 1962 by Gerry Patrick Hemming and Frank Sturgis at the request of the New Orleans branch of the Cuban Revolutionary Council. Sergio Arcacha Smith was the leader of the CRC in New Orleans, so the request must have come from him. The MDC occupied the camp, but various groups used it as well. The DRE, November 30 (Masferrer's group), and the MIRR of Orlando Bosch were all known to frequent the camp.[1102]

One of the men active in training exiles there was David Ferrie. Delphine Roberts claimed he took Oswald there on at least one occasion "to train with rifles." Colonel Bishop also said he was aware that Oswald had visited the camp. "I did look into Oswald's background," Bishop stated. "I never met him, but I'd seen him in a training film in New Orleans the past summer [in 1963]. He just happened to be in the group out there at the Pontchartrain camp. Trying to get in with the anti-Castro exiles...."[1103]

On July 31, as part of the federal crackdown against exile activity, federal agents raided a cottage owned by Mafioso William McLaney. They confiscated a significant supply of explosives and bomb casings. The site was located near the Lake Pontchartrain camp and sent the inhabitants scurrying for safety. In 1976, the Senate Intelligence Committee disclosed that the camp "was directed by the same individuals who were involved in procuring the dynamite the FBI seized." Eleven men were arrested, including Rich Lauchi, the ex-Minutemen turned gun supplier. The FBI released them all without being charged. According to one source, some material confiscated had been part of the Schlumberger arms cache that involved Banister and Gordon Novel two years earlier. FBI interviews in Miami uncovered that some of the explosives were for a bombing run on Cuba.[1104]

Five days prior to the raid on the McLaney cottage, someone other than Oswald signed "Lee H. Oswald, USSR, Dallas Road, Dallas, Texas," into the register at the Atomic Energy Museum in Oak Ridge, Tennessee. There is no rational explanation for this, for Oswald was not in Tennessee, nor was he living in Dallas. It was a signal to someone – maybe to meet with Oswald or to keep an eye on what he was up to in New Orleans, with the JFK assassination in mind. Not coincidentally, it was around this time that Lee Harvey Oswald accelerated his interest in Cuba.[1105]

Oswald, who had not contacted the FPCC since he wrote the undated letter to Vincent Lee sometime prior to June 16, wrote Lee again on August

1, reconfirming his support. The spelling errors make the letter unmistakably Oswald's and are a stark contrast to the letters he had supposedly written earlier that summer.

> I rented an office as I planned and was promply [sic] closed three days later for some obsure [sic] reasons by the renters. They said something about remodeling ect., [sic] I'm sure you understand...i [sic] worked out of a post office box and by useing [sic] street demonstrations and some circular work have substained [sic] a great deal of interest but no new members.
>
> Through the efforts of some cuban-exial [sic] "gusanos" a street demonstration was attacked and we were officially cautioned by police. this incident robbed me of what support I had leaving me alone.
>
> never-the-less thousands of circulars were distrubed [sic] and many, many pamphlets [sic] which your office supplied.
>
> We also manged [sic] to picket the fleet when it came in and I was surprised at the number of officers who were interested in our literature.
>
> I continue to recive [sic] through my post office box inquires [sic] and questions which I shall endeavor to keep ansewering [sic] to the best of my ability."[1106]

Though seemingly innocent, the letter is revealing. The office Oswald said he rented and was closed three days later must have been the Newman Building office referred to by Arnesto Rodriguez. It suggests Oswald arrived at Banister's door only after the effort with Rodriguez fell through, which would have been in early August. Since David Ferrie was already working out of Banister's office, he probably brought Oswald there. Unknown to Banister, he may have unwittingly become a peripheral figure in the JFK assassination.

***

Jack Ruby was in financial trouble as 1963 began. In March, the IRS was after him for unpaid taxes for the previous six years totaling $21,000. By the summer, the sum ballooned to nearly twice that figure. The Warren Commission reported that his financial records were "chaotic," and he owed an additional $20,000. His "pockets and the trunk of his car served as his bank." Yet, on June 6, Ruby's lawyer, Graham R. E. Koch, notified the IRS that his client would settle his account as soon as he arranged to borrow money. "We will contact this office not later than June 14," Koch wrote. On November 19, just three days before the assassination, the story gets increasingly suspicious, for on that day, Ruby told his lawyer that he now had a "connection" who would supply him with the money needed to settle his tax debt. Ruby didn't have the money to make such a claim, for his bank account showed $246.[1107] An FBI check of over fifty banks in the Dallas area revealed Ruby did not contact any of them in 1963. The implication was clear – around the time of the assassination, Jack Ruby was in an enterprise that was profitable to the extent that he could pay off his enormous debt.[1108]

The initial warning sign that Jack Ruby was involved in something sinister came on May 7, 1963, when he telephoned the Sho-Bar on Bourbon Street in New Orleans. Peter Marcello, Carlos's brother, owned the bar. It was the beginning of a series of calls between Ruby and leading mobsters throughout the country that would continue until the assassination. It was also around the time that Oswald left Dallas for New Orleans.

On May 10, three days after his call to the Sho-Bar, and the day Lafitte's datebook entry cautioned, "T says tail LO – no direct contact – calls No. Report to Angleton," Ruby shipped a .38 Smith & Wesson revolver to his old friend Lewis McWillie, who now resided in Las Vegas. Ruby explained after his arrest that McWillie requested him to purchase four Cobra pistols and mail them to him. McWillie offered a weak excuse: "I didn't even know you could buy a gun in a store." It was a ridiculous attempt to minimize an event that undoubtedly was significant, for McWillie never picked up the gun after it was delivered. The gesture was symbolic, perhaps a signal to McWillie that a proposed gun deal was about to be completed, which could imply that Ruby's interest at this time was gun running and not the JFK assassination.

In relation to the McWillie gun purchase, Ruby claimed he contacted a gun dealer named Ray Brantley, who had previous dealings with McWillie. However, according to Ruby, Brantley wouldn't sell guns to him because "he feels it would be illegal to send guns out of the country." It meant the guns were going overseas, and Las Vegas was not the intended destination. As we will see, Ruby allegedly visited Cuba during this period on more than one occasion, and the guns were probably for the Cuban underground. As Ruby cryptically said regarding this deal with McWillie, it "was the only relationship I had of any mention, outside of phone calls, to Mr. McWillie, or any person from Havana, Cuba." It was an admission that the gun deal involved Cuba. However, Ruby and Thomas Davis were trafficking weapons together; therefore, the arms may have been for Haiti and an attack against Cuba. Lafitte's datebook for March 26 reads: "McWillie – GUNS with Davis-Oswald." Regardless, during his polygraph exam hearing, Ruby underscored the importance of the deal, stating, "This is incriminating against me...."[1109]

As previously discussed, it was also around this time that Paulino Sierra established a coalition of Cuban exiles, right-wingers, mercenaries, and organized crime figures in a final attempt to eliminate Castro. Carlos Prio was to head the new government. We know Ruby and Prio were linked, which inevitably leads to speculation that Ruby's involvement with McWillie may have been part of the Sierra affair. And considering what was going on at 544 Camp Street with guns destined for the war against Castro, financed in part by Carlos Marcello, it is hard to believe that Ruby's new-found interest in New Orleans was not related to the "Cuban Grand Central Station."

On May 12, Ruby placed a 6-minute call to the Thunderbird Hotel in Las Vegas, where McWillie worked. He then traveled to New Orleans and visited the Old French Opera House on Bourbon Street. The establishment was owned by Frank Caracci, a New Orleans mobster closely affiliated with Carlos Marcello. Ruby visited New Orleans several more times prior to the assassination and called the Old Opera House eight times during the next three months.[1110]

On May 27, the U.S. Supreme Court declined to review Marcello's deportation appeal, which was his last chance to stay in America. Meanwhile, Trafficante had his operations busted, and the IRS placed tax liens against him and his wife while the FBI hounded Roselli and Giancana. The pressure was on to do something fast to stop this.[1111]

Returning to Dallas after his brief stint in New Orleans, Ruby placed a 28-minute call to the Old French Opera House on June 5. The following day, he instructed his lawyer to tell the IRS he had an arrangement to borrow money, so whatever Ruby was involved in with Caracci, it included a means for him to pay off his debt. The following day, June 7, Lafitte's datebook reads: "Else and W's wife = shipment $ – John 'Wilson-H' – Ruby."[1112] The name "Mr. Hodson" appears in Oswald's address book (More about Hudson later. I mention it here because of the significance of a relationship between Hudson and Ruby that references money at a time when Ruby was going back and forth to New Orleans and calling mobsters around the country). Ruby then drove to New Orleans and visited another Caracci establishment, the 500 Club. According to the FBI, Ruby met Caracci there. Ruby also met with Caracci's brother-in-law, Nick Graffagnini, at the Sho-Gun Bar during this trip.[1113]

Ruby was back in Dallas on June 9, the day after many out-of-state mobsters descended on the city. According to a confidential report written by

Lieutenant Robert L. May Jr. of the Dallas Police Department, they were at the Carousel Club and two other nearby strip joints. The purpose of the gathering was to establish syndicate control of local prostitution and gambling by introducing hired killers to rid Dallas of independent pimps and bookies. However, Ruby's simultaneous interest in running guns, visiting New Orleans, and the Paulino Sierra affair may have been why organized crime figures were in Dallas. The mobsters also met at a Howard Johnson's in Arlington, and Ruby placed a one-minute call there on June 10, then another call that lasted seven minutes on June 13. In between, he again called Peter Marcello's Sho-Bar, a three-minute call on June 11.[1114]

Amidst all this mob activity, on June 10, Ruby made a 16-minute call to stripper Candy Barr in Edna, Texas. Twenty-eight years old and separated from her third husband, Barr had been released from a Texas state prison in April, and Ruby had been in contact with her since, calling her five times and visiting her at home. However, she was strictly forbidden to strip according to the provisions of her parole, and she was not even allowed to visit Dallas, so that wasn't why Ruby was interested in her. Most likely, it was Barr's companion, California mobster Mickey Cohen, whom Ruby was talking to through Barr. So, whatever Ruby was up to, it involved gangsters nationwide.

Later that day, Ruby telephoned convicted extortionist Rudy Eichenbaum in San Francisco. Eichenbaum had served time and ran an investment and loan business without employees and no listing in the phone directory. The two men talked for twenty minutes.[1115]

On June 14, Ruby called the Old French Opera House again and talked for seven minutes. It was the first of four calls he made there that week. On June 24, "[mobster Nofio] Pecora received a telephone call from Marcello…at the very same Tropical Court phone from which Pecora called Ruby a month earlier." Three days later, Ruby called McWillie at his Las Vegas home and talked to him for seven minutes. Finally, he again called the Old French Opera House on the 6th and 24th of July.[1116]

In between all this activity, Jack Ruby secretly traveled to Cuba. Warren Commission counsel Lee Rankin told CIA Deputy Director Richard Helms in March 1964 that he received information that Ruby had used an alias and a Czechoslovakian passport to reach Havana via Mexico City in 1963. It explained Ruby's mysterious absences during April and June of that year. Ruby was also reportedly seen in Houston's Escapade Club in April, bragging that he was on his way to Havana and would return with boxes of cigars. He was with a pilot who talked about having flown pipeline inspections over West Texas.[1117]

On January 29, 1964, the DRE issued a press release in Miami, which claimed that "Jack Ruby, the man accused of killing President Kennedy's assassin, Lee H. Oswald, stayed in Cuba during 1962 and the beginning of 1963. Ruby flew to Havana from Mexico City...." They wrote this before anyone was aware that Ruby may have traveled there.[1118]

In 1976, four Dallas deputy constables reported that, after the assassination, a woman with a Latin American boyfriend gave them a box containing papers that linked Jack Ruby and Oswald. "She was really scared because she had all that stuff...." There were newspaper clippings from Mexico and a press card issued to Ruby for the *Daily Worker*; a receipt from a motel near New Orleans with both Oswald's and Ruby's names on it; references to telephone calls to Mexico City; a reference to a landing strip somewhere in Mexico; the mention of "agents" in the border towns of McAllen and Laredo; and a church brochure with markings referring to a trip to Cuba.[1119] According to a Dallas Police informant, Ruby told his physician he "was going to Cuba to 'collect' his income tax and take a 'breather.'"[1120]

Ruby's activity that summer involving mobsters was related to his trips to Cuba. Still, it is hard to imagine he would have bragged about going there to strangers if it involved helping Fidel Castro or if Ruby was involved in a plot to assassinate JFK. It was gunrunning Ruby was involved in, with anti-Castro Cuban exiles who were part of the Sierra group, funded by the Mafia.

Delphine Roberts said David Ferrie acted undercover at times as a Castro supporter. Oswald was doing just that with his bogus FPCC chapter. It returns us to the story of Richard Case Nagell, whose interest in Oswald peaked during July and August when Oswald was "exploited by various individuals for their own reasons." Nagell claimed that in New Orleans, Oswald was approached by two men named Angel and Leopoldo. They claimed to be agents of Castro and were going to deliver a "Christmas present" to Kennedy in retaliation for the various assassination attempts perpetrated against Fidel Castro. Did Oswald try to infiltrate this group, not knowing they were setting him up as the patsy in the JFK assassination, or was he already in league with the assassination conspirators? A lot was going on, with many moving parts, and as the next chapter will show, Lee Harvey Oswald's work in New Orleans was far from done.[1121]

CHAPTER TWENTY

LIVING HARD IN THE BIG EASY

When Lee Harvey Oswald first arrived in New Orleans, he was closely watched, based on the May 10 Lafitte datebook entry: "T. says tail LO – no direct contact – calls No. Report to Angleton and not here..." By September 16, there was uncertainty about him, for that entry reads: "T says L.O is 'idiot' But can be led regardless set-up complete J W-H [John Wilson – Hudson]." On November 9: "On the wings of murder. The pigeon way for unsuspecting Lee. Clip Clip his wings."[1122] The latter entry suggests Oswald was working undercover as an informant, aka stool pigeon, probably for the FBI, and the conspirators knew what he was up to.

In New Orleans in the summer of 1963, Oswald encountered two men named Angel and Leopoldo who believed Cuba deserved to be independent of Soviet or American oversight, which was in line with Oswald's political philosophy. Both were reportedly former CIA employees. Leopoldo was about 200 lbs., 5'10"-5'-11" tall, heavily built, with black hair. He was of Mexican ancestry and between 27 and 29 years old. He had received training from the U.S. military at Fort Jackson, South Carolina. Angel was between 28 and 30 years old, weighed a stocky 180 pounds, was roughly 5'-11" to 6'-0" tall, and had black hair and hazel eyes. According to Richard Nagell, "Both men were said to be connected with a violence-prone faction of a CIA-financed group operating in Mexico City and elsewhere. Both were said to be well known to Mexican and Cuban authorities and, of course, to the CIA. They were affiliated with Alpha 66...There were past ties to the Movement to Free Cuba, cryptically known as 'Cuba Libre.'"[1123]

New Orleans attorney Dean Andrews had previously worked for Carlos Marcello. He told the Warren Commission that Oswald appeared at his law office several times in the summer of 1963 to get his undesirable Marine discharge changed. Andrews testified that Oswald "was accompanied by a Mexican and at times by apparent homosexuals." The Mexican closely resembled Leopoldo. "He's stocky [and] has what they call an athletic build. He could go to fist city pretty good if he had to... About 26 [years old], hard to tell...."[1124]

In the spring of 1963, Nagell's assignment was to determine if rumors about a plot to assassinate the President were true. He told Jim Garrison that his contact at the CIA (which would have been his case officer, Henry Hecksher) was "curious about a project involving a fellow named Lee Oswald and some other men, [and he] was assigned to spend time establishing the necessary relationships and observing."[1125] So, Nagell traveled to New Orleans to join an affiliate of Alpha 66 "to find out if things were real," which eventually led him to Dallas. According to Robert Morrow, Tracy Barnes, whom Hecksher worked for, was the one who sent Nagell to New Orleans. In the Garrison files, as reported in *The Man Who Knew Too Much*, there is a memorandum of an assassination researcher's conversation with Nagell in 1969, recording Nagell as saying that the "Movement to Free Cuba [was] headed by Tracy Barnes," to which both Angel and Leopoldo belonged. The same memo said Ferrie also knew Angel and Leopoldo.[1126]

Recall that according to John Newman, by this time, Antonio Veciana had steered Alpha 66 away from the CIA, whom he no longer trusted, into the open arms of Army Intelligence and General Lansdale. The military was still interested in launching an invasion of Cuba and thought Alpha 66 could be of service by organizing an underground army that would assist the U.S. military during the invasion.

A May 2, 1969, Military Intelligence report, prepared by Special Agent Thomas J. Hench of the 766th Military Intelligence Department, described that "During July, August, September [1963], and on one occasion prior to this, SUBJECT [Nagell] conducted an inquiry into the activities of Lee Harvey Oswald, and the allegation that he had established a Fair Play For Cuba Committee in New Orleans, Louisiana…. He was primarily concerned with investigating activities of Anti-Castro organizations and their personnel in the United States and Mexico."[1127]

Michael Kurtz wrote that Oswald "made several trips to Baton Rouge in the summer of 1963. According to witnesses, he accompanied a prominent leader of the White Citizens' Council [Kent Courtney]…to Baton Rouge six or eight times in July and August….Oswald and his companion engaged in discussions which included criticism of American foreign policy as being 'soft on Communism' and of United States civil rights programs. On their last visit to Baton Rouge, *the two men were accompanied by two 'Latins,' neither of whom said anything to them.*" (Author's italics)

Richard Nagell stumbled upon the assassination plot that was already in the works and intended to use JFK's assassination as a catalyst to invade Cuba. Barnes, who had sent Nagell to New Orleans to investigate, was part

352

of the Lafitte/Skorzeny/Harvey/Angleton group that wanted to ensure a second invasion of Cuba did not happen, and they would sabotage the operation to control the narrative. They thought Cuba was not that important, and the ramifications for West Berlin and Europe would have been catastrophic. We will discuss this in more detail later.

**

On July 27, Oswald spoke at the Jesuit House of Studies at Spring Hill College, where his cousin Eugene was a seminarian. "Americans are apt to scoff at the idea that a military coup in the U.S., as so often happens in Latin American countries, could ever replace our government," Oswald told those in attendance. "But that is an idea that has grounds for consideration." Four months before the assassination, Oswald spoke publicly about a potential military takeover, so he must have been aware this was in the works. The question is, was he already a willing participant in the plot and freely accepted his role as the assassination patsy?[1128]

That Lee Harvey Oswald traveled to Mexico in the latter part of September 1963 is well documented. However, there is evidence that he made at least one other trip south of the border earlier that summer, and it was here where Oswald's participation in the assassination plot began. The timing would have been around the end of July or the beginning of August when, for five days, his whereabouts were unknown.

Delphine Roberts told Anthony Summers that "on the basis of what Banister told her – she knew Oswald had made more than one trip to Mexico in the summer of 1963."[1129] According to what Dick Russell wrote in *The Man Who Knew Too Much*, a 1975 file from the *Time-Life* library stated that "Lee Harvey Oswald had made two trips to Mexico, calling at the Castro Cuban Embassy both times and also attempting to visit the Soviet Embassy." The source was someone inside the State Department. Also, the March 1964 newsletter, *Manion Forum*, stated: "Oswald made two trips to Mexico, the last one from September 26 to October 3, 1963, and visited the Cuban Embassy there." The editor of the newsletter was Dean Manion, a strong supporter of right-wing causes. He received his information from a Cuban exile named Leopoldo Aguilera, Jr.[1130]

The FBI's legal attaché in Mexico City at the time of the assassination, Clark Anderson, recalled having heard about a second Oswald trip to Mexico. Thomas Mann, the U.S. ambassador to Mexico, also said there was a rumor that there had been more than one Oswald trip to Mexico. Richard Nagell told Russell that he had met Oswald in Mexico but not in September 1963. Nagell told a friend, John Margain, that he was in Mexico City with

Oswald. "He wouldn't tell me what it was," Margain said, "but it was something like a mission. He said he thought the plot was people from CIA and the Cubans." Reporter Lonnie Hudkins, who was close to the intelligence community, told Russell: "There was a meeting in Mexico sometime in the summer of '63. There were no Americans present other than Oswald and one CIA man..."[1131]

If Oswald became privy to the assassination plot around the end of July 1963 during a secret trip to Mexico City, how he acted after that should be viewed differently from the period that preceded it. It brings us to the next wave of Oswald's interest in Cuba that summer, nearly two months after his original display of support for Castro had ended. It was now much more open and visible than it had been before.

***

On August 2, two Cubans appeared unannounced at Carlos Bringuier's clothing store, the Cosa Roca, on Decatur Street in New Orleans. They claimed to have deserted the "training camp that was across Lake Pontchartrain" and that "there was a Castro agent inside that training camp," Bringuier said. The FBI raided the camp, which led to agents interviewing Victor Batista of the MDC on August 3. According to Batista, in June, a man named Fernando Fernandez approached the MDC in Miami, who turned out to be a pro-Castro infiltrator. A letter he had written on August 1 to the Cuban ambassador in Mexico said he "had infiltrated a commando group who was preparing to engage in an operation in Cuba."[1132]

On August 5, the FBI learned Oswald was living in New Orleans on Magazine Street, which was the same day he approached Carlos Bringuier in his store. It was the first time Oswald ever used his real name publicly in conjunction with anything related to Cuba.

Bringuier was the New Orleans head of the DRE. He had entered the war against Castro in 1961 as propaganda secretary for the CRC and was suspicious of strangers looking to help the Cuban exile cause. He told the Warren Commission that when Oswald walked into his clothing store, he "told me that he was against Castro...he asked me first for some English literature against Castro, and I gave him some copies of the Cuban report printed by the Cuban Student Directorate. After that, Oswald told me he had been in the Marine Corps...had training in guerrilla warfare, and that he was willing to train Cubans to fight against Castro. Even more, he told me that he was willing to go himself to fight Castro."[1133]

The unemployed Oswald offered Bringuier money to support the exile cause, which he could not afford to do if he was acting alone. Bringuier turned him down. "I had inside myself the feeling, well, maybe this is from the FBI, or maybe this is a Communist." The following day, Oswald returned to the Casa Roca and dropped off his Marine Corps training manual.[1134]

On August 7, FBI SAC New Orleans wrote to J. Edgar Hoover that there was no "known branch of the FPCC ... of any branch of the July 26th Movement, [and] there are no pro-Castro groups ... in the New Orleans area." The CRC was the "only anti-Castro organization as a group [that] exists in the New Orleans area ... .headed by Frank Bartes ..."[1135]

It was a timely memo, considering Oswald was about to go public with his support for Fidel Castro, and the person keeping tabs on him, who undoubtedly provided the above information, was FBI agent Warren de Brueys. De Brueys had worked with a radio intelligence unit deciphering Japanese codes during World War II, worked undercover with the FBI in Mexico City, served as an assistant legal attaché at U.S. embassies in Mexico City and Buenos Aires, and as a legal attaché at embassies in Rio de Janeiro and Brasilia, Brazil. Oswald's address book contained his name, disguised as two Russian words, which meant Oswald tried to hide that he knew de Brueys. A copy of the address book entry was sent to de Brueys in July 1993 by author Alan Jules Weberman, and de Brueys did not deny that it was his name. "I find it interesting," he said, "but I think [that] obviously he put my name in his address book because I had investigated him prior to the assassination ... I talked to his landlady on Magazine Street. The idea was to confirm if he had any employment that placed him in contact with sensitive material, as far as national security was concerned. And, of course, I gave her my name and showed her identification."[1136]

Oswald's landlady at Magazine Street, Mrs. Jesse Garner, said it was FBI agent Milton Kaack who questioned her about Oswald, not de Brueys. She told the Secret Service that "an FBI Agent, believed to be Milton Kooch or Koach, was investigating Oswald during the time he lived at 4907 Magazine Street, that he had interviewed her four or five times about Oswald."

De Brueys also said, "I got the impression that he [Oswald] fancied himself as a spook ... I never met him ever, and to my knowledge, I never spoke to him." Still, how could de Brueys say that Oswald "fancied himself as a spook" if he had not met him until after the assassination in the Dallas police station?

De Brueys was more truthful later when he testified before the HSCA. "Oswald was never an asset," he said. "He was never an informant. I am disinclined to believe he was ever recorded as a source, but that possibility exists ... He would be somebody who would be in the area, somebody else who could tell us about what went on in the [Habana] bar. We may have talked to him." It sounded like an admission.

FBI Agent William Walter testified before HSCA about a report written by de Brueys that established Oswald as an FBI informant but was repeatedly interrupted by Harold Leap, one of the interviewers, which made Walter indignant. "I know what I know, and I know what I saw," he said. Oswald had "an informant's status with our office."

In the late 1950s/early 1960s, de Brueys was involved in monitoring Cuban exiles, and in doing so, he worked closely with Howard Hunt as a member of PROJECT SEAL, the CIA's attempt to create a Cuban Government-in-exile. David Phillips was asked if he had ever met de Brueys: "Yes. I remember having been in touch with him ... I knew a lot of FBI people." De Brueys told author Alan Jules Weberman: "I knew David Phillips when I was undercover and assigned to the Dominican Republic revolution for about six months in Santo Domingo, and Dave was the CIA Station Chief ... I think, maybe when I was in Brazil, he may have been there [for] a short period of time. I never thought of this before." However, as Howard Hunt told the HSCA, "The DRE. Dave Phillips ran that for us." De Brueys was clearly hiding something. [1137]

The Habana Bar, which de Brueys referred to, was located two doors from the Casa Roca. On August 8, two nights after dropping off his manual, Oswald was seen there at 3:00 A.M. by the proprietor, Orest Pena, and a waiter. In 1975, Pena publicly claimed he had seen de Brueys with Oswald on "numerous occasions" and reported that de Brueys had threatened him physically if he mentioned that while testifying before the Warren Commission.

Pena told Bringuier about an incident at the Habana Bar and wrote the FBI about it: "Oswald asked for a lemonade, and when they collected for it, he said that surely the owner had to be a Cuban capitalist ... Oswald was [with] a Mexican. After that, the Mexican returned with another Mexican to the Habana Bar." These two men may have been Angel and Leopoldo. The descriptions were consistent with what Nagell, Dean Andrews, and people in Baton Rouge provided of the two men they had seen with Oswald. The FBI was concerned, for they inquired at the bar "and left word that if they saw them [Angel and Leopoldo] again, to call there."[1138]

It was not a coincidence that on the afternoon of August 9, the day following the incident at the Habana Bar, Oswald began to distribute FPCC literature publicly for the first time in almost two months. Although the handbills were the same, there was a distinct difference in how Oswald op-

356

erated compared to what he had done back in June. Abandoned was his desire to maintain anonymity by using the name Hidell and falsifying his PO box. For his new crusade, Oswald brazenly stamped L.H. Oswald, 4907 Magazine St., New Orleans, La., on each handbill. He now wanted to attract attention to himself and his support for Fidel Castro by making it possible for anyone interested to find him at home.

Carlos Bringuier was in his store when he learned Oswald was distributing pro-Castro literature on Canal Street. The confrontation that followed was inevitable. Bringuier was irate and called Oswald a "Castro agent." The crowd shouted: "Traitor! Communist! Go to Cuba! Kill him!" One of Bringuier's associates grabbed the leaflets and threw them in the air. Bringuier approached Oswald as if he was going to attack him physically. Oswald only smiled and said, "Okay, Carlos, if you want to hit me, hit me." The New Orleans police soon arrived and arrested Bringuier, his two companions, and Oswald.

Former DRE leader Isadro Borja thought it was a staged event. He knew "the CIA had Oswald under surveillance for a long time. Why would someone come to tell Bringuier that Oswald was in the street handing out pro-Castro leaflets? And who was that person?" William Gaudet agreed and called it "a sort of PR operation...I think Carlos went there on purpose." Tourist Matt O. Wilson told Garrison he had seen Bringuier and two colleagues emerge out of nowhere as if "they must have been standing right there in front of one of the buildings." A "funny look" came onto Oswald's face, a "sneery look," as if "he didn't care what happened." Harry Dean, who infiltrated the FPCC on behalf of the CIA in Chicago, told both Garrison and Marguerite Oswald that Oswald was "doing the same job as I was."[1139]

Orest Pena swore under oath that during the altercation, he saw the FBI taking photographs, which meant de Brueys knew it was going to happen. Pena also said he knew Gaudet was a "CIA-FBI agent." Then there was John Martin, a Minnesota Minutemen member who served under General Walker in Germany in 1960, who just happened to be in town filming the Oswald-Bringuier encounter after first traveling to Dallas to film the bullet hole in Walker's home. It seems Walker also knew about the incident in advance.[1140]

Pena posted bail for Bringuier, but Oswald spent the night in jail. He was interviewed extensively at the police station by Lieutenant Francis Martello, who concluded that he "seemed to have set them up to create an incident." Sergeant Horace Austin said Oswald "is being used by these people...

and knows very little about this [FPCC] organization that he belongs to and its ultimate purpose or goal."[1141]

After Oswald answered Martello's questions, he said he was "desirous of seeing an [FBI] agent and supplying to him information with regard to his activities with the FPCC in New Orleans." Officially, he had no prior contact with the FBI. "Just call the FBI," Oswald told Martello. "Tell them you have Lee Oswald in custody. When they arrive, hand them this note." And he added that he wished to talk to Warren de Brueys.

***

The FBI's William Walter took Martello's call in the middle of the night. The only agent present was John Quigley, who ordered Walter to search the office files for any record of a "Lee Oswald." He found 105 Oswald files related to espionage and Cuba and 134 (Informant) files. There was also a security file in the locked file cabinet of SAC Harry Maynor, with two names on the file jacket: "Lee Oswald" and "Warren de Brueys." The files had to do with ongoing surveillance and paid informants and were locked up "for some security purpose." Walter would later tell Jim Garrison that during the summer of 1963, the FBI had two distinct sets of files on Oswald and were communicating with him on a regular basis.[1142]

A concerned Quigley called de Brueys, who refused to leave home because he had to attend a barbeque later that day, a somewhat weak excuse. Most likely, he did not want the police to know he and Oswald had a working relationship. So, Quigley was left to interview Oswald, which he did at the police station for an hour and a half. And just like Dr. Humes would do after JFK's autopsy, Quigley burned his notes when the interview was over, so there is no official record of what they discussed. Quigley claimed he had never heard of Oswald prior to the interview, which is hard to believe considering the large number of Oswald FBI files Walter found in their office. It was also Quigley who handled the Oswald case for the New Orleans FBI after Oswald defected to the Soviet Union. According to Quigley's account of the interview, Oswald did not tell him anything of importance, which is unlikely considering how long they talked. Why would a man who was allegedly acting undercover for the FBI and would be out of jail in twenty-four hours call for an FBI agent and essentially blow his cover? Up until then, Oswald had tried to separate himself from the FBI. He used an incorrect P.O. box number on the handbills, changed his place of residence repeatedly to stay one step ahead of them, employed aliases, etc. Now, at a time when Oswald began stamping his real name and address on FPCC handbills, he brought the FBI directly to him.

Consider also that Oswald waited until after the FBI interview to call his family for help in posting bail, something he could have done at the time of his arrest. He obviously wanted to remain in jail until he was able to talk to the FBI, and the literature he gave to Quigley during the interview may provide the answer. In addition to FPCC pamphlets, he also gave the FBI agent a copy of *The Crime Against Cuba*, which had the name FPCC stamped inside the back cover, along with Guy Banister's 544 Camp Street address. For the trained eye of the FBI, it was a bombshell of information. The alleged leftist Oswald was working out of the den of right-wing activism, and Oswald intentionally wanted Quigley to know this. He had just renewed his public support for Cuba and wanted his connection to Banister known.

Before they parted, Oswald handed Martello a note he wanted given to the FBI. Martello transcribed part of it, gave it to Quigley, and kept the original for himself. The day after the assassination, he turned his file on Oswald over to Agent A.G. Vial of the Secret Service, which included "a small white piece of paper containing handwritten notes." Martello told the Warren Commission that Oswald purposely left it. It "was inadvertently picked up with the [FPCC] literature, and I put it in a file folder, and it remained there." "This piece of paper, which was folded over twice and was about 2" x 3" in size, contained some English writing and some writing which appeared to me to be in a foreign language which I could not identify. Before I gave this paper to Mr. Vial, I made a copy of the information...." On one side were street addresses for relatives in Dallas and New Orleans. On the back, handwritten in Russian, was the name "Leo Setyaev."[1143]

As described in Chapter Two, Leo Setyaev was a contact of Oswald's in Russia. The FBI and CIA both knew of him, and Oswald must have been aware of that because by leaving Setyaev's name, he let the local FBI know that he was not just your run-of-the-mill informant – he had connections to U.S. intelligence. But they must have known that already, for why else would Quigley have rushed to the police station in the middle of the night instead of waiting until a reasonable hour the following day to meet with a Communist who was distributing pro-Castro literature on the streets of New Orleans?

On August 11, the day after he posted bailed, Oswald continued his quest for publicity by asking the city editor of the *New Orleans States-Item* to provide coverage of his FPCC campaign. Three days later, he telephoned a prominent New York radio reporter named Long John Nebel, offering to appear on Nebel's radio show at his own expense. Meanwhile, Bringuier invited a WDSU-TV camera crew to the trial on August 12 and angrily described Oswald's attempt to infiltrate his group, holding up his Marine Corps manual for the entire courtroom to see. Oswald quietly sat on the "colored side" of the room, something the southerners in attendance would have construed as a Communist act. He pleaded guilty to "disturbing the peace by creating a scene." His uncle, accompanied by a Carlos Marcello associate, paid the fine. The judge dropped the charges against the Cubans.

Bringuier was accompanied to the courtroom by Frank Bartes, whose name appeared five days before in an FBI report about the CRC. After the trial, Bartes became very vocal as the news media surrounded Oswald in search of a statement. According to Bartes, he "got into an argument with the media and Oswald because the Cubans were not being given an opportunity to present their views." Later that day, Bartes warned the FBI about Oswald, saying he was a dangerous man. A month later, he told the FBI that he had never met Oswald before the trial, which may have been a lie because Bartes was instrumental in establishing the training camp at Lake Pontchartrain that Oswald allegedly visited.

Bartes had good reason to want to overthrow Castro. He had been a wealthy man in Cuba, the owner of a private railroad company that employed thousands and had assets of $100 million. According to Hemming, "Bartes was a very distinguished guy, a close friend of Bill Pawley. He was of Spanish descent [and] very patrician. This ain't no flat-nosed beaner, tortilla roller. This is a goddamn aristocrat. The guy is honorable."

Bartes was also an informant for the FBI and the CIA. A July 2, 1962, CIA memo from the New Orleans office of the Domestic Contacts Division included information from Bartes: "On 25 June 1962, Laurence Joseph Laborde and two other men had called on him [Bartes]. He had met Laborde earlier in Miami. The men said that they wanted to train Cuban refugees as guerrilla fighters and demolition experts who would then go to Cuba. The other men were Gerald P. Hemming, Jr. and Howard Kenneth Davis."[1144]

Laborde had also given Bartes a letter of recommendation from Carlos Rodriguez Quesada, a leader of the 30th of November, Rolando Masferrer's group, whom he also knew. Bartes was a significant player in the war against Castro, which is why the word "Bardes" appears in Oswald's notebook, an apparent reference to Bartes.[1145]

According to Robert Morrow, Rodriguez Quesada was a one-time bodyguard for Rolando Masferrer and a lieutenant of Mario Garcia Kohly. He was killed in 1964 by a CIA mercenary named John O'Hare because he planned to go public with what he knew about the Kennedy assassination.[1146]

Frank Bartes and Gerry Patrick Hemming were involved in the Lake Pontchartrain camp that trained Cuban exiles, and Hemming was a member of a caravan that traveled to Dallas with a car full of weapons on the day prior to the JFK assassination if Marita Lorenz's story is true. Lorenz was the one-time mistress of Fidel Castro, a friend of June Cobb, and a Frank Sturgis associate. They tried to assassinate Castro by having Lorenz return to Cuba and drop poison pills into Castro's drink. Sturgis, Howard Hunt, and Oswald were all part of the caravan. Sturgis' involvement also suggests Operation 40, and Morrow claimed Quesada was a lieutenant of Mario Garcia Kohly, which again points to Operation 40. Quesada was close to Rolando Masferrer, whom Colonel Bishop said was the bagman for Alpha 66 and a critical liaison between the Cuban exile community and Jimmy Hoffa and Santo Trafficante.[1147]

On the evening of the trial, Oswald again wrote to Vincent Lee of the FPCC, enclosing a copy of his summons and a newspaper clipping regarding his sentencing. "Continuing my efforts on behalf of the F.P.C.C. I find that I have incurred the displeasure of the Cuban exile 'worms' here. I was attacked by three of them as the copy of the enclosed summons indicates. I was fined $10 and the three Cubans were not fined because of [a] 'lack of evidence' as the judge said. I am very glad I am stirring things up and shall continue to do so. The incident was given considerable coverage in the press and local TV news broadcasts. I am sure it will be to the good of the Fair Play for Cuba Committee."[1148]

The fact that Oswald mentioned his altercation with Bringuier proves beyond doubt that his previous letter of July 31 described a separate street altercation and not the Bringuier affair that had not yet occurred.

On August 16, Oswald once again took to the streets, handing out FPCC leaflets near the International Trade Mart. This time, he hired three or four men at two dollars apiece to assist him. Although they were there for only a short time, local TV station WDSU-TV filmed Oswald and his companions. Someone had alerted them ahead of time. Miguel Cruz, an associate of Carlos Bringuier, stood by and watched quietly. He later told a Garrison investigator there was "a strong looking Latin-American type person around 25 or 30 years old who was a little taller than OSWALD and who weighed close to 200 pounds, standing in front of the Maison Blanche Building with a camera and taking pictures of OSWALD and other people."[1149]

361

It was a similar description to Nagell's Leopoldo and the man previously seen in Oswald's company by Richard Nagell, Dean Andrews, Orest Pena, and the people from Baton Rouge. According to Cruz's report, the man was with Oswald and perhaps directed him.

Also present was Warren de Brueys, standing just inside the doors of the Trade Mart. Oswald entered the Press Club, where he asked for a glass of ice water. Seated at the bar was *States-Item* reporter on the police beat, Jack Dempsey. Still holding one of Oswald's FPCC leaflets, Dempsey offered Oswald a beer. "No, thank you, sir," Oswald said. "Water would do me better than a beer or a coke." "Have you read the leaflet?" Oswald asked.[1150]

That evening, Carlos Quiroga paid Oswald a visit at his Magazine Street home. He later told the Secret Service on November 30 that Bringuier wanted him "to infiltrate Oswald's organization if he could." According to a December 3 Secret Service report:

> Quiroga spent about an hour talking to Oswald who told him he learned to speak Russian at Tulane University....Oswald had not mentioned to him that he had defected to Russia. He said Oswald asked him to join the Fair Play for Cuba group and had given him an application form... Oswald stated that if the United States should invade Cuba, he, Oswald, would fight on the side of the Castro Government....
>
> Carlos said he had been willing to join the Fair Play for Cuba group provided it was done with the backing of the FBI or the local police force. He said he had made this known to Lt. Martello, NOPD, who apparently forgot about it. He said he did not contact the FBI for the reason on a previous occasion he had notified their office that Oswald was handing out what he assumed to be pro-communist literature in front of the International Trade Mart... and the FBI had given him the cold shoulder.[1151]

Carlos Bringuier confirmed Quiroga's story when he testified before the Warren Commission. "My friend [Quiroga] asked to [sic] me if I think that it would be good that he will go to Oswald's house posing as a pro-Castro..." Bringuier agreed it was a good idea, "and there was when we found that Oswald had some connection with Russia...."[1152]

Left out of this credible explanation was that a CIA memo reported that while a student at Tulane University, Quiroga was "a candidate for the CIA Student Recruitment Program, designed to recruit Cuban students to return to Cuba as agents in place," and he "reportedly had homosexual tendencies..." Recall that Dean Andrews claimed to have seen Oswald in the company of gay Cubans earlier that summer.

The December 3 Secret Service report also added that a "Rodriguez Sr." told them Quiroga "knew Arcacha well and was with him frequently at 544 Camp Street." Rodriguez Sr. was the father of Arnesto Rodriguez, who was part of the Crusade to Free Cuba, had tried to rent space at 544 Camp Street, and was "well acquainted with Oswald." We know Arcacha was familiar with Oswald, Ferrie, and Banister. Another report by Garrison investigator David Lewis claimed he had witnessed Quiroga, Banister, and Ferrie in Banister's office with a man introduced as Leon Oswald. Considering that Banister employed students at Tulane University to act undercover to weed out Communists, his relationship with Quiroga is believable.[1153]

Returning to the real purpose of Quiroga's visit to Oswald's home, landlady Jesse Garner told the Warren Commission, "Well, there was that Cuban or Spanish-looking guy [who] one time rang my bell in the late afternoon... And he had a stack of them [FPCC pamphlets], and he asked me about Oswald, and I said he was living around on that side where the screen porch is ... and I said, 'You are not going to spread those things on my porch....'"[1154]

Mrs. Garner obviously believed Quiroga was a fellow supporter of the FPCC. The Warren Commission was equally concerned, for her testimony did not coincide with the story Bringuier and Quiroga were telling. Quiroga claimed he had picked up FPCC pamphlets off the street after Oswald left and brought them to Oswald's home as proof of his support for the FPCC. However, it was not just a few pamphlets Mrs. Garner observed, for she testified it was a stack about the width of her hand. It defies logic that Quiroga would have taken the time to pick up so many pamphlets to demonstrate his support for the FPCC. There must be another explanation.

Quiroga said he visited Oswald to infiltrate his FPCC chapter, but when Oswald gave him the opportunity to become a member, he declined. And if Quiroga wanted to ensure he had police or FBI approval before infiltrating Oswald's group, as he claimed, why didn't he do that before visiting Oswald? The whole explanation seems designed to hide a connection between Quiroga and Oswald that the Cuban exile didn't want to reveal. Considering Mrs. Garner's testimony, Quiroga's and Oswald's independent association with 544 Camp Street, and Banister's acknowledgment that he was aware that Oswald handed out pro-Castro literature, it appears that Quiroga was delivering the pamphlets to Oswald for his use. Why else would he have had such a large stack in his hands when he arrived? It confirms what we already suspected to be true – that Bringuier and Oswald staged the street altercation to furnish Oswald with publicity as a Castro supporter.[1155]

Quiroga would fail a lie detector test given to him by Jim Garrison, and when asked if he knew that Oswald was not a Communist and that his FPCC activity was a cover, he pleaded the Fifth. When asked if he was aware that the assassination of JFK involved a conspiracy, he again took the Fifth. "Would you be surprised if I told you that Oswald was not a Communist at all," Garrison said to him. There was no response.[1156]

***

Arnesto Rodriguez, Sr., who was with the Crusade to Free Cuba Committee, the group created by Guy Banister and Sergio Arcacha Smith, was an FBI informant in 1967 who reported to de Brueys. At the time, he suggested that the District Attorney's office in New Orleans contact a man named Piedra about the JFK assassination since Piedra possessed files on exiles suspected of being double agents. In 1963, Orlando Piedra owned a clothing rental store at 117 Camp Street. Before Castro took over Cuba, he had been Chief of the Investigations Bureau of the Cuban National Police and worked closely with the Mafia and the CIA. According to the FBI, "Orlando Piedra enjoys the distinction of being considered by the Castro regime as one of the principal war criminals in the United States." A CIA report stated that "Orlando Piedra…is one of the main organizers and exponents of political propaganda in favor of Batista; close to him and enjoying his trust." He was also an associate of Enriqie Fernandez Parajon, the former Chief of Batista's Secret Police, and was a friend of Bringuier and Sergio Arcacha.

On December 20, 1963, FBI SAC James J. O'Conner questioned Piedra because his store's address was in Oswald's address book, and Piedra claimed he "never had any personal contact with Oswald." It's incredulous that seemingly everyone listed in Oswald's address book claimed to have never met the man.

Gerry Patrick Hemming also knew Piedra in the early 1960s. "Piedra was a Godfather kind of guy who had a private detective agency," Hemming said. "Very personable. He belonged to the Junta of National Liberation. William K. Harvey's people supported it. William K. Harvey was setting up this team of people, which a lot of people call OPERATION FORTY, which is an erroneous name. They were setting up this team of people to eliminate Fidelista without Fidel, like Manuel Ray. They were to eliminate everybody in place if accidentally the former Castro people got into power militarily or civilly during the anarchy that would follow a victory over

Castro. Frank Sturgis was kept on tap to blow a few fucking people away. It was an extension of ZR RIFLE. [It was] ethnic cleansing of the new government after the Bay of Pigs. It would be impossible for him [Oswald] to get Piedra's address. Piedra did not advertise where the fuck he was. He was in business but didn't advertise where the fuck he was. If you wanted to see him, you had to make an appointment...There was kidnap money out on him. Juan Orta [June Cobb's boss in Cuba] set up a couple of operations to snatch all these people. These people were fucking war criminals. So, how would Oswald come up with this? Somebody in the government had to give it to him."[1157]

The information probably originated with Orta, who was known to be an agent of Castro's who worked with Cuban intelligence agents in Miami. Considering that Orta was the one Santo Trafficante turned to in 1959 to slip poison pills to Castro, it tells us where the Mafia boss's allegiance lay.[1158]

The August 6, 1963 entry in Lafitte's datebook reads: "Harvey with me [Lafitte in New Orleans]." This, along with what Hemming said above, means William Harvey was involved in Cuban affairs in New Orleans, as well as being part of the JFK assassination conspiracy, and it all began in 1961 with an intent to kill the leftist Cuban government in exile after they arrived in Cuba. Apparently, if the Omega Plan/AMWORLD were allowed to go forward, Operation 40 would have done the same thing to the Robert Kennedy/Enrique Williams hand-picked government in exile, and this would still have been Harvey's responsibility.

On May 8, 1973, a CIA memo titled "Cuban Involvement in Watergate Case and Attitudes in Miami Area" included individual bios of "Sidney Gottlieb, Renaldo Pico, Orlando Piedra, Rolando Masferrer, Joaquin Pedromo Sanjenis, Juan A. Paula, Edgardo Buttari, Charles 'Bebe' Reboso, James Flannery."

Piedra, Masferrer, and Pedromo were ex-Batistaites. Howard Hunt referred to Juan Paula in *Give Us This Day*. He was an accountant who served as treasurer of the Frente in April 1963. Buttari was an ex-Batista Minister of Commerce and a Director of Social Welfare of the Association of the Veterans of the Bay of Pigs Brigade 2056. Bernardo Torres was Vice Director of Military Affairs. Flannery was a colleague of David Atlee Phillips, and Gottlieb was MK/ULTRA's "Doctor Death." These men were all hardcore right-wing anti-Castro Fascists. So, how did their names wind up in a CIA memo related to Watergate ten years after the JFK assassination?[1159]

***

Whatever Oswald was up to in the summer of 1963, he was no stranger to Lieutenant Francis Martello, who told the Warren Commission that in the course of his duties in the Intelligence Division, he investigated Tulane professor Dr. Leonard Reissman. Reissman was at the center of Communist-front activity in New Orleans and was involved with the FPCC. FPCC pamphlets were found on Pine Street near Reissman's home, according to Martello. It was prior to the Oswald/Bringuier incident when Oswald told Martello that the FPCC held meetings on Pine Street. Martello asked Oswald if the FPCC held meetings at Reissman's, but he refused to answer. Captain James Arnold, who was present during Martello's interview of Oswald, thought the expression on Oswald's face revealed that he knew Reissman.

Martello told the Secret Service eight days after the assassination that he had asked Oswald if he was acquainted with Reissman, and "Oswald replied he was." According to Oswald's aunt, Lillian Murret, Oswald admitted he knew Tulane professor Reissman and had been to his home. She was under the impression that Oswald had met him through Ruth Paine when she visited New Orleans, which would have been near the end of September, right before Oswald left the city. Reissman was certainly someone Paine would have been interested in. Richard Steele, who Oswald paid to hand out FPCC leaflets, told the Warren Commission he got the impression from Oswald that the FPCC had a connection to Tulane.

William W. Barker, Jr. of the Louisiana National Guard, worked at Lakefront Airport. He contacted New Orleans FBI Agent James R. Riordan on November 25, 1963, because he was reasonably sure he had seen Oswald come out of the office of Leonard Krimmerman, a professor of Symbolic Logic at Louisiana State University in New Orleans, where he was a student. Krimmerman frequently invited Barker to meetings or seminars at Tulane and distributed literature Barker considered "detrimental to the United States."

Vereen Alexander was a student at Newcombe College, the women's division of Tulane. She was from a prominent political family – her grandfather was chief justice of the Louisiana Supreme Court. She published a liberal newspaper called *The Reed*. In the summer of 1963, Alexander attended a party at an apartment near Slogan's bar on Magazine Street. The FBI memo from Agent Don Adams noted, "Miss Alexander has the strong belief that Lee Harvey Oswald was also possibly present at this party."

Lieutenant John R. Knight of the Louisiana State Police prepared a forty-one-page report on Oswald's activities for the Warren Commission, which he gave to State Police Superintendent Thomas Burbank and Governor Jimmie Davis in the form of a booklet. Years later, when Garrison investigator Sciambra asked Knight to look over the report, he noticed that "many photographs of LEE HARVEY OSWALD at different stages of his residency down here" were missing. He said the booklet had contained a photograph of Oswald marching down Canal Street with a group of people, several pictures of Oswald in front of the Trade Mart, and some taken at the time of his arrest. They were all gone.[1160]

***

Understanding Lee Harvey Oswald's New Orleans experience is one of the keys to unraveling the assassination riddle. Oswald was the perfect patsy candidate for the conspirators. An avowed Marxist who was associated with radical right-wingers, Oswald's desire for worldwide revolution and his belief that a war between the United States and the Soviet Union was inevitable made him a willing participant. Perhaps a desire to ignite a war that would lead to the political system he longed for was what motivated him.

Oswald was sent to New Orleans from Dallas because the conspirators were considering him for the role of assassination patsy. The initial handbill caper involving the Hidell alias and the phony P.O. box was obviously a scam, but for what purpose? Perhaps he was being tested so others had an opportunity to observe him. Recall the May 10th entry in Lafitte's datebook reads: "T says tail LO – no direct contact – calls No. Report to Angleton and not here…"[1161]

There can be little doubt that Banister was instrumental in Oswald's handbill schemes. Handing out handbills to attract the attention of the left was a Banister standby and could explain his involvement with Oswald. Still, it does not necessarily mean Banister was involved in the assassination. Banister's anger when he discovered that Oswald had stamped the 544 Camp St. address on some of the handbills he distributed was proof of that. He ordered Oswald never to connect his office with pro-Castro activity again.

Oswald was brought into the assassination plot around the end of July by Angel and Leopoldo, who were posing as Castro agents. One thing is sure – one-time supporters of Castro who opposed the involvement of the Soviet Union and the United States in Cuban affairs would have appealed to Oswald. They undoubtedly convinced Oswald that to help Cuba, it was necessary to create an incident that would turn the Soviet Union and the United States against each other.

We know Oswald's handling of the FPCC leaflets changed when Angel and Leopoldo brought him into the assassination plot, for he was now willing to attract attention to himself. The Bringuier incident was another scam, and shortly after that, as will be shown in the next chapter, Oswald once again lost interest in Cuba, as the Communist Party USA became the focus of his attention. It was a significant step in the creation of Oswald's leftist profile, for the conspirators needed him to be branded a Communist, not just a supporter of Fidel Castro. By the fall of 1963, Lee Oswald was on a collision course with destiny, and unknown to him, what was in store for him was already pre-determined.

CHAPTER TWENTY-ONE

WITH FRIENDS LIKE THESE, WHO NEEDS ENEMIES

It was quite a gathering at Antoine's Room, a famous New Orleans restaurant. On August 16, 1963, the entry in Lafitte's datebook reads: "Antoine's Room – Martello, E. Joan. and Labadie. Quigley interview [illegible] demonstration. Call Holdout."[1162]

The people mentioned had one thing in common – an interest in Cuban affairs. Lieutenant Francis Martello was the policeman who interviewed Oswald after the altercation on August 9 with Carlos Bringuier, who was head of the DRE in New Orleans. E. Joan. was shorthand for Efythron Joannides, the chief of Psychological Warfare for the CIA at the JM/WAVE station, who the CIA recently put in charge of the DRE. Labadie was Special Agent Stephen J. Labadie, who worked out of the FBI office in Tampa, Florida. FBI agent John Quigley interviewed Oswald at the New Orleans police station after the Bringuier incident, which occurred on August 9. This meeting, which took place one week later, must have been to discuss Oswald, the FPCC chapter he was allegedly looking to promote in New Orleans, and what exactly Oswald was up to, considering his other relationships New Orleans law enforcement and the local FBI were aware of.

Three days prior, on August 13, a Lafitte datebook entry reads: "T w/ Silverthorne – T flying here with Harvey – meet Trafficante tomorrow." It had something to do with the Labadie meeting in New Orleans with representatives from the New Orleans police department, the FBI, and the CIA, respectively, presumably to talk about Oswald, because four days after that, on August 20, Labadie wrote a five-page FBI report titled "Santo Trafficante, Jr., aka."

The significance was that Labadie's focus was on Trafficante before and after the gathering at Antoine's, which had to do with Oswald. It makes one ponder the possibility that Trafficante was also an item of discussion. Recall that J. Edgar Hoover had told the New Orleans, Dallas, and Miami FBI offices to start producing meaningful reports on the Mafia, so the gathering at Antoine's may have had something to do with that as well. However, it does not explain why William Harvey, who was supposed to be in Rome, was meeting with Lafitte, the mysterious "T", a pilot named Joseph Silverthorne, who was a former member of the OSS, a CIA asset, and an occasional assassin, and Santo Trafficante in New Orleans three months before the JFK assassination.[1163]

According to Lamar Waldron and Thom Hartmann, the authors of *Ultimate Sacrifice: John and Robert Kennedy, the Plan for a Coup in Cuba, and the murder of JFK*, just six weeks prior, on June 26, 1963, the first AMWORLD document, a five-page memo listed as SECRET, EYES ONLY, was sent by J.C. King, Chief of the CIA's Western Hemisphere Division, to the "Chiefs of Certain [CIA] Stations." The title of the memo was "AMWORLD Background of Program, Operational Support Requirements and Procedural Rules," and the point of the memo was to "serve to alert you to the inception of AMWORLD, a new CIA program targeted against Cuba. Some manifestations of activity resulting from this program may come to your notice before long."[1164]

As we know, AMWORLD was the CIA's name for the Omega Plan, the Bobby Kennedy/U.S. military's joint operation to take back Cuba, from which the CIA's role was limited. The CIA's dissatisfaction with their role is evident in the low-key and unenthusiastic description of the plan provided by J.C. King. Still, some essential points provided in the memo support the meeting at Antoine's and what was happening in the early weeks of August 1963.

As described in *Coup in Dallas*, recently released CIA documents contain a memorandum titled "AMWORLD MEETING IN MIAMI, 28-29 June 1964" include the following: "AMBIDDY [Manuel Artime] claims to have been contacted in the past by the Mafia for the sale of arms," and that the Dominican Republic was mentioned as a possible source of support for AMWORLD. We know that Trafficante had previously visited the DR, so a connection here is not out of the question. And according to *Coup in Dallas*:

> In light of Lafitte's entry to indicate that Santo Trafficante arrived in New Orleans to meet with William King Harvey on August 13, the possibility exists that the meeting at Antoine's on August 16, and subsequent communication between Lafitte and Joannides [who by now was involved with the DRE] and discussions with J.C. King, George Hunter White and Charles Siragusa, may have surpassed plans for Lee Harvey Oswald's involvement in the forthcoming assassination of the president...but were equally, if not more, focused on deliberations at the highest level of AMWORLD, an operation that had been in play for months."[1165]

It is more probable that AMWORLD was the codename for the CIA's involvement with Paulino Sierra and their plan to assassinate JFK, which certainly was different than what Bobby Kennedy had in mind with the Omega Plan.

***

It was around this time that things began to move fast for Lee Oswald. On August 17, he received a telephone call from William Stuckey of WDSU Radio, who had been told about Oswald by Carlos Bringuier. Lee agreed to an interview, of which only four-and-one-half minutes aired on Stuckey's radio show. There was a follow-up debate on August 21, with Oswald opposing Bringuier and Edward Butler, the head of a right-wing propaganda organization known as the Information Council of the Americas (INCA). INCA's office was in the International Trade Mart. Butler and Clay Shaw knew each other well.[1166]

Stuckey called New Orleans FBI SAC Harry Maynor to tell him about the Oswald interview and the upcoming debate. Maynor passed that information on to SA Milton Kaack.[1167]

Edward Butler, a frequent visitor to 544 Camp Street, may have already known Oswald. On September 11, he testified before the House of Representatives that he trained individuals to infiltrate Communist groups. "We have been privately counseling certain individuals…on specific 'how to' methods for counteracting the party and destroying it in individual cases."[1168]

Financing for INCA came from right-wing radicals in the New Orleans area like Dr. Alton Ochsner. Eustis Reily of Reily Coffee Company donated thousands of dollars. The owners of WDSU radio and television, Edgar and Edith Stern, hosted the radio debate and were INCA members. INCA's "Chief of Security," Robert R. Rainold, was a "Past President of the National Society of Former Special Agents of the FBI." And Reily Vice President William I. Monaghan, an ex-FBI agent, was also a member.[1169]

"I believe it was mentioned that you at one time asked to renounce your American citizenship and become a Soviet citizen…," Stuckey asked during the debate. "I don't think that has any particular import to this discussion," Oswald said. Asked if he was a Marxist, he responded: "Yes, I am a Marxist."

When asked how he supported himself in the Soviet Union for three years, Oswald replied: "I worked in Russia. I was under uh, the protection of the uh… of the uh…that is to say, I was not under the protection of the uh… American government. But that is, I was at all times considered an American citizen."[1170]

Oswald said he was under the protection of the U.S. government and inadvertently revealed too much about the nature of his trip to Russia. The

Warren Commission was concerned and inserted the word "not" in their debate transcript to falsify what Oswald had said.

Falsely asserting that Oswald was a Communist to connect the FPCC to the Soviet Union was the intent of the debaters. Eventually, the discussion returned to the FPCC and Cuba. "We do not support the man," Oswald said, referring to Castro. "We support the idea of an independent revolution in the Western Hemisphere, free from American intervention," which was in line with what he had previously written. Notice how he always said we, which was an indication he was not acting alone. Regardless, the debaters destroyed Oswald's credibility by exposing his defection, and the radio debate was likely a staged event, just as the street altercation with Bringuier had been. After writing to Vincent Lee of the FPCC on August 17, Lee Oswald would never correspond with them again. His focus of attention was now the CPUSA.[1171]

A week after the debate, Oswald wrote to the CPUSA, a group he detested. The letter opened with the greeting, "Comrades," and closed, "With Freternal [sic] Greeting." Oswald was not entitled to use either salutation since he was not a party member. He explained he had started an FPCC branch in New Orleans, "a position which, frankly, I have used to foster communist ideals." Referring to the debate, Oswald wrote: "Our opponents could use my background of residence in the U.S.S.R. against any case which I join." He complained that "by association, they could say the organization of which I am a member, is Russian controlled, ect [sic]. I am sure you see my point." The letter closed "time fighters for progress. Please advise."[1172]

Oswald acted like he was already working for the Communists. He asked if he should work above ground after disclosing he had tried to "legally dissolve my United States citizenship" while in Russia [which Oswald vehemently insisted he did not do], or was it better to "remain in the background, i.e., underground." Knowing the FBI was monitoring their correspondence, the CPUSA carefully worded their reply. He was told, "It is advisable for some people to remain in the background, not underground."[1173]

Oswald initially corresponded with the CPUSA on August 12, after the critical end of July period when the conspirators brought him into the assassination plot. He sent a clipping of his street altercation arrest to Arnold Johnson in New York, the party's information director. Two weeks before, Oswald had spoken at his cousin's Mobile, Alabama, monastery, where he denounced the Soviet way of life. Just days before, Lieutenant Martello asked him following the Bringuier incident if he was a Communist. He said he was not. Martello "asked him if he was a socialist, and he said 'guilty.'" Oswald told him, "There was not true communism in Russia....they have 'fat, stinking politicians over there just like we have over here....'" His new-found interest in communism was insincere and done with an ulterior motive in mind.

On August 31, Oswald wrote to the CPUSA newspaper, *The Worker*, allegedly looking for a job as a commercial photographer. "I have, in the past made blow-ups, reverses and other types of photo work for the 'Worker'... My family and I shall, in a few weeks, be relocating into your area."[1174] To support the claim that he was moving north, Oswald acquired the Bulletin of the New York School for Marxist Study for the fall term of 1963. However, on September 1, the day after writing to *The Worker* in New York, Oswald wrote to the CPUSA again, asking, "How can I contact the Party in the Baltimore-Washington area, to which I shall relocate in October." That same day, he also wrote to the Socialist Workers Party: "Please advise me as to how I can get into direct contact with S.W.P. representatives in the Washington-Baltimore area. I and my family are moving to that area in October."[1175]

By this time, the FBI in Washington, Dallas, New York, New Orleans, and Miami were tracking Oswald. Various divisions within the CIA, Naval Intelligence, Military Intelligence, Post Offices, and U.S. Customs were doing the same. His writings to subversive groups, public support for the FPCC, and radio debate made finding him easy, but it was all a deception.

On August 25, Ruth Paine mailed a letter to Marina from Paoli, Pennsylvania, promising to be in New Orleans on September 20. Ruth wanted Marina and her child to accompany her back to Dallas, which would leave Oswald alone and unemployed in New Orleans to come and go as he pleased. Oswald likely knew he was headed for Mexico as soon as Marina and June returned to Dallas with Ruth. Hence, the purpose of his letters was to mislead authorities into thinking he was heading north. Whatever relationship he may have had with the FBI was now over.

After writing to the CPUSA, Oswald did not correspond with a left-wing organization until November 1, three weeks prior to the assassination. And for the first two-and-one-half weeks of September, his whereabouts are unknown, except for an incident at the beginning of the month in Clinton, Louisiana. Of interest is that just before his extended disappearance, the Lafitte datebook entry for August 29 reads: "Call George W.[Hunter White] for shipment of LSD for New Orleans & Dallas – Texas laws?"

***

Clinton is a small town ninety miles north of New Orleans, where, for years, Guy Banister and his colleagues looked to keep the number of eligible black voters to a minimum. After Henry Earl Palmer became voter registrar, the number of blacks registered in East Feliciana Parish dropped from 1,027 to 50. The FBI intervened and discovered that of 2,000 parish voters, only eight were black, in a parish that was 60-65 percent African American.[1176]

Things got ugly in the summer of 1963 with the unlawful arrest of CORE volunteer Michael Lesser. When CORE National Director James Farmer spoke in Plaquemines on August 19, the police used tear gas to disperse an unruly mob. Lesser was freed on August 27, but tensions remained high just prior to Oswald's appearance in Clinton in early September.[1177]

Oswald's story begins in the adjacent town of Jackson. Edwin Lea McGehee testified during the Clay Shaw trial that Oswald entered his barbershop and said he wanted a job at the nearby East Louisiana State Hospital. McGehee told him he needed to visit State Representative Reeves Morgan at his home. Garrison investigators Andrew Sciambra and Lieutenant Francis Fruge interviewed Morgan in 1967, who said Oswald wanted a job in the hospital's electrical department. Morgan told Oswald he needed to be a registered voter, and his daughter Mary remembered there was a woman in the car waiting for him.

The next day, Oswald went to Clinton to register to vote. According to eyewitnesses, a late-model black Cadillac with three white occupants parked near the registrar's office in clear view of those waiting in line. Due to the recent racial turbulence, the town marshal checked the license plate number. The car was registered to the International Trade Mart. He spoke with the driver, who was "a big man, gray-haired, with a ruddy complexion." He and others testified at Clay Shaw's trial that it was the defendant sitting in the parked car that day.[1178]

Core chairman Corrie Collins recalled the man sitting on the passenger side of the vehicle: "The most outstanding thing about him was his eyebrows and hair... they were unnatural, didn't seem as if they were real hair." It could only have been David Ferrie. There was a third occupant, a young white man, who left the car and was seen by various people.[1179]

Thomas Williams owned a store across from the registrar's office and was sure it was Oswald. Henry Palmer identified Ferrie from a picture shown to him. William Dunn, Sr., an African American who was registering voters for CORE, identified Shaw and Oswald during his testimony. Henry Burnell Clark recognized Ferrie by his hair. "It was bushy and stood up in all directions on his head..." He also identified Shaw as the driver.[1180]

Oswald waited for several hours on the voter registration line. Being the only white man, he was easily remembered by those who were likely unnerved by his presence. When he finally reached Henry Palmer's registrar desk, Palmer told him he had not been in the area long enough to register. Oswald thanked him and left.[1181]

In its final report, the HSCA concluded that "the Clinton witnesses were credible [and] establish an association of an undetermined nature between Ferrie, Shaw, and Oswald less than three months before the assassination."[1182]

The next day, Oswald arrived at the infamous East Louisiana State Hospital in Jackson, where almost every patient they treated came through the criminal justice system. They were all expendable, and the hospital subjected many to mind-altering drug experimentation.

Oswald walked in wearing a T-shirt and talked loudly to call attention to himself, which was out of character. Receptionist Bobby Dedon spoke to him. Maxine Kemp Drane, who worked in personnel, told Garrison that after the assassination, she came across Oswald's application filed as "Oswald, Harvey." She later discovered the file was missing. Aline Woodside also said she had seen Oswald's application.[1183]

Oswald spoke to hospital attendants about Cuba and what it would take to bring Castro down, and one of them called over Cuban Dr. Silva. "I'm involved with getting rid of Fidel Castro," Oswald allegedly said. "I'm using my skills as a Marine."

Born in Cuba in 1929, Silva came to the U.S. and graduated from Tulane University School of Medicine in 1958, where he was an associate professor of clinical psychiatry from 1959 to 1972. He coauthored at least two widely read medical papers with Dr. Robert G. Heath of Tulane. One was titled *Comparative Effects of the Administration of taraxein d-LSD. Mescaline, and Psilocybin to Human Volunteers.* The introduction to the paper stated, "The patient donors [were] housed in a special Tulane University Research Unit at the East Louisiana State Hospital, Jackson." The Commonwealth Fund financed the project, which was a CIA front. The other paper was titled *Comparative Effects of the Administration of Taraxein, d-LSD, Mescaline, and Psilocybin to Human Volunteers.* At a meeting of the Society of Biological Psychiatry, it was discussed along with "a 16-mm sound movie film depicting brief excerpts of the reaction of the subjects to each of four compounds" of LSD and other hallucinogens. There were "four volunteer subjects: one psychiatrist; and three prisoners at the Louisiana State Penitentiary at Angola [Louisiana]." Dr. Silva was one of the subjects. He was given an injection of taraxein and, within about ten minutes, was "experiencing symptoms… associated with the disease, schizophrenia." In a day or two, Silva was tested with LSD.[1184]

Dr. Robert Heath performed experiments involving electrical stimulation of patients by surgically implanting electrodes in their brains. The CIA and the military provided funding. He also experimented with LSD, using unwitting prisoners from Louisiana State Penitentiary as guinea pigs. He practiced gay conversion therapy by implanting electrodes into a subject's brain. Heath then stimulated the electrodes while he subjected the patient to heterosexual pornographic material. He then forced the subject to have intercourse with a female prostitute recruited for the study. Today, the good Dr. Heath might be considered certifiably insane.[1185]

Dr. Alfred T. Butterworth, who arrived at East Louisiana after Oswald's visit, had also taken part in LSD experiments at Angola State Prison. He had previously worked with Sidney Gottlieb at Fort Detrick under Project MK/NAOMI, and Drs. Harris Isbell and Abraham Wikler at the NIMH Kentucky Addiction Farm. His job in his early years at State Hospital was "instructing other doctors in the use of LSD for the treatment of mental disorders."[1186]

Recall the August 29 entry in Lafitte's datebook noted above that mentions LSD, which was days before Oswald showed up at Lousiana State Hospital. It was also a time when Oswald's whereabouts were unknown for weeks. It leads one to believe he may have been subject to mind-altering drug experimentation once again, for why else would he make this mysterious visit to Clinton while disappearing for an extended period?[1187]

Erick Crouchet was a CAP cadet who served under David Ferrie. On August 21, 1961, he submitted a statement that Ferrie had committed "acts of crimes against nature on him on two separate occasions." Subsequently, the New Orleans Police Department sent Crouchet and other boys who had been CAP members under Ferrie to Louisiana State Hospital for a brief period.

In 1968, Jim Garrison interviewed Crouchet, who revealed that in the early 1960s, he had attended a party at Dr. Heath's home. Dr. Silva was also in attendance and introduced Crouchet to Sergio Arcacha Smith, who we know was closely tied to Ferrie, Banister, and Oswald in the months leading up to the assassination. For some reason, Crouchet was returned to East Louisiana State Hospital from August 1963 through JFK's assassination in November. The timing is odd, but there is no proof that any assassination-related motive was behind this.[1188]

East Louisiana State Hospital and Tulane University were up to no good. They were involved with drug experimentation on young boys, including CAP cadets, which may explain Oswald's involvement with Ferrie and Banister as far back as 1955. And how was it that the specter of drug experimentation continued to hover over Oswald? It existed in New York, at the Bordentown Reformatory; it was in New Orleans when David Ferrie delivered CAP boys to East Louisiana State Hospital; it was with Oswald in the Marines; and in 1963 when Ferrie and Shaw drove Oswald to East Louisiana State for no apparent reason.

***

One other Oswald sighting occurred in the late summer of 1963. It was in the small town of Bay Cliff, Texas, at the home of convicted gunrunner Robert McKeown. In 1975, McKeown told Dan Rather of CBS News that Oswald and a Latin man came to see him regarding the purchase of several high-powered rifles. The following year McKeown told Dick Russell that the Cuban's name was Hernandez and that the other man said, "My name's Oswald. Just call me Lee. My contacts have a big opportunity to take over Salvador. I want to know if you'd be interested in furnishing some arms." McKeown claimed he turned Oswald down, but the encounter is still intriguing because of McKeown's other known associates. One was Carlos Prio, arrested with McKeown for running guns to Castro while Batista was still in power and was whom the Paulino Sierra group wanted to take over Cuba after they removed Castro. Another was Jack Ruby, who had contacted McKeown in 1959 regarding a potential sale of jeeps to Castro. It strengthens the possibility that Oswald and Ruby already knew each other in the summer of 1963 and were possibly running guns together, maybe with Thomas Eli Davis. Someone had to have told Oswald about McKeown.[1189]

Robert Morrow claimed that on July 1, 1963, Tracy Barnes ordered him to purchase four Mannlicher 7.35 mm surplus rifles (the rifle found in the Book Depository was a 6.5 mm Mannlicher), which he did. During the first week of August, David Ferrie allegedly picked up the rifles in a private plane at a local airstrip. Barnes told Morrow the guns were to be used to assassinate Juan Bosch of the Dominican Republic. From what we know, the assassination would probably have been blamed on Castro to get the U.S. military to invade Cuba.[1190]

On September 25, the Dominican military and local police overthrew Juan Bosch and accused him of catering to Communists, but they did not kill him. The timing coincided with Nagell's assertion that the JFK assassination was to occur around the 26th or 27th of September.

***

On September 17, Lee Oswald reappeared after a prolonged absence at the Mexican consulate. He obtained a fifteen-day tourist entry permit for travel to Mexico. As previously stated, Oswald bypassed proper channels when he traveled to Mexico earlier that summer, and we must assume he could have done so again here if he desired. Traveling legally now indicated he wanted it on record that the trip had occurred, or at least that it appeared that way.

On his application, Oswald listed his occupation as a photographer with a business address at 640 Rampart Street. An FBI investigation revealed, "there is no 640 Rampart Street in New Orleans..." We should consider that the street got its name from the wall, or "Rampart" (Rempart in French), that was built on the north side of the street in the city's early years to fortify the French colonial city. The last address Oswald falsified was French Street, and this was all done while Oswald was allegedly part of an assassination plot with Frenchman Jean Pierre Lafitte, who also used the alias Hidell. One wonders if Oswald used these cryptic French references to reveal who he was working for in the JFK assassination conspiracy.

More critical is that directly ahead of Oswald in line at the consulate was William Gaudet of the CIA, who, as we know, later connected Oswald to David Ferrie, Guy Banister, and Sergio Arcacha Smith. His presence must have alarmed the Warren Commission, for they left Gaudet's name off the list of those applying for Mexican travel visas on the same day that Oswald did. It was a blatant attempt to withhold evidence from the public. That Gaudet was in front of Oswald became known eleven years later when someone inadvertently declassified an FBI report. Gaudet insisted it was a coincidence, but it is hard to believe that was the case. Here was a CIA operative who warned the FBI that Jack Ruby was in New Orleans in 1959, who knew Ferrie, Banister, and Arcacha were aware of Oswald throughout the summer of 1963, and who knew Clay Shaw. That he and Oswald were together on line by accident defies logic. Either Gaudet was working with Oswald or he was keeping an eye on him. The latter is more probable, for if Gaudet had any direct involvement with Oswald, he would not have disclosed what he knew about the relationship between Oswald and those associated with 544 Camp Street. Therefore, just two months prior to the assassination, we can assume that William Gaudet of the CIA was keeping a close eye on the actions of Lee Harvey Oswald.[1191]

While Gaudet was watching Oswald, Richard Nagell was telling Oswald that he was lied to by Angel and Leopoldo about the JFK assassination plot. According to Nagell:

Oswald was told that neither Leopoldo nor Angel were agents of Cuban G-2, a story they had strapped on Oswald the previous month...the two were, in fact, counterrevolutionaries... with a violence-prone faction of a CIA-financed group (Alpha 66) operating in Mexico City... that both were well known to Cuban and Mexican authorities and, of course, to the CIA. He was informed in so many words that *he was being "used" by fascist elements* in an attempt to disrupt the Cuban revolution, to ruin chances for a contemplated rapprochement between Cuba and the United States, probably *to incite the U.S. government to initiate severe retaliatory measures against Cuba (in the form of an invasion)*, etc... He seemed genuinely upset and visibly shaken...."(Author's Italics)[1192]

By this time, Alpha 66 was working with the U.S. military and intended to disrupt the Cuban revolution. The JFK administration was pursuing an attempt at rapprochement with the Cuban government. According to Lafitte's datebook, Fascists were using Oswald in the JFK assassination plot. Everything Nagell said supported the idea that initially, the JFK assassination was to be a catalyst for a second invasion of Cuba, possibly involving Oswald traveling to Cuba and being charged as the patsy who assassinated Castro, which would have led to an invasion of Cuba involving the U.S. military. However, unknown to Nagell, the Lafitte plotters real agenda was to sabotage that plan so that Kennedy's death would prevent the second invasion from occurring.

On September 20, while Oswald pondered what Nagell had told him and prepared for his upcoming trip to Mexico, Nagell quietly walked into a bank in El Paso, Texas. He asked a teller for one hundred dollars in American Express traveler's checks, then fired two shots harmlessly into the bank's ceiling (The traveler's checks were symbolic. Recall from Chapter Six, Oswald's encounter with Michael Jelisavcic and American Express in Moscow and that "Am Ex" appeared six times in Oswald's notebook). Nagell left the bank, and the police arrested him without a struggle. In his wallet was a mimeographed newsletter from the FPCC addressed to him, which suggests a connection with Oswald and possibly June Cobb related to the FPCC. In the trunk of his car were two briefcases filled with documents detailing his outstanding military record, including that he had received the Purple Heart three times and had graduated with honors from the Army Intelligence School. Apparently, Nagell wanted it known that he had served his country well, just as Oswald had wished to have his military papers saved in the letter he wrote prior to the attempt on General Walker's life. There was a Minolta 16-millimeter camera, a complete film development laboratory, a suit jacket bearing the label of a clothing store in Mexico City, and two tourist cards for entry into Mexico. One card was in the name of "Joseph Kramer," an alias Nagell had previously used when writing to J. Edgar Hoover about Oswald and the assassination. The other was either in the name of "Albert Hidel" or "Aleksei Hidel," aliases used by Nagell, Oswald, and Lafitte. The discovery of FPCC literature and the Hidell alias should have created a stir within the FBI, but it did not, at least not publicly. Perhaps Oswald told the truth after the assassination when he said Hidell was not an alias but someone else.

Nagell issued only one statement to the FBI after his arrest: "I would rather be arrested than commit murder and treason." The first FBI report regarding the bank incident quoted Nagell as saying, "All of my problems have been solved for a long time, and now I won't have to go to Cuba," which was where Oswald intended to go.

According to Nagell, in the summer of 1963, he became aware of "a domestic-inspired, domestic-formulated, and domestic-sponsored" plan to assassinate President Kennedy, and he was sent to New Orleans to investigate by Tracy Barnes. However, when Nagell tried to reach Barnes to say the plot was a reality, Barnes was nowhere to be found, and Nagell suspected he had been double-crossed and possibly set up to take the fall along with Oswald.

As previously discussed, Nagell's CIA handler's name was "Bob," whom Dick Russell believed was Henry Hecksher. In any event, it appears that Barnes and Hecksher may have used Nagell to find out what was really happening regarding the assassination plot. Nagell later said this led to his "indirect involvement in a conspiracy to assassinate President Kennedy and other highly placed government officials in September 1963." He was sure he had become part of "the Pentagon hopes" to spark a military conflict with Cuba, which was the military's plan.[1193]

What is interesting is that Nagell told Dick Russell, "The conspiracy I was cognizant of, I'm not saying is the same one that resulted in the president's death, although I'm sure the same people were involved." In other words, the assassination plot changed after Nagell shot up the bank in El Paso and Oswald traveled to Mexico City, which is consistent with our thesis that the JFK assassination was to abort a second invasion of Cuba, not to serve as a catalyst to remove Castro, which appears to have been the original intent of the conspirators.

Recall the September 16 Lafitte datebook entry: "See J.R. Dallas, T [Barnes] says L.O. [Oswald] is idiot but can be led regardless set-up complete JW-H [John Wilson Hudson]." With the change in plans for the operation and Oswald now aware the conspirators were setting him up, there were those who wanted to abort the JFK assassination plot. However, the Lafitte entry says "T" remained confident that they could still manipulate Oswald." So, they continued to move forward. Still, as late as October 20, Lafitte wrote, "Hard to believe that it will go forward ... but it will, it is me?"[1194]

***

Ruth Paine arrived in New Orleans on September 20, and three days later, she and Marina drove back to Irving, Texas. Lee Oswald was alone again, but a late September assassination attempt that could have become a reality had Nagell not gotten himself arrested was no longer feasible. Four days later, David Ferrie made a fifteen-minute phone call to Chicago number WH4-4970, which was the apartment building where a woman named Jean West resided. On the night before the assassination, West would be in Dallas with Lawrence Meyers, a Chicago businessman, in town for a convention. The two checked into the Cabana Motel, and Ruby visited Meyers at the Cabana and stayed well into the morning. A Ruby/Meyers/Ferrie relationship must have existed, for it was common practice for organized crime figures, whose phones the FBI had tapped, to use intermediaries to pass messages between themselves. It does not mean the call was related to the assassination, considering the gun-running activities that were going on. Still, the timing of the call from Ferrie in relation to Nagell's action makes it suspicious.[1195]

Regarding Ferrie, Nagell said he "and his friends were nothing but peripheral characters, always expendable, who really didn't know the scheme of things, and couldn't tell you anything even if they were around to do so ... and that while you people may have set sail in the right direction you are now (from what I hear) about 180 degrees off course ... but then, that is how it was meant to be." What Nagell meant was that initially, Jim Garrison thought it was the ultraright that killed JFK, and he had been on the right track but failed to pursue it.

***

A curious incident occurred just after the late summer activity in Clinton, as described above. Thirty-eight-year-old Edward G. Gillin worked at Juvenile Court in New Orleans as an assistant district attorney in the fall of 1963. A young man approached his desk who "gave every indication of emotional disturbance and lack of personal conviction or sense of security." The visitor had a question regarding a book he had read, *Brave New World*

381

by Aldous Huxley, which involved a drug the author stated would enable the reader to see into the future. The man wanted to know if the drug was legal and what its name was, for he could not remember.

Gillin later recalled that part of the man's name was Oswald because it reminded him of a comedian on the Milton Berle radio show. After the assassination, he recognized Oswald as the visitor, so he called the FBI. Years later, Judge Gillin said he never received a reply.

New Orleans library records confirm that Oswald checked out *Brave New World* on September 19, 1963, just before Gillin's encounter with him. It was also a couple of weeks after Oswald appeared at East Louisiana State Hospital, where doctors performed mind-altering drug experiments on unsuspecting individuals. The public at the time was unaware that the CIA and military were involved in such things, so Gillen had no reason to fabricate such a story. The likely explanation is that Oswald approached Gillin searching for answers to something he was involved in but could not understand.[1196]

It is also interesting that Kerry Thornley, who probably picked up the handbills at Jones Printing on Oswald's behalf, had suggested that Oswald read *Brave New World* when the two served in the Marines at El Toro in California in 1959. Could it be a coincidence that *Brave New World* popped up again in 1963 when Thornley once again reentered Oswald's life?

Thornley and Oswald resided at the Hotel McBeath in New Orleans for a while and frequented the Ryder Coffee House. Oswald's signature was in their guest book. Barbara Reid provided a sworn statement saying that she had seen Thornley and Oswald together at the Bourbon House. "I am positive that the person sitting at the table with Kerry Thornley was Lee Harvey Oswald," Reid said, and she called them "the gold dust twins." Peter Deageano was at Reid's table and saw Oswald walk in and join Thornley. He had also seen the two together on another occasion, "in either August or September," and saw Oswald distributing leaflets on Canal Street. Deageano identified him as "being identical" to the person he had seen at the Bourbon House. L.P. Davis also saw Oswald and Thornley at the Bourbon House, each wearing the same black pants and white shirts, which suggests they both belonged to the same radical group, which remains unknown. Newsman Cliff Hall reported that Thornley admitted to him shortly after the assassination that he had seen Oswald during the summer of 1963. Another witness, Jeanne Hack, said Thornley knew about Oswald's FPCC activity. On the day of the assassination, he told her, "Oswald did not do it alone but had help."[1197]

Doris Dowell, the assistant manager of an apartment complex in Arlington, Virginia, where Thornley worked from December 1963 until mid-1964, claimed he told her he had known Oswald in New Orleans the previous summer. The official report of her interview with Garrison's office stated that Thornley and Oswald "were buddies in New Orleans. He [Thornley] said that he had met Oswald again in New Orleans and that they had met at a place in the French Quarter that she would probably not like."[1198] Saying they met again in New Orleans suggests they had met prior to the 1963 encounter, which could only have been in the mid-1950s when Oswald had previously lived in New Orleans.

At the Clay Shaw trial, LSU professor Martin McAuliffe remembered that Thornley had mentioned Oswald to him at the Bourbon House that summer. Jeanne Hack had been surprised that Thornley, like Oswald, had a post office box at the Lafayette Square station, far from his customary venues. Thornley had also once taken her to a meeting at the back of Bringuier's store. John Schwegmann Jr. told Garrison he had seen Thornley at Oswald's residence on Magazine Street. Myrtle and Tony LaSavia were both "positive" they had seen Thornley walking past their house at 919 Upperline with Marina on the way to the Winn-Dixie supermarket on Prytania Street. Tony LaSavia was sure it was not Oswald but "another man" with Marina. When he saw Thornley on television, as well as in the newspaper, he immediately recognized him "as being the person who used to walk with Marina to the Winn-Dixie food store."[1199] His words indicate this occurred multiple times.

Judith Baker mentioned something similar in *Me and Lee*. She wrote, "The apartment manager said he saw Thornley with Marina. Neighbors testified to the Warren Commission that Thornley was there so often that they were unsure as to which one was really Marina's husband. Garrison's investigation confirmed the same point. What was Kerry Thornley doing spending so much time with Marina Oswald? Had he taken the place of Ruth Paine, who was still stuck in Dallas and could no longer babysit Marina? Maybe so."[1200]

Speaking of babysitters, when Marina first left Dallas for New Orleans, Ruth Paine contacted Ruth Kloepfer, a local Quaker whom she did not know, to check on Marina and her daughter June. She was married to a Tulane professor, Dr. Henry Warner Kloepfer, and not long after they met Marina, the couple moved from Pine Street to Louisiana Avenue Parkway, which was close to David Ferrie. Their first visit to 4905 Magazine involved only Mrs. Kloepfer and her daughters. Marina was unaware that Dr. Kloepfer was a geneticist (i.e., eugenicist) at Tulane Medical School, whose name, address, and phone number were in Lee's address book. Why their sudden interest in Marina?

Meanwhile, Thornley was on good terms with people from Banister's office. On the night of the assassination, he was with Allen Campbell, who worked for Banister and knew Oswald. Thornley admitted to Campbell that he had known Oswald that summer in New Orleans. Regarding Oswald's arrest, Thornley said, "It could not have happened to a nicer guy."[1201]

Jim Garrison discovered that at the time of the assassination, Thornley was living in a New Orleans apartment that he had rented from a friend of Clay Shaw's named John Spencer. Several days after the assassination, Spencer came to his house to find Thornley suspiciously gone, even though his rent was not due for a week. Thornley left a note for Spencer stating: "I must leave. I am going to the Washington, D.C. area, probably Alexandria, Virginia..."

Thornley hinted that he may have known what transpired in a letter he wrote to a friend just months after the assassination. "The whole thing was very interesting for a while," Thornley wrote, "the assassination, because – on the surface – there was good reason for the unenlightened SS [sic] and F.B.I. to suspect I might've had a hand in it. We had some political conversations and finally, I guess, I was cleared. No word from them lately... When it is all over, though, I may yet go piss on JFK's grave, RIP."[1202]

***

It was around the time of David Ferrie's phone call to Jean West that Oswald left New Orleans and never returned. Neighbors last saw him at his apartment on the evening of September 23. The Warren Commission concluded he went by bus to Houston on the night of September 24, even though they could not produce documentary evidence to support this, nor were there any bus line personnel or passengers who had seen him. It was a critical point since eyewitnesses had identified a man who looked like Oswald boarding a bus from Houston to Laredo at 6:00 A.M. on the 26th. Since he did not know how to drive a car, they needed to prove Oswald got to Houston without assistance, so they assumed it was by bus. Anything else would point to a conspiracy. Despite what the Commission claimed, the HSCA later concluded that Oswald left New Orleans during the last week of September and that, based on his movements, he had access to a car.[1203]

In *Reasonable Doubt*, author Henry Hurt posited that a man named Robert Easterling drove Oswald out of New Orleans. Easterling claimed that

Oswald was under constant surveillance by the FBI, so they set a diversionary fire in an African-American neighborhood, and he had to drive his car over fire hoses because the fire hydrant was across the street. With Oswald lying hidden in the back seat, Easterling was pursued by an unmarked car as they drove off at a high rate of speed. They eventually lost their pursuers and were off to Houston.[1204]

Hurt had difficulty finding a record of the fire Easterling described. The New Orleans Fire Department's records were nowhere to be found, and newspapers did not report such a fire. Then Hurt discovered the original firehouse fire-report ledgers in the basement of the New Orleans Public Library. One referenced a fire at 9:22 A.M. on September 24, 1963. The structure was a wooden apartment building in an African American section of town, diagonally across the street from a church and fire hydrant, just where Easterling said it was. The address was a two-minute drive from where he picked up Oswald. The fire was suspicious and "under investigation."[1205]

Hurt's confirmation suggests Easterling's story was true. The problem is Easterling was not a credible person. He was a lifelong criminal with a history of severe mental illness. Still, Oswald's landlady, Nina Garner, confirmed that the FBI hounded Oswald, as Easterling said they did. She stated Oswald was under heavy surveillance by FBI men in "a car which used to park there at night and watch him and the house, round the corner by the drugstore." New Orleans FBI agent Milton Kaack was one of those agents. When Anthony Summers contacted Kaack, he cried, "No. No. I'm not talking. You won't get anything out of me."[1206]

What was it about Oswald, who lived unemployed in New Orleans, who floated between the FPCC and Banister's office, who was involved in a street altercation, appeared on a radio debate, who had the aura of illicit drug experimentation hover over him throughout his adult life, who had the FBI, CIA, Military Intelligence, and U.S. Customs follow his every move, that worried FBI agent Milton Kaack so? The answer is there was plenty for Kaack to worry about – which anyone who took the time to look into Lee Oswald's story, then or now, could easily see.

CHAPTER TWENTY-TWO

WHERE'S OSWALD?

Lee Harvey Oswald's departure from New Orleans did not go unnoticed. The day after he was killed by Jack Ruby, a *New York Times* article quoted William M. Kline, assistant United States Customs Agent-in-Charge of the Bureau's Investigative Service at Laredo, Texas, as saying that when Oswald crossed the border into Mexico, his "movements were watched at the request of a 'federal agency at Washington.'" When asked to elaborate, Kline said, "'I'm not at liberty to say,'" The *New York Herald-Tribune* reported that another "US Customs official, Oran Pugh, had said that…US Immigration has a folder on Oswald's trip."[1207]

In *Oswald and the CIA*, John Newman wrote that as Oswald made his way to Mexico, the CIA put information pertaining to his FPCC activities in a different file from his existing CIA 201 file, and they were kept separate until after the assassination. CIA documents list a September 10, 1963, report by James Hosty that connected Oswald to the FPCC, which they filed in Oswald's CI/SIG soft file as well as his security file. In addition, three major FBI reports on Oswald, all from the New Orleans office, were placed in the security file. Why was it so essential to keep Oswald's FPCC information separate from everything else?

Even though Customs had files on Oswald traveling to Mexico City on October 2, FBI agents were still searching for him in New Orleans. Six days prior to that, FBI headquarters informed its New York office that the CIA had asked for the FPCC's mailing list and "other documents," which the FBI could only obtain if they broke into the FPCC office in New York. The CIA wanted to know if the man traveling on the bus to Mexico was Lee Harvey Oswald.

Something was not right. Another FBI report, written on September 24, was received at the CIA on October 2. This report contained details of Oswald's New Orleans FPCC activities but did not include the Quigley jailhouse interview, which was a critical omission. On October 9, the CIA's Mexico City station informed headquarters only that an Oswald impostor had appeared at the Soviet Embassy gate. The next day, the CIA sent a cable to the FBI, State, and Navy, informing them of this with a misleading physical description of the man. It was clear from the beginning that the CIA wanted people to think an impostor had traveled to Mexico.[1208]

***

After Oswald arrived in Houston on September 25, he called the Houston home of Howard Twiford, a member of the Socialist Labor Party. Twiford's wife took the call "sometime between 7:00 pm and 10:00 pm." She believed it was a local call because an operator was not involved. The FBI would interview her about it on December 2, 1963.

We know that Oswald, or a man claiming to be him, left Houston by bus on the morning of the 26th. The day before, a man calling himself "Harvey Oswald," which matched the name on Oswald's application file at the East Louisiana State Hospital the month before, walked into the Selective Service office in Austin, Texas, unhappy with the undesirable discharge he had received from the Marines. He told Mrs. Lee Dannelly that he wanted his status upgraded based on two years of good behavior. She could not help him because she did not have a Harvey Oswald listing in her files, but since he said he was from Fort Worth, she suggested he check with the Selective Service office there. After the assassination, Mrs. Dannelly reported her encounter with "Harvey Oswald."[1209]

Meanwhile, as Joan Mellen wrote in *A Farewell to Justice*, there were incidents in Louisiana that defy explanation. A brawl broke out at a Holiday Inn lounge in Lafayette, as reported by columnist Robert J. Angers, who was a longtime CIA asset who also wrote for William Gaudet's *Latin American Reports*. A visitor who introduced himself as "Lee Harvey Oswald" created a disturbance, and in the ensuing skirmish "over another queer at the lounge," a knife fell to the floor. The man had signed his bar slip "Hidell," then fled without paying, but there was no "Hidell" registered. Jessie Romero, who worked the front desk, remembered a man named "Oswald." Witness Ernie Broussard was sure the man had previously been there in September.

Cedric Rolleston said a man in the lobby of the Bentley Hotel in Alexandria on October 11th or 12th said his name was "Lee Harvey Oswald." He predicted, "A lot of Catholic rulers are going to be killed in a few months." The FBI dismissed the story as "unreliable." There were reports of a "traveling Oswald" causing disturbances all along the route to Texas, according to the state police. There were also Jack Ruby sightings with an Oswald impostor.

Oswald's decision to go to Mexico occurred after Nagell warned him that the assassination plot was not what Oswald thought it was. The evidence shows the conspirators were worried by this turn of events, and it appears they purposely cast doubt on Oswald's trip to make it seem he never left the United States.[1210]

Returning to the Selective Service incident in Austin, the city is approximately 150 miles west of Houston and 195 miles from Dallas. One could drive from Houston to Austin and then to Dallas all on the same day. It means it was feasible for Oswald, or an impostor, to stop at the home of Cuban exile Silvia Odio in Dallas late that night. We will return to the Odio visit shortly, but for now, we should consider what Silvia told author Dick Russell: "I know this was part of something big, and for some reason, I was made a part of it. All I can tell you is that what came out in the Warren Report was distorted. *I know it was Lee Harvey Oswald, not someone posing as Oswald, at my door.*" (Authors italics)[1211]

***

Early on the morning of September 26, 1963, Lee Oswald, or someone posing as him, boarded Continental Trailways bus 5133 in Houston, headed for the border town of Laredo. John and Meryl McFarland, a British couple, later signed a Warren Commission affidavit attesting that they had seen Oswald on the bus. "He said he was secretary of the New Orleans branch of the Fair Play for Cuba organization," the McFarlands said, "and that he was on his way to Cuba to see Castro if he could."[1212]

By mid-afternoon, "Oswald" boarded another bus at Laredo, bound for Mexico City. During the trip, he left his seat to talk to two Australian girls at great length about his time in the Marines and his stay in the Soviet Union. He showed them his old passport to prove he had been to Russia. The girls recalled that an elderly Englishman sat next to Oswald for the duration of the trip. Oswald recommended the Hotel Cuba to the girls as an excellent place to stay. "This young man appears to have been in Mexico before," the Englishman commented.[1213]

A few weeks after the assassination, authorities attempted to determine the identity of the Englishman who appeared to be Oswald's companion. The FBI finally tracked him down in the early part of 1964. His real name was Albert Osborne, but on the trip to Mexico, he traveled under the name John Howard Bowen. Like almost everyone in the Oswald saga, Osborne, aka Bowen, did not have a typical story to tell. We will revisit him in the next chapter.

It was odd that "Oswald" openly discussed his Soviet defection since the real Oswald tried to hide this during his radio debate with Carlos Bringuier and rarely publicized it. After the assassination, the FBI was concerned it may have been an impostor on the bus, and on December 5, 1963, the San Antonio office sent the following cable to Director Hoover:

> Investigation to date has failed to establish subject [Oswald] returned to [the] US on October 3 last or entered Mexico on September 26 last, although Mexican immigration records reflect person using [the] name Lee Harvey Oswald entered and left Mexico on those dates.
>
> Request Legat, Mexico City obtain list...of all persons riding La Frontera bus leaving Mexico City October 2 last en route for Nuevo Laredo on which person using [the] name of Oswald was passenger...."[1214]

San Antonio cabled Hoover again on December 12, saying that they could find "no information at this time concerning means by which ticket from Nuevo Laredo... was obtained by [a] man using name Oswald."[1215] It is interesting that in both cables, the FBI carefully chose its words to refer to the rider as a man using the name Oswald, not Oswald himself. Was this another sign they already suspected there was an Oswald impostor on the bus?

A curious exchange took place during Oswald's interrogation after the assassination when James Hosty asked him if he had ever been to Mexico. Oswald said he had been to Tijuana while stationed in San Diego with the Marines. "No, not Tijuana. Mexico City... have you ever been to Mexico City," Hosty persisted, which made Oswald visibly upset. "What makes you think I've been to Mexico City," Oswald replied. "I've never been there. I deny that. He was shaking his head, and he was starting to sweat now. I knew I had touched a nerve."[1216]

The man on the bus claiming to be Oswald did not attempt to hide who he was and went out of his way to ensure other passengers would remember him. Why, then, did the real Oswald so vehemently deny he ever went to Mexico City? The answer is the man on the bus was an impostor, and the real Oswald traveled to Mexico secretly by other means, as he had previously done during the summer. The conspirators' intent was damage control – to get the impostor to Mexico City before the real Oswald got there.

***

The question then becomes, who could that impostor have been? One possibility is Kerry Thornley, but there is no evidence that he was in Mexico City. Another is Thomas Eli Davis, even though they do not look the same. As described in Chapter Four, Davis was recruiting mercenaries for

389

an invasion of Haiti, which involved Loran Hall, while George de Mohren-schildt was also in Haiti at the same time. Davis was also close to Jean Pierre Lafitte, George Hunter White, and Charles Siragusa. Davis had extensive mob and intelligence connections, making him a prime candidate for being on the periphery of the JFK assassination conspiracy, as does the fact that he is mentioned prominently in Lafitte's datebook.

According to *Coup in Dallas*, Davis "regularly used 'Oswald' as an alias during his travels." Davis also said he was "worried about being dragged into the assassination," and "what made it look so bad for me was that I was using the name of 'Oswald'" when arrested in Algiers on the day of the assassination.[1217] Lafitte's datebook also tells us that Davis was in Mexico City that September when Oswald was there. According to his wife, Carolyn Hawley Davis, "Tom knew [Victor] Oswald...The other Oswald, the man they said that killed the President...I had no idea who he was until his name was in the newspapers. But when I saw his picture, I remembered him right away from being in Mexico at a hotel thing with Tommy. He and Tom had been together for a few days. That frightened me a lot, but Tommy said to forget about it."[1218]

According to June Cobb: "At the time, I don't think I knew what his name was; only that he was an American. He was easy to remember. [He was] tall, lanky, blond hair, that lethargic, drawling manner, easy-going cowboy-like. In Mexico, he stood out like a lone orchid among thorny cacti...I saw him at the Hotel Luma before Elena spotted him at the Duran's party, but I knew who she was talking with right away. He [Davis] and Oswald made quite the pair, I would imagine." The fact that Carolyn Davis and June Cobb saw Oswald and Thomas Davis together in Mexico City does not mean it was not Thomas Davis impersonating Oswald on the bus.[1219]

On December 20, 1963, J. Edgar Hoover sent a memorandum to the deputy assistant secretary of Security at the State Department with the subject: "Lee Harvey Oswald, Internal Security." The document focused mainly on Thomas Eli Davis. *Dallas Times Herald* police reporter George Carter wrote: "He [Davis] used the name Oswald in his anti-Castro activities in the period 1959-1962 while the real Lee Harvey Oswald was in the USSR..." Carter's lead on this came from Jack Ruby's attorney, Tom Howard. Howard must have gotten his information from Ruby, who ran guns with Davis. It means Ruby was aware of Oswald years before the assassination.[1220]

Davis using Oswald's name while he was in Russia is reminiscent of the Bolton car dealership story and the man named Oswald, who may have been Davis, who was looking to buy jeeps on behalf of Guy Banister's Friends of a Democratic Cuba. There is also evidence that Davis spent time in New Orleans. As described in *Reasonable Doubt*, Henry Hurt uncovered that on August 8 and 9, 1963, a "T.E. Davis" signed the registry book at the La Salle Hotel, and a November 27, 1963, FBI document stated agents checked the La Salle Hotel to see if Oswald had stayed there but came up empty. Jean Pierre Lafitte, like Oswald, used the alias Hidell, and he lived in New Orleans at the time and knew Davis. There was a good chance that Oswald and Davis met, which was when Oswald was presenting himself as a Communist supporter of the FPCC. So, Davis may have impersonated Oswald on the bus to Mexico City.

***

Silvia Odio was a Cuban exile whose family was one of the wealthiest in Cuba prior to the revolution. Her father owned the island's largest trucking business and was known as the "transport tycoon" of Latin America. Despite their wealth, the Odios supported Castro early on but turned against him when he betrayed the revolution. In October 1961, as an Alpha 66 plot to assassinate Castro unraveled, the Cuban police arrested one of the conspirators, Reinaldo Gonzalez, who was hiding at the Odio home outside Havana. Cuban authorities accused Silvia's parents of harboring a fugitive, and their house became a woman's prison. Silvia's mother was confined there for eight years. Her father, Amador, was imprisoned on the infamous Isle of Pines.[1221]

Silvia was a 24-year-old mother of four living in Puerto Rico when Castro imprisoned her parents. Around the same time, her husband abandoned her, leaving her alone to support their children. Her parent's plight and a radical shift in financial and social status resulted in emotional problems for Silvia, who struggled to cope with what fate had wrought.

Silvia had two sisters, Annie and Sarita, who lived in Dallas. Annie was seventeen, and Sarita was a student at the University of Dallas. Sarita was involved in Cuban affairs and befriended Lucille Connell, a local socialite who was active with the Cuban Refugee Center. It was with Connell's assistance that Silvia was able to move to Dallas in March 1963. Soon, she found a good job and began seeing a psychiatrist who helped her cope. Still, her apartment was small for her and her four children, which was why she planned to move into a bigger place on October 1. That week, Annie stayed with Silvia to watch the children and help her pack. It would later prove to be helpful in pinpointing when they encountered Lee Harvey Oswald.[1222]

Manola Ray was the leader of JURE, one of the groups the Kennedys approved of for AMWORLD. Silvia told the Warren Commission, "We had been trying to establish a contact in Dallas with Mr. Johnny Martin... [who] had heard I was involved in this movement. And he [Martin] said that he had a lot of contacts in Latin America to buy arms... and that if he were in contact with one of our chief leaders of the underground, he would be able to sell him second-hand arms that we could use in our revolution.... So I called Eugenio [war name of Rogelio Cisneros] long distance from Dallas... Eugenio arrived from Miami to see Johnny Martin [and] they went to my house..."[1223]

On May 4, 1964, Cisneros confirmed to the Secret Service that he went to Dallas from Miami in June 1963 to meet with Silvia Odio, who was to introduce him to a gun dealer. He was with Jorge Rodriguez Alvareda, JURE's Dallas delegate, and no one else. Rodriguez also confirmed to the FBI on September 8, 1964, that a late June meeting took place in Odio's apartment. Antonio Alentado Leon, who had succeeded Rodriguez as president of Jure in Dallas, said so as well. In the same FBI interview, Alentado mentioned that Silvia "had done some translation work" for JURE and "could be useful in the translation of propaganda material..."

The meeting with Johnny Martin was unsuccessful, but it provides insight into what Silvia was up to in 1963. It brings us to the evening of the 25th, 26th, or 27th of September when Lee Oswald was supposed to be on a bus headed to Mexico. Three strangers, two Latins, and one Anglo, appeared unannounced at Silvia's front door and were greeted by Annie. Although initially reluctant, Silvia agreed to talk to them. They were unkempt and unshaven and remained in the well-lit vestibule outside the front door. They said they were members of JURE who had just arrived from New Orleans and needed help translating a fund-raising letter into English.

Silvia spoke primarily with the leader of the group, who called himself Leopoldo. She wasn't sure of the other Latin's name, but it sounded something like Angel. Both sisters described him as "looking more Mexican than anything else." He was shorter, heavyset, with dark, shiny hair. The Anglo called himself Leon Oswald. These were not their real names but "war names," a common practice among exile activists. They knew the proper code names, including those of Silvia's father and mother. Despite this, they frightened Silvia, and she refused to let them into the house. They stayed only briefly and soon departed.[1224]

Within forty-eight hours, Silvia received a call from Leopoldo. "What do you think of the American?" he asked. Since she had limited conversation with him, she said she had nothing upon which to form an opinion. "Well, you know, he's a Marine, an ex-Marine," Leopoldo said, "and an expert marksman. He would be a tremendous asset to anyone, except that you never know how to take him. He's kind of loco, kind of nuts ... He could do anything – like getting underground in Cuba, like killing Castro. The American says we Cubans don't have any guts. He says we should have shot President Kennedy after the Bay of Pigs..."[1225]

On the afternoon of the assassination, Silvia returned to work after lunch to learn that the office was closing early. She recalled the phone call from Leopoldo two months earlier and his remarks about the American Marine who had threatened to kill Kennedy. It made Silvia nervous, and she fainted on the way to her car, something she was prone to do in times of stress. Meanwhile, Annie saw Oswald's face on television and was sure she had seen him before, but exactly where she couldn't remember. She said this to Silvia when she visited her in the hospital later that day, which made Silvia remember Oswald and the other two visitors who had come to her home in September.

Silvia's psychiatrist, Dr. Burton Einspruch, confirmed that prior to the assassination, Silvia had told him about the three men who visited her. She also wrote about it to her father prior to the assassination. He wrote back, saying she should exercise caution since he had never heard of Angel and Leopoldo. "I do not have any friend who might be here through Dallas, so reject his friendship until you give me his [real] name."[1226]

The Odio sisters wanted to keep their Oswald encounter a secret, but Sarita told the story to Lucille Connell. After Ruby shot Oswald, Connell spoke to a friend who happened to work for Ruby's attorney, Graham Koch. Later that day, Connell told another friend, Marcella Insua, the daughter of the man who headed the Cuban Relief Committee, that a friend of hers had dealings with Ruby. By coincidence, Insua taught a Spanish class to American students, one of whom was the son of FBI agent James Hosty. It was this connection that brought the FBI to Connell's door and subsequently to Silvia Odio's as well.[1227]

In September 1964, Warren Commission Chief Council J. Lee Rankin wrote to J. Edgar Hoover, "It is a matter of some importance to the Commission that Mrs. Odio's allegations either be proved or disproved." Assistant Counsel Wesley Liebeler, who had taken Odio's testimony, stated: "There really is no evidence at all that Oswald left Houston on that bus. Odio may well be right. The Commission will look bad if it turns out she is."[1228]

393

Without any evidence, the FBI concluded that the three men who visited Silvia Odio that night were Loran Hall, Lawrence Howard, Jr., and William Seymour. All were heavily involved in anti-Castro activities and were members of Interpen, the Gerry Patrick Hemming group that had aligned itself with Frank Sturgis' International Anti-Communist Brigade. Hall initially said he did visit Silvia Odio but later retracted his story, claiming the FBI had concocted the whole thing. A week later, in an interview, Seymour and Howard both denied ever having met Odio. Undaunted, the Warren Commission wrote that it was Hall, Seymour, and Howard who had visited Silvia. They surmised it could not have been Oswald because he was on a bus to Mexico at that time and could not have been in two places at once. The proof was never a prerequisite when they needed to support a narrative they wanted to promote.[1229]

***

Loran Hall knew Thomas Davis. They first met in New Orleans about two years before the assassination and came together again in Los Angeles when Davis was recruiting mercenaries for his Haitian operation. Both had a connection to Norman, Oklahoma, along with Lee Oswald and June Cobb.

Hall drove to Dallas for a third time in June 1963 on his way to California. He stayed briefly with Wally Yeats, who was looking to form a racist, anti-Semitic group in Dallas, where the Minutemen were already active. Hall attended a meeting with wealthy Dallas oilman Lester Logue and some well-heeled Texans. One man stood up and said, "Here's $50,000, and if the rest of you will match it, we'll give it to this man to blow Kennedy's ass off. With Kennedy dead, we'll have a Texan in office, and Texans take care of Texans." Hall said he might blow someone's head off outside the country, but "I don't pull that shit here." Logue told the HSCA in 1978 that he denied this took place but did admit meeting Hall several times during 1963.[1230]

Hall left Dallas and spent the next few months in southern California. He told the HSCA he became involved with a very right-wing anti-Castro organization, the American Committee to Free Cuba (Dallas DA Henry Wade said Oswald belonged to the Free Cuba Committee). He then began speaking at John Birch Society fundraisers and was in close touch with various exile groups. His objective was to publicize that the Kennedy brothers had thrown their support behind leftist Cuban exiles like Manola Ray and had turned their back on the rest.[1231]

On September 18, Hall was looking to fund an invasion of Cuba independent of the Kennedys. He passed a lie-detector test given at the request of Bill Tennyson, one of his John Birch Society associates. The person who administered the test gave the results to a U.S. Treasury investigator. That person then shared the results with the local CIA Domestic Contacts office, which Tracy Barnes headed. Meanwhile, Hall had raised enough money to buy a trailer full of arms and medical supplies for his proposed Cuban operation. He left California for Florida but stopped in Dallas to raise more money. With him were a Mexican American named Lawrence Howard and a Cuban named Celio Castro Alba. Howard would later state they left California "on or about" September 17. Castro Alba added that before reaching Dallas, Hall and Howard spent a day in Juarez, Mexico, while he remained in El Paso.

The three men left the trailer at Lester Logue's house when they left Dallas, and Hall returned in mid-October with William Seymour to pick it up. Around the same time, John Martino was in Dallas promoting his book. Meanwhile, the DRE was also attempting to procure weapons in Dallas through an Oswald-look-alike gun dealer named John Thomas Masen. More about Masen later, but for now, it is important to know he was a member of the Minutemen and said there was a small "elite group" of patriots in Dallas who were armed and willing to defend their country from the Communists who had infiltrated their government. On February 11, 1964, an Irving police officer reported that Masen had told him that "Minutemen and Birchers in Dallas had contacted him for the purposes of buying ammunition."

According to a 1967 report from Jim Garrison's investigation, two members of the Dallas Minutemen, Ronnie A. Wisk and Harold L. Helm, were issued permanent pass cards numbered 238 and 239 to Jack Ruby's Carousel Club. Wisk was allegedly at a Minutemen Patriotic Party meeting at 3510 Greenville Avenue, Dallas, where they discussed assassinating Stanley Marcus, the Jewish owner of the Neiman Marcus department store. There was also a flier with the same Greenville Avenue address announcing a speech by Minutemen leader Robert DePugh. The press reported that the Minutemen were responsible for the mug-shot-style "Wanted for Murder – Khrushchev" posters plastered on downtown Dallas windows on August 31.[1232]

Hall and Seymour returned to Dallas in mid-October. A policeman stopped them and discovered a large cache of amphetamines in their car. After their arrest, Hall called University of Dallas president Robert Morris, who had ties to right-wing extremist groups, H.L. Hunt, and the Schmidt brothers, who worked for General Walker. Larry Schmidt was involved with the "Welcome Mr. President" advertisement that criticized JFK in the *Dallas Morning News* on the day of the assassination. The advertisement contained mug-shot photos of JFK like the Minutemen poster of Khrushchev mentioned above.[1233]

After hearing from Hall, Morris called Lester Logue, who hired a young attorney named Michael Rhode. Then Hall asked to see an FBI agent, which led to J. Harlan Brown of the Dallas FBI interviewing him on October 18 (Shades of Lee Harvey Oswald and Agent Quigley in New Orleans two months before). Rhode got Hall released on $200 bond and told the HSCA in 1977 that officials from the CIA and military intelligence visited Hall after his arrest.[1234]

Returning to Thomas Eli Davis, he also knew Logan Logue. H.P. Albarelli wrote in *A Secret Order* that following Davis's death in 1973, "his widow Carolyn...described Logue as 'a wealthy guy Tom did some work for in Texas' and 'a Cuban guy, I think, named Lauren, that Tom met in L.A.' It's safe to assume that Lauren was Loran Eugene Hall who, like Davis, was a soldier of fortune who was in California at the same time Davis was recruiting for his invasion of Haiti." The fact that Carolyn mentioned Lauren Hall in the same sentence as Logan Logue implies Davis and these two men were working together on the Haitian operation.[1235]

Silvia Odio's cousin Orlando Nunez was a former mid-level official in Castro's government who was married to former CIA employee Deborah Fitzgerald. According to Nunez, "In 1963, Sylvia was being courted by the right-wing in Dallas, and I believe [she] was made a target of people who needed her association. Who those people were, I have no idea. [They were] possibly CIA, or right-wing, or adventurers, or even Castro agents pretending to fly the flag of being right-wing extremists. Any of these might have sought out my cousin because she was fashionable. She spoke languages and went to finishing school in Pennsylvania. She had connections back in Cuba because her father was in prison there at that time...Was she used? Yes, categorically."[1236]

On October 1, 1964, four days after the Warren Report was released, the FBI showed Silvia and Annie Odio photos of Hall, Seymour, and Castro Alba. Both denied having ever seen these men before. As Lawrence Howard told Dick Russell: "I feel personally that Loran Hall got me into this mess...We went through the Dallas area, holed up for a few days...Then somebody signed my name in the register of the Dallas YMCA on November 22....I'd like to see the handwriting on that signature..."[1237]

Gerry Patrick Hemming told *Argosy* magazine that he thought Loran Hall was involved in the assassination. "Yes, the day of the assassination, I made a call to Texas from Miami," Hemming said. "And I pointedly asked, is Lorenzo Hall in Dallas? I made the call [at] about 1:30 or 2:00 in the afternoon. He was there. My contact had seen him in Dallas the day before." Hemming explained that Hall "siphoned off a couple of people who had worked with me in the past and started organizing his own operation with Sturgis and some other guys... I think somebody was trying to put him there [Dallas] so he'd be one of the patsies."[1238]

***

There were also reports that Silvia Odio knew Lee Oswald. Burt W. Griffin of the Warren Commission interviewed Dr. Einspruch, who stated "that, in the course of psychotherapy, Miss Odio told him that she had seen Oswald at more than one anti-Castro meeting. One of these meetings was apparently at her house, he believed, and Miss Odio's sister also saw Oswald at the house... Miss Odio reported to him that Oswald made inflammatory comments about Cuba...."[1239]

Lucille Connell recalled that Silvia told her she "personally considered Oswald brilliant and clever, and that he had captivated the groups to whom he spoke... [but] Oswald was considered by a source in New Orleans to be a 'double agent.' The source stated that Oswald was probably trying to infiltrate the Dallas Cuban refugee group."[1240]

The men Oswald was with when they initially visited Silvia's home said they were with JURE. One of them later called to say Oswald talked of killing the President, which potentially implicated her father. So, Silvia would not have said Oswald came to her home if it were not true. And why would she say Oswald spoke at gatherings if it did not happen? She told the Warren Commission that "we did have some meetings, yes. John Martino spoke, who was... one of the men who was in Isle of Pines for three years... knew Mr. Odio [her father], that Mr. Odio's daughters were in Dallas, and [that] she [Sarita] went to the meeting. I did not go because they kept it quiet from me so I would not get upset about it. I don't know if you know who John Martino is." So, Silvia was aware of what was going on.[1241]

Of the three Odio sisters, Sarita was the most active in the Cuban exile cause and was reportedly a member of the DRE, the group the CIA had trouble controlling. She was also a student at the University of Dallas in the fall of 1963, where Robert Morris was president. Fermin de Goicochea

Sanchez was a student there as well, and Sarita must have known him. De Goicochea was a Bay of Pigs veteran and DRE member who met with DRE military leader Salvat when he traveled to Dallas from Miami in October 1963. De Goicochea admitted to the FBI that Salvat recruited him at that time to serve as DRE "secretary for military affairs" in Dallas. It meant it was his responsibility to locate arms for guerilla strikes against Castro.

James Hosty received an airtel on November 1 instructing him to find exile George Perrel, who the FBI believed was in the Dallas area. By the spring of 1964, the Secret Service was also looking for Parrel. The FBI would finally interview him in September 1964 after LBJ received the Warren Report. By that time, based on the information given to ATF agent Frank Ellsworth by John Thomas Masen, the FBI knew that the DRE's de Goicochea Sanchez was George Perrel. However, they kept this from the Warren Commission because, just before the assassination, de Goicochea was part of a stolen arms deal from Fort Hood that may have involved Oswald.

Silvia Odio denied to the Warren Commission that she had a connection to the DRE, but she did admit that family members in New Orleans knew about the group. John Martino admitted he knew of "a woman in Dallas who knew a lot of things" about the assassination. Later, he learned this was Silvia.[1242]

Twelve years later, Silvia told the HSCA that she had no idea her uncle was at Oswald's court hearing in New Orleans. She claimed her association was with the more liberal JURE. However, Felix Guillermo Othon Pacho, an exile who in October 1963 was named the Dallas DRE delegate by Salvat, told the FBI he knew of Silvia Odio and was "acquainted with her sister Sarita."

Silvia told the Warren Commission's Wesley Liebeler that she knew "about the directorate in New Orleans, because I have family there and they told me about all the incidents about him [Oswald] in New Orleans, about Oswald giving propaganda in the street and how he was down in front of a judge and caused a fight with Carlos Bringuier, and that, of course, this man [Oswald] had been working pro-Castro in this Fair Play for Cuba."[1243] Silvia's uncle Agustin Guitart, a physics professor at Loyola, was her source, and he was the one who attended Oswald's courtroom hearing. He can be seen in a photograph leaving the courtroom. Recall that Frank Bartes was also there.[1244]

So, it appears both Silvia and Sarita Odio had an association with the right-wing DRE, but their father was close to the left-wing JURE. There must be an explanation for this. As we know, various exile groups came

398

together under Paulino Sierra's umbrella with the help of the Mafia. One group affiliated with the DRE was Alpha 66, which started as part of JURE. It could explain how the men at Silvia's door knew so much about her father, even though they may have been with the DRE or Alpha 66.

Antonio Veciana founded Alpha 66. Exactly when that occurred is questionable since Veciana provided contradictory information through the years regarding when that happened. Regardless, he eventually came to Miami and worked with the CIA's Maurice Bishop. As described in Chapter Eight, HSCA investigator Gaeton Fonzi had a police artist sketch Bishop based on Veciana's recollection. When Fonzi showed the sketch to Senator Schweiker, he immediately recognized him as David Atlee Phillips, who had recently testified before the Church Committee.[1245]

There is sufficient reason to believe Phillips was Maurice Bishop. In his autobiography, *The Night Watch*, Phillips mentioned a favorite Cuban restaurant in Havana where Veciana said they first met. Veciana told Fonzi this one year before Phillips' book was published, and he also said Bishop spoke with a Texas accent and was fluent in French and Spanish, as did Phillips. Finally, there were the physical similarities. In the early 1960's, Phillips was a dead ringer for the Bishop sketch. In his book *The Last Investigation*, Fonzi wrote, "'Maurice Bishop' was David Atlee Phillips...believe me, I know that he was...."[1246]

In early September 1963, Veciana saw Bishop in downtown Dallas, and according to what he told author Anthony Summers, "A young man accompanied Maurice...rather strange and preoccupied..." Veciana was adamant the man with Bishop was Oswald.[1247] At the time, Oswald's whereabouts were unknown; therefore, it could be true, and researchers have generally believed it did happen. However, by this time, Alpha 66 was working with the U.S. military, not the CIA, and it is unlikely Phillips would still be meeting with Veciana. As a result, Veciana's truthfulness has been brought into question. Still, Alpha 66 brings us to the story of Garrett Trapnell, as told by Dick Russell in *The Man Who Knew Too Much*. In 1958, Trapnell traveled to Cuba to help train Castro's forces, only to be arrested by Batista's men. He was imprisoned and eventually deported to Miami. It was there, in the early 1960s, that he began working undercover for Cuban G-2 intelligence, infiltrating various exile groups, including Alpha 66. An FBI file confirmed that Trapnell contacted the Bureau on August 19, 1963, claiming that while infiltrating Alpha 66, he learned of an assassination plot against Robert Kennedy planned by a group of Cubans (he later said JFK was the actual target) in September of that year. "The men who attempted to involve me in the assassination of JFK in the spring-summer of 1963," he wrote, "were not Cuban G2 nationals...they were exiles with the assistance of white adult males whom I assumed were US nationals...." He also said someone "referred to as Oswaldo was there at the second meeting."[1248]

Trapnell said that in May or June 1963, he met four Cubans in Miami's Little Havana who claimed to be supporters of Castro. They wanted to kill Robert Kennedy to "sabotage any relationship between the Cuban Revolutionary Movement and the United States." One of the conspirators was a Hispanic male, twenty-eight years old, medium height, roughly two hundred pounds, a description that matched Leopoldo. In a letter to Dick Russell, Trapnell asked, "Why don't you write David Atlee Phillips and ask him if he knows Trapnell? I met him in 1963 during one of the interviews after I had stated what I knew... we spoke in Spanish, and he was very solicitive. He's a gin and tonic drinker and also a Cuba-libre imbiber. He knows all about the place on Flagler [the street in Miami where assassination planning took place]."[1249]

The meeting Trapnell referred to must have occurred around the beginning of August, which is consistent with the timing of Oswald's first trip to Mexico City when he allegedly was brought into the plot. That it involved American males and Cuban exiles is also in line with what we have discussed. Nagell said Angel and Leopoldo both belonged to Alpha 66, and it was this group that he was investigating when he was looking into rumors of a potential assassination plot.

Richard Case Nagell wrote that the conspiracy was "neither Communist inspired nor was it instigated by any foreign government or organization or individual representative of any foreign government...." Rather, it was a "domestic-inspired, domestic-formulated, and domestic-sponsored act of violence." Nagell was careful to state that a foreign government or a group connected to a foreign government was not involved, but this did not preclude the involvement of a foreign group or foreign individuals who acted on their own, such as Jean Pierre Lafitte, Otto Skorzeny, and their Fascist group which operated out of Madrid. In addition, Nagell claimed that Oswald was the "indispensable tool" of the conspiracy plot.[1250]

David Morales was a "husky, dark bronze skin, Latin-looking but maybe part Mexican" individual who fit the description of the man frequently seen with Oswald in the months leading up to the assassination. Jim Garrison's staff received an anonymous tip that he was known as "Indio." Gaeton Fonzi later discovered that "Indio," or "El Indio," was David Morales. As we know, David Phillips was well acquainted with Morales. He referred to "El

Indio" in his autobiography as "a massive American of Mexican and Indian extraction I had seen only briefly during the revolt but was to work with on other operations over the years."[1251]

In *The War That Never Was*, the CIA's Bradley Ayers, recalling his time at the JM/WAVE station, wrote: "Dave, the big New Mexican Indian who ran it, was the only branch chief who treated us less than respectfully. He ran all the station's activities with a heavy hand and was famous for his temper. We soon learned that no one...argued with Dave, and to cross him in any way was to invite trouble." Morales was Chief of Operations at JM/WAVE. In later years, he was in Vietnam, involved with Operation Phoenix, the ruthless program of trained assassins organized by William Colby. A Marine officer who knew him there said Morales was "a fairly heavy drinker when I met him. He was a 'macho' kind of guy, strongly opinionated, an enforcer type...I wouldn't want to cross him."[1252]

The description matched the one given by Dean Andrews of the man he had seen in Oswald's company in the summer of 1963 in New Orleans. He was "a Mexican... stocky, has what they call an athletic build. He could go to fist city pretty good if he had to... About 26 [years old]...." There is no definitive proof, but possibly, the man referred to by Andrews, Silvia Odio, Garrett Trapnell, Bradley Ayers, Orest Pena, the people in Baton Rouge, Richard Nagell, and the man outside the International Trade Mart in New Orleans when Oswald distributed FPCC literature was David Morales.

"Morales was a hit man for the CIA," wrote Fonzi. "He was a killer. He said it himself... he had killed people for the CIA in Vietnam, in Venezuela, in Uruguay, and other places... these were assassinations of individuals or groups selected for annihilation."

Morales's boyhood friend Ruben Carbajal and another man named Bob Walton visited Morales in Washington DC years after the assassination. When Walton spoke favorably of JFK, it enraged Morales. "I remember he was lying down, and he jumped up screaming," Walton said. "'That no good son of a bitch motherfucker!' He started yelling about what a wimp Kennedy was and talking about how he had worked on the Bay of Pigs and how he had to watch all the men he had recruited and trained get wiped out because of Kennedy." Morales added a singular postscript to his tirade. "Well, we took care of that son of a bitch, didn't we?" Cabarel confirmed that what Walton remembered was true.[1253]

***

Lee Oswald spent the summer of 1963 in New Orleans in the company of Cuban exiles and American mercenaries who wanted to overthrow

Castro. He allegedly made a trip to Mexico at the beginning of August and was brought into the assassination plot. Returning to New Orleans after that, he used his real name and address in his FPCC endeavors, which he had never done before; he had a street altercation with Carlos Bringuier; he appeared on a radio debate about Cuba; and he contacted the media to expand his exposure. It has propaganda specialist David Phillips's handiwork written all over it, and the description of Leopoldo matched David Morales. It means the CIA was now directing Oswald as he continued to portray himself as a Castro supporter and a Communist, and this must have been their responsibility in the assassination plot.

It is this author's opinion that an Oswald impostor was on the bus to Mexico City, and the real Oswald was at Silvia Odio's house with Angel and Leopoldo. Something had changed in Oswald when Nagell told him it was not Castro supporters who were looking to assassinate JFK but a right-wing domestic group. Perhaps Oswald went to Mexico on his own to find out what was happening. It is also possible that the conspirators told Oswald to go to Mexico because he was upset and could potentially become a liability. They needed to determine if Oswald was still a viable candidate for the assassination patsy. As we know, they would conclude he was.

CHAPTER TWENTY-THREE

AN IMPOSTOR IN MEXICO CITY

In early September 1963, Richard Case Nagell warned Oswald that Fascists were using him in a plot to assassinate President Kennedy. Oswald took Nagell seriously and obtained a visa on September 17 for entry into Mexico, with William Gaudet standing in line in front of him. A week later, the police in El Paso arrested Nagell for firing a gun into the ceiling of a bank. He did so because he wanted an airtight alibi. Shortly after that, Oswald, who may or may not have been aware of what Nagell had done, left New Orleans.[1254]

In Lafitte's datebook, the entry for September 27 reads, "Algur – Mex. City Ilya." Followed by "Oswald – Comercio Hotel – To Meet With Tom D at Luma – T says yes." It was the day that Oswald arrived in Mexico City.[1255]

Ten years before the assassination, Algur Meadows' company, General American Oil of Texas, signed a highly lucrative Spanish oil deal with Otto Skorzeny, which required the approval of Spain's President, Francisco Franco. Meadows was born in Vidalia, Georgia, and was very much anti-Communist. Ilya Mamantov was the White Russian whom Jack Crichton contacted after the assassination to act as Marina's interpreter. Tom D was Thomas Eli Davis. The appearance of these men in Mexico City coincided with the conspirators' concerns about Oswald, who may have been having second thoughts after what Nagell told him.

Another critical datebook entry occurred the following day, September 28. It reads: "Bowen & Hudson – Mc City. School cover – wife Spanish (Rene [Lafitte's wife] to see her next week)."

John Howard Bowen, aka Albert Osborne, sat next to "Oswald" on the bus to Mexico City and ran a school in Mexico. John Wilson Hudson was an intelligence operative who is mentioned many times in the Lafitte datebook. After Jack Ruby killed Oswald, Wilson-Hudson called the U.S. Embassy in London to report that when he was in a Cuban prison in the summer of 1959, a fellow prisoner, an American gangster named Santo, was visited by "an American gangster type named Ruby." Wilson-Hudson just happened to remember Jack Ruby four years later. His memory was just as good as William Gaudet's.

***

In March 1959, Frank Sturgis left Cuba for Washington to let the FBI know Castro planned to eliminate President Somoza of Nicaragua and then send troops to the Dominican Republic to spread communism throughout Latin America. Sturgis said that "various revolutionary groups in Havana ... were having a difficult time contacting Castro... [who] was too busy with Cuban affairs to deal with them directly."[1256] The truth was these revolutionary groups, made up of Cubans and American mercenaries, were looking to overthrow Castro. They intended to stage an attack that made it appear Castro was trying to expand his revolution in Latin America so that President Eisenhower would be justified to invade Cuba with the U.S. military.

In 1976, assassination researcher Bernard Fensterwald, Jr. uncovered documents related to Wilson-Hudson through the Freedom of Information Act. According to a confidential memo from Richard Helms to the FBI dated November 28, 1963, the CIA maintained a file on Wilson-Hudson dating back to 1951. He "was a contact of one Bert Sucharov, a suspected Soviet agent in Santiago, Chile." In addition, British authorities had tried to have Wilson-Hudson expelled from Chile because he had impersonated a British Royal Air Force officer. A CIA source in Chile said he was "very probably an intelligence agent." Everything about this man pointed in that direction. Hudson was in a Cuban jail because he and three Americans were involved in a foiled aerial bombing raid on Nicaragua, the same operation that got Loran Hall arrested.

The name "Hodson" appears in Lee Oswald's address book, an apparent reference to John Wilson-Hudson. The authors of *Coup in Dallas* wrote that Wilson Hudson "was involved with the World Commerce Corporation (WCC) and had direct dealings with Otto Skorzeny." They cite a CIA report, which reads: "Another report dated 20 June 1959 from a usually reliable source stated that PAUL HUGHES, an American soldier of fortune, claimed to have at his disposal three aircraft, including one bomber, and planned to launch an attack on Puerto Cabanas, Nicaragua, during the weekend of 27-28 June 1959. Hughes said that Carl WILSON [HUDSON], a British journalist, and about 65 volunteers would join him in the attack. Sources commented that HUGHES also vaguely spoke of possibly bombing Managua for the psychological effect. WILSON said that Castro had no knowledge of HUGHES' plan."

A *United Press International* report dated July 1, 1959, said that the Cuban home of Capt. Paul Hughes was raided, leading to the seizure of a large arms cache and air-sea invasion plans and the detention of two other Americans, a British journalist, several Cubans, and nearly 200 would-be members of an expeditionary force against the regime of Nicaraguan President Luis Somoza.[1257]

Prior to the Nicaragua affair, on April 22, 1959, eighty-seven Cubans and Panamanians landed at a remote beach in Panama. At the time, Castro was visiting the United States, and as soon as he learned of the invasion, he said he had nothing to do with it. On May 31, a month later, Cuban soldiers landed by plane in the mountains of Nicaragua. According to Paul Bethel, the U.S. Embassy in Havana was aware of the invasion prior to it happening, which tells us they probably were involved in the invasion planning. On June 28, a group of Havana-trained Nicaraguans was captured trying to cross into Nicaragua from Honduras. The Cuban government insisted the U.S. was behind these invasions, and they may have been right. Loran Hall and Gerry Patrick Hemming were involved in the second invasion from Honduras that looked to overthrow Nicaraguan President Somoza. Cuban army chief of staff Camilo Cienfuegos, who was anti-Communist, was the one who organized the attack.[1258]

It tells us where John Wilson-Hudson's allegiances lay after Castro came to power. It all had to do with blaming Castro for an invasion of another Latin American country that could be a catalyst for the United States to justify using its military to invade Cuba in retaliation to remove Castro. It involved John Wilson-Hudson in 1959, and his name reappeared in Oswald's address book four years later, probably in relation to a similar operation. The fact that his name is also in Lafitte's datebook in 1963, alongside the name Bowen, in relation to Oswald, and he knew about Ruby, tells us that John Wilson-Hudson was involved in the JFK assassination conspiracy in some capacity, perhaps unknowingly.

***

After the assassination, investigators tried to determine the identity of the Englishman who sat next to Oswald on the bus to Mexico City. The FBI tracked him down in the early part of 1964. His name was Albert Osborne, but on this trip, he traveled under the alias John Howard Bowen. He initially insisted he and Oswald did not sit together, but the McFarlands, who were seated directly in front of the pair, were sure they did. They recalled that Osborne told them he was a retired schoolteacher and was writing a book about the Lisbon earthquake of 1775.

The FBI learned that Osborne was a missionary and preacher who traveled extensively. For the past twenty-five years, he had run a school for poor Mexican children, and the donations he received through his mission in Oaxaca, Mexico, were allegedly his only source of income. And like so many of Oswald's associates, Osborne was a passionate supporter of Nazi Germany during World War II. When he traveled to Canada in 1958, Mexican officials asked the Canadians to investigate him. An FBI file stated he "had apparently effected many entries into the United States, most of them from Mexico, but there is no indication that he was ever in possession of a valid immigrant visa... or re-entry permit."[1259] After the Warren Report was released, lawyers in the southwest recalled the murder of Jake Floyd, whose father, District Judge Floyd, was the intended target. Two suspects testified Osborne had hired them. It was alleged that Osborne was part of Division V of the FBI, which was involved in domestic intelligence, and he was also connected to Clay Shaw's Centro Mondiale Commerciale.[1260]

There was a missionary named John Howard Bowen, with whom Osborne was acquainted, who died around 1958. They were similar in appearance and about the same age, so Osborne assumed Bowen's identity and used a counterfeit birth certificate in Bowen's name to obtain a Mexican tourist card. During World War II, Bowen had operated a camp for boys in Henderson Springs, Tennessee, and neighbors complained about the pro-Nazi activities that went on there.There is no evidence that Osborne and Oswald were together in Mexico, although they departed within twenty-four hours of each other. Osborne left for New Orleans on October 2 and appeared at the Canadian Consulate on October 10. Using his actual birth certificate, he obtained a passport in his real name, saying he had just arrived by bus from Montreal and was on his way to Mexico City. In truth, he was about to embark on a lengthy trip across the southern United States. On November 14, just eight days before the assassination, he wrote an article for the *Knoxville Journal* that stated, "John Howard Bowen... left New York yesterday for a speaking tour in England, Spain, Portugal and Italy." Osborne/Bowen wanted it known he would be out of the county at the time of the assassination.[1261]

Osborne wrote to American Express in Mexico, asking that all letters to Bowen be forwarded to him in New York, probably to stay clear of FBI informants working in U.S. post offices. He then left for Europe, but there weren't any speaking engagements. He traveled to Grimsby, England, to stay with his sister and visit his brother, whom he hadn't seen for forty years. Shortly before the assassination, he left for London, and twenty-five minutes before the assassination, a newspaper in Cambridge received a mysterious call from an unidentified man. "The caller said only that the reporter should call the American Embassy in London for some big news and then rang off," stated a CIA cable released in 1976.[1262]

After he returned to the U.S., Osborne denied using the name Bowen when questioned by the FBI but finally admitted that he had. Despite this, the FBI dropped their investigation, claiming they could not link him to Oswald, but they were probably afraid of what they might uncover were they to dig deeper. They knew Oswald had used the name Osborne when purchasing FPCC handbills in New Orleans, so it was safer to let the preacher be. One impostor on the bus was sufficient, even if two impostors happened to be sitting next to each other.

On December 2, Harvey Cash, the American Consul at Nuevo Laredo, gave the FBI a list of persons who had entered Mexico from there on September 26. It contained the names of Dr. John McFarland, Maryl McFarland, and John H. Bowen, but not Lee Harvey Oswald.[1263] The FBI was justifiably concerned, and as previously mentioned, the San Antonio FBI office cabled Hoover on two occasions that they could not prove that Oswald traveled to or from Mexico by bus.[1264]

Hotel records show that a person calling himself Lee Oswald checked into the Hotel Comercio in Mexico City on the morning of September 27, within an hour after the bus arrived. The signature "Lee, Harvey Oswald" was written on line 18, his room number, but for the three nights after that, only the name "Lee Harvey" appeared. It was the hotel's practice to write in a guest's name after the day of arrival, which explained the change to "Lee Harvey." However, each guest's name was written in longhand, other than Oswald's, which was printed. It may mean his name was added later. And what about him signing in as Harvey Oswald Lee? Soon, he would be back in Dallas, renting a room under the name O.H. Lee. Was this another coincidence?[1265]

Around 11:00 A.M., a man claiming to be Oswald visited the Cuban Consulate, requesting an in-transit visa for travel through Cuba to the Soviet Union. As he had done on the bus, the man produced a passport, old Soviet documents, correspondence with the CPUSA, a membership card for the FPCC, and a newspaper clipping detailing his arrest in New Orleans. The real Oswald always said he was a Marxist, not a Communist, so this was out of character for him. Silvia Duran, to whom he spoke, claimed she told him that she could not issue a visa without the submittal of passport-type photographs. She claimed the man left and later returned with photographs, and Duran filled out Oswald's application, which he signed in her presence. After the assassination, the FBI's effort to find a shop nearby that could take such photos proved unsuccessful.

Cuban consul Alfredo Mirabal was surprised by the man claiming to be Oswald. "I have also been a Communist for a number of years, and that generally, we do not use credentials or a card to identify ourselves as members of the party," he said. "Rather, we are identified to ourselves as Communists by our own behavior and by our own ideas...I think it would be interesting to know how he obtained the card. It did not have his name, and it did coincide with the same name that appeared in the other documents." The last two sentences are puzzling. What did Mirabal mean by saying that the Communist card did not have Oswald's name, but it was the same name as shown on other documents? Does that mean the visa request was for Oswald, but the card and documents were under a different name, Hidell, perhaps? Or was the visa request under another name, and the documents pertained to Oswald? Either way, the Cubans would not give an entry visa to a person whose name did not match. It means the Oswald impostor's role here was to create doubt at the Cuban Consulate in advance of the real Oswald's arrival to ensure he would not be able to obtain an entry visa to Cuba or the Soviet Union.[1266]

On November 9, when Oswald was back in Dallas at Ruth Paine's house, he left a typed letter he had written to the Russian Embassy in Washington in a place she was sure to find it. The letter contained the following passage: "I was unable to remain in Mexico undefinily [sic] because of my Mexican visa restrictions which was for 15 days only. *I could not take a chance on requesting a new visa unless I used my real name, so I returned to the United States.*" (Author's italics). When considered alongside what Mirabal said, and other evidence pointing towards an impostor, which we will discuss shortly, it is clear the intent was that later, everyone would believe there was an Oswald impersonator in Mexico City who may have been a Soviet sleeper agent.[1267]

Duran later recalled that their exchange took place around 1:00 P.M. Meanwhile, an unidentified man phoned the Soviet Military Attache asking about getting a visa to Odesa in Russia. They told him to contact the Soviet Consulate. At 10:37 A.M., the same man phoned the Consulate. The Consul was not there, so he called back at 11:30 A.M. Neither call came from the Hotel del Comercio, which means this was not the Harvey Oswald Lee who had checked into the hotel and was at the Cuban Embassy. At 12:30 P.M., Lee Harvey Oswald appeared at the Soviet Consulate. The timing suggests two men were visiting the embassies in Mexico City, each claiming to be Lee Oswald.

***

Winston Scott was the longtime chief of the CIA Mexico City station. He was close to William Harvey and James Angleton, going back to when he oversaw all intelligence operations in West Germany, France, and Great Britain. "He was the chief of the most important division in the agency," recalled Cleveland Cram, a career officer who served under him. "He really had things going his own way. He was a big deal in the Agency."[1268]

After he left the CIA, Scott wrote a manuscript about his career, which included the following passage:

> Lee Harvey Oswald, having just arrived in Mexico City, made his first contact with the Soviet Embassy in Mexico... saying that the Soviet Embassy in Mexico should have received word from the Soviet Embassy in Washington that he (Oswald) would contact them about a visit for himself, his wife, who he said was a Soviet citizen, and their child."[1269]

Scott confirmed that while someone was at the Cuban Embassy claiming to be Oswald, the real Oswald went to the Soviet Embassy first. He spoke briefly with Valery Kostikov before being handed over to Oleg Nechiporenko. The CIA was watching and listening in, and his encounter with Kostikov must have caused quite a stir. Kostikov was "a staff officer of the KGB... whose responsibilities include assassination and sabotage." Nechiporenko was also KGB with a private detective force in Mexico City composed of corrupt police officials.[1270]

In his book *Passport to Assassination*, written after the Soviet Union fell, Nechiporenko wrote that he was aware that Oswald had already contacted the Soviet Embassy in Washington about him, Marina, and their child returning to Russia. Nechiporenko wrote that Oswald was afraid "the FBI would arrest him for establishing contact... [so], he decided to come to Mexico to follow through on his plan." He explained to Oswald that travel to the USSR was "handled by the embassies or consulates in the country in which a person lived. As far as his case was concerned, we could make an exception and give him the necessary papers to fill out, which we would then send on to Moscow, but the answer would still be sent to his permanent residence, and it would take, at the very least, four months."[1271]

According to Nechiporenko, Oswald was quite upset and shouted, "This won't do for me! This is not my case! For me, it's going to end in tragedy."

After the outburst, Nechiporenko abruptly ended the meeting and led Oswald out to the sentry at the front gate.[1272]

After leaving the Soviet Embassy, the real Oswald went to the Cuban Consulate after closing hours. The people there must have been confused, considering a different Oswald was there earlier, which explains why they were willing to talk to the real Oswald after their office was closed. He met with Silvia Duran, who had earlier helped the Oswald impostor. He lied and told her the Soviets had agreed to give him his visa, which she found suspicious, so she phoned the Soviets to see if it was true. Kostikov called her back at 4:26 P.M., and according to the CIA transcript of their conversation, the Russian said, "The Cubans cannot give him a visa without his first getting a Russian visa. I do not know what to do with him. I have to wait for an answer from Washington." Duran replied, "We have to wait too, because he knows no one in Cuba and therefore, it's difficult to give him a visa."[1273]

Duran told Oswald it would take four months, which made him angry. She told Anthony Summers, "He didn't want to listen. His face reddened, his eyes flashed, and he shouted, 'Impossible! I can't wait that long!'" Oswald was so obnoxious that Cuban consul Eusebio Azcue intervened and told him he needed to be patient, but he remained excited. When Oswald called him a bureaucrat, Azcue ordered him to leave.[1274]

That evening, Kostikov and Nechiporenko met at a local cantina to have a beer and discuss the events of the day. Regarding Oswald, Nechiporenko wrote that Kostikov told him the following:

> As soon as I came back from lunch and the sentry passed on your message to me, I got a call from the Cubans. It was Silvia Duran from the Consulate. It turned out that our "friend" had been to see them after us and supposedly told them that we had promised him a visa, so she decided to call and double-check...I told her we hadn't promised him anything and...it would take at least four months. She thanked me, and that's it.[1275]

The following morning, Oswald returned to the Soviet Consulate and met with Soviet Consul Pavel Yatskov, who the CIA believed was the KGB's chief in Mexico City. When Kostikov arrived at 9:30 A.M., he found Oswald and Yatskov together. In *Passport to Assassination*, Nechiporenko describes what happened next:

> Throughout his story, Oswald was extremely agitated and clearly nervous, especially whenever he mentioned the FBI, but he suddenly became hysterical, began to sob, and through his tears cried, "I am

afraid... they'll kill me. Let me in." Repeating over and over that he was being persecuted and that he was being followed even here in Mexico, he stuck his right hand into the left pocket of his jacket and pulled out a revolver, saying, "See? This is what I must now carry to protect my life," and placed the revolver on the desk where we were sitting opposite one another.[1276]

Oswald eventually calmed down. He was offered a visa application but did not take it. A four-month wait was too long for him. He was escorted off the premises and would never return. The three officials who had met with him sent a coded cable to Moscow. The Cubans had sent their cable to Havana the previous evening.

As previously mentioned, Nechiporenko knew about the letter Oswald had sent to the Soviet Embassy in Washington, but why would the Embassy in Washington have contacted Mexico City about him? The only logical explanation is that the Mexico City Consulate had a previous encounter with Oswald that summer and had notified Washington about what had occurred. Washington then advised Mexico City that they had also heard from Oswald and forwarded his letter back to them. It confirms that Oswald had previously traveled to Mexico City in August and had contacted the Soviet Consulate at that time. This is why, during the conversation between Kostikov and Nechiporenko at the cantina, Kostikov referred to Oswald as "our friend." Officially, their only encounter with Oswald had occurred earlier that day when Oswald was at the Embassy for approximately one hour. Referring to Oswald as "our friend" suggests a familiarity with him beyond this short visit and implies they were already aware of Oswald from a previous August encounter.

***

We know the FBI was very concerned that the man who had traveled to Mexico by bus was not Oswald. They "checked all travel permits issued during... September 1963, under the name Lee Harvey Oswald and H.O. Lee..." They checked all persons entering and leaving Mexico from August 10, 1963, to November 22, 1963, under the true name and known aliases of Oswald....," but came up empty.[1277]

The fact that the FBI checked as far back as August 10 suggests they were aware of another Oswald trip to Mexico City around that date. They also checked under the alias H.O. Lee, which matched the name written in September in the registry of the Hotel Comercio, Lee, Harvey Oswald. However, they did not check the O.H. Lee he would use at 1026 N. Beckley boardinghouse when he returned to Dallas. Also, why did they check up until the day of the assassination when they knew Oswald was in custody that day? Did the FBI fear that Oswald had made it out of Dallas and had returned to Mexico City that night, and the police had apprehended an impostor? As we will see, it is not so far-fetched. After the assassination, the FBI and the CIA suspected there were two Oswalds and tried hard to prove or disprove what was happening.

According to Gaeton Fonzi of the HSCA, the report written for the Committee by Ed Lopez stated "that the consensus among employees within the Cuban Consulate after the Kennedy assassination was that it wasn't Oswald who had been there. Two assets said that they reported that to the Agency, but there were no documents in the CIA file noting that fact."[1278]

Oscar Contreras was a law student in Mexico City in September 1963. He belonged to a left-wing student group that supported Castro, so he knew people who worked at the Cuban Consulate. One night, a man at a nearby table in the university cafeteria struck up a conversation with him and three friends who shared his political views. The man spelled out his entire name – "Lee Harvey Oswald." The name made the young men laugh, for "Harvey" and "Oswald" were rabbits in a popular cartoon in Mexico. It was a foolish thing, but it made the name stick in their minds. Oswald told his new acquaintances that he was a painter who had to leave Texas because the FBI was bothering him, and he wanted to go to Cuba, but the Consulate denied his visa request. He asked Contreras if he and his friends could intervene on his behalf, and Contreras said they would do what they could. That night, they talked to their Cuban friends, including Azcue, and were told to break off contact with Oswald immediately. The Cubans believed Oswald was "highly suspect as being some sort of provocateur, sent by the United States to go to Cuba with evil intent." Why would they think that? Probably because they met two different Oswalds on the same day. Alfredo Mirabal later told the HSCA that his "impression from the very first moment was that it was, in fact, a provocation."[1279]

Contreras said Oswald was around thirty years old. He believed he was approximately 5'-6" tall because he recalled looking down at Oswald. Contreras was 5' - 9". One thing that puzzled him was why Oswald contacted him in the first place. There was nothing he and his companions had done that evening to give the impression they were supporters of the revolution and had contacts inside the Cuban Consulate. Yet, the man claiming to be Oswald knew to approach them.[1280]

***

The Cubans were understandably concerned about Oswald, and they may have used Silvia Duran to learn what he was up to. Her story begins in the fall of 1962 and involves Carlos Lechuga, who at the time was the Cuban ambassador to the U.N. A February 18, 1963, CIA memo reported that: "In late December 1962, Carlos Lechuga Hevia, described as an ambitious, evasive and not overly intelligent man, was unhappy in New York, as Cuban Ambassador to the UN, because neither the United States nor the USSR paid any attention to him. In spite of being in love with his wife, Lechuga had denounced her...as being a passive enemy of the revolution."

According to a CIA informant, Lechuga's comment about his wife "was allegedly made under pressure by certain members of the Cuban Embassy in Mexico, who, in their attempts to persuade Lechuga, had employed the influences of Ana Maria Blanco, the first Secretary at the Embassy, and Silvia Duran, a Mexican married woman employed at the Cuban-Mexican Cultural Institute. Lechuga had offered to marry Duran after divorcing his wife since she was ready to accompany him to Cuba, and Lechuga considered this a requisite indispensable to his revolutionary spirit...."[1281]

That Lechuga offered to marry Duran means their relationship was serious, but her intent was solely to separate him from his wife for the good of the revolution. In 1963, she showed a similar interest in Oswald. Fifteen years after the assassination, David Phillips told Congress that "Duran was possibly an agent or source" for the CIA. He later told his friend, reporter Lonnie Hudkins, about a meeting attended by Oswald, a CIA undercover man, and Silvia Duran, who was posing as a prostitute. Phillips admitted he had often bought information from Duran.[1282]

New Orleans attorney Dean Andrews told the New Orleans District Attorney's office after the assassination that he learned Oswald had "befriended a CIA whore" in Mexico City. A confidential source told the HSCA that "all that would have to be done to recruit Silvia Duran, whom he referred to by using the Spanish word for 'whore,' would be to get a blond, blue-eyed American into bed with her." The HSCA received many other reports of Duran's promiscuity.[1283]

That the CIA knew of an Oswald/Duran relationship comes as no surprise. According to Lamar Waldron and Tom Hartmann in *Legacy of Secrecy*, William Gaudet said he was with Oswald in Mexico for the CIA, and a Naval Intelligence source said Oswald was under surveillance while he was there.[1284] Win Scott confirmed this:

413

> Every piece of information concerning Lee Harvey Oswald was re-
> ported immediately after it was received to: US Ambassador Thomas
> C. Mann, by memorandum; the FBI Chief in Mexico, by memoran-
> dum; and to my headquarters by cable; and included in each and
> every one of these reports was the entire conversation Oswald had,
> so far as it was known. These reports were made on all his contacts
> with both the Cuban Consulate and with the Soviets.
>
> Because we thought at first that Lee Harvey Oswald might be a
> dangerous potential defector from the USA to the Soviet Union, he
> was of great interest to us, so we kept a special watch on him and
> his activities. He was observed on all his visits to each of the two
> communist embassies; and his conversations with [the] personnel
> of these embassies were studied in detail, so far as we knew them.

Scott seemed to be alluding to multiple visits by Oswald to Mexico City, not just the one in September, and they kept "a special watch" on him, which must have been extensive. It is not surprising. An internal CIA memo dated June 13, 1967, prepared for Scott by an agent on the ground, stated he was "doing his best to keep active certain contacts...One of those contacts was Silvia Duran, who is well-known to headquarters." Laurence Keenan, the FBI agent who coordinated the Mexico City investigation after the assas-sination, said, "Silvia Duran was possibly a source of information for the Agency [CIA] or the Bureau [FBI]."

Pedro Gutierrez was a credit investigator for a Mexican department store. He told a CIA contact that he saw an American, who he later identi-fied as Oswald, and a tall Cuban leaving the Cuban Embassy. They drove off together in a Renault, and when the FBI traced the car, it turned out to be owned by Silvia Duran's family.[1285]

***

After the assassination, Elena Garro de Paz, a playwright and wife of Mexican poet Octavio Paz, alleged she had attended a Twist dance party at the home of Silvia Duran's brother, Ruben, and that Oswald was there. The State Department's Charles Thomas learned about the party after the assassination and contacted Elena Garro to learn more. As he wrote in his letter to Secretary of State William Rodgers, Garro told him:

> At the party, the man she assumes was Oswald wore a black sweater.
> He tended to be silent and stared a lot at the floor. Of his two young
> American companions, one was very tall and slender and had long
> blond hair which hung across his forehead. He had a gaunt face and
> a rather long protruding chin. The other was also rather tall and had

short, light brown hair, but he had no real distinguishing characteristics. All three were obviously Americans and did not dance or mix with the other people. The three were evidently friends, because she saw them by chance the next day walking down the street together.[1286]

June Cobb worked for David Phillips in Mexico City station at the time. As previously described, she probably knew Oswald in the U.S. and had a Norman, Oklahoma, connection to him that may have included Thomas Davis and Loren Hall. On October 5, 1964, eleven days after the release of the Warren Report, Elena's story alleging Oswald's presence at a party attended by Cuban government personnel was provided to the CIA by June Cobb. "Ms. Cobb was sent to her [Garro's] house shortly after the assassination for a few days by a mutual friend ... [and] that while at her house, Ms. Cobb expressed interest in the Kennedy assassination. One night, Elena's sister Deva, who was visiting, got drunk and told the whole story."

The account is misleading because the CIA put Elena into a safe house immediately after the assassination, which suggests the CIA already knew of the Twist party. The HSCA tried to learn more but was frustrated by Cobb's explanation. She said, "A quick social gathering had been slapped together for a purpose. Elena had concluded that the Cubans were in on the assassination ...," and the party was set up by Cubans involved "so they could provide an underground for Oswald after the assassination ..."[1287]

The Lopez Report also stated that Cobb told the CIA that Oswald was allegedly at this party "in the company of two other beatnik-looking boys. The Americans remained together the entire evening and did not dance. When Elena tried to speak with the Americans, she was 'shifted' to another room by one of her cousins...One of Elena's cousins told her...that Silvia Duran...had brought them to the party."[1288]

The authors of *Coup in Dallas* interviewed Cobb in 2015, and she said Thomas Eli Davis was with Oswald at the party. "At the time, I don't think I knew what his name was; only that he was an American. He was easy to remember. Tall, lanky, blond hair, that lethargic, drawling manner, easy-going cowboy-like. In Mexico, he stood out like a lone orchid among thorny cacti ... I saw him at the Hotel Luma before Elena spotted him at the Duran's party, but I knew who she was talking about right away. He and Oswald made quite the pair, I would imagine."[1289]

Bill Mannix, a CIA pseudonym, was Cobb's handler and Chief of Cuban Operations at the Mexico City station and reported directly to Win Scott. He confirmed that Cobb saw a man "who turned out to be Davis." The CIA told her not to discuss Davis or commit anything to writing because "June saw Davis in MC at the Luma with Oswald" and "she wasn't the only person who reported him being there." Mannix refused to reveal who the others were.[1290]

"I did what I always did with all such new information," Cobb said. "I wrote it up, with all the details, on a small index card and passed it on to my handler... Scott was much less than a fan of mine... There was a tremendous amount of game playing around Oswald in Mexico and at the party with Elena and her daughter. He was there, no doubt about it, but I think that Davis being with him caused a lot of consternation and agony in the Embassy."[1291]

Cobb said she saw Davis "at the Hotel Luma before Elena spotted him at the Duran's party, but she didn't know his name, which means they had never met before. Oswald was probably there as well, who Cobb likely already knew. As described above, Silvia Duran was, at the very least, a CIA informant. Cobb also told the HSCA that "a quick social gathering had been slapped together for a purpose," which suggests the CIA instructed Silvia Duran to initiate the party to find out what Oswald was up to, which was why Silvia's brother Ruben put the party together so quickly. It would seem that the assassination conspirators were unsure of Oswald and wanted to observe him in the presence of Cuban and Mexican Communists.

June was right about how Win Scott felt about her. In 1964, he wrote: "June Cobb is promiscuous and sleeps with a large number of men [and] sometimes spends several nights (consecutively) with a man in his apartment."[1292] Whether this was true or not is irrelevant. The fact is Scott was looking to discredit Cobb, which, in this author's opinion, was because she disclosed that Davis and Oswald were together in Mexico City. And since their relationship caused "a lot of consternation and agony in the embassy," we can assume the Embassy and the CIA were already familiar with Davis and probably Oswald as well, which returns us to the alleged relationship between Oswald and Silvia Duran.

***

On June 18, 1967, the CIA Mexico City station wrote to J.C. King, chief of the Western Hemisphere Division, "that Silvia Duran had sexual intercourse with Lee Harvey Oswald on several occasions when the latter was in Mexico City...The Mexican police did not report the extent of the Duran-Oswald relationship to this Station." The last sentence was to let J.C. King know the Mexican police were not forthcoming about the Duran/ Oswald relationship and that the CIA knew about this on their own, which confirms they had been tracking Oswald closely. Considering that Duran was a CIA asset, the CIA Mexico City office may have instructed her to approach Oswald and develop a close relationship to find out what he was up to. If that were true, the appearance of a second Oswald in September would have caught them by surprise.

Confirmation that there was an affair came from Luis Alberu, the cultural attache at the Cuban Embassy. He told the CIA that "Silvia Duran [deleted] had first met Oswald when he applied for a visa and had gone out with him several times since she liked him from the start. She admitted that she had sexual relations with him but insisted that she had no idea of his plans. When the news of the assassination broke ... she was immediately taken into custody by the Mexican police and interrogated thoroughly until she admitted that she had an affair with Oswald."[1293]

The news about the relationship between Duran and Oswald caused concern among Mexican authorities, and a CIA headquarters memo to the Mexico City station cautioned them to tread slowly. "Arrest of Silvia Duran is extremely serious matter," the memo stated, "which could prejudice U.S. freedom of action on [the] entire question of Cuban responsibility [in the JFK assassination]." Apparently, the U.S. did not want to be too aggressive, which could have jeopardized a second military invasion of Cuba, which they were still considering. [1294]

The Cuban government issued an official complaint to the Mexicans over the harsh treatment Duran received. Then, as she was about to depart for Havana, she was picked up again at the behest of Richard Helms, who cabled Win Scott, "We want to ensure that neither Silvia Duran nor Cubans get [the] impression that Americans behind her rearrest..."[1295]

The memo to J.C. King and the account of Luis Alberu both described the affair between Duran and Oswald as a fact. Alberu was with the Cuban Embassy, so we can assume his report was accurate, and a relationship between Duran and Oswald existed that included Duran admitting to going out with Oswald several times. The J.C. King memo similarly claimed they had sex "on several occasions." We know Oswald arrived in Mexico City on September 27th and supposedly departed on October 3rd, so he was there for only six nights. He spent at least one night with Oscar Contreras and another in the company of Contreras and his friends. It is hard to believe that this passionate relationship between Duran and Oswald, with multiple encounters, could have occurred over such a limited period. However, if Oswald had traveled to Mexico at least once in August, and perhaps more, he probably visited the Cuban Consulate at that time (recall Kostikov's description of Oswald as "our friend"), so, probably, the Oswald/ Duran relationship began then. Alberu said Duran met Oswald when he first arrived and had applied for a visa, which would have been in August. It supports the idea that an Oswald impostor appeared at the Cuban Consulate first in September, and it explains how Oswald's visa application had his signature and photograph on it because he had already submitted it in August. It also explains why Oswald initially went to the Soviet Consulate in September and only visited the Cuban Consulate after he knew the Soviets would not issue him a visa. When Duran encountered the real Oswald that afternoon, after meeting the impostor in the morning, she handled him calmly and rejected his request for an entry visa into Cuba. Then, when confronted by Oswald and Davis together at the party, she handled that the same way. The bottom line is that the purpose of the Oswald impostor was to create confusion so the Cubans and the Soviets would not allow him to enter Cuba under any circumstances. It thwarted Oswald's attempt to escape, which meant he would still be available to fulfill his role as the assassination patsy, even if he were beginning to have doubts about doing that.

***

Carolyn Davis's comment that she met Lee Oswald "in Mexico at a hotel thing with Tom" referred to the Hotel Luma, which seemed to be the center of covert activity. We first learn of the significance of the hotel through June Cobb, who left New York for Mexico City on May 26, 1961. One of the first contacts she made there was her old friend from Manhattan, Warren Broglie, who now managed the Hotel Luma. Broglie would play a role in what Cobb was doing in Mexico City in 1963 and beyond, and she would pass important intelligence information received from him to Win Scott.[1296]

The reader may recall that Broglie, Allen Dulles, and Conrad Hilton were all members of the Knights of Malta. This secretive Roman Catholic group also included U.S. military officers, CIA officials, European Fascists and Monarchists, and some of the wealthiest men in the world who all leaned to the far right (see *It Did Not Start With JFK, Volume 1*). They were more concerned with preventing the spread of communism throughout Western Europe than the dispute the United States was having with an insignificant country like Cuba.

According to colleagues of attorney Thomas Proctor, he had associated with Broglie and Cobb in New York City "since at least 1959…maybe having met Cobb at the Hotel Iroquois, when she lived there before going briefly to Cuba." Proctor also traveled several times to Mexico City in the early 1960s. As described in Chapter Four, when Thomas Eli Davis was arrested in Tangiers after the assassination, he had in his possession a letter that referred to Victor Oswald in Madrid and the JFK assassination, and Davis was supposed to forward the letter to Proctor.

June Cobb said that New York City politician Paul O'Dwyer, the brother of former New York City mayor William O'Dwyer, accompanied Proctor to Mexico City. A former policeman, lawyer, and judge, William O'Dwyer was Mafia-connected, most notably to Frank Costello, to whom he owed political favors. He repaid them by appointing Costello friends to important municipal positions.[1297]

If William O'Dwyer had a connection to Thomas Proctor, it is safe to assume he was familiar with Thomas Eli Davis and June Cobb as well. We know Cobb had ties to notable Mafia figures such as Carlos Marcello and Santo Trafficante from her days working for the FBN in Colombia and Cuba. As did Thomas Davis, who was close with Loran Hall, the man incarcerated in Cuba with Trafficante, and John Wilson Hudson, who was also in Mexico City that September, according to the Lafitte datebook. Davis also knew Lafitte, whom he first encountered when he was an informant for the FBN. According to a letter from Charles Siragusa to George Hunter White, Davis once met with French drug traffickers in Algiers, including drug dealer and assassin Jean Souetre. Then there was Davis's gunrunning relationship with Jack Ruby. So, it seems that two months before the JFK assassination, there was a Hotel Luma gathering of leading intelligence operatives who were presumably there to discuss the JFK assassination plot and to decide what to do about Oswald, who was becoming a problem and possibly looking for a way out of the operation by escaping the country.[1298]

Richard Case Nagell also knew the Hotel Luma well, having stayed there as early as August 1962. In *The Man Who Kew Too Much*, Dick Russell included a letter from a friend of Nagell's, Richard Von Kleist, who described a meeting at the "Hotel Luna[sic], Mexico City, July 1963," which was attended by "Alex Hydell, otherwise known as Lee Harvey Oswald; a female attorney who is a well known Communist in Los Angeles… [and] hotel headwaiter, Frity [sic: Franz Waehauf]… who owned a launch believed to be shuttling between Mexico and Cuba. Also believed to be involved – Richard Case Nagell."[1299] It was around the time of this meeting that June Cobb was approved by CIA security "as an informant" for "WH [Western Hemisphere]/3-Mexico, D.F."[1300]

When Nagell was arrested, in his wallet was a newsletter from the Fair Play for Cuba Committee addressed to him. Found in the trunk of his car were two tourist cards for entry into Mexico. One was in the name of "Joseph Kramer," an alias Nagell used. The other was in the name of either "Albert or Aleksei Hidel," both Oswald aliases. Nagell had left everything they found by design, and it should have raised eyebrows at the FBI. It didn't, at least not publicly. In particular, the FPCC literature and Hidell reference should have connected Nagell to Oswald's activity in New Orleans. His notebook contained the names of congressmen, attorneys, American leftists, officials in Far East governments, a Soviet military attaché, six names under the heading "CIA," and two listings for the "Fair Play for Cuba Committee." The FBI kept the notebook hidden for eleven years. After it was released, it contained the following entry:

C.E. MEXICO D.F.
PHONE:
11-28-47
MEET
JUFER REST
CALLE VERSALLE
LAREDO, TEXAS"

Oswald's notebook had a similar entry and should confirm a connection to Nagell and Mexico City.

Mexico City
Consulada de Cuba
Zamora Y F Marquez
11-28-47
Sylvia Duran[1301]

Robert Buick was an American bullfighter in Mexico City who hung around the Hotel Luma. As proof, he showed researcher Bernard Fensterwald, Jr. his spring 1962 hotel receipts and posters proving he was a bullfighter while Oswald was there. Buick claimed he "happened to stumble on meetings and accidental things and ... something too big for me to handle was in the making. In 1963, summer, *Hydell [Oswald] was in Mexico before September 1963. Hydell went once by bus and once by plane.* Hydell was mixed up in it to the hilt. The man was used as a pawn all the way through." (Author's italics)[1302]

In his book *Reflection: Behind the Rain*, Buick claimed David Phillips and Howard Hunt asked him to keep track of the mysterious characters he met at the Hotel Luma. Hunt told him, "You're looking for any subversive activity, strong anti-American sentiments," Buick recalled. Hunt later asked for specific information on the Luma's cocktail waiter, Franz Waehauf, a Czech national whom Nagell had previously kept an eye on. He also made a point of running into Alek Hidell, who bragged he was planning to go to Cuba by boat. "Hidell" also told Buick that he was first going to "hit" Kennedy: "It's all set, the machinery is already in gear." Buick had also seen Hidell two months before, sitting in a booth with a tall man with a scar across his face, who would have been Nagell. Meanwhile, Warren Broglie was passing along information that Buick was drawing attention to himself.[1303]

***

On October 9, almost one week after Oswald left Mexico for the United States, the CIA's Mexico City station sent a cable to Washington that on October 1, an "American Male who spoke broken Russian said his name Lee Oswald (phonetic), stated he at Sovemb on 28 Sept when spoke with consul whom he believed be Valeriy Vladimirovich Kostikov…" The cable described Oswald as "age 35, athletic build, circa 6 feet, receding hairline, balding top. Wore khakis and sports shirt."[1304]

The man obviously was not Oswald, nor did he fit the description of the impostor who appeared at the Cuban Embassy, which the cable did not mention. The following day, the CIA in Washington replied to Mexico City: "Lee Oswald who contacted Sovemb 1 Oct probably identical Lee Henry Oswald (201-289248) born 18 Oct 1939, New Orleans, Louisiana, [a] former radar operator in United States Marines who defected to USSR in Oct 1959. Oswald is five feet ten inches, one hundred sixty-five pounds, light brown wavy hair, blue eyes."[1305]

Washington subtly advised the Mexico City station that the man in their cable who appeared at the Soviet Embassy was not Lee Oswald, who they stated was only 24 years old. It is also interesting that they said Oswald was 5'-10" tall. We know his Department of Defense ID card and passport when he left the Marines recorded his height as 5'-11", while the man who returned from the Soviet Union and Jack Ruby killed was 5'-9". Apparently, Washington could not reconcile this discrepancy, so they elected to split the difference.

The CIA's reply that Oswald's middle name was Henry was not an accident. In 1975, the chief of the Agency's Counterintelligence Staff, George Kalaris, wrote a memo whose first sentence read: "Lee Harvey Oswald's 201 file was first opened under the name of Lee Henry Oswald on 9 December 1960 as a result of his "defection" to the USSR on 31 October 1959…" Quotes around the word "defection" jump off the page because they support the idea that Oswald's defection was fake and a CIA operation, which we suspect to be the case. As we will see in the following pages, a faked defection and a possible Oswald impostor have everything to do with Oswald's appearance in Mexico City.[1306]

On May 17, 1978, HSCA Staff Counsel Michael Goldsmith deposed CIA Counter-intelligence Staff Officer Ann Egerter about the Oswald 201 file she had opened.

> Mr. Goldsmith: Coincidentally, is that your handwriting?
>
> Mrs. Egerter: That is. If I wrote Henry, which looks like my writing, I did it at a later time because this is much more carefully done than that.
>
> Mr. Goldsmith: For the record, you just pointed to the name Henry. You are indicating that the word Henry was written in at a later time than "Oswald Lee."
>
> Mrs. Ann: I think so. It looks that way to me. Maybe not. That is just a guess. I have a feeling I may have stopped but I do not know whether there was another document that showed the name Henry or not.
>
> Mr. Goldsmith: So you were aware that his middle name was Harvey
>
> Mrs. Egerter: Yes.[1307]

Egerter claimed she had written in the correct middle name, Harvey, but saw another document with the name Henry and changed it, even though she knew Harvey was correct. She would only do that for one reason. She suspected that Henry was a pseudonym, a cryptic clue that identified Lee Henry Oswald as an alias for the impostor, and according to Kalaris, this also applied to Oswald's Mexico City trip. Something was terribly amiss here.

Also, on October 10, the CIA in Washington cabled the FBI, INS, the State Department, and the Navy that "On 1 October 1963, a reliable and sensitive source in Mexico reported that an American male, *who identified himself as Lee Oswald,* contacted the Soviet Embassy in Mexico City…The American was described as approximately 35 years old, with an athletic build, about six feet tall, with a receding hairline…Oswald may be identical to Lee *Henry* Oswald, born on 18 October 1939 in New Orleans, Louisiana, a former US Marine who defected to the Soviet Union in October 1959…"[1308] (Author's italics)

Notice how carefully Washington worded the phrase that it was not Oswald but a man who claimed to be him who was 35 years old but then said he might be identical to Lee Henry Oswald, who was 24 years old. An impostor Oswald present in Mexico City would remain the CIA's secret for the time being. After the assassination, they would try to make it appear that the real Oswald never traveled south of the border at all.

The Mexico City station had transcripts of all conversations between Oswald, or an Oswald impostor, with anyone inside the Cuban or Soviet Consulates who dealt with either one. On the day after the assassination, Richard Helms launched an investigation to determine if Oswald was part of a foreign conspiracy. If it were the Soviets or Cuba who were concerned about him, rest assured he would have said so directly. So, was it the foreign group consist of ex-Nazis that included Otto Skorzeny, Madrid Fascists like Victor Oswald, French Fascists like Jean Souetre and Jean Pierre Lafitte, and their American counterparts at the CIA that concerned Helms?

Helms assigned John Whitten to investigate what happened in Mexico City. Whitten said Win Scott oversaw the CIA's most extensive and sophisticated electronic surveillance operation in the world. The CIA tapped every phone line going in and out of the Soviet and Cuban embassies, and there were banks of CIA surveillance cameras around both embassies.[1309] According to Scott, "Oswald was under constant surveillance during his visit to Mexico City… persons watching these embassies photographed Oswald as he entered and left each one, and clocked the time on each visit."[1310]

So, what do we make of this? The first question that comes to mind is, with all the taping of conversations and surveillance cameras, why didn't the CIA provide proof of Oswald's presence at the two consulates? If Oswald was really there, and they wanted to blame him after the assassination as the lone gunman, it would have served them well to release the photos. It would have added to his guilt without accusing the Cubans or Soviets of involvement.

Furthermore, why didn't they mention that Oswald appeared at the Cuban Consulate if he actually did? It was because an Oswald impostor appeared there in the morning, and the CIA could never reveal that. However, the real Oswald did appear at the Soviet Consulate, so why didn't the CIA provide photos showing him there? The CIA knew what the Soviets discussed with Oswald, and some of it probably contained damaging disclosures that the Soviets could have revealed later if they had to. In short, the minute that Oswald left New Orleans and decided to go to Mexico City, after being warned by Nagell, the CIA went into damage control to make it look like he was never there.

The CIA, FBI, and Naval Intelligence were very much aware of who Lee Oswald was and were following his every move. They knew he was a defector, how old he was, and what his physical description was. They also knew that talk of an Oswald impostor began when he defected in 1959 and that J. Edgar Hoover and Secretary of State Dean Rusk were both concerned someone was impersonating Oswald while he was in Russia. They knew the man who left the Marines was 5'-11" and the man who returned from Russia was 5'-9", which explains why the CIA did not mention Oswald's physical description in the cable they sent to the other agencies. They said he "may be identical," which did not specifically say it was Oswald but implied that it was. It was a purposeful deception.[1311] So, CIA headquarters misled the FBI, State Department, and the Navy into believing it was really Oswald in Mexico City, and they created a ridiculous Oswald impostor scenario that would only become known after the assassination.

On the day of the assassination, a CIA memo stated: "Reference is made to our conversation of 22 November in which I requested permission to give the [FBI] Legal Attache´ copies of photographs of a certain person who is known to you." The photos were of the 35-year-old man who appeared at the Soviet Embassy at the end of Oswald's trip, claiming to be him. And since the memo referred to the man as "a person who is known to you," and not Oswald, he was not a stranger to CIA HQS, and they knew from the beginning he was not Oswald.[1312]

According to a memo written by J. Edgar Hoover, FBI agents in Dallas looked at the photos and "listened to a recording of [his] voice." They quickly reached "the opinion that the above-referred-to-individual was not Lee Harvey Oswald." The FBI must have been confused as to what had occurred in Mexico. They were having difficulty proving Oswald had made the trip there, and now there was proof of an Oswald impostor who did not look or sound like him.

The CIA's handling of the matter gets stranger still. Three CIA officials told the Assassinations Committee they had seen a surveillance photo of the real Oswald at either the Russian or Cuban Embassy. If true, there would have been audio tapes of Oswald made after he had entered the building. The person who provided the CIA's explanation for why none of this was available was none other than David Atlee Phillips, who said, "A capability for such photographic coverage existed, but it was not a twenty-four-hour-a-day, Saturday and Sunday, capability. [We] spent several days studying literally hundreds of photographs available to the CIA before and during Oswald's trip to Mexico City. He did not appear in any of them."[1313]

To say that the CIA turned the cameras off on weekends was insulting. Even if true, it did not explain why Oswald was not photographed on Friday at the Cuban Embassy if it was really him. Richard Sprague of the Assassinations Committee did not accept the CIA's explanation. "When I heard all that," he said, "I wanted to talk to the CIA camera people. I wanted to find out if it was true. And that's where we got stopped."[1314]

Proof that the CIA was behind the Oswald impostor illusion is evident from a phone transcript allegedly involving Oswald, Silvia Duran, and the Soviet Embassy. As previously mentioned, Oswald met with Soviet officials for the last time on the morning of Saturday, September 28. There is no record of him returning to the Cuban Embassy later that day, which makes sense since the Cuban Embassy was closed on Saturdays. Yet, an hour after Oswald left the Soviet Embassy, the CIA alleged they intercepted a phone call sent to the Soviet Embassy, reportedly from Silvia Duran. The transcript of the conversation is as follows:

> Duran: There is an American here who says he has been to the Russian Consulate.
>
> Russian Consulate: Wait a minute. [Duran is heard speaking to someone sitting with her in English.]
>
> Duran: He said wait. Do you speak Russian?
>
> "Oswald": Yes
>
> Duran: Why don't you speak with him then?
>
> "Oswald": I don't know...[The person claiming to be Oswald gets on the line. He speaks "terrible, hardly recognizable Russian."]
>
> "Oswald": I was in your Embassy and spoke to your Consul.
>
> Russian Embassy: What else do you want?
>
> "Oswald": I was just now at your Embassy, and they took my address.
>
> Russian Embassy: I know that.
>
> "Oswald": I did not know it then. I went to the Cuban Embassy to ask them for my address because they have it.
>
> Russian Embassy: Why don't you come by and leave it then. We're not far.
>
> "Oswald": Well, I'll be there right away.[1315]

The CIA obviously staged the conversation. The real Oswald did not need Duran to tell him his address, and why would she say she was with an American who claimed he had been at the Russian Embassy when, the previous day, the real Silvia Duran had spoken to the Russians about him? The real Duran confirmed after the assassination that after Oswald's visit

425

on September 27, "he never called again." This impostor Oswald spoke in broken Russian, which coincided with the October 9 CIA cable regarding the man who visited the Soviet Embassy posing as him.

In a 1974 letter to researcher Bernard Fensterwald Jr., Richard Nagell claimed that Oswald "definitely visited the USSR Embassy at D.F. [Mexico] in September 1963, the first time on the morning of the 27th, where he was photographed, seated and standing, inside the visitors waiting room. Please accept this as fact."[1316]

We know Nagell warned Oswald that the conspirators were setting him up, which raises the possibility that Oswald approached the Soviets looking for help to extricate himself from a situation that would not end well for him. In 1976, David Phillips told the *Washington Post* that Oswald told the Soviets at the Consulate, "I have information you would be interested in, and I know you can pay my way [to Russia]." The translator and typist of the intercepted call confirmed this was true. The typist recalled: "He [Oswald] said he had some information to tell them. His main concern was in getting to one of the countries, and he wanted them to pay for it."[1317]

When Oswald walked into the Soviet Consulate, let's consider the possibility that he provided details of the assassination plot to them. If true, one could hardly expect the Soviet officials involved to admit this. Considering Nagell's warning, Oswald was seeking asylum in either Cuba or the Soviet Union to remove himself from the plot, but the Soviets turned him away. Recall Nechiporenko's account of their encounter: "Oswald was extremely agitated and clearly nervous... he [was] hysterical, began to sob, and through his tears cried, 'I am afraid... they'll kill me. Let me in....'"

It's plausible that Oswald was flown to Mexico City by plane by the conspirators to appease him because they knew he was upset, and they had to decide what to do with him. So, they put an impostor on a bus next to Osborne/Bowen and had him visit the Cuban Consulate while the real Oswald was at the Soviet Consulate. Then, after Oswald left Mexico, an impostor who looked nothing like him inquired about Oswald's visa status at the Soviet Consulate. It was necessary to instill doubt that the real Lee Oswald, who had appeared at the Soviet Consulate earlier, may have been an impostor as well. Had the Soviets approached the U.S. government about a potential JFK assassination attempt, there was a need to discredit the story. After the assassination, it lessened the chance of a military retaliation against Cuba or Russia with all the confusion surrounding Oswald impostors and no record of him traveling to Mexico or returning to the U.S.

After the assassination, investigators also had to deal with evidence that made it appear an Oswald impostor "sleeper agent" had returned from the Soviet Union in his place. Oswald left the Marines with a DOD ID card and passport that said he was 5'-11" tall, which he also listed on his Albert Schweitzer College application. In Moscow, two reporters interviewed him. They recorded different heights, 5'-9" and 5'-11", respectively. On June 3, 1960, J. Edgar Hoover wrote to the State Department that "there is a possibility that an impostor is using Oswald's birth certificate." In January 1961, while Oswald was still in Russia, the Bolton Ford incident took place in New Orleans involving Guy Banister's group, the Friends of a Democratic Cuba. It included the name "Oswald" on the pending sale documents. The FBI was concerned and conducted interviews to "obtain background data" because it seems they connected the Bolton incident to an Oswald impostor in Russia. At the same time, Thomas Davis claimed he used the name Oswald while he was still in Russia.

On March 31, Edward J. Hickey, Deputy Chief of the Passport Office, wrote that "there is an impostor using Oswald's ID data …" In July, Secretary of State Dean Rusk wrote to the Embassy in Moscow that, "It is assumed that the person who has been in communication with the Embassy is the person who was issued a passport in the name of Lee Harvey Oswald."

After Oswald returned to the United States, he always gave his height as 5'-9", two inches shorter than when he left the Marines. When he went to Mexico City in 1963, the FBI could not prove he traveled by bus to get there or return home. Meanwhile, there was someone at Silvia Odio's home in Dallas at the same time, and the Odio sisters said it was Oswald. In Mexico City, those who met Oswald at the Cuban Consulate claimed he was not the man who shot JFK. At the Soviet Consulate, there are photographs and audio recordings of a man claiming to be Oswald, who does not look or sound anything like him. Back in Dallas, Oswald wrote to the Soviet Consulate in Washington that he had left Mexico to avoid using his real name.

As we will see, investigators will uncover many reports of Oswald sightings around Dallas at times when the real Oswald was at work. They will learn that Oswald used the name Hidell to buy his rifle and pistol and in connection with his FPCC chapter in New Orleans. They will discover a second Oswald wallet at the Tippit shooting with information pertaining to Oswald and Hidell. Digging deeper, they will learn that Richard Nagell also had a Hidell DOD ID card in his trunk at the time of his arrest.

Oswald's autopsy will show the body was 5'-9", and the FBI misled the Warren Commission by hiding that there were photos of two different people on Oswald's ID cards. On December 3, 1963, an FBI agent went to Harris Hospital in Fort Worth to examine Oswald's early medical history because there was no mention of scars or bone removal in Oswald's post-mortem. On February 18, 1964, Richard Helms asked the FBI if Oswald's body had a scar on his left wrist, which was due to his attempted suicide in Moscow. Helms wanted the body exhumed if necessary. He wanted to verify that the real Oswald was in his grave. A week after Helms' request, two Dallas FBI agents contacted C.J. Price, the Administrator at Parkland Memorial Hospital, where the coroner performed Oswald's autopsy. Price said no one, including himself, "commented on a scar on OSWALD'S inner left wrist."[1318]

The impostor in Mexico City fit a pattern that followed Oswald from when he left the Marines until after he was dead and buried. It was all an illusion to make it appear the Soviets had killed Oswald while he was in Russia and had installed an impostor "sleeper agent" in his place. It was why Nagell called Oswald the "indispensable tool" in the assassination plot. The questions surrounding his defection to the Soviet Union ensured the U.S. would not seriously investigate the assassination, nor would the Soviets disclose what they knew because they faced being implicated with Oswald by association.

On September 16, 1963, shortly after Nagell warned Oswald that he was the assassination patsy, the following appears in Lafitte's datebook: "T says L.O is [an] idiot but can be led regardless set-up complete."[1319] The conspirators were onto Oswald and his attempt to escape to Cuba or Russia and convinced him to remain a part of the assassination plot.

CHAPTER TWENTY-FOUR

THE POINT OF NO RETURN

In 1961, British Secretary of State John Profumo began an affair with a 19-year-old London dancer named Christine Keeler. In March 1963, he lied about it to Parliament, claiming there was "no impropriety whatsoever," and on June 4, he resigned. There was also talk about Keeler being a pawn of the KGB. Her lover was Russian military attaché Eugene Ivanov, and she was introduced to Profumo by Stephen Ward, who had connections to the underworld. Ivanov was recalled to the Soviet Union before the scandal became public, and Ward committed suicide on the last day of his trial for pimping. The scandal also led to the downfall of Prime Minister Macmillan, whom the opposition party would defeat in October 1963.[1320]

Arthur Schlesinger spent three days in London that spring and alerted Kennedy about the scandal. According to JFK's friend Ben Bradlee of the *Washington Post*, "Kennedy had devoured every word written about the Profumo case; it combined so many of the things that interested him: low dongs in high places, the British nobility, sex, and spying." Kennedy's ongoing affair with Ellen Rometsch was why he was so interested; he told Schlesinger that the Bobby Baker scandal "might be the Profumo Affair of the administration." Schlesinger told his diary "that Bobby [Baker] had been running a kind of high-class whorehouse for the Senate" and "that a number of our friends – i.e., liberal Democrats-might be involved."[1321]

In the summer of 1962, Lyndon Johnson's protégé Bobby Baker opened the Carousel Club in Ocean City, Maryland. It catered to members of Congress and their wealthy supporters who enjoyed "spending time" with beautiful women. One such woman was Ellen Rometsch, an East German beauty believed to be a Communist spy.

On October 28, 1963, Robert Kennedy and J. Edgar Hoover discussed Rometsch. As Hoover described in his report: "I outlined to the Attorney General the details of the situation and the ramifications of it." He also wrote about a conversation he had "with the President on the preceding Sunday by phone in which the President expressed concern about the possible involvement of personnel at the White House" with Rometsch. JFK said nothing about his affair with her, but how could he? Most likely, it was what concerned him most. Hoover told JFK that FBI agents "had immediately interviewed the Rometsch woman," but they redacted the following paragraph. So, we don't know what Hoover and JFK discussed, but we can certainly surmise that she described her relationship with the President. Why else would Hoover have confronted JFK about this if it had not involved him?

On that same day, FBI official C.D. DeLoach wrote to the FBI's John P. Mohr about a newspaper article written by Clark Mollenhoff that stated Rometsch "was involved with a number of Administration officials, including White House personnel." Deloach's memo said that Edwin O. Guthman, Bobby Kennedy's press secretary, contacted the FBI five times on October 26. "The first call was a request to kill Mollenhoff's story in the *New York Daily News*; the second, third, fourth, and fifth calls were requests to kill the story with the *Associated Press*; on the fifth occasion, Guthman told me the President was personally interested in having the story killed." In all instances, the FBI refused to get involved. DeLoach added that "the results of our interview [with Rometsch] had been furnished to the Attorney General," which probably explains why she was deported to East Germany two days later.

Rometsch's name appears in Lafitte's datebook between June 15 and October 18. Bobby Baker's Quorum Club is also listed. One wonders if the assassination conspirators hoped to use Rometsch to blackmail JFK into resigning based on his behavior, which would have been a bloodless coup. Once Bobby had her deported, they had no choice but to proceed with the assassination plot as planned. Either way, the Kennedy brothers continued to play with fire.[1322]

***

On June 9, JFK was in Hawaii, speaking to the nation's mayors about civil rights. "The cause is just," he said. "The question is whether you and I will do nothing…inviting possible violence, or whether you will…move to fulfill the rights of your Negro citizens in a peaceful and constructive manner." That month, there were 162 racial incidents reported across the country. Black unemployment was three times that of whites, and housing and employment inequity was rampant. One thousand five hundred white-robed white supremacists gathered in a field near Tuscaloosa days before at a KKK rally, and Alabama Governor George Wallace did nothing to stop it. Meanwhile, civil unrest had also spread to northern cities like Chicago, Detroit, Pittsburgh, and New York.[1323]

Previously, on April 25, Robert Kennedy visited Wallace to talk about allowing black students to enroll at the University of Alabama. The people of Alabama treated him like a foreign dignitary, and demonstrators held up signs saying, "Mississippi Murderer" and "Kosher Team-Kennedy/Kastro/Khrushchev." Six hundred state troopers surrounded the State Capitol, and one put a billy club in Bobby's belly when he entered the Rotunda. Southern segregationist groups had warned there would be hell to pay if he tried to integrate Alabama. Wallace knew of an estimated fifty thousand Klansmen who were ready to storm the campus on the governor's command, and three thousand state soldiers were prepared to deploy. It was a powder keg waiting to explode.[1324]

Nuclear warfare also occupied Kennedy's thoughts. On June 5, he was in Colorado Springs visiting the operational center of NORAD to watch a simulation where Soviet "intercontinental missiles … erupted in white ovals as they struck American cities," wrote *New York Times* correspondent Hugh Sidey. He then flew to the White Sands Missile Range in New Mexico to see seven missiles launched. The next day, he was aboard the attack carrier USS Kitty Hawk for a naval demonstration, followed by a visit to a test station northeast of Los Angeles "where scientists conceive, build, and test the weapons of tomorrow." It prompted him to give a speech on the need to roll back the nuclear arsenal, a draft of which he showed to significant members of the administration, including Joint Chiefs Chairman Maxwell Taylor, who criticized the speech as political. It was an insight into what the military believed motivated the President. Interestingly, JFK did not consult the CIA, LBJ, or the Congressional leadership.[1325]

On June 10, JFK gave his famous commencement speech at American University, calling for coexistence with the Soviet Union. It was a controversial position for him to take, but he believed the time was right. "No government or social system is so evil that its people must be considered as lacking in virtue," Kennedy said, "and if we cannot end now our differences, at least we can help make the world safe for diversity. For, in the final analysis … we all inhabit this small planet. We all breathe the same air. We all cherish our children's future. And we are all mortal." The speech would lead to the signing of a test ban treaty with the Soviets in August.

Internationally, the reaction to the speech was encouraging. The Soviets allowed the Voice of America to broadcast the speech, an unprecedented move. The state newspaper, *Izvestia*, planned to publish the Peace Speech in full on June 12, and *Pravda* devoted thirteen column inches to a report on the speech by TASS, the government news agency. In Holland, *de Volk-*

skrant said: "This new initiative may be the first historical step toward easing international tensions," and other European newspapers were equally enthusiastic.

At home, the *Washington Post* called it a "bid for an end to the Cold War," but critics, like the *Wall Street Journal,* warned: "We have already conceded much in the test ban talks; if the Soviets... should agree to a treaty this summer it might not be a safe treaty for us, and the Soviet treaty record indicated they would evade it if it suited them." Goldwater called JFK "naïve" and "foolish."[1326] The Joint Chiefs told Kennedy they were against any test ban treaty with the Soviets.[1327]

Kennedy desperately wanted, some might say needed, to use his speech as a springboard that would lead to nuclear test ban treaty discussions. It was why when Khrushchev announced on July 2 that he would not accept any inspections by the UN because Moscow would not "open its doors to NATO spies," Kennedy told Averell Harriman to accept the proposal. It was an indication that JFK was desperate to sign a treaty with Khrushchev, which did not go unnoticed by those who thought you could not trust the Soviets and were already plotting his assassination.[1328]

The day after the speech, the first African American students ever to attend the University of Alabama were to arrive, and racist governor George Wallace threatened to resist. Kennedy federalized the Alabama National Guard, and Wallace backed down, but racial tensions remained high. There were African American protests in Virginia, where police turned fire hoses on 150 demonstrators in Danville. The mayor, Julian Stinson, blamed the trouble on "hoodlums" from out of state. There were tensions on the eastern shore of Maryland that resulted in twenty-five nights of near martial law.

That night, JFK delivered a civil rights speech on national television: "The Negro baby born in America today... has about one-half as much chance of completing high school as a white baby... one-third as much chance of completing college, one-third as much chance of becoming a professional man, twice as much chance of becoming unemployed... a life expectancy which is seven years shorter, and the prospects of earning only half as much."[1329]

The next day, Medgar Evers of the NAACP was shot and killed in front of his wife and three children in Mississippi by white supremacist Byron De La Beckwith. Twice in 1964, hung juries let him go free, and it took until 1994 for him to be convicted. The FBI received a letter on July 8 addressed to JFK from the Citizens' Council of America, Atlanta, Georgia, which read: "The execution of one of your unlawful agitators, Medgar Evers, is only the beginning of events such as you have never anticipated...This is not so much a threat as it is a solemn promise to defend our way of life by whatever means becomes necessary..."[1330]

***

Averill Harriman traveled to Moscow on July 14 to negotiate the test ban treaty. Apparently not trusting anyone but himself, President Kennedy spent hours in the cramped White House Situation Room editing the U.S. position as if he were at the negotiating table in Moscow. On July 25, just six weeks after the American University address, Harriman put his initials on the Limited Test Ban Treaty.[1331] Maxwell Taylor warned the treaty would allow the Soviets to "make important gains through clandestine testing." Nuclear physicist Edward Teller, the most boisterous voice in favor of testing, argued that ending testing prevented the U.S. from developing a shield against ballistic missiles.[1332]

Prior to Senate treaty ratification, on September 20, JFK took his case to the United Nations: "Today we may have reached a pause in the cold war – but that is not a lasting peace...And if we fail to make the most of this moment and this momentum...then the indictment of posterity will rightly point its finger at us all..."[1333] Five days later, the U.S. Senate ratified the treaty by a vote of eighty to nineteen. LBJ refused to sign despite its passage. Dean Rusk and John McCone were against it. Nelson Rockefeller wondered if Kennedy was following a policy of appeasement.[1334] West German Chancellor Konrad Adenauer publicly criticized Kennedy for negotiating with the Soviets. The Germans and Western Europe were the first line of defense and would suffer the consequences if JFK's gambit for peaceful coexistence with the Soviets proved to be a mistake.[1335]

Although nationwide President Kennedy's popularity was high three months before the assassination, the combination of a test ban treaty with Moscow and a push towards coexistence with the Soviet Union, along with racial desegregation and equal rights under the law, were signs he had gone too far for those who opposed him.

***

As described in Chapter Fourteen, in the spring of 1963, Kennedy began to consider the removal of U.S. troops from Southeast Asia. In September, he still thought Vietnam was a hopeless situation, and he told Walter Cronkite during an interview: "I don't think that unless a greater effort is made by the [South Vietnam] government to win popular support that the war can be won out there. In the final analysis, it is their war...We can help them, we can give them equipment, we can send our men out there as advisers, but they have to win it...."[1336]

The military continued its deception that the war was going well, and at the same time, the JCS continued to resist withdrawing troops. On August 20, they wrote McNamara that they should wait "until the political and religious tensions now confronting the Government of Vietnam have eased." They argued that "the withdrawal plan should be withheld until late October"- one month before Kennedy was assassinated.[1337]

On September 10, General Krulak and Joseph Mendenhall, a State Department Asian expert, reported to President Kennedy on their four-day visit to Vietnam. Krulak described a war that was going great. Mendenhall saw "a virtual breakdown of the civil government in Saigon as well as a pervasive atmosphere of fear and hate arising from the police reign of terror and the arrest of students. The war against the Viet Cong was secondary to the war against the regime," and he concluded that if Diem's brother Nhu remained in power, South Vietnam would lose the war. An astonished Kennedy asked, "The two of you did visit the same country, didn't you?"[1338]

In need of answers, at the end of September, Kennedy sent Maxwell Taylor and Robert McNamara to Vietnam to assess the situation. Their report, received by the President on October 2, 1963, maintained the military's optimistic view of the war and recommended that "a program be established...so that essential functions now performed by U.S. military personnel can be carried out by Vietnamese by the end of 1965....the Defense Department should announce in the very near future presently prepared plans to withdraw 1,000 U.S. military personnel by the end of 1963....the U.S. part of the task can be completed by the end of 1965."

That same day, Pierre Salinger publicly announced JFK's endorsement of the McNamara-Taylor recommendations. He accepted "their judgment that the major part of the U.S. military task can be completed by the end of 1965..."[1339]

The report supposedly represented Taylor's and McNamara's position after their first-hand inspection of the situation in Vietnam, but that was not true. It was the Kennedys who wrote the report. Taylor and McNamara sent preliminary drafts from Vietnam to General Krulak in Washington, as well as an outline of what their final report would be. Then, almost daily prior to their return, Krulak visited with Robert Kennedy, going over the copies he received, and Krulak was given recommendations as to what the President wanted to see. The result was not a report that Taylor and McNamara had prepared. General Taylor, who supported the escalation of the war, would not have returned from Vietnam with a recommendation that the U.S. should withdraw the bulk of its forces by the end of 1965. It was what the President wanted based upon his belief it was Vietnam's responsibility to carry the burden because the favorable conditions observed by Taylor and McNamara did not exist. Kennedy's motivation for his deception was strictly political. The Taylor/McNamara report offered JFK an excuse when conservatives objected to the removal of 1,000 troops later that year and the significant withdrawal that was to occur during his second term. It was not his idea – the Secretary of Defense and Chairman of the JCS recommended it. Kennedy's plan was evident in an October 31 press conference, where he said: "Well, as you know, when Secretary McNamara and General Taylor came back, they announced that we would expect to withdraw a thousand men from South Vietnam before the end of the year and there has been some reference to that by General Harkins...."[1340]

Kennedy was playing a dangerous game less than two months before the assassination. Once again, he played politics with the military, and the stakes this time were higher than ever, for the military's position was opposite of what the President believed should be done. They thought that to curtail the spread of communism, the battle had to be in Vietnam, with the intervention of U.S. troops on a large scale, and delay could potentially place the United States in mortal danger. It was one of the reasons why it was necessary to remove Kennedy in the fall of 1963 and shift the focus away from Cuba to Southeast Asia.

The McNamara and Taylor report became NSAM 263 on October 11. Written by the Kennedy brothers, they approved the recommendations contained therein. Throughout October and November, the military still maintained that the war was going well, despite reports by the State Department that the war was going wrong. Kennedy seemed inclined to want to pull out of Vietnam unless conditions appreciably improved. As Robert Dallek wrote in *An Unfinished Life, John F. Kennedy, 1917-1963*:

> The lesson Kennedy seemed to take from all this was the U.S. involvement in so unstable a country was a poor idea. He was immediately dismissive of the new [Vietnamese] government and its prospects for survival. And having been so concerned, as he had told McNamara on November 5, not to get "bogged down" in Cuba as the British, the Russians, and the Americans had in South Africa, Finland, and North Korea, respectively, it was hardly conceivable that Kennedy would have sent tens of thousands more Americans to

fight in so inhospitable a place as Vietnam. Reduced commitments, especially of military personnel, during a second Kennedy term were a more likely development. The failed coup had – just as the Bay of Pigs had in Cuba – pushed Kennedy further away from direct engagement.[1341]

At a November 14th press conference, Kennedy stated that the Honolulu conference on November 20 would be an "attempt to assess the situation in Vietnam: what American policy should be, and what our aid policy should be, how we can intensify the struggle, how we can bring Americans out of there. Now that is our objective, to bring Americans home, permit the South Vietnamese to maintain themselves as a free and independent country, and permit democratic forces within the country to operate." On November 16, the Department of Defense officially announced that 1,000 troops would return by year's end. However, six days later, the President was assassinated, resulting in a complete reversal of America's position.[1342]

Two days after the assassination, it was clear that Johnson intended to approach Vietnam differently. "I am not going to lose Vietnam," he said. "I am not going to be the President who saw Southeast Asia go the way that China went." He told aide Bill Moyers, "They'll think with Kennedy dead, we've lost heart. So, they'll think we're yellow and don't mean what we say...The Chinese. The fellas in the Kremlin. They'll be taking the measure of us... I'm not going to let Vietnam go the way of China. I told them to go back and tell those generals in Saigon that Lyndon Johnson intends to stand by our word."[1343]

The change from Cuba to Vietnam was a tradeoff the CIA was willing to accept. Cuba was too dangerous to allow the military to go forward with a second invasion because West Berlin would be compromised. Vietnam supported George Kennan's policy of containment, which the CIA adhered to, and they could live with that. *Washington Daily News* reporter Richard Starne wrote about the CIA's "unrestrained thirst for power" in Vietnam. He cited a "very high American official" in Saigon who "likened the CIA's growth to a malignancy, and added he was not sure even the White House could control it any longer." He cited an unnamed U.S. official who spoke of a possible CIA coup in Washington. "If the United States ever experiences a *Seven Days in May*," the source said, "it will come from the CIA, and not the Pentagon."

The CIA had penetrated every branch of the American operation in Saigon. According to Colonel Fletcher Prouty, Allen Dulles told him, "I want an office that's cleared to do what we have to have done...But the system will not be aware of what initiated the request – they'll think it came from the Secretary of Defense. They won't realize it came from the Director of Central Intelligence." Prouty created a network of subordinate offices throughout the entire U.S. government. Each office was led by a "cleared" CIA employee who took orders from the CIA while working under cover of his branch of government, including the State Department, FBI, and the White House.[1344]

In 1960, JFK appointed Averell Harriman ambassador-at-large to operate "with the full confidence of the president and an intimate knowledge of all aspects of United States policy." By 1963, he was making decisions regarding "Vietnam without consulting the president or the attorney general."[1345]

Kennedy worried that his government was "coming apart," especially the rift between the Pentagon and the State Department. Generals Krulak and Taylor, and to a lesser extent McNamara, believed in President Diem, while the State Department faction of Harriman, Ball, Hilsman, and Lodge wanted him out. It was true that since May 1962, the Department of Defense ran all primary paramilitary operations. Still, General Harkins intended the war to be what the military always wanted it to be, which was a large-scale military action. Two days before the assassination, McNamara outlined the military position that Special Forces would train and arm irregular Vietnamese units to be used only in support of traditional military operations by gathering intelligence and harassing the enemy. Another European-type war was what the JCS wanted.[1346]

Regardless of the spin put on the war by some, the press continued to paint a dim picture. In an August 15 *New York Times* article, David Halberstam wrote that "South Vietnam's military situation in the vital Mekong Delta has deteriorated in the last year, and informed officials are warning of ominous signs…a Communist Vietcong build-up is taking place in the delta." "In the first six months of this year," Halberstam continued, "military statistics showed an increase of about 33 percent over the [South] Vietnamese Army losses…At the same time, Vietcong personnel losses fell 30 percent."[1347] Things did not bode well.

***

In the summer of 1963, Diem's regime began to unravel over a dispute with Vietnam's majority Buddhist community. During an anti-Diem demonstration in early May, a mysterious explosion in the city of Hue killed a woman and seven children. In the ensuing chaos, Diem's troops fired into the crowd, which resulted in more casualties. Civil disturbances escalated across the country in response. On June 11, an elderly Buddhist monk set himself on fire in protest, and journalists around the world showed photos of the grotesque suicide. On August 21, despite strong warnings from the Kennedy administration, Diem and his brother Nhu launched a series of violent, repressive strikes against Buddhists, including the Xa Loi Temple, the most sacred Buddhist shrine in Saigon. Soldiers plundered pagodas and arrested thousands of monks and nuns. Monks continued setting themselves on fire, and the United States faced worldwide criticism for supporting such a repressive government.[1348]

As early as August 16, 1962, Joseph A. Mendenhall, the political counselor in Saigon, sent out a memorandum that said, "There is no chance of changing Diem and Nhu's political ways or methods of organization and governing..." The answer was to "get rid of Diem... and the rest of the Ngo family."[1349]

Nhu used systematic corruption to finance intelligence and counterinsurgency operations. When the U.S. urged him to initiate "reforms," Diem refused and reneged on his promise to have his brother leave the country. Roger Hilsman, Assistant Secretary of State for Far Eastern Affairs, declared that "we must face the possibility that Diem himself cannot be preserved." This message was given to new Ambassador Henry Cabot Lodge on August 24, only two days after he assumed his post. On August 29, Lodge posted the following message to the White House: "We are launched on a course from which there is no respectable turning back: the overthrow of the Diem government."[1350]

Harriman asked Richard Helms to approve an August 24 telegram to Lodge since CIA Director McCone, who supported Diem, was out of town. "It's about time we bit the bullet," Helms told Harriman, which was in direct conflict with what McCone had said to JFK on his return. According to *The Pentagon Papers*, the military told Lodge we would "back you to the hilt on actions you take to achieve our objectives," which was code for the forcible removal of Diem.[1351]

JFK was in Hyannis Port and learned of the backroom discussions about getting rid of Diem. "This shit has got to stop!" he said upon his return to Washington. He still thought Diem might remove the Nhus. Still, Lodge disagreed, saying he believed "that such a step... would have the very serious effect of being regarded by the [coup] Generals as a sign of American indecision and delay." The reality was that Lodge and JFK were political enemies with different agendas. "The best chance of doing it is by the Generals taking over the government lock, stock, and barrel," Lodge wrote, and "I am contemplating no further talks with Diem at this time."[1352]

Harriman, Hilsman, and Ball from the State Department and Forrestal from the NSC thought Diem should go. A Pentagon faction of McNamara, Taylor, and Krulak believed Diem had to remain. In *The Dark Side of Camelot*, Seymour Hersh cited Lodge's unpublished memoirs as stating: "I was instructed to send my telegrams directly to [President Kennedy]" and bypass everyone else. In other words, Kennedy intended to use this back-channel communication to keep the U.S. military and others who supported Diem out of the loop.[1353]

In September, Hilsman attended a meeting of the Senate Foreign Relations Committee and reported to Lodge that its members had "far-reaching doubts regarding [the] advisability of continued US participation in [the] Viet-Nam war," and that "it is the sense of the Senate that the American people are no longer willing to support a regime in South Viet-Nam that oppresses the people and religious sects." In an NSC meeting two days later, Bobby Kennedy wondered why they hadn't cut their losses and pulled out now. Rusk called pulling out "very serious," saying we would be in "real trouble" if the Vietcong took over, but it was clear the Kennedy brothers were ready to pull out as soon as it was politically practical to do so.[1354]

***

The coup to oust Diem and his brother was supposed to be bloodless. Kennedy gave the order that the two men and their families were to be evacuated safely from Vietnam. When it was over, and the Diem brothers were dead, JFK learned that "the orders that ended in the deaths of Diem and his brother originated with Harriman and Henry Cabot Lodge's military assistant carried them out."[1355] Kennedy leaped to his feet and rushed from the room with a look of shock and dismay on his face, which I had never seen before," said General Taylor. When JFK left the room, NSC members were amused by the President's naivete in encouraging a coup without thinking assassination was a possibility.[1356]

Lodge's military assistant was Lucien Conein. As described in Chapter Four, Conein was a former OSS liaison officer with the French Resistance during WWII. He was a shadowy figure and honorary member of the Union Course, the European branch of the international crime syndicate. Regarding William Harvey's ZR/RIFLE assassination program: "QJ/WIN was first contacted in [deleted], in conjunction with an illegal narcotics operation into the United States. For a period of a year and a half, he was contacted sporadically by CIS Lucien Conein on behalf of the Bureau of Narcotics."[1357]

During World War II, Conein was a member of the Jedburgs, Bill Donovan's elite paramilitary force that parachuted into France to organize resistance against the Nazis. When the European theater ended, Conein moved to China and worked closely with U.S. Army Major General Gallagher, who was cooperating with Ho Chi Minh.[1358]

In *The Best and the Brightest,* David Halberstam described Conein as "Shrewd, irreverent, colorful, he seemed an American version of the audacious French paratrooper, someone sprung to life from a pulp adventure thriller. He knew the country, and the people, and he flirted with danger, it was danger that made life more exciting. Two fingers were missing from one hand, and stories were told all over Saigon as to how those fingers had disappeared, in what noble or ignoble cause..."[1359]

The head of the CIA's Far East Division in 1963 at the time of Diem's overthrow was William Colby, a fellow Jedburg. In his autobiography, he referred to Conein as "my old Jedburg buddy." One of Colby's claims to fame was the infamous Phoenix program during the Vietnam War, which was a murderous operation where as many as 60,000 villagers suspected of aiding the Vietcong were tortured and executed. According to Colby, "My experience as a Jedburg made me a natural recruit for the CIA's world of espionage, sabotage, covert operations, and intelligence." David Morales was allegedly involved in the Phoenix Program as well.[1360]

Tracy Barnes was also a Jedburg. After the war, he was stationed in Germany for the CIA at the time of the Berlin Tunnel, which put him in contact with William Harvey. He was familiar with Conein, who brought QJ/WIN to Harvey's and the CIA's attention.[1361]

Conein's first assignment with QJ/WIN was on behalf of the Federal Bureau of Narcotics, which put him in contact with Lafitte and George Hunter White. It was when Sheffield Edwards, the CIA's security officer for Project Artichoke, was working with the FBN's liaison to the CIA, Charles Siragusa, who also was an ex-military intelligence officer during World War II. Edwards wanted Siragusa to find organized crime figures to assassinate foreign leaders. Conein often bragged about his affiliation with the Corsican Mafia, whose involvement in the drug trade in Indochina is well known. Then, there is the relationship between Conein, Harvey, and Barnes. It was Harvey who wrote "Corsicans recommended" as potential assassination candidates.[1362]

Conein had experience working with many of Saigon's Corsican gangsters. When he left Vietnam, the Corsicans gave him a heavy gold medallion embossed with the Napoleonic eagle and the Corsican crest. Engraved on the back was *Per Tu Amicu Conein* (For your friendship, Conein). He proudly explained that the medallion served as an identification badge for secret meetings, narcotics drops, etc., for influential Corsican syndicate leaders around the world. "The Corsicans are smarter, tougher, and better organized than the Sicilians," he said. "They are absolutely ruthless and are the equal of anything we know about the Sicilians, but they hide their internal fighting better." He was involved with Corsican smugglers in Saigon who purchased morphine base through Corsican contacts in Vientiane, Laos, and shipped it on French merchant vessels to Marseille, where they processed it into heroin.[1363]

Conein knew most of the Vietnam coup generals for years, ever since he conducted the CIA's sabotage operations against the Viet Minh in the mid-1950s. On October 24, General Tran Van Don informed Conein that the coup was imminent. Conein and the CIA passed the word to Lodge, who notified the State Department. The day before, Kennedy had said, "We can discourage a coup in ways other than telling Diem of the rebel Generals' plans." Bundy wired Kennedy's position to Lodge. Lodge ignored him.[1364]

At 1 P.M. on November 1, a coup d'etat commenced against the Diem government, led by South Vietnamese General Duong Vasn Minh (a.k.a. "Big Minh"). He immediately ordered the execution of key Diem military leaders, followed by strikes against Diem's presidential palace and key military sites. Diem and Nhu managed to escape through an underground passageway and made it to Cholon, where Nhu's opium network contacts kept them hidden. The brothers agreed to surrender in exchange for safe passage out of the country. Minh agreed and dispatched troops who shot them to death instead.

Lodge chose Conein because he was French by birth and knew their language and customs. Conein was given a direct line of communication to the Saigon CIA outpost, and he was in steady cable contact with McGeorge Bundy at the White House Situation Room. Conein provided Minh and his insurgents with money, weapons, and intelligence information. Allegedly, Minh asked Conein for a plane to fly Diem and Nhu out of the country, but that did not happen. On August 30, Roger Hilsman had written a top-secret memo; the last page read as follows: "Under no circumstances should the Ngo's be permitted to remain in Southeast Asia in close proximity to Viet-Nam because of the plots they will try to mount to regain power."[1365]

"The overthrow of the Diem regime was purely a Vietnamese affair," Lodge wrote in a *New York Times* article on June 30, 1964. "We never participated in the planning. We never gave any advice. We had nothing whatever to do with it." Lodge did not fool Senator Mike Gravel. "For the military coup d'etat against Ngo Dinh Diem," he wrote, "the U.S. must accept its full share of responsibility. Beginning in August of 1963, we variously authorized, sanctioned, and encouraged the coup efforts of the Vietnamese generals...In October, we cut off aid to Diem...We maintained clandestine contact with them throughout the planning and execution of the coup..."[1366]

Three weeks later, another combined CIA/European operation would assassinate JFK. Maybe Diem's murder was a warning the young president failed to heed. Whatever the case, the center of gravity would shift to Vietnam, but first, loose ends in Cuba needed to be secured, such as preventing the Omega Plan from initiating World War III.

CHAPTER TWENTY-FIVE

BY ANY MEANS POSSIBLE

On June 8, 1963, the CIA's Desmond FitzGerald submitted a paper to the Standing Group that stated the CIA assumed the "current U.S. policy does not contemplate outright military intervention in Cuba or a provocation…as a pretext for an invasion of Cuba by the United States military forces…the U.S. policy calls for the exertion of maximum pressure by all means available to the U.S. Government, short of military intervention." It was the opposite of what McCone and FitzGerald had told the Special Group on April 25, when they said the CIA might require the use of the U.S. military to overthrow Castro. Something changed between April 25 and June 8. Perhaps FitzGerald and the CIA recognized that using the military against Cuba threatened West Berlin and jeopardized world peace.

At the beginning of June, the CIA sent army intelligence a report that Manuel Artime was in Nicaragua and Costa Rica looking for bases to launch raids against Cuba. Artime was the leader of MRR, one of the left-wing exile groups brought into the Omega Plan operation by Harry Williams. It is noteworthy that the CIA provided military intelligence with information about Artime, who still had one foot in the right-wing camp even though he was part of Bobby's group.

On June 19, FitzGerald met with President Kennedy, Robert McNamara, Averill Harriman, McGeorge Bundy, and John McCone to discuss what to do about Cuba. FitzGerald did not think sabotage raids would work, but as he wrote in a memorandum to McCone, a "Higher Authority," meaning Bobby Kennedy, was interested in sabotage and asked when it would begin. FitzGerald said sometime in July, and the plan was to launch two or three raids per month.[1367]

Averill Harriman, who was on his way to Moscow to negotiate a nuclear test ban treaty, was against this, thinking sabotage raids could ruin negotiations with the Russians. Rusk agreed, but for a different reason. He believed a reproachment with Castro was possible and did not want to do anything to prevent that from happening.[1368]

John and Bobby Kennedy liked the Ivy League FitzGerald, who was a stark contrast to the rough and tumble William Harvey, whom he replaced. After six months on the job, FitzGerald demonstrated a willingness to listen to the Kennedys and give them what they wanted, even if he disagreed. At times, they pressured him relentlessly, which in this case applied to increased sabotage raids, which resulted in twenty-five Cuban exiles killed or captured in five raids against Cuba in 1963. It did not sit well with Fitz-Gerald and others at the Agency who thought the raids were pointless, and privately, they considered the Kennedys amateurs who should have kept their noses out of intelligence affairs.[1369]

Nicaraguan President Anastasio Somoza came to the U.S. in July to meet with Cuban exiles in Florida. On July 14, Hal Hendrix of the *Miami News* reported that Somoza wished to instigate a Cuban attack against his own country, similar to what was tried in 1959, after which the U.S. would feel compelled to help Nicaragua by invading Cuba. FitzGerald thought the plan could derail what they were trying to accomplish. By August, he asked Artime to relocate his base from Nicaragua to Costa Rica and focus on building an internal uprising within Cuba, even though the CIA had already decided that was pointless. At the same time, FitzGerald briefed the Joint Chiefs and told them to be prepared for a quick invasion in the event of an uprising in Cuba, even though he had told JFK that military invasion was off the table.[1370]

***

On June 19, a CIA cable referenced an attempt to establish contact with Rolando Cubela after a year and a half of silence. FitzGerald felt Cubela was the one Cuban working on the inside who might be willing to assassinate Castro. The CIA had lost touch with him, but they now wanted to reestablish a relationship.

On September 7, Cubela met two CIA agents in Porto Alegre, Brazil. One was Nestor Sanchez, who had worked with both William Harvey and FitzGerald in the war against Cuba. Harvey was now stationed in Rome and was no longer officially part of any Cuban operation, so his continued involvement must have been done without McCone or the Kennedys knowing. Sanchez had previously worked for Harvey in the propaganda section of the Cuba Desk for Tasks Force W "to develop assets inside Cuba that could be used in a coup against Castro."[1371]

That same day, Fitzgerald received a cable from Brazil that stated, "AM-LASH [Cubela] still feels there only two ways accomplish change either

BY ANY MEANS POSSIBLE

inside job or invasion he realistic enough to realize latter out of question... AMLASH still waiting for U.S. [to] reveal plan of action."[1372]

Cubela told Sanchez he was willing to assassinate Castro if it was part of a more significant coup d'etat to take back Cuba. After Bobby's Cuban Coordinating Group met privately on September 12, it was clear this interested the group because the frequency of their gatherings increased from this point on. Cubela later claimed FitzGerald told him Robert Kennedy approved the operation, which Sanchez confirmed. "FitzGerald gave assurance that the United States not only would support the government which emerged after a successful coup," Sanchez said, "but also gave assurances that the United States would help in bringing about that coup."[1373]

Cubela did not know that his demand for a coup, of which the assassination of Castro was only a part, was already in the works, and the Agency had bigger plans for him. FitzGerald and Sanchez were referring to Operation AMTRUNK, which was part of the AMWORLD Operation. They wanted Cubela "to penetrate the Cuban military to encourage either defections... or perhaps even to forming a group which would be capable of replacing the then government in Cuba." The CIA's Inspector General Report of 1967 recalled that "Cubela discussed a group of Cuban military officers known to him... [and] although many of them were anti-Communist, they were either loyal to Fidel or so afraid of him that they were reluctant to discuss any conspiracies for fear there might be provocations..."[1374]

***

As Dick Russell wrote in *On the Trail of the JFK Assassins*, "[Henry] Hecksher soon became FitzGerald's main deputy charged with AMWORLD, as well as Manuel Artime's case officer. Around the same time, Nagell was given a list of Cuban exiles, including Artime, whose activities he proceeded to monitor in various locations [New Orleans, Miami, and Dallas]."[1375]

According to Arthur Schlesinger, "The CIA wished to organize Castro's overthrow from outside Cuba, as against the White House, the Attorney General's office and State who wished to support an anti-Castro movement inside Cuba [with a general uprising of the people]. The CIA's idea was to fight a war; the others hoped to promote a revolution. Any successful anti-Castro movement inside Cuba would have to draw on disenchanted Castroites and aim to rescue the revolution from the Communists. This approach, stigmatized as Fidelismo sin Fidel, was opposed by businessmen, both Cuban and American, who dreamed of the restoration of nationalized properties. But the CIA alternative was probably dictated less by business

445

interests than by the agency's preference for operations it could completely control…"[1376]

The differences between the CIA and Bobby Kennedy complicated matters, and the problem FitzGerald and the CIA faced was keeping tabs on the various Cuban exile groups that were independent of Robert Kennedy's group. Clare Boothe Luce and William Pawley, both members of the Citizens Committee to Free Cuba, financed various right-wing exile groups, most notably the DRE. As early as June 1960, then Secretary of State Christian Herter complained to President Eisenhower that Pawley was working with a right-wing group of Cubans, including former Batista police. Eisenhower told Herter to "call up Mr. Pawley and tell him to get out of this operation." By 1963, nothing had changed.[1377]

Washington Post editor Jefferson Morley wrote that in the early 1960s, "In Miami, the DRE quickly attracted the support of CIA covert operations officers such as David Phillips and Howard Hunt…" Hunt stated under oath that Phillips ran the DRE. Still, by 1963, he handed that responsibility to George Joannides, who by July was focusing his attention exclusively on the DRE and was part of the Special Affairs Staff (SAS) under FitzGerald.[1378]

There was also Paulino Sierra's organization, which involved many Cuban exile groups financed by organized crime and big business and aligned with ex-Cuban President Carlos Prio, who was trying to stay relevant with any group that might show some interest.

These Cuban exile groups, supported by private interests, worked outside Bobby Kennedy's control and expected the JFK assassination to be the catalyst for launching an invasion of Cuba that would eliminate Fidel Castro. It eventually included Manuel Artime, who operated a training camp for AMWORLD near New Orleans until it was closed in August. The problem was, with so many groups with different agendas, it was impossible to keep everyone on the same page, and the potential for disaster was ever-present.

When Artime passed through Mexico City on his way to the exiles' military bases in Nicaragua, David Phillips placed him in a safe house and kept his profile low. In a CIA memo written by Hecksher in October 1963, he described plans "to activate our media capabilities in Mexico City on promoting a more acceptable image for AMBIDDY-1 [Artime's codename]. This was briefly discussed with Michael CHOEDEN [Phillips] on October 4." According to another CIA document, Phillips was to arrive at the JM/WAVE station "for consultation" on October 4, which was likely when he met with Hecksher, just two days after Oswald left Mexico City. Four days later, Lafitte's datebook lists "848" (Hecksher) with Angleton, Harvey, and Charles "Boots" Askins, a known assassin.[1379]

Phillips, Hunt, and Hecksher had good reason to be interested in Artime for, even though he was part of Bobby Kennedy's group, he was still the CIA's "Golden Boy," receiving $170,000 during August and $47,000 in the first part of September from the Agency, according to a State Department memorandum. A separate Hecksher memo described a meeting that took place between November 7 and 10 where one of Artime's leading advisors opined that while JFK remained in power, it would be impossible to defeat Castro. Rafael "Chi Chi" Quintero, who also worked closely with Artime, was quoted as saying that Hecksher did not believe AMWORLD was going to work.[1380]

Then, there was a "Memorandum for the Record" that Hecksher wrote on July 10 about a meeting he had with Artime in Washington. Artime described "the irreparability of his break with [leftist] Manuel RAY….at a later stage, this relationship may become a pivotal factor in determining the political complexion of a successorship [to Castro]..." A CIA dispatch followed this on July 22 regarding Ray, the leader of JURE: "Manola Ray himself was personally critical of the CIA and told one JURE associate that he thought CIA agents 'were more dangerous than the Kennedy administration.'" The left-leaning Ray was one of Bobby Kennedy's boys, and he was supposed to play a leading role in the Cuban government that would take over for Castro, which the CIA would never accept. So, the Agency had to do something to prevent that from happening.

In February 1964, Hecksher described that, at an AMWORLD meeting in New York, they discussed that JURE was under surveillance and that Hecksher had authorized Artime's boats to fire on Ray's boats should they encounter them. By this point, with JFK dead, Robert Kennedy and Ray no longer had any clout, but Hecksher's animosity for RAY remained just as strong as it was before the assassination.[1381]

***

Henry Hecksher was perhaps the most secretive character in a world of secret characters. Why did he continue to pursue AMWORLD, even though he had no faith the operation would succeed? Is it possible that Hecksher and those he worked with wanted the operation to fail because they considered a forcible takeover of Cuba by the United States was a reward not worth the risk when weighed against the Soviet retaliation that might follow in Europe?

According to Hecksher's formal resume, "From 1960 to Present-in charge of desk in ARA, [the State Department's Bureau of Inter-American Affairs]. Supervises the collection of data and the writing of scheduled and spot reports on Latin America." Working for the State Department was a cover, for during this same period, Hecksher's signature appeared on numerous reports related to AM/WORLD, Manuel Artime, and anti-Castro operations. Yet, there was no specific mention of Cuba in his resume. Why the secrecy?

Hecksher, whose real name was Heinrich Detlev Heckscher, was born in Hamburg, Germany, in 1910. His father served in the government of Kaiser Wilhelm II, so it is safe to assume Henry was a Monarchist. He came to the United States in 1938, served in the U.S. Army during World War II, and then joined the OSS, where he interrogated some of the top leaders of the Nazi Party after the war. One can assume he got to know Otto Skorzeny.

He next became part of the War Department's Secret Intelligence (SI). In 1946, he headed its counterintelligence section in Berlin, where he worked with Ted Shackley, David Morales, and William Harvey. Being part of counterintelligence meant he crossed paths with James Angleton as well. Hecksher joined the CIA in 1947, and during the 1953 Berlin Riots following Stalin's death, he asked headquarters in Washington for permission to arm the rioters with rifles and stun guns. He was already a staunch anti-Communist and probably supportive of the Nazis prisoners he got to know from his many years in Germany.

In 1954, Hecksher worked with David Phillips, Tracy Barnes, and Howard Hunt in the overthrow of Arbenz in Guatemala, which was where he became familiar with Nicaraguan President Somoza. By 1958, he was CIA Chief of Station in Laos, promoting covert operations. He then moved to Thailand and supervised transborder covert activities around the Golden Triangle.[1382]

Constantine Broutsas was a CIA official and close friend of Hecksher's from the time they met in Berlin in the early 1950s, but he knew nothing about Hecksher's involvement in the war against Cuba. "When I think of Cuba, I think of Bill Harvey and Ted Shackley," Broutsas said, "but I didn't know Henry was involved…" Peter Sichel, who worked with Hecksher in Germany, told Dick Russell: "I knew very little about it because it was after I left the agency…They ended up with a lot of the old German hands in the Cuba thing. Like William Harvey, who'd been Henry's boss for a while in Berlin…Henry became, as he got older, extremely right-wing. He became an absolutist, and I think he got retired a little too late. That should have happened... before he got involved in this whole mess in Cuba and what-have-yous."[1383] Why did so many people who knew Hecksher professionally not know about his involvement in the war against Castro?

Regarding his CIA career, Hecksher said: "My intelligence specialty is political action, but not to the exclusion of related pursuits, such as counterintelligence. The dominant focus of my professional interests has at all times been the Soviet Union, its satellites, and its surrogates...I always considered myself targeted against the KGB (active measures) and the International Department of the Central Committee of the CPSU."

According to files declassified by the CIA years later, Hecksher's signature appeared on numerous reports relating to AM/WORLD, Manuel Artime, and anti-Castro operations. One wonders why he needed to purge his Cuban experience from the official record. And what happened in Cuba that was so potentially dangerous that it had to remain hidden? Was it the JFK assassination?

As described above, Peter Sichel said Hecksher "got involved in this whole mess in Cuba and what-have-yous." What does that mean? There were numerous intelligence agents and military personnel involved in Cuban operations, but this did not define who they were. But Hecksher's Cuban experience seemed to define him negatively. We know a deep hatred for communism, particularly the Soviet Union, drove Hecksher. The question is, was there no limit to what he might do to contain the spread of communism, especially if it involved preventing communism from spreading into Germany, where he was born?

Hecksher's first involvement with Cuba was in 1958 in connection with the CIA's interest in anti-Batista groups like Menoyo's SNFE, members of the DRE, and a small contingent from Che Guevera's July 26 Movement. When Castro took control on January 1, 1959, Hecksher was on the ground in Cuba. He submitted reports on the fighting going on in the streets of Santiago de Cuba to the CIA base in that city. By September, Hecksher was reporting on security issues related to Michael Choaden (David Atlee Phillips) and Douglas Freapane (David U. Groves) to CIA headquarters. He also spent some time in the Dominican Republic and Mike. K. Holbik, who worked with Hecksher on AMWORLD, characterized him as a "wild man."[1384]

Henry D. Hecksher may have been who Lafitte referred to as 848 because the numbers correspond to his initials, but why the secrecy? Author John Newman provided a clue in his book *Countdown To Darkness*.

449

In the CIA cable and dispatches from Cuba that discuss the ... activities of Henry Hecksher, *"his true name was never mentioned.* The first appearance of the name Hecksher in a CIA document – that I [Newman] have found so far – is a November 1955 recommendation by him for his subordinate, Anne Goodpasture...That document, however, was different from the Havana Station cables and dispatches that were sent electronically or placed in diplomatic pouches – and the same is true for the cables and dispatches of the CIA's Miami JMASH (later JMWAVE) Station. The Goodpasture recommendation was an internal memorandum and, as such, not as exposed to the risks of interception and prying eyes. The next time Hecksher enters the record is not until 1963 and 1964 when the name is ubiquitous among internal CIA HQS memoranda concerning the AM-WORLD project.[1385] (Author's italics)

Newman continues: "The activities of Henry Hecksher were always protected by pseudonyms in cables and dispatches sent from CIA sites to HQS and in cables from HQS to those sites. These pseudonyms fragmented AMWORLD activities into several compartments...The importance of Hecksher to the history of the JFK case – beginning in Cuba and ending at CIA HQS – increased over time..."[1386]

As described in Chapter Fifteen, Richard Nagell said that while in Miami in January 1963 which, according to *Coup in Dallas,* was when "848" first appeared in Lafitte's datebook, "I conducted surveillance on a man, said to have been an ex-CIA employee, observed talking to [exile] leader Manuel Artime and former Cuban senator/racketeer Rolando Masferrer." Another CIA man, who he knew as "Bob," was also involved. Nagell first met Bob in Japan, where he also met Lee Oswald for the first time. That was when he followed Oswald to the Soviet Embassy in Tokyo related to the Colonel Eroshkin incident. Nagell would run into Bob again in Mexico City in September 1962, and Oswald would mysteriously show up there the following year. For the next year, Bob, who reported to Desmond FitzGerald, became Nagell's CIA point of contact.[1387]

Dick Russell believes "Bob" was Henry Hecksher, which meant Hecksher was involved with Nagell and Oswald in Japan and again throughout 1963 while Nagell investigated Cuban exiles, as well as Lee and Marina Oswald.

In Chapter Twenty-Three, we discussed how CIA documents related to Oswald in Mexico used "Lee Henry Oswald" to describe him. CIA Counterintelligence Staff Officer Ann Egerter admitted she wrote the middle name

"Henry" but did not know why. I understand that this may be a stretch, but did someone at CIA Counterintelligence change Oswald's middle name to "Henry" to provide a cryptic connection to Henry Hecksher?

The bottom line is that Hecksher's name only appears in internal CIA cable dispatches and was never used in correspondence outside the Agency. You could not say that about anyone else at the CIA. So, it was not by accident that Hecksher wanted this part of his career expunged from his record. From this, we can deduce that this pro-German, anti-Communist, right-wing Monarchist, who associated with the group operating out of Madrid, which included Otto Skorzeny, Victor Oswald, Charles Willoughby, and other ex-Nazis, was part of the group who conspired to kill JFK.

***

On August 23, Desmond FitzGerald wrote the Miami station that he "sees [Carlos] Prio's main role is one of creating a nuisance," and if he wanted to help, he should "cough up some of the millions he stole from the Cuban people while President…" Recall it was Paulino Sierra's group who planned on making Prio the next Cuban president if they successfully overthrew Castro. One could argue that Fitzgerald would only be concerned with Prio being a nuisance if the CIA was working with Sierra's group.

Rejected by FitzGerald, Prio turned to Artime, but a CIA "Telegram Information Report" dated September 27 stated that Artime did not want to join with Prio. It also makes sense since Artime was now working with the CIA. So, Prio had to remain close to Tony Varona. The importance of this disclosure is that the sabotage raids FitzGerald agreed to were privately financed outside regular CIA funding sources, using Cuban and mercenary assets operating within America's borders, which Robert Kennedy objected to but was powerless to stop.

Meanwhile, Cuban exile groups in Miami and New Orleans, who were frequently meeting with Bobby Kennedy, were talking openly about a U.S-supported invasion that would start in late 1963 and culminate in 1964, which coincided with the Joint Chiefs invasion timetable.[1388]

James Hosty claimed he first heard about a possible second invasion of Cuba on or around October 25, according to an FBI document.[1389]

Then, a critical CIA "Telegram Information Report" dated October 7 categorically stated that operations against Cuba would "begin in November or December 1963." It was a reference to the Omega Plan, for which the Castro assassination was to be a catalyst to justify a military invasion of Cuba and result in a new leftist Cuban government taking charge in Cuba that was favorable to the Kennedy brothers. The report stated that "Prio is trying to convince wealthy Cubans in exile that, if they want to recoup their riches in Cuba in the future, they must contribute some of their wealth" to him. "If they do not, they will allow the United States to utilize a few Cubans to topple Castro and establish a government of their choosing." Another CIA document sent to John McCone on November 6 quoted Prio as saying that "evidence exists" that "President Kennedy secretly plans [to] replace Fidel Castro with more acceptable Cuban leader... coup... would pu[r] port[edely] be Tito-type thus paving [the] way for US recognition [of] Communist regime in Cuba."[1390] Unknown to Prio, the Kennedy brothers, and others, there was a right-wing elitist group in the U.S., headed by the CIA, in league with the group in Madrid and French Monarchists, that was not going to let that happen.

***

On September 7, while Sanchez was meeting with Cubela in Brazil, Castro attended a reception at the Brazilian embassy in Havana. Daniel Harker of the *Associated Press* interviewed him, and the article appeared in most major newspapers. Castro told Harker that "United States leaders would be in danger if they helped in any attempt to do away with the leaders of Cuba...United States leaders should be mindful that if they are aiding terrorist plans to eliminate Cuban leaders, they themselves will not be safe."[1391]

Around the same time, a close friend of Cubela's named Victor Espinosa Hernandez contacted the INS with information regarding Cubela. Espinosa was an anti-Castro arms dealer who had twenty-four hundred pounds of dynamite and twenty bomb casings seized at the Lake Pontchartrain raid on July 31. The INS notified the FBI, who contacted the CIA, which led Fitzgerald's Counterintelligence chief to write: "The AM/LASH circle is wide and each new friend of whom we learn seems to have knowledge of plan. I believe the problem is a more serious and basic one. Fidel reportedly knew that this group was plotting against him and once enlisted its support. Hence, we cannot rule out the possibility of provocation."[1392]

So, the die was cast. If JFK were to be assassinated by a supporter of Fidel Castro, America would be justified in attacking Cuba and removing Castro once and for all. It was why, on September 30, the Defense Department's International Security Affairs section prepared a draft of its "State-Defense Contingency Plan for a Coup in Cuba" for the Joint Chiefs. Once the JCS agreed to the plan, the coup was good to go. The military did not need Cubela or Almeida – these two men were part of the CIA's operation. The Joint Chiefs were ready to proceed without them. They just needed a justifiable reason to invade.

By Any Means Possible

***

Around the same time, things got more complicated. It began in January 1963, when the NSA intercepted a diplomatic cable regarding a ten-hour interview Castro gave to reporter Lisa Howard of ABC News, where he clearly stated he was interested in a possible rapprochement with the United States.[1393]

By the spring, as the potential for talks with Castro progressed, CIA officials were not pleased, especially since normalizing relations was never part of their agenda. An alliance with Castro, which was against George Kennan's policy of containment, was the opposite of what they expected from their President. In a memo on May 2, 1963, John McCone asked that the "Lisa Howard report be handled in the most limited and sensitive manner" and "that no active steps be taken on the rapprochement matter at this time." They even considered trying to block ABC's airing of her interview.

Unknown to Lisa Howard and William Attwood, who was working with her on behalf of JFK to try and bring the talks to fruition, while they were on the phone in her apartment speaking with the Cubans, the CIA was listening in. In one call to Havana, agents overheard Howard describing Kennedy's enthusiasm for rapprochement, which she had no right to do. She did not understand the powers that were working against her and their motives. The CIA wanted to sabotage JFK's secret bid for peace. They had done it to Eisenhower, and they would do it again. At a White House meeting pertaining to Cuba as late as November 5, Helms urged that they slow down the Attwood initiative.[1394]

Also on November 5, Attwood met with McGeorge Bundy and Gordon Chase of the NSC to explain Castro's eagerness to facilitate a dialogue with Kennedy. On November 11, Dr. Rene Vallejo, Castro's aide and personal physician, phoned Lisa Howard and said Castro would go along with any arrangements Kennedy's representatives wanted. The next day, Bundy said there should be preliminary talks with Vallejo at the UN before they met with Castro directly. Three days later, Lisa Howard relayed this to Vallejo. On November 18, Howard called Vallejo again and then passed the phone to Attwood (Castro was listening in, as he told Attwood many years later). They decided to send instructions to Lechuga at the UN to propose an agenda for a later meeting with Castro.[1395]

Right before the final call, Kennedy signed off on several sabotage operations scheduled for the weekend of November 16-17. He canceled the raids a few hours later. It was a sign that the talks with Castro interested him. Bundy called Attwood to discuss a sensitive message from the Presi-

453

dent that he could only deliver in person. Kennedy said he wanted to begin discussions by having Vallejo visit the U.S. and deliver any messages from Castro directly to Attwood. More importantly, JFK wanted to know if Castro was willing to modify his position on two critical issues: the reduction of Communist influence in Cuba and the end of Castro spreading his revolution throughout Latin America. Without resolving these issues, normalizing relations would not be accomplished. However, it did not matter. Kennedy was just days away from being assassinated.[1396]

***

On October 5, after meeting with Cubela in Paris, and as things progressed slowly, Sanchez cabled headquarters that Cubela might get fed up and return to Cuba. He talked about assassinating Castro, then switched to organizing a military coup to get rid of him. Cubela also wanted to meet a high-level US government official, "preferably Robert F. Kennedy," to confirm that the U.S. government supported him. Bobby's telephone logs show he took a call from FitzGerald within the hour. Between September 1 and November 21, Bobby received 477 calls, but only this one call from FitzGerald, so we know what they discussed. On October 13, Cubela again demanded a meeting with Robert Kennedy to ensure JFK supported the coup. Sanchez suggested they fly Cubela to Washington by military plane for a short meeting with RFK, but others at headquarters did not approve. Some were concerned Cubela was a double agent keeping Castro updated on what the Kennedy brothers were up to, and they had not forgotten Castro's September 7 threat.[1397]

FitzGerald decided that instead of having Cubela meet with Bobby Kennedy, he would travel to Paris to meet Cubela himself. The Special Affairs Staff (SAS) objected to this. As SAS counterintelligence officer Joseph Langoscsh warned, Cubela might be a "dangle"- a double agent recruited by Castro to penetrate the American plots against him...Cubela was regarded by the CIA as unstable..."[1398]

Ted Shackley told author Evan Thomas: "I told Des that it was something he shouldn't do. 'If AMLASH [Cubela] does do something,' I told him, 'it's quite likely they'll track you down. You have a high profile. What are you going to get out of this? The only thing you'll get is the satisfaction of saying you saw the guy!" FitzGerald's security chief, Harold Swenson, was also against the meeting and later told the Church Committee: "I didn't consider it a good operation on security grounds or any grounds... we were dealing with people whose bona fides were subject to question, and I felt that if they had succeeded in killing Castro, that he might have been succeeded by his brother, for example, who would be worse... I thought it was a lot of nonsense."[1399]

FitzGerald's boss, Richard Helms, agreed with the SAS staff and could have vetoed the trip. "But I was also getting my ass beaten," he later said. "You should have enjoyed the experience of Bobby Kennedy rampant on your back." Helms agreed to let FitzGerald meet with Cubela.[1400]

The CIA probably suspected Cubela was a double agent and was using him to justify a second invasion of Cuba. After the JFK assassination, it would appear that Castro had penetrated the plan to assassinate him, and he got Kennedy first, just as he said he would do in Brazil.

On October 10, an FBI informant in Miami reported that the CIA had been meeting with "a Cuban official" identified as Cubela, and he knew the date and location of one of the meetings. Castro's agents had penetrated the exile community, so he probably knew what was happening. Jose Aleman would also tell the FBI that Santo Trafficante was working for Castro.[1401]

Meanwhile, the sabotage raids continued. CIA documents show that on September 30, U.S.-backed exiles blew up the Marabi, a Cuban lumber mill, and three weeks later, the exiles blew up two Cuban patrol boats and two oil storage tanks. In retaliation, one week before Kennedy's assassination, Cuba executed thirteen Cubans accused of spying for the CIA.[1402]

As late as November 12, the last memo declassified from the Cuban Contingency planning showed the subcommittee was still working on "the preparation of contingency plans to counter possible actions by Castro," which included the attempted "assassination of American officials." Declassified files show that Robert Kennedy was to meet with coup leaders Harry Williams and Artime in Washington on November 17, 1963, the day before JFK was to give a speech with a cryptic message to let Almeida know his administration was backing the coup. Around the same time, Khrushchev publicly warned the "US that [an] attack on Cuba will lead to war."[1403]

The warnings from Castro and Khrushchev must have alleviated any concerns that the CIA and the Skorzeny Madrid group may have had about killing JFK to prevent the second invasion of Cuba from occurring. It was the only way to avoid World War III.

The meeting in Paris between Cubela and FitzGerald took place on October 29, just four days before the coup in Vietnam, and the same day that the Army Chief of Staff, General Wheeler, sent Robert McNamara an updated draft of the "State-Defense Contingency Plan for a coup in Cuba." Nestor Sanchez served as interpreter, and according to the CIA's Inspector General Report, "FitzGerald will present self as personal representative of

455

Robert F. Kennedy who traveled Paris for specific purpose meeting Cubela and giving him assurances of full U.S. support if there is [a] change of the present government in Cuba." Sanchez's report said FitzGerald told Cubela that U.S. support "will be forthcoming only after a real coup has been affected and the group involved is in a position to request U.S.....recognition and support." It was precisely how the U.S. Government went about overthrowing leaders they wanted out. Cubela told FitzGerald that assassinating Castro was all they needed for regime change in Cuba, which was all the CIA expected of him.

Incredibly, the CIA had chosen to have a senior officer meet with a questionable operative without a cutout to maintain plausible deniability. Furthermore, Robert Kennedy's Cuban coup operation did not include the CIA as a major player, so for the Agency to meet with Cubela and say they were speaking for the Attorney General was unconscionable. As Peter Dale Scott wrote in *Deep Politics*, "From this point on the AMLASH initiative had the look of an anti-Kennedy provocation. One thing was clear: Stevenson was right when he told me back in September that 'the CIA is in charge of Cuba'; or, anyway, acted as if it thought it was, and to hell with the President it was pledged to serve."[1404]

***

As the December date for the invasion of Cuba approached, Castro's Army Commander Juan Almeida started to get cold feet about betraying the revolution. He contacted Robert Kennedy's man, Harry Williams, because, like Cubela, he wanted JFK's assurance that the President would fully support the coup once it began. He did not want another Bay of Pigs fiasco. So, on November 18 in Miami, JFK delivered a speech with several lines specifically written to reassure Almeida that his administration supported the coup. A 1963 CIA report uncovered by Congressional investigators years later confirmed that "the CIA intended President Kennedy's speech to serve as a signal to dissident elements in Cuba that the US would support a coup." JFK specifically chose the words for "dissident elements in the Cuban Armed Forces [who] must have solemn assurances from high-level US spokesmen, especially the President, that the United States will exert its decisive influence during and immediately after the coup."[1405]

Meanwhile, on November 19, just three days before the JFK assassination, Cubela again demanded proof that Washington was backing him, or the deal was off, and he would return to Cuba. On that same day, exile leader Tony Varona received a phone call from fellow exile Erneido Oliva. He told Varona to go immediately to Washington to attend a meeting with

Bobby Kennedy. In Havana, the CIA advised AM/TRUNK infiltrators within Castro's army to monitor the Voice of America radio network on the coming night for an important message that would "inspire the rebel army to unite and rise in a coup against Fidel." The broadcast would also "carry two major guarantees from the U.S. Government."[1406]

The next day, Sanchez told Cubela that the meeting with FitzGerald would take place on November 22. He would receive a ballpoint pen inserted with a hypodermic needle loaded with a poison called Black Leaf 40, and a cache of arms, including high-powered rifles with scopes, would be delivered to him in Cuba.[1407]

On November 22, Robert Kennedy arranged for Harry Williams to meet with a group of CIA officials for final planning for the Almeida coup. Williams was to be secretly flown to Guantanamo the next day, where he would meet with Almeida and await the coup scheduled to begin on December 1. Meanwhile, also on the 22nd, McCone sent a memo to Ted Shackley confirming that the "general uprising scheduled for December 1" was "planned as [a] result of [the] Mi[litary] Service Act" because "in [the] opinion of" the coup "leaders [it] would tremendously" impact the "clandestine movement in Cuba." The CIA did not give the memo to the Warren Commission. It was declassified in 1993.[1408]

On the afternoon of November 22, after JFK was pronounced dead, Robert Kennedy called Harry Williams and asked him to pass the phone to Haynes Johnson. "Robert Kennedy was utterly in control of his emotions when he came on the line," Johnson later recalled, "and sounded almost studiously brisk as he said, 'One of your [Cuban] boys did it.'"[1409]

***

In the days immediately after the assassination, Secretary of State Dean Rusk signed off on a joint Defense Department-State Department contingency plan for the invasion of Cuba. The Defense Department had revised the plan numerous times throughout 1963 and finalized it in late October. Both departments agreed not to submit the contingency plan to President Johnson. Lieutenant Colonel Alexander Haig then rushed the plan to Secretary of the Army Cyrus Vance and McNamara for each man's approval.

Before the Rockefeller Commission in 1975, John McCone talked about what would have happened if they knew Castro was involved in the assassination. "The indignation of this country would have been so great that the Marines would have taken over Cuba..." It begs the question, how much more evidence did they need? As mentioned in the Introduction, it was simple enough to fabricate a false narrative around an Oswald/Castro connection to justify an invasion of Cuba after Kennedy's assassination. So why wasn't it done?[1410]

If Bobby Kennedy's plan to assassinate Castro, simultaneous with a military revolt led by Almeida, was a catalyst to justify an invasion of Cuba with the U.S. military after the Almeida government asked for help, shouldn't the assassination of John F. Kennedy have accomplished the same thing? Of course, it should have. In fact, the murder of a U.S. President was even more reason to invade Cuba to avenge his death, and the evidence immediately after the assassination looked like JFK's murder was Cuban retaliation for the attempts on Castro's life. That the U.S. military did not invade Cuba is more convincing that a conspiracy assassinated JFK than if the full might of the U.S. Government had forcibly overthrown Castro. Something spooked the Pentagon and compelled them to stand down.

***

A lot was going on at the time of the JFK assassination. Cubela was looking to kill Castro; Almeida claimed he could organize a military coup; the U.S. military was planning a significant invasion of Cuba; Robert Kennedy's hand-picked Cuban exiles ran sabotage raids against Cuba and believed they would be the new government once Castro was gone; private entities in the U.S were sponsoring other Cuban exile groups; the military was supporting Alpha 66 and other violent groups to keep the pressure on; there seemed to be two Lee Harvey Oswald's in Mexico City; and it appeared part of the plan was to justify an invasion of Cuba by making it appear Castro was behind the JFK assassination. To understand fully what was happening, we must also add the French connection to the evidence already discussed.

***

Algeria became a French military colony in 1834 and officially part of France in 1848. Algerians fought for France during World War II. After the war, when a desire for self-determination began to take hold in third-world countries, Algeria wanted its freedom. Hostilities began on November 1, 1954, with attacks on various French military and civilian targets, as bombs detonated simultaneously in numerous Algerian cities. The official French response was that Algeria would remain part of France.

"We have not come here to defend colonialism," declared Radio-Bigeard on the military's radio station. "We have nothing in common with the rich clons [short for colonists, the European population in Algeria] who exploit the Muslims. We are the defenders of liberty and...*a new order.*".[1411] (Author's italics).

A new world order was what the French military wanted. In 1960, during the Barricades Trial, which had to do with the military's attempt to take control of Algiers without the approval of the French government, Colonel Antoine Argoud explained that the military wanted "to halt the decadence of the West and the march of Communism. That is our duty, the real duty of the army. That is why we must win the war in Algeria."[1412] Like their counterparts in the United States, the Nazis in Madrid, and Lee Harvey Oswald, the French military wanted a new world order based upon a more socially conscious form of capitalism and the elimination of communism.

Oswald Mosley was England's leading Fascist and Nazi supporter prior to and during World War II. His beliefs grew stronger after the war as his notoriety among international fascist circles grew. He believed that an alliance of Fascist governments would result in world peace and banish both communism and capitalism from the face of the earth. Mosley wrote in 1948 that a united Europe would "insure [sic] that Europeans shall never be slaves either of West or East; either of finance or of bolshevism. We shall neither be bought by Wall Street nor conquered by the Kremlin." In addition, Mosley said it would be necessary to maintain African colonies to serve the needs of Europeans, which was precisely what the OAS was fighting to preserve a decade later.[1413]

As previously mentioned, Oswald believed there were "two world systems, one twisted beyond recognition (communism)...the other decadent and dying (capitalism)." A democratic system "would combine the better qualities of the two upon an American foundation." After the final "conflict between the two world systems leaves the country without defense or foundation of government..." the survivors would "seek an alternative to those systems which have brought them misery."

Oswald's philosophy mirrored the words of Argoud and Mosley. Lee Oswald and Argoud both used the term decadent to describe the United States. They looked to initiate a war between the U.S. and the Soviet Union that would lead to a new world order based on the better parts of each political system.

Meanwhile, Mosley, along with Otto Skorzeny, was one of the leaders behind the Gladio stay-behind army network. He placed great importance on international links and arranged gatherings of European Fascists, including Nazis Hans-Ulrich Rudel and Skorzeny. Mosley also worked for a Spanish travel agency associated with Aginter Press, a Gladio unit, and personally organized Skorzeny's travel.[1414] The travel agency endeavor is of interest, considering Skorzeny's wife Ilse, who a CIA informant described as a "very attractive and highly intelligent woman," was in touch with several intelligence services, most notably in France, and invested in tourism in the Bahama Islands.[1415]

Rudel is also a person of interest. Stephen Dorril wrote in *Blackshirt: Sir Oswald Mosley and British Fascism*: "At the end of May 1951...Fascist and neo-Nazi groups from across Europe assembled in Malmo, Sweden, to found a new international... movement affiliated to the 'Malmo International,' and a secretariate was set up in Rome. Activists tried to establish national branches for their pan-European umbrella movement. *The New York Times* claimed that one of its main objectives was "to penetrate [the] United States and British democratic organizations by taking advantage of the rising tide of anti-communism." They established contacts with forty extremist organizations in Europe and a coordinating body for twenty neo-Nazi groups under the leadership of Rudel.[1416]

Rudel, who was part of the international Fascist movement, shared a similar sentiment. As described in Chapter Sixteen, a State Department report stated that Rudel "is primarily interested in the reconstitution of an independent Germany with its own army separate from a Western Army... this can be accomplished by German action with international Fascist support..." There was another State Department report that described how in Germany, there were "plans for an "International Waffen-SS," composed of Nazi veterans scattered throughout the world, presumably were outlined before the last days of the war.... [by] *Otto SKORZENY*, with Gauleiters KAUFMAN."[1417]

Stephen Dorril continued that "MAC [Movement d'Action Civique, a far-right movement in Belgium in the 1960s] linked to Mosley's Union Movement which...had launched the Young Britain Movement...Other JE [Jeune Europe, Young Europe] linked groups included Mouvement Jeune Nation and ultras in Spain and Portugal. Thiriart [founder of MAC] forged connections with Skorzeny, Rudel, and to Jean-Marie Le Pen's pro-Algerie Francaise movement in France, which made MAC into a 'principal-agent' of the OAS in Belgium."[1418]

Regarding the situation in Algeria, many Nazis naturally supported the traditional European pro-colonialism "white" France against its unruly natives. In addition, twenty-thousand Wehrmacht and Waffen SS veterans volunteered for the French Foreign Legion to earn money, look for adventure, and fight the "war of the white race" in Algeria. So, early in the 1950s, there was a connection between France, Nazis, European Monarchists, and American Fascists in Algeria. This alliance would continue after de Gaulle granted Algeria independence, with the OAS replacing the French government in this alliance.[1419]

There were similarities between the new world order philosophies that the Nazis in Madrid, the rebellious OAS French military, and Lee Harvey Oswald espoused. It raises the question: Was the assassination of JFK originally supposed to be the catalyst to bring about a confrontation between the world's two superpowers, but something changed? Was Oswald, an American "Communist" who had previously "defected" to Russia, willingly prepared to take the blame for assassinating JFK, which was the spark to initiate World War III?

When de Gaulle called for "an emancipated Algeria" in November 1960, French General Raoul Salan responded that "the time for evasions is over." When de Gaulle visited Algeria in December, four unsuccessful plots to assassinate him occurred, and the military was ready to revolt. In March 1961, posters bearing the initials OAS (Organisation Armee Secrete) appeared on the walls of Algiers for the first time, followed by multiple bombings and at least one plan to assassinate de Gaulle with a telescopic rifle. The OAS reign of terror had begun.[1420]

Ruthless killers filled their ranks. Many were Legionnaires who were drug dealers, bank robbers, and petty criminals when not serving France. As described in *Age of the Guerilla*, the OAS "had plenty of men to use, mainly deserters who were ready to assassinate for a price…plastic bombs exploded nightly in Algiers. Arabs were killed indiscriminately, simply to frighten the Muslim population into submission." Their terror did not occur in Algeria alone. Though numbering only 600 in metropolitan France, after 1961, the OAS was joined by 800,000 Algerian French that poured into the country.[1421]

The OAS was in a civil war with France and engaged in political assassinations and bombings that left thousands of civilians dead. In October 1961, the government imposed a curfew on Muslim Algerians living in and around Paris. On October 17, nearly 30,000 Algerians took to the streets to peacefully demonstrate their support for independence. Maurice Papon, the head of the Paris police, ordered his men to attack the demonstrators. Thousands were injured, and the police detained 14,000 Muslims. There was no official death toll, but witnesses estimated the police shot and killed around 400 Algerians. The police threw some into the Seine River. It was

461

a massacre and proved that many in France, including the police, did not support Algerian independence.[1422]

Independence came on July 5, 1962, but it did not stop the assassination attempts against de Gaulle or the terrorism the OAS engaged in. Eventually, the OSS became part of a larger anti-Communist, Monarchist movement to save Europe, which was how the likes of Souetre and General Salan became aligned with the Fascist Nazi group in Madrid that wanted the same thing. In *A Savage War For Peace,* author Alistair Horne writes that in Madrid, Salan "set up court at the Hotel Princesa, a veritable colony for exiled right-wingers – Belgian Rexists, Argentinian [sic] Peronists, French Patainists and former collabos... One of Salan's first contacts had been Otto Skorzeny."[1423] Madrid was where like-minded, violence-prone individuals and groups came together to create a new world order by any means possible.

***

The CIA financed OAS through its front companies like PERMINDEX and the Centro Mondiale Comerciale, which involved Clay Shaw and his New Orleans associates, who were all familiar with Lee Harvey Oswald. President Kennedy had been a strong supporter of Algerian independence since his Senate days, which was one more reason to make him an enemy of the old guard in Europe.

As described in Chapter Sixteen, Philippe de Vosjoli, France's liaison with CIA counterintelligence, was close to James Angleton. Although de Vosjoli technically worked for France, assignments came to him directly from the CIA. In August 1962, he traveled to Cuba at the request of Allen Dulles to investigate missiles the Soviet Union was secretly delivering there. "What I have learned," he wrote, "I passed on to Paris and shared with the American intelligence authorities." James Angleton's biographer, Tom Mangold, was told by Walt Elder, a special assistant to John McCone at the CIA, that "de Vosjoli was recruited and worked for us. It was a CI (Counterintelligence) operation run by Angleton..." De Vosjoli remained at his post at the French Embassy, working for de Gaulle while simultaneously providing the CIA with classified information. CIA officer Newton ("Scotty") Miler confirmed Walt Elder's statements. "De Vosjoli was Jim's [Angleton's] operation... with the knowledge of the DCI."

De Vosjoli resigned from the SDECE on October 18, 1963, because France asked him to spy against the U.S. "I am probably the only French intelligence officer in history to defect to the United States," de Vosjoli said. De Gaulle denounced him as a "defector to the CIA."[1424]

As described in *Coup in Dallas*, in his 1970 memoir, *LAMIA*, de Vosjoli wrote: "Solving political difficulties [in the early 1960s] by assassination had become a habit in Paris..." He continued that "an hour after the assassination of President Kennedy, I received a cable from SDECE ordering me to fly at once to Paris...That night, a very dear friend called me from Paris with a serious warning, 'You are now in a free country. The minute you are sent back to France, you will no longer be free. Orders have been given to silence you by any means.'"[1425]

De Vosjoli went to Mexico, where he spent several months with Frank Brandsetter at a resort in Acapulco. As previously discussed, Brandsetter ran the Havana Hilton for Santo Trafficante before Castro took over and was involved in the 1959 anti-Castro coup run out of the U.S. Embassy in Havana that involved June Cobb, David Phillips, David Morales, Frank Sturgis, Henry Hecksher, and others. He is in Lafitte's financial ledger along with Conrad Hilton, James Angleton, and ex-Generals Walker and del Valle. De Vosjoli is mentioned twice in Lafitte's datebook.

As the authors of *Coup in Dallas* continued, "Lafitte's record in the spring of 1963 indicated that he knew Vosjoli was, at the very least, acquainted with actors that he...was directing, including Thomas Eli Davis and wife Carolyn." A connection to Davis and his wife leads to Victor Oswald, Thomas Proctor, Loran Hall, June Cobb, James Angleton, Tracy Barnes, Allen Dulles, the Knights of Malta, Otto Skozeny, other ex-Nazis, Charles Willoughby, the right-wing activities run out of Madrid, Texas oilmen like Clint Murchison, and William Pawley. It was the heart of the international right-wing movement and ground zero for the JFK assassination conspirators.

The pieces slowly come into focus. Lucien Conein, who was at the center of the coup that resulted in the assassination of the Diem brothers in Vietnam on November 2, 1963, knew Otto Skorzeny well. Their relationship began with La Cagoule, the French Resistance. It led to Guerin-Serac, the poster child for European assassination and terrorism in the early 1960s, who envisioned a Christian-Fascist New World Order. Guerin-Serac wrote that "two forms of terrorism can provoke [the breakdown of the state]: blind terrorism (committing massacres indiscriminately which cause a large number of victims), and selective terrorism (eliminate chosen persons)..." More importantly, he believed "this destruction of the state must be carried out under the cover of 'communist activities,' which clearly explains why using Lee Oswald as a patsy was such an integral part of the JFK assassination plot.[1426]

463

Guerin-Serac spent his life dedicated to promoting the advancement of fascism that combined the divinity of the Roman church with the United States and Europe as a successor to the Holy Roman Empire, which explains the coming together of many ex-Nazis like Skorzeny with leading members of the CIA and other American Fascists. Guerin-Serac also belonged to a veteran clan of French officers who served in the Indochina, Korean, and Algerian struggles and was a member of the elite troop of the 1éme Demi-Brigade Parachutiste du Choc, which worked with the SDECE. His connection to French Intelligence would be the key to his becoming a founding member of the OAS.[1427]

Not surprisingly, Jean Souetre, the French OAS assassin who was in Dallas on November 22, 1963, was part of this group and met with CIA and OAS representatives in Lisbon, Portugal, on May 23, 1963. It was around the time that Lafitte mentioned de Vosjoli in his datebook. Souetre later told the U.S. State Department's Intelligence Bureau that "he intended to provide some information about the activities of [the OAS] which would be of interest to the U.S." What that was, he did not say, but the JFK assassination plot was just beginning, and considering the OAS's preoccupation with assassination, one can assume it was related to that. In 1980, Dick Russell spoke to Mike Ewing, an investigator for the HSCA. Ewing told him that Jean Souetre "was connected with people involved with murders or political assassinations in Europe," such as QJ/WIN, WI/ROGUE, which leads us to William Harvey's attempt to find Corsican assassins in Europe for ZR/RIFLE.[1428]

A June 25, 1963, CIA file on Souetre said he offered them a "list of the Communist penetrations of the French government" and expressed the OAS's belief "that the de Gaulle government was aiding the Communist takeover by seeking a rapprochement with the USSR." De Gaulle "was an old man [who] could easily meet with an accident," Souetre said, and the OAS was "prepared to counter a Communist plot at any time." Even to "the expedient of preventing the [next French] election from taking place." Soviet defector Golitsin told Angleton in 1963 that the KGB had penetrated the SDECE with a spy ring of some twelve agents, and more KGB agents were in the top echelons of the French government. The result was Angleton's recruitment of Vosjoli.[1429]

There was a core of hardened French, German, and American intelligence veterans whose primary goal was to prevent the spread of communism. These men and women worked together for years and did not get caught up in local hostilities like Cuba, a country that meant nothing in the big international picture. They did not consider Cuba an essential pawn in the struggle for world dominance. Considering that 60 years later, Cuba has caused few problems for the United States, one would have to say they were right. Losing West Berlin was a different story, for it could have led to attempted Soviet territorial expansion and World War III. The people who killed Kennedy were more interested in creating a new world order based on a right-wing, authoritarian, anti-Communist, Nazi sans-Hitler way of life. President Kennedy and the Omega Plan/AMWORLD stood in their way.

Chapter Twenty-Six

Countdown To Assassination

After leaving Mexico City, one would have expected Lee Harvey Oswald to return to New Orleans to continue his public support of the FPCC. However, he would never return to the Big Easy again. Nor would he ever again publicly support Cuba as he had previously done. Radio debates and street demonstrations designed to draw attention to himself were over. The Oswald who graced the streets of New Orleans was gone forever. He had less than two months to live when he arrived in Dallas on October 3. A new Oswald was about to emerge who was content to maintain a low profile, for there was no reason to resurrect the old one. The work done in New Orleans and Mexico City was sufficient to paint him as a Communist supporter of Fidel Castro after the assassination of JFK.

Arriving in Dallas, Oswald first went to the Texas Unemployment Commission to look for a job. It was out of character, considering Oswald had been fired from Reilly in July and had made no effort to find work until now. After the assassination, Dallas Western Union employees C.A. Hamblen and Aubrey Lewis recalled that "Oswald was a customer who had collected money orders several times….one of the money orders had been delivered to the YMCA and that the customer had identified himself with a Navy ID card and a library card." Lewis remembered a Latin individual accompanied him. [1430]

Oswald spent his first night at the local YMCA without telling his wife he was in town. The following day, he visited the employment agency JOB-CO and applied for work at Padgett Printing Corporation as a typesetter. The plant superintendent who interviewed him said he was "well dressed and neat" and "made a favorable impression." Still, he turned Oswald down after calling his former employer, Jaggars-Chiles-Stovall. The notation at the bottom of his job application read: "Bob Stovall does not recommend this man. He was released because of his record as a troublemaker. Has communistic tendencies."[1431]

Eventually, Oswald telephoned his wife, who was still living with Ruth Paine. He spent the weekend at the Paine home, and even though he did not yet have a job, on Monday, he rented an apartment from Mary Bledsoe in the Oak Cliff section of Dallas for $7 per week. She would state that Oswald left the rooming house at 9:00 A.M. each morning and returned at 1:30 P.M.

Oswald applied for a job at Burton-Dixie on a referral from the Texas Employment Commission, but they also turned him down. The Weiner Lumber Company rejected him because Sam Weiner did not believe he had received an honorable discharge from the Marine Corps. Finding a job was hard for the one-time defector to the Soviet Union.

Perhaps it was a coincidence, but on the day that Oswald arrived in Dallas, FBI agent James Hosty received a report from the New Orleans FBI that Oswald and his wife had left their city. A woman who could speak Russian had picked up Marina and her 2-year-old child in a station wagon with Texas license plates.[1432]

By week's end, Mrs. Bledsoe told Oswald to leave. Against her wishes, he was keeping food in her refrigerator, and he had spoken to Marina on the phone in Russian. As Bledsoe told a friend, "I don't like anybody talking in a foreign language."[1433]

In early October, a high school teacher named Lovell Penn was startled by the sound of a high-powered rifle from the cow pasture behind her house. She confronted the three men who had fired the gun, one of whom was Latin. They departed after she threatened to call the police, but they left an ejected cartridge behind. The FBI determined it was for a 6.5 caliber Mannlicher Carcano, the same as Oswald's rifle, but it had not been fired from Oswald's gun. That ended the FBI's interest, even though Mrs. Penn said one of the men was Oswald.[1434]

Around the same time, Ruth Paine's estranged husband, Michael, took an interest in Oswald and brought him to an ACLU meeting. Oswald wrote to *The Worker*: "Through a friend, I have been introduced into the American Civil Liberties Union Local chapter...The first meeting I attended was on October 5, a film was shown and afterwards, a very critical discussion of the ultra-right in Dallas."[1435]

***

Roscoe White began working for the Dallas Police Department as an apprentice policeman on October 7. His wife Geneva worked for Jack Ruby as a hostess at the Carousel Club. Beverly Oliver, a friend of the couple, claimed to have seen Roscoe on the Grassy Knoll at the time of the assassination. As described in Chapter Twelve, White may have something to do with the backyard photos taken of Oswald. It all makes Roscoe a person of interest.

Cables found among Roscoe's possessions after the assassination were addressed to MANDARIN, Roscoe's code name. They point to a Naval Intelligence connection. The first cable, sent in February 1963, stated, in part, "The next assignment is to eliminate a National Security threat to world peace...Destination will be Houston, Austin or Dallas."[1436]

The second cable was in September: "Dallas destination chosen. Your place hidden within the department...Continue as planned." The third cable was in December and read in part: "Stay within department, witness have eyes, ears and mouths...Stay as planned, wait for further orders."

The cables potentially provide crucial information when considered in the context of what else we know. The first cable in February described that they intended to eliminate a threat to world peace. It was clearly a reference to President Kennedy, for this was around the time that JFK instructed Bobby to lead the AMWORLD operation, which involved a second invasion of Cuba. The September cable says the JFK assassination was to take place in Dallas, which was the month Richard Nagell told Oswald the conspirators were setting him up as the designated patsy. A concerned Oswald went to Mexico City, and according to Lafitte's datebook, the conspirators began to reconsider if they should use Oswald because he had potentially become a liability. The October 6 entry, written three days after Oswald's return to Dallas, reads: "Oswald-Issue (!) with Caretaker." The final Mandarin cable written after the assassination tells Roscoe to stay at the police department because there were problems that needed to be addressed.

There was one other person at the time who was nicknamed Mandarin – French OAS chief, General Raoul Salan. According to author Alistair Horne in *A Savage War of Peace*, Salan was called Mandarin because of his service in Indochina, where he had exploited the drug traffic to the benefit of French Intelligence. Which meant he must have had a connection to the Union Corse. As described in the previous chapter, Salan was living in exile in Madrid. He had arrived in the Spanish capital in November 1960, just a few months before the OAS would rear its ugly head for the first time. One of Salan's first contacts in Madrid was Otto Skorzeny.[1437]

The references to Madrid and Otto Skorzeny placed Salan at the center of the international Fascist, Monarchist, and anti-communist community. It explains how the OAS became part of the JFK assassination plot. Furthermore, as described in *The Man Who Knew Too Much*, Dick Russell received an anonymous letter in 1975 from an American who claimed the Chinese had brainwashed him. The letter referenced "Mandarin Chinese." Possibly, this was a cryptic reference to Salan and Roscoe White. The writer also included a ten-year-old attachment with his letter, which stated that a German named TSCHEPPE-WEIDENBACH "MASTERMINDED THE ASSASSINATION WITH THE APPROVAL. 'THE' MAN WHO COULD DO NO WRONG IN AMERICA HISTORY?"

Russell correctly determined that Weidenbach is Charles Willoughby, but the man who could do no wrong remains a mystery. I have narrowed it down to either Allen Dulles or Douglas MacArthur. Irrefutable proof remains elusive, but I am inclined to believe the reference was to MacArthur. Regardless, the attachment also contained the paragraph: "THE TITLE 'MANCHURIAN CANDIDATE' COMES OUT LINKED TO THE WORD 'BIBLE' AND SOMETHING NAMED 'WHITE.'" The connection to the word "Bible" is unknown, but considering the writer's reference to Mandarin, could the mention of "White" be a reference to Roscoe White?

Interestingly, the Roscoe White documents referred to three shooters named Mandarin, Saul, and Lebanon. We know that Saul was the first king of Israel and has a biblical connection. Perhaps it applies to Christian David since David was the second king of Israel. Meanwhile, Lebanon could be relevant because the word means "white" when transmitted from the Semitic root Lbn. And Mandarin connects to Raoul Salan, which means this shooter was part of the OAS.

Once again, Lafitte's datebook may provide the answer. The April 7 entry refers to the backyard photos and reads: "Walker – Lee and pictures – Planned soon – Can He Do It? Won't." The entry for the following day, on April 8, two days before the Walker shooting attempt, the datebook mentions Salan: "Hal du Berrier (Salan R)." Is it a coincidence that the name Salan, who shared the codename Mandarin with Roscoe White, appears in the datebook the day after Lafitte references the backyard photos, which Roscoe White may have had something to do with? Hilaire du Berrier was an American intelligence agent who was an ultra-right anti-Communist and European Monarchist. He served the Axis during World War II and wrote articles for the John Birch Society.

Then, on April 12, the datebook reads: "Congress meet. – Willoughby soldier kill squads, Rene will meet with Crichton – Dallas." So, Charles Willoughby, aka Tscheppe-Weidenbach, who, according to the letter, masterminded the JFK assassination with the approval of Allen Dulles or General MacArthur, is listed in the datebook at the same time as Raoul Salan and Roscoe White, along with a reference to "kill squads." Was this all a coincidence or a cryptic attempt to tie Salan, Skorzeny, White, Willoughby, and kill squads together in relation to Oswald at the time of the Walker shooting?

***

From the moment Oswald returned to the United States, by all appearances, he had a working relationship with the FBI, and this was still true after his return to Dallas from Mexico City. On October 9, the Bureau canceled their "WANTED NOTICE CARD" on Oswald, which meant from that point forward, he would not be detained or placed under surveillance by the FBI or Secret Service, which included during President Kennedy's visit to Dallas. It happened the day before the FBI received the cable from the CIA stating: "On 1 October 1963, a reliable and sensitive source in Mexico reported that an American male, who identified himself as Lee Oswald, contacted the Soviet Embassy in Mexico City... It is believed that Oswald may be identical to Lee Henry Oswald, born on 18 October 1939 in New Orleans, Louisiana, a former US Marine who defected to the Soviet Union in October 1959..."

The Wanted Notice Card had been active since November 10, 1959, shortly after Oswald relinquished his passport at the U.S. Embassy in Moscow, and after that, the FBI monitored his movements. They continued to do so after October 9, 1963, so why was the card discontinued? A logical explanation is that J. Edgar Hoover knew the assassination was going to take place, or at the very least, that something unexplainable had occurred in Mexico City, and he wanted it on record that Oswald was not on their radar. Since it happened the day before the FBI received the CIA cable, it means the FBI was following Oswald while he was in Mexico City, which points toward Willaim Gaudet, who had been following Oswald in New Orleans. The Lafitte datebook entry for September 22, two days before Oswald left New Orleans, reads: "Oswald-Mexico City Gaudet?"[1438]

After the assassination, a Dallas citizen recalled seeing a man "identical" to Oswald at an October 13 meeting of the DRE. General Walker was in attendance, as was Oswald. He wrote he had gone to "a [sic] ultra-right meeting headed by Gen. Edwin A. Walker...." If Silvia Odio was also in attendance, or at least aware that Oswald was associated with the DRE in Dallas, it explains why she fainted upon hearing of the assassination.[1439]

On Monday, October 14, Oswald rented a room at 1026 North Beckley under the name O.H. Lee. It was the first time he used an alias when renting a place to live, a sign he wanted to make it difficult for authorities to locate him. Housekeeper Earlene Roberts said Oswald kept to himself. She told the Warren Commission that he only watched television "if someone in the other rooms had it on…he would come and stand at the back of the couch – not over 5 minutes and go to his room and shut the door and never say a word …." It was typical behavior for Oswald and reminiscent of the Minutemen magazine, *On Target,* which counseled readers to blend into the surroundings, remain "anonymous," and avoid being called a "fear monger [or] racist." "Revolutionary upheaval could arrive at any time, so it was important not to bind yourself to one area…you can leave a rented house faster than one you own…." *On Target* instructed readers to find a job that did not require too much responsibility and would not take up too much free time. Live frugally, to do so "might mean the difference between life and death." It described Oswald's life from the spring of 1963 until the day he died and added to the possibility that he belonged to the Minutemen.[1440]

According to the manager of the garage across the street from Oswald's apartment, he made at least two long-distance phone calls from the pay phone there. Each time, Oswald asked the garage manager for change to make the call.[1441]

Officially, Oswald happened upon this apartment by chance, but someone may have directed him there. Earlene Roberts had a younger sister named Bertha Cheek, who met with Jack Ruby at the Carousel Club for several hours four nights prior to the assassination. Ruby had Bertha's phone number written on a slip of paper in his possession after killing Oswald, which was perhaps a clue for the police, who ignored it. Cheek was also the landlady of Harry Olsen, a Dallas police officer who dated Kathy Kay, a stripper at the Carousel Club. Olsen was one of the few people in America who couldn't recall where he was at the time of the Kennedy assassination, and Olsen, Kay, and Ruby had a 2 to 3-hour-long meeting in the parking lot of Simon's Garage around 1:00 to 2:00 A.M. in the early morning hours of November 23. Kay never returned to the Carousel Club after the assassination, and within a week, she left Dallas for Oklahoma City. Tom Palmer, a Dallas union official, testified, "She was afraid... and wanted to get out of town." Olsen was seriously injured in a car crash on December 7, about two weeks after the assassination, when his car veered off the road and struck a telephone pole. He spent two weeks in a hospital, and shortly after that, he and Kay moved to California. There is good reason to think Olsen and Kay knew something about the assassination or at least learned something from their discussion with Ruby that frightened them into leaving town.[1442]

Bertha Cheek had a young boyfriend named Wilburn Waldon Litchfield, who was at her house when the FBI knocked five days after the assassination. On December 2, Litchfield contacted the FBI to report that in the first two weeks of November, he had seen a man closely resembling Oswald at the Carousel Club. Ruby acknowledged that Litchfield had been in his club but that he had seen someone else, not Oswald.

County records showed that Bertha acquired more than a dozen apartment buildings in 1963, and she moved to an upscale Park Cities address in Dallas. "We went as far as we could with some of these questions at the time [in the form of tenant records]," said Burt Griffin of the Warren Commission, "but we weren't conducting the investigation. That was being done by the FBI." She also failed to tell Griffin about her relationship with Olsen.[1443]

By 1968, Bertha realized a dramatic increase in wealth and purchased a Dallas hotel for more than $900,000. Ruby was involved in gunrunning in 1963, so maybe Bertha was as well. Perhaps it was Oswald's involvement with Cuban exiles in Dallas familiar with Cheek that led him to the boardinghouse with an available room.[1444]

It is also odd that even after she saw Oswald's picture on television, housekeeper Earlene Roberts never called the police, so they did not search his room until 4:30 or 5:00 P.M. There is also a question as to how the police learned Oswald lived there since he had told no one. Police Officers Adamcik, Rose, and Stovall said Captain Fritz dispatched them to Ruth Paine's home at 2:30 P.M., and they waited 35-40 minutes for the deputy sheriffs to arrive since Irving was outside their jurisdiction. Harry Weatherford, Buddy Walthers, and J. L. Oxford were the deputy sheriffs, and they said Ruth gave them Oswald's phone number, which was how they came up with the Beckley St. address. However, according to Captain Will Fritz's Warren Commission testimony, "just before I started to talk to him [Oswald, around 2:00 P.M.], some officer told me outside of my office that he had a room on Beckley." That indicates someone was feeding the Dallas police department information about Oswald, perhaps Roscoe White.

On October 14, General Walker wrote a letter to J. Evetts Haley, a wealthy Texas rancher with ties to the Hunt family and other radicals like Joseph Milteer, Dan Smoot, and Robert Surrey. He also had a working relationship with General Pedro del Valle dating back to 1956.

"We started a good one," Walker wrote Haley. "10,000 fliers going all over Dallas. [I] hope you can come in for it. There may be some fun on the 24th...Our mutual friend Sarah Hughes [who swore in LBJ on Air Force One] is sponsoring U.N. week and Adlai [Stevenson]." Walker was joking when he called Sarah Hughes a friend.[1445]

Also, on the 14th, Ruth Paine mentioned to a neighbor that Lee was having trouble finding work. Linnie Mae Randle said there were jobs available where her brother Wesley Frazier worked. The next day, a presumptuous Ruth called Superintendent Roy Truly on Oswald's behalf, which was how he obtained a job at the Texas School Book Depository. Oswald gave Ruth's address and phone number as his own on his job application, making it impossible for anyone to find him, as the Minutemen recommended.[1446]

Later that day, Robert Adams of the Texas Employment Commission called Ruth Paine's home about a potential job at Trans-Texas Airways that paid $310 per month, much more than Oswald would earn at the TSBD. Ruth said she would tell Oswald, but she never did. Ruth initially testified to the Warren Commission that she did not know about the call but eventually relented. "I do recall some reference of that sort," Ruth said, "which fell through – that there was not that possibility," which was a lie. She wanted Oswald to take the job at the TSBD.[1447]

On October 15, confidential informant "T-2," who was familiar with Communist Party activities in New Orleans told the FBI he did not know Oswald or his wife or what they were involved in. The importance here is that the FBI was still making inquiries about Oswald in New Orleans three weeks after he had left for Mexico City.[1448]

Oswald began work at the Book Depository on October 16th. His twenty-fourth birthday was two days after that, which was why Wesley Frazier drove him to Ruth Paine's house after work. There was a celebration, which moved Lee to tears. Later, he and Marina watched two movies on television, *Suddenly* and *We Were Strangers*. The former starred Frank Sinatra as an unbalanced ex-serviceman hired to assassinate the President. The latter was about a revolution in Cuba where an assassination marked the beginning of the overthrow of the Machado dictatorship in 1933. It was interesting viewing, considering what Oswald was involved in.[1449]

Back in February, Oswald had met pro-Nazi Volkmar Schmidt at a dinner party hosted by Everett Glover, who was a roommate of Schmidt's. Schmidt was friends with de Mohrenchildt. On October 16, Volkmar and Glover's names appear in Lafitte's datebook. There was no reason for these two men to have reentered Oswald's life again eight months after they had parted ways except to help with Oswald in some capacity, who had become a problem. The next day, an entry says James Angleton called about a high-level meeting in Washington, followed by: "Lancelot – Go – OK – Oswald – Others." OK may have referred to Oklahoma, considering the inclusion of Volkmar and Glover in the entry the previous day. Apparently, there were still questions about Oswald being part of the plot approximately one month before the assassination.[1450]

***

Operation Lancelot may also have had something to do with Haiti. At the time of the assassination, George de Mohrenschildt was still there, associating with "foreign traders, gunrunners, Euro-trash... a veritable ship of fools." Port-au-Prince CIA station chief Joseph G. Benson appointed "Conrad V. Rubricius," a pseudonym, to spy on de Mohrenschildt. He reported directly to Desmond FitzGerald, who was busy with Rolando Cubela in Paris and his attempt to assassinate Castro prior to the second invasion of Cuba. The CIA's Joseph Dryer was part of this Haitian group. He found de Mohrenschildt distasteful and later told the HSCA that he reported all he knew about de Mohrenschildt to the CIA and Army Intelligence.

Sometimes de Mohrenschildt, his Haitian business associate Clemard Charles, and Dryer would meet at *Le Picardie*, a restaurant owned by a beautiful fortyish mulatto named Jacqueline Lancelot, who had CIA connections. Her importance is that Lafitte used the name Lancelot in his date-book, either as an acronym for the JFK assassination or a separate operation in Haiti related to Kennedy's murder.

De Mohrenschildt resided at the Hotel Oloffson, owned by a former New York stockbroker named Maurice de Young, who was part of the Caribbean Legion, whose primary goal was to "topple tyrants." The Legion was formed in 1948, one year after the CIA came into existence. Among its members were Fidel Castro and Che Guevera, as well as their nemesis Rolando Masferrer. According to a CIA document, they called the Legion a "clandestine and important instrument through which the 'democracies' are pursuing their 'anti-dictatorship' policy."

"If I were you," Lancelot told Dryer, "I would not be talking to that person...You wait and see. De Mohrenschildt is up to no good...There's something bad about him." After JFK's assassination, she told Dryer that a bank acquaintance told her that between $200,000 and $250,000 had been deposited in de Mohrenschildt's account in Port-au-Prince, drawn on a Bahamian bank. She also said, "You're going to find out that de Mohrenschildt had something to do with the Kennedy assassination...You're going to find that the Warren Report will have his name all over it." At the time, few people knew of his relationship with Oswald. The question is, how did a CIA asset in Haiti know about it?

It was not long before Lancelot drew Dryer into her intelligence network. She gave him the phone number of Philippe de Vosjoli, the French SDECE officer who had befriended James Angleton and other CIA bigwigs, as described in the previous chapter. De Vosjoli's name appears in the datebook on May 20 with Thomas and Carolyn Davis, Proctor, and Otto Skorzeny, and again on May 26 with Angleton, Frank Wisner, and L.O, who was probably not Oswald but Colonel Lawrence Orlov. It was from de Vosjoli that Lancelot learned of de Mohrenschildt's connection to the JFK assassination, and it was on de Vosjoli's behalf that Lancelot enlisted one of her many sources to monitor his bank account. According to Joan Mellon, "Lancelot was de Vosjoli's favorite, his most astute and reliable Haitian informant."

De Mohrenschildt's Haitian banker friend Clemard Charles enlisted Joe Dryer to contact people in Washington on his behalf. One was the Pentagon's Dorothy Matlack, Army Intelligence's chief liaison with the CIA, with whom de Mohrenschildt and Charles met, along with the Army's Sam Kail and Frank Brandsetter, prior to coming to Haiti. In Haiti, Dryer created a cadre of informants, including one-time CIA asset Jack Cogswell, who had reported to David Atlee Phillips when he served in Cuba. Among other things, Cogswell kept an eye on de Mohrenschildt for Dryer. The CIA and Military Intelligence would keep a watchful eye on de Mohrenschildt for the remainder of his life.[1451]

There was something about the activities happening in Haiti that suggested they were related to the JFK assassination. Thomas Davis and Loran Hall were looking to raise a mercenary army to allegedly overthrow Papa Doc, probably making it appear Castro's soldiers were responsible. Or, maybe they intended to attack Cuba from Haiti, hoping to instigate a response from Castro against Haiti in return. De Mohrenschildt may have been there as part of a plot to assassinate Papa Doc. The objective was to provide the U.S. military justification to launch an invasion of Cuba, and any of the above scenarios could have accomplished that.

***

On October 18, James Hosty interviewed Edith Shannon, Oswald's former neighbor on Mercedes Street in Fort Worth. She could not remember him, but her importance is that the FBI was still trying to track down Lee Oswald.[1452]

On October 22, in Metz, France, Army private first-class Eugene B. Dinkin wrote a letter to Robert Kennedy warning of an impending assassination attempt against the President. It was to "occur on November 28th, 1963; that if it were to succeed, [the] blame would then be placed upon a Communist or Negro, who would be designated the assassin; and believing that the conspiracy was being engineered by elements of the Military, I did speculate that a military coup might ensue..." Dinkin was a crypto operator with a high-security clearance. One of his duties was to break the code of telegrams that originated with the OAS in France. It explains how Dinkin learned about the plot to kill JFK, considering Jean Souetre of the OAS was in Dallas on November 22 and the possible involvement of Raoul Salan. An FBI report dated April 3, 1964, stated that "a conspiracy was in the making by the 'military' of the United States, perhaps combined with an 'ultra-right economic group.'"[1453] It implies that with the second invasion of Cuba scheduled for the end of December, the military was involved in a conspiracy to kill JFK, which would be the catalyst they needed to justify that invasion.

On October 24, UN Ambassador Adlai Stevenson arrived in Dallas. According to the *New York Times*, he was "shoved, booed, beat and spat in the face...." The mood in Dallas was hostile to anyone who was considered a left-wing Communist sympathizer.[1454]

Also, on the 24th, FBI Agent Milton Kaack, who had been keeping an eye on Oswald in New Orleans, visited the Bureau of Vital Statistics to review Oswald's birth records. Why this sudden interest by the FBI a month before the assassination? Did they suspect an Oswald impostor was roaming about after the shenanigans in Mexico City?[1455]

On the night of October 25, Oswald accompanied Michael Paine to another ACLU meeting. Oswald spoke briefly and afterward conversed with other attendees. Raymond Krystinic later told the FBI that Oswald said Walker was responsible for the trouble at the Stevenson meeting, and he and Oswald engaged in a heated discussion after Oswald said he was a Marxist.[1456]

On October 27, the *Dallas Times Herald* identified Larrie Schmidt as the leader of the student demonstration against Stevenson. As described in Chapter Thirteen, Schmidt had worked with Charles Willoughby and had organized Conservatism-USA to work against Walker. In 1963 it was neo-Nazi Robert Surrey who introduced Walker to the Schmidt brothers so they could infiltrate Walker's inner circle to spy on him for the CUSA.[1457]

Also on the 27th, businessman Jim Allison was in Chicago meeting with the Mafia's A. Gordon Hardy, who introduced him to Jimmy Hoffa at the Bismark Hotel. Allison saw Hardy hand a "little guy" an envelope containing a thick stack of $100 bills. Allison identified the "little guy" as Jack Ruby after Ruby shot Oswald. Two or three months later, Hardy died of a sudden heart attack. Suspiciously, neither the Warren Commission nor the HSCA could find a record of Ruby being in Dallas on October 27, one of the few days prior to the assassination, when his whereabouts were unknown. The day before, Ruby had called the number of an associate of corrupt Teamster official and mobster Allen Dorfman in Chicago. The FBI knew about a rumored payoff to Ruby prior to JFK's death involving Dorfman.[1458]

Gali Sherbatoff and Colonel Lawrence Orlov mysteriously appear in Lafitte's datebook on October 27. As described in Chapter Twelve, Gali was a White Russian who was married to Max Clark, who worked for General Dynamics and had a CIA security clearance. Orlov had intelligence connections and was handball partners with J. Walton Moore, who worked for Tracy Barnes at the CIA. Orlov was in the oil business and an associate of George de Mohrenschildt.[1459]

It is interesting that Volkmar Schmidt, Lawrence Glover, Gali Sherbatoff, and Lawrence Orlov, all of whom had at least a passing relationship with Ruth Paine, Michael Paine, or George de Mohrenschildt, reappeared during this period, at the same time that Michael Paine began spending time with Oswald. These were all people whom Oswald had associated with at the beginning of the year, and their reappearance likely had to do with Oswald's state of mind, who remained disgruntled after his return from Mexico City.

On October 29th, Larry Schmidt wrote the following to his military base in Munich: "The town [Dallas] is a battleground ... I am a hero to the right, a stormtrooper to the left ... Kennedy is scheduled in Dallas on November 24 [sic]. All big things are happening now."[1460]

***

Lee Oswald managed to elude the FBI when he fled New Orleans on his way to Mexico, leaving them unsure of his whereabouts. On October 1, agents visited the home of Oswald's aunt, Lillian Murret, hoping she might know where he was. She didn't, but she told them Ruth Paine had brought Marina to New Orleans after Lee had found a job, so maybe Ruth knew something. On October 7, FBI informant T-1, who worked in the New Orleans post office, "advised that there is no such Post Office Box as 30016 in the New Orleans area," an investigation undoubtedly prompted by the incorrect P.O. box on Oswald's FPCC handbill. However, the handbill referred to Hidell, not Oswald, which was likely why, on that same day, the "New Orleans Retailers' Credit Bureau... failed to indicate that there was anyone with a credit record in New Orleans by the name of A.J. Hidell. The city directory in New Orleans contained no record in the name of A.J. Hidell." The FBI assumed Hidell was an Oswald associate and had reached a dead end trying to find him. Also, on October 7, Mrs. Garner, Oswald's landlady at Magazine Street, told the FBI, "Oswald and his wife did not have any meetings to her knowledge when he was residing at 4907 Magazine Street. She advised that they did have some friends... who used to visit them on occasions. She stated she had not learned where Oswald had gone but presumed [sic] he had returned to Texas."[1461]

Garner's comments were clearly in response to questions posed by the FBI, who were trying to find out if Oswald or Marina were holding meetings with Communists in their home.

On October 10, the CIA sent their report to the FBI regarding the impostor Oswald being at the Russian embassy in Mexico City, who looked nothing like Oswald. On October 15, the New Orleans FBI office, still trying to figure out what Oswald was up to, was notified by informant T-2, who was familiar with Communist Party members in their city, that there was no knowledge of either Oswald or his wife engaging in Communist activities. Considering the FBI was also in possession of a pro-Castro pamphlet stamped 544 Camp Street, it is safe to assume they were somewhat bewildered. On October 25, based on the October 10th report they received from the CIA, the New Orleans FBI notified Dallas that Oswald had been to the Russian Embassy in Mexico City. Because of what the CIA failed to disclose, the FBI was unaware that the man referred to did not resemble Oswald. Knowledge of the Mexico City affair placed a higher priority in finding Oswald in Hosty's mind, as did the change-of-address card filed in New Orleans early in October that told the FBI Oswald had settled in Dallas. New Orleans also notified Hosty of Ruth Paine's address, which brought him there on November 1.

According to Hosty, he "was working the right-wing extremists, like General Walker, etc.," but Oswald had publicly shown he was a Marxist supporter of Fidel Castro. Perhaps the Dallas FBI knew more about Oswald than they let on, for sending an agent to see him who specialized in right-wing activism was the proper thing to do.[1462]

Prior to Hosty visiting the Paine home in search of the illusive Oswald, the FBI investigated Ruth and Michael Paine. On October 31, the Irving Credit Bureau told them Michael worked for Bell Helicopter, and Ruth was a housewife who taught Russian on a part-time basis at St. Mark's School. On that same day, the Dallas County Sheriff's Office and the Irving Police Department told the FBI that Ruth did not have a criminal record. Meanwhile, Ted Schurman, a security officer at Bell Helicopter, said Michael Paine had a security clearance. The FBI wanted to ensure the people Lee Oswald associated with were not Communists.[1463]

478

Armed with the knowledge that there was nothing suspicious about the Paines, on November 1st, Hosty visited Ruth's home. He was disappointed to learn that Oswald lived elsewhere, but where Ruth did not know. She told Hosty that Lee worked at the Book Depository and that he visited periodically on weekends to see his family. Hosty left his phone number, which Ruth gave to Oswald when he arrived that evening. Near the end of the interview, Marina appeared. She was alarmed that the visitor was from the FBI, and Hosty reassured her that it was not their policy to hurt people. Nevertheless, she made a note of Hosty's license plate number.

Also, on November 1, Lafitte wrote, "Trial run – mistakes aplenty – Not Good." That the conspirators wanted to rehearse their plan would be expected, which may explain why Oswald opened a post office box during his lunch break that day, almost a month after he was back in Dallas. The conspirators instructed Oswald to do this so he would be out of the building when they did their trial run. It meant they did not want him to know the details of the plan or who was involved. It was a sign that the conspirators still questioned if Oswald should be the assassination patsy.

Oswald listed Fair Play for Cuba Committee and American Civil Liberties Union on his post office application as nonprofit organizations permitted to receive mail. He failed to refer to Hidell for the first time in quite a while, and the fact that Richard Nagell was now behind bars might have been the reason.[1464]

Oswald also mailed three letters that day. One was a change-of-address card to the Russian Embassy in Washington. Another was to notify the Communist Party USA that he did not move to Baltimore but had settled in Dallas. The third was a membership application to the ACLU, and Oswald asked how he could get in touch with "ACLU groups in my area." It was a curious request, considering he had attended an ACLU meeting with Michael Paine only days before. A possible explanation is that Oswald knew all three letters would let FBI post office informants know he was in Dallas.[1465]

That same day, George Senator moved in with Jack Ruby, and Ruby asked Larry Crafard to work at the Carousel Club for room and board only. These were signs that Ruby was scared. Seven days later, Ruby also opened a post office box about twelve feet away from Oswald's.[1466]

Meanwhile, an FBI airtel, dated November 1, 1963, stated that the planned second invasion of Cuba was to "begin with the last week of November against the Cuban mainland," initially with an "extended series of small size commando-type raids," followed by "a large-scale amphibious operation." As the JFK assassination approached, the U.S. military, the

479

CIA, Cuban exiles, American mercenaries, and members of the Mafia all were aware of a significant invasion of Cuba that was to occur in the weeks ahead.[1467]

On November 2, the day after Hosty visited Ruth Paine's home, an entry in Lafitte's datebook reads: "Runner Runner (FBI) w/T 4 pm." Alone, the entry means nothing, but an ad placed in the *Dallas Morning News* on October 15 may provide some clarity. That ad read, "Running Man, please call me. Please. Please." It was signed, "Lee." The ad was a frantic plea for Running Man to call Lee at a time when Oswald was nervous about his role in the assassination plot. It had appeared the day after Lee moved into the 1026 N. Beckley home. Who was this mysterious Running Man?[1468]

An FBI memo on April 6, 1964, stating that the Capri Theater in Dallas ran the ad to promote the movie The Running Man, which starred Lee Remick. However, it makes no sense that a theater would put a movie promotion in the classified ads and then not mention the name of the movie or the Capri Theater. It is more likely another example of FBI subterfuge, for no one ever investigated the ad or spoke to those involved to find out what really happened. It is my opinion that Lee Oswald wrote the ad, possibly with the intent of meeting a contact in the Capri Theater

From the datebook entry, we know Runner Runner was with the FBI. We also know that Oswald listed Hosty in his address book as "James P. Hasty [sic]." Did Oswald purposely write "Hasty" as a reminder he was "Running Man?" Perhaps, but a more logical explanation is that it referred to another Dallas FBI agent, Bardwell Odum. According to Odum's obituary, Odum "was a lifelong runner and competed as a member of The University of Texas track team."

Obviously, this alone does not make Odum a person of interest. Consider that on the same page in Oswald's address book as the "Hasty" listing is the name "Burton Dixie," where Robert Adams sent Oswald to look for a job. However, an entry for "Dallas Texas State" and "Robert Adum" is listed on a different page from the "Burton Dixie" reference, which is odd. One would have expected them to be on the same page. And did Oswald misspell Adams as Adum on purpose? Maybe so. If we replace the letter "a" with "o" and change "Adum" to "Odum," as Oswald did with Hosty and "Hasty," we wind up with Robert Odum. In *The Oswald Code*, author Alan Weberman believes this is what Oswald did. He cryptically referred to Bardwell Odum, and I agree with him. Odum investigated the Walker shooting, collected evidence at Ruth Paine's home, interviewed assassination witnesses, handled the most significant parts of the FBI's investigation of the Kennedy assassination, and was their liaison to the CIA. It explains the connection between the "Hasty" page and the "Odum" page and cryptically ties together the two FBI agents who were very closely involved in the Oswald investigation.[1469]

There is more. On the same page as the Hasty listing in Oswald's address book is the notation "Mr. Hodson," who was John Wilson-Hudson. The letter "u" has been similarly replaced with the letter "o." Why is Hudson's name, whom we previously discussed in Chapter Twenty-Three regarding a connection to Oswald's Mexico City trip related to Bowen on September 28 and an attempt to invade Nicaragua from Cuba in 1959, on the same page as the Hasty notation and referred to with the salutation Mister? Does this imply that Oswald believed this man warranted some respect? And why is Hudson mentioned in conjunction with Ruby in the Lafitte datebook on June 7 and October 30, the latter being the day before Hosty showed up at Ruth Paine's house?

On November 4th, Hosty called the Book Depository to verify Oswald's employment and learned Oswald had provided Ruth Paine's address as his own. "I then sent a communication," Hosty wrote, "instructing the New Orleans office to make the Dallas office the office of origin. We are now assuming control because he has now been verified in our division." It was the prudent thing for Hosty to do. However, one thing is hard to understand. Hosty had been searching for Oswald for quite some time when he learned Oswald had given a false address to his new employer. Hosty knew Oswald was in Mexico City and admitted this created an urgent need to find him. Why, then, didn't Hosty ask TSBD superintendent Roy Truly if he could speak to Oswald directly so he could ask him what his address was and why he lied about it? Something was terribly odd about the way Hosty conducted his search for Oswald.[1470]

The next day, Hosty and fellow agent Gary Wilson returned to Ruth Paine's home. She told them again she had no idea where Lee was living. One would think Hosty would have told Ruth that Oswald had given her address to his new employer. Maybe he didn't because he was afraid she would tell Lee, and he didn't want Lee to know that he was still looking for him. That's possible, but how does one explain how Hosty could write that because he had a heavy caseload and "had now established that Oswald was not employed in a sensitive industry," he ended his investigation. How was that possible? The FBI had been searching for Oswald in multiple cities for weeks until Hosty told them to stop doing so the previous day. Hosty had been trying to find him since March, and he allegedly still did not know where Oswald lived. So how could Hosty end his investigation of a returned defector to the Soviet Union who had traveled to Mexico City and visited the Russian Embassy there? That alone should have warranted Oswald's arrest for questioning, especially considering JFK would arrive in Dallas in a couple of weeks.

There was something odd about the way Hosty acted after the assassination. He must have known JFK was shot within 5 minutes after it happened. Yet, in *Assignment Oswald,* Hosty wrote that he got in his car and drove to the Trade Mart. Why did he do that? Wouldn't an FBI agent first ask where JFK was shot and head to that location? Hosty eventually left the Trade Mart and turned on his car radio as he returned downtown. When he heard that JFK was taken to Parkland Hospital, he went there. Again, the question is, was that a logical place for him to go? He eventually called his office from Parkland and was told to go back to the office. However, while driving back, Dallas FBI agent Bob Barrett came on the radio and said a cop was shot and killed in Oak Cliff. Hosty wrote: "Now that's odd, I thought. A cop is shot in broad daylight in a nice, quiet neighborhood." Seriously? The President and a policeman were shot and killed within 45 minutes of each other, and he doesn't make a connection? One can't help but think that Hosty was covering up something, and his story gets stranger still. "I passed Dealey Plaza and noticed a commotion down on Elm and Houston," he wrote. "There was a fire truck with its hook and ladder extended to the roof of a seven-story building on Elm Street. Police were surrounding the building. I said to myself, so that's where the bastard shot from, the roof of that building."

His explanation defies logic. He had to know that it was the Texas School Book Depository building. He knew Oswald, a returned defector to Russia, worked there, and that he had provided his employer with a false home address. He knew Oswald was purposely avoiding the FBI in Dallas and New Orleans and had dropped off a note for Hosty at the FBI office saying he would blow up the building if Hosty did not stop bothering his wife. Instead, Hosty casually returned to the FBI office and at 2:15 pm was told that the police had arrested a guy named Oswald, and that's when the lightbulb lit in Hosty's head. No way can this be a valid account of what happened. In this author's opinion, Hosty had a relationship with Oswald prior to the assassination. Perhaps Oswald was an informant for Hosty, and he created an alibi after the fact to cover up that relationship because it would have been damning to Hosty's reputation and career if it had become known that he was aware of Oswald. It was much more self-serving to say he was trying hard to find Oswald but was having trouble locating him.[1471]

This author believes Hosty knew where Oswald lived, but he visited Ruth Paine's home and where Oswald worked to find out what he could about who Oswald associated with and what he was doing. Or, Oswald had become an informant for either Hosty or Odum, and he was not providing information fast enough to suit them. Either way, Hosty never revealed all he knew.

It explains why, according to Marina, Oswald became very agitated when he learned that Hosty had visited a second time to inquire about him. Around November 6th or 7th, it compelled Oswald to make a surprise appearance at the FBI's Dallas office. When notified by the receptionist, Nanny Fenner, that Hosty was out to lunch, Oswald handed her an envelope. "Get this to him," he said and then departed. After the assassination, the FBI remained silent about the incident. A journalist learned about it in 1975 from a contact within the FBI, and the story became known only after the HSCA elected to investigate further. Hosty testified that within hours after the assassination, Special Agent-in-Charge Gordon Shanklin asked him to account for the note. Hosty explained his recent interviews with Ruth Paine and how Oswald had dropped off the note while he was out to lunch. After Ruby killed Oswald, Shanklin told Hosty, "Oswald's dead now. There can be no trial. Here- get rid of this." Hosty then "flushed it down the drain."

During his testimony in 1975, Shanklin denied seeing the letter, but FBI Assistant Director William Sullivan said Shanklin often discussed an "internal problem" regarding a message from Oswald. Agent Howe of the

483

Dallas office confirmed that Shanklin had seen the note. All this suggests the letter was serious, but Hosty maintained that all it said was, "If you have anything you want to learn about me, come talk to me directly. If you don't cease bothering my wife, I will take appropriate action and report this to the proper authorities." Nanny Fenner claimed to have caught a glimpse of the note before handing it to Hosty. "Let this be a warning," she said it read. "I will blow up the FBI and the Dallas Police Department if you don't stop bothering my wife. Lee Harvey Oswald." [1472]

The FBI knew where Oswald worked and could have arrested him based on what the note said, especially if Fenner's recollection was correct. However, if Oswald were an FBI informant, he had good reason to be upset, especially considering his involvement in the assassination plot. Hosty was putting his family in danger. Consider also the November 9th Lafitte entry, which reads: *"On the wings of murder. The pigeon way for unsuspecting Lee. Clip Clip his wings."* Did Lafitte and the assassination conspirators know Oswald was an FBI informant (stool pigeon), and they intended to clip the wings of the designated patsy? It looks like they did. [1473]

On November 8, a day or two after he visited the FBI office, Oswald wrote another letter that showed he was nervous, just like his "Runner Runner" ad. It reads as follows:

> Dear Mr. Hunt,
> I would like information concerding [sic] my position.
>   I am asking only for information. I am suggesting that we discuss the matter fully before any steps are taken by me or anyone else.
> Thank you,
> Lee Harvy [sic] Oswald

The letter was sent anonymously to assassination researcher Penn Jones, Jr. on August 18, 1975. The envelope had a Mexico City postmark. Jones gave a copy to Dallas reporter Earl Golz, and The *Dallas Morning News* hired three handwriting experts, all of whom concluded the signature on the note was Oswald's (Analysts hired by the HSCA "were unable to come to any firm conclusion.") Golz also gave a copy to ex-H.L. Hunt security chief Paul Rothermel, who passed it along to the FBI, who came to see Golz to try and determine its authenticity. [1474]

H.L. Hunt and his sons, Lamar and Nelson Bunker, were all candidates to be the letter's Mr. Hunt. Jack Ruby and Mafia figure Jim Braden, whom the police arrested in Dealey Plaza immediately after the assassination, both visited the H.L. Hunt offices on the day prior to the assassination. Investigators found Lamar Hunt's name in Ruby's notebook. The Hunt family were well-known supporters of the ultra-right and made no secret of their hatred for the President. It was also logical to assume that Hunt financed gunrunning operations against Castro, which could explain his relationship with both Ruby and Braden. And if Oswald was involved in gunrunning with Ruby, he also had reason to associate with Hunt.

Another possible candidate was the CIA's Howard Hunt, who was Tracy Barnes's right-hand man in the Domestic Contacts Division. He was also close to David Atlee Phillips and a supporter of the hardline Cuban exiles. However, this author believes Oswald would not have referred to him so formally as Mr. Hunt, so an H.L. Hunt family member is a more logical possibility.

The letter begins with a request for information, indicating that whatever the plot entailed, Oswald was not privy to what his role was to be. He needed answers, which was especially true if he was an FBI informant. Oswald then repeated that it was information he was interested in to emphasize the point. He was not looking to solicit money or anything else.

On November 9, the day after he wrote to Mr. Hunt, Oswald was at it again, writing the previously discussed suspicious letter to the Soviet Embassy in Washington. He left a draft on Ruth Paine's desk, where she found it. She later claimed she intended to give a copy to the FBI the next time they visited, which never occurred. So, Ruth handed her copy to them the day after the assassination. "This is to inform you of recent events since my meetings with comrade Kostin in the Embassy of the Soviet Union, Mexico City, Mexico," the letter began. "I was unable to remain in Mexico undefini-ly [sic] because of my Mexican visa restrictions which was for 15 days only. *I could not take a chance on requesting a new visa unless I used my real name, so I returned to the United States*... had I been able to reach the Soviet Embassy in Havana as planned, the embassy there would have had time to complete our business..." (Author's Italics)[1475]

The Kostin referred to was clearly Kostikov, one of the three Russians Oswald met at the Russian Embassy in Mexico City, which proves the real Oswald was there. Kostikov was with the KGB's Department 13 assassination group, which potentially implicated the Soviets in the JFK assassination. The letter mentioned that the Russian Embassy in Havana was already aware of some business concerning Oswald, and he was using an alias in Mexico City.

The letter fits nicely with all the other evidence pointing to Oswald being a phony "sleeper agent" who was really a CIA operative to make it appear the Soviets had killed Oswald while he was in the Soviet Union. However, there is another possibility for the letter when considered in its proper context with the November 2 "Runner Runner" datebook entry, Oswald's November 6 or 7 surprise visit to the FBI office, the references to "Hasty," "Hodson," and "Odum" in Oswald's address book, and the mysterious letter to Mr. Hunt. When Oswald wrote the letter, Hosty had been to the Paine home twice, and Ruth freely told Hosty everything she knew about him, including where Lee worked. Since Oswald left the letter in a place where Ruth was sure to find it, one could assume he expected her to give it to the FBI right away, and they would have arrested him immediately based on its contents. Considering the Nagell warning, Oswald's attempt to get to Cuba via Mexico City, and his somewhat frantic pleas for knowledge of what he was involved in and his general nervousness, was this another attempt by Oswald to remove himself from the assassination plot, as Nagell had done?

Some have suggested that Ruth Paine wrote the letter, which was proven to have been typed on her typewriter. However, in his 1978 book *Legend: The Secret World of Lee Harvey Oswald*, Edward Jay Epstein wrote that Oswald took a typing class from January to March 1963. It was also a typical Oswald letter with multiple misspellings, which suggests that Oswald likely wrote the letter.[1476]

What is hard to understand is why Ruth didn't immediately give the letter to the FBI when she found it because she admitted Oswald worried her. She testified to the Warren Commission that as early as September 1963, when she learned that Oswald was going to leave New Orleans and go to Texas to meet a contact, she thought Oswald might be a spy. As she testified, "I may say, also, I wondered, as I have already indicated for the Commission, I had wondered, from time to time, whether this was a man who was working as a spy or in any way a threat to the Nation, and I thought, 'This is the first I have heard anything about a contact. I am interested to know if this is a real thing or something unreal.'" She repeated similar concerns about Lee throughout her testimony regarding the time she lived with Marina in Dallas.[1477]

So, Ruth expects us to believe she thought Lee Oswald might be a spy. She then finds a letter where Oswald wrote he was at the Cuban Embassy in Mexico City using an alias and could not go to Havana to complete his business. One would think Ruth would have immediately driven to the FBI office and handed over the letter. The problem is Ruth was never truthful and had everyone fooled. In his book, Hosty calls Ruth Paine "the kindly Quaker woman who was letting Marina and the Oswald children live with her in Irving." This kindly woman threw Oswald under the bus after the assassination. When the police first arrived at her house, she said we've been expecting you. Imagine how different things would have been if Marina had never met Ruth. There was really nothing incriminating Marina could have said. Instead, we have Ruth Paine parading the police and FBI around her house, speaking in English and translating for Marina, maybe falsely. She had an important role to play in creating Oswald's persona after the fact. All the while, she acted like an innocent lamb that was looking to help, and everyone bought it.

On November 11, two days after the letter was dated, the CIA's Bruce Solie asked Marguerite D. Stevens of the Office of Security to do a security search for Sylvia Hyde Hoke and Carl Hyde, Ruth Paine's sister and brother. The reader may recall that Marguerite Stevens investigated Oswald and other military men who defected to the Soviet Union in the late 1950s. Marguerite learned that Sylvia worked for the CIA and Carl also had intelligence connections. An FBI Post Office informant probably intercepted Oswald's November 9 letter to the Russian Embassy, which explains what prompted this investigation of Ruth's family the next day.[1478]

It was also on November 9 that Joseph Milteer told FBI informant William Somersett in Miami that plans were in the works to assassinate JFK and the government would blame a Communist. Somersett alerted the FBI, and because of Kennedy's impending trip to Miami on November 18, they notified the Secret Service.

So many individuals knew of the pending assassination, like Milteer and Private Dinkin, while others, like the FBI, were probably using Oswald to find out what he was involved in. Meanwhile, there was a plot going on to kill JFK, and the city of Dallas was a powder keg waiting to explode.

CHAPTER TWENTY-SEVEN

A NOVEMBER TO REMEMBER

On November 13, based on information provided by William Somersett, FBI agent Don Adams was told to investigate Joseph Milteer. Milteer had been present at an October 18-20 Constitution Party meeting in Indianapolis, where talk of assassinating President Kennedy had taken place. On that same day, Admiral John G. Crommelin, an associate of Milteer, visited Wesley Swift at a strategy conference where they discussed mass violence by "inner dens" of the Christian Knights of the Invisible Empire. American Nazi Party leader George Lincoln Rockwell told the FBI on March 7, 1964, that Crommelin, Colonel William Potter Gale, and General Pedro del Valle had planned to overthrow the government.[1479]

A Secret Service report dated November 15, 1963, described "information received by phone from FBI headquarters, Washington, D.C.," that involved the arrest of an unnamed person who had stolen three automobiles on September 30 in Piedras Negras, Mexico. On November 14, the accused car thief told the FBI "that he is a member of the Ku Klux Klan; that during his travels throughout the country, his sources have told him that a militant group of the National States Rights Party plans to assassinate the President and other high-level officials…"[1480]

The FBI report went on to state there was "no information developed that would indicate any danger to the President in the near future or during his trip to Texas." Perhaps the writer of the report believed this, but the hierarchy at the FBI and Secret Service should have taken it more seriously. In addition to Milteer, the FBI was aware of the warnings of Garret Trapnell, Army Private Eugene B. Dinkin, and Richard Case Nagell. All pointed to a domestic right-wing conspiracy involving the military. Considering that Nagell specifically mentioned Oswald in his letter to the FBI as being an integral part of that conspiracy, it is hard to understand why Oswald was not a priority risk during the President's trip to Dallas. Hosty may have been kept in the dark by Hoover, who likely knew about the assassination plot and allowed it to happen.

On Saturday, November 16, Oswald was interviewed by the FBI, according to a *Dallas Morning News* article posted two days after the assassination. Written by James Ewell and based on information provided by anonymous sources, the article read: "Lee Harvey Oswald, charged with murdering President Kennedy, was interviewed by the FBI here six days before the Friday assassination. But word of the interview with the former defector to Russia was not conveyed to the U.S. Secret Service and Dallas police, reliable sources told *The Dallas News* Saturday. An FBI agent referred all inquiries to Agent-in-Charge Gordon Shanklin, who could not be immediately reached for comment."[1481]

Years later, Ewell revealed that his source was Dallas Police Chief Jesse Curry and his police intelligence unit, which explains why the story appeared in print on November 24. The day before, on Saturday afternoon, Chief Curry made a public statement: "I understand the FBI did know that he [Oswald] was in Dallas," and Curry must have provided additional details privately to Ewell. However, word traveled quickly, and within minutes, someone at the FBI called Curry to minimize the damage, which prompted the chief to call a press conference hastily. "I'm certainly not saying that the FBI knew something that we should have known and didn't tell us," he said. When asked by reporters if he had any doubt that Oswald was the assassin, Curry replied, "I think this is the man who killed the President." Not exactly a ringing endorsement. By that time, Curry had viewed the Zapruder film, had spoken to eyewitnesses, knew the evidence was flimsy, and the FBI had briefed him. Curry knew the official story was a lie and that, most likely, Oswald was an FBI informant. On Sunday morning, Curry was asked by the press: "Sir, could you tell us whether or not there is a possibility of other people being involved?" "I'm not making no more comments," was his response.[1482]

It was also on Sunday, November 17, that Harold Reynolds, a commercial photographer in Abilene, Texas, was showing photographs to his neighbor, Pedro Gonzales. Gonzales was president of the Cuban Liberation Committee, an anti-Castro Cuban exile group. According to Reynolds, their landlady knocked on the door and handed Gonzales a note that she had seen wedged in his mailbox for a couple of days. It said something like, "Call me immediately, urgent," and had two Dallas phone numbers on it. It was signed "Lee Oswald," who apparently was still in a state of panic five days before the assassination and was reaching out to others for information. Gonzales told Reynolds that Oswald was an attorney from Dallas. Despite the disclaimer, Reynolds noticed Gonzales "looked nervous, and sweat started appearing on his forehead." Shortly after that, Reynolds saw Gonzales' car parked a few blocks from his house "and him standing in a pay phone booth." After the assassination, he disappeared. Reynolds tried to alert the FBI about the note and the frequency of Cuban visitors with Louisiana and Florida license plates to Gonzales' home, but they were uninterested.[1483]

Also on the 17th, New Orleans FBI agent William Walter received a teletype sent to all FBI offices warning about a plot to kill JFK on November 22 in Dallas. The FBI had "determined that a militant revolutionary group..." was behind the plot. The memo advised that all "race and hate groups" should be investigated to determine if there was a basis for the threat. It explains why FBI agents would later question Sumner and De Lapara about race and hate groups, even though these two witnesses had contacted the Bureau about a potential Mafia/ Carlos Marcello involvement in the assassination (see Chapter Eighteen).

After the assassination, Walter told the HSCA, "I was curious and went back to look and see what the files would indicate that had been done by the New Orleans [FBI] office to Oswald, curious as to whether or not our office had an ongoing investigation before the assassination. What I found was a file in the Special Agent in Charge's safe or his locked file cabinet, and I don't recall the file number, but I recall on the jacket of the file a Special Agent [Warren] DeBrueys' name."

As for FBI employees corroborating Walter's story, agents had to sign affidavits – not that the teletype did not exist, but that they would not disclose confidential information. Walter remembered agents discussed it openly, the "phantom teletype," "information contacts," and "Oswald's relationships with agents in the New Orleans office."

William Sullivan, who directed the Bureau's domestic intelligence operations, supported Walter's story. In October 1977, as Sullivan was preparing to testify before the HSCA (which never occurred), he called Walter, and they agreed that Oswald was an informant for the FBI. Sullivan had already told a government committee about Oswald being an FBI informant: "I think there may be something on that. I don't recall having seen anything like that, but I think there is something on that point."

As far as Walter, he told HSCA counsels Robert W. Genzman, Michael Goldsmith, and Gary Cornwall "that Mr. Hoover sent them down, two agents down, to set me straight, and they wanted me to admit that I had had – was going through an emotional trauma, change of jobs, and I had all these problems..." "My answer to all that is I have had every opportunity to back out. I could have said, 'Okay, Mr. Hoover and Mr. Bureau, what I did is confuse the teletype of the 17th with the teletype of the 22nd. In good conscience, I am not going to do that..."

William Walter was a principled man, and he was not going to let the FBI bully him into saying something he knew to be untrue. He also went on to become senior vice president of Patterson State Bank in Morgan City, Louisiana. Undoubtedly, he was telling the truth.[1484]

***

During November, while for the most part, Oswald remained isolated in his room, working or visiting family on weekends, someone was impersonating him, a continuance of the charade that began in Mexico City. After the assassination, the people of Dallas would recall their encounters with Lee Oswald.

It started on November 1, when a young man buying rifle ammunition caught the attention of people at Morgan's Gun shop in Fort Worth. He was "rude and impertinent" and boasted about having been in the Marines. After the assassination, three who witnessed the spectacle believed the man looked like Oswald. The real Oswald was at work in Dallas and not in Fort Worth.

A couple of days later, a man resembling Oswald, accompanied by a woman and two children, entered a furniture store with a sign "Guns" posted in the outside window. He wanted to have the firing pin on his rifle repaired, so the store manager directed him to Irving Sports Shop, located nearby. The couple stayed a while to look at furniture. Marina later insisted she was never in the store. The incident became known after the assassination when a *London Evening Standard* reporter was checking all gun shops in the area where Ruth Paine lived and came across the same sign in the furniture store window. The manager told the reporter about the Oswald look-alike, which a witness corroborated, and that the husband spoke to his wife in a foreign language.[1485]

The Irving Sports Shop received notoriety two days after the assassination when an anonymous caller told the Dallas police that Oswald had a rifle sighted there. No one at the store could recall a visit by Oswald, but a check of their records revealed a customer ticket with the name "Oswald" on it. However, no Oswald in the Dallas area had a gun repaired at Irving Sports Shop at that time. The customer ticket noted that the shop had mounted a telescopic sight onto the rifle between November 4 and 8. The work performed was to drill three holes, yet Oswald's rifle scope had only two holes, indicating the rifle serviced was different from the assassination weapon. Someone had submitted a gun in Oswald's name to have a scope sighted a couple of weeks before the assassination to plant evidence in support of Oswald's guilt.

Around November 9, there were numerous sightings at the Sports Drome Rifle Range of an obnoxious man, who later was identified as Lee Oswald. The most notable event occurred on the 16th when Dr. Homer Wood and his young son were practicing at the range. Dr. Wood recalled, "As soon as I saw Oswald on TV, I said to my wife, 'He looks like the man who was sitting in the next booth to our son, out at the rifle range.' When my son came home from school…he also looked at the television, and he spoke to me quickly, saying, 'Daddy, that looks just like that man that we saw at the range when we were sighting in our rifles.'"

There were other things about the man that the young Wood remembered. He was an excellent shot and told the thirteen-year-old boy that his rifle was a 6.5-mm Italian rifle with a four-power scope, which was different from the assassination weapon. It emitted a "ball of fire" when fired. He also recalled that the man was with another "man in a newer model car."[1486]

On November 8, a man identifying himself as "Harvey Oswald" entered a grocery store in Irving, Texas, and asked the proprietor, Leonard Hutchinson, to cash a check made out in his name for $189. Hutchinson declined but recalled seeing the man again, sometimes accompanied by two women. He returned to the store once or twice a week in the early morning and always bought a gallon of milk and cinnamon rolls. Both Marina and Ruth Paine stated these were not items the real Oswald would have purchased. Oswald's landlady confirmed this. She remembered him buying lunch meats and jellies and nothing else.[1487]

The Warren Commission chose not to believe Hutchinson because Oswald could not have been in Irving at the time specified. They also ignored a barber who had a shop near Hutchinson's store, who claimed he had cut the hair of a man who looked like Oswald. The man was with a fourteen-year-old boy, and the two made leftist remarks. He told the barber he was visiting his wife, and the barber saw Oswald and a woman entering Hutchinson's store together.

On November 9, around 2:00 P.M., when the real Oswald was at work, a man calling himself Lee Oswald visited the showroom of Downtown Lincoln-Mercury. Salesman Albert Bogard took him for a test drive of a Mercury Comet, an improbable circumstance for the real Oswald, who did not know how to drive. The impostor drove recklessly on Stemmons Freeway at speeds up to eighty miles per hour and told Bogard he would receive "a lot of money in the next two or three weeks." Co-workers corroborated the story. One remembered Oswald protesting about the high price of automobiles and complaining that he might have to go "back to Russia where they treat workers like men."[1488]

These incidents were well choreographed. Oswald was seen at the shooting range, had a scope sighted, and made leftist comments in public. The Hutchinson and Albert Bogard encounters involved money. After the assassination, it looked like Oswald was a Russian agent who anticipated the pending assassination and was to get paid a large sum.

One more incident occurred on that eventful Saturday of November 9. A man identifying himself as Oswald applied for a job as a parking attendant for Allright Parking Systems at the Southland Hotel in downtown Dallas. Manager Hubert Morrow first wrote down the man's name as "Lee Harvey Osborn" but was corrected that the name was "Oswald." He recalled that "Oswald" wanted to know how high the Southland building was and if it offered a good view of Dallas. "I was working here at night, Morrow said. "It was around ten o'clock when he came into the garage, and he asked me if he could see Main Street from the top of the roof. I said, you probably can, but you're not allowed up on that roof… He asked would the motorcade be going down Elm Street or Main Street? I said it would be going down Main Street… He was carrying a long item that appeared to be about as long as a rifle…wrapped up in a brown paper or canvas sack…Only the muzzle was sticking out of the end…The next time I saw him was when he assassinated the President."[1489]

On the weekend of November 16, other than the newspaper article claiming the FBI interviewed Oswald, his whereabouts are unknown. Marina admitted he did not spend this weekend at Ruth Paine's home because the previous weekend was a three-day holiday, and he had overstayed his welcome. His landlady also said he was absent the entire weekend. Therefore, from the evening of Friday, November 15, just one week before the assassination, until Monday morning, November 18, it is uncertain where Lee Oswald was.

"There's no doubt it was Oswald," gunsmith Howard Price told Dallas newsman Hugh Aynesworth. After the assassination, Price said he saw Lee Oswald practicing with his rifle at the Sportsdrome Gun Range in Grand Prairie, thirteen miles from Oswald's North Beckley Street apartment, starting on October 26, then on November 9 or 10, and again on November 17. More importantly, "Other people were with him."

Mrs. Price recalled her husband's reaction when he first saw Oswald's face on television: "Howard jumped out of his chair, and before the suspect's name was mentioned, said, 'That's Oswald! He comes to the rifle range. I sighted his scope.'" When the FBI interviewed Price, he didn't say he knew Oswald by name. "He didn't want to get involved," recalled his widow. Price told newsman Aynesworth that Oswald was not alone and that someone passed a wrapped-up rifle over the five-foot fence to him.

Also at the range on November 17 was Garland Slack, who was firing from the stall next to Oswald. He remembered Oswald well, and they got into a shouting match because Oswald was shooting rapid fire at the targets assigned to other shooters, including Slack. He also remembered that the person with Oswald was "25 years old or younger, [and] passed a rifle over the fence to Oswald wrapped in 'rags or something.'" After the assassination, the *Dallas Morning News* reported that the police had found the man who had driven Oswald to the rifle range. Their source was an investigator in the police department, who said, "A man who knew Oswald stated he drove the 24-year-old suspect to the range area." When Garland Slack's wife, Lucille, was interviewed by the FBI in 1964, she volunteered that her husband told her Oswald was driven to the range by a man named "Frazier." The only Frazier known to associate with Oswald was Wesley Frazier, who worked at the TSBD and drove Oswald to work the morning of the assassination. The police were suspicious of Frazier and subjected him to an intense interview after the assassination. Frazier denied being with Oswald at the shooting range, but it remains a strong possibility that Frazier did not tell authorities all he knew about Oswald.[1490]

Oswald phoned Marina on Monday, November 18, and he learned she had called him over the weekend. No one knew Lee Oswald there because he had registered as O.H. Lee. He explained that he used an alias because he did not want his landlady to learn he had gone to Russia. It was a weak excuse, but one Marina had no choice but to accept.[1491]

Five days after the assassination, Ralph Leon Yates told the FBI that he also encountered Oswald. He was driving near Beckley Street on Wednesday, November 20, when he picked up a young man hitchhiking into downtown Dallas who was carrying an extended package that the man said contained curtain rods. They talked about JFK's upcoming trip. The man asked Yates if they had changed the President's motorcade route and if Yates believed a person with a rifle could shoot the President from the top of a building or an open window. He dropped off his passenger at Elm and

Houston Streets, the site of the TSBD. Yates returned to his place of work and described the incident to a co-worker, Dempsey Jones.

The above are not the only examples of an Oswald impersonator, but they are sufficient to make the point. Unknown to Oswald, the conspirators were planting the seed in Dallas the week before the assassination that Lee Oswald was preparing to assassinate JFK.

***

It was indeed an exciting time to be in Dallas and concerned with Cuban affairs in the fall of 1963, and the time for Robert Kennedy's second invasion of Cuba approached. FBI and Treasury Department memos from October quoted a Dallas gun dealer saying that in "the last week of November 1963 ... a large scale amphibious operation would take place against the Cuba mainland" and "United States military forces or government agencies would possibly be involved in this operation [which] involved an attack by rebel Cuban forces."[1492]

In a speech given in October, the leader of SNFE (Second National Front Escambray, the Alpha 66 offshoot), Eloy Gutierrez Menoyo, said they would be "in Cuba in less than six months." The month before, a letter intercepted by the FBI revealed that SNFE/Alpha 66/MRP was "training... men for a specialized reserve brigade in various types of guerrilla warfare." The day prior to the assassination, Menoyo boasted that "something very big would happen soon that would advance the Cuban cause."[1493]

Menoyo was not the only one anticipating the assassination of JFK. According to a Secret Service Report, an informant reported that Homer Echevarria of the 30th of November Movement and the DRE said the day before the assassination that "we now have plenty of money – our new backers are Jews – as soon as 'we' (or 'they') take care of Kennedy..." The informant claimed "he had heard that one Thomas Mosley allegedly had been attempting to negotiate a sale of machine guns to Homer S. Echevarria..." Secret Service agent Walt Rogers stated that "one Paulino Sierra, an attorney in the Chicago area who became interested in the anti-Castro movement, could possibly be the contact for Mosley."[1494]

Back in June, Andres Sargen of Alpha 66 had written to Manuel Rodriguez in Miami suggesting they open a local chapter in Dallas. Rodriguez agreed and established a Dallas SNFE/Alpha 66/MRP chapter at 3128 Harlandale Avenue. Lee Harvey Oswald was a frequent visitor to this den of right-wing anti-Castroism that November.

Like Menoyo, Rodriguez had fought with Castro during the revolution but defected to the United States after Castro's turn to communism. And like many Cuban exiles, he felt betrayed by Kennedy. An FBI report dated November 24, 1963, stated that Rodriguez "was known to be violently anti-President Kennedy...." The Secret Service included his name on a Protective Research Referral Memoranda of people suspected of being capable of assassinating the President. A Warren Commission document said Rodriguez was "apparently a Cuban survivor of the Bay of Pigs episode, [who] was attempting to purchase arms in Dallas for Alpha 66. Rodriguez is also a member of the DRE."[1495] A collaboration between the DRE and Alpha 66 and the other groups huddled under Paulino Sierra's umbrella should not come as a surprise. Bobby Kennedy had cut them out, and they had no choice but to work together. They planned to assassinate JFK, which would be the catalyst to lead to a U.S. military invasion of Cuba.

On the day after the assassination, Dallas deputy sheriff Buddy Walthers filed a police report that stated "some Cubans" had conducted secret meetings at 3128 Harlandale, and they were "possibly connected with the 'Freedom for Cuba Party' of which Oswald was a member." Walthers submitted a follow-up report three days later, stating that sometime between November 15 and 23, "these Cubans moved from this house," and his informant "stated that subject Oswald had been to this house before." If true, it connected Oswald directly to SNFE/Alpha 66/MRP, the DRE, and anti-Castro activities involving the U.S. military. As previously described, on the night of the assassination, Dallas DA Henry Wade told the press that Oswald was a member of the Free Cuba Committee, a similar name to the one Walthers said Oswald belonged to, and Jack Ruby immediately corrected him. It meant Ruby must have been familiar with the Cubans from the house on Harlandale Avenue as well.

On the day after the assassination, the FBI interviewed a gas station owner in Sulphur, Oklahoma, who claimed that on November 17, 1963, "a male who resembled Lee Oswald had been in ...[the] service station in the company of people who appeared to be Cubans." The report stated that "a light-complexioned man who resembled Lee Oswald, drove up... in about a 1958 Ford station wagon...of white and tan color with a white center and tan bottom...." Also in the car were Cuban men, women, and some young children. The man he thought was Oswald "was of light complexion, pale, appeared to be in his late 20's or early 30's, about 6' tall, 170 pounds, thin and slender, light brown hair., reasonably high forehead, thin lips...."[1496]

A follow-up investigation by the FBI revealed the following:

496

MIGUEL L. de SOCARRAZ, M.D., at Oklahoma Veterans Hospital... advised he is a Cuban refugee and very anti-Communist. The following people contacted him on Sunday, November 17, 1963: MANOLITO RODRIGUEZ, with his wife and two or three-year-old baby; two other men, both of whom were of dark complexion, one having the name of SALAZAR and the other CHITO RIVERO. With SALAZAR and RIVERO were their wives, and a girl about thirteen or fourteen years of age... All of these people were in an older Ford station wagon of cream color...

SOCARRAZ advised from the descriptions of the Cubans visiting the FINA service station on November 17, 1963 and their vehicle, he feels certainly they are the Cubans, described above, who visited him on that date."

The Rodriguez referred to was Manuel Rodriguez, who did not deny there was someone in the car who looked like Oswald. He told one of the authors of *Coup D'Etat In America*, Michael Canfield, that "someone thought one of [his] friends was Oswald" and that "it was just one big mistake that was soon cleared up."[1497]

One would not have expected Rodriguez to tell the truth if Lee Harvey Oswald was a passenger in his car. However, there was a Dallas gunrunner who looked a lot like Oswald, who associated with Rodriguez, and it may have been him. His name was John Thomas Masen.

***

"If I saw a picture of Lee Harvey Oswald," Masen told author Dick Russell, "I could probably pick it out. But I can't really visualize his face." It was an absurd comment, for anyone alive at the time of the assassination would recognize Oswald. Yet, here was a man who could have passed for Oswald's twin, owned a gun shop in the city where the assassination took place, and claimed he would have trouble recognizing him. It brings us to a story involving Masen and a federal agent named Frank Ellsworth. As Ellsworth recalled, "I do remember two instances where Oswald was supposed to have been at someone's house in North Dallas, and I was able to ascertain after the assassination that it was actually the look-alike... there were instances where witnesses thought they saw Oswald in the company of several Minutemen. One of these times did involve a group of Minutemen at a rifle range. The look-alike knew all these people."[1498]

According to Ellsworth, Masen was "an ardent member of the Minutemen," and as previously discussed, Oswald may have been one as well. It is intriguing that an FBI file dated March 27, 1964, reported that Masen "purchased about ten boxes of 6.5 mm Mannlicher-Carcano, Western Cartridge Company ammunition from Johnny Brinegar in early 1963 and that he sold these ten boxes to individuals. He stated that he was not able to recall the identity of any persons to whom he sold the ammunition...." The FBI also reported that "during the summer of 1963, he made an extensive vacation trip to Mexico, visiting friends in various places."[1499]

Frank Ellsworth was an agent with the Treasury Department's Alcohol, Tobacco, and Firearms Division in Dallas in 1963. Testifying before the Warren Commission, Ellsworth stated, "An organization known as the Minutemen is the right-wing group in Dallas most likely to have been associated with any effort to assassinate the President. The Minutemen are closely tied to General Walker and H.L. Hunt."

As mentioned previously, Oswald was involved in an illegal gun transaction days before the assassination that went wrong. It also included Frank Ellsworth, whose investigative work brought him into close contact with the radical right in Dallas, which may have also involved Lee Oswald and Jack Ruby. Ellsworth had set up a sting operation to try and catch Manuel Rodriguez of Alpha 66 and John Thomas Masen. On the evening of Monday, November 18, he patiently waited in Dallas for the arrival of a car carrying a cache of illegal weapons. Working undercover as an Irving policeman looking to make extra money illegally running guns, Ellsworth had convinced Masen that he represented a New Mexican veterinarian who was "very much in the market for military ordinance..." Masen told him the transaction would take place on the 18th and when and where it was going to occur. However, the car transporting the weapons never arrived, and Ellsworth had to call off the sting.

That same evening, the FBI and local Dallas detectives, acting on a tip from an informant, staked out an empty lot in Dallas where the transaction of weapons stolen from a Texas National Guard armory on November 14 was supposed to occur. While they waited, a white 1963 Dodge entered the lot, and the driver remained inside the car. In the backseat were the guns Ellsworth was waiting for blocks away.

As the FBI and Dallas detectives remained hidden, a blue 1962 Thunderbird convertible carrying two men pulled into the vacant lot. The Thunderbird stopped alongside the Dodge, and the two men began transferring the weapons from the Dodge to their car. When done, the two cars left in opposite directions. The Dallas police pursued the Thunderbird, not wanting the car with the guns to get away. A car chase resulted in a crash that injured an occupant of the Thunderbird, Lawrence Reginald Miller. Also arrested was the second man in the car, Donald Whitter.

According to Ellsworth, Army Captain George Charles Nonte, Jr., stationed at Fort Hood, was involved in the gun robbery. Ellsworth, who was keeping the FBI informed, told them about Nonte and his involvement with the stolen weapons, but they were already aware of what Nonte was up to. In fact, the circumstances suggest that the arrest of Whitter and Miller was to sabotage Ellsworth's sting operation and keep Nonte and Masen in business. It was how things turned out. After their arrest, Ellsworth had blown his cover.

Meanwhile, as described in *Oswald Talked* by authors Ray and Mary La Fontaine, Nonte was also keeping the FBI informed. The Bureau was aware that Cuban exiles were planning a second invasion of Cuba for "the last week of November against the Cuba mainland." Nonte learned about this from Masen, who heard of it from a man named Martinez, a Miami-based "weapons buyer" who had come "through Dallas on [a] recent buying trip." The man, whose full name was Joaquin Martinez de Pinillos, was a member of the DRE.

In August 1964, a man named John Elrod walked into the Shelby County Sheriff's Office in downtown Memphis, Tennessee, claiming to have information about the JFK assassination. He said he was walking near a railroad track by Harry Hines Boulevard in Dallas on the afternoon of November 22, and even though he was not carrying a gun, Elrod was arrested "for investigation of conspiracy to commit murder." He was placed in a cell on the fifth floor of the Dallas jail with Lee Harvey Oswald, whom the police had not yet accused of killing the President. Meanwhile, Lawrence Reginald Miller entered with a horribly battered face. Oswald told Elrod that he recognized the injured man, whom he had previously met at a motel room with four others, and they all had been advanced money. The man drove a Thunderbird filled with guns, Oswald claimed, and he also revealed that the name of one of the men in the motel room was Jack Ruby.

The Memphis police contacted the FBI regarding Elrod's story and discovered he had five offenses on his record. Still, regarding the weekend of the assassination, their report "does not reflect incarceration of ELROD in the Dallas City Jail, as claimed." As a result, his story lay dormant until February 1992, when Mary La Fontaine uncovered Elrod's arrest report in Dallas police files. It proved Elrod had told the truth, and the Dallas PD withheld information from the FBI.

Various relatives recalled Elrod saying he was in the same cell as Oswald. Phone records show that Oswald was in cell F-2 of the three-cell F block when first incarcerated, and cell F-1 contained a young man named Daniel Douglas. Elrod accurately described Douglas in a 1993 interview as a "kid from Tennessee who had stolen a car in Memphis," information he could only have known if he was in jail with him. It all leads one to believe Elrod's story, which suggests that Oswald and Ruby were involved in smuggling guns from Fort Hood just days before the assassination. And Oswald may have kept Hosty informed about the operation.

***

As we have seen, independent of all gunrunning and Cuban exile activity and Robert Kennedy's plan for a second invasion of Cuba, in the fall of 1963, there were credible reports that members of the radical right were planning to take over the U.S. government. The FBI learned that months prior to the October 1963 Constitution Party meeting attended by Joseph Milteer, retired army Colonel William Gale and his colleague Wesley A. Swift were part of an assassination plot. In April and June, an informant had told the FBI their group planned to assassinate 300 public officials in high positions in government and industry. The FBI investigated both men after the assassination and concluded they were not involved in the JFK assassination. The FBI had already interviewed Gale on November 16, six days before the assassination, so he was on their radar. George Lincoln Rockwell later told the FBI on March 7, 1964, that Crommelin, Gale, and del Valle planned to overthrow the government.[1500]

As described in the previous chapter, Charles Willoughby was one of the masterminds of the JFK assassination plot. Around the same time as this right-wing call for violent insurrection was happening, from October 14 through 16, Charles Willoughby's International Committee for the Defense of Christian Culture (ICDCC) met in Lucerne, Switzerland. Presiding over the affair was Jose Solis Ruiz, a minister in the Spanish cabinet of dictator Francisco Franco and a leading member of a secret Catholic order called Opus Dei. Among the speakers was Dr. Theodor Oberlander, a former German officer who had led the Ukrainian Nightingales, which was part of an American intelligence program of former Nazi sympathizers who infiltrated Ukraine after World War II as part of Operation Gladio that could have involved Skorzeny.[1501] Oberlander also served as West Germany's minister of refugee affairs until 1960, when he resigned after his Nazi past became public. He was also a delegate to the Asian People's Anti-Communist League. Herman Punder, the ICDCC's outgoing international president, was an ex-Nazi Abwehr agent.

At the same time, Willoughby was corresponding with Colonel Charles Thourot Pichel. When Hitler first came to power, Pichel had written to Ernst Hanfstaengl, a member of Hitler's inner circle, requesting that he be appointed official American liaison to Hitler. In 1963, Pichel became grand chancellor of the Shickshinny Knights, who claimed to be the legitimate heirs of the Knights of Malta, a Catholic order dating back to the Crusades. Their potential importance was that the Catholic Church permitted assassination if the victim was a tyrant. As author Mark Riebling explains in *Church of Spies*:

> Church teaching stated the conditions under which citizens could kill tyrants. Catholic doctrine permitted capital punishment; and though a priest himself could not shed blood, a Christian knight could wield the sword of justice at the bidding of a priest...They divided tyrants into two classes: usurpers, who seized power illegally, and oppressors, who used power unjustly.
>
> [In addition], the tyrant's executioners must have good grounds for believing his death would actually [sic] improve conditions and would not cause a bloody civil war...[and] his assassins must have sufficient reason to believe that those unjust policies would end with the tyrant's life.[1502]

As I described in Volume 1 of *It Did Not Start With JFK*, "the Church still had a legendary military society that dated back to the Crusades, called the Sovereign Military Order of Malta. One had to be knighted by the Church to become a member of this secret society." There were numerous American military and intelligence leaders in the years leading up to the JFK assassination who were knighted into this group by the Vatican. The bond they shared was an intense hatred for communism. "The list included CIA Counterintelligence chief James Angleton and ex-Nazi spy chief Reinhard Gehlen.[1503]

A similar group was the Shickshinny Knights of the Order of St. John of Jerusalem, a radical right-wing Catholic organization founded in 1956, headquartered in Shickshinny, Pa., who claimed to be the real Knights of Malta. Many members of the armed services belonged to this group: Generals Charles Willoughby, Pedro del Valle, Bonner Fellers, Lemuel Shepard, and Colonels Phillip Corso and Benjamin F. von Stahl. Sir Edward Domvile, an admiral in the British Royal Navy and a Nazi sympathizer, was also a member. As described throughout this book, these men were all Fascists who had an intense hatred for communism.[1504]

How Willoughby became involved with Pichel and the Shickshinny Knights is unknown, but by September 1963, he had become the Order's "security general." "I shall be honored to be of service," Willoughby wrote Pichel. I am familiar with the tradition and ethical purposes of your Order.[1505]

Recall that Willoughby received approval from his mentor, Douglas MacArthur, to proceed with the assassination plot. His name is mentioned often in the Lafitte datebook, including a reference to "soldier kill squads." So are General Pedro del Valle, Frank Wisner, and ex-Nazi Otto Skorzeny. All had good reason to protect Europe and would not have wanted the second invasion of Cuba to occur. Fortunately for them, Lyndon Johnson was the perfect candidate waiting in the wings for what they wanted to accomplish.

***

On November 20, two men and a woman approached Wayne January at his plane rental business at Red Bird Airport, located on the outskirts of Dallas. They wanted to rent a plane to take them to Mexico on Friday, the day of the assassination. He refused, for there was something about them he didn't like. He came forward after seeing Oswald on television, telling the FBI that one of the men he had talked to looked like Oswald.

On November 21, the day that Eloy Gutierrez Menoyo said, "Something very big would happen soon that would advance Cuban cause," Marita Lorenz was at a meeting in Dallas where Howard Hunt paid Frank Sturgis for guns they had just transported from Miami. Lee Oswald, Jack Ruby, Jerry Patrick Hemming, Pedro Diaz Lanz, and the Novo brothers were also present.

That same day, Lee Oswald approached Wesley Frazier at work and asked him for a ride to Ruth Paine's home after work. Oswald surprised both Marina and Ruth, who had not been expecting him until the next day. He told Marina that since he had come on Thursday, he would not see her on Friday, as was his practice. Unknown to Marina, on this Friday, he was involved in something that would keep him away for good.

CHAPTER TWENTY-EIGHT

INTERLUDE

The writing was on the wall as the hatred directed against President Kennedy reached epic proportions in the fall of 1963. A *New Republic* September article titled "Rebellion in the Air Force?" began, "The Air Force's ruling hierarchy is in open defiance of its Constitutional Commander-in-Chief, and in some ways, the situation bears a growing resemblance to the fictional storyline of last year's best-seller *Seven Days in May*, the account of a nearly successful military coup by an Air Force general in protest against a nuclear arms treaty just concluded with the Russians." The article's author, Raymond Senter, reported that at a recent convention, the Air Force Association (AFA), made up of retired and active-duty Air Force personnel, aerospace contractors, and lobbyists, had issued a blistering statement opposing the test ban treaty.[1506]

The military was dead set against the treaty. Many preferred that the United States launch a surprise nuclear first strike against the Soviet Union because the country enjoyed a massive nuclear weapons superiority over the Soviets in 1963, but that would not last forever. So, if war with the Soviets was inevitable, as many at the Pentagon believed, why not engage when conditions were most favorable?[1507]

Regarding Cuba, the Missile Crisis had weakened Kennedy's resolve. On October 10, he told Soviet Minister of Foreign Affairs Andrei Gromyko: "I don't deny that the Cuban problem is a serious one, but I am restraining those who are in favor of actions which could lead to war." U.S. militarism since the Crisis was on the rise, and JFK admitted he was doing all he could to control the hawks in his government. Ten days later, the State Department drafted a letter from Kennedy to Khrushchev that read, "I am convinced that the possibilities for an improvement in the international situation are real." The opportunities might be "fragile ones," he said, but they should "move forward, lest our hopes of progress be jeopardized." Kennedy signed off on the letter, and McGeorge Bundy scrawled on its bottom, "Approved. Let's get it out," but the State Department did not send it. Dean Rusk later blamed it on a "clerical misunderstanding." As Arthur Schlesinger told JFK earlier that year, lest you think you control the U.S. government, the subject is up for debate. In truth, no debate was necessary, for JFK had lost control.[1508]

At an October 24 meeting with Rusk, Maxwell Taylor, and Roswell Gilpatric, Kennedy approved a schedule for redeploying U.S. forces from Europe. He agreed to a reduction of 30,000 from U.S. logistical forces, 10 percent from headquarters staff, and the return of units sent during the 1961 Berlin crisis. An NSA memo summarized that the "possible redeployment of US forces... should not be discussed publicly nor with our allies until a decision has been made and politico-military plan for action approved."

JFK did not want it known that he was reducing the number of troops in Europe. He knew American forces would be needed in West Berlin to defend against Soviet aggression after a second invasion of Cuba. Hence, he wanted to avoid the inevitable confrontation that would ensue, and he was willing to sacrifice West Berlin to advance his political agenda.[1509]

On that same day, during a White House interview, Kennedy told reporter Jean Daniel, who was soon to meet with Castro, that: "I believe that there is no country in the world... where economic colonization, humiliation, and exploitation were worse than in Cuba, in part owing to my country's policies during the Batista regime... I will go even further: to some extent, it is as though Batista was the incarnation of a number of sins on the part of the United States. Now, we shall have to pay for those sins."[1510]

On October 28, the CIA asked the FBI for information on Manuel Artime. It was odd since the Agency knew very well who Artime was and what he was up to. It took until November 14 for the FBI to reply that they had not investigated him, which seems impossible. As previously mentioned in Chapter Twenty-Six, the FBI had canceled Oswald's WANTED NOTICE CARD on October 9, which was an indication the Bureau was very familiar with what was going on. At any rate, on that same day, the Department of the Army's Joseph Califano wrote to the DIA thanking them for loaning two men to the CIA to write personal bios of Cuban exiles they needed for the second invasion. It was a sign the military was now in control of Cuban exile groups while the CIA was on the outside, looking in. [1511]

On November 8, the Venezuelan government discovered a large cache of arms, with serial numbers removed, on one of its beaches. They accused Castro of exporting his revolution into Venezuela, and an OAS delegation later confirmed they were Cuban weapons. However, it is more likely the CIA planted the arms to satisfy President Kennedy's mandate that proof Castro exported his revolution was required to justify a second invasion of Cuba. It was what the Kennedy brothers needed to hear.

INTERLUDE

On September 11, 1975, Richard Helms testified before the Church Committee that "in the summer or fall of 1963, talking to Mr. Robert Kennedy about the problem of Castro's efforts to send arms and trained guerillas and so forth into other Latin American and Central American countries…it just seemed to me that this was dangerous indeed, particularly after the difficulties we had with Castro and the Cuban Missile Crisis, and my general recollection is that Mr. Kennedy said yes, but what can the President do? If you can bring him evidence that Castro is sending arms and trained guerillas and so forth to Latin American countries…sometime after that….the Venezuelan authorities found a large arms cache…and they also found, through some penetration or agent, rather, a plan of some guerillas, Venezuelan guerillas, in touch with the Cubans to tie off certain sections of Caracas with armed men and so forth and bring the city to a halt…"[1512]

Helms brought Robert Kennedy one of the Cuban submachine guns found and said, "Here's the evidence you are looking for." A short time later, Helms was in the White House briefing the President. There are no known tapes of this or any other White House meetings after early November, even though there was a taping system that recorded everything. Hours after JFK died, Bobby took possession of all the tapes. He donated some to the Kennedy Library, but not everything. What Bobby wanted to keep hidden is anyone's guess, but one must assume it was in some way connected to Cuba and his brother's assassination. As the architect of the second invasion of Cuba, he probably held himself responsible.[1513]

On November 12, JFK issued NSAM-271, titled "Cooperation with the USSR on Outer Space Matters," which had to do with a potential joint space exploration between the United States and the Soviet Union. For those who believed the Soviet Union could not be trusted and opposed any collaboration with them, this was too much.[1514]

On November 18, during a speech at the New York Economic Club, Robert McNamara advised that a significant cut in defense spending was "in the works," calling it "a fundamental strategic shift…not just a temporary slash." The hawks who opposed Kennedy were not pleased, and any doubt among the assassination plotters quickly went by the wayside.[1515]

On the following day, the U.S. ambassador to Ghana, William Mahoney, complained he was tired of asking President Kwame Nkrumah before the beginning of every General Assembly session to vote against admitting Communist China to the UN. President Kennedy was undeterred by this because he hoped to improve relations with China during his second term. He showed Mahoney a draft of Assistant Secretary of State for Far East-

505

ern Affairs Roger Hilsman's speech, which he planned to give the following month. It called for improved relations with China if they ceased exporting revolution and communism to third-world countries. What JFK intended to do was not a secret. He had told journalist Marie Ridder it was on his agenda for his second term. Secretary of State Dean Rusk said they often discussed it, and he thought Kennedy would have reached out to the Chinese in 1965, even though the military and the CIA distrusted the Chinese as much as they did the Soviets.[1516]

Clearly, there was strong opposition to President Kennedy throughout 1963, especially among American militarists, civilian and military alike, and right-wing mercenary and Fascist groups, domestic and foreign. So, it was no wonder that by the end of December 1963, the KGB concluded that the JFK assassination was a coup d'etat. Their December 23 internal report included the following: "The assassination of JFK on November 22 of this year in Dallas was organized by a circle of reactionary monopolists in league with pro-fascist groups of the U.S. with the objective of strengthening the reactionary and aggressive aspects of U.S. policy."[1517]

The Russians were close to the truth but not entirely correct. They were unaware that the assassination of JFK was to shift attention away from Cuba and Western Europe and redirect it to Southeast Asia. The American monopolists could always find another Cuba, an insignificant country that they could deal with. More critical was protecting their interests in Europe and containing the spread of communism in accordance with George Kennan's Containment Policy. Europe would have remained safe if West Berlin had stayed in the sphere of influence of the Western Allies. However, Southeast Asia, which included countries like Vietnam, Laos, and Indonesia, remained up for grabs, and that had to change. So, the Russians were unaware that the Kennedy assassination was to prevent a second invasion of Cuba from occurring, not to initiate one, but how could they have known this? It was counter to everything the United States looked to do since Castro came to power.

Meanwhile, as described in Chapter Twenty-Five, through the efforts of ABC reporter Lisa Howard, the Kennedy administration considered normalizing relations with Castro. That would die on the vine when Lyndon Johnson became President.

The new U.S. ambassador to Vietnam, Henry Lodge, was a pro-military Republican and political nemesis of President Kennedy. He orchestrated a coup with the help of the CIA's Lucien Conein, who was a protégé of General Lansdale and a friend of the OAS and the Corsican Unione Corse. The intent was to remove Vietnam's President Diem from power and replace him with a right-wing military government. Lodge had support from the State Department, the military, and the CIA. President Kennedy knew a coup was in the works. Still, when he learned that Diem and his brother were murdered on November 2, less than three weeks before he would suffer a similar fate, he was almost catatonic because he knew forces in his administration had misled him. However, he should have seen it coming. For years, the military had been lying to him about the state of the war in Vietnam, and he knew that. Still, he ordered them to make plans for the removal of all U.S. troops by 1965, something they believed threatened the security of the United States. The Kennedy brothers feared the Pentagon might take over the government during the Missile Crisis. What made them think the military would sit idly by and allow them to pull out of Vietnam? They were naïve.

Meanwhile, Bobby had organized a Cuban exile left-wing army that intended to invade Cuba that December with the support of the U.S. military. There is no doubt that Allen Dulles and his supporters at the CIA worried that this would lead to a Soviet takeover of West Berlin, as Dulles had believed in 1959 when he sabotaged a coup to oust Castro run out of the U.S. Embassy in Havana. So, to prevent that from happening, a group among the conspirators chose the only option that remained for them, which was to assassinate the President.

To make things worse, the CIA's Desmond FitzGerald was in Paris on November 22, meeting with Rolando Cubela, who had allegedly turned against Castro and was willing to kill him. However, many at the CIA thought he was a Castro agent working undercover against the U.S., and the CIA would have used this to implicate Castro in JFK's assassination.

Despite all the opposition they faced, John and Bobby Kennedy were still willing to proceed with the second invasion of Cuba, but not because they thought it was in the best interest of the United States. Their decision was politically motivated. How they handled Castro was going to play a pivotal role in the 1964 presidential election, and in order to win, the Kennedys believed they needed to do something big, even sacrificing West Berlin to the Communists. Castro had to go by any means possible.

President Kennedy had lost control of his government by the fall of 1963. He must have known this was the case because the signs were clear. His downfall was that he did not realize to what extent those who opposed him would go to stop him.

CHAPTER TWENTY-NINE

THE DARKEST DAY –
AN AMERICAN TRAGEDY

Dallas police lieutenant Jack Revill headed the Criminal Intelligence Division. He told the Warren Commission that an Army Intelligence officer rode with him from Dealey Plaza to the Dallas police station after the JFK assassination. We know Army Intelligence was at the scene because agent James Powell was locked in the Dal-Tex Building after the police sealed it off, and he had to provide credentials to prove who he was to get out.[1518]

In Revill's possession was a list of employees from the Book Depository. At the top was the name "Lee Harvey Oswald," which is highly suspect since the address listed alongside Oswald's name was 605 Elsbeth Street. Oswald lived at 602 Elsbeth in late 1962 and early 1963, not 605. Stranger still, the Book Depository did not know that Oswald had lived there since he had given them Ruth Paine's address as his own, so Revill must have received his information from someone else. His source, without question, was the Military Intelligence officer riding in the car with him.

The 112th Military Intelligence Group maintained an office in Dallas. It kept a file on "Harvey Lee Oswald," which described him as a Communist who was involved in pro-Castro activity in New Orleans. The file listed Oswald's address as 605 Elsbeth Street, the same error that appeared on Revill's list. The question is, why was Military Intelligence even aware of Oswald's old address, and why were they concerned with him so quickly after the assassination, long before he was considered a suspect?

Forty-five minutes prior to the assassination, a meeting took place in Dallas at the office of ATF agent Frank Ellsworth. Also in attendance were FBI Agent James Hosty and Agent Ed J. Coyle of Army Counterintelligence, who was the army's liaison for Presidential protection in Dallas that day. Hosty later told the Warren Commission that the meeting had nothing to do with the President's visit. Ellsworth wanted to discuss with Army Intelligence the continued theft of arms from Fort Hood and his recent blown cover in the John Thomas Masen affair described in Chapter Twenty-Seven. Because he believed members of the Minutemen and supporters of General Walker might have been responsible, Ellsworth wanted Hosty there too, who was the FBI's specialist on right-wing groups.

According to Hosty, he first learned about guns being stolen from Fort Hood the previous day when he met with Coyle and Revill to begin working on the case. Yet, we know the FBI was aware of the operation as early as October when Ellsworth told them he suspected George Nonte was the one at Fort Hood responsible for the arms thefts. Unknown to Ellsworth, Nonte was working undercover and kept the FBI informed. Recall it was the FBI and Dallas police detectives who thwarted Ellsworth's attempt to upend the operation, which resulted in Nonte remaining in business.[1519]

FBI agent Joe Abernathy, who was hiding with two Burglary and Theft Division detectives, disrupted the arms deal involving Whitter and Miller based on a tip they received from a police informant. On April 29, 1964, Arnold Sagalyn, the director of law-enforcement coordination for the U.S. Treasury, wrote a letter to Secret Service inspector Thomas J. Kelley, which stated that "Alcohol & Tobacco Tax was not involved in any way" in the arms transaction gone wrong, and they "only learned about this when it received a telephone call from the US Attorney concerned," who was presumably B.H. Timmins, Jr. However, Timmins filed a motion claiming Abernathy's source was the ATF and not the police, which explains why detectives did not appear in court to testify. One wonders why the Secret Service official investigating the assassination took an interest in what seemed to be an unrelated gun-running operation unless Oswald was involved.

On April 17, 1964, Dallas police deputy chief M.W. Stevenson sent a memo to Texas Attorney General Waggoner Carr, who was investigating the assassination on behalf of LBJ, concurrent with the Warren Commission investigation. The subject of the memo, "Check of Garages and Service Stations Patronized by Jack Ruby," described that "Donnell D. Whitter... formerly worked at the Texaco Service Station... [that] serviced Ruby's car." A memo from police Lt. E.L. Cunningham to Chief of Police Jesse Curry had said the same thing two weeks earlier. It suggests Ruby was involved in the gunrunning operation. Oswald had told John Elrod that Ruby was involved, and the police were aware of his connection to Whitter.

There is also evidence that sabotaging Ellsworth's sting operation was not an accident. An FBI Teletype dated October 25, 1963, said the FBI interviewed Nonte the day before and "briefed [him] as to scope of discreet inquiry to be made of Masen on contact." In other words, Nonte was an FBI informant they wanted to protect.

509

Hosty, Revill, and Coyle met on November 21, which was followed by a three-hour meeting between Ellsworth, Hosty, and Coyle the next day. We know Coyle and Hosty were working on the DRE's attempt to purchase arms in Dallas, and they probably were aware that Oswald was involved with the DRE in New Orleans. It explains why Hosty visited Ruth Paine's home, trying to find Oswald. In addition, the DRE Intelligence Officer in Miami, Jose Antonion Lanusa, later "described Oswald [as] definitely a Communist and supporter of Castro," and the Miami FBI files have DRE chief Manuel Salvat referring to a "Harvey Lee Oswald," which matched the Military Intelligence file's name described above.[1520]

The meetings held by Ellsworth, Hosty, Coyle, and Revill dealt with the Fort Hood arms operation, which involved Whitter and Miller, and Oswald told John Elrod he knew these men. As previously discussed, the references to Running Man and Runner Runner possibly connected Oswald to gun-running activity, so it is not surprising if Military Intelligence and the FBI were already aware of Oswald and focused their attention on him so quickly after the assassination, knowing he worked at the Book Depository. It is especially true if Oswald was an FBI informant providing information on the Fort Hood arms deal. It is also understandable that none of the men involved would admit this later, which was why Army Counterintelligence agent Coyle was sent to Korea shortly after the assassination before reporters could question him.[1521]

Lt. Colonel Robert E. Jones was an operating officer for the 112th Military Intelligence Group, stationed at Fort Sam Houston in San Antonio. Even though Jack Revill was given the past address of Oswald by a Military Intelligence officer on the scene, Jones said that one of his agents in Dallas reported that the police had arrested an A.J. Hidell. When Oswald was apprehended, he had in his wallet documents containing both names. Yet, it did not take long for authorities to ascertain that his real name was Oswald, especially since he was missing from the Depository Building. So, in addition to being aware of Oswald's Elsbeth Street address, Military Intelligence knew of the alias Hidell before anyone else on the ground could make the connection. According to Jones, he checked his office files to see if there was information on Hidell and found a file that also referenced Oswald, his defection to the Soviet Union, and his involvement in pro-Castro activities in New Orleans. The files said Hidell was an Oswald alias and that Military Intelligence became aware of him the previous summer in New Orleans when the New Orleans Police contacted them following Oswald's arrest after the Bringuier incident.[1522] However, this does not explain how they knew Oswald used the alias Hidell. Recall that Oswald began his charade by passing out FPCC handbills with a phony post office box without anything connecting himself to it. Three days after the assassination, Major Robert H. Erdrich of the 112th Army Intelligence Group told the FBI that one of his men picked up a handbill with Hidell's name on it at Tulane University. Still, there was no known link between Oswald and the handbill.[1523]

By the time Oswald was arrested in New Orleans in August 1963, he had started stamping handbills with his real name and address. The FPCC membership card found in Oswald's wallet was in his name and signed by the chapter president, A.J. Hidell. New Orleans FBI agent Quigley's report after his jailhouse interview with Oswald contained this passage: "Since receiving his membership card... he [Oswald] had spoken with Hidell on the telephone on several occasions... He said he has never personally met Hidell..."[1524] The FBI believed that Hidell and Oswald were two different people, and maybe they were. Recall from Chapter Twenty-Five that the FBI ran a check on Hidell with the New Orleans Retailers' Credit Bureau and the New Orleans City Directory in October, trying to learn who Hidell was, but came up empty. Why, then, did Military Intelligence categorically state that Hidell was Oswald's alias at a time when no one else did? What evidence did they have to believe this?

According to eyewitnesses, Oswald used the name Hidell in the summer of 1963 when he secretly visited Mexico. It was when the conspirators brought Oswald into the assassination plot, which involved Richard Nagell. Nagell was with Military Intelligence, and he also used the alias Hidell, as did Jean Pierre Lafitte. It seems Mexico City was an Army Intelligence gathering, which explains how they knew so much about Oswald, his previous address, and the alias Hidell.

We know either Oswald or an impostor used the name Hidell when purchasing the rifle and pistol through the mail in March 1963. That was when he was living on Elsbeth Street, the last known Oswald address that Army Intelligence had in their files, so it is conceivable they were aware of him when the gun purchase occurred. It was also around that time that Nagell showed up in Dallas to check on what Oswald and his wife were up to. And since we know Nagell was aware of the assassination plot and that Oswald was the designated fall guy, it makes sense that he kept Army Intelligence informed of what he learned. It explains why Oswald became a suspect so soon after the assassination and why Army Intelligence knew about Hidell.

The House Select Committee on Assassinations was troubled by the discovery of Army Intelligence files on Oswald and said, "It raised the possibil-

511

ity that he had intelligence associations of some kind." In 1978, the Committee asked to see the Oswald files, but Army Intelligence claimed to have destroyed them in 1973. The HSCA found this "extremely troublesome, especially when viewed in light of the Department of Defense's failure to make the files available to the Warren Commission. Despite the credibility of Jones' testimony, without access to the file he referenced, the HSCA could not confirm Oswald's connection to Army Intelligence."[1525]

There were other suspicious incidents involving the military that day. As described in Chapter Sixteen, former OSS officer Jack Crichton was the head of the 488th Military Intelligence Detachment in Dallas, which included around fifty members of the Dallas police. Crichton was part of the Texas oil community, and in July 1963, he became director of the board of the H.L. Hunt Foundation. Crichton served as President of the Dallas Petroleum Engineers Club and had a connection to Madrid through Clint Murchison and the Du Ponts when they looked to obtain oil drilling rights in Spain during the 1950s. He knew George Bush very well and was a director of Dorchester Gas Producing along with oilman David Harold Boyd, who owned the Texas School Book Depository Building. After the assassination, it was Crichton who asked Ilya Mamantov to become Marina Oswald's interpreter, which exemplifies the strong relationship Crichton had with the Dallas police. When Khrushchev referred to the involvement of moneyed interests in the assassination, he was referring to the likes of Jack Crichton.

Crichton's diary revealed "his unit's participation" and "concealed involvement" during Kennedy's trip to Dallas. We know Frank Brandsetter was in Dallas the day before the assassination, reportedly conducting a similar service for Army Intelligence, as was William Bishop, who said he was assigned to the Texas Trade Mart while working for Military Intelligence. Both men must have associated with Crichton and his 488th Military Intelligence group that day. Lafitte's datebook mentions Crichton three times. On November 5: "Meet with Crichton at Tech building. O says Lancelot go;" November 11: "Terry says call + [illegible] 7436 Kenshire, Dallas J. Crichton;" and on November 14: "Crichton w T. (Caretaker)."[1526] So, the fact that Lafitte mentioned Crichton three times in November in his datebook confirms that Crichton played a role in the JFK assassination.

Meanwhile, in Washington, D.C., the telephone system broke down. Overloaded phone lines were the reason given, and it took almost an hour for the phone company to restore service. By that time, the Pentagon had placed American troops on worldwide alert, and a military man grabbed the phone at the White House switchboard and said the Secretary of Defense and the Joint Chiefs of Staff "are now the President." Was this all a coincidence, or was this really a military coup, which Private Eugene Dinkin had warned about? One thing was for sure. The evidence was clear that Lee Harvey Oswald did not shoot President Kennedy, although he undoubtedly was involved. And as Oswald made his escape from Dealey Plaza, the evidence left behind would eventually lead police in his direction. Unfortunately, circumstances beyond his control would make him a suspect before he anticipated.

***

That President Kennedy intended to visit Dallas in the fall of 1963 was publicly announced on April 24 of that year. The purpose was to settle a political dispute between conservative and liberal factions of the Democratic party in Texas. If allowed to continue, the battle waged between conservative Governor John Connally and liberal Senator Ralph Yarborough had the potential to divide Democratic voters in the 1964 Presidential election. It had a paralyzing effect on Texas politics, with Vice President Lyndon Johnson embroiled in the conflict as well. Johnson believed Yarborough was trying to get him removed from the Kennedy ticket in 1964. As a result, he privately offered financial backing to one of his supporters, Representative James Wright, to try and unseat Yarborough in the upcoming election.

Kennedy may have intended to drop Johnson from the ticket in 1964, but he also knew he needed him to carry Texas and its twenty-five electoral votes. In 1960, Kennedy managed to win Texas by the narrowest margin- only 46,233 votes. A poll taken in 1963 showed that only 38 percent of all Texans had a favorable view of the President. There was concern that problems within the party could cost Kennedy Texas. As a result, Johnson and Kennedy both traveled to the Lone Star State and, along with Connally and Yarborough, put on a display that was supposed to unite the party and ensure a Democratic victory in 1964. By the afternoon of November 22, it no longer mattered.

The importance of political harmony notwithstanding, not everyone thought the trip to Dallas was a good idea. In October, Kennedy met with Marquis Childs of the *St. Louis Post-Dispatch*, who had authored a book titled *They Hate Roosevelt*. Having recently returned from a trip throughout the south and southwest, Childs was alarmed by the hostility he saw directed at the President. "From smug editorial writers to filling station attendants, I heard hatred," Childs told Kennedy. "The rich and privileged were again excoriating that son of a bitch in Washington, and not only the rich and privileged this time. It was for me a deeply disturbing phenomenon." "I don't believe it," the President responded. "I just don't believe that's true... I don't think they feel toward me the way they felt toward Roosevelt. I can't believe that."[1527]

The Texas National Democratic Committeeman, Byron Skelton, was deeply concerned. On November 4, he wrote to the Attorney General, stating, "Frankly, I am worried about President Kennedy's proposed trip to Dallas." He quoted a prominent Dallas resident who had recently declared that "Kennedy is a liability to the free world." "A man who would make this kind of statement," Skelton commented, "is capable of doing harm to the President." He would have [felt] better "if the President's itinerary did not include Dallas." Senator William Fulbright, a liberal from Arkansas who was a frequent target of the extreme right, warned the President that "Dallas is a very dangerous place. I wouldn't go there. Don't you go." Adlai Stevenson, who had been spat upon in Dallas the previous month, was shocked at the level of hatred in the city. He seriously questioned the wisdom of going to Dallas. U.S. Attorney H. Barefoot Sanders, Lyndon Johnson's contact man in Dallas, said the city's political climate made the trip "inadvisable." Senator Hubert Humphrey told him not to go. Congressman Hale Boggs said, "Mr. President, you're going into a hornet's nest."[1528]

In the election of 1960, Kennedy and Nixon ran close in seventy-one of the seventy-two counties in northeast Texas. Only in Dallas did Kennedy get soundly defeated by an overwhelming 62.5 percent, and there was no reason to believe things would be different in 1964. By the fall of 1963, the hatred for the President in Dallas had reached a climax. Treason and Communist were the two words most associated with the liberal President from the north. Racial integration, nonintervention in Vietnam, the Cuban problem, the Berlin Wall, a nuclear test ban treaty, and coexistence with Communists were JFK policies for which the citizenry of Dallas had little tolerance. It seemed an atmosphere of hatred and bigotry had engulfed the city.

It was not a coincidence that Dallas led the nation in homicides. In 1963, there were 110 murders in the city by the time of the Kennedy assassination. "Impeach Earl Warren" appeared on billboards in giant letters. To a certain extent, lawlessness was prevalent. When Congressman Henry Gonzales returned to Washington after a trip to Texas, he told the President that "Dallas is like the Congo. It isn't ready for self-government."[1529]

That an element of the radical right might try to assassinate Kennedy was a concern as the time for the trip to Dallas approached. In Chicago on No-

THE DARKEST DAY – AN AMERICAN TRAGEDY

vember 2, the Secret Service learned of a possible threat to the President's life, which led to the arrest of a former Marine with a history of mental illness named Thomas Vallee. He was a member of the John Birch Society and an outspoken opponent of the President who arranged to take time off from work on the day Kennedy was to visit. They found in his possession an M-1 rifle and three thousand rounds of ammunition. However, according to Secret Service agent Abraham Bolden, who came forward after the assassination, the plot the Secret Service was aware of was more complex, involving a four-man team with high-powered rifles. Bolden stated that two of the men were in custody on the night prior to Kennedy's scheduled arrival, but the two others remained free. At the last moment, the White House canceled Kennedy's Chicago trip.[1530]

On November 9, Joseph Milteer was caught on tape describing a possible assassination attempt that was to occur during Kennedy's trip to Miami on November 18. Charles Sapp, the head of Miami's Police Intelligence Bureau, believed the threat was real. "From an office building with a high-powered rifle," was how Milteer described it would happen. When Kennedy arrived, they canceled a planned motorcade. He took a helicopter to Miami Beach instead. The following day, perhaps an indication he was aware of the danger that existed in Miami, Kennedy told an aide, "Last night would have been a hell of a night to assassinate a President... Anyone perched above the crowd with a rifle could do it."[1531]

***

President Kennedy left for Texas on November 21. His first stop was San Antonio, followed by Houston. By the time he arrived in Fort Worth at midnight, he had traveled safely in four motorcades. November 22 began with a speech in the rain outside Kennedy's hotel. Returning to his room, the President noticed a copy of the *Dallas Morning News* that included an advertisement by The American Fact-Finding Committee titled *Welcome Mr. Kennedy To Dallas*. "Why have you scrapped the Monroe Doctrine," it read, "in favor of the 'Spirit of Moscow'...Because of your policy, thousands of Cubans have been imprisoned, are starving and being persecuted – with thousands already murdered and thousands more awaiting execution..."

In all, there were twelve questions insinuating the President was soft on communism. Lamar Hunt was among the ad's sponsors. After reading it, Kennedy said to Jackie with disgust: "You know, we're heading into nut country today." He was so right.[1532]

Protesters were also distributing flyers on the streets of Dallas, with the heading "Wanted for Treason" and two photos of JFK in the style of an FBI wanted poster. It accused him of "turning the sovereignty of the U.S. over to the communist-controlled United Nations," of "betraying our friends (Cuba, Katanga, Portugal) and befriending our enemies (Russia, Yugoslavia, Poland)," and of being "WRONG on innumerable issues affecting the security of the U.S. (United Nations- Berlin wall- Missile removal- Cuba-Wheat deals- Test Ban Treaty, etc.)."[1533]

Air Force One touched down at Love Field in Dallas at 11:38 A.M. A Confederate flag held high above the crowd greeted them. Many held signs aloft with hateful messages. "YOUR [sic] A TRAITOR," read one. "MR. PRESIDENT, BECAUSE OF YOUR SOCIALIST TENDENCIES AND BECAUSE OF YOUR SURRENDER TO COMMUNISM I HOLD YOU IN COMPLETE CONTEMPT," read another.[1534]

Despite everything, the crowds were large and responsive, and as the motorcade wound its way through the streets, the people cheered. Seated in front of the Kennedys in the limousine were Governor John Connally and his wife, Nellie. Obviously pleased, she turned and said, "Mr. Kennedy, you can't say Dallas doesn't love you." "That is very obvious," he replied as he continued to wave to the crowd. The time was 12:29. A minute later, they were making the awkward turn at Houston and Elm in front of the Texas School Book Depository Building.[1535]

***

Lee Harvey Oswald rose early on Friday morning, November 22, at Ruth Paine's home. He usually arrived on Friday and spent the weekend, but this time, he unexpectedly appeared on Thursday night. Marina said Lee was pleasant that morning, kissing the children goodbye as they slept. He left his wedding ring and $170 in a dresser drawer, which was almost everything he owned and a sign he would not be returning.[1536]

Oswald walked to the home of coworker Wesley Frazier, who was to drive him to work. Linnie Mae Randle, Frazier's sister, noticed Oswald carrying a lengthy brown paper package, which he placed in the back seat of her brother's car. Oswald told Frazier the package contained curtain rods, and Frazier remembered him saying something about that the night before when he had driven him home. When they arrived at work, Oswald quickly walked ahead with the package tucked under his right arm. Still, it was 35" long when disassembled, too long to be held that way. As described in Chapter Twenty-Seven, Garland Slack's wife, Lucille, told the FBI in 1964 that "her husband told her Oswald was driven to the [shooting] range by a man named Frazier," so Wesley may have had a reason not to be totally truthful after Oswald's arrest. A PSE (Psychological Stress Evaluator) test indicated he was lying. When HSCA investigators tried to interview him in 1977, he stalled repeatedly. The investigator wrote, "Frazier continues to procrastinate. Now [he] wants to meet in [his] lawyer's office next Friday. Definite resistance…"[1537]

His sister may also have lied to protect him. Linnie Mae Randle could not have seen Oswald or her brother's car in her driveway that morning from her vantage point, as she testified, because a carport attached to the house blocked her vision.

Depository worker Jack Dougherty saw Oswald enter the building after he left Frazier's car, but he did not recall him carrying a package. No one else saw it either. So, something was amiss. Oswald would have had to enter the building holding the rifle and punched in while waiting in line with others without being seen by anyone. Or, he handed the rifle to another conspirator on the street. Still, only Frazier and his sister provided any evidence that Oswald carried a rifle from Ruth Paine's garage to Frazier's car and then into the building that day.[1538]

***

As Oswald went about his regular work duties that morning, others on the street noticed suspicious activity. Just before 11:00 A.M., twenty-three-year-old Julia Ann Mercer was driving west on Elm Street, just beyond the point where President Kennedy's assassination would occur. She had to stop her car when a green Ford pickup truck with Texas plates and the words "AIR CONDITIONING" painted on the side blocked her lane. She waited for perhaps three minutes and saw a young man exit the passenger side and retrieve what appeared to be a rifle wrapped in a paper package from the rear of the truck. He then walked towards the grassy knoll with the package in hand. As she maneuvered her car around the pickup truck, she passed and locked eyes with the driver, who had a heavy build and a round face. She later told acquaintances what she had seen, which led to her being questioned by the police later that day. At four o'clock the following morning, the FBI came to her home and brought her back to Dallas to look at photographs of potential suspects. She picked out two, which she believed were the men she had seen the previous morning. On Sunday, she watched Ruby shoot Oswald on television with some friends and immediately shouted that these were the two men whose photos she had picked out.[1539]

At about the time that Mercer said the truck incident occurred, Dallas policeman Joe Murphy radioed from Dealey Plaza, "Could you send a city wrecker to the triple underpass …to clear a stalled truck from the route of the escort?" A few minutes later, he said, "Disregard…We got a truck to push him out of here."[1540] It confirmed that what Mercer claimed she had seen was true.

That the FBI showed Mercer a photo of Ruby before he killed Oswald is possible since, just days before that, the foiled gun transaction with Lawrence Miller and Donald Whitter occurred, which may have involved both Oswald and Ruby, so they were already persons of interest.

Lee Bowers watched the assassination from a 14-foot tower behind the wooden fence atop the grassy knoll. During the hour prior to the assassination, he noticed three unfamiliar cars enter the parking lot behind the Book Depository. The first was a blue-and-white 1959 Oldsmobile station wagon splattered with dirt, with an out-of-state license plate and "Goldwater for President" bumper sticker. The second was a black 1957 Ford. The driver appeared to be speaking into a microphone as he steered with one hand. The third was a 1961 white Chevy Impala, also with a Goldwater bumper sticker, which entered the lot about ten minutes prior to the assassination. At the time of the shooting, Bowers noticed two men near the wooden fence. One was middle-aged and heavy-set. The other was in his mid-twenties and wore a plaid shirt. They were the only two strangers in the area and bore a resemblance to the two men Julia Ann Mercer had seen.[1541]

Gordon Arnold was a young soldier who was home from Army basic training. He planned to take a movie of the motorcade, but as he walked behind the fence at the top of the grassy knoll, a man in a suit wearing a side arm said he was a Secret Service agent and told him to leave. There were no Secret Service agents on duty in Dealey Plaza that day.[1542]

Meanwhile, in front of the Depository Building, people noticed peculiar activity on the building's 6th floor. Arnold and Barbara Rowland were standing at the west entrance of the Dallas County Records Building on Houston Street, which had an excellent view of the Depository Building. Rowland saw a man with a rifle at a Depository window just as he heard a police radio report that the motorcade had reached Cedar Springs Road. Police records showed this occurred between 12:15 P.M. and 12:16 P.M. Rowland described the man as 140 to 150 lbs., light-skinned with short-cropped dark hair, with a light-colored shirt over a T-shirt and dark pants. He told the FBI the man was at the far-left window. At the far-right 6th-floor window at the alleged sniper's nest, he saw an African American man, about 55 years old, balding, and thin.[1543]

Ruby Henderson also saw two men on the 6th floor, right after an ambulance left that had attended to a man having an apparent seizure in front of the Depository Building. Records show the ambulance left at 12:24 P.M., just six minutes before the assassination. She said one of the men "had dark hair... a darker complexion than the other." He was "possibly a Mexican but could have been a Negro." The second man was taller and lighter.[1544]

Fifteen-year-old Amos Euins was standing on the other side of Elm Street. He also saw a dark-skinned man with a rifle at the southeast corner window, at the opposite end of the building from the sniper's nest, confirming what Rowland had seen.[1545] John Powell was an inmate on the 6th floor of the Dallas County Jail, which offered an excellent view of the sniper's nest. For years, he told friends and family members that he and his cellmates could see two men with a gun in the sniper's nest window. His vantage point was so clear that Powell could see them "fooling with the scope" on the gun. "Quite a few of us saw them," he said. Powell recalled that one of the men appeared to be Latin.[1546]

Carolyn Walther also saw two men with a rifle. "I saw this man in a window," she said, "and he had a gun in his hands, pointed downwards. The man evidently was in a kneeling position because his forearms were resting on the windowsill. Another man was standing beside him, but I only saw a portion of his body because he was standing partly up against the window... only halfway in the window; and the window was dirty, and I couldn't see his face... because the window was pushed up..." The man with the gun "was wearing a white shirt and had blond or light brown hair." The second man wore "a brown suit coat."[1547]

Construction worker Richard Carr watched the activities from the upper floor of a building he was working in near Dealey Plaza. He saw a heavy-set man wearing a hat, a tan sports coat, and horn-rimmed glasses on the 6th floor shortly before the shooting.[1548]

James Worrell was walking along Houston Street. After the shooting, he saw a man run suspiciously from the back of the Book Depository wearing a brown sports coat. Carr, Worrell, and Carolyn Walther likely all saw the same man.[1549]

Employee Charles Givens was inside the Book Depository and later testified that he saw Oswald on the 6th floor at 11:55 A.M. It was critical testimony because finding an eyewitness who placed Oswald there was needed to contradict the recollections of those on the street who claimed to have seen two men. However, when first questioned, Givens never mentioned that he saw Oswald on the 6th floor. Instead, he said he "observed Lee reading a newspaper in the Domino Room [on the first floor] where the employees eat lunch about 11:50 A.M." In fact, he signed a notarized

519

affidavit, dated the day of the assassination, that never mentioned Oswald. He said that at noon, he went on his lunch break, left the building, and was in a parking lot at the corner of Record and Elm Streets when he heard the shots.[1550]

Foreman Bill Shelley saw Oswald on the first floor, near a telephone, ten or fifteen minutes before noon. Another employee, Eddie Piper, said he spoke to Oswald "just at twelve o'clock, down on the first floor." These men knew Oswald and would have recognized him. Givens, Shelley and Piper all saw him on the first floor 5-10 minutes before noon, which was corroborated by Oswald after his arrest when he said he had followed his coworkers down to eat on the first floor. He also remembered two African American workers walking through the Domino Room while he was eating. One of them, Oswald recalled, was called "Junior." He could not remember the name of the second man but knew he was "short."[1551]

Two African American employees, "Junior" Jarman and Harold Norman (who was short), usually ate lunch together. According to Norman, he was in the Domino Room between 12:00 and 12:15 P.M. and thought "there was someone else in there," but he couldn't remember who that was. Around 12:15 P.M., Jarman and Norman walked out of the Domino Room together, just as Oswald described, and left the building for a few minutes. Between 12:20 and 12:25 P.M., they went upstairs to the 5th floor to watch the motorcade. Oswald could not have known that they were in the Domino Room unless he had seen them there. It indicates that as late as 12:15, possibly 12:20 P.M., Lee Oswald was still on the first floor.[1552]

During questioning, Oswald stated he left the Domino Room to go to the second-floor lunchroom where the Coke machine was. It would have been around 12:15 P.M. Carolyn Arnold, whose FBI interview the Warren Commission omitted from their report, was secretary to the vice president of the Book Depository. In 1978, she recalled for Anthony Summers that she told the FBI, "I went into the lunchroom on the second floor for a moment...Oswald was sitting in one of the booth seats on the right-hand side of the room...I did not speak to him, but I recognized him clearly." She claimed the time was "about 12:15. It may have been slightly later."[1553]

Oswald was seen by Givens, Shelley, and Piper on the first floor when Oswald claimed to be on the first floor. Oswald confirmed the presence of Jarmen and Norman in the Domino Room at the precise time that Norman said they were there. Carolyn Arnold saw Oswald in the second-floor lunchroom around 12:15 P.M., which is when Oswald left the first floor to go upstairs. No one else recalled seeing Oswald in the half-hour leading up to the assassination, yet what these people claimed was entirely rejected by the Warren Commission.

Arnold Rowland saw two men with a rifle on the 6th floor shortly after 12:15 P.M. Ruby Henderson's sighting occurred around 12:25 P.M., establishing Rowland's sighting as the earliest time anyone saw a gunman on the 6th floor. It makes sense since another employee, Bonny Ray Williams, did not leave the sixth floor until around 12:15 P.M. Mrs. Arnold claimed she did not leave the lunchroom until 12:25 P.M., which was after the Rowland sighting. Since she did not mention seeing Oswald leave the lunchroom before she did, it is safe to assume that Oswald was still there at 12:25 P.M. when she left. It obviously precludes Oswald from being on the 6th floor at 12:15 P.M., which means he did not shoot President John F. Kennedy.

The Warren Commission disregarded these witnesses. Instead, they elected to believe Howard Brennan, who had poor eyesight and was standing at the southwest corner of Houston and Elm. Brennan claimed he saw a man moving in the sniper's nest before the assassination and looked up in time to see the final shot. However, he failed to identify Oswald in a lineup, even though he had already seen Oswald's picture on television. A month later, Brennan told the FBI he was sure the man in the window was Oswald, but later still, he said he couldn't be sure. He eventually claimed he did not identify Oswald out of fear of reprisal from Communists. In 1979, the HSCA, recognizing that Brennan's testimony was useless, ignored him completely.[1554]

In 1978, photographic expert Robert Groden, working for the HSCA, enhanced a film taken by amateur photographer Charles Bronson six minutes prior to the assassination. It shows the 6th floor and captures what appears to be movement in two separate windows at the same time, which corroborates the claims of those who saw two men on the 6th floor. According to Groden, "The fact that there is movement in two windows that are separated by a good eight feet indicates beyond question that there was more than one person up there."[1555]

After eating their lunch on the 1st floor, Harold Norman and James "Junior" Jarman went up to the 5th floor to watch the motorcade pass. They positioned themselves in the window directly below the sniper's nest. Norman told the Warren Commission in March 1964 that he heard shells being ejected from the rifle hitting the floor above him. He also said dirt particles from above, caused by the impact of shells hitting the floor, fell into the hair of his coworker standing next to him. However, just four days after the

521

assassination, Norman was interviewed by the FBI and did not mention anything about ejected shells hitting the floor.

On the contrary, Norman said that after the first shot, he stuck his head outside the window, and as he looked up, he was hit with falling dirt particles. Five witnesses corroborated this: James Jarman and four people on the street who saw him look out the window. What Norman initially said had to be the truth, and like Givens, he lied to the Warren Commission. Yet, people continue to ignore his FBI interview and quote Norman's Warren Commission testimony as proof that Oswald killed JFK. Maybe Norman lied because he was intimidated by the police into changing his story, for by the spring of 1964, there were already reports of mysterious deaths. Norman was African American, and a majority of the Dallas PD belonged to the KKK, so he had a reason to be evasive. The real question is why the Warren Commission didn't call out Norman and Givens for lying; they must have known what they had initially said.[1556]

***

Motorcycle patrolman Marrion Baker was riding several car lengths behind the President and was approaching the Book Depository as shots rang out. He looked up and saw pigeons flying off the Depository roof, which made him think the shots had originated from there. Maybe so, but we can assume the pigeons would have flown off the roof after the first shot, which means Baker should have seen a gun protruding from the sniper's nest window as the pigeons flew away. He did not, which makes his account somewhat suspect. Regardless, he charged into the building, gun in hand, supposedly not having seen the gunman in the window. He was met almost immediately by TSBD superintendent Roy Truly, who led Baker to the elevators, but both were stuck on an upper floor. Undaunted, the two men ran up the stairs, and when Baker reached the second floor, he caught movement out of the corner of his eye through the window of the door leading to the lunchroom. Baker entered and summoned Oswald, who was standing near the Coke machine. According to Truly, Oswald remained calm, even though Baker had his gun pressed against his stomach. After Truly told Baker that Oswald was an employee, they left him alone and continued up the stairs.

Carolyn Arnold had seen Oswald in the lunchroom as late as 12:25 P.M. Minutes later, Baker and Truly found him in the same place, so it is fair to say Oswald never left. However, the Warren Commission needed him to be on the 6th floor, so they ignored Arnold's statement and determined that Oswald had enough time to shoot JFK, hide the gun, and run down to the second floor for Baker to confront him. So improbable was their conclusion that it hinged upon Oswald buying a Coke and not having already purchased one because time would not permit the latter. It was why Baker crossed out in his report that he "saw a man standing in the lunchroom drinking a Coke" to Oswald was in the process of buying the soft drink from a vending machine. Ignored was that Police Chief Curry reported that Baker and Truly saw Oswald carrying a Coke, and he could only have been given this information by them. Oswald confirmed what Curry said, saying he was "drinking a Coca-Cola when the officer came in." Therefore, the confrontation with Baker supports the evidence that Oswald never left the second floor and was not the assassin.[1557]

Thomas Dillard, chief photographer for the *Dallas Morning News,* was about fifty yards from the Book Depository when shots rang out. A photograph of the sniper's nest taken by Dillard, compared with one taken later by Army Intelligence agent Powell, showed someone had rearranged the boxes in the window. The HSCA was sure this was true, which took time to do, something Oswald did not have if he was to make it to the second floor before Baker did. Someone else had moved the boxes to create the sniper's nest.[1558]

John Martino had worked for Santo Trafficante in Havana before Castro came to power. He was imprisoned by Castro and released with the Bay of Pigs prisoners. He wrote a book about his experience titled *I Was Castro's Prisoner,* and he became an active participant in the war against Castro. In 1978, a business associate of Martino, Fred Claasen, contacted journalist Earl Golz with information that Martino had said he was a CIA contract agent. In addition, Martino stated: "The anti-Castro people put Oswald together. Oswald didn't know who he was working for...Oswald was to meet his contact at the Texas Theater. They were to meet Oswald in the theater and get him out of the country, then eliminate him. Oswald made a mistake... There was no way we could get to him. They had Ruby kill him."[1559]

Getting Oswald out of the country made sense and must have been the plan. However, Oswald lingered at work, likely waiting on the 2nd-floor lunchroom for the assassins to make their way down to help them get out of the building. He was close to elevators, the stairway, and the exit to the rear of the building, and no one would question him because he worked there. The arrival of Baker so soon changed things, and the layout of the second floor is critical in understanding how Baker happened to notice Oswald.

The stairs are in the northwest corner of the building. They are "L" shaped, so once Baker and Truly reached the second floor, they had to walk around the stairs to get to the next flight to go up to the third. Fifteen feet from the stairs towards the southeast was a door at a 45-degree angle to the stairs. Through that door was a small vestibule, which led through a second door to the second-floor lunchroom where the Coke machine was. [1560]

Baker could not have spotted Oswald in the lunchroom from the stairway, for he would have had to look through two sets of doors that were at different angles. So, he must have seen Oswald in the vestibule between the two doors, looking out the door window towards the stairs. Roy Truly had not seen anyone, but Baker, who was following behind, did. As he told the Warren Commission, "There is a door there with a glass... and then there is another door ... and there is a hallway over there and a hallway entering into a lunchroom, and when I got to where I could see him, he was walking away from me about 20 feet away from me in the lunchroom." [1561]

What Baker said made sense. He saw Oswald walking away from him through the vestibule door window, and since Truly did not see him, we can assume Oswald saw Truly coming and had backed away. After Truly moved on, Oswald returned to the vestibule, and Baker's arrival caught him by surprise. He returned to the security of the lunchroom, but not in time to go unnoticed by Baker. It all took time, and Oswald did not have time if he had to run down from the 6th floor.

Leaving Oswald, Baker and Truly took the stairs to the 5th floor and were able to take the east elevator up to the seventh, bypassing the sixth. They then walked to the roof, where they searched for several minutes. While this went on, there was plenty of time for the assassins to make their escape, for it was some time before the police sealed off the building.

Victoria Adams watched the motorcade pass from a 4th-floor window with co-worker Sandra Styles. Immediately after the shooting, they left their office and hurried through the stockroom toward the stairs and freight elevators at the back of the building. They did not see or hear Truly and Baker coming up the old and rickety wooden stairs, and the two men would have heard the women descending the stairs if they were in the lunchroom with Oswald, so Adams and Styles must have reached the first floor before Truly and Baker began their assent. Most likely, the assassins from the 6th floor waited on an intermediate level as Adams and Styles made their way down and as Baker and Truly made their way up to the roof, or they managed to hurry down the stairs before anyone had seen them.[1562] Either way, Oswald likely helped them escape the building out the rear door on the first floor via the back staircase, which was where eyewitness James Worrell saw the man in the tan coat leave the building. Oswald then left the building on his own. On his way to the front stairway that led to the 1st floor, fellow employee Elizabeth Reid confronted him. She had entered the Book Depository office and saw Oswald wearing a white shirt and carrying a Coke bottle. Oswald had entered the office through the rear door, which was close to the lunchroom and the back stairs. "I had no thoughts or anything of him having any connection with it at all because he was very calm." She told Oswald that someone had shot the President, and he mumbled something she could not understand and walked through the office towards the front door. Considering what Reid told him right after patrolman Baker had thrust a gun against his body, Oswald's calm demeanor suggests he was not at all surprised by circumstances that should have excited him were he not involved in the assassination plot.[1563]

Around fifteen minutes after the assassination, Deputy Sheriff Roger Craig was standing on the east side of Elm Street, across from the Book Depository, when he heard someone whistle. He turned to see a man running down the grassy knoll get into a light-colored Nash Rambler station wagon with a luggage rack on top, driven by either an African American or dark-skinned Latin. Craig said the man who entered the car was 5'-9", 140-150 lbs., with medium brown sandy hair, and wearing a white shirt. He later identified the man as Lee Harvey Oswald at the police station after the accused assassin was in custody.[1564]

The station wagon had come to a halt on Elm Street, about one-half block away. Directly behind was a Cadillac driven by Marvin Robinson, who had to slam on his brakes to prevent hitting the car when it suddenly stopped. He noticed a white man running down the grassy slope enter the station wagon. Robinson's employer, Roy Cooper, was driving directly behind him in a different vehicle. He also saw a white male, 20-30 years old, wave at the driver and enter the station wagon. Mrs. Helen Forrest saw the same man in a white shirt run from the side of the Depository Building and enter the station wagon. She later said, "If it wasn't Oswald, it was his identical twin." James Pennington saw a man in a white shirt run from the side of the Depository Building and enter the station wagon. He later identified the man as "Lee Harvey Oswald." All said it was Oswald wearing a white shirt, as did Mrs. Reid when she confronted him inside.[1565]

Richard Carr had climbed down from his construction site perch in time to see the man he had seen in the sniper's nest, the one wearing the tan sports coat, and two other men quickly moving away from the scene on Commerce Street. As he told the FBI, "The man got into a 1961 or 1962 gray Rambler station wagon parked just north of Commerce Street on Record Street. The station wagon, which had Texas license plates and was driven by a young Negro man, drove off in a northerly direction." James Worrell was walking on Houston Street and saw the man in the tan sports coat running from the back of the Depository south on Houston Street. He told the Commission he was running "like a bat out of hell."[1566]

Off-duty policeman Tom Tilson was driving nearby and arrived in time to see the President's "limousine come under the underpass...Well, the limousine just sped past [this] car parked on the grass on the north side of Elm Street near the west side of the underpass. Here's one guy coming from the railroad tracks. He came down that grassy slope on the west side of the Triple Underpass, on the Elm Street side. He had [this] car parked there, a black car...he threw something in the back seat and went around the front hurriedly and got in the car and took off... I saw all this, and I said, 'That doesn't make sense, everybody running to the scene and one person running from it....'" Tilson gave chase but lost the car on Interstate 30 heading toward Fort Worth. He gave a description of the man, the car, and the license plate number to Homicide detectives, but they never contacted him. As Tilson said in 1978, "Homicide...had arrested a suspect in one day... They didn't want to have to look for anybody else...They wanted to clear up the case."[1567]

***

While Tilson, Craig, Robinson, Cooper, Forrest, Pennington, Carr, and Worrell noticed the expeditious departure of suspicious characters from Dealey Plaza, other equally suspect persons went undetected. Two men stood near the Stemmons Freeway sign along Elm Street, and before the assassination, one was holding a closed umbrella. The second man was Hispanic and quietly stood near the other. As the President's car turned onto Elm, the first man inexplicably opened his umbrella, even though it was not raining. As the car approached where the two men were standing, where the first shot hit Kennedy, the man began pumping the umbrella in the air. He was the only person in Dealey Plaza that day with an open umbrella. The second man simultaneously raised his right arm with a clenched fist defiantly over his head as Kennedy passed. As pandemonium reigned and people scurried about, these two men, unaffected by what had transpired within feet from where they stood, sat down next to each other on the curb on the north side of Elm Street. In one photo, the dark-complected man is putting a walkie-talkie up to his mouth, and what appears to be an antenna can be seen behind his head. Moments later, the "umbrella man" got up, took a last look at the motorcade passing under the Triple Underpass, and began walking east toward the Book Depository. The Hispanic man walked in the opposite direction, towards the Triple Underpass, past people charging up the grassy knoll. He appeared to be stuffing an object into

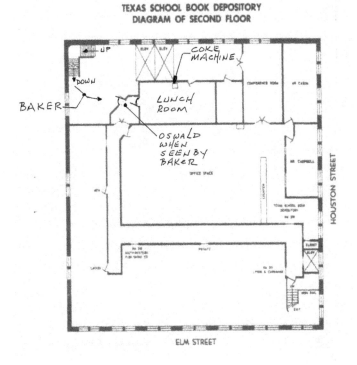

the back of his pants.

In 1978, the HSCA conducted a nationwide search to determine the identity of the "umbrella man." A former Dallas insurance salesman named Louis Steven Witt admitted he was who they were looking for. He said he opened the umbrella to upset JFK. As Witt told the HSCA interviewer, "It had something to do with the – when the senior Mr. Kennedy was Ambassador to England, and the Prime Minister, some activity they had had in appeasing Hitler. The umbrella that the Prime Minister of England came back with got to be a symbol in some manner with the British people. By association, it got transferred to the Kennedy family, and, as I understood, it was a sore spot with the Kennedy family…"[1568]

Joseph Kennedy was Ambassador to England from 1938 to 1940. So, twenty-three years later, Witt decided to use an umbrella to heckle JFK. It is a ridiculous explanation. What makes it worse is that this student of history claimed he was unaware that he was a person of interest for fifteen years and knew nothing about the JFK assassination, even though he lived in Dallas.

His credibility becomes even more suspect when he describes what happened next. "I think I got up and started fiddling with that umbrella, trying to get it open.... Whereas other people I understand saw the President shot and his movements; I did not see this because of this thing [the umbrella] in front of me... My view of the car during that length of time was blocked by the umbrella being open."[1569]

Photos show that Witt was not telling the truth. As Kennedy's car passed in front of him, he stared directly at the car with the umbrella held high over his head. His vision was not restricted in the least by the umbrella. Was he one of the assassination conspirators? Probably. He and the other man could be seen from the Book Depository and Dal-Tex Buildings in the rear and from the grassy knoll in the front. They must have maintained radio contact with shooters at various locations, coordinating shots. As for the open umbrella, it provided a visible signal that the assassination was on. The exposure of the President and the location of Secret Service agents and motorcycle policemen were factors that needed to be confirmed before they proceeded. It is speculation, but it offers a logical explanation for illogical behavior, something Witt was unable to do.

Jack Lawrence worked at Downtown Lincoln-Mercury, the car dealership where the Oswald impostor had test-driven a car weeks before. That day, Lawrence arrived late for work, around thirty minutes after the assassination. Muddy and sweating profusely, he went into the bathroom and vomited. Lawrence told fellow employees he had a hangover from the previous night. His car, which he had borrowed from the dealership the day before, was found parked behind the wooden fence on the Grassy Knoll. His strange behavior prompted other employees to call the police, and he was arrested, jailed for twenty-four hours, and then released. Lawrence was a right-winger who had recently come to Dallas from Los Angeles and warranted more attention.[1570]

The Dal-Tex building was located across the street from the Book Depository and offered an excellent view of the kill zone. Moments after the assassination, an elevator operator saw a man in the building whom he did not know and summoned Deputy Sheriff Lummie Lewis. He was arrested and taken to the sheriff's office for questioning. His name was Jim Braden, and he was in Dallas working on an oil-related business. He was "walking down Elm Street trying to get a cab" when he heard people saying someone had shot JFK. He ran into the Dal-Tex building and took a freight elevator to the third floor to find a telephone. His interrogators believed his unlikely story, and he was released, which was unfortunate. His real name was Eugene Hale Brading, and he had a long list of criminal offenses against him. In 1951, he used the name "James Bradley Lee" and knew James Dolan. Dolan knew Jack Ruby well and, as reported by the HSCA, was "an acquaintance of both Carlos Marcello and Santos Trafficante."

Brading had changed his name to Braden on September 9, 1963, and in November, he received permission from his parole officer to travel to Texas. He arrived in Dallas on November 21 and checked into the Cabana Motel with an associate named Morgan Brown. That afternoon, they visited the offices of H.L. Hunt at about the same time that Jack Ruby did. Also staying at the Cabana Motel that night was Lawrence Meyers, a friend of Ruby's. Meyers had traveled to Dallas from Chicago with Jean West, whom he described as a "rather dumb but accommodating broad." Recall that on September 24, the day Oswald left New Orleans, David Ferrie phoned the house where Jean West lived, a fantastic coincidence. Equally suspicious was that in the weeks leading up to the assassination, Braden worked out of Room 1701 of the Pere Marquette Building in New Orleans. Down the hall, in Room 1707, David Ferrie was busy working on Carlos Marcello's defense.

Braden lied to the authorities, for he was not just passing through Dealey Plaza. Photos clearly show him among the spectators watching the motorcade. His presence is a mystery and may have had something to do with either the assassination or Ruby's gun-running activities. As for Morgan Brown, he abruptly left the Cabana Motel at 2:00 P.M., leaving Braden in the custody of police.[1571]

John Curington, a former H.L. Hunt employee, thought Braden was involved with Nelson Bunker Hunt (whose name was in Jack Ruby's notebook) in "financing certain conservative causes," such as the AVG group. Dallas newspaper reporter Earl Gotz learned from sources that Nelson Bunker contributed money to AVG to purchase weapons for a California anti-Communist group. An AVG newsletter, with Pedro Del Valle on the cover, alleged there was a "kill squad" funded by Nelson Bunker through Brading/Braden. Curington confirmed to the FBI that Hunt had organized a "kill squad" to eliminate liberal and Communist world leaders and that Braden was in Hunt's office in the period of 1962-1963.[1572]

There are two references to "kill squads" in the Lafitte datebook. The first is dated April 12, and it is related to Charles Willoughby. It was around the time of the Walker shooting. The second is on October 9 and referenced Jean Souetre, the OAS assassin who was flown out of Dallas secretly on a private plane shortly after the assassination.[1573]

Nelson Bunker more than equaled his father's hatred for the Kennedys. According to ex-FBI agent and former Hunt security man Paul Rothermeil, the younger Hunt's desire to purge America of Communists had no limits. He tried to establish a killer paramilitary force that would eliminate victims with a gas gun that made it appear they had a heart attack. He recruited killers from General Walker's group.[1574] Amazingly, Lafitte's datebook also mentioned gas guns on July 18: "Del Valle and Walker....$ Rothermeil says no on Gas Guns..." Then again on September 7: "O.S. [Otto Skorzeny] – gas guns."[1575]

It is interesting that on February 2, 1963, seven months earlier, the Austrian government put out a warrant for Skorzeny's arrest because, during the spring of 1944, he had tested an experimental "poison gas gun" on inmates of Sachsenhausen concentration camp.[1576]

There was also a reference to gas guns in the Minutemen magazine, *On Target*, dated March 15, 1963: "That extra fountain pen in the pocket of the insurance salesman that calls on you might be a cyanide-gas gun... Traitors beware! Even now the cross hairs are on the back of your necks...."[1577]

There was a close working relationship involving Pedro del Valle, Walker, Willoughby, Braden/Brading, and the Hunt family that involved kill squads and gas guns. Lafitte thought it was important enough to mention in his datebook.

***

The commotion in the period immediately following the assassination centered around the grassy knoll, just right and to the front of the President where the fatal shot came from. Of the 178 witnesses in Dealey Plaza that day, 61 believed that at least some shots came from there. As people rushed up the grassy knoll, men claiming to be Secret Service agents met them, but there were no Secret Service agents in the area at the time of the assassination.

An alleged Secret Service agent told Gordon Arnold to move, so he positioned himself in front of the picket fence. "Just after the car turned onto Elm and started toward me," he said, "a shot went off from over my left shoulder. I felt the bullet rather than heard it, and it went right past my left ear...It was being fired over my head. And I hit the dirt... I heard two shots, and then there was a blend... The next thing I knew, someone was kicking my butt and telling me to get up. It was a policeman... And then this other guy – a policeman – comes up with a gun... And he was crying...One of them asked me if I had taken any film, and I said yes. He told me to give him my film, so I tossed him my camera...."[1578]

Mary Moorman was standing on the opposite side of Elm Street from the grassy knoll. She photographed the President at the exact moment he was struck by the fatal headshot. Her photo supported Arnold's story. An enlargement revealed two figures, one of whom has been dubbed "Badge Man." He appears to be wearing a dark shirt with a semicircular patch on the left shoulder and what looks to be a badge on his left chest. His head is visible, except for around his mouth, which a bright flash from the muzzle blast of a rifle obscured.[1579]

Patrolman Joe Smith was one of the first to reach the parking lot behind the wooden fence above the grassy knoll. An impostor Secret Service agent also confronted him. Smith said: "I should have checked the man closer, but at the time, I didn't snap on it...." Malcolm Summers "ran across Elm Street to run up there toward the knoll. And we were stopped by a man in a suit, and he had an overcoat over his arm. I saw a gun under the coat. And his comment was, 'Don't you all come up here any further, you could get shot...or killed....'"[1580]

Constable Seymour Weitzman and police sergeant D.V. Harkness also confronted Secret Service agents. Harkness told the Warren Commission that he ran to the rear of the Depository Building moments after the shooting and "there were some Secret Service agents there." He said he didn't ask them for identification. "They told me they are Secret Service." In later years, Harkness elaborated that they "were all armed."[1581] James Romack saw them as well. "There was [sic] two other gentlemen which I never said anything about that [had] taken over," he said. "They were FBI or something standing right here at the very [back] entrance and just stood there."[1582]

It is not surprising that the real assassins did not have difficulty escaping with the assistance they had on the street. In the commotion of the moment, no one would question a man's credentials. People expected the Secret Service to be there.

***

Meanwhile, while most people ran to the grassy knoll, the Book Depository became the focal point of the police investigation. A rifle was found on the 6th floor within one hour, as was the brown paper bag allegedly used to conceal it. The police discovered the sniper's nest, and they accepted that the assassin had methodically positioned boxes ahead of time to shield what he intended to do. They found two spent cartridge shells and one unfired bullet on the floor beneath the sniper's window. They would soon learn that an A. Hidell had purchased the rifle, and it was delivered to Oswald's P.O. box the previous March. Eventually, the police and FBI connected the cartridge shells to the assassin's rifle. A further FBI investigation revealed that Hidell was an alias Oswald used in New Orleans in the summer of 1963. The police had their evidence and focused their attention on Oswald. The problem was the evidence was flimsy at best.

Deputy Eugene Boone, who worked for Bill Decker in the Sheriff's Department, was on the 6th floor when he found the rifle hidden behind a stack of boxes far away from the sniper's nest. Captain Fritz ejected a live round from the rifle, and Lt. J.C. Day of the Dallas Police arrived next to examine the weapon. Soon, Deputy Constable Seymour Weitzman joined them. He was familiar with rifles, having once owned a sporting goods store, and he identified it as a 7.65 Mauser. He signed a notarized affidavit on November 23, 1963, that stated, "This rifle was a 7.65 Mauser bolt action equipped with a 4/18 scope, a thick leather brownish-black sling on it…" It was a precise description, suggesting Weitzman had examined the weapon closely. An FBI report on that same day stated: "Mr. Weitzman described the rifle which was found as a 7.65 caliber Mauser bolt-action rifle, which loads from a five-shot clip which is locked on the underside of the receiver forward of the receiver guard." Eugene Boone's report, written to Sheriff Decker on the day of the assassination, also said the rifle was "a 7.65 Mauser with a telescopic sight on the rifle." A CIA report, dated November 25, 1963, stated, "The rifle he [Oswald] used was a Mauser which OSWALD had ordered…from Klein's Mail Order House, Chicago, Illinois…"[1583]

In the early morning hours of November 23, Dallas District Attorney Henry Wade told a press conference that the murder weapon was a Mauser. Later that day, the FBI reported that Oswald had purchased a 6.5 Italian-made rifle through the mail under the name A.J. Hidell. After that, all references to the Mauser disappeared, and the murder weapon became a Manlicher-Carcano. There were no signed affidavits from police officers or sheriff deputies explaining why the rifle changed. The Carcano rifle had stamped on the barrel: "Made Italy" and "Cal 6.5." How was it that so many qualified people handled this rifle and examined it closely on the 22nd and the 23rd, but no one noticed this? It is hard to imagine that would have happened unless they were determined to blame Oswald for the crime, even if it meant misrepresenting the facts.

Also of interest is the story of a man who eventually became director of the Marine Corps in the Intelligence Center at Quantico, Virginia. In November 1963, he worked as a clerk for the Dallas FBI. Agent Vincent Drain asked him to build a box large enough to ship the Mannlicher Carcano rifle to Washington for testing. The clerk's name is in the Warren Report, his fingerprints were on boxes on the 6th floor, and Drain said two clerks had packed the rifle, so the story is credible.

The unnamed clerk stated, "The rifle had a dirty bore…an exceptionally dirty bore," which meant the gun had not been fired for some time and was wrapped in something that collected dust particles inside the barrel. With this in mind, let's consider the testimony of FBI firearms expert Robert Frazier, who examined the rifle in Washington. Warren Commission member John McCloy asked him if he found metal fragments in the barrel of the rifle. Frazier replied, "I did not examine it for that," which was odd. Frazier needed to determine if metal fragments in the rifle matched fragments removed from JFK's and Connally's bodies. So, he dodged the question, which suggests he did not honestly want to answer what the barrel looked like.[1584]

At Ruth Paine's house after the assassination, Marina directed police to the garage where she said Oswald kept his rifle, and they found the blanket used to wrap the rifle but not the gun. If true, the homemade brown bag located on the 6th floor, which Oswald allegedly used to carry the rifle from Ruth's garage to the Depository Building, should have had oil stains and carpet fibers inside that were transferred from the rifle. However, as James DiEugenio wrote in *The JFK Assassination*, "FBI agent Paul Stombaugh could not find enough of the fibers to make a positive identification since there were too many types of fibers in the blanket that were not found on the paper."[1585]

Deputy Sheriff Luke Mooney entered the 6th floor and went directly to the sniper's nest, where he found spent shell casings. Sheriff Bill Decker, Captain Will Fritz, and Police Lieutenant Carl Day soon joined him, and Day photographed two empty cartridges and one live round of ammunition. The photo was identified as CE 716 and appeared on page 500 of Volume 17 of the Warren Report. Lieutenant Day and R.L. Studebaker removed the evidence and turned it over to the Dallas PD identification bureau at 2:15 P.M. Later that afternoon, they transferred the evidence to FBI agents Charles T. Brown and Vincent Drain. FBI agent J. Doyle Williams then also took two photographs of the two empty cartridges and one live round of ammunition. He sent a report to Washington: "Two photographs were also made on November 22, 1963, of two 6.5 mm ammunition hulls obtained from the Dallas Police Department Crime Laboratory. Also photographed along with the two above items was one 'live' round of 6.5 mm ammunition obtained from Captain Will Fritz of the Dallas Police Department." T Joe Pearce developed the FBI film and placed it in an envelope that read: "2 negatives & 4 prints of each of two 6.5 mm bullet hulls & 1 live round of 6.5 ammunition from [the] rifle found on 6th floor..."

The following day, J. Edgar Hoover signed a report sent to Dallas Police Chief Jesse Curry identifying two cartridge casings (Q6 & Q7) and one live cartridge (Q8) turned over to SA Vincent Drain. The FBI tested the cartridges for latent fingerprints, with negative results.

Meanwhile, the FBI and Dallas police soon learned that one shot had missed JFK's limo, which meant three shots had to have been fired from the sniper's nest for Oswald to have been the lone assassin. It was why, on November 27, the Dallas police miraculously discovered a third empty cartridge casing (CE 543), which they gave to FBI Special Agent Vincent Drain. The next day, Drain wrote in his report that he had received from Lieutenant Day "one spent hull of 6.5 mm shell believed to have been fired from [the rifle], SN C2766, believed to have been the gun used in the assassination." The HSCA examined the 3rd hull and reported, "Perhaps the most remarkable mark on this casing (CE 543) is a dent in the lip that would prevent it from being fired. The second most remarkable thing is the conspicuous absence of the seating mark found on all the rounds that were known to have come from the rifle...[and] marks indicating loading and extracting at least three times from an unidentifiable weapon...[and] three sets of marks on the base that were not found on any other cartridges that came from LHO's rifle..." The HSCA thought the police planted the third cartridge because, by the time it appeared, the FBI had concluded three shots were fired at JFK, and they needed three spent cartridges near the 6th-floor window to support this. Clearly, the shell evidence is suspect.[1586]

One final point. If the Dallas Police, FBI, and Warren Commission were so sure it was Oswald's gun the police found on the 6th floor, why did Police Chief Jesse Curry tell Dallas reporter Tom Johnson on July 16, 1964, "We don't have any proof that Oswald fired the rifle, and never did. Nobody's yet been able to put him in that building with a gun in his hand."

***

Although it was some time before police sealed off the Book Depository, it took no time at all to generate a description of a suspect. Just fourteen minutes after the assassination, the police radio broadcast the following: "Attention all squads. The suspect in the shooting at Elm and Houston is supposed to be an unknown white male, approximately 30, 165 pounds,

THE DARKEST DAY – AN AMERICAN TRAGEDY

slender build, armed with what is thought to be a 30-30 rifle... no further description at this time."[1587]

Who gave the police this description, and why were they looking for only one suspect when it appeared shots had come from multiple directions? The official story was that Roy Truly made a roll call to Book Depository employees, and Oswald was the only one not present, which was not valid. Many employees remained outside, caught up in the events that were unfolding. It was not until 2:30 P.M., after Oswald was already in custody, that they learned he was missing from work. It seems that while the conspirators wanted to remove Oswald from the scene and get him out of the country, others were leading investigators in his direction. The evidence suggests it was most likely Military Intelligence who made the police aware of Oswald.[1588]

If Oswald had made it out of the country, almost certainly, the evidence left in his wake would have justified a second invasion of Cuba. However, the fact that Military Intelligence steered the FBI and police toward Oswald does not imply they did not want the second invasion of Cuba to happen. Most likely, Oswald was already supposed to be out of town. So, what went wrong?

CHAPTER THIRTY

NOWHERE TO RUN, NOWHERE TO HIDE

Lee Harvey Oswald left the Book Depository building shortly after his confrontation with Patrolman Baker. Credible witnesses had already seen someone who looked like him enter a station wagon, but the real Oswald, whom Baker confronted, was still in the second-floor lunchroom when that occurred. He left through the front door of the TSBD and walked seven blocks northeast to board the Marsalis Street bus that would have left him one mile from his rooming house in Oak Cliff. Also on the bus was his ex-landlady, Mary Bledsoe, who had asked him to move out after only one week. She told the Warren Commission she recognized him immediately. Undoubtedly, he recognized her as well. So, we have two Oswalds, each identified by credible witnesses, one leaving by car and the other by bus. We cannot ignore this contradiction, especially when one considers the multiple sightings of an Oswald impostor prior to the assassination, going all the way back to his Mexico City trip. The only logical explanation is that this was part of the plan to set up Oswald.

As the bus approached Dealey Plaza, it became embroiled in traffic that placed a stranglehold around the area. A passing motorist told the bus driver that the President had been shot in the head, which created a stir among the passengers. Whether it was hearing this, the encounter with Mrs. Bledsoe, who could identify him, or the traffic that slowed him down, after approximately four minutes, Oswald got off the bus at the general scene of the crime. Mrs. Bledsoe's testimony, a bus transfer ticket found on Oswald at the time of his arrest, dated November 22, 1963, and Oswald's testimony while in custody corroborate that this is what happened.[1589]

After exiting the bus, Oswald walked toward the Greyhound bus station in search of a taxi. He remained calm, offering to give the first cab he approached to an older woman. She declined, so Oswald took the cab himself, electing to sit in the front seat beside cab driver William Whaley. As he approached his home, he told Whaley to drop him off four blocks beyond the rooming house, closer to the Texas Theater and 10th and Patton, where

Officer Tippit was shot shortly after that. Most likely, Oswald did not want Whaley to know the location of his home, which, according to the testimony of housekeeper Earlene Roberts, he entered around 1:00 P.M.[1590]

One wonders why Oswald chose the Marsalis Street bus when he lived on Beckley. It did not go unnoticed by the Warren Commission, which reported, "Marsalis Street is seven blocks from Beckley. Oswald lived at 1026 North Beckley. He could not reach his rooming house on the Marsalis bus, but the Beckley bus was behind the Marsalis bus...."[1591]

The Commission concluded that Oswald was in a hurry and "boarded the first Oak Cliff bus that came along." Their explanation was foolish. Getting on the right bus was not complicated, and Oswald did it many times because the Beckley bus dropped him off across the street from where he lived. And since Oswald calmly walked several blocks to get on the Marsalis bus instead of taking a cab right from the beginning, it indicates he wasn't as rushed as the Commission theorized. The fact is Oswald initially did not plan to go home.

The bus ride from Dealey Plaza to the corner of Marsalis and 11th was normally about 11 minutes. The distance from there to the Texas Theater is less than a mile, so that might have been his destination. Some have suggested that since Jack Ruby's apartment was only two blocks from Marsalis and 11th, Oswald planned to go there. It is possible, but there is no evidence to support that. It is more likely that Oswald was supposed to meet his contact in the Texas Theater, and the quickest way to get there was via the Marsalis Street bus. However, something happened that made him change his original plan.[1592]

***

The Good Luck Oil Company gas station was at 1502 N. Zang Boulevard, where the south end of Houston Street crosses the Trinity River into Oak Cliff. Officer J.D. Tippit parked his patrol car there around 12:40 P.M. and sat watching the cars leaving downtown Dallas. Photographer Al Volkland and his wife Lou, who both knew Tippit, saw him, and they waved. Three employees of GLOCO also knew Tippit and saw him waiting for about ten minutes, which was around the time that the Marsalis Street bus passed Tippit's car. As the bus made a left and continued south on Marsalis, several witnesses saw Tippit's car leave the station towards Jefferson Boulevard. Chances are he followed the bus all the way to Marsalis and 11th, and when his charge for that afternoon, Lee Harvey Oswald, did not get off, Tippit began to panic.[1593]

537

***

Earlene Roberts was watching a televised report of the shooting of President Kennedy when the man she knew as O.H. Lee hurriedly entered through the front door at 1026 North Beckley. She spoke to him briefly, but Oswald grunted something and ignored her as he quickly walked across the room. He entered the small bedroom that he rented and closed the door behind him.

It was while Oswald was in his room that Mrs. Roberts heard an automobile honk twice outside the house. She looked through the window and saw a Dallas police car parked in front with two uniformed police officers inside, which was odd. During the day, officers patrolled alone. Some have suggested it was Tippit, but there is insufficient evidence to state with any degree of certainty that it was him, though it might have been. He certainly had enough time to drive there from Marsalis and 11th after discovering Oswald was not on the bus. What we do know is that Tippit was patrolling a section of town he was not supposed to be in, and the police never adequately explained why this was so. It is beyond the scope of this book to investigate the evidence pertaining to the Tippit killing in detail. I will cover this in a subsequent book. However, I will cover facts herein that are necessary to fill in the blanks applicable to what happened as Oswald tried to escape.

***

That there were two Oswalds at the Book Depository becomes even more plausible when we realize there may have been two Oswalds at the Texas Theater when Oswald was apprehended.

"Butch" Burroughs was the concession stand operator at the theater that day. A double feature was showing, *Cry of Battle* and *War is Hell*, and the first movie began at 1:15 p.m. Burroughs testified before the Warren Commission and explained what he knew about a man who had snuck into the theater.

> Mr. Ball: *Did you see that man come in the theatre?*
>
> Mr. Burroughs: *No, sir; I didn't.*
>
> Mr. Ball: *Do you have any idea what you were doing when he came in?*
>
> Mr. Burroughs: *Well, I was----I had a lot of stock candy to count and put in the candy case for the coming night, and if he had came [sic] around in front of the concession out there, I would have seen him, even though I was bent down, I would have seen him, but otherwise I think he sneaked up the stairs real fast.*

Mr. Ball: *Up to the balcony?*

Mr. Burroughs: *Yes, sir----first, I think he was up there.*

Mr. Ball: *At least there was a stairway there?*

Mr. Burroughs: *Yes, there was two.*

Mr. Ball: *Is there a stairway near the entry?*

Mr. Burroughs: *Of the door----yes. Yes, it goes straight----you come through the door and go straight----you go upstairs to the balcony.*

Burroughs said he did not see the man who entered the theater at 1:35 P.M., which was officially the time the alleged killer of Tippit entered without paying. However, Burroughs, who was unaware there were possibly two Oswalds, later said the Oswald on the main floor of the theater (where police arrested him) had entered much earlier, around when the first feature started. A few minutes later, Oswald came to his concession stand to buy popcorn. He then returned to watch the movie and sat down next to a pregnant woman. Several minutes later, she went upstairs to the ladies' room, and Burroughs heard the restroom door close behind her.[1594]

Jack Davis, a patron at the theater, told a similar story. He was sitting in the right rear section. When the opening credits of the first film began, he was startled by a man who squeezed past to sit right next to him, even though the nine-hundred-seat theater had only twenty seats occupied. The man did not say a word. In short order, he got up and took a seat next to another person, then got up and walked into the theater's lobby. It was around the time Burroughs said Oswald was at the concession stand. Davis vaguely remembered the man returning to the main floor theater section a few minutes later.[1595]

Recall that Earlene Roberts testified that Oswald arrived at his rooming house around 1:00 P.M. It was a mile walk, or a 4-minute drive, to the Texas Theater. Either option was doable for Oswald to get to the theater around 1:15 when Burroughs and Davis said they saw him.

The accounts of Burroughs and Davis corroborate each other, and the actions of Oswald, as described by Davis, were consistent with an individual who was looking for his contact but did not know who that was. Was Oswald sitting next to different people expecting to receive some signal in return?

Lamar Waldron and Thom Hartmann wrote in *Legacy of Secrecy*, "In David Atlee Phillips's autobiography, *The Night Watch* ... Phillips wrote about his own experience meeting contacts at movie theaters ... using 'recognition procedures' that included code phrases. In Oswald's pocket on November 22 was half a torn box top, as if Oswald expected to meet someone who had the other half at the theater. [Antonio] Veciana told us about meeting the CIA official who first recruited Phillips, who gave Veciana half of a torn dollar bill to use as a recognition procedure later. Oswald had a couple of torn dollar bills in his room, and the torn-bill technique was also used in the Texas arm of the French connection heroin ring."[1596]

Mary Tollerton had joined the Minutemen "for kicks," which led to her arrest for carrying a gun when the police stopped her for a routine traffic violation. In *The Minutemen,* author J. Harry Jones, Jr. wrote, "When Mary entered the office of Detective John Jamison that night, Jamison was later to relate, she quickly stuffed pieces of paper in her mouth, chewed them up, and swallowed them. She eventually told me the pieces of paper had been three halves of dollar bills, the serial numbers of which would have identified her to contacts in Florida. On another occasion, Minutemen leader Robert DePugh had given a Minutemen member "half of a dollar bill – serial number J56077322A – and told him a courier would use the other half to identify himself to him when he arrived some time in the future with instructions." Also, "When he returned to Kansas City, he said he was to insert a Help Wanted ad in the [*Kansas City*] *Star* for several days. It would be his signal to the Minutemen he was back in town … [and] it was suggested that he move into a certain apartment complex in south Kansas City."[1597]

It was not just the torn one-dollar bills that may have mirrored Oswald's behavior in the theater that are of interest here. The Help Wanted ad in the *Kansas City Star* is reminiscent of Oswald placing an ad in the *Dallas Morning News* when he returned from Mexico City to Dallas, which included the reference to "running man." Did Oswald let others know in the ad that he was back in town? There were also instructions for the person in question to move to a specific apartment complex. When Oswald arrived in Dallas, he went to 1026 N. Beckley first, but nothing was available. Later, after leaving Mary Bledsoe's apartment, he went back to 1026 N. Beckley, and there was a vacant room. What was so important about 1026 N. Beckley? Was he also told to find a room there? As previously discussed, Earlene Roberts' sister, Bertha Cheek, had strong connections to the radical right in Dallas, as well as to Jack Ruby. There are too many connections between the Minutemen and Oswald for this all to be a coincidence.

***

There were two sets of doors separated by a breezeway that one passed through to enter the Texas Theater. In the breezeway was a staircase that led to the balcony. About twenty minutes after the first movie started, from his concession stand, Burroughs heard the front doors to the theater open, but the interior doors remained closed, which meant someone had gone up to the balcony. It was something he listened for because young people had been sneaking into the theater and going directly to the balcony to avoid detection.[1598]

Ticket seller Julia Postal called the police to report that a suspicious man was hiding in the balcony after Johnny Brewer, who had followed the suspect, told her the man had entered without paying. At 1:46 P.M., the Dallas Police dispatcher broadcast the following message: "Have information a suspect just went in the Texas Theater on West Jefferson....supposed to be hiding in balcony." FBI Special Agent Bob Barrett arrived shortly after that, and soon Detective Paul Bentley, Patrolman Bob Apple, Sergeant Gerald Hill, and reporter Jim Ewell joined him at the theater entrance. Bentley ran upstairs and searched the men's and women's restrooms with another officer while Hill searched the balcony. Officers Bob Carroll and K.E. Lyons entered through the front doors and headed to the balcony as well, as did Deputy Sheriff Bill Courson. He hurried up the stairs and was "reasonably satisfied in his own mind" that he met Lee Harvey Oswald coming down the front stairs from the balcony. A few moments later, Lieutenant Cunningham, Detective E.E. Taylor, and Detective J.B. Toney entered the front of the theater and were told by Julia Postal, "There's a young man upstairs in the balcony. He just went up there." They met him sitting on the stairs, smoking a cigarette. Deputy Sheriff Buddy Walthers arrived and saw police officers questioning the man as he rushed up the stairs. The man was released when they were told by the "manager on duty" that he "had been in the theater since around 12:05 P.M.," which was before the JFK assassination happened.

The encounter with the young man on the second floor should have been straightforward, but like everything else that day, it was not. The theater only opened its doors at 12:45 P.M., which makes sense since the first movie started around 1:15 P.M. So why did the manager on duty say the man entered the theater at 12:05 P.M.? The answer is there was no manager on duty that afternoon.

When SA Barrett arrived, he asked a man who identified himself as the assistant manager to turn up the lights. The man replied, "I don't know. This is my first day on the job." The FBI and police later learned there was no assistant manager at the Texas Theater on November 22. There was theater manager John Callahan (who left before the police arrived), Julia Postal and Butch Burroughs. So, it appears that the intervention by the so-called "assistant manager" with the police allowed the man in the balcony section to go free.[1599] It was part of the plan, reminiscent of the people who were confronted by Secret Service agents in Dealey Plaza, even though there were not any Secret Service agents there.

The Dallas police homicide report regarding Tippit's killing stated: "Suspect was later arrested in the balcony of the Texas Theater..." Even police officer M.N. McDonald, who was standing in front of the screen and would arrest Oswald on the main level, described how someone tipped him off that Oswald "was sitting in the third row from the rear of the ground floor and not in the balcony." Who was that mystery man? Was he another accomplice? He probably was, and based on what we know, it seems the conspirators were willing to sacrifice Oswald on the main level so the man in the balcony could go free. It coincided with what John Martino said: "Oswald was to meet his contact at the Texas Theater. They were to meet Oswald in the theater and get him out of the country, then eliminate him. Oswald made a mistake... There was no way we could get to him. They had Ruby kill him."[1600]

Shoe store manager Johnny Brewer was listening to the radio when he learned of Tippit's shooting. Hearing police sirens, he saw a man suspiciously duck into the store entryway as a police car drove by. Brewer followed him towards the Texas Theater and asked Julia Postal if she had just sold a ticket to anyone, and she said she had not. Brewer entered the theater, and Butch Burroughs told him that no one had entered.[1601] Now, if the second Oswald had not attracted Brewer's attention, he would have entered the theater undetected. There would have been no one to direct the police towards Oswald on the main floor, and he could have found his contact, waited for things to die down, and quietly left the area, as was his plan. Unfortunately for him, it was not how things played out, and one wonders if the man Brewer saw acted suspiciously on purpose so Brewer would follow him to the Texas Theater and lead police there.

***

One of the most significant pieces of evidence pointing to the setup of Oswald, as well as proof there was an impostor Oswald, was the discovery of a second Oswald wallet at the Tippit murder scene. According to the Warren Commission testimony of Dallas Police Captain W.R. Westbrook, he arrived at the Tippit murder after the ambulance had left with Tippit's body. According to ambulance driver Jasper Clayton Butler, Tippit was pronounced dead at Methodist Hospital four minutes after he received the call, so Westbrook arrived at the murder scene within a few minutes after it happened. Shortly after that, Westbrook learned that a potential suspect had entered a nearby library, so Westbrook left to investigate that. When he returned to the Tippit murder scene, he met up with FBI Special Agent Bob Barrett.

The first policeman to arrive at the Tippit scene was Sergeant Kenneth H. Croy. He was handed a wallet by an unidentified civilian, which he later gave to Sergeant Calvin "Bud" Owens.[1602] Decades later, news footage from 1963 was discovered by a local Dallas television station, showing Owens holding a man's leather wallet as he stood next to Captain George Doughty near Tippit's car. The wallet is open as Doughty examines an item that was removed from the wallet, just as a plainclothes officer, most likely Westbrook, joined the two men. We know the wallet was not Tippit's. That was among the effects taken from him at Methodist Hospital after his death.[1603]

Westbrook "had this wallet in his hand," Barrett recalled years later. "Westbrook asked me, 'Do you know who Lee Harvey Oswald is?' 'Do you know who Alex Hidell is?' And I said, 'No, I never heard of them.'" FBI agent James Hosty discussed the wallet incident in his 1995 book, *Assignment Oswald*. "Westbrook called Barrett over and showed him the wallet and [the] identifications...Westbrook took the wallet into his custody [and] Barrett told me [Hosty] that if I had been at the scene with Westbrook, I would have immediately known who Oswald was."[1604]

There must be an explanation for why a second Oswald wallet was intentionally left where Tippit died, considering the police had apprehended Oswald in the theater with another wallet in his possession. The only logical explanation is that the conspirators killed Tippet to draw the police to Oak Cliff. Not knowing when Oswald would be apprehended, the wallet at the scene would make Oswald an immediate person of interest. Authorities would soon discover that Lee Harvey Oswald worked at the Book Depository, had defected to Russia, had started a Fair Play for Cuba chapter in New Orleans, supported Fidel Castro, was arrested in a street altercation handing out FPCC literature, was considered a Communist, and had traveled to Mexico City two months before the assassination trying to get into Cuba. They would learn that Hidell was the name used to purchase Oswald's Mannlicher Carcano rifle and was an alleged alias Oswald used in New Orleans when promoting the FPCC. They would learn about the letter Oswald wrote to the Soviet Embassy in Washington, mentioning he had to leave Mexico unless he used his real name.

543

Meanwhile, Oswald was sitting in the Texas Theater waiting to meet his contact, who would never appear. The scenario only made sense if getting Oswald arrested was what the conspirators wanted. And if that were the case, then the assassination plot was purposely sabotaged by a cabal within the conspiracy group because they needed Oswald alive and in custody.

Let's remember that the purpose of killing Kennedy was supposed to be so his death could be a catalyst for AMWORLD, resulting in the second invasion of Cuba. It was what those who were part of the Sierra group expected to happen. Still, we also know that the CIA, Skorzeny's Nazi group operating out of Madrid, the French OAS, and European Monarchists did not want that to happen. They worried that an invasion of Cuba involving the U.S. military would lead to the loss of West Berlin and initiate a confrontation between the United States and the Soviet Union that potentially could have resulted in World War III.

This cabal within the conspiracy knew they could not stop the JFK assassination even if they wanted to. Still, they could create a scenario where the United States would have to back down and make sure that the second invasion of Cuba never occurred. And in this operation, Lee Harvey Oswald was a critical component if they were to be successful.

Consider that Oswald was privy to a lot of information U.S. intelligence preferred remained hidden. His Marine tour of duty that included mind-altering drug experimentation; his Russian defection, which was an intelligence operation; the possibility that he was an FBI informant; his penetration of Communist groups through Guy Banister; his involvement in gunrunning, which probably included Jack Ruby; and his knowledge of the JFK assassination plot, and who many of the conspirators were, made him a liability. It was why Nagell called Oswald "the indispensable tool" in the assassination conspiracy. The Russians also knew a great deal about Oswald, which further guaranteed that his arrest would result in the aborting of the invasion of Cuba.

It was also why Lafittes' datebook entry for November 9 reads: "On the wings of murder. The pigeon way for unsuspecting Lee. Clip Clip his wings." Dictionary.com defines clip his wings as: "Restrain or reduce someone's freedom, as in *Hiding his car keys—you're really clipping his wings*. This metaphor for clipping a bird's wings to prevent it from flying away dates from ancient Roman times. Christopher Marlowe used it in *The Massacre at Paris* (1590): 'Away to prison with him, I'll clip his wings.'"[1605]

So, Lafitte's reference to "clip his wings" confirms that the plan was for Oswald to be arrested. And if Oswald was an informant, in other words, a stool pigeon, "the pigeon way" tells us why this became Oswald's fate. That Oswald was an informant could refer to the FBI or even the CIA, considering that Richard Nagell was working undercover, infiltrating anti-Castro groups and trying to find out what he could about the assassination plot. Maybe Oswald was doing the same, and the conspirators turned the tables on him.

Interestingly, Jean Lafitte's entry for November 22 reads: "Merde, Merde, [Murder, Murder], Fuck, Fuck – O Tippett [sic]/why? Run Sparrow Run, Fly! Ask JA [James Angleton] who is Tippet!"[1606] It means Lafitte had no idea who Tippit was and the mention of Angleton's name implies the CIA was responsible for controlling Oswald after his return from Mexico City. They set him up and created the Oswald impostor scenario. They supervised the operation on the ground in Dallas, arranged Tippit's death to lure the police to the Texas Theater, and planted Oswald's wallet at the Tippit murder scene, which set off a series of events that resulted in Oswald's arrest.

***

For the two Oswalds in the Texas Theater and the second wallet at the Tippit murder scene scenario to work, the timeline from when Oswald left the Book Depository until his arrest in the Texas Theater must comply with the available evidence. In the opinion of this author, it does.

> 1. Oswald left the second-floor lunchroom in the TSBD and got on the Marsalis Street bus, while the impostor Oswald got into the Nash Rambler station wagon on Elm Street, as witnessed by numerous people.
>
> 2. The real Oswald got off the bus around 12:40 P.M. and took a cab that dropped him four blocks past his rooming house at 1026 N. Beckley, which was a 5-minute ride under normal conditions.
>
> 3. Oswald walked the four blocks to the rooming house. Housekeeper Earlene Roberts said he arrived around 1:00 P.M., which makes sense. Oswald left the rooming house around 1:05 P.M. with his revolver.
>
> 4. Oswald walked directly to the Texas Theater, which was 1.0 miles away, about a 10-minute walk from the rooming house. He arrived at the theater around 1:15 P.M., around when the first movie started, which agrees with when Burroughs and Davis say they saw Oswald for the first time inside the theater.

5. The Oswald impostor was on the 6th floor of the TSBD at the time of the shooting. A fellow conspirator drove him to Oak Cliff. He arrived there probably around 12:45 P.M., with ample time to cross paths with Tippit.

6. Officer J.D. Tippit left the intersection of Marsalis and 11th, worried because Oswald was not on the bus and was nowhere to be found. Perhaps his responsibility was to kill Oswald or get him out of town. Tippit parked his patrol car about a block west of the Texas Theater, at the corner of Bishop and Jefferson, near the Top Ten Record Store. It was around 1:05 P.M., the time the real Oswald was leaving his rooming house. Tippit ran into the record store to make a phone call, which he did on occasion at that shop. Whoever he called did not pick up, so he hurried back to his car and headed toward Jefferson Boulevard.[1607]

7. A few minutes later, a couple of blocks from the record store, James A. Andrews was forced to the curb when Tippit cut in front of Andrews' car, forcing him to stop. Tippit jumped out of his patrol car, checked the front and back seats in Andrews's car, saw no one, then quickly returned to his car and sped off, driving east on 10th Street. Andrews recalled that Tippit looked upset and was acting wildly. Tippit was clearly looking for Lee Oswald.

8. Around 1:15 P.M., Tippit came across the Oswald impostor walking west on 10th Street from Marsalis towards Tippit's patrol car. The impostor noticed Tippit's car coming toward him.

9. Tippit stopped the Oswald impostor and got out of his car after speaking to him through the small window on the passenger side, which one would have expected him to do if he wanted to know why Oswald had deviated from his original plan. Tippit was unaware that the Oswald impostor was probably searching for him.

10. The Oswald impostor shot Tippit, and he, or an accomplice, dropped the second Oswald wallet at the scene. The time was around 1:15 P.M. The impostor ran towards the Texas Theater, dropping a jacket along the way to tie Oswald to Tippet's murder. The killer made sure Brewer saw him enter the theater without paying around 1:40 P.M., then headed to the balcony.

11. The killing of Tippit brought the police to Oak Cliff and the Texas Theater, which resulted in the arrest on the main floor of the assassination patsy, the real Lee Harvey Oswald.

There are also other facts to take into account.

12. If Butch Burroughs and Jack Davis were correct that they saw Oswald at the Texas Theater at around 1:15 P.M., the timing is such that he could not have been Tippit's killer.

13. Someone was impersonating Oswald prior to the assassination. Two Oswalds were in Mexico City, there was an Oswald impersonator in Dallas in the weeks leading up to the assassination, there were two Oswalds at the Book Depository at the time of the JFK assassination, and two Oswalds were at the Texas Theater when the police arrested the real Oswald. It is logical that the setup of the real Oswald, which tied the crime and the arrest together, would have involved the impostor Oswald.

14. Oswald's revolver misfired while he was struggling with police inside the Texas Theater after allegedly firing multiple bullets into Tippet, allegedly with the same gun, less than an hour before without an issue.

15. The jacket allegedly dropped by Tippit's killer did not match any jacket Oswald owned and could not be purchased from any store in the Dallas vicinity. The jacket contained a label that indicated it was manufactured in California and was sold almost exclusively on the West Coast, except for a large department store in Philadelphia. Oswald was never in California or Philadelphia.

16. The police discovered a laundry mark and a dry cleaning tag on the jacket. The FBI checked all dry cleaning establishments in the Dallas-Fort Worth area to see if one of the two identifying marks matched what they used. The FBI investigated 1424 establishments without a successful match. The FBI then went to New Orleans and checked 293 establishments there, but again, this did not produce a positive match.

17. The police identified the bullet shells found at the scene as having been fired from an automatic pistol. Oswald's gun was a standard revolver.

***

Lee Harvey Oswald was taken from the Texas Theater around 2:00 P.M., driven to police headquarters, and brought to the third-floor office of Captain Will Fritz. The police did not yet know that he worked at the Book Depository. His arrest was for the murder of Tippit, but he soon became the prime suspect in the assassination of the President. Detective Gus Rose found two pieces of identification in his possession: a Department of Defense ID card in the name of Lee Harvey Oswald and a Selective Service card made out to Alek Hidell. Rose asked the prisoner to explain which one he was. "You're the cop. You figure it out," Oswald told him.[1608]

Oswald was charged with the Tippit murder around 7:00 P.M., five hours after his arrest, and formally charged with the murder of the President in the early morning hours of the following day. Oswald spent most of his time in custody, answering questions from a variety of local, state, and federal investigators. Even though they were interrogating the alleged murderer of the President, they did not take notes, nor did a stenographer record what transpired.

As mentioned in Chapter Twenty-Two, Hosty asked Oswald if he had been to Mexico City, which made Oswald visibly upset. When Oswald found out he was talking to Hosty, he got extremely agitated and told him to stop bothering his wife.[1609]

If Oswald had been on the bus to Mexico City, he would have known there was a bus manifest with his name on it, and we can assume he would not have denied having gone there so vigorously when Hosty asked him about it. It confirms that Oswald traveled secretly to Mexico City and that there was an Oswald impostor on the bus.

During another interrogation, Captain Fritz asked police officer Roger Craig to confirm it was Oswald he had seen get into the Nash Rambler station wagon. Craig said, "Yes, it was." Oswald interrupted him and said, "That station wagon belongs to Mrs. Paine. Don't try to tie her into this. She had nothing to do with it."

Oswald's response indicated he knew nothing about the station wagon in Dealey Plaza that Roger Craig and other witnesses saw an Oswald impostor enter. Oswald thought they were referring to Ruth Paine's car, the only station wagon he was aware of. However, unknowingly, Oswald still revealed a great deal. By saying Ruth Paine had "nothing to do with it" and "Don't try to tie her into this," Oswald admitted he was involved in something that day that warranted his arrest. When the police approached him in the theater and he yelled, "It's all over now," he also admitted he was involved in the assassination plot. [1610]

While the police and FBI questioned Oswald, J. Edgar Hoover and LBJ's minions in Washington were pushing the lone gunman scenario, as authorities in Dallas suspected Oswald was part of an international conspiracy. Calls to prevent a conspiracy-based indictment of Oswald from being filed were made in the late afternoon and evening hours by Lyndon Johnson aides Cliff Carter and Barefoot Sanders to Dallas District Attorney Henry Wade and Texas Attorney General Waggoner Carr. Hoover's aides also contacted Dallas FBI SAC Gordon Shanklin to solicit his help in burying the conspiracy angle. Henry Wade admitted to the Warren Commission that on the night of the assassination, Lyndon Johnson's advisers pressured him to drop conspiracy allegations and charge Oswald as the lone assassin, which Wade did. When asked by reporters if Oswald was "simply a nut or a middleman" involved in a conspiracy, Wade answered, "I'll put it this way: I don't think he's a nut."[1611]

Support that Wade was telling the truth came in November 1993, when the PBS show *Frontline* interviewed James Hosty, who admitted that Assistant District Attorney Bill Alexander's original indictment had charged Oswald "in furtherance of an international conspiracy."[1612]

Wade and Alexander were prosecutors on the ground in Dallas who were privy to the actual evidence. They would not believe that Oswald was part of an international conspiracy unless they had proof to support the allegation. That LBJ's people stopped them is troubling because the new President knew more than he was willing to tell, and he was trying to circumvent the investigation and hide the truth. "This is the time when our whole public system could go awry," Johnson said just three days after the assassination. "Not just the Republican party and Democratic party, but the American system of government."[1613] It was a peculiar thing for Johnson to say, considering that by that time, the FBI had already concluded that Oswald had assassinated JFK by himself, so what was LBJ afraid of revealing?

J. Edgar Hoover reportedly said something similar. A year after the assassination, Hoover discussed the crime with the son of Texas oilman Billy Byars, who claimed Hoover told him the following: "If I told you what I really know, it would be very dangerous to this country. Our whole political system could be disrupted."[1614]

The intimidation of Carr and Wade by LBJ's people on the evening of November 22 was the primary subject of questioning months later by the Warren Commission.

> Allen Dulles: In your talks … with Mr. Carter at the White House … did any questions come up … about not raising the issue that … there might be a conspiracy
>
> Wade: I'm rather sure sometime Friday afternoon … he called me and said, "Are they making any progress on the case?" You see, Cliff Carter and I are close personal friends. [And] they were all upset, and I said, "I don't know. I have heard they got some pretty good evidence." I think that is the only conversation I had with him … I … saw it come on the radio that they are [sic] going to file on Oswald

as part of an international conspiracy in murdering the US President, and I think I talked to Barefoot Sanders.

Rankin: Well, did [Sanders] say anything to you about that point?

Wade: [H]e said he had heard it on the radio and…he did not think it ought to be done…so I went down there to be sure they didn't…I talked to…Carr that night…

Rankin: Why did you not include…a charge of an international conspiracy?

Wade: The US attorney and the [Texas] attorney general had called me and said that if it wasn't absolutely necessary, they thought it shouldn't be done.

Cooper: [C]onspiracy is a crime in Texas, isn't it, conspiracy to commit a crime?

Wade: Yes, sir…

Rankin: Have you ever had any evidence that Oswald was involved with anyone else in actually shooting the President?

Wade: I have always felt that [at] the minimum [there] was an inspiration from some cause, and [at] the maximum was actual pay [to Oswald]…

Rankin: Was there anyone either from the State or Federal Government that urged you not to state…international conspiracy if you found one was present?

Wade: It is like I mentioned to you what Mr. Carr and Mr. Sanders both inquired…and I told them right off that whether it was so or not doesn't make any difference. It wouldn't be alleged.

Rankin: Now, going back to the telephone conversation with Mr. Carr…

Wade: [He] said that he had a call from Washington….I remember he said…This would be a bad situation, if you allege it as part of a… conspiracy, and it may affect your international relations, a lot of things of the country…"

On the night of the assassination, Wade told reporters: "It is this man and this man alone. As far as I know, there was no one else involved." Over the next thirty-six hours, Wade told reporters, "We, we're just interested in proving that he did it….I can't describe him any other than – the murderer of the President."[1615]

550

One can sense the frustration Wade felt in being forced to submit to Washington's pressure to charge Oswald as the lone gunman. If it were a Fidel Castro connection that Wade alluded to, considering it was only one year after the Cuban Missile Crisis, Wade would have explicitly mentioned that Oswald conspired with Castro to assassinate JFK. The same logic applies if Wade thought Khrushchev and the Soviet Union were responsible. An international conspiracy would be more broad, such as a collaboration of French anti-Communists, ex-Nazis, a Fascist group operating in Madrid, European Monarchists, and a right-wing Fascist American group made up of right-wing leaders at the CIA. That was the definition of an international conspiracy.

Chapter Thirty-One

Epilogue

One could argue that President John F. Kennedy's inconsistent foreign policy led to his assassination. On the one hand, he strongly supported self-determination for third-world countries that had obtained their freedom from European colonialism. Whether it was in the Congo, Algeria, Indonesia, Vietnam, or anywhere else – the people had a right to choose the type of government they wanted to live under. Kennedy consistently supported this, from 1951 when, as a congressman, he traveled to Southeast Asia with Bobby and their sister, Patricia, until the day he died. Yet, on the other hand, he had no qualms about sending military advisers and equipment to third-world countries and providing those nations with financial aid to stave off Communist infiltration, even if that was not what the people wanted. In *An Unfinished Life*, author and JFK historian Robert Dallek wrote about this: "How could he [JFK] square professions of self-determination – a central principle of the Alliance – with the reality of secret American interventions in Cuba, Brazil, British Guiana, Peru, Haiti, the Dominican Republic, and every country that seemed vulnerable to left-wing subversion? (And that was just the beginning: A June National Security directive approved by the President had listed four additional Latin American countries' sufficiently threatened by Communist-inspired insurgency-Ecuador, Colombia, Guatemala, and Venezuela.)"[1616]

In Brazil, JFK prepared to back a military coup when he learned the Soviets might look to establish a presence there. He was willing to assassinate authoritarian leaders in Haiti and the Dominican Republic to prevent a Communist government from taking over. In Laos, he was content to keep the U.S. on the sidelines if Khrushchev abided by their agreement not to get involved. In South Vietnam, he knowingly overthrew Diem so that a Vietnamese military regime would take control. In Indonesia, JFK was willing to support Sukarno and buy the Indonesian leader's allegiance because he understood the advantages of establishing an alliance with a nation of 100 million people that was rich in raw materials.

With such a track record, it was not surprising that President Kennedy was willing to launch a second invasion of Cuba to get rid of Fidel Castro in December 1963, even if it resulted in a confrontation with the Soviets in West Berlin. Meanwhile, the Pentagon, the CIA, and many at the State Department considered the Soviet Union an evil empire with whom there could be no accommodation or compromise. They were understandably furious when Kennedy waited until October 1962 to publicly acknowledge there were Russian offensive nuclear weapons in Cuba, knowing JFK delayed because it would help the Democrats in the midterm elections. Still, having survived this, I believe the military and U.S. intelligence were willing to tolerate Kennedy's policies in the post-Missile Crisis world as long as his administration did not place the United States and the world in danger once again. Unfortunately, he had not learned his lesson.

At the beginning of 1963, after cracking down on right-wing Cuban exiles, American mercenaries, and the CIA, Robert Kennedy was placed in charge of the Omega Plan/ AMWORLD operation to mount a second invasion of Cuba in December of that year. It was irresponsible and reckless to give the Attorney General such responsibility and was probably the last straw for many who opposed the Kennedy brothers. Bobby was not qualified to head such an operation, and the fact that politics was the motivating factor behind it made it that much worse. Assassinating JFK was the only recourse left for the conspirators who wanted Kennedy removed from power by any means possible.

President Eisenhower wanted to remove Castro in 1959 after the Cuban leader declared himself a Communist. Still, Ike knew he could not replace Castro with someone as oppressive and corrupt as Batista because it would have offended the other Latin American countries. Cuba needed a democratic government that would serve the Cuban people fairly, and it was understandable that Bobby pursued the same agenda in 1963, for the basic premise had not changed. However, he went about it all wrong.

The war against Castro had always been a CIA operation, so President Kennedy made a significant mistake by shutting down Operation Mongoose and essentially cutting the Agency out of the Omega Plan/AMWORLD plan in 1963. Consider that in 2017, when President-elect Donald Trump criticized the CIA, the seasoned Washington insider, Senate Minority Leader Chuck Schumer, warned him to tread carefully. Trump is "being really dumb," Schumer said. "Let me tell you, you take on the intelligence community, they have six ways from Sunday at getting back at you."[1617]

The same rule applied in 1963, and JFK was equally blind to the slippery slope he was following. Especially since, by that time, the CIA considered the President a national security risk and a threat to democracy and the American way of life. He had fired Allen Dulles and banished William Harvey to Rome; he placed his inexperienced brother in charge of a paramilitary operation just months after a tense showdown with the Soviet Union during the Cuban Missile Crisis; he looked to normalize relations with Castro and Russia; and JFK split hairs by planning a second invasion of Cuba for political reasons that violated the agreement he had made with Khrushchev.

Henry Hecksher was on record as saying the Omega/AMWORLD plan was not going to work, and there were very few at the CIA who thought it would. It simply was not worth the risk. What made things worse was that Bobby Kennedy's plan was contingent on three premises coming to fruition, all of which the CIA and the Pentagon considered impossible as far back as the Bay of Pigs invasion.

The first was that an active underground in Cuba would support a second invasion and help topple Castro. The second was that assassinating Castro would turn the people against the government. The third was that an internal Cuban military coup was feasible. None of the three had any chance of succeeding. Rolando Cubela, the Cuban assassin Desmond Fitz-Gerald was meeting with, and Cuban General Juan Almeida, who was supposed to orchestrate the military coup, were both probably double agents, which meant Castro was privy to Bobby's plan to invade Cuba once again, which was why most people at the CIA were against the operation.

For the Omega Plan/AMWORLD operation to succeed, it needed a catalyst to justify invading Cuba because the United States could not just march into a foreign country without facing international repercussions. After the Trujillo assassination on May 30, 1961, the Kennedy brothers considered sending the Marines into the Dominican Republic to control the narrative. President Kennedy thought better of it because he would have to deal with accusations of American imperialism. Robert Kennedy then suggested they burn down the U.S. consulate and blame it on rebels, which could have been used to rationalize sending troops to the DR. Fortunately, Bobby's suggestion fell on deaf ears, but it provides an insight into his recklessness.[1618]

In 1963, Bobby knew he needed to involve the U.S. military in a Cuban invasion. That required a catalyst, such as a staged invasion of Haiti with troops dressed as Castro's army, which was what Thomas Eli Davis and Loran Hall were probably doing. Another option was to assassinate Papa Doc Duvalier and blame it on Cuba. The latter may have involved Jacqueline

Lancelot, as well as George de Mohrenschildt, who was in Haiti. A third was a staged attack against Guantanamo Bay with troops dressed as Castro's army, which Bobby had been pushing for years. It is hard to imagine that the CIA and the Pentagon supported any of these schemes. The Pentagon wanted a Normandy-type amphibious invasion run by them, and they welcomed the opportunity to take the fight to the Soviets directly. However, the CIA was ready to walk away from Cuba. They knew the chance of success was remote, and Khrushchev would have retaliated in Europe with a force that would have devastating consequences.

The Pentagon had been waiting since 1959 to send troops into Cuba. All they needed was Presidential authorization to do so. It was going to happen in December 1963, and the military prepared for that eventuality. That is, unless the Kennedy brothers got cold feet, which they were prone to do. Nevertheless, the Pentagon appeared willing to play along and made preparations to invade Cuba as part of the Omega Plan. But how serious were they? What the military really wanted was to engage Communists in Vietnam, not Cuba, and that could only happen if John F. Kennedy were no longer President.

***

The right-wing Cuban exiles and the American mercenaries who supported them had good reason to hate the Kennedys. They were left out of the Omega Plan/AMWORLD operation and subject to arrest if they engaged in any sabotage raids or paramilitary activity against Cuba from the same government that had trained them to do that. Harry Williams and a group of left-wing Cuban exiles were whom Bobby Kennedy approved of, and they would spearhead the invasion and make up the new Cuban government once they removed Castro from power.

It was why groups like Alpha 66, SNFE, Commandos L, MIRR, and the DRE gravitated towards Paulino Sierra's coalition government. Sierra had Mafia financing, and organized crime had a motive for wanting Castro removed from power, which was a problem for the CIA. As William Harvey said, "They [CIA] couldn't tell those Mafia types to go to hell. They were in bed with 'em," and there was "a very pregnant possibility... of this government being blackmailed either by Cubans for political purposes or by figures in organized crime for their own self-protection or aggrandizement."[1619] So, an alliance of Cuban exiles and the Mafia concerned the CIA. Still, we know Harvey maintained close ties to Johnny Roselli and, to a lesser extent, Santo Trafficante after the CIA transferred him to Rome. Hence, the CIA was still part of this unholy Alliance, and they supported the Sierra group. However, while the Cuban exiles and the Mafia wanted to invade Cuba and get rid of Castro, the CIA's real intent was to sabotage that effort to prevent a war between the United States and the Soviet Union.

Private financing backed Sierra along with organized crime. We know that on April 15, 1963, Sierra met with Allen Dulles and retired Army General Lucius Clay, who two years earlier had wanted to take on the Soviets in West Berlin during the Checkpoint Charlie standoff, but President Kennedy got cold feet. Clay now represented the interests of large corporations. It proved there was a much closer alliance between Sierra's group, the CIA, and the U.S. military than has previously been revealed.[1620]

The Dulles/Clay meeting with Sierra took place five days after the failed assassination attempt of General Walker at his home on April 10. On April 12, Lafitte referenced Charles Willoughby in connection with "soldier kill squads." Something big was in the offing immediately after the Walker shooting, and a month later, Sierra approached various exile groups as the representative of a coalition of American businessmen who wanted to see Castro overthrown. Sierra was also an ex-Batista supporter, which naturally attracted the attention of the Mafia, Texas oilmen, wealthy donors like William Pawley and Clare Booth Luce, disgruntled cattle ranchers, American mercenaries, and right-wing Cuban exile groups who wanted Cuba returned to how it had been under Batista. They were all willing to support Sierra's coalition. Still, it is crucial to keep in mind that not everyone was involved in the JFK's assassination plot.

By this time, Alpha 66 and the Cuban exile groups affiliated with them were working with General Lansdale and the U.S. Army, and Richard Nagell was investigating Alpha 66 regarding a conspiracy to assassinate JFK in the summer of 1963. Meanwhile, Batista's ex-strongman, Rolando Masferrer, was Alpha 66's Mafia contact and key bagman. It created a connection between Allen Dulles and elements of the CIA, the U.S. Army through Lucius Clay and Edward Landsdale, right-wing Cuban exiles, ex-Batista supporters, and the Mafia, which was not out of the question because these groups had worked together for years.

At the same time, Manuel Artime, who was the military leader for Bobby Kennedy's second invasion of Cuba, was still receiving monthly financial support from the CIA. It was an indication that Artime was unhappy with his role in the Omega Plan and that, based on his experience, he did not trust the Kennedys to follow through on their promise to invade Cuba again. A Hecksher memo described a meeting that took place between November 7 and 10, 1963, where one of Artime's leading advisors said that

556

EPILOGUE

while JFK remained in power, it would be impossible to defeat Castro. In a CIA memo written by Hecksher in October, he described plans "to activate our media capabilities in Mexico City on promoting a more acceptable image for AMBIDDY-1 [Artime's codename]. He discussed this with David Atlee Phillips on October 4, just two days after Oswald left Mexico City.

On September 25, just prior to Hecksher's meeting with Phillips and the day after Oswald left New Orleans for Mexico City, Hecksher met with Sam Papich, the FBI's liaison to the CIA. The FBI was concerned about a "high-level meeting of Cuban exiles" that had been "held in New York City in July 1963." An FBI report stated that "the meeting involved American and Cuban businessmen, which may have included "William Caldwell, a CIA intelligence officer who had been assigned to Cuba at one time."[1621] Caldwell was more than just an intelligence officer. On March 20, 1978, Frank Sturgis testified before the House Selection Committee on Assassination that Caldwell had been Chief of Station in Havana around 1958 while Batista was in power.[1622]

Hecksher told Papich the CIA knew nothing about the meeting in New York, which seems unlikely. The FBI liaison also wanted to know what the CIA knew about Manuel Artime organizing Cuban exiles and spending considerable time in Nicaragua. Hecksher advised that the CIA was "not involved in any intelligence operation with [Nicaraguan President] Somoza." It was part of Bobby Kennedy's operation. He emphasized that the CIA was not organizing a Cuban invasion force in any foreign countries. Hecksher added that "CIA has received numerous reports and rumors regarding Somoza's activities and his alleged connection with the U.S. Government. He advised that for several months, Somoza had been championing a plan, allegedly designed by him, which has as its objective to overthrow the Castro Government."

Regarding CIA operations, "Hecksher advised that his agency follows only programs which have been approved by the White House," which we know was an outright lie. He continued that "CIA still has the responsibility of running intelligence operations inside Cuba ... which continue to include the necessity of maintaining contact with Cuban exiles who possibly might be useful ... CIA is making a point of maintaining liaison with Cuban exile leaders and organizations who are in a position to assist in obtaining intelligence information inside Cuba and who have the potential to organize forces for the penetration or possible invasion of the country."[1623]

Hecksher was one of the few people at the CIA who kept his involvement in the war against Castro hidden for the remainder of his life. In his

557

discussion with Papich, he skirted around the Castro assassination operation involving Cubela and the Almeida effort to create a military coup. The intent was to keep the FBI in the dark. Hecksher added that the CIA was not furnishing arms, planes, or ammunition to Artime, and that "Somoza had been in regular contact with Carlos Prio...and with William Pauley [sic]," and that "CIA definitely is not utilizing Prio or Pauley in any capacity..." The inclusion of William Pawley suggests he was at the "high-level" meeting in New York with Cuban exiles, and Prio, we know, had designs on replacing Castro and was involved with Sierra's group. Therefore, the high-level meeting likely pertained to the Sierra group's plan to wrest control of the Cuban operation away from Bobby Kennedy after the JFK assassination. Hecksher's knowledge of this meant a group within the CIA was also involved with the Sierra group. They were likely operatives at a lower level, such as David Morales, David Phillips, and Howard Hunt. Hecksher's group, which included Allen Dulles, James Angleton, William Harvey, Frank Wisner, Tracy Barnes, Otto Skorzeny, Charles Willoughby, and Jean Pierre Lafitte, were against the second invasion and had bigger fish to fry. They knew AMWORLD was not going to work, and more importantly, they knew it was not going to end well.[1624]

As the months passed in 1963, JFK did not instill confidence that the second invasion of Cuba Bobby was planning would come to fruition. Not only did he crack down on Cuban exile activity, he looked to normalize relations with Castro. In Vietnam, he had the Pentagon prepare for a complete troop removal within two years. He signed a nuclear test ban treaty with the Soviets, was working towards a mutual nuclear arms reduction and a joint space program, and wanted to normalize relations with them as well. Domestically, his position on civil rights and his social programs were considered a violation of the Constitution and Communist-inspired by his critics, a position right-wing American elites had supported since FDR introduced the New Deal.

It is unclear if JFK was serious about invading Cuba, considering he was simultaneously looking to normalize relations with Castro. However, we do know he would only approve an invasion if it suited him politically, but this had no bearing on the Sierra group coalition, which was acting independently of Bobby's Omega Plan/ AMWORLD operation. Right-wing Cuban exiles, American mercenaries, the Mafia, Cuban and American businessmen, and members of the military, retired and active, did not want a *left-wing Fidelisimo without Fidel* government replacement for Castro. These groups longed for a return to the days of Batista. And the only way that was going to happen was with Lyndon Johnson as President, whom they could control, and with Bobby Kennedy no longer a factor. So, for them to be satisfied, JFK had to be removed from office.

There was a great deal of chatter about the assassination happening as November 22 drew closer. The day prior, Eloy Gutierrez Menoyo, the leader of the Second National Front of the Escambray, boasted that "something very big would happen soon that would advance the Cuban cause." In a Secret Service Report, informant Homer Echevarria of the November 30 Movement and the DRE reported that "we now have plenty of money – our new backers are Jews – as soon as 'we' (or 'they') take care of Kennedy..."[1625] In October, far-right racist and ant-Communist Joseph Milteer was caught on tape saying Kennedy was going to be killed by an assassin with a rifle from a tall building and a Communist would take the fall for the crime.

As early as April 4-6, 1963, at the Congress of Freedom in New Orleans, they discussed "the overthrow of the present government of the United States" and the establishment "of criminal activity to assassinate particular persons...high-ranking members of the Armed Forces... secretly belonged to the organization."

Garrett Trapnell claimed that while infiltrating Alpha 66, he learned of an assassination plot against JFK planned by a group of Cubans.

Prior to the October 1963 Constitution Party meeting attended by Joseph Milteer, retired army Colonel William Gale and his colleague Wesley A. Swift were part of an assassination plot. The FBI knew their group planned to assassinate three hundred public officials in high positions in government and industry.

On October 22, 1963, in Metz, France, Army private first-class Eugene B. Dinkin wrote a letter to Robert Kennedy warning of an impending assassination attempt against the President that would be blamed on a Communist or an African American. It was a military conspiracy, and Dinkin speculated that a military coup might ensue.[1626] Another FBI report stated that "a conspiracy was in the making by the 'military' of the United States, perhaps combined with an 'ultra-right economic group.'"[1627]

Meanwhile, many people knew that a second invasion of Cuba was going to happen at the end of 1963.

> • On November 1, an FBI airtel stated that a planned second invasion of Cuba was to "begin in the last week of November against the Cuban mainland."

559

- Fort Hood's Army Captain George Charles Nonte knew Cuban exiles were planning a second invasion of Cuba, and he probably informed the FBI. Nonte learned about it from John Thomas Masen, who heard of it from a Miami-based "weapons buyer" named Martinez, who had come "through Dallas on [a] recent buying trip." The man, Joaquin Martinez de Pinillos, was a member of the DRE.

- James Hosty claimed he first heard about a possible second invasion of Cuba on or around October 25, according to an FBI document.

- A critical CIA "Telegram Information Report" dated October 7 categorically stated that operations against Cuba would "begin in November or December 1963."

- An FBI report written just weeks after JFK's assassination said Jack Ruby stated, "the United States Government was sponsoring an invasion of Cuba."

- Another FBI memo later revealed that a close associate of David Ferrie told the Bureau about Ferrie's "dealings with the late Attorney General Robert Kennedy [and] plans for a Cuban second invasion."

- A friend of Banister wrote in the summer of 1963 that there was secret "Kennedy Administration planning" where Castro "would be the fall guy in a complete reorganization for the regime which will [then] be free of Soviet influence." Banister wrote that following Castro's removal, "a new government [would be] set up with such men as ...Manola Ray..."

- According to investigator Dr. Michael L. Kurtz, John Martino worked with Guy Banister and Carlos Marcello in the summer of 1963. He quoted the former Superintendent of the New Orleans Police Department saying that Martino "met with Marcello himself at the Town and Country Motel." FBI files also show that Martino knew the Kennedys intended to use Almeida in a military revolt within Cuba and that "President Kennedy was engaged in a plot to overthrow the Castro regime by preparing another invasion attempt against Cuba." Then, according to an FBI file not revealed until 1998, Martino told a small-time newspaper two months after the assassination that "Kennedy was embarked on a plan to get rid of Castro. There was to be another invasion and uprising in Cuba."

How did so many, including people in Dallas and New Orleans who were close to Lee Oswald, know so much about the Omega Plan/AMWORLD operation, unless it was a real operation that was going to happen? And how did these far-right wingers and Mafia figures know about a plan that involved Robert Kennedy and left-leaning Cuban exiles?

In addition, a Secret Service report dated November 15, 1963, involved the arrest of a car thief who told the FBI "that he is a member of the Ku Klux Klan; that during his travels throughout the country, his sources have told him that a militant group of the National States Rights Party plans to assassinate the President and other high-level officials."

On November 17, New Orleans FBI agent William Walter received a teletype sent to all FBI offices warning about a plot to kill JFK on November 22 in Dallas. The FBI had "determined that a militant revolutionary group…" was behind the plot. The memo advised that they should keep an eye on all "race and hate groups." Recall that shortly after the assassination, two men named Sumner and DeLaparra independently contacted the FBI to report that in the summer of 1963, each learned of a possible Carlos Marcello crime family involvement in the JFK assassination. The FBI agents who interviewed the two eyewitnesses were concerned about "race and hate groups," not organized crime. The previous October, informants had told the FBI that Carlos Marcello, Santos Trafficante, and Jimmy Hoffa had all said that the JFK assassination was in the works, so an alarm bell should have gone off at the Bureau.

By November 22, 1963, the FBI knew that the Mafia, right-wing Cuban exiles, radical right-wing groups, which included Southern racists, American mercenaries, retired and active high-level ex-officers of the U.S. military, and a militant revolutionary group were aware of the plot to assassinate JFK. The common denominator that united these groups was the Sierra group.

Noticeably absent were reports regarding the CIA, which was not surprising. Dulles, Angleton, Harvey, Hecksher, Barnes, Wisner, Skorzeny, Willoughby, Lafitte, Souetre, and de Vosjoli, who were the conspirators in charge of the assassination plot, intended to sabotage the operation after they killed JFK to ensure the second invasion of Cuba never happened.

***

Tracy Barnes had worked with Howard Hunt in Guatemala and on the Bay of Pigs operation. In 1963, Barnes asked Hunt to join him at the Domestic Operations Division, in charge of covert action. In addition to being connected to the Cuban exile community, Hunt was reportedly in contact with OAS assassin Jean Souetre, according to Gilbert Le Cavelier, who had conducted research in France for Bernard Fensterwald. Le Cavelier said Souetre's official residence was Madrid. "Extremely close ties have always existed between the anti-Castroites in Florida and the French extreme right through the intermediary of ex-O.A.S. members who emigrated to Argentina, Paraguay, and Venezuela," Le Cavelier wrote Fensterwald in 1982. "In March-April 1963, Souetre met Howard Hunt in Madrid." Also at the meeting were OAS intelligence director Jean Claude Perez and several anti-Communist Hungarians. Hungarians had taken part in an assassination attempt against de Gaulle the previous year, so their presence at the meeting was not a surprise.[1628]

There is additional evidence pointing to a French connection to the JFK assassination, which is consistent with our thesis. Virgil Bailey, an INS investigator in 1963, told researcher Gary Shaw years later about "picking up a Frenchman in Dallas shortly after the assassination of President Kennedy." Bailey's supervisor at the time, Hal Norwood, described the arrest of an "individual who might have been French, which occurred shortly after the killing of the President." The man in question was a wanted criminal, and shortly after INS took him into custody, the head of Washington INS investigations called requesting a pickup on the man. [1629]

As reported by Lamar Waldron in *The Hidden History of the JFK Assassination*, "The two European shooters...trained at [Carlos] Marcello's huge, secluded Churchill Farms estate outside New Orleans...were taken to Dallas by Joe Campisi, Sr., Marcello's number-two underboss in that city. Twenty-two years later, Marcello explained the key role Campisi played in his plot to his cellmate Jack Van Laningham. Campisi hid the two hitmen at his restaurant until it was time for them to go to Dealey Plaza before JFK's motorcade passed through that park-like part of downtown Dallas." [1630]

The Mafia was part of the Sierra group, so their involvement in the assassination is believable, but the role they played was minor at best. As previously described, William Harvey was adamant that the CIA was accountable to the Mafia because they could blackmail the Agency. It explains why the conspirators involved the Mafia, who also provided a degree of separation and plausible deniability if something went wrong. Harvey also insisted that assassins should come from Europe.

That there were multiple shooters is a fact based on eyewitness testimony, ballistic evidence, the recollection of Parkland Hospital doctors and nurses, and the information derived from JFK's autopsy. In fact, all reliable reports that Robert Kennedy received after the assassination supported that conclusion.

Secret Service agent Roy Kellerman, who was sitting in the front seat of JFK's limo, told Bobby he did not believe "it was one man." Kellerman later told the Warren Commission that "there have got to be more than three shots, gentlemen" and that a "flurry of shells" flew into the vehicle. Kellerman's widow, June, said he always "accepted that there was a conspiracy."

Secret Service head James Rowley told Bobby the evening of the assassination that a crossfire from three or four gunmen killed his brother. The President was "the victim of a powerful organization," Rowley told Bobby. Rowley must have been privy to sensitive information to have made a statement like that so quickly. However, when he testified before the Warren Commission months later, he succumbed to pressure and testified that Oswald had acted alone.[1631]

Secret Service Agents David Powers and Kenneth O'Donnell, riding in the follow-up limousine, were confident the first shot came from the right front of their limo, from the grassy knoll. Powers felt they were "riding into an ambush." Agent Lem Johns, two cars behind Powers, was also sure the first shot came from the grassy knoll. Dave Powers said that "the same bullet that hit JFK did not hit John Connally." Agent Forrest Sorrels said he "looked towards the top of the terrace to my right, as the sound of the shots seemed to come from that direction." Chief Curry, driving the lead car, radioed to "get a man on top of that triple underpass and see what happened up there." Sheriff Bill Decker, sitting beside Sorrels, sent the order to "move all available men out of my office [and] into the railroad yard to try to determine what happened in there."[1632]

ABC television affiliate WFAA had two reporters stationed near Dealey Plaza as the motorcade passed – Jay Watson and Jerry Haynes. On camera, Haynes reported that "some of the Secret Service agents thought the gunfire was from a ... weapon fired... from a grassy knoll to which the police rushed," and added, "In other words, they fired into the car as it came down the hill."[1633]

Dr. George Burkley, JFK's physician, was present at Parkland Hospital and the autopsy in Bethesda, Maryland. He told researcher Henry Hurt in 1982 that JFK was the target of a conspiracy.

Peter Lawford told a friend that during the last weekend at the White House, Bobby revealed that a powerful plot grew out of one of the government's secret anti-Castro operations and assassinated JFK, which is what we believe to be true. Bobby told Lawford and other family members there was nothing he could do at the moment because they were facing a formidable enemy, and they no longer controlled the government.[1634]

Bobby must have wondered how a staged invasion of Cuban exiles dressed as Castro's soldiers that would lead to a second Cuban invasion

563

morphed into the assassination of his brother. The Attorney General may have speculated that a loss of confidence in his and the President's commitment to carry through with the Omega Plan was why the assassination happened. They had betrayed the Cuban exiles, the Pentagon, the CIA, and their supporters during the Bay of Pigs invasion. They had the chance to invade Cuba before Russian missiles were in place but failed to do so because it was politically expedient to wait until the month before the midterm elections to address the crisis, and then it was too late. They cracked down on all exile sabotage raids and covert activity after the Missile Crisis was over and disbanded Operation Mongoose. They looked to normalize relations with Castro in 1963, which meant the Kennedy brothers did not care if the exiles never returned to their homeland or if Cuban and American businessmen would ever recoup the fortunes they lost after Castro took their businesses away from them. How could the Kennedy brothers be trusted to follow through on the Omega Plan with such a track record?

Bobby's plan was reliant upon Cuban General Juan Almeida orchestrating a coup against Castro and Rolando Cubela assassinating Castro to jump-start an internal uprising. Then, once the Cuban exile invasion force landed, they would ask the United States for help to establish their new government, which was when the U.S. military would invade Cuba to support them. This plan had been on the table since the Bay of Pigs, and the Pentagon knew the chances of this being successful were remote and would have led to a military confrontation with the Soviets. There were those at the Pentagon who would have welcomed this confrontation, but most level-headed military brass understood this was counterproductive. The objective was to get boots on the ground in Southeast Asia.

Meanwhile, there was Sierra's coalition of right-wing Cuban exiles, the Mafia, Texas oilmen, and American and Cuban businessmen who had lost their homeland and a great deal of money when Castro ousted Batista. They wanted Castro gone, but Bobby cut them out of his left-wing coalition anyway.

***

A lot was happening in April 1963, the pivotal month when the assassination planning began.

- CIA assassin Jean Souetre met with Howard Hunt in Madrid, the home of Otto Skorzeny and his Nazi cohorts.

EPILOGUE

- The Congress of Freedom met in New Orleans and discussed "the overthrow of the present government of the United States" and the establishment "of criminal activity to assassinate particular persons..."

- Paulino Sierra met with Allen Dulles and retired Army General Lucius Clay.

- The United States removed Jupiter missiles from Italy and Turkey.

- The United States and Great Britain signed the Nassau Agreement, which allowed the mounting of British nuclear warheads on Polaris missiles in times of "supreme peril." De Gaulle refused the same deal because he believed JFK would let Western Europe fall rather than risk a Soviet nuclear attack on American cities. Germany's Adenauer agreed. He also did not think Kennedy was strong enough to stand up to the Soviets.

- On election day in Italy, the Communists gained twenty-five percent of the votes while all other parties lost seats. In response, Prime Minister Aldo Morro named Socialists to cabinet posts, and President Kennedy supported his decision.

- Minutemen leader Robert DePugh said in an interview that "we could very easily be sitting on the edge of a bloodbath in this country" if a Communist killed him.

- There was an attempt on the life of General Walker involving Lee Harvey Oswald.

- On Easter Sunday, neo-Nazis swept through Dallas during the night and vandalized the homes of several prominent Jews with a custom-printed decal that was blood red with a black swastika and the words, "WE ARE BACK." The next night, vandals plastered Jewish-owned businesses in downtown Dallas with swastikas.

- Lee Harvey Oswald left a letter for his wife as if he were a soldier going behind enemy lines, telling her what to do if he were alive and taken prisoner.

It was also in April 1963 that Richard Case Nagell entered the picture. He had been investigating Cuban exile groups like Alpha 66 and individuals like Rolando Masferrer on behalf of the CIA. In conjunction with that, he also investigated Lee and Marina Oswald. Oswald was already affiliated with the Minutemen by then, which placed him at the center of the neo-Nazi racist and anti-Communist hate groups in Dallas that were beginning to come together. There was talk about "kill squads" and executing traitors and Communists in the U.S. government, which included President Kennedy. Oswald's philosophy mirrored what these groups stood for and what they wanted to accomplish, which was to initiate a third world war between the United States and the Soviet Union. What Oswald wrote made it clear that the objective was to create a new world order because there were "two world systems, one twisted beyond recognition (communism)... the other decadent and dying (capitalism). A truly democratic system would combine the better qualities of the two upon an American foundation."[1635]

Oswald's new world-order philosophy was what the ex-Nazis in Madrid believed, which is not surprising. Recall the involvement of George de Mohrenschild and Volkmar Schmidt in the Nazi indoctrination of Oswald early in 1963.

We learned in Chapter Sixteen that a State Department report stated that Otto Skorzeny's associate Hans-Ulrich Rudel "is primarily interested in the reconstitution of an independent Germany with its own army separate from a Western Army...this can be accomplished by German action with international Fascist support..." There was another State Department report that described how in Germany, there were "plans for an "International Waffen-SS," composed of Nazi veterans scattered throughout the world, presumably were outlined before the last days of the war....*OTTO SKORZENY*, with Gauleiters KAUFMAN, KREBS, and LAUTERBACH, was involved in the first of these manifestations in Germany."[1636]

The OSS philosophy mirrored what Oswald and the Nazis believed. Colonel Antoine Argoud of the OSS explained that the military wanted "to halt the decadence of the West and the march of Communism. That is our duty, the real duty of the army. That is why we must win the war in Algeria." "We have not come here to defend colonialism," declared Radio-Bigeard on the OSS military's radio station. "We are the defenders of liberty and...a new order.".[1637]

A new world order is what Lee Oswald, Otto Skorzeny, Rudel and their Nazi cohorts, European Monarchists, Fascists, and the French OSS wanted to achieve. There was also a long history of a similar sentiment in the United States.

In his 2002 book *Memoirs*, David Rockefeller wrote that "ideological extremists at either end of the political spectrum have seized upon well-publicized incidents...to attack the Rockefeller family for the inordinate influence they claim we have over American political and economic institutions. Some even believe we are part of a secret cabal working against the best interests of the United States, characterizing my family and me as 'internationalists' and conspiring with others around the world to build a more

EPILOGUE

integrated global political and economic structure – one world if you will. If that's the charge, I stand guilty, and I am proud of it."

The Warren Commission's John McCloy wrote: "I would take a chance on this country using its strength *tyrannously*...We need, if you will, a Pax Americana, and in the course of it, the world will become more receptive to the Bill of Rights viewpoint than if we do no more than devoutly wish for peace and freedom."[1638]

Josef Muller was a go-between for the Vatican and Nazi generals looking to assassinate Hitler. He envisioned "a [united] European Economic Union, which would make war between separate states seemingly impossible." It would be a Union formed on Christian values. "We must think like Christians and must plan and prepare to rebuild again....German Jesuit and Dominican leadership concurred, pledging "to endure and preserve our Catholic honor, before our consciences, before the people, before history, the Church and the Lord God." They were proposing a new world order, a united Europe that included Western Christians but excluded Communists and Jews. It was similar to what was being considered by right-wing groups in the United States. As a result, it was inevitable that anti-Communists and Fascists from both sides of the Atlantic would be drawn together after the war to pursue their common goal. And that still included the Vatican.[1639]

To those interested in establishing an international Fascist new world order supported by European colonialism throughout the world, it was clear President John F. Kennedy was a deterrent to their vision. As early as July 1957, Senator Kennedy stated, "The most powerful single force in the world today is neither communism nor capitalism, neither the H-bomb nor the guided missile – it is man's eternal desire to be free and independent. The great enemy of that tremendous force of freedom is called, for want of a better term, imperialism – and today that means Soviet imperialism and, whether we like it or not, and though they are not to be equated, Western imperialism. Thus, the single most important test of American foreign policy today is how we meet the challenge of imperialism [and] what we do to further man's desire to be free...If we fail to meet the challenge of either Soviet or Western imperialism, then no amount of foreign aid, no aggrandizement of armaments, no new pacts or doctrines or high-level conferences can prevent further setbacks to our course and to our security."

To accuse Western Europe and the United States of imperialism in 1957 was blasphemous to those who considered the Soviet Union a Godless enemy. Still, it was clear this was what JFK stood for. He reconfirmed his position on October 12, 1960, when he spoke at the Hotel Theresa in Harlem,

567

where Castro and Khrushchev had just met, demonstrating that he had not changed his opinion in the least.

> "Behind the fact of Castro coming to this hotel, [and] Khrushchev coming to Castro," JFK said, "there is another great traveler in the world, and that is the travel of a world revolution, a world in turmoil... We should not fear the 20th century, for this worldwide revolution which we see all around us is part of the original American Revolution. When the Indonesians revolted after the end of World War II, they scrawled on the walls, 'Give me liberty or give me death.' They scrawled on the walls, 'All men are created equal.' When they had a meeting for independence in Northern Rhodesia, they called it a Boston Tea Party... This is the unfinished business that we have. Woodrow Wilson, Franklin Roosevelt, [and] Harry Truman, each of their generations met their responsibilities. Now, it is ours. Now it is ours to finish the job... What has happened to America? We are the great revolutionary people. We believe in freedom. We believe in independence... What is wrong? I believe it is important that the President of the United States personify the ideals of our society, speak out on this, [and] associate ourselves with the great fight for equality.... The white people are a minority in the world. We want to hold our hand out in friendship... How many members of the Foreign Service are of African descent? There are over 6,000 people involved in the whole Foreign Service – 23 out of 6,000. That is not very many, when Africa will poll one-fourth of all the votes in the General Assembly by 1962. One-fourth of all the votes of the General Assembly by 1962 will be African... So, I come to Harlem today to ask you to join us... to move, to go forward, until the United States achieves this great goal of practicing what it preaches.

What JFK failed to understand was that the worldwide revolution he was promoting was different from what others had in mind. Four days after he was sworn in, on January 26, 1961, Allen Dulles sent President Kennedy a report that stated:

> A pre-revolutionary atmosphere reigns in France... The Army and the Air Force are staunchly opposed to de Gaulle... At least 80 percent of the officers are violently against him. They haven't forgotten that in 1958, he had given his word of honor that he would never abandon Algeria. He is now reneging on his promise, and they hate him for that. De Gaulle surely won't last if he tries to let go of Algeria. Everything will probably be over for him by the end of the year – he will be either deposed or assassinated.

It may have been a warning from Dulles to Kennedy. After the failed coup d'etat, de Gaulle purged his security forces and removed General Paul Grossin, the chief of SDECE. Grossin was close to the CIA and told Frank Wisner that the return of de Gaulle to power was equivalent to the Communists taking over in Paris. [1640]

Henrik Kruger wrote in *The Great Heroin Coup, Intelligence & International Fascism*, that "Internacional Fascista is the outgrowth of many years of planning in Madrid by the late Nazi, Otto Skorzeny, who in the fifties had worked for the CIA. On its rolls are former SS agents, OAS terrorists, hatchet men for Portugal's dreaded secret police (PIDE), terrorists from Spain's Fuerza Nueva, Argentine and Italian Facists, Cuban exiles, French gangsters from SAC, and former CIA agents hardened by terror campaigns in Operation 40, Guatemala, Brazil and Argentina. International Fascista's militants have at various times numbered the Army for the Liberation of Portugal (ELP) and its Aginter Press contingent under Guerin-Serac, the Italian Ordine Nuovo led by Salvatore Francia, and Pierluigi Concutelli; Spain's Guerillas of Christ the King, Associacion Anticommmunista Iberica and Alianz Anticommunista Apostolica (AAA) ..."[1641]

Miami was part of international fascism, stretching across the Atlantic to the Aginter operation, originally in Lisbon, with Skorzeny in Madrid at the center of this arms smuggling web. The Miami-Lisbon-Madrid-Rome axis was a continuation of the CIA's alliance with ex-Nazis. The Fascist Paladin Group, as well as the Spanish intelligence agency, Direccion General de Seguridad (DGS), were both run by Skorzeny.

William Harvey was the one person at the CIA who checked all the boxes. He was station chief in Berlin at a time when he would have gotten to know Otto Skorzeny. He ran the Cuban operation and the CIA's assassinations operation while Mongoose was going on and the CIA was trying to kill Castro. He was on record looking for assassins in Europe. He was in Rome at the time of the JFK assassination when Gladio's stay-behind armies were still flourishing throughout Europe and had the opportunity to work with NATO chief General Lyman Lemnitzer while still maintaining ties to the Mafia and Johnny Roselli. Finally, he is mentioned many times in Lafitte's datebook.

"I wouldn't be surprised to learn that Harvey was in Dallas in November 1963," HSCA investigator Dan Hardway said. "We considered Harvey to be one of our prime suspects from the very start. He had all the key connections – to organized crime, to the CIA station in Miami where the plots against Castro were run...We tried to get Harvey's travel vouchers and

569

security file from the CIA, but they always blocked us. But we did come across a lot of memos that suggested he was traveling a lot in the months leading up to the assassination."[1642]

***

It is not surprising that Oswald felt at home with groups that were espousing a philosophy promoting a worldwide revolution similar to what he believed in, albeit from a different political perspective. He was not the only one to equate Marxism with fascism and feel comfortable in both camps. In the 1930s, James Burnham was a Marxist who, like Lee Oswald, was a proponent of Leon Trotsky's teachings and was against capitalism and Soviet communism. He believed that should the Capitalists start a war, the "AWP [American Worker's Party] would act to turn the conflict into a workers' revolt against the war makers. Similarly, if the USSR came under capitalist attack, the AWP would come to its defense, joining with the workers to overthrow the U.S. government. But Burnham also criticized the Soviet policy [under Stalin] of 'socialism in one country,' charging it with abandoning the principle of 'proletarian internationalism' and the goal of world revolution." Later, Burnam did an about-face and worked for the OPC under Frank Wisner and Allen Dulles. He backed Nelson Rockefeller's nomination for president in 1968 and Ronald Reagan as vice president, he approved when Rockefeller was selected as vice president by Gerald Ford and supported the decision by Ford to name Henry Kissinger Secretary of State.[1643]

So, Oswald was not the first Marxist to call for worldwide revolution and still find a home dealing with American Fascists like Wisner and Dulles. However, what Oswald did not realize was that the groups he was involved with intended to use him, and it began with the shooting attempt against General Walker in April 1963. By all indications, Walker's assassination was supposed to be a catalyst that would have led to a general right-wing uprising that spring. That never materialized, so Oswald traveled to New Orleans and wound up working with Guy Banister, David Ferrie, and the anti-Communist, anti-Castro group centered around the Cuban Grand Central Station. It was likely that his relationship with the New Orleans group, which included Carlos Marcello, was to connect them to Oswald after the assassination when there would be allegations of guilt by association. We do know the time he spent in New Orleans had nothing to do with the JFK assassination plot, at least not at the beginning, for Lafitte instructed the conspirators to watch Oswald but not to make contact with him. Then, sometime in the summer of 1963, the conspirators brought Oswald into the assassination plot during a meeting in Mexico City, and he may have willingly agreed to become the assassination patsy to bring about the new world order he was looking for. However, in September, Richard Nagell let Oswald know the assassination conspirators had misled him, which changed everything.

Oswald returned to Mexico City at the end of September with the intent of going to Cuba to escape what fate had in store for him, similar to what Nagell had done. However, the CIA was not going to let that happen. They sent an Oswald impostor to Mexico City who appeared at the Cuban Embassy first to ensure the Russians and Cubans would never grant the real Oswald an entry visa into Cuba.

Oswald was clearly nervous when he returned to Dallas. On October 15, a classified ad in the *Dallas Morning News* read, "Running Man, please call me. Please. Please," signed by "Lee." On November 6 or 7, Oswald appeared at the FBI office and delivered a letter for James Hosty, which said he was going to blow up the FBI building if Hosty did not stop bothering his wife. He should have been arrested for this alone. On November 8, he wrote a letter to Mr. Hunt, writing, "I am asking only for information. I am suggesting that we discuss the matter fully before any steps are taken by me or anyone else." The next day, knowing the letter he left at the FBI office did not have the desired effect, Oswald wrote a suspicious letter to the Soviet Embassy in Washington and left a draft on Ruth Paine's desk, where she was sure to find it. The letter included the passage, "I could not take a chance on requesting a new visa unless I used my real name, so I returned to the United States…had I been able to reach the Soviet Embassy in Havana as planned, the embassy there would have had time to complete our business…" Undoubtedly, someone helped him write the letter. Oswald was hoping Ruth would immediately give it to the FBI, which would have resulted in his arrest. Unfortunately for Oswald, there was no escape for him.

The Lafitte datebook tells us the conspirators were aware of Oswald's anxiety. On October 6, three days after Oswald returned from Mexico City, the entry reads, "Oswald – Issue (!) with Caretaker." Then, on October 16, the names "[Everett] Glover" and "Volkmar [Schmidt]" inexplicably reappear after a ten-month hiatus, probably because they needed to calm Oswald down. On the following day, the entry refers to a "High-level gathering in D.C.," [that] the "Lancelot [Operation]" was a "Go – Ok – Oswald – Others." Three days later, a concerned Lafitte wrote, "Hard to believe that it will go forward…but it will, it is me?" The name "Volkmar" appears again on October 24, and on the following day, the entry reads, "Oswald set in place." However, there was still concern regarding Oswald, which was why two days later, on October 27, the names" Gali Sherbatoff" and "L.O (Orlov),"

571

two other names from the past mysteriously reappeared. On November 5, Lafitte wrote again, "O [Otto] says Lancelot = go," which suggests some still questioned if the assassination should move forward, but Skorzeny overruled them. The concern was because Oswald was probably talking to the FBI, for the November 9 entry reads, 'On the wings of murder. The pigeon way for unsuspecting Lee. Clip Clip his wings."[1644]

***

Unknown to the right-wing Sierra group coalition that believed the JFK assassination would be a catalyst to justify a second invasion of Cuba, the CIA had other plans, and there was a history as to how they handled operations they wanted to destroy. Allen Dulles had sabotaged the 1959 coup to overthrow Castro, which resulted in William Morgan's execution. Dulles headed the CIA when the Agency sabotaged the U-2 flight over the Soviet Union in 1960 to prevent a nuclear test ban treaty from happening. He was the one who kept JFK in the dark about the strategic importance of Indonesia and orchestrated a failed military coup to remove Sukarno, which would eventually be successful in 1965. It was Dulles who delayed the initial Bay of Pigs invasion, which was supposed to take place before the 1960 election and catapult Richard Nixon into the Presidency. That would have led to a Soviet invasion of West Berlin, which Dulles wanted to avoid. Finally, Dulles knew the Bay of Pigs invasion was bound to fail, which is what he wanted, so he and Richard Bissell misled JFK into believing it would work.

Even though Dulles no longer ran the CIA in 1963, he was still the puppet master pulling the strings behind the scenes, and the narrative had not changed for Dulles and the CIA from what it had been since 1959, although the stakes were higher this time. Sabotaging JFK was no longer feasible because things had progressed too far. Hence, Dulles and his cohorts knew they had to assassinate the President to prevent a second invasion of Cuba from occurring, as opposed to being a catalyst to promote an invasion, which the right-wing Cuban exile/Mafia Sierra coalition wanted. If allowed to happen, the invasion of Cuba involving the U.S. military would have resulted in Europe taking the brunt of the Soviet retaliation. West Berlin would have been the first domino to fall, followed by a Red Army advance across Western Europe. Nuclear war would have been unavoidable, especially since the hardline military faction in Moscow was still smarting over their defeat during the Cuban Missile Crisis. The extent of their dissatisfaction became apparent when Khrushchev was forcibly removed from power on October 14, 1964, less than a year after the JFK assassination. It was a sign that Russian militarists blamed Khrushchev for his failure to stand up to the United States, and that was not going to happen again.

Keeping Western Europe free from communism was essential to the CIA. In addition to Dulles, James Angleton had served in Italy and prevented the Communists from taking control of the Italian government. William Harvey, who was now station chief in Rome, had been station chief in West Berlin before heading ZR/RIFLE. Tracy Barnes, Ted Shackley, Henry Hecksher, and David Morales all worked for Harvey in West Berlin, and there were powerful money interests in the United States with strong ties to Germany that wanted it protected. Frank Wisner had strong ties to Germany as well, having served there under Allen Dulles at the end of World War II.

It was a critical time, as explained by a National Intelligence Estimate on Soviet nuclear missile capabilities. There was concern that a shift in the balance of power could threaten to undermine the American position in Berlin by the end of Kennedy's first term. The prediction was that the Soviets would match the United States intercontinental ballistic missile force and nuclear defense systems by 1965, and the Soviets could challenge the West in Berlin or anywhere else around the world without fear of repercussions.

There was no doubt how important Berlin was to the Soviets. Khrushchev promised he would "eradicate this splinter from the heart of Europe." After the Bay of Pigs, Khrushchev alluded to a link between Berlin and Cuba when he said, "Military armament and the world political situation are such at this time that any so-called 'little war' can touch off a chain reaction in all parts of the globe."[1645]

Henry Kissinger was an advisor to President Kennedy on foreign policy. He understood how important protecting Berlin was to the security of the Western world. He warned JFK that: "A defeat over Berlin, that is a deterioration of Berlin's possibility to live in freedom, would inevitably demoralize the Federal Republic... All other NATO nations would be bound to draw the indicated conclusions from such a demonstration of the West's impotence. For other parts of the world, the irresistible nature of the Communist movement would be underlined. Coming on top of the Communist gains of the past five years, it would teach a clear lesson even to neutralists. Western guarantees, already degraded in significance, would mean little in the future. The realization of the Communist proposal that Berlin become a 'free city' could well be the decisive turn in the struggle of freedom against tyranny. Any consideration of policy must start from the premise that the West simply cannot afford a defeat in Berlin." Kissinger further warned JFK not to take West Berlin for granted. "We should give them some tangible demonstration of our confidence to maintain their hope and courage," he wrote.

There was no ambiguity here. JFK understood how important Berlin was. After the Berlin Wall went up on August 13, 1961, Kennedy gave a speech at the United Nations the following month. He said that "the decisions of the next ten months may well decide the fate of man for the next ten thousand years....And we in this hall shall be remembered either as part of the generation that turned this planet into a flaming funeral pyre or the generation that met its vow to 'save succeeding generations from the scourge of war.'"[1646]

The Pentagon had made it clear throughout the Cold War that they welcomed a confrontation with the Soviets. However, their main objective was to initiate hostilities in Southeast Asia, not in Europe, which they wanted to protect. So, one can make a case that the Joint Chiefs were on board with the plan to assassinate JFK and sabotage the Omega Plan/AMWORLD operation, knowing LBJ would take action to curtail the spread of communism in Southeast Asia.

Otto Skorzeny's Nazi group in Madrid, the French OAS, and European Monarchists did not like what was happening in Algeria. They wanted a return to European colonialism and a continent free from communism, and they had worked with the CIA for years to ensure Europe remained that way. They wanted a unified Germany, but not one controlled by the Soviet Union.

William Harvey had looked to Europe to find assassins when he started ZR/RIFLE, Frank Wisner had worked with Eastern European émigré groups since the end of World War II, and James Angleton was instrumental in keeping Communists from controlling Italian and French politics. Angleton later employed the services of Philippe de Vosjoli to fight communism during Kennedy's presidency. In the 1950s, Otto Skorzeny had set up a Nazi network of stay-behind armies to hold back the Soviets. At the same time, Allen Dulles and William Donovan had their own stay-behind armies, and Paix et Liberté, the French intelligence group, also had anti-Communist armies throughout Europe. It was all financed privately, mostly with Mafia drug money laundered through the Vatican. So, it was natural for the CIA to turn to men like Skorzeny, Lafitte, Souetre, and de Vosjoli, who were already working with the Agency, to orchestrate the assassination plot in a manner that would prevent the second invasion of Cuba from occurring and provide plausible deniability.

EPILOGUE

We know that as early as January 1951, the U.S. High Commissioner in Germany, and future Warren Commission member, John McCloy, wrote the U.S. Secretary of State that President Franco in Spain was "utilizing Skorseny, former Nazi intelligence chief, for [the] purpose of organizing military units in Spain." He was "recruiting former Nazi officers and specialists among German refugees." German Chancellor Adenauer was concerned that this was supported and encouraged by America. If it became public, "it would have [the] most serious effect upon opinion, not only in Germany but elsewhere in Western Europe, as obviously, it would result in the creation of revival Nazi force."[1647]

So, it is logical that at some point, the CIA brought Otto Skorzeny into the assassination plot.

As Richard Nagell said, "The conspiracy I was cognizant of, I'm not saying, is the same one that resulted in the president's death, although I'm sure the same people were involved."[1648]

***

The key to controlling the narrative related to the JFK assassination operation was Lee Harvey Oswald, "the indispensable tool." After the assassination, the plan was to lure the police to Oak Cliff and have Oswald arrested, which they accomplished by killing Tippit and leaving a second wallet at the murder scene containing Oswald's identification information for the police to find. The CIA was aware that Oswald's defection to the Soviet Union had been an American military intelligence operation and that the Russians knew that as well. They knew part of the operation was to create the illusion that the Soviets had killed Oswald behind the Iron Curtain, and an impostor 2" shorter had taken his place. They knew about the mind control and illicit drugs Oswald was subjected to while he was in the Marines. They knew the truth about the Walker shooting, Oswald's FPCC scam in New Orleans, his relationship with the Mafia in that city, and the hijinks they had perpetrated in Mexico City to make it seem Oswald was never there.

As mentioned in the Introduction, any justification the United States needed to invade Cuba with the U.S. military was handed to them on a silver platter with President Kennedy's assassination. The world would soon learn that the accused assassin, Lee Harvey Oswald, had defected to the Soviet Union and had strong ties to Cuba and even tried to enter Cuba from Mexico City two months before the assassination. It was not hard to make a case that Cuba was involved with Oswald in the assassination, whether it was true or not, and the people responsible knew that President Lyndon

Johnson and the powers that be would never let the truth about Oswald be publicly known. If the American people knew about Oswald's height discrepancy, forged identification cards, and that it looked like the Soviets had murdered him in Russia, the clamor for revenge would have compelled LBJ to react against the Soviet Union with force. Preventing World War III was the argument Johnson used to convince Earl Warren and others to join an investigative commission designed to conclude Oswald was the lone assassin. It was not a coincidence that the FBI came to the same conclusion the very day Hoover learned about the Cubela/Kostikov relationship.

So, Oswald was left out in the cold at the Texas Theater, waiting for someone who would never arrive. It was only a matter of time before the police arrested him. Once Oswald was in custody, the fear of who he really was and that he might talk and reveal everything he knew resulted in the cancelation of the second invasion of Cuba, and the whitewash coverup of what really transpired in Dallas began.

The Mafia had a lot to lose if Oswald talked. They had a connection to him in New Orleans, and they must have feared they would be accused of being responsible for the JFK assassination if Oswald revealed his association with the mob. So, Jack Ruby silenced Oswald on national television, which resulted in the majority of the nation questioning who really killed their beloved President. After that, there was no chance for AMWORLD to move forward. However, we should seriously consider that it may not have been the mob that had Ruby kill Oswald. Recall William Harvey's testimony that the Mafia had the potential to blackmail the CIA, and the Agency needed leverage over the Mafia, which they got when Ruby killed Oswald. Recall also that Ruby told the Warren Commission that Fascists and Nazis placed him in the position he was in. So, it is more likely that it was the radical right that compelled Ruby to shoot Oswald.

The bottom line is the JFK assassination was a coup d'etat, and any open-minded person around the world at the time clearly understood that. The innocence of the United States died that day; however, what people did not understand and continue to ignore today is that the assassination was not a sign of American imperialist aggression. It was precisely the opposite because the JFK assassination prevented American expansionist forces from taking over Cuba and removing a world leader who was an insignificant threat to the security of the United States. That is not to say America turned into an angelic world savior in the years to come. History shows the truth is far from that, but it does show that the nation's priority was still to protect Europe from Soviet aggression, and George Kennan's Policy of

576

Containment was still in place. It was how disciples of Kennan wanted it to be, and the CIA certainly fit that category. The next arena of confrontation would be Southeast Asia, where the battle waged by the good democratic forces of America and Europe against the evil Communist totalitarian governments, which began with the Korean War, was about to expand. Vietnam was to take center stage, which satisfied the Pentagon and the Military Industrial Complex, and concerns about Cuba became a thing of the past. That was what the Pentagon really wanted and would never achieve while Kennedy was President.

***

On the afternoon of November 22, 1963, after JFK was dead, Robert Kennedy called Harry Williams and asked him to pass the phone to the Cuban exile-connected writer, Haynes Johnson. "Robert Kennedy was utterly in control of his emotions when he came on the line," Johnson later recalled, "and sounded almost studiously brisk as he said, 'One of your [Cuban] boys did it.'" Haynes wrote that he "stumbled out of the Ebbitt [Hotel] lobby shaken by… what Robert Kennedy had said to me."[1649]

Bobby Kennedy was beside himself, knowing his aggressive plan to take over Cuba had led to his brother's murder, which meant he was responsible. Bobby said it was "impossible that Oswald and Ruby hadn't known one another," and he was angry at Cuban exiles who were "working for the mob. They blame us for the Bay of Pigs, and they're trying to make this look like a Castro Communist hit. I don't buy it. And I don't trust those guys at the CIA. They're worse than the Mafia."[1650]

Returning from Kennedy's funeral, Charles de Gaulle said the following to his Information Minister, Alain Peyrefitte: "What happened to Kennedy is what nearly happened to me. His story is the same as mine. It looks like a cowboy story, but it's only an OAS story. The security forces were in cahoots with the extremists. They got their hands on this Communist who wasn't one while still being one. He had a subpar intellect and was an exalted fanatic – just the man they needed, the perfect one to be accused. The guy ran away because he probably became suspicious. They wanted to kill him on the spot before he could be grabbed by the judicial system. Unfortunately, it didn't happen exactly the way they had probably planned it would… But a trial, you realize, is just terrible. People would have talked. They would have dug up so much! They would have unearthed everything. Then the security forces went looking for [a man named Jack Ruby] they totally controlled, and who couldn't refuse their offer, and that guy sacrificed himself to kill the fake assassin – supposedly in defense of Kennedy's memory!"[1651]

Charles de Gaulle left out the connection between French Monarchists and Madrid Nazis to the CIA, but his description of what he thought happened was right on the mark.

In the final analysis, JFK was just collateral damage to those responsible. The conspirators could easily rationalize his assassination because, for their way of thinking, sacrificing a single person, no matter how important, was a small price to pay to save Europe and protect the Western World from the Red Menace. At least, that is what they probably told themselves.

Considering everything they knew about Oswald, the Russians were eerily silent after the assassination. On February 4, 1964, Yuri Nosenko, an officer of the KGB, defected to the CIA in Geneva, Switzerland. By April, he was in the United States, claiming he had been in charge of Oswald's file while he was in the Soviet Union and that the KGB had nothing to do with Oswald. He was almost certainly a KGB plant whose job was to provide the CIA with sufficient information to ensure that the United States did not blame the Soviet Union for JFK's assassination. It was a sign the Kremlin was scared.

On October 1, 1965, a right-wing military coup assassinated six Indonesian army generals, took over the government and replaced President Sukarno. Working with CIA analysts, American Embassy political officer Robert Martens provided a list of names of thousands of Communists and people they suspected to be Communists. The Army generals who were now in charge of the new Indonesian government systematically murdered those on the list. Within days, a nationwide slaughter of innocent civilians was underway. By the time it was over, U.S. Ambassador Marshall Green cabled Washington that the PKI, the Indonesian Communist Party, "has ceased for the foreseeable future to be an important power element... Most Politburo and Central Committee members have been killed or arrested, and estimates of the number of party members killed range up to several hundred thousand." They tortured most people, then macheted or bound them and threw them in a river. The actual number of killed was estimated to be between one and three million. Once again, the Soviets remained quiet. There were no denunciations at the U.N. or threats of retaliation, as the United States did nothing to stop the slaughter.[1652]

Frank Wisner was severely troubled by the time of the Indonesian military coup. He had witnessed firsthand thousands of Romanians loaded into rail cars at the end of World War II and sent to Russian labor camps. He

578

was in Germany when the Communists forcibly crushed an East German labor strike. In 1956, he was beside himself with anguish as a CIA-instigated Hungarian uprising was overwhelmed by Russian tanks. It was probably the reason Wisner conspired to assassinate JFK. He knew that the innocent lives in Berlin and throughout Europe the Soviets would slaughter if the United States invaded Cuba would far exceed what he had already seen. He did not want any more innocent blood on his hands.

On October 24, 1964, during the heart of the Indonesian slaughter, Frank Wisner took one of his sons' shotguns and killed himself at the family farm in Galena, Maryland. Perhaps his involvement in the JFK assassination, followed by the events in Indonesia, compelled him to do this. No one knows for sure, but it is possible, for Frank Wisner could not take anymore. He was just another case of collateral damage. It was exactly one month after the Warren Commission submitted its report to President Johnson.

On April 3, 1964, Paraguayan dictator Alfredo Stroessner sent a personal letter instructing his ambassador in Madrid to issue Otto Skorzeny a Paraguayan passport immediately. The person who told Stroessner to do this was Skorzeny's old Nazi friend Hans Rudel. Skorzeny admitted in his biography, *My Commando Operations*, that he took up the offer, and the stamped passport still exists. Was Rudel afraid that the Warren Commission was going to expose Skorzeny's role in the assassination plot, and he had better relocate to a country that would protect him? Perhaps, but we do not know. For the Warren Commission, it was better to let sleeping dogs lie.[1653]

ENDNOTES

1   Russo, Gus, *Live By the Sword, The Secret War Against Castro and the Death of JFK*, Baltimore, Maryland, Bancroft Press, 1998.

2   Trento, Joseph J., *The Secret History of the CIA*, New York, New York, MJF Books, 2001.

3   Johnston, *Murder Inc.: The CIA Under John F. Kennedy*.

4   Newman, John M., *Where Angels Tread Lightly: The Assassination of President Kennedy, Volume I*, North Charleston, South Carolina, CreateSpace Independent Publishing Platform, 2017, and Newman, John M., *Countdown to Darkness: The Assassination Of President Kennedy, Volume II*, North Charleston, South Carolina, CreateSpace Independent Publishing Platform, 2017.

5   Johnston, James, H., *Murder Inc.: The CIA Under John F. Kennedy*, Lincoln Nebraska, Potomac Books, an imprint of the University of Nebraska Press, 2019.

6   Kempe, Frederick, *Berlin 1961: Kennedy, Khrushchev, And The Most Dangerous Place On Earth*, New York, New York, G.P Putnam's Sons, 2011.

7   Mellen, Joan, *The Great Game in Cuba, How the CIA Sabotaged Its Own Plot to Unseat Fidel Castro*, New York, New York, Skyhorse Publishing, 2013.

8   Smith Stuart, *Otto Skorzeny: The Devil's Disciple*, Oxford, England, Ospry Publishing, 2018.

9   Albarelli, H.P. Jr., with Sharp, Leslie and Kent, Alan, *Coup in Dallas: The Decisive Investigation into Who Killed JFK*, New York, New York, Skyhorse Publishing, 2021.

10   Ibid

11   Ranelagh, John, *The Agency, The Rise and Decline of the CIA*, New York, New York, Simon and Schuster, 1986

12   Ibid

13   Anderson, Scott, *The Quiet Americans: Four CIA Spies at the Dawn of the Cold War – A Tragedy in Three Acts*, New York, New York, Doubleday Publishing, 2020.

14   Leffler, *For the Soul of Mankind, The United States, the Soviet Union, and The Cold War*.

15   Nichols, David A., *Eisenhower 1956, The President's Year of Crisis, Suez and the Brink of War*, New York, New York, Simon & Schuster, 2011.

16   Leffler, *For the Soul of Mankind, The United States, the Soviet Union, and The Cold War*.

17   Leffler, *For the Soul of Mankind, The United States, the Soviet Union, and The Cold War*.

18   Thomas, Evan, *Ike's Bluff, President Eisenhower's Secret Battle to Save the World*, New York, New York, Little, Brown and Company, 2012.

19   Ibid, and Gaddis, *Strategies of Containment, A Critical Appraisal of Postwar American National Security Policy*.

20   Ibid

21   Ibid

22   Kempe, *Berlin 1961: Kennedy, Khrushchev, And The Most Dangerous Place On Earth*.

23   Thomas, Evan, *The Very Best Men, Four Who Dared: The Early Years of the CIA*, New York, New York, Simon & Schuster, 1995.

24   Woods, Randall B., *Shadow Warrior, William Egan Colby and the CIA*, New York, New York, Basic Books, 2013.

25   Ibid

26   Anderson, *The Quiet Americans: Four CIA Spies at the Dawn of the Cold War – A Tragedy in Three Acts*.

LAST RESORT BEYOND LAST RESORT

27   Prados, John, *Safe for Democracy: The Secret Wars Of The CIA*, Chicago, Illinois, Ivan R. Dee, 2006.

Chapter One

28   Kempe, Frederick, *Berlin 1961, Kennedy, Khrushchev And The Most Dangerous Place On Earth*, New York, New York, G.P. Putnam's Sons, 2011.

29   Kempe, Berlin 1961, *Kennedy, Khrushchev And The Most Dangerous Place On Earth*.

30   Taubman, William, *Khrushchev: The Man And His Era*, New York, New York, W.M. Norton & Company, 2003.

31   Bird, Kai, *The Color of Truth, McGeorge Bundy and William Bundy: Brothers In Arms*, New York, New York, Simon & Schuster, 1998.

32   Ibid

33   Jacobsen, Annie, *The Pentagon's Brain: An Uncensored History Of DARPA, America's Top Secret Military Research Agency*, New York, New York, Little, Brown and Company, 2015.

34   Dallek, Robert, *Camelot's Court: Inside the Kennedy White House*, New York, New York, Harper Collins, 2013.

35   Beisner, Robert L., *Dean Acheson: a Life in the Cold War*, New York, New York, Oxford University Press, 2006.

36   Swanson, Michael, *The War State: The Cold War Origins Of The Military-Industrial Complex And The Power Elite, 1945-1963*, North Charleston, South Carolina, CreateSpace Independent Publishing Platform, 2013.

37   Bamford, James, *Body of Secrets: Anatomy Of The Ultra-Secret National Security Agency*, New York, New York, Doubleday, 2001.

38   Binder, L. James, *Lemnitzer: A Soldier for His Time*, Washington, D.C., Brassey's, 1997.

39   Ibid

40   Ibid

41   Bamford, *Body of Secrets: Anatomy Of The Ultra-Secret National Security Agency*.

42   Ibid

43   Swanson, *The War State: The Cold War Origins Of The Military-Industrial Complex And The Power Elite, 1945-1963*.

44   Newman, John M., *Countdown to Darkness: The Assassination of President Kennedy, Volume II*, North Charleston, South Carolina, CreateSpace Independent Publishing Platform, 2017.

45   Talbot, David, *Brothers: The Hidden History Of The Kennedy Years*, New York, New York, Free Press, 2007; Rasenberger, Jim, *The Brilliant Disaster: JFK, Castro, And America's Doomed Invasion of Cuba's Bay Of Pigs*, New York, New York, Scribner, 2011; Kaiser, David, *The Road to Dallas: The Assassination Of John F. Kennedy*, Cambridge, Massachusetts, The Belknap Press of Harvard University Press, 2008; and https://www.historynet.com/bay-of-pigs-the-perfect-failure.htm

46   Newman, John M., *Where Angels Tread Lightly: The Assassination of President Kennedy, Volume I*, North Charleston, South Carolina, CreateSpace Independent Publishing Platform, 2017.

47   Kaiser, *The Road to Dallas: The Assassination Of John F. Kennedy*.

48   Mellen, Joan, *The Great Game in Cuba: How The CIA Sabotaged Its Own Plot To Unseat Fidel Castro*, New York, New York, Skyhorse Publishing, 2013.

49   Bamford, *Body of Secrets: Anatomy Of The Ultra-Secret National Security Agency*.

50   Dallek, Robert, *An Unfinished Life: John F. Kennedy, 1917-1963*, New York, New York, Little, Brown and Company, 2003.

51   Bamford, *Body of Secrets: Anatomy Of The Ultra-Secret National Security Agency*.

52   DiEugenio, James, *Destiny Betrayed: JFK, Cuba, and the Garrison Case*, New York, New York, Sheridan Square Press, 1992.

53   Bamford, *Body of Secrets: Anatomy Of The Ultra-Secret National Security Agency*.

54   Grose, Peter, Gentleman *Spy-The Life of Allen Dulles*, New York, New York, Houghton Mifflin Company, 1994.

Endnotes

55   Bird, *The Color of Truth, McGeorge Bundy and William Bundy: Brothers In Arms*; Mellen, *The Great Game in Cuba: How The CIA Sabotaged Its Own Plot To Unseat Fidel Castro*; And Binder, *Lemnitzer: A Soldier for His Time*.

56   Morrow, Robert D., *First Hand Knowledge: How I Participated In The CIA-Mafia Murder Of President Kennedy*, New York, New York, S.P.i. Books, 1992.

57   Rasenberger, *The Brilliant Disaster: JFK, Castro, And America's Doomed Invasion Of Cuba's Bay Of Pigs*.

58   Waldron, Lamar, with Hartman, Thom, *Ultimate Sacrifice: John and Robert Kennedy, the Plan for a Coup in Cuba, and the Murder of JFK*, New York, New York, Carroll & Graf Publishers, 2005; Russo, Gus, *Live By The Sword: The Secret War Against Castro And The Death Of JFK*, Baltimore, Maryland, Bancroft Press, 1998.

59   Waldron, Lamar, *The Hidden History of the JFK Assassination: The Definitive Account of the Most Controversial Crime of the Twentieth Century*, Berkeley, California, Counterpoint, 2013.

60   Morrow, *First Hand Knowledge: How I Participated In The CIA-Mafia Murder Of President Kennedy*.

61   Albarelli, H.P. Jr., with Sharp, Leslie and Kent, Alan, *Coup in Dallas: The Decisive Investigation into Who Killed JFK*, New York, New York, Skyhorse Publishing, 2021.

62   Herbst, Walter, *It Did Not Start With JFK: The Decades Of Events That Led To The Assassination Of John F. Kennedy, Volume One*, Harrisburg, Pennsylvania, Sunbury Press, 2021.

63   Waldron, *The Hidden History of the JFK Assassination: The Definitive Account of the Most Controversial Crime of the Twentieth Century*.

64   Blakey, G. Robert, and Billings, Richard N., *The Plot to Kill the President: Organized Crime Assassinated J.F.K., The Definitive Story*, New York, New York, Times Books, 1981; Hinckle, Warren, and Turner, William, *The Fish Is Red: The Story Of The Secret War Against Castro*, New York, New York, Harper & Row, Publishers, 1981.

65   Fensterwald, Bernard Jr., *Assassination of JFK By Coincidence or Conspiracy?*, New York, New York, Kensington Publishing Corp., 1977.

66   Russo, *Live By The Sword: The Secret War Against Castro And The Death Of JFK*; Johnson, Haynes, *The Bay of Pigs – The Leaders' Story of Brigade 2506*,New York, New York, W.W.Norton & Co., 1964.

67   Waldron, *The Hidden History of the JFK Assassination: The Definitive Account of the Most Controversial Crime of the Twentieth Century*.

68   https://archive.org/stream/CoupDetatInAmerica/NODULE%2014%20THE%20CUBAN%20E XILE%20MILITIAS%20C

69   English, T.J., *Havana Nocturnal: How The Mob Owned Cuba…And Then Lost It To The Revolution*, New York, New York, William Morrow, 2007.

70   https://archive.org/stream/CoupDetatInAmerica/NODULE%2014%20THE%20CUBAN%20 EXILE%20MILITIAS%20C ASTRATED%20BY%20KENNEDY_djvu.txt

71   Rasenberger, *The Brilliant Disaster: JFK, Castro, And America's Doomed Invasion Of Cuba's Bay Of Pigs*.

72   Ibid; and Kempe, Berlin 1961, *Kennedy, Khrushchev And The Most Dangerous Place On Earth Berlin* 1961.

73   Kempe, *Berlin 1961, Kennedy, Khrushchev And The Most Dangerous Place On Earth*.

74   Rasenberger, *The Brilliant Disaster: JFK, Castro, And America's Doomed Invasion Of Cuba's Bay Of Pigs*.

75   Kempe, *Berlin 1961, Kennedy, Khrushchev And The Most Dangerous Place On Earth*.

76   Fursenko, Aleksandr, and Naftali, Timonty, *Krhushchev's Cold War: The Inside Story Of An American Adversary*, New York, New York, W.W. Norton & Company, 2006

77   Carrozza, Anthony R., William D. Pawley: *The Extraordinary Life Of The Adventurer, Entrepreneur, And Diplomat Who Cofounded The Flying Tigers*, Washington D.C., Potomac Books, 2012.

78   Thomas, Evan, *The Very Best Men, Four Who Dared: The Early Years Of The CIA*, New York, New York, Simon & Schuster, 1995.

79   Swanson, *The War State: The Cold War Origins Of The Military-Industrial Complex And The Power Elite, 1945-1963*.

80   Carrozza, William D. Pawley: *The Extraordinary Life Of The Adventurer, Entrepreneur, And Diplomat Who Cofounded The Flying Tigers*.

81 Schlesinger, Arthur M. Jr., *Robert Kennedy and his Times*, Boston, Massachusetts, Houghton Mifflin Company, 1978.

82 Prouty, L. Fletcher, *JFK, The CIA, Vietnam And The Plot to Assassinate John F. Kennedy*, New York, New York, Carol Publishing Group, 1992.

83 Schlesinger, Arthur M. Jr., *Robert Kennedy and His Times*, Boston, Massachusetts, Houghton, Mifflin Company, 1978.

84 Binder, *Lemnitzer: A Soldier for His Time*.

Chapter Two

85 Nechiporenko, Col. Oleg Maximovich, *Passport to Assassination: The Never-Before-Told Story Of Lee Harvey Oswald By The KGB Colonel Who Knew Him*, New York, New York, Carol Publishing Group, 1993.

86 Russell, Dick, On the Trail of the JFK Assassins, *A Groundbreaking look at America's Most Infamous Conspiracy*, New York, New York, Skyhorse Publishing, 2008.

87 CE No. 833, FBI report entitled *"Lee Harvey Oswald" April 6, 1964, Vol. XVII, p. 789*, from Newman, John, *Oswald and the CIA, New York*, New York, Carroll & Graf Publishers, Inc., 1995, and Evica, George Michael, *A Certain Arrogance; The Sacrificing of Lee Harvey Oswald and the Cold War Manipulation of Religious Groups by US Intelligence*, Walterville, Oregon, TrineDay, 2011.

88 Russell, On the Trail of the JFK Assassins, *A Groundbreaking look at America's Most Infamous Conspiracy*

89 Eddowes, Michael, *The Oswald File, New York*, New York, Clarkson N. Potter, Inc., 1977.

90 Ibid

91 Russell, On the Trail of the JFK Assassins, *A Groundbreaking look at America's Most Infamous Conspiracy*.

92 Newman, *Oswald and the CIA*

93 Ibid

94 Ibid

95 Epstein, Edward Jay, Legend, *The Secret World of Lee Harvey Oswald, New York*, New York, McGraw-Hill Book Company, 1978.

96 Newman, *Oswald and the CIA*

97 Russell, On the Trail of the JFK Assassins, *A Groundbreaking look at America's Most Infamous Conspiracy*.

98 Epstein, Legend, *The Secret World of Lee Harvey Oswald*.

99 Ibid

100 Weberman, Alan Jules, *The Oswald Code*, Createspace Independent Publishers, 2014.

101 Ibid

102 Newman, *Oswald and the CIA*.

103 Talbot, David, *The Devil's Chessboard, Allen Dulles, the CIA, and the Rise of America's Secret Government, New York*, New York, Harper Collins Publishers, 2015.

104 De Mey, Flip, *The Lee Harvey Oswald Files: Why The CIA Killed Kennedy, Belgium*, Lannoo Publishing, 2016, and Titovets, Ernst, *Oswald: Russian Episode*, Washington, DC, Eagle View Books, 2013.

105 Titovets, *Oswald: Russian Episode*.

106 Russell, Dick, *The Man Who Knew Too Much, New York*, New York, Carroll & Graf Publishers/Richard Gallen, 1992.

107 Barron, John, *KGB: The Secret Work of Soviet Secret Agents, New York*, New York, Reader's Digest Association Publishers, 1974.

108 Summers, Anthony, *Conspiracy, New York*, New York, McGraw-Hill Book Company, 1980.

109 Ibid

110 Ibid

111 De Gramont, Sanche, *The Secret War, New York*, New York, Dell Publishing, 1962.

112 Russell, *The Man Who Knew Too Much*.

Endnotes

113 Weberman, Alan J., and Canfield, Michael, Coup D'Etat In America, *The CIA and the Assassination of John F. Kennedy,* San Francisco, The Third Press, 1975.

114 Fisher, Seymour, *The Use of Hypnosis in Intelligence and Related Military Situations,* Study SSR 177-D, Contract AF 18 (600) 1797, Technical Report No. 4, Washington D.C.: Bureau of Social Science Research, 1958, from Russell, *The Man Who Knew Too Much.*

115 Newman, *Oswald and the CIA*

116 Weberman and Canfield, Coup D'Etat In America, *The CIA and the Assassination of John F. Kennedy,* and Russell, *The Man Who Knew Too Much.*

117 RIF # 124-90080-10027, from Haverstick, Mary, *A Woman I Know: Female Spies, Double Identities, and A New Story of the Kennedy Assassination, New York,* New York, crown Publishing, 2023.

118 Mellen, Joan, *Our Man in Haiti,* George de Mohrenschildt and the CIA in the Nightmare Republic, Walterville, Oregon, Trine Day, 2012.

119 Newman, *Oswald and the CIA.*

120 Summers, *Conspiracy.*

121 De Mey, *The Lee Harvey Oswald Files: Why The CIA Killed Kennedy.*

122 Summers, *Conspiracy.*

123 Russell, *The Man Who Knew Too Much,* and Oswald, Marguerite, Warren Commission Testimony, Washington DC, Warren Report Volume I, 1964.

124 Weberman, *The Oswald Code.*

125 Newman, *Oswald and the CIA.*

126 Weberman, *The Oswald Code.*

127 Russell, *On the Trail of the JFK Assassins.*

128 Newman, *Oswald and the CIA.*

129 Evica, *A Certain Arrogance.*

130 Ibid

131 *Warren Commission Report, Volume XVII,* Exhibit CE823.

132 https://www.law.cornell.edu/uscode/text/18/1544

133 https://www.forbes.com/sites/robertwood/2023/01/12/fee-to-renounce-citizenship-to-drop-422/?sh=13c501455a2b.

134 Weberman, *The Oswald Code.*

135 Weberman, *The Oswald Code.*

136 Ibid

137 Ibid

138 Ibid and Mellen, Joan, *A Farewell to Justice,* Jim Garrison, *JFK's Assassination, and the Case That Should Have Changed History, New York,* New York, Skyhorse Publishing, 2013.

139 Mellen, *A Farewell to Justice,* Jim Garrison, *JFK's Assassination, and the Case That Should Have Changed History,* and Russell, *On the Trail of the JFK Assassins.*

140 Russell, *On the Trail of the JFK Assassins.*

141 Weberman, *The Oswald Code,* and Mellen, *A Farewell to Justice.*

142 Weberman, *The Oswald Code.*

Chapter Three

143 Minutaglio, Bill, and Davis, Steven L., *Dallas 1963, New York,* New York, Hachette Book Group, 2013.

144 Caufield, M.D., Jeffrey H., *General Walker and the Murder of President Kennedy, The Extensive New Evidence of a Radical-Right Conspiracy,* Moreland Press, 2015.

145 Talbot, David, Brothers, *The Hidden History of the Kennedy Years, New York,* New York, Free Press, 2007.

146 Bamford, James, *Body of Secrets, Anatomy of the Ultra-Secret National Security Agency, From the Cold War Through the Dawn of a New Century, New York,* New York, Doubleday, 2001.

147 Ibid

148 Minutaglio and Davis, *Dallas 1963,* and Talbot, *Brothers.*

149 Talbot, *Brothers.*

150 North, Mark, *Act of Treason, The Role of J. Edgar Hoover in the Assassination of President Kennedy, New York,* New York, Carroll & Graf Publishers, 1991.

151 Ibid

152 Ibid

153 Ibid

154 Minutaglio and Davis, *Dallas 1963.*

155 JFK Speech, November 18, 1963, https://www.jfklibrary.org/asset_viewer/_archives/_JFKPOF/036/JFKPOF-036-020

156 Ibid

157 Dallek, Robert, *An Unfinished Life: John F. Kennedy, 1917-1963, New York,* New York, Little, Brown and Company, 2003.

158 *History of the Joint Chiefs of Staff The Joint Chiefs of Staff and National Policy Volume VIII 1961-1964* Walter S. Poole, *Office of Joint History Office of the Chairman of the Joint Chiefs of Staff,* Washington, DC, 2011, https://www.jcs.mil/Portals/36/Documents/History/Policy/Policy_V008.pdf

159 Ibid

160 Ibid

161 Kempe, Frederick, *Berlin 1961: Kennedy, Khrushchev, and the Most Dangerous Place on Earth, New York,* New York, G.P Putnam's Sons, 2011.

162 Dallek, Robert, *Camelot's Court: Inside The Kennedy White House, New York,* New York, Harper Collins, 2013.

163 Ibid

164 Dallek, Robert, *An Unfinished Life: John F. Kennedy, 1917-1963, New York,* New York, Little, Brown and Company, 2003.

165 *Berlin 1961*

166 *Camelot's Court*

167 Poole, *History of the Joint Chiefs of Staff The Joint Chiefs of Staff and National Policy Volume VIII 1961-1964.*

168 Kempe, *Berlin 1961: Kennedy, Khrushchev, and the Most Dangerous Place on Earth.*

169 Dallek, *An Unfinished Life: John F. Kennedy, 1917-1963.*

170 Kurlantzick, Joshua, *A Great Place to Have a War: American In Laos And The Birth Of A Military CIA, New York,* New York, Simon & Schuster, 2016.

171 Scott, Peter Dale, *American War Machine – Deep Politics, the CIA Global Drug Connection, and the Road to Afghanistan, New York,* New York, Rowman & Littlefield, 2010.

172 Kurlantzick, *A Great Place to Have a War,* and https://history.state.gov/milestones/1961-1968/laos-crisis.

173 Newman, John M., *Countdown to Darkness: The Assassination Of President Kennedy, Volume II,* North Charleston, South Carolina, CreateSpace Independent Publishing Platform, 2017.

174 Schlesinger, Arthur M. Jr., *A Thousand Days,* Greenwich, Connecticut, Fawcett Publications, Inc., 1965.

175 Newman, *Countdown to Darkness: The Assassination Of President Kennedy, Volume II.*

176 Newman, John M., *JFK and Vietnam, New York,* New York, Warner Books, 1992.

177 Ibid

178 Schlesinger, *A Thousand Days.*

179 Newman, *JFK and Vietnam.*

180 Sheehan, Neil, *The Pentagon Papers: The Secret History of the Vietnam War, New York,* New York, Racehorwse Publishing, 2017.

181 Dallek, *Camelot's Court: Inside The Kennedy White House.*

182 Ibid

183 Newman, *JFK and Vietnam.*

184 Ibid

Endnotes

185   Ibid

186   Sheehan, *The Pentagon Papers: The Secret History of the Vietnam War.*

187   Jacobsen, Annie, *The Pentagon's Brain, An Uncensored History of DARPA, America's Top Secret Military Research Agency, New York,* New York, Little, Brown and Company, 2015.

188   Schlesinger, Arthur M. Jr., *Robert Kennedy and His Times, Boston, Massachusetts, Houghton Mifflin Company, 1978.*

189   Sheehan, *The Pentagon Papers: The Secret History of the Vietnam War.*

190   Halberstam, David, *The Best And the Brightest, New York,* New York, Ballentine Boks, 1993.

191   Sheehan, *The Pentagon Papers: The Secret History of the Vietnam War.*

192   Dallek, *An Unfinished Life: John F. Kennedy, 1917-1963.*

193   Ibid

194   Sheehan, *The Pentagon Papers: The Secret History of the Vietnam War.*

195   Bird, Kai, *The Color of Truth, McGeorge Bundy and William Bundy: Brothers In Arms, New York,* New York, Simon & Schuster, 1998.

196   Williams, Susan, *Who Killed Hammarskjold? The UN, The Cold War And The White Supremacy In Africa, New York,* New York, Oxford University Press, 2014.

197   Ibid

198   Dallek, *Camelot's Court: Inside The Kennedy White House.*

199   Fursenko, Aleksandr, and Naftali, Timothy, *Khrushchev's Cold War, The Inside Story of an American Adversary, New York,* New York, W.W. Norton & Company, 2006.

200   Williams, *Who Killed Hammarskjold? The UN, The Cold War And The White Supremacy In Africa.*

201   Ibid

202   Dallek, *An Unfinished Life: John F. Kennedy, 1917-1963.*

203   MacGregor, Iain, *Checkpoint Charlie: The Cold War, The Berlin Wall, And The Most Dangerous Place On Earth, New York,* New York, Scribner, 2019.

204   Newman, John M., *Into The Storm: The Assassination of President Kennedy, Volume III,* North Charleston, South Carolina, CreateSpace Independent Publishing Platform, 2019.

205   MacGregor, *Checkpoint Charlie: The Cold War, The Berlin Wall, And The Most Dangerous Place On Earth.*

206   Bevins, Vincent, *The Jakarta Method: Washington's Anticommunist Crusade & the Mass Murder Program that Shaped Our World, New York,* New York, Public Affairs, Hatchett Book Group, 2021.

207   Poulgrain, Dr. Greg, *JFK vs. Allen Dulles: Battleground Indonesia, New York,* New York, Skyhorse Publishing, 2020.

208   Newman, *JFK and Vietnam.*

209   Dallek, *An Unfinished Life: John F. Kennedy, 1917-1963.*

210   Miller, Nathan, *Spying for America, the Hidden History of U.S. Intelligence, New York,* New York, Paragon House, 1989.

211   Prouty, L. Fletcher, *JFK, The CIA, Vietnam And The Plot to Assassinate John F. Kennedy, New York,* New York, Carol Publishing Group, 1992.

Chapter Four

212   Del Hierro, Pablo, *The Neofascist Network and Madrid, 1945–1953: From City of Refuge to Transnational Hub and Centre of Operations,* Cambridge University Press, https://doi.org/10.1017/S0960777321000114.

213   Lorenz-Meyer, Martin, *Safehaven: The Allied Pursuit of Nazi Assets Abroad,* Columbia, Missouri, University of Missouri Press, 2007.

214   Del Hierro, *The Neofascist Network and Madrid, 1945–1953: From City of Refuge to Transnational Hub and Centre of Operations.*

215   Smith Stuart, *Otto Skorzeny: The Devil's Disciple,* Oxford, England, Ospry Publishing, 2018.

216   Del Hierro, *The Neofascist Network and Madrid, 1945–1953: From City of Refuge to Transnational Hub and Centre of Operations,* and Lee, Martin A., *The Beast Reawakens: Fascism's Resurgence*

from Hitler's Spymasters to Today's Neo-Nazi Groups and Right- Wing Extremists, New York, New York, Routledge, 2000.

217 Smith, *Otto Skorzeny: The Devil's Disciple.*

218 Del Hierro, Pablo, *The Neofascist Network and Madrid, 1945–1953: From City of Refuge to Transnational Hub and Centre of Operations.*

219 Orbach, Danny, *Fugitives: A History of Nazi Mercenaries During the Cold War, New York,* New York, Pegasus Books, 2022.

220 Smith, *Otto Skorzeny: The Devil's Disciple.*

221 Bedard, Paul, *Revealed: Post-World War II Secret Nazi, Vatican Army, US News and World Report, 2011,* https://www.usnews.com/news/blogs/washingtonwhispers/2011/12/02/revealed- post-world-war-ii-secret-nazi-vatican-army.

222 Del Hierro, Pablo, *The Neofascist Network and Madrid, 1945–1953: From City of Refuge to Transnational Hub and Centre of Operations.*

223 Trento, Joseph J., *The Secret History of the CIA, New York,* New York, MJF Books, 2001, and Stockton, Bayard, *Flawed Patriot: The Rise And Fall Of CIA Legend Bill Harvey,* Washington DC, Potomac Book, Inc., 2006.

224 Stockton, *Flawed Patriot: The Rise And Fall Of CIA Legend Bill Harvey.*

225 Trento, *The Secret History of the CIA.*

226 Woods, Randall B., *Shadow Warrior, William Egan Colby and the CIA, New York,* New York, Basic Books, 2013.

227 Ganis, Major Ralph P., USAF, Ret., *The Skorzeny Papers, Evidence for the Plot to Kill JFK, New York,* New York, Skyhorse Publishing, 2018.

228 Ibid, and Lee, Martin A., *The Beast Reawakens: Fascism's Resourgence from Hitler's Spymasters to Today's Neo-Nazi Groups and Right-Wing Extremists, New York,* New York, Routledge, 2000.

229 Ganis, *The Skorzeny Papers, Evidence for the Plot to Kill JFK,* and Duhamel, Eric, *Jean-Paul David et el movement Paix et Liberte, un anticommunisme radical, in Jean Delmas and Kessler 9eds, Renseignement et propaganda pendant la guerre froide, 1947-1953, Brussels: Editions Complexe, 1999,* from https://link.springer.com/chapter/10.1057/9781137388803_6.

230 Corsi, Jerome R., P.H.D., *Who Really Killed Kennedy?, 50 Years Later, Stunning New Revelations about the JFK Assassination,* Washington, D.C., WND Books, 2013.

231 Ganis, *The Skorzeny Papers, Evidence for the Plot to Kill JFK.*

232 Talbot, *The Devil's Chessboard, Allen Dulles, the CIA, and the Rise of America's Secret Government.*

233 Smith, *Otto Skorzeny: The Devil's Disciple.*

234 Talbot, *The Devil's Chessboard, Allen Dulles, the CIA, and the Rise of America's Secret Government.*

235 Trento, *The Secret History of the CIA.*

236 Predos, John, *Safe for Democracy: The Secret Wars Of The CIA,* Chicago, Illinois, Ivan R. Dee, Publisher, 2006.

237 Trento, Joseph J., *Prelude to Terror: The Rogue CIA and the Legacy of America's Private Intelligence Network,* New York, New York, Carroll & Graf Publishers, 2005, and Trento, *The Secret History of the CIA.*

238 Ibid, and Thomas, Evan, *The Very Best Men, Four Who Dared: The Early Years Of The CIA, New York,* New York, Simon & Schuster, 1995.

239 Anderson, Scott, *The Quiet Americans: Four CIA Spies at the Dawn of the Cold War – A Tragedy in Three Acts, New York,* New York, Doubleday Publishing, 2020.

240 Thomas, *The Very Best Men, Four Who Dared: The Early Years of the CIA.*

241 Simpson, Christopher, *Blowback: The First Full Account of America's Recruitment of Nazis, and its Disastrous Effect on Our Domestic and Foreign Policy, New York,* New York, Collier's Books – Macmillan, 1989.

242 McCallion, Kenetth Foard, *The Marseille Connection: The Major Unsolved Crime of the Twentieth Century – Finally Solved!, New York,* New York, HHI Media, 2023.

243 Simpson, *Blowback, The First Full Account of America's Recruitment of Nazis, and its Disastrous Effect on Our Domestic and Foreign Policy.*

244 Ganis, *The Skorzeny Papers, Evidence for the Plot to Kill JFK.*

ENDNOTES

245 Orbach, Danny, *Fugitives: A History of Nazi Mercenaries During the Cold War, New York,* +New York, Pegasus Books, 2022.

246 Stockton, Flawed Patriot: *The Rise And Fall Of CIA Legend Bill Harvey.*

247 McCallion, *The Marseille Connection: The Major Unsolved Crime of the Twentieth Century – Finally Solved!*

248 Albarelli, H.P. Jr., *A Secret Order, Investigating the High Strangeness and Synchronicity in the JFK Assassination,* Walterville, Oregon, Trine Day, 2013.

249 Ganis, *The Skorzeny Papers, Evidence for the Plot to Kill JFK.*

250 Ibid and Albarelli, *A Secret Order, Investigating the High Strangeness and Synchronicity in the JFK Assassination.*

251 Stockton, *Flawed Patriot: The Rise And Fall Of CIA Legend Bill Harvey.*

252 Trento, *The Secret History of the CIA.*

253 Russo, Gus, *Live By the Sword, The Secret War Against Castro and the Death of JFK,* Baltimore, Maryland, Bancroft Press, 1998.

254 Ibid

255 Ibid

256 Ibid

257 Ibid

258 Prouty, L. Fletcher, JFK, *The CIA, Vietnam And The Plot to Assassinate John F. Kennedy, New York,* New York, Carol Publishing Group, 1992, and Miller, Nathan, *Spying for America: The Hidden History of U.S. Intelligence, Brooklyn,* New York, Paragon House, 1989.

259 Schlesinger, Arthur M. Jr., *Robert Kennedy and His Times,* Boston, Massachusetts, Houghton Mifflin Company, 1978.

260 Talbot, David, Brothers, *The Hidden History of the Kennedy Years, New York,* New York, Free Press, 2007.

261 Ibid

262 Schlesinger, *Robert Kennedy and his Times.*

263 Trento, *The Secret History of the CIA.*

264 Albarelli, H.P. Jr., with Sharp, Leslie and Kent, Alan, *Coup in Dallas: The Decisive Investigation into Who Killed JFK, New York,* New York, Skyhorse Publishing, 2021.

265 *CIA Record Number 104-10182-10098, CIA Report February 18, 1963.*

266 Albarelli, with Sharp and Kent, *Coup in Dallas: The Decisive Investigation into Who Killed JFK.*

267 McCallion, *The Marseille Connection: The Major Unsolved Crime of the Twentieth Century – Finally Solved!*

268 Albarelli, with Sharp and Kent, *Coup in Dallas: The Decisive Investigation into Who Killed JFK.*

269 Ibid

270 Albarelli, *A Secret Order, Investigating the High Strangeness and Synchronicity in the JFK Assassination.*

271 Ibid

272 Ibid

273 Talbot, Brothers, *The Hidden History of the Kennedy Years.*

274 Ibid

275 Fonzi, Gaeton, *The Last Investigation, New York,* New York, Thunder's Mouth Press, 1993.

276 Mahoney, *Richard, Sons and Brothers, New York,* New York, Arcade Publishing, 1999.

277 Stockton, *Flawed Patriot: The Rise And Fall Of CIA Legend Bill Harvey.*

278 Ibid

279 Ibid

280 Ibid

281 CIA document 632-796, April 1, 1964, from Marrs, Jim, *Crossfire, The Plot That Killed Kennedy, New York,* New York, Carroll & Graf Publishers, Inc., 1989., and Russell, Dick, *The Man Who Knew Too Much, New York,* New York, Carroll & Graf Publishers/Richard Gallen, 1992.

282 Marrs, *Crossfire*, and Russell, *The Man Who Knew Too Much.*

283 Russell, *The Man Who Knew Too Much.*

284 Ibid

285 Marrs, *Crossfire.*

286 Marrs, *Crossfire*, and Russell, *The Man Who Knew Too Much.*

287 Kruger, Henrik, *The Great Heroin Coup: Drugs, Intelligence & International Fascism,* Walterville, Oregon, Trine Day Publishing, 2016.

288 Marrs, *Crossfire.*

289 Marrs, *Crossfire*, and Russell, *The Man Who Knew Too Much.*

290 *The Man Who Knew Too Much*

291 O'Leary, Brad, and Seymour, Lee, *Triangle of Death: The Shocking Trith About the Role of South Vietnam and the French Mafia in the Assassination of JFK,* Nashville, Tennessee, W Publishing Group, 2003.

292 Dallek, Robert, *Camelot's Court: Inside The Kennedy White House, New York,* New York, Harper Collins, 2013.

293 Russo, Gus, *Live By the Sword, The Secret War Against Castro and the Death of JFK,* Baltimore, Maryland, Bancroft Press, 1998.

294 Newman, John M., *Countdown to Darkness: The Assassination Of President Kennedy, Volume II,* North Charleston, South Carolina, CreateSpace Independent Publishing Platform, 2017.

295 Talbot, David, Brothers, *The Hidden History of the Kennedy Years.*

296 Newman, *Countdown to Darkness.*

297 Martin, David, *Wilderness of Mirrors, New York,* New York, Harper & Row, 1980.

298 Ibid

299 Trento, *The Secret History of the CIA.*

Chapter Five

300 Martin, John Bartlow, *Overtaken By Events, Garden City, New York, Doubleday & Company, Inc., 1966.*

301 Ibid

302 Newman, John M., *Countdown to Darkness*: *The Assassination Of President Kennedy, Volume II,* North Charleston, South Carolina, CreateSpace Independent Publishing Platform, 2017.

303 Ibid

304 Carrozza, Anthony R., William D. Pawley, *The Extraordinary Life of the Adventurer, Entrepreneur, and Diplomat Who Cofounded the Flying Tigers,* Washington D.C., Potomac Books, 2012.

305 Ibid

306 Schlesinger, Arthur M. Jr., *Robert Kennedy and His Times,* Boston, Massachusetts, Houghton Mifflin Company, 1978, and Anderson, Scott, *The Quiet Americans: Four CIA Spies at the Dawn of the Cold War – A Tragedy in Three Acts, New York,* New York, Doubleday Publishing, 2020.

307 Ameringer, Charles D., *U.S. Foreign Intelligence: The Secret Side of American History,* New York, New York Lexington Books, 1990.

308 Russell, Dick, *The Man Who Knew Too Much, New York,* New York, Carroll & Graf Publishers/Richard Gallen, 1992.

309 https://nsarchive2.gwu.edu/NSAEBB/NSAEBB222/family_jewels_full_ocr.pdf, CIA Family Jewels Memo, May 16, 1973.

310 Williams, Susan, *Spies In The Congo: America's Atomic Mission In World War II, New York,* New York, PublicAffairs, 2016.

311 Williams, Susan, *Who Killed Hammarskjold? The UN, The Cold War And The White Supremacy In Africa, New York,* New York, Oxford University Press, 2014.

312 Williams, Susan, *White Malice: The CIA and the Covert Recolonization of Africa, New York,* New York, PublicAffairs, 2021.

313 Williams, *Spies in the Congo: America's Atomic Mission In World War II,* and Williams, *White Malice: The CIA and the Covert Recolonization of Africa.*

ENDNOTES

314 Williams, *White Malice: The CIA and the Covert Recolonization of Africa.*

315 Ibid and Williams, *Who Killed Hammarskjold? The UN, The Cold War And The White Supremacy In Africa.*

316 Williams, *Who Killed Hammarskjold? The UN, The Cold War And The White Supremacy In Africa.*

317 Ibid

318 Ganis, Major Ralph P., USAF, Ret., *The Skorzeny Papers, Evidence for the Plot to Kill JFK, New York,* New York, Skyhorse Publishing, 2018.

319 Ranelagh, John, *The Agency, The Rise and Decline of the CIA, New York,* New York, Simon and Schuster, 1986

320 Fursenko, Aleksandr, and Naftali, Timothy, *Khrushchev's Cold War, The Inside Story of an American Adversary, New York,* New York, W.W. Norton & Company, 2006.

321 Ibid and Williams, *Who Killed Hammarskjold? The UN, The Cold War And The White Supremacy In Africa.*

322 Williams, *White Malice: The CIA and the Covert Recolonization of Africa.*

323 Ranelagh, *The Agency, The Rise and Decline of the CIA.*

324 Williams, *White Malice: The CIA and the Covert Recolonization of Africa.*

325 Williams, *White Malice: The CIA and the Covert Recolonization of Africa.* and Williams, *Who Killed Hammarskjold? The UN, The Cold War And The White Supremacy In Africa.*

326 Williams, *Who Killed Hammarskjold? The UN, The Cold War And The White Supremacy In Africa.*

327 Williams, *White Malice: The CIA and the Covert Recolonization of Africa.*

328 Kalb, Madeleine G., The Congo Cables, *The Cold War in Africa-From Eisenhower to Kennedy, New York,* New York, Macmillan Publishing Co., Inc., 1982.

329 Ibid

330 Ibid & Williams, *Who Killed Hammarskjold? The UN, The Cold War And The White Supremacy In Africa.*

331 Poulgrain, Dr. Greg, *JFK vs. Allen Dulles: Battleground Indonesia, New York,* New York, Skyhorse Publishing, 2020.

332 Ibid

333 Kalb, The Congo Cables, *The Cold War in Africa – From Eisenhower to Kennedy.*

334 Marrs, Jim, *Crossfire, The Plot That Killed Kennedy, New York,* New York, Carroll & Graf Publishers, Inc., 1989.

335 Kalb, The Congo Cables, *The Cold War in Africa – From Eisenhower to Kennedy.*

336 Williams, *White Malice: The CIA and the Covert Recolonization of Africa.*

337 Newman, *Countdown to Darkness: The Assassination Of President Kennedy, Volume II.*

338 Smith Stuart, *Otto Skorzeny: The Devil's Disciple,* Oxford, England, Ospry Publishing, 2018

339 Ibid.

340 Kalb, The Congo Cables, *The Cold War in Africa – From Eisenhower to Kennedy.*

341 *Senate Intelligence Report on Foreign Assassinations.*

342 Williams, *White Malice: The CIA and the Covert Recolonization of Africa.*

343 *Alleged Assassination Plots Involving Foreign Leaders, An Interim Report of the Select Committee to Study Governmental Operations with respect to Intelligence Activites,* United States Senate, Washington Dc, U.S. Government Printing Office, November 18, 1975.

344 Weberman, Alan J., and Canfield, Michael, *Coup D'Etat In America,* San Francisco, California, The Third Press, 1975.

345 Williams, *White Malice: The CIA and the Covert Recolonization of Africa.*

346 Williams, *Who Killed Hammarskjold? The UN, The Cold War And The White Supremacy In Africa.*

347 Ganis, The Skorzeny Papers, *Evidence for the Plot to Kill JFK.*

348 Williams, *Who Killed Hammarskjold? The UN, The Cold War And The White Supremacy In Africa.*

349 Ibid

350 Bellamy, Alex J., Paul Williams, and Stuart Griffin, *Understanding Peacekeeping,* Cambridge, UK, Polity, 2010.

LAST RESORT BEYOND LAST RESORT

351 Williams, *Who Killed Hammarskjold? The UN, The Cold War And The White Supremacy In Africa.*

352 Caufield, M.D., Jeffrey H., *General Walker and the Murder of President Kennedy, The Extensive New Evidence of a Radical-Right Conspiracy,* Moreland Press, 2015.

353 Williams, *Who Killed Hammarskjold? The UN, The Cold War And The White Supremacy In Africa.*

354 Ibid

355 Ibid

356 Ibid

357 Ibid

358 Ibid

359 Poulgrain, *JFK vs. Allen Dulles: Battleground Indonesia.*

360 Ibid

361 Ibid

362 Ibid

363 June 19, 1961 New York Times article, and Wilkepedia, *1961 Vitry-Francois Train Bombing.*

364 October 18, 1961 New York Times article, and Wilkepdia, *Paris Massacre of 1961.*

Chapter Six

365 Marrs, Jim, *Crossfire, The Plot That Killed Kennedy, New York,* New York, Carroll & Graf Publishers, Inc., 1989, and Summers, Anthony, *Conspiracy, New York,* New York, McGraw-Hill Book Company, 1980.

366 Hinckle, Warren, and Turner, William, *The Fish is Red, The Story of the Secret War Against Castro, New York,* New York, Harper & Row Publishers, 1981.

367 Weberman, Alan Jules, *The Oswald Code,* Createspace Independent Publishers, 2014, and *The San Francisco Sunday Examiner article, June 22, 1975.*

368 De Gramont, Sanche, *The Secret War, New York,* New York, Dell Publishing, 1962.

369 Russell, Dick, *The Man Who Knew Too Much, New York,* New York, Carroll & Graf Publishers/Richard Gallen, 1992.

370 Morrow, Robert, *First Hand Knowledge, How I Participated in the CIA-Mafia Murder of President Kennedy, New York,* New York, Shapolsky Publishers, Inc., 1992.

371 Summers, *Conspiracy.*

372 Groden, Robert J., and Livingston, Harrison Edward, *High Treason: The Assassination Of President John F. Kennedy, What Really Happpened, New York,* New York, The Conservatory Press, 1989.

373 Fensterwald, Bernard Jr. *Assassination of JFK by Coincidence or Conspiracy?, New York,* New York, Kensington Publishing Corp., 1977, and Russell, *The Man Who Knew Too Much.*

374 Caufield, M.D., Jeffrey H., *General Walker and the Murder of President Kennedy, The Extensive New Evidence of a Radical-Right Conspiracy,* Moreland Press, 2015, and Russell, *The Man Who Knew Too Much.*

375 Albarelli, H.P. Jr., *A Secret Order, Investigating the High Strangeness and Synchronicity in the JFK Assassination,* Walterville, Oregon, Trine Day, 2013.

376 Ibid & Herbst, Walter, *It Did Not Start With JFK: The Decades Of Events That Led To The Assassination Of John F. Kennedy, Volume Two,* Harrisburg, Pennsylvania, Sunbury Press, 2021.

377 Russell, *The Man Who Knew Too Much.*

378 Weberman, *Oswald Code.*

379 Epstein, Edward Jay, Legend, *The Secret World of Lee Harvey Oswald, New York,* New York, McGraw-Hill Book Company, 1978.

380 McMillan, Priscilla Johnson, *Marina and Lee, New York,* New York, Harper & Row, 1977.

381 Epstein, Legend, *The Secret World of Lee Harvey Oswald.*

382 Russell, *The Man Who Knew Too Much.*

383 Gaddis, John Lewis, *George F. Kennan: An American Life, New York,* New York, The Penguin Press, 2011.

Endnotes

384 Simpson, Christopher, *Blowback: The First Full Account of America's Recruitment of Nazis, and its Disastrous Effect on Our Domestic and Foreign Policy, New York,* New York, Collier's Books – Macmillan, 1989.

385 Ibid

386 Ibid

387 *The Russian Fascists, Tragedy and Farce in Exile, 1925-1945,* John J. Stephan, *Harper & Row, New York,* New York, 1978

388 Ibid

389 Swastika, Charles Higham, *Doubleday & Company, Inc.,* Garden City, New York, 1985.

390 Summers, *Conspiracy.*

391 Parsons, Talcon, *Essays in Sociological Theory,* Glencoe, Illinois, The Free Press, 1954.

Chapter Seven

392 Epstein, Edward Jay, Legend, *The Secret World of Lee Harvey Oswald, New York,* New York, McGraw-Hill Book Company, 1978.

393 Newman, John, *Oswald and the CIA, New York,* New York, Carroll & Graf Publishers, Inc., 1995.

394 *National Archives Record No. 157-10014-101378, 1975, J. Edgar Hoover FBI memo dated May 31, 1962*

395 Eddows, Michael, *The Oswald File: Startling New Evidence and Undeniable Conclusions on the Man Sent to Kill Kennedy, New York,* New York, Clarkson N. Potter, Inc./Publisher, 1977.

396 Epstein, Legend, *The Secret World of Lee Harvey Oswald.*

397 McMillan, Priscilla Johnson, *Marina and Lee, New York,* New York, Harper & Row, 1977.

398 Ibid

399 Ibid

400 Ibid

401 Ibid

402 Russell, Dick, *The Man Who Knew Too Much, New York,* New York, Carroll & Graf Publishers/Richard Gallen, 1992.

403 Ibid

404 Ibid and Eddows, *The Oswald File: Startling New Evidence and Undeniable Conclusions on the Man Sent to Kill Kennedy.*

405 Epstein, Legend, *The Secret World of Lee Harvey Oswald.*

406 *CIA Record No, 157-10003-10494, FBI report dated September 24, 1963 on Lee Harvey Oswald.*

407 Newman, *Oswald and the CIA.*

408 Ibid

409 Epstein, Legend, *The Secret World of Lee Harvey Oswald.*

410 Summers, Anthony, *Conspiracy, New York,* New York, McGraw-Hill Book Company, 1980.

411 McMillan, *Marina and Lee.*

412 Ibid

413 Epstein, Legend, *The Secret World of Lee Harvey Oswald.*

414 Ibid

415 Russell, *The Man Who Knew Too Much.*

416 Epstein, Legend, *The Secret World of Lee Harvey Oswald.*

417 Anderson, Scott, *The Quiet Americans: Four CIA Spies at the Dawn of the Cold War, New York,* New York, Anchor Publishing, 2021.

418 Lane, Mark, Plausible Denial, *Was the CIA Involved in the Assassination of JFK?, New York,* New York, Thunder's Mouth Press, 1991.

419 Ibid

420 Ibid

421 Ibid

422 Summers, *Conspiracy.*

423 Ibid

424 Epstein, Legend, *The Secret World of Lee Harvey Oswald.*

425 Lateer, J.W., *The Three Barons, The Organizational Chart of the Kennedy Assassination,* Walterville, Oregon, Trine Day, 2017.

426 Ballen, Samuel, *Warren Commission Testimony, March 24, 1964,* Washington DC, *Warren Report Volume IX, 1964.*

427 Oswald, Marina, *Warren Commission Testimony, February 3, 1964,* Washington DC, Warren Report Volume 1, 1964.

428 Epstein, Legend, *The Secret World of Lee Harvey Oswald.*

429 McMillan, *Marina & Lee.*

430 Ibid

431 Summers, *Conspiracy.*

432 Eddows, *The Oswald File: Startling New Evidence and Undeniable Conclusions on the Man Sent to Kill Kennedy.*

433 Epstein, Legend, *The Secret World of Lee Harvey Oswald.*

434 Russell, *The Man Who Knew Too Much.*

435 Epstein, Legend, *The Secret World of Lee Harvey Oswald.*

Chapter Eight

436 Douglas, James, W., *JFK and the Unspeakable, Why He Died & Why It Matters,* Maryknoll, New York, Orbis Books, 2008.

437 Taubman, William, *Khrushchev, The Man and His Era, New York,* New York, W.W. Norton & Company, 2003.

438 Dallek, Robert, *Camelot's Court: Inside The Kennedy White House, New York,* New York, Harper Collins, 2013.

439 Morley, Jefferson, *Our Man in Mexico: Winston Scott and the Hidden History of the CIA, Lawrence,* Kansas, University Press of Kansas, 2008.

440 Douglas, *JFK and the Unspeakable, Why He Died & Why It Matters.*

441 Dallek, Robert, *Camelot's Court: Inside The Kennedy White House.*

442 Ibid

443 Fursenko, Aleksandr, and Naftali, Timothy, *One Hell of a Gamble, The Secret History of the Cuban Missile Crisis, Khrushchev, Castro & Kennedy, 1958-1964, New York,* New York, W.W. Norton & Company, 1997.

444 Mellen, Joan, *The Great Game in Cuba, How the CIA Sabotaged Its Own Plot to Unseat Fidel Castro, New York,* New York, Skyhorse Publishing, 2013.

445 Johnston, James, H., *Murder Inc.: The CIA Under John F. Kennedy,* Lincoln Nebraska, Potomac Books, an imprint of the University of Nebraska Press, 2019.

446 Mahoney, Richard D., *Sons and Brothers: The Days Of Jack And Bobby Kennedy, New York,* New York, Arcade Publishing, 1999.

447 Fursenko and Naftali, *One Hell of a Gamble, The Secret History of the Cuban Missile Crisis,* Khrushchev, Castro & Kennedy, 1958-1964.

448 Johnston, *Murder Inc.: The CIA Under John F. Kennedy.*

449 Kaiser, David, *The Road to Dallas, The Assassination of John F. Kennedy,* Cambridge, Massachusetts, The Belknap Press of Harvard University Press, 2008.

450 *FBI Record No. 124-10226-10458, July 2, 1962, FBI Airtel to J. Edgar Hoover from SAC New York.*

451 Kaiser, *The Road to Dallas, The Assassination of John F. Kennedy.*

452 Ibid

453 Blakey, G. Robert, and Billings, Richard N., *The Plot to Kill the President, Organized Crimed Assassinated J.F.K., The Definitive Story, New York,* New York, Times Books, 1981.

454 Russell, Dick, *The Man Who Knew Too Much, New York,* New York, Carroll & Graf Publishers/Richard Gallen, 1992.

455 Fonzi, Gaeton, *The Last Investigation, New York,* New York, Thunder's Mouth Press, 1993.

ENDNOTES

456 Ibid

457 Hinckle, Warren, and Turner, William, *The Fish is Red, The Story of the Secret War Against Castro, New York,* New York, Harper & Row Publishers, 1981.

458 Waldron, Lamar, and Hartmann, Thom, *Ultimate Sacrifice, John and Robert Kennedy, the Plan for a Coup in Cuba, and the Murder of JFK, New York,* New York, Carroll & Graf Publishers, 2005.

459 Kaiser, *The Road to Dallas, The Assassination of John F. Kennedy.*

460 Mellen, *The Great Game in Cuba, How the CIA Sabotaged Its Own Plot to Unseat Fidel Castro,* and *The San Francisco Sunday Examiner article, June 22, 1975.*

461 Morrow, Robert, *First Hand Knowledge, How I Participated In The CIA-Mafia Murder Of President Kennedy, New York,* New York, Shapolsky Publishers Inc., 1992.

462 Newman, *John M., Into The Storm: The Assassination of President Kennedy, Volume III,* North Charleston, South Carolina, CreateSpace Independent Publishing Platform, 2019.

463 Kaiser, *The Road to Dallas, The Assassination of John F. Kennedy.*

464 Ibid and Morrow, First Hand Knowledge, *How I Participated In The CIA-Mafia Murder Of President Kennedy.*

465 Waldron and Hartmann, *Ultimate Sacrifice, John and Robert Kennedy, the Plan for a Coup in Cuba, and the Murder of JFK.*

466 Morley, *Our Man in Mexico: Winston Scott and the Hidden History of the CIA,* and Kaiser, *The Road to Dallas, The Assassination of John F. Kennedy.*

467 Ibid

468 Ibid

469 Kaiser, *The Road to Dallas, The Assassination of John F. Kennedy.*

470 Weberman, Alan Jules, *The Oswald Code,* Createspace Independent Publishers, 2014, and *The San Francisco Sunday Examiner article, June 22, 1975.*

471 Albarelli, H.P. Jr., with Sharp, Leslie and Kent, Alan, *Coup in Dallas: The Decisive Investigation into Who Killed JFK, New York,* New York, Skyhorse Publishing, 2021, and Mellen, Joan, *Our Man in Haiti, George de Mohrenschildt and the CIA in the Nightmare Republic,* Walterville, Oregon, Trine Day, 2012.

472 Quinn, Ruth, *This Week in History, Dorothy K. Matlack, A Pioneer and Champion of Army HUMINT,* U.S. Army website, https://www.army.mil/article/97889, March 6, 1963.

473 Weberman, *The Oswald Code.*

474 Ibid

475 Russell, Dick, *On the Trail of the JFK Assassins, A Groundbreaking Look at America's Most Infamous Conspiracy, New York,* New York, Skyhorse Publishing, 2008, and Waldron and Hartmann, *Ultimate Sacrifice,* John and Robert Kennedy, *the Plan for a Coup in Cuba, and Albarelli,* H.P. Jr., *A Secret Order, Investigating the High Strangeness and Synchronicity in the JFK Assassination,* Walterville, Oregon, Trine Day, 2013.

476 Stockton, Bayard, *Flawed Patriot: The Rise And Fall Of CIA Legend Bill Harvey,* Washington DC, Potomac Book, Inc., 2006.

477 Ibid

478 Ibid and Prados, John, *Safe for Democracy: The Secret Wars Of The CIA,* Chicago, Illinois, Ivan R. Dee, 2006.

479 Dallek, Robert, *Camelot's Court: Inside The Kennedy White House.*

480 Prouty, L. Fletcher, *The Secret Team, The CIA and Its Allies in Control of the United States and the World, New York,* New York, Skyhorse Publishing, 2011

481 Trento, Joseph J., *The Secret History of the CIA, New York,* New York, MJF Books, 2001.

482 Douglas, *JFK and the Unspeakable, Why He Died & Why It Matters.*

483 Dallek, Robert, *Camelot's Court: Inside The Kennedy White House.*

484 Douglas, *JFK and the Unspeakable, Why He Died & Why It Matters.*

485 Mahoney, Sons and Brothers: *The Days Of Jack And Bobby Kennedy.*

486 Douglas, *JFK and the Unspeakable, Why He Died & Why It Matters.*

487 Clarke, Thurston, *JFK's Last Hundred Days: The Transformation of a Man and the Emergence of a Great President, New York,* New York, The Penguin Press, 2013.

488 Ibid

489 Ibid

490 Dallek, Robert, *An Unfinished Life: John F. Kennedy, 1917-1963, New York,* New York, Little, Brown and Company, 2003.

491 Sheehan, Neil, *The Pentagon Papers: The Secret History of the Vietnam War, New York,* New York, Racehorwse Publishing, 2017.

492 Ibid

493 Douglas, *JFK and the Unspeakable, Why He Died & Why It Matters.*

494 Ibid

495 Poulgrain, Dr. Greg, *JFK vs. Allen Dulles: Battleground Indonesia, New York,* New York, Skyhorse Publishing, 2020.

496 Ibid

497 Douglas, *JFK and the Unspeakable, Why He Died & Why It Matters.*

498 Ibid

499 Talbot, David, *The Devil's Chessboard, Allen Dulles, the CIA, and the Rise of America's Secret Government, New York,* New York, Harper Collins Publishers, 2015.

500 Ibid

501 Newman, John M., *Countdown to Darkness: The Assassination of President Kennedy, Volume II,* North Charleston, South Carolina, CreateSpace Independent Publishing Platform, 2017.

502 Cottrell, Richard, Gladio, *Nato's Dagger at the Heart of Europe, The Pentagon-Nazi-Mafia Terror Axis,* San Diego, California, Progressive Press, 2015.

Chapter Nine

503 Kessler, Ronald, *Sins of the Fathers: Joseph P. Kennedy and the Dynasty He Founded, New York,* New York, Warner Books, 1996, and Raab, Selwyn, *Five Families: The Rise, Decline, And Resurgence Of America's Most Powerful Mafia Empires, New York,* New York, Thomas Dunne Books, 2016.

504 Kessler, *Sins of the Fathers: Joseph P. Kennedy and the Dynasty He Founded.*

505 Ibid

506 Ibid

507 Ibid

508 North, Mark, *Act of Treason. The Role of J. Edgar Hoover in the Assassination of President Kennedy, New York,* New York, Carroll & Graf Publishers, Inc., 1991.

509 Server, Lee, Handsome Johnny, *The Life And Death Of Johnny Rosselli: Gentleman, Gangster, Hollywood Producer, CIA Assassin, New York,* New York, St. Martin's Press, 2018.

510 Ibid

511 Ibid

512 Blakey, G. Robert, and Billings, Richard N., *The Plot to Kill the President, Organized Crime Assassinated J.F.K., The Definitive Story, New York,* New York, Times Books, 1981.

513 North, Act of Treason. *The Role of J. Edgar Hoover in the Assassination of President Kennedy.*

514 Blakey and Billings, *The Plot to Kill the President, Organized Crime Assassinated J.F.K., The Definitive Story,* and Kessler, *Sins of the Fathers: Joseph P. Kennedy and the Dynasty He Founded.*

515 Blakey and Billings, *The Plot to Kill the President, Organized Crime Assassinated J.F.K., The Definitive Story.*

516 Marrs, Jim, *Crossfire, The Plot That Killed Kennedy, New York,* New York, Carroll & Graf Publishers, Inc., 1989; Scheim, David E., Contract on America, *The Mafia Murder of President John F. Kennedy, New York,* New York, Shapolsky Publishers, Inc., 1988.

517 Ibid

518 Server, Handsome Johnny, *The Life And Death Of Johnny Rosselli: Gentleman, Gangster, Hollywood Producer, CIA Assassin.*

519 Blakey and Billings, *The Plot to Kill the President, Organized Crime Assassinated J.F.K., The Definitive Story.*

ENDNOTES

520 Ibid

521 Hougan, Jim, *Spooks: The Haunting of America – The Private Use of Secret Agents, New York,* New York, William Morrow And Company, Inc., 1978.

522 Hersh, Seymour M., *The Dark Side of Camelot, Boston, Massachusetts, Little Brown And Company, 1997.*

523 Ibid

524 Hinckle, Warren, and Turner, William, *The Fish is Red, The Story of the Secret War Against Castro, New York,* New York, Harper & Row Publishers, 1981.

525 Server, Handsome Johnny, *The Life And Death Of Johnny Rosselli: Gentleman, Gangster, Hollywood Producer, CIA Assassin.*

526 Hinckle and Turner, *The Fish is Red, The Story of the Secret War Against Castro.*

527 Blakey and Billings, *The Plot to Kill the President, Organized Crime Assassinated J.F.K., The Definitive Story.*

528 Davis, John H., *Mafia Kingfish, Carlos Marcello and the Assassination of John F. Kennedy, New York,* New York, Penguin Books USA Inc., 1989.

529 Ibid

530 Maier, Thomas, *Mafia Spies: The Inside Story Of The CIA, Gangsters, JFK, And Castro, New York,* New York, Skyhorse Publishing, 2019.

531 Davis, Mafia Kingfish, *Carlos Marcello and the Assassination of John F. Kennedy.*

532 Margolis, Jay, and Buskin, Richard, *The Murder of Marilyn Monroe: Case Closed, New York,* New York, Skyhorse, 2014.

533 Hughes-Wilson, Colonel John, *JFK An American Coup d'Etat: The Truth Behind The Kennedy Assassination,* London, England, John Blake Publishing, Ltd, 2013.

534 North, Act of Treason. *The Role of J. Edgar Hoover in the Assassination of President Kennedy*, and Hughes-Wilson, *JFK An American Coup d'Etat: The Truth Behind The Kennedy Assassination.*

535 *The Secret Life of Marilyn Monroe*

536 *Mafia Spies*

537 *The Reporter Who Kew Too Much*

538 Taraborrelli, J. Randy, *The Secret Life of Marilyn Monroe, New York,* New York, Grand Central Publishing, 2010.

539 Ibid

540 Ibid

541 Ibid

542 Ibid

543 Ibid

544 Ibid

545 Davis, Mafia Kingfish, *Carlos Marcello and the Assassination of John F. Kennedy.*

546 Summers, Anthony, *Conspiracy, New York,* New York, McGraw-Hill Book Company, 1980.

547 Scheim, David E., Contract on America, *The Mafia Murder of President John F. Kennedy, New York,* New York, Shapolsky Publishers, Inc., 1988

548 Summers, *Conspiracy.*

549 North, Act of Treason. *The Role of J. Edgar Hoover in the Assassination of President Kennedy.*

550 Ibid

551 Russell, Dick, *The Man Who Knew Too Much, New York,* New York, Carroll & Graf Publishers, 1992.

552 Ibid

553 Gentry, Curt, *J. Edgar Hoover: The Man and the Secrets, New York,* New York, W W Norton & Co Inc., 1991.

554 *J. Edgar Hoover speech to Washington Hebrew Congregation,* December 4, 1963, from North, Act of Treason. *The Role of J. Edgar Hoover in the Assassination of President Kennedy.*

Chapter Ten

555 Fursenko, Aleksandr, and Naftali, Timothy, *One Hell of a Gamble, The Secret History of the Cuban Missile Crisis, Khrushchev, Castro & Kennedy, 1958-1964, New York,* New York, W.W. Norton & Company, 1997.

556 Russo, Gus, *Live By the Sword, The Secret War Against Castro and the Death of JFK,* Baltimore, Maryland, Bancroft Press, 1998.

557 Fursenko, Aleksandr, and Naftali, Timothy, *Khrushchev's Cold War, The Inside Story of an American Adversary, New York,* New York, W.W. Norton & Company, 2006.

558 Fursenko and Naftali, *One Hell of a Gamble, The Secret History of the Cuban Missile Crisis, Khrushchev, Castro & Kennedy.*

559 Stockton, Bayard, *Flawed Patriot: The Rise And Fall Of CIA Legend Bill Harvey,* Washington DC, Potomac Book, Inc., 2006.

560 Russo, *Live By the Sword, The Secret War Against Castro and the Death of JFK.*

561 Ibid

562 Fursenko and Naftali, *One Hell of a Gamble, The Secret History of the Cuban Missile Crisis, Khrushchev, Castro & Kennedy.*

563 Ibid

564 Russo, *Live By the Sword, The Secret War Against Castro and the Death of JFK.*

565 Galbraith, James, *Did the U.S. Military Plan a Nuclear First Strike for 1963?* The American Prospect, Fall 1994, from Newman, John M., *Into The Storm: The Assassination of President Kennedy, Volume III,* North Charleston, South Carolina, CreateSpace Independent Publishing Platform, 2019.

566 Bamford, James, *Body of Secrets, Anatomy of the Ultra-Secret National Security Agency, From the Cold War Through the Dawn of a New Century, New York,* New York, Doubleday, 2001.

567 Taubman, William, *Khrushchev: The Man And His Era, New York,* New York, W.W. Norton & Company, 2003.

568 Bamford, *Body of Secrets, Anatomy of the Ultra-Secret National Security Agency, From the Cold War Through the Dawn of a New Century.*

569 Taubman, *Khrushchev: The Man And His Era.*

570 Newman, *Into The Storm: The Assassination of President Kennedy, Volume III.*

571 Bamford, *Body of Secrets, Anatomy of the Ultra-Secret National Security Agency, From the Cold War Through the Dawn of a New Century.*

572 Bird, Kai, *The Color of Truth,* McGeorge Bundy and William Bundy: *Brothers in Arms, New York* New York, Simon & Schuster, 1998.

573 Taubman, *Khrushchev: The Man And His Era.*

574 Ibid

575 Albarelli, H.P. Jr., with Sharp, Leslie and Kent, Alan, *Coup in Dallas: The Decisive Investigation into Who Killed JFK, New York,* New York, Skyhorse Publishing, 2021.

576 Mellen, Joan, *Our Man in Haiti, George de Mohrenschildt and the CIA in the Nightmare Republic,* Walterville, Oregon, Trine Day, 2012.

577 Fursenko and Naftali, *One Hell of a Gamble, The Secret History of the Cuban Missile Crisis, Khrushchev, Castro & Kennedy.*

578 September 19, 1962, CIA National Estimate, *The Military Buildup in Cuba; from Chang, Laurence and Peter Kornbluh, The Cuban Missile Crisis, 1962,* New Press, New York, New York, 1992.

579 Newman, *Into The Storm: The Assassination of President Kennedy, Volume III.*

580 Fursenko and Naftali, *One Hell of a Gamble, The Secret History of the Cuban Missile Crisis, Khrushchev, Castro & Kennedy.*

581 Taubman, *Khrushchev: The Man And His Era.*

582 Schlesinger, Arthur M. Jr, *A Thousand Days: John F. Kennedy in the White House, New York,* New York, Houghton Mifflin, 1965.

583 *Life Magazine October 5, 1962.*

584 Taubman, *Khrushchev: The Man And His Era.*

585 Ibid

Endnotes

586   Fursenko and Naftali, *One Hell of a Gamble, The Secret History of the Cuban Missile Crisis, Khrushchev, Castro & Kennedy.*

587   Taubman, *Khrushchev: The Man And His Era, and Dallek,* Robert, *An Unfinished Life: John F. Kennedy, 1917-1963, New York,* New York, Little, Brown and Company, 2003.

588   Fursenko and Naftali, *Khrushchev's Cold War, The Inside Story of an American Adversary.*

589   Dallek, Robert, *An Unfinished Life: John F. Kennedy, 1917-1963, New York,* New York, Little, Brown and Company, 2003.

590   Bamford, *Body of Secrets, Anatomy of the Ultra-Secret National Security Agency, From the Cold War Through the Dawn of a New Century.*

591   Ibid

592   Fursenko and Naftali, *One Hell of a Gamble, The Secret History of the Cuban Missile Crisis, Khrushchev, Castro & Kennedy.*

593   Newman, *Into The Storm: The Assassination of President Kennedy, Volume III.*

594   Ibid

595   Carrozza, Anthony R., William D. Pawley, *The Extraordinary Life of the Adventurer, Entrepreneur, and Diplomat Who Cofounded the Flying Tigers,* Washington D.C., Potomac Books, 2012.

596   Dallek, Robert, *Camelot's Court: Inside The Kennedy White House, New York,* New York, Harper Collins, 2013.

597   Newman, *Into The Storm: The Assassination of President Kennedy, Volume III.*

598   Bird, *The Color of Truth, McGeorge Bundy and William Bundy: Brothers in Arms.*

599   Ibid

600   Dallek, *An Unfinished Life: John F. Kennedy, 1917-1963.*

601   Dallek, *Camelot's Court: Inside The Kennedy White House.*

602   Dallek, *An Unfinished Life: John F. Kennedy, 1917-1963.*

603   Talbot, David, Brothers, *The Hidden History of the Kennedy Years, New York,* New York, Free Press, 2007, and Dallek, *Camelot's Court: Inside The Kennedy White House.*

604   Dallek, *Camelot's Court: Inside The Kennedy White House.*

605   Bird, *The Color of Truth, McGeorge Bundy and William Bundy: Brothers in Arms.*

606   Bamford, *Body of Secrets, Anatomy of the Ultra-Secret National Security Agency, From the Cold War Through the Dawn of a New Century.*

607   Taubman, *Khrushchev: The Man And His Era.*

608   Stockton, *Flawed Patriot: The Rise And Fall Of CIA Legend Bill Harvey.*

609   Waldron, Lamar, *The Hidden History of the JFK Assassination, The Definitive Account of the Most Controversial Crime of the Twentieth Century,* Berkeley, California, Counterpoint, 2013.

610   Douglas, James, W., *JFK and the Unspeakable, Why He Died & Why It Matters,* Maryknoll, New York, Orbis Books, 2008.

611   Bird, *The Color of Truth, McGeorge Bundy and William Bundy: Brothers in Arms.*

612   Talbot, Brothers, *The Hidden History of the Kennedy Years.*

613   Ibid

614   Douglas, *JFK and the Unspeakable, Why He Died & Why It Matters.*

615   Ibid

616   Taubman, *Khrushchev: The Man And His Era.*

617   Dallek, *An Unfinished Life: John F. Kennedy, 1917-1963.*

618   Newman, *Into The Storm: The Assassination of President Kennedy, Volume III.*

619   Swanson, Michael, *The War State, The Cold War Origins of the Military-Industrial Complex and The Power Elite, 1945-1963,* North Charleston, South Carolina, CreateSpace Independent Publishing Platform, 2013.

620   Ibid

621   Talbot, Brothers, *The Hidden History of the Kennedy Years.*

622   Clarke, Thurston, *JFK's Last Hundred Days, The Transformation of a Man and the Emergence of a Great President, New York,* New York, The Penguin Press, 2013.

623 Marrs, Jim, *Crossfire, The Plot That Killed Kennedy, New York,* New York, Carroll & Graf Publishers, Inc., 1989.

624 Douglas, *JFK and the Unspeakable, Why He Died & Why It Matters.*

625 Herbst, Walter, *It Did Not Start With JFK: The Decades Of Events That Led To The Assassination Of John F. Kennedy, Volume One,* Harrisburg, Pennsylvania, Sunbury Press, 2021.

Chapter Eleven

626 Wicker, Tom, *Kennedy Asks For Inquiry On 'Excessive' Stockpile; He Hints At Profiteering,* New York Times, February 1, 1962.

627 Lewis, Anthony, *Robert Kennedy Begins One-Month Goodwill Trip Around The World,* New York Times, February 2, 1962

628 Giniger, Henry, *Salan Is Indicted: Lays Terrorism To 'Insane' Aides,* New York Times, April 22, 1962, and Albarelli, H.P. Jr., with Sharp, Leslie and Kent, Alan, *Coup in Dallas: The Decisive Investigation into Who Killed JFK, New York,* New York, Skyhorse Publishing, 2021.

629 Albarelli, with Sharp and Kent, *Coup in Dallas: The Decisive Investigation into Who Killed JFK.*

630 *Terrorists Shoot Up French Police station,* New York Times, April 28, 1962

631 Ibid

632 Prouty, L. Fletcher, *JFK, The CIA, Vietnam and the Plot to Assassinate John F. Kennedy, New York,* New York, Carol Publishing Group, 1992.

633 Ibid

634 Hersh, Seymour M., *The Dark Side of Camelot,* Boston, Massachusetts, Little Brown And Company, 1997.

635 Janney, Peter, *Mary's Mosaic, The CIA Conspiracy to Murder John F. Kennedy, Mary Pinchot Meyer, and Their Vision for World Peace, New York,* New York, Skyhorse Publishing, 2012.

636 Kantor, Seth, *Fort Worth Press, October 24, 1962,* from www.spartacus-educational.com.

637 Albarelli, with Sharp and Kent, *Coup in Dallas: The Decisive Investigation into Who Killed JFK.*

638 Marrs, Jim, *Crossfire, The Plot That Killed Kennedy, New York,* New York, Carroll & Graf Publishers, Inc., 1989, and Valentine, Douglas, *The Strength of the Wolf, The Secret History of America's War on Drugs,* London, England, Verso, 2004.

639 De Mey, Flip, *The Lee Harvey Oswald Files: Why The CIA Killed Kennedy,* Belgium, Lannoo Publishing, 2016, and Titovets, Ernst, *Oswald: Russian Episode,* Washington, DC, Eagle View Books, 2013.

640 Russell, Dick, *The Man Who Knew Too Much, New York,* New York, Carroll & Graf Publishers, 1992.

641 Minutaglio, Bill, and Davis, Steven L., *Dallas 1963, New York,* New York, Hachette Book Group, 2013, and Marrs, *Crossfire, The Plot That Killed Kennedy.*

642 Minutaglio and Davis, *Dallas 1963.*

643 https://fee.org/articles/the-shame-of-medicine-the-case-of-general-edwin-walker/

644 Minutaglio and Davis, *Dallas 1963.* and Marrs, Jim, *Crossfire, The Plot That Killed Kennedy.*

645 Fursenko, Aleksandr, and Naftali, Timothy, *One Hell of a Gamble, The Secret History of the Cuban Missile Crisis, Khrushchev, Castro & Kennedy, 1958-1964, New York,* New York, W.W. Norton & Company, 1997.

646 Ibid

647 Schlesinger, Arthur M. Jr., *Robert Kennedy and His Times,* Boston, Massachusetts, Houghton Mifflin Company, 1978.

648 Kaiser, David, *The Road to Dallas, The Assassination of John F. Kennedy,* Cambridge, Massachusetts, The Belknap Press of Harvard University Press, 2008.

649 Summers, Anthony, *Conspiracy, New York,* New York, McGraw-Hill Book Company, 1980.

650 Ibid

651 Talbot, David, Brothers, *The Hidden History of the Kennedy Years. New York,* New York, Free Press, 2007

652 Weberman, Alan J., and Canfield, Michael, *Coup D' Etat In America, The CIA and the Assassination of John F. Kennedy,* San Francisco, The Third Press, 1975.

653 Kaiser, *The Road to Dallas, The Assassination of John F. Kennedy.*

ENDNOTES

654 Ibid

655 Morley, Jefferson, *Our Man in Mexico: Winston Scott and the Hidden History of the CIA*, Lawrence, Kansas, University Press of Kansas, 2008.

656 Waldron, Lamar, and Hartmann, Thom, *Ultimate Sacrifice, John and Robert Kennedy, the Plan for a Coup in Cuba, and the Murder of JFK, New York,* New York, Carroll & Graf Publishers, 2005.

657 Fursenko and Naftali, *One Hell of a Gamble, The Secret History of the Cuban Missile Crisis, Khrushchev, Castro & Kennedy, 1958-1964.*

658 Valentine, *The Strength of the Wolf, The Secret History of America's War on Drugs.*

659 Kaiser, *The Road to Dallas, The Assassination of John F. Kennedy.*

Chapter Twelve

660 Ofstein, Dennis, Hyman, *Warren Commission Testimony,* Washington DC, March 30, 1964, Warren Report, Volume X, 1964.

661 Lateer, J.W., *The Three Barons, The Organizational Chart of the Kennedy Assassination,* Walterville, Oregon, Trine Day, 2017, and Simpich, Bill, *The Twelve Who Built the Oswald Legend* from the Mary Ferrell Foundation website, maryferrell.org/ pages/Oswald_ Legend. html.

662 Epstein, Edward Jay, Legend, *The Secret World of Lee Harvey Oswald, New York,* New York, McGraw-Hill Book Company, 1978.

663 McMillan, Priscilla Johnson, *Marina & Lee, New York,* New York, Harper & Row, 1977.

664 Fonzi, Gaeton, *The Last Investigation, New York,* New York, Thunder's Mouth Press, 1993.

665 Newman, John, *Oswald and the CIA, New York,* New York, Carroll & Graf Publishers, Inc., 1995.

666 Hosty, James P., *Assignment Oswald, New York,* New York, Arcade Publishing, 1996.

667 Mellen, Joan, *Our Man in Haiti, George de Mohrenschildt and the CIA in the Nightmare Republic,* Walterville, Oregon, Trine Day, 2012.

668 Ibid

669 Ibid

670 Weberman, Alan Jules, *The Oswald Code*, Lexington, Kentucky, Createspace Independent Publishers, 2014, and *The San Francisco Sunday Examiner article, June 22, 1975.*

671 Warren Commission Volume X, *Testimony of Everett D. Glover*

672 *Sparticus International*

673 Glover, Everett D., *Warren Commission Testimony,* Washington DC, March 24, 1964, *Warren Report, Volume X,* 1964.

674 Epstein, Legend, *The Secret World of Lee Harvey Oswald.*

675 Evica, George Michael, *A Certain Arrogance; The Sacrificing of Lee Harvey Oswald and the Cold War Manipulation of Religious Groups by US Intelligence,* Walterville, Oregon, TrineDay, 2011.

676 Weberman, *The Oswald Code.*

677 Newman, John M., *Where Angels Tread Lightly: The Assassination of President Kennedy, Volume I,* North Charleston, South Carolina, CreateSpace Independent Publishing Platform, 2017.

678 Haverstick, Mary, *A Woman I Know: Female Spies, Double Identities, and A New Story of The Kennedy Assassination, New York,* New York, Crown Publishing, 2023.

679 Hilts, Philip, Louis J. West, 74, *Psychiatrist Who Studied Extremes, Dies, The New York Times article, January 9, 1999,* and Albarelli, H.P. Jr., *A Secret Order, Investigating the High Strangeness and Synchronicity in the JFK Assassination,* Walterville, Oregon, Trine Day, 2013.

680 Albarelli, *A Secret Order, Investigating the High Strangeness and Synchronicity in the JFK Assassination.*

681 Albarelli, H.P. Jr., with Sharp, Leslie and Kent, Alan, *Coup in Dallas: The Decisive Investigation into Who Killed JFK, New York,* New York, Skyhorse Publishing, 2021.

682 Glover, *Warren Commission Testimony.*

683 Evica, *A Certain Arrogance; The Sacrificing of Lee Harvey Oswald and the Cold War Manipulation of Religious Groups by US Intelligence.*

684 Summers, Anthony, *Conspiracy, New York,* New York, McGraw-Hill Book Company, 1980.

685 https://en.wikipedia.org/wiki/Norman_Thomas

686 Evica, *A Certain Arrogance; The Sacrificing of Lee Harvey Oswald and the Cold War Manipulation of Religious Groups by US Intelligence*.

687 Ibid

688 Douglas, James W., *JFK And The Unspeakable, Why He Died And Why It Matters,* Maryknoll, New York, Orbis Books, 2013.

689 Fensterwald, Bernard Jr. *Assassination of JFK by Coincidence or Conspiracy?, New York,* New York, Kensington Publishing Corp., 1977.

690 Plesko, Les, *Oswald: The Secret Files (Controversial Documents from the Secret Censored Archives of the FBI, CIA and more),* Single Issue Magazine, Las Vegas, Nevada, Goldstein & Associates, 1992.

691 Oswald, Marina, *Warren Commission Testimony, February 3, 1964,* Washington DC, *Warren Report Volume 1,* 1964.

692 Plesko, *Oswald: The Secret Files (Controversial Documents from the Secret Censored Archives of the FBI, CIA and more).*

693 Evica, A Certain Arrogance; *The Sacrificing of Lee Harvey Oswald and the Cold War Manipulation of Religious Groups by US Intelligence.*

694 Epstein, Legend, *The Secret World of Lee Harvey Oswald.*

695 Russell, Dick, *The Man Who Knew Too Much, New York,* New York, Carroll & Graf Publishers, 1992.

696 Jones, J. Harry Jr., *The Minutemen,* Garden City, New York, Doubleday & Company, 1968.

697 Ibid

698 Ibid

699 Ibid

700 Summers, *Conspiracy.*

701 Jones, *The Minutemen.*

702 Ibid

703 *Warren Commission Report, Volume XVI,* Exhibit CE97, 1964.

704 Ibid

705 Ibid

706 Russell, *The Man Who Knew Too Much.*

707 *Washington Post article, February 16, 1963.*

708 Middleton, Drew, *French Seize 5 In Plot To Take De Gaulle's Life,* New York Times February 16, 1963

709 Giniger, Henry, *French Break Up Plot On Premier,* New York Times, March 1, 1963.

710 McMillan, Priscilla Johnson, *Marina & Lee, New York,* New York, Harper & Row, 1977.

711 Newman, John, *Oswald and the CIA, New York,* New York, Carroll & Graf Publishers, Inc., 1995.

712 LaFontaine, Ray and Mary, *Oswald Talked, The New Evidence in the JFK Assassination,* Gretna, Louisiana, Pelican Publishing Company, 1996.

713 *On Target article,* April 4/1963, from Jones, *The Minutemen.*

714 McMillan, *Marina & Lee.*

715 Blakey, G. Robert, and Billings, Richard N., *The Plot to Kill the President, Organized Crimed Assassinated J.F.K., The Definitive Story, New York,* New York, Times Books, 1981., North, Mark, *Act of Treason, The Role of J. Edgar Hoover in the Assassination of President Kennedy, New York,* New York, Carroll & Graf Publishers, 1991, and Jones, *The Minutemen.*

716 Summers, *Conspiracy.*

717 DiEugenio, James, *The JFK Assassination, New York,* New York, Skyhorse Publishing, 2016, and Armstrong, John, *Harvey and Lee: How The CIA Framed Oswald,* Berkeley, California, Quasar Books, 2003.

718 *On Target article,* March 15, 1963

719 Russell, *The Man Who Knew Too Much.*

720 Ibid

721 Livingstone, Harrison Edward, High Treason 2, *The Great Cover-Up,: The Assassination Of President John F. Kennedy, New York,* New York, Carroll & Graf Publishers, Inc., 1992.

722 Russell, *The Man Who Knew Too Much*

ENDNOTES

723 Ibid

724 Peterson, Sara, and Zachry, K.W., *The Lone Star Speaks: Untold Texas Stories about the JFK Assassination,* Baltimore Maryland, Bancroft Press, 2020.

725 Marrs, Jim, *Crossfire, The Plot That Killed Kennedy, New York,* New York, Carroll & Graf Publishers, Inc., 1989.

726 Groden, Robert J., *The Killing of a President: The Complete Photographic Record of the JFK Assassination,* Studio Publishing, 1993, and Benson, Michael, *Who's Who in the JFK Assassination, An A-to-Z Encyclopedia, New York,* New York, Carol Publishing Group, 1993.

727 White, Ricky, J. Gary Shaw & Brian K. Edwards, *Admitted Assassin, Roscoe White and the Murder of President Kennedy*, Canyon Lake, Texas, Peniel Unlimited, LLC, 2023..

728 Marrs, *Crossfire, The Plot That Killed Kennedy.*

729 Bookhout, James, *FBI report,* November 25, 1963, *Warren Commission Volume XIV,* CE1986.

730 Fritz, Captain J.W., *Warren Commission Testimony*, Washington DC, July 14, 1964, *Warren Report, Volume XV*, 1964, and Livingstone, Harrison Edward, and Groden, Robert J., High Treason, *The Assassination Of President John F. Kennedy: What Really Happened, New York,* New York, The Conservatory Press, 1989.

731 Caufield, M.D., Jeffrey H., *General Walker and the Murder of President Kennedy, The Extensive New Evidence of a Radical-Right Conspiracy*, Moreland Press, 2015.

732 Eddowes, Michael, *The Oswald File, New York,* New York, Clarkson N. Potter, Inc., 1977.

Chapter Thirteen

733 Minutaglio, Bill, and Davis, Steven L., *Dallas 1963, New York,* New York, Hachette Book Group, 2013.

734 North, Mark, Act of Treason. *The Role of J. Edgar Hoover in the Assassination of President Kennedy, New York,* New York, Carroll & Graf Publishers, Inc., 1991.

735 Ibid

736 Ibid

737 Sherwin, Mark, *The Extremists, New York,* New York, St Martin's Press, 1963.

738 Ibid

739 Martin, Seymour, and Raab, *Earl, The Politics OF Unreason, Right-Wing Extremism in America, 1790-1970, Harper & Row, New York,* New York, 1970.

740 Sherwin, *The Extremists.*

741 Russell, Dick, *The Man Who Knew Too Much, New York,* New York, Carroll & Graf Publishers, 1992.

742 Livingstone, Harrison Edward, and Groden, Robert J., *High Treason, The Assassination Of President John F. Kennedy: What Really Happened, New York,* New York, The Conservatory Press, 1989.

743 Caufield, M.D., Jeffrey H., *General Walker and the Murder of President Kennedy, The Extensive New Evidence of a Radical-Right Conspiracy,* Moreland Press, 2015.

744 Ibid

745 Ibid

746 Ibid

747 Russell, *The Man Who Knew Too Much.*

748 Caufield, *General Walker and the Murder of President Kennedy, The Extensive New Evidence of a Radical-Right Conspiracy.*

749 Summers, Anthony, *Conspiracy, New York,* New York, McGraw-Hill Book Company, 1980.

750 Caufield, *General Walker and the Murder of President Kennedy, The Extensive New Evidence of a Radical-Right Conspiracy.*

751 Ibid

752 Ibid

753 Ibid

754 Ibid

755 Minutaglio and Davis, *Dallas 1963.*

603

Last Resort Beyond Last Resort

756 Ibid

757 Ibid

758 Jones, J. Harry Jr., *The Minutemen*, Garden City, New York, Doubleday & Company, 1968.

759 Russell, *The Man Who Knew Too Much*.

760 McMillan, Priscilla Johnson, *Marina & Lee, New York*, New York, Harper & Row, 1977.

761 Ibid

762 Ibid

763 Marrs, Jim, *Crossfire, The Plot That Killed Kennedy, New York*, New York, Carroll & Graf Publishers, Inc., 1989.

764 McMillan, *Marina & Lee*.

765 Hosty, James P., *Assignment Oswald, New York*, New York, Arcade Publishing, 1996.

766 Ibid

767 Minutaglio and Davis, *Dallas 1963*.

768 Albarelli, H.P. Jr., with Sharp, Leslie and Kent, Alan, *Coup in Dallas: The Decisive Investigation into Who Killed JFK, New York*, New York, Skyhorse Publishing, 2021.

769 Weberman, Alan Jules, *The Oswald Code*, Lexington, Kentucky, Createspace Independent Publishers, 2014, and Caufield, *General Walker and the Murder of President Kennedy, The Extensive New Evidence of a Radical-Right Conspiracy*.

770 Caufield, *General Walker and the Murder of President Kennedy, The Extensive New Evidence of a Radical-Right Conspiracy*.

771 Ibid

772 Ibid

773 North, Act of Treason. *The Role of J. Edgar Hoover in the Assassination of President Kennedy*.

774 Ibid

775 *New York Times article,* April 11, 1963, from North, Act of Treason. *The Role of J. Edgar Hoover in the Assassination of President Kennedy*.

776 Summers, *Conspiracy*, Russell, *The Man Who Knew Too Much*, North, *Act of Treason. The Role of J. Edgar Hoover in the Assassination of President Kennedy*, and Caufield, *General Walker and the Murder of President Kennedy, The Extensive New Evidence of a Radical-Right Conspiracy*.

777 Marrs, *Crossfire* and Summers, *Conspiracy*.

778 Marrs, *Crossfire*.

779 Summers, *Conspiracy*.

780 De Mey, Flip, *The Lee Harvey Oswald Files: Why The CIA Killed Kennedy,* Belgium, Lannoo Publishing, 2016.

781 Russell, *The Man Who Knew Too Much*, and McMillan, *Marina & Lee*.

782 Minutaglio and Davis, *Dallas 1963*.

783 Russell, *The Man Who Knew Too Much*.

784 Caufield, *General Walker and the Murder of President Kennedy, The Extensive New Evidence of a Radical-Right Conspiracy*.

785 Ibid

786 Summers, *Conspiracy*

787 *Richard Case Nagell letter to Senator Russell,* January 3, 1967, from Russell, *The Man Who Knew Too Much*.

788 *Nagel interview with Dick Russell,* from Russell, *The Man Who Knew Too Much*.

789 McMillan, *Marina and Lee*.

Chapter Fourteen

790 Swanson, Michael, The War State, *The Cold War Origins of the Military-Industrial Complex and the Power Elite, 1945-1963*, North Charleston, South Carolina, CreateSpace Independent Publishing Platform, 2013.

791 Ibid

ENDNOTES

792   Cottrell, Richard, Gladio, *Nato's Dagger at the Heart of Europe, The Pentagon-Nazi-Mafia Terror Axis,* San Diego, California, Progressive Press, 2015.

793   Fursenko, Aleksandr, and Naftali, Timothy, *Khrushchev's Cold War, The Inside Story of an American Adversary, New York,* New York, W.W. Norton & Company, 2006.

794   Ibid

795   Ibid

796   Ibid

797   Cohen, Andrew, *Two Days in June, John F. Kennedy and the 48 Hours That Made History,* Canada, McClelland & Stewart, 2014.

798   Caufield, M.D., Jeffrey H., *General Walker and the Murder of President Kennedy, The Extensive New Evidence of a Radical-Right Conspiracy*, Moreland Press, 2015.

799   Hughes-Wilson, Colonel John, *JFK, An American Coup D'Etat, The Truth Behind the Kennedy Assassination,* London, England, John Blake Publishing Ltd., 2015

800   Ibid

801   Ibid

802   Kurlantzick, Joshua, *A Great Place to Have a War: American In Laos And The Birth Of A Military CIA, New York,* New York, Simon & Schuster, 2016.

803   Ibid

804   Talbot, David, *The Devil's Chessboard, Allen Dulles, the CIA, and the Rise of America's Secret Government, New York,* New York, Harper Collins Publishers, 2015.

805   Kaiser, David, *The Road to Dallas, The Assassination of John F. Kennedy,* Cambridge, Massachusetts, The Belknap Press of Harvard University Press, 2008.

806   Mellen, Joan, *Our Man in Haiti, George de Mohrenschildt and the CIA in the Nightmare Republic,* Walterville, Oregon, Trine Day, 2012.

807   Ibid

808   Ibid

809   Ibid

810   Ibid

811   Kaiser, *The Road to Dallas, The Assassination of John F. Kennedy.*

812   Paget, Karen M., *Patriotic Betrayal, New Haven Connecticut,* Yale University Press, 2015.

813   Ibid

814   Fursenko and Naftali, *Khrushchev's Cold War, The Inside Story of an American Adversary.*

815   Paget, *Patriotic Betrayal*

816   https://nsarchive.gwu.edu/briefing-book/intelligence/2020-04-06/cia-covert-operations-overthrow-cheddi-jagan-british-guiana-1964

817   Prados, John, *Safe for Democracy: The Secret Wars Of The CIA,* Chicago, Illinois, Ivan R. Dee, 2006.

818   Ibid

819   Williams, Paul L., Operation Gladio, *The Unholy Alliance between The Vatican, The CIA, And The Mafia,* Amherst, New York, Prometheus Books, 2015.

820   Ibid

821   Ibid

822   Valentine, Douglas, *The Strength of the Wolf, The Secret History of America's War on Drugs*, London, England, Verso, 2004.

823   Williams, Operation Gladio, *The Unholy Alliance between The Vatican, The CIA, And The Mafia,* and https://en.wikipedia.org/wiki/U.S._Army_Field_Manual_30-31B.

824   Talbot, *The Devil's Chessboard, Allen Dulles, the CIA, and the Rise of America's Secret Government.*

825   Hinckle, Warren, and Turner, William, *The Fish is Red, The Story of the Secret War Against Castro, New York,* New York, Harper & Row Publishers, 1981.

826   Schlesinger, Arthur M. Jr., *A Thousand Days,* Fawcett Publications, Inc., Greenwich, Connecticut, 1965.

827   Talbot, *The Devil's Chessboard, Allen Dulles, the CIA, and the Rise of America's Secret Government.*

828   Cohen, *Two Days in June, John F. Kennedy and the 48 Hours That Made History.*

LAST RESORT BEYOND LAST RESORT

829 Poulgrain, Dr. Greg, *JFK vs. Allen Dulles: Battleground Indonesia, New York,* New York, Skyhorse Publishing, 2020.

830 Ibid

831 Bevins, Vincent, *The Jakarta Method: Washington's Anticommunist Crusade & the Mass Murder Program that Shaped Our World, New York,* New York, Public Affairs, Hatchett Book Group, 2021.

832 Ibid

833 Huchthausen, James P., *Imperialism, Corporatism, Militarism, An American Tragedy,* North Charleston, South Carolina, Createspace Publishing Platform, 2014.

834 Ibid

835 Dallek, Robert, *Camelot's Court: Inside The Kennedy White House, New York,* New York, Harper Collins, 2013.

836 Bird, Kai, *The Color of Truth, McGeorge Bundy and William Bundy: Brothers in Arms. New York,* New York, Simon & Schuster, 1998.

837 Dallek, *Camelot's Court: Inside The Kennedy White House.*

838 *JFK and Vietnam*

839 Ibid

840 *The Best and the Brightest*

841 Newman, John M., *JFK and Vietnam, New York,* New York, Warner Books, 1992.

842 O'Donnell, Kenneth P., and Powers, David F., *Johnny, We Hardly Knew Ya: Memoirs Of John Fitzgerald Kennedy, New York,* New York, Little, Brown Publishers, 1972.

843 Douglas, James, W., *JFK and the Unspeakable, Why He Died & Why It Matters,* Maryknoll, New York, Orbis Books, 2008.

844 Newman, *JFK and Vietnam.*

845 Ibid

846 Ibid

847 Trento, Joseph J., *The Secret History of the CIA, New York,* New York, MJF Books, 2001.

848 Douglas, *JFK and the Unspeakable, Why He Died & Why It Matters.*

849 Sheehan, Neil, *The Pentagon Papers: The Secret History of the Vietnam War, New York,* New York, Racehorse Publishing, 2017.

Chapter Fifteen

850 Hinckle, Warren, and Turner, William, *The Fish is Red, The Story of the Secret War Against Castro, New York,* New York, Harper & Row Publishers, 1981.

851 Ibid

852 Ibid

853 Ibid

854 Ibid

855 Ibid

856 Bamford, James, *Body of Secrets, Anatomy of the Ultra-Secret National Security Agency, From the Cold War Through the Dawn of a New Century, New York,* New York, Doubleday, 2001.

857 Ibid

858 Prados, John, *Safe for Democracy: The Secret Wars Of The CIA,* Chicago, Illinois, Ivan R. Dee, 2006.

859 Ibid

860 Russo, Gus, *Live By the Sword, The Secret War Against Castro and the Death of JFK,* Baltimore, Maryland, Bancroft Press, 1998.

861 Ibid

862 Ibid

863 Ibid

864 Ibid

865 Hinckle and Turner, *The Fish is Red, The Story of the Secret War Against Castro.*

866 Russo, *Live By The Sword, The Secret War Against Castro and the Death of JFK.*

Endnotes

867 Mellen, *The Great Game in Cuba, How the CIA Sabotaged Its Own Plot to Unseat Fidel Castro, New York,* New York, Skyhorse Publishing, 2013.

868 Russell, Dick, *The Man Who Knew Too Much, New York,* New York, Carroll & Graf Publishers/Richard Gallen, 1992.

869 Mellen, *The Great Game in Cuba, How the CIA Sabotaged Its Own Plot to Unseat Fidel Castro.*

870 Hinckle and Turner, *The Fish is Red, The Story of the Secret War Against Castro.*

871 Kaiser, David, *The Road to Dallas, The Assassination of John F. Kennedy,* Cambridge, Massachusetts, The Belknap Press of Harvard University Press, 2008.

872 Hinckle and Turner, *The Fish is Red, The Story of the Secret War Against Castro.*

873 Fonzi, Gaeton, *The Last Investigation, New York,* New York, Thunder's Mouth Press, 1993.

874 Summers, Anthony, *Conspiracy, New York,* New York, McGraw-Hill Book Company, 1980.

875 Hinckle and Turner, *The Fish is Red, The Story of the Secret War Against Castro.*

876 Weberman, Alan Jules, The *Oswald Code*, Createspace Independent Publishers, 2014, and *The San Francisco Sunday Examiner article,* June 22, 1975.

877 Albarelli, H.P. Jr., with Sharp, Leslie and Kent, Alan, *Coup in Dallas: The Decisive Investigation into Who Killed JFK, New York,* New York, Skyhorse Publishing, 2021.

878 Kruse, Kevin M., *One Nation Under God, How Corporate America Invented Christian America, New York,* New York, Basic Books, 2015.

879 Mellen, *The Great Game in Cuba, How the CIA Sabotaged Its Own Plot to Unseat Fidel Castro.*

880 Colby, Gerard, with Bennett, Charlotte, *Thy Will Be Done, The Conquest Of The Amazon: Nelson Rockefeller and Evangilism in the Age of Oil, New York,* New York, HarperCollins, 1995.

881 Hurt, Henry, *Reasonable Doubt: An Investigation Into The Assassination Of John F. Kennedy, New York,* New York, Holt, Rinehart and Winston, 1985.

882 *U.S. Curbs Miami Exiles To Prevent Raids on Cuba,* NY Times article, April 1, 1963.

883 Waldron, Lamar, *The Hidden History of the JFK Assassination, The Definitive Account of the Most Controversial Crime of the Twentieth Century,* Berkeley, California, Counterpoint, 2013.

884 Schlesinger, Arthur M. Jr., *Robert Kennedy and His Times,* Boston, Massachusetts, Houghton Mifflin Company, 1978.

885 Russell, *The Man Who Knew Too Much.*

886 Ibid

887 National Archives Document released on March 25, 2010.

888 Ibid

889 Ibid

890 Ibid

891 Waldron, Lamar, and Hartmann, Thom, *Ultimate Sacrifice, John and Robert Kennedy, the Plan for a Coup in Cuba, and the Murder of JFK, New York,* New York, Carroll & Graf Publishers, 2005.

892 Ibid

893 Kaiser, *The Road to Dallas, The Assassination of John F. Kennedy.*

894 Waldron and Hartmann, *Ultimate Sacrifice,* John and Robert Kennedy, *the Plan for a Coup in Cuba, and the Murder of JFK.*

895 Stockton, Bayard, *Flawed Patriot: The Rise And Fall Of CIA Legend Bill Harvey*, Washington DC, Potomac Book, Inc., 2006.

896 Ibid

897 Talbot, David, *The Devil's Chessboard, Allen Dulles, the CIA, and the Rise of America's Secret Government, New York,* New York, Harper Collins Publishers, 2015.

898 Ibid

899 Mellen, *The Great Game in Cuba, How the CIA Sabotaged Its Own Plot to Unseat Fidel Castro.*

900 Hinckle and Turner, *The Fish is Red, The Story of the Secret War Against Castro.*

901 Waldron, *The Hidden History of the JFK Assassination, The Definitive Account of the Most Controversial Crime of the Twentieth Century.*

902 Ibid

903 Ibid

904 Russel, *The Man Who Knew Too Much*.

905 Ibid

906 Kaiser, *The Road to Dallas, The Assassination of John F. Kennedy*.

907 Hinckle and Turner, *The Fish is Red, The Story of the Secret War Against Castro*.

908 Schlesinger, *Robert Kennedy and His Times*.

909 Ibid

910 Ibid

Chapter Sixteen

911 Coudenhove-Kalergi, Richard, *An Idea Conquers The World, New York,* Breat Britain, Purcell & Sons, Ltd., 1954.

912 Chung, Cynthia, *The Empire On Which The Black Sun Never Set: The Birth of International Fascism & Anglo_American Foreign Policy, Canada, 2022.*

913 *CIA-RDP62-00865R000300030004-4 CIA Report, July 22, 1953,* https://www.cia.gov/reading-room/docs/CIA-RDP62-00865R000300030004-4.pdf

914 *Warren Commission Report, Volume XVI,* Exhibit CE97

915 *CIA Report,* July 22, 1953

916 Binder, L. James, Lemnitzer, *A Soldier for His Time,* Washington, D.C., Brassey's, 1997, and https://larouchepub.com/other/2004/3114_terror_legacy.html

917 Stephen Dorril, *MI: Inside the Covert World of her Majesty's Secret Intelligence Service,* Touchstone, 2000.

918 *CIA Department Report,* July 22, 1953.

919 https://en.wikipedia.org/wiki/Hans-Ulrich_Rudel

920 *State Department Report,* July 22, 1953.

921 Ibid

922 Russell, Dick, *The Man Who Knew Too Much, New York,* New York, Carroll & Graf Publishers/Richard Gallen, 1992.

923 Carrozza, Anthony R., *William D. Pawley, The Extraordinary Life of the Adventurer, Entrepreneur, and Diplomat Who Cofounded the Flying Tigers,* Washington D.C., Potomac Books, 2012.

924 Ibid

925 Russell. *The Man Who Knew Too Much*.

926 Ganis, Major Ralph P., USAF, Ret., *The Skorzeny Papers, Evidence for the Plot to Kill JFK, New York,* New York, Skyhorse Publishing, 2018.

927 Russell, *The Man Who Knew Too Much*.

928 Ibid

929 Smith Stuart, *Otto Skorzeny: The Devil's Disciple,* Oxford, England, Ospry Publishing, 2018.

930 Baker, Russ, *Family of Secrets, The Bush Dynasty, America's Invisible Government, and the Hidden History of the Last Fifty Years,* London, United Kingdom, Bloomsbury Publishing, 2009.

931 Albarelli, H.P. Jr., with Sharp, Leslie and Kent, Alan, *Coup in Dallas: The Decisive Investigation into Who Killed JFK, New York,* New York, Skyhorse Publishing, 2021.

932 Escalante, Fabian, *The Secret War: CIA Covert Operations Against Cuba,* 1959-62, Ocean Press, 1995.

933 Baker, *Family Secrets, The Bush Dynasty, America's Invisible Government, and the Hidden History of the Last Fifty Years*.

934 Evica, George Michael, *A Certain Arrogance; The Sacrificing of Lee Harvey Oswald and the Cold War Manipulation of Religious Groups by US Intelligence,* Walterville, Oregon, TrineDay, 2011, and Ganis, *The Skorzeny Papers, Evidence for the Plot to Kill JFK*.

935 Ganis, *The Skorzeny Papers, Evidence for the Plot to Kill JFK*.

936 Ibid

937 Ibid

Endnotes

938 Farrell, Joseph P., *The Third Way, The Nazi International, European Union, and Corporate Fascism,* Kempton, Illinois, Adventure Unlimited Press, 2015.

939 Albarelli, with Sharp and Kent, *Coup in Dallas: The Decisive Investigation into Who Killed JFK.*

940 Ibid, and Ganis, *The Skorzeny Papers, Evidence for the Plot to Kill JFK.*

941 Smith Stuart, *Otto Skorzeny: The Devil's Disciple*

942 The National Security Archive, April 2o, 1963, https://nsarchive.gwu.edu/briefing book/cuban-missile-crisis-nuclear-vault/2023-04-20/jupiter-missiles-and-cuban-missile.

943 Dallek, Robert, *An Unfinished Life: John F. Kennedy, 1917-1963. New York,* New York, Little, Brown and Company, 2003, and https://en.wikipedia.org/wiki/Nassau_Agreement.

944 Albarelli, with Sharp and Kent, *Coup in Dallas: The Decisive Investigation into Who Killed JFK.*

945 DiEugenio, James, *Destiny Betrayed, JFK, Cuba, and the Garrison Case, New York,* New York, Sheridan Square Press, 1992, and Mellen, *A Farewell to Justice*, Jim Garrison, *JFK's Assassination, and the Case That Should Have Changed History.*

946 Mellen, Joan, *Our Man in Haiti, George de Mohrenschildt and the CIA in the Nightmare Republic,* Walterville, Oregon, Trine Day, 2012.

947 Albarelli, with Sharp and Kent, *Coup in Dallas: The Decisive Investigation into Who Killed JFK.*

948 Ganis, *The Skorzeny Papers, Evidence for the Plot to Kill JFK.*

Chapter Seventeen

949 Johnston, James, H., *Murder Inc.: The CIA Under John F. Kennedy,* Lincoln Nebraska, Potomac Books, an imprint of the University of Nebraska Press, 2019.

950 Morley, Jefferson, *Our Man in Mexico: Winston Scott and the Hidden History of the CIA,* Lawrence, Kansas, University Press of Kansas, 2008.

951 Ibid

952 Colby, Gerard, with Bennett, Charlotte, *Thy Will Be Done, The Conquest Of The Amazon: Nelson Rockefeller and Evangilism in the Age of Oil, New York,* New York, HarperCollins, 1995.

953 Ibid

954 Johnston, *Murder Inc.: The CIA Under John F. Kennedy.*

955 Ibid

956 Scott, Peter Dale, *Deep Politics and the Death of JFK,* Berkely, California, University of California Press, 1996.

957 Russell, Dick, *On the Trail of the JFK Assassins, A Groundbreaking Look at America's Most Infamous Conspiracy, New York,* New York, Skyhorse Publishing, 2008

958 Russo, Gus, *Live By the Sword, The Secret War Against Castro and the Death of JFK,* Baltimore, Maryland, Bancroft Press, 1998.

959 Ibid

960 Ibid

961 Ibid

962 Scott, *Deep Politics and the Death of JFK.*

963 Schlesinger, Arthur M. Jr., *Robert Kennedy and His Times,* Boston, Massachusetts, Houghton Mifflin Company, 1978.

964 Scott, *Deep Politics and the Death of JFK.*

965 Morley, *Our Man in Mexico: Winston Scott and the Hidden History of the CIA.*

966 Johnston, *Murder Inc.: The CIA Under John F. Kennedy.*

967 Ibid

968 Dallek, Robert, *Camelot's Court: Inside The Kennedy White House, New York,* New York, Harper Collins, 2013.

969 Johnston, *Murder Inc.: The CIA Under John F. Kennedy.*

970 Ibid

971 Ibid

972 Ibid

973 Ibid

974 Ibid

975 Ibid

976 Ibid

977 Ibid

978 Waldron, Lamar, *The Hidden History of the JFK Assassination, The Definitive Account of the Most Controversial Crime of the Twentieth Century*, Berkeley, California, Counterpoint, 2013.

979 Ibid

980 Ibid

981 Ibid

982 Ibid

983 Ibid

984 Ibid

985 Waldron, Lemar, and Hartmann, Thom, *Legacy of Secrecy: The Long Shadow of the JFK Assassination,* Berkeley, California, Counterpoint Press, 2008.

986 Waldron, *The Hidden History of the JFK Assassination, The Definitive Account of the Most Controversial Crime of the Twentieth Century.*

987 Morley, *Our Man in Mexico: Winston Scott and the Hidden History of the CIA.*

988 Waldron, Lamar, and Hartmann, Thom, *Ultimate Sacrifice, John and Robert Kennedy, the Plan for a Coup in Cuba, and the Murder of JFK, New York,* New York, Carroll & Graf Publishers, 2005.

989 Waldron, *The Hidden History of the JFK Assassination, The Definitive Account of the Most Controversial Crime of the Twentieth Century.*

990 Ibid

991 Ibid

992 Riebling, Mark, *The Wedge: The Secret War Between The FBI and CIA, New York,* New York, Knopf, 1994.

993 Janney, Peter, Mary's Mosaic, *The CIA Conspiracy to Murder John F. Kennedy, Mary Pinchot Meyer, and Their Vision for World Peace, New York,* New York, Skyhorse Publishing, 2012

994 Ibid

995 Waldron, *The Hidden History of the JFK Assassination, The Definitive Account of the Most Controversial Crime of the Twentieth Century.*

996 Waldron and Hartmann, *Ultimate Sacrifice,* John and Robert Kennedy, *the Plan for a Coup in Cuba, and the Murder of JFK.*

997 Ibid

998 Ibid

999 Morley, *Our Man in Mexico: Winston Scott and the Hidden History of the CIA.*

1000 Ibid

Chapter Eighteen

1001 North, Mark, Act of Treason. *The Role of J. Edgar Hoover in the Assassination of President Kennedy*, New York, New York, Carroll & Graf Publishers, Inc., 1991.

1002 Benson, Michael, *Who's Who in the JFK Assassination: An A-to-Z Encyclopedia. New York,* New York, Carol Publishing Group,1993.

1003 Waldron, Lamar, *The Hidden History of the JFK Assassination, The Definitive Account of the Most Controversial Crime of the Twentieth Century*, Berkeley, California, Counterpoint, 2013.

1004 Edward Jay, Legend: *The Secret World of Lee Harvey Oswald, New York,* New York, McGraw-Hill Book Company, 1978.

1005 Garrison, Jim, *On the Trail of the Assassins: One Man's Quest To Solve The Murder Of President Kennedy, New York,* New York, Warner Books, 1988.

1006 Albarelli, H.P. Jr., with Sharp, Leslie and Kent, Alan, *Coup in Dallas: The Decisive Investigation into Who Killed JFK, New York,* New York, Skyhorse Publishing, 2021.

ENDNOTES

1007 Epstein, Legend: *The Secret World of Lee Harvey Oswald.*

1008 *FBI Report from Znew Orleans, January 26, 1963,* from North, Mark, *Act of Treason. The Role of J. Edgar Hoover in the Assassination of President Kennedy.*

1009 *House Select Committee On Assassinations, Vol. 10,* from North, Mark, *Act of Treason. The Role of J. Edgar Hoover in the Assassination of President Kennedy.*

1010 Summers, Anthony, *Conspiracy, New York,* New York, McGraw-Hill Book Company, 1980.

1011 Ibid

1012 *House Select Committee on Assassinations Vol. X,* p.128, from Newman, John, *Oswald and the CIA, New York,* New York, Carroll & Graf Publishers, Inc., 1995.

1013 *House Select Committee on Assassinations Vol. X,* p.219, from Newman, *Oswald and the CIA.*

1014 Mellen, Joan, *A Farewell to Justice,* Jim Garrison, *JFK's Assassination, and the Case That Should Have Changed History, New York,* New York, Skyhorse Publishing, 2013.

1015 Caufield, M.D., Jeffrey H., *General Walker and the Murder of President Kennedy, The Extensive New Evidence of a Radical-Right Conspiracy,* Moreland Press, 2015.

1016 Mellen, *A Farewell to Justice,* Jim Garrison, *JFK's Assassination, and the Case That Should Have Changed History.*

1017 Waldron, Lemar, and Hartmann, Thom, *Legacy of Secrecy: The Long Shadow of the JFK Assassination,* Berkeley, California, Counterpoint Press, 2008.

1018 Carpenter, Donald, H., *Man of a Million Fragments: The True Story of Clay Shaw, Publisher: Donald H. Carpenter, LLC, 2014.*

1019 Summers, *Conspiracy.*

1020 Ibid

1021 Caufield, *General Walker and the Murder of President Kennedy, The Extensive New Evidence of a Radical-Right Conspiracy.*

1022 Russell, Dick, *The Man Who Knew Too Much, New York,* New York, Carroll & Graf Publishers/Richard Gallen, 1992.

1023 Blakey, G. Robert, and Billings, Richard N., *The Plot to Kill the President, Organized Crimed Assassinated J.F.K., The Definitive Story, New York,* New York, Times Books, 1981.

1024 Davis, John H., Mafia Kingfish, *Carlos Marcello and the Assassination of John F. Kennedy, New York,* New York, Penguin Books USA Inc., 1989, and Summers, *Conspiracy.*

1025 Summers, *Conspiracy.*

1026 Caufield, *General Walker and the Murder of President Kennedy, The Extensive New Evidence of a Radical-Right Conspiracy.*

1027 Hinckle, Warren, and Turner, William, *The Fish is Red, The Story of the Secret War Against Castro, New York,* New York, Harper & Row Publishers, 1981.

1028 Weberman, Alan J., and Canfield, Michael, *Coup D'Etat In America,* San Francisco, California, The Third Press, 1975.

1029 Hunt, Howard, E., *Undercover: Memoirs of an American Secret Agent,* Berkeley, California, Berkeley Publishing Corporation, 1974.

1030 Fonzi, Gaeton, *The Last Investigation, New York,* New York, Thunder's Mouth Press, 1993.

1031 Benson, Michael, *Who's Who in the JFK Assassination, An A-to-Z Encyclopedia, New York,* New York, Carol Publishing Group, 1993.

1032 Summers, *Conspiracy.*

1033 Waldron, *The Hidden History of the JFK Assassination, The Definitive Account of the Most Controversial Crime of the Twentieth Century.*

1034 Waldron and Hartmann, *Legacy of Secrecy: The Long Shadow of the JFK Assassination.*

1035 Ibid

1036 Caufield, *General Walker and the Murder of President Kennedy, The Extensive New Evidence of a Radical-Right Conspiracy.*

1037 Summers, *Conspiracy.*

1038 Wise, David, and Ross, Thomas B., *The Invisible Government, New York,* New York, Random House Inc., 1964.

1039 Russell, *The Man Who Knew Too Much*, and Garrison, *On the Trail of the Assassins: One Man's Quest To Solve The Murder Of President Kennedy*.

1040 Fensterwald, *Bernard Jr. Assassination of JFK by Coincidence or Conspiracy?, New York*, New York, Kensington Publishing Corp., 1977

1041 Caufield, *General Walker and the Murder of President Kennedy, The Extensive New Evidence of a Radical-Right Conspiracy*.

1042 Russell, *The Man Who Knew Too Much*, and Hinckle and Turner, *The Fish is Red, The Story of the Secret War Against Castro*.

1043 Hinckle and Turner, *The Fish is Red, The Story of the Secret War Against Castro*.

1044 Benson, *Who's Who in the JFK Assassination: An A-to-Z Encyclopedia*.

1045 Albarelli, H.P. Jr., *A Terrible Mistake, The Murder of Frank Olson and the CIA's Secret Cold War Experiments*, Walterville, Oregon, Trine Day, 2009.

1046 Waldron, *The Hidden History of the JFK Assassination, The Definitive Account of the Most Controversial Crime of the Twentieth Century*.

1047 Davis, Mafia Kingfish, *Carlos Marcello and the Assassination of John F. Kennedy*.

1048 Benson, *Who's Who in the JFK Assassination: An A-to-Z Encyclopedia*.

1049 Davis, Mafia Kingfish, *Carlos Marcello and the Assassination of John F. Kennedy*.

1050 Ibid

1051 Ibid

1052 Ibid

1053 Ibid

1054 Albarelli, with Sharp and Kent, *Coup in Dallas: The Decisive Investigation into Who Killed JFK*.

1055 Newman, *Oswald and the CIA*.

1056 Ibid

1057 Mellen, *A Farewell to Justice*, Jim Garrison, *JFK's Assassination, and the Case That Should Have Changed History*.

1058 Caufield, *General Walker and the Murder of President Kennedy, The Extensive New Evidence of a Radical-Right Conspiracy*.

Chapter Nineteen

1059 Caufield, M.D., Jeffrey H., *General Walker and the Murder of President Kennedy, The Extensive New Evidence of a Radical-Right Conspiracy*, Moreland Press, 2015.

1060 Russell, Dick, *The Man Who Knew Too Much, New York*, New York, Carroll & Graf Publishers/Richard Gallen, 1992.

1061 Newman, John, *Oswald and the CIA, New York*, New York, Carroll & Graf Publishers, Inc., 1995, and North, Mark, Act of Treason, *The Role of J. Edgar Hoover in the Assassination of President Kennedy, New York*, New York, Carroll & Graf Publishers, Inc., 1991.

1062 McMillan, Priscilla Johnson, *Marina & Lee, New York*, New York, Harper & Row, 1977.

1063 Summers, Anthony, *Conspiracy, New York*, New York, McGraw-Hill Book Company, 1980.

1064 North, Act of Treason, *The Role of J. Edgar Hoover in the Assassination of President Kennedy*.

1065 Caufield, M.D., Jeffrey H., *General Walker and the Murder of President Kennedy, The Extensive New Evidence of a Radical-Right Conspiracy*

1066 McMillan, *Marina & Lee*.

1067 Albarelli, H.P. Jr., with Sharp, Leslie and Kent, Alan, *Coup in Dallas: The Decisive Investigation into Who Killed JFK, New York*, New York, Skyhorse Publishing, 2021.

1068 *Oswald letter to Vincent Lee, Warren Commission Report Vol. XX*, Lee exhibit 4, p. 518-521.

1069 Newman, *Oswald and the CIA*.

1070 Ibid

1071 Ibid

1072 Ibid

1073 Ibid

ENDNOTES

1074 Kaiser, David, *The Road to Dallas, The Assassination of John F. Kennedy*, Cambridge, Massachusetts, The Belknap Press of Harvard University Press, 2008.

1075 North, Act of Treason, *The Role of J. Edgar Hoover in the Assassination of President Kennedy*.

1076 Summers, *Conspiracy*.

1077 *Warren Commission Report Vol. XVIII*, Exhibit no. 986, p. 520-525.

1078 *Warren Commission Report Vol. XVI*, Exhibit no. 90.

1079 Johnston, James, H., *Murder Inc.: The CIA Under John F. Kennedy*, Lincoln Nebraska, Potomac Books, an imprint of the University of Nebraska Press, 2019.

1080 Hurt, Henry, *Reasonable Doubt, New York*, New York, Rinehart and Winston, 1985.

1081 Summers, *Conspiracy*

1082 *FBI letter, April 6, 1964, Warren Commission Report Vol. XXVI*, exhibit 2718, p.92-99.

1083 Garrison, Jim, *On the Trail of the Assassins: One Man's Quest to Solve the Murder of President Kennedy, New York*, New York, Warner Books, 1988.

1084 Caufield, *General Walker and the Murder of President Kennedy, The Extensive New Evidence of a Radical-Right Conspiracy*.

1085 Mellen, Joan, *A Farewell to Justice, Jim Garrison, JFK's Assassination, and the Case That Should Have Changed History, New York*, New York, Skyhorse Publishing, 2013.

1086 Valentine, Douglas, *The Strength of the Wolf, The Secret History of America's War on Drugs*, London, England, Verso, 2004.

1087 Garrison, *On the Trail of the Assassins: One Man's Quest to Solve the Murder of President Kennedy*.

1088 Albarelli, with Sharp and Kent, *Coup in Dallas: The Decisive Investigation into Who Killed J JFK*.

1089 Ibid

1090 Caufield, *General Walker and the Murder of President Kennedy, The Extensive New Evidence of a Radical-Right Conspiracy*.

1091 Mellen, *A Farewell to Justice, Jim Garrison, JFK's Assassination, and the Case That Should Have Changed History*.

1092 Carpenter, Donald, H., *Man of a Million Fragments: The True Story of Clay Shaw*, Publisher: Donald H. Carpenter, LLC, 2014.

1093 Mellen, *A Farewell to Justice, Jim Garrison, JFK's Assassination, and the Case That Should Have Changed History*.

1094 Carpenter, *Man of a Million Fragments: The True Story of Clay Shaw*, Publisher: Donald H. Carpenter, LLC, 2014.

1095 Russell, Dick, *On the Trail of the JFK Assassins, A Groundbreaking Look at America's Most Infamous Conspiracy, New York*, New York, Skyhorse Publishing, 2008.

1096 Corsi, Jerome R., P.H.D., *Who Really Killed Kennedy?, 50 Years Later, Stunning New Revelations about the JFK Assassination*, Washington, D.C., WND Books, 2013.

1097 *Warren Commission Report Vol. XXII*, Exhibit no. 1414, from Weberman, Alan J., and Canfield, Michael, *Coup D'Etat In America, San Francisco*, California, The Third Press, 1975, and Scheim, David E., *Contract On America, The Mafia Murder of President John F. Kennedy, New York*, New York, Shapolsky Publishers, Inc., 1988.

1098 Summers, *Conspiracy*

1099 Newman, *Oswald and the CIA*, and Russell, *The Man Who Knew Too Much*.

1100 Summers, *Conspiracy*

1101 Newman, *Oswald and the CIA*.

1102 Hinckle, Warren, and Turner, William, *The Fish Is Red, The Story of the Secret War Against Castro, New York*, New York, Harper & Row, 1981.

1103 Russell, *The Man Who Knew Too Much*.

1104 Russo, Gus, *Live By the Sword, The Secret War Against Castro and the Death of JFK*, Baltimore, Maryland, Bancroft Press, 1998.

1105 Warren Commission document 1066.612; 8897.506, from Russell, *The Man Who Knew Too Much*.

1106 *Oswald letter*, August 1, 1963, from *Oswald: the Secret Files*, Las Vegas, Nevada, Goldstein & Associates, Inc., 1992.

613

LAST RESORT BEYOND LAST RESORT

1107 Summers, *Conspiracy*

1108 Blakey, G. Robert, and Billings, Richard N., *The Plot to Kill the President, Organized Crimed Assassinated J.F.K., The Definitive Story, New York,* New York, Times Books, 1981.

1109 Weberman and Canfield, *Coup D' Etat In America.*

1110 Scheim, David E., *Contract On America, The Mafia Murder of President John F. Kennedy.*

1111 Waldron, Lamar, and Hartmann, Thom, *Ultimate Sacrifice, John and Robert Kennedy, the Plan for a Coup in Cuba, and the Murder of JFK, New York,* New York, Carroll & Graf Publishers, 2005.

1112 Albarelli, H.P. Jr., with Sharp and Kent, *Coup in Dallas: The Decisive Investigation into Who Killed JFK.*

1113 Kantor, Seth, *The Ruby Cover-Up, New York,* New York, Kensington Pub Corp, 1992.

1114 Kantor, *The Ruby Cover-up,* and Scheim, *Contract on America, The Mafia Murder of President John F. Kennedy.*

1115 Kantor, *The Ruby Cover-Up.*

1116 Scheim, *Contract on America, The Mafia Murder of President John F. Kennedy,* and North, Act of Treason, *The Role of J. Edgar Hoover in the Assassination of President Kennedy.*

1117 Kantor, *The Ruby Cover-Up.*

1118 Ibid

1119 Marrs, Jim, *Crossfire, The Plot That Killed Kennedy, New York,* New York, Carroll & Graf Publishers, Inc., 1989, and Summers, Anthony, *Conspiracy, New York,* New York, McGraw-Hill Book Company, 1980.

1120 Scheim, *Contract on America, The Mafia Murder of President John F. Kennedy.*

1121 Russell, *The Man Who Knew Too Much.*

Chapter Twenty

1122 Albarelli, H.P. Jr., with Sharp, Leslie and Kent, Alan, *Coup in Dallas: The Decisive Investigation into Who Killed JFK, New York,* New York, Skyhorse Publishing, 2021.

1123 Russell, Dick, *The Man Who Knew Too Much, New York,* New York, Carroll & Graf Publishers, 1992.

1124 Benson, Michael, *Who's Who in the JFK: Assassination, An A-to-Z Encyclopedia, New York,* New York, Carol Publishing Group, 1993.

1125 Garrison, Jim, *On the Trail of the Assassins: One Man's Quest To Solve The Murder Of President Kennedy, New York,* New York, Warner Books, 1988.

1126 Russell, *The Man Who Knew Too Much.*

1127 Ibid

1128 Douglass, James W., *JFK and the Unspeakable, Why He Died and Why it Matters,* Marknoll, New York, Orbis Books, 2014.

1129 Summers, Anthony, *Conspiracy, New York,* New York, McGraw-Hill Book Company, 1980.

1130 Russell, *The Man Who Knew Too Much.*

1131 Ibid

1132 Newman, John, *Oswald and the CIA, New York,* New York, Carroll & Graf Publishers, Inc., 1995.

1133 *Warren Commission Report Volume X*, Carlos Bringuier testimony, April 7 & 8, 1964..

1134 Newman, *Oswald and the CIA.*

1135 Weberman, Alan Jules, The *Oswald Code,* Createspace Independent Publishers, 2014, and *The San Francisco Sunday Examiner article, June 22, 1975.*

1136 Ibid

1137 Ibid

1138 Russell, *The Man Who Knew Too Much.*

1139 Mellen, Joan, *A Farewell to Justice,* Jim Garrison, *JFK's Assassination, and the Case That Should Have Changed History, New York,* New York, Skyhorse Publishing, 2013.

1140 Caufield, M.D., Jeffrey H., *General Walker and the Murder of President Kennedy, The Extensive New Evidence of a Radical-Right Conspiracy*, Moreland Press, 2015.

1141 Summers, *Conspiracy.*

Endnotes

1142 Mellen, *A Farewell to Justice, Jim Garrison, JFK's Assassination, and the Case That Should Have Changed History.*

1143 Newman, *Oswald and the CIA.*

1144 Ibid

1145 Ibid

1146 Morrow, Robert, *First Hand Knowledge, How I Participated in the CIA-Mafia Murder of President Kennedy, New York,* New York, Shapolsky Publishers, Inc., 1992.

1147 Russell, *The Man Who Knew Too Much.*

1148 Ibid

1149 *Memo to Jim Garrison from Andrew J. Sciambra, interview with Miguel Cruz,* March 19, 1967, from Russell, *The Man Who Knew Too Much.*

1150 Mellen, *A Farewell to Justice, Jim Garrison, JFK's Assassination, and the Case That Should Have Changed History.*

1151 Ibid

1152 Ibid

1153 Ibid and Benson, *Who's Who in the JFK: Assassination, An A-to-Z Encyclopedia.*

1154 Newman, *Oswald and the CIA.*

1155 Ibid

1156 Caufield, M.D., Jeffrey H., *General Walker and the Murder of President Kennedy, The Extensive New Evidence of a Radical-Right Conspiracy.*

1157 Weberman, *The Oswald Code.*

1158 NARA RIF # 124-90137-10079.

1159 Ibid

1160 Caufield, M.D., Jeffrey H., *General Walker and the Murder of President Kennedy, The Extensive New Evidence of a Radical-Right Conspiracy.*

1161 Albarelli, with Sharp and Kent, Alan, *Coup in Dallas: The Decisive Investigation into Who Killed JFK.*

Chapter Twenty-One

1162 Albarelli, H.P. Jr., with Sharp, Leslie and Kent, Alan, *Coup in Dallas: The Decisive Investigation into Who Killed JFK, New York,* New York, Skyhorse Publishing, 2021.

1163 Ibid and North, Mark, Act of Treason, *The Role of J. Edgar Hoover in the Assassination of President Kennedy, New York,* New York, Carroll & Graf Publishers, Inc., 1991.

1164 Waldron, Lamar, and Hartmann, Thom, *Ultimate Sacrifice, John and Robert Kennedy, the Plan for a Coup in Cuba, and the Murder of JFK, New York,* New York, Carroll & Graf Publishers, 2005

1165 Albarelli, with Shar and Kent, *Coup in Dallas: The Decisive Investigation into Who Killed JFK.*

1166 Carpenter, Donald, H., *Man of a Million Fragments: The True Story of Clay Shaw,* Publisher: Donald H. Carpenter, LLC, 2014.

1167 Newman, John, *Oswald and the CIA, New York,* New York, Carroll & Graf Publishers, Inc., 1995.

1168 Caufield, M.D., Jeffrey H., *General Walker and the Murder of President Kennedy, The Extensive New Evidence of a Radical-Right Conspiracy,* Moreland Press, 2015.

1169 Haslam, Edward T., *Dr. Mary's Monkey: How the Unsolved Murder of a Doctor, a Secret in New Orleans and Cancer-Causing Monkey Viruses Are Linked to Lee Harvey, the JFK Assassination and Emerging Global Epidemics,* Walterville, Oregon, Trine Day, 2015.

1170 Newman, *Oswald and the CIA.*

1171 Kaiser, David, *The Road to Dallas, The Assassination of John F. Kennedy,* Cambridge, Massachusetts, The Belknap Press of Harvard University Press, 2008.

1172 Newman, *Oswald and the CIA,* and McMillan, Priscilla Johnson, *Marina & Lee,* New York, New York, Harper & Row, 1977.

1173 *Report of the Warren Commission on the Assassination of President Kennedy, New York,* New York, Bantam Books, 1964.

1174 Newman, *Oswald and the CIA,* and Fensterwald, Bernard Jr., *Assassination of JFK by Coincidence or Conspiracy?, New York,* New York, Kensington Publishing Corp., 1977.

1175 *Warren Commission Report ,Vol. XIX*. p.577 and Vol. XX. p.270.

1176 Caufield, *General Walker and the Murder of President Kennedy, The New Evidence of a Radical-Right Conspiracy*.

1177 Ibid

1178 LaFontaine, Ray and Mary, Oswald Talked, *The New Evidence in the JFK Assassination,* Gretna, Louisiana, Pelican Publishing Company, 1996.

1179 Caufield, *General Walker and the Murder of President Kennedy, The New Evidence of a Radical-Right Conspiracy*.

1180 Ibid

1181 Summers, Anthony, *Conspiracy, New York,* New York, McGraw-Hill Book Company, 1980, and LaFontaine, Oswald Talked, *The New Evidence in the JFK Assassination*.

1182 *House Select Committee Assassinations Report,* p. 142-143, from Hurt, Henry, *Reasonable Doubt, New York,* New York, Rinehart and Winston, 1985.

1183 Ibid

1184 Ibid

1185 Albarelli, H.P. Jr., *A Secret Order, Investigating the High Strangeness and Synchronicity in the JFK Assassination,* Walterville, Oregon, Trine Day, 2013.

1186 Ibid

1187 Albarelli, with Sharp and Kent, Alan, *Coup in Dallas: The Decisive Investigation into Who Killed JFK*.

1188 Albarelli, *A Secret Order, Investigating the High Strangeness and Synchronicity in the JFK Assassination*.

1189 Russell, Dick, *The Man Who Knew Too Much, New York,* New York, Carroll & Graf Publishers/Richard Gallen, 1992.

1190 Ibid and Morrow, Robert, *First Hand Knowledge, How I Participated in the CIA-Mafia Murder of President Kennedy, New York,* New York, Shapolsky Publishers, Inc., 1992.

1191 Fensterwald, *Assassination of JFK by Coincidence or Conspiracy?*

1192 Russell, *The Man Who Knew Too Much*.

1193 Ibid

1194 Albarelli, with Sharp and Kent, Alan, *Coup in Dallas: The Decisive Investigation into Who Killed JFK*.

1195 Summers, *Conspiracy*.

1196 Albarelli, *A Secret Order, Investigating the High Strangeness and Synchronicity in the JFK Assassination*.

1197 Mellen, Joan, *A Farewell to Justice, Jim Garrison, JFK's Assassination, and the Case That Should Have Changed History, New York,* New York, Skyhorse Publishing, 2013.

1198 Fensterwald, Bernard Jr., *Assassination of JFK by Coincidence or Conspiracy?*

1199 Mellen, Joan, *A Farewell to Justice, Jim Garrison, JFK's Assassination, and the Case That Should Have Changed History*

1200 Baker, Judyth Vary, Me & Lee, *How I Came To Know, Love And Lose Lee Harvey Oswald,* Walterville, Oregon, Trine Day, 2011.

1201 Caufield, *General Walker and the Murder of President Kennedy, The New Evidence of a Radical-Right Conspiracy*.

1202 Garrison, Jim, *On The Trail Of The Assassins, New York,* New York, Warner Books, 1988.

1203 Fonzi, Gaeton, *The Last Investigation, New York,* New York, Thunder's Mouth Press, 1993.

1204 Hurt, *Reasonable Doubt*.

1205 Ibid

1206 Summers, *Conspiracy*.

Chapter Twenty-Two

1207 Waldron, Lamar, and Hartmann, Thom, *Ultimate Sacrifice, John and Robert Kennedy, the Plan for a Coup in Cuba, and the Murder of JFK, New York,* New York, Carroll & Graf Publishers, 2005, and New York Times article, *Oswald Made a Visit In September to Mexico,* November 25, 1963.

ENDNOTES

1208 Newman, John, *Oswald and the CIA, New York,* New York, Carroll & Graf Publishers, Inc., 1995.

1209 Summers, Anthony, *Conspiracy, New York,* New York, McGraw-Hill Book Company, 1980.

1210 Mellen, Joan, *A Farewell to Justice,* Jim Garrison, *JFK's Assassination, and the Case That Should Have Changed History, New York,* New York, Skyhorse Publishing, 2013.

1211 Russell, Dick, *The Man Who Knew Too Much, New York,* New York, Carroll & Graf Publishers/Richard Gallen, 1992.

1212 *Warren Commission Report Vol. XI,* p. 214-15.

1213 *Warren Commission Report Vol. XI,* p. 215-17.

1214 *Oswald: The Secret Files,* Las Vegas, Nevada, Goldstein & Associates Inc., 1992.

1215 Ibid

1216 Hosty, James P. Jr., *Assignment Oswald, New York,* New York, Arcade Publishing, 1996.

1217 Albarelli, H.P. Jr., with Sharp, Leslie and Kent, Alan, *Coup in Dallas: The Decisive Investigation into Who Killed JFK, New York,* New York, Skyhorse Publishing, 2021.

1218 Ibid

1219 Ibid

1220 Ibid

1221 Fonzi, Gaeton, *The Last Investigation, New York,* New York, Thunder's Mouth Press, 1993.

1222 Ibid

1223 LaFontaine, Ray and Mary, Oswald Talked, *The New Evidence in the JFK Assassination,* Gretna, Louisiana, Pelican Publishing Company, 1996.

1224 Ibid and Blakey, G. Robert, and Billings, Richard N., *The Plot To Kill the President, Organized Crime Assassinated J.F.K., New York,* New York, Times Books, 1981.

1225 Summers, *Conspiracy.*

1226 Russell, *The Man Who Knew Too Much.*

1227 *House Select Committee on Assassinations document* 180-10101-10283, *Memorandum from Gaeton Fonzi to Dave Marston,* April 4, 1976, from Fonzi, *The Last Investigation.*

1228 Blakey, G. Robert, and Billings, Richard N., *The Plot to Kill the President,* Organized Crimed Assassinated J.F.K., *The Definitive Story, New York,* New York, Times Books, 1981.

1229 Weberman, Alan J., and Canfield, Michael, *Coup D'Etat In America,* San Francisco, California, The Third Press, 1975.

1230 Kaiser, David, *The Road to Dallas, The Assassination of John F. Kennedy,* Cambridge, Massachusetts, The Belknap Press of Harvard University Press, 2008.

1231 Ibid

1232 Caufield, M.D., Jeffrey H., *General Walker and the Murder of President Kennedy, The Extensive New Evidence of a Radical-Right Conspiracy,* Moreland Press, 2015.

1233 Albarelli, with Sharp and Kent, *Coup in Dallas: The Decisive Investigation into Who Killed J JFK.*

1234 Kaiser, *The Road to Dallas, The Assassination of John F. Kennedy.*

1235 Albarelli, H.P. Jr., *A Secret Order, Investigating the High Strangeness and Synchronicity in the JFK Assassination,* Walterville, Oregon, Trine Day, 2013.

1236 Russell, Dick, *On the Trail of the JFK Assassins, A Groundbreaking Look at America's Most Infamous Conspiracy, New York,* New York, Skyhorse Publishing, 2008.

1237 Ibid

1238 Ibid

1239 LaFontaine, Oswald Talked, *The New Evidence in the JFK Assassination.*

1240 Ibid

1241 Kaiser, *The Road to Dallas, The Assassination of John F. Kennedy.*

1242 Ibid

1243 *Warren Commission Report Vol. XI*

1244 Oswald Talked, *The New Evidence in the JFK Assassination.*

1245 Rappleye, Charles and Becker, *Ed, All American Mafioso, New York,* New York, Doubleday Books, 1991.

Last Resort Beyond Last Resort

1246 Fonzi, *The Last Investigation.*

1247 Summers, *Conspiracy*

1248 Russell, *The Man Who Knew Too Much.*

1249 Ibid

1250 Ibid

1251 Phillips, David Atlee, *The Night Watch: 25 Years Of Peculiar Service, New York,* New York, Atheneum Books, 1977.

1252 Fonzi, *The Last Investigation.*

1253 Ibid

Chapter Twenty-Three

1254 Russell, Dick, *On the Trail of the JFK Assassins, A Groundbreaking Look at America's Most Infamous Conspiracy, New York,* New York, Skyhorse Publishing, 2008.

1255 Albarelli, H.P. Jr., with Sharp, Leslie and Kent, Alan, *Coup in Dallas: The Decisive Investigation into Who Killed JFK, New York,* New York, Skyhorse Publishing, 2021.

1256 Newman, John M., *Where Angels Tread Lightly: The Assassination of President Kennedy, Volume I,* North Charleston, South Carolina, CreateSpace Independent Publishing Platform, 2017.

1257 Albarelli, with Sharp and Kent, *Coup in Dallas: The Decisive Investigation into Who Killed JFK.*

1258 Newman, *Where Angels Tread Lightly: The Assassination of President Kennedy.*

1259 Russell, Dick, *The Man Who Knew Too Much, New York,* New York, Carroll & Graf Publishers/Richard Gallen, 1992.

1260 Albarelli, with Sharp and Kent, *Coup in Dallas: The Decisive Investigation into Who Killed JFK.*

1261 Russell, *The Man Who Knew Too Much.*

1262 Ibid

1263 Armstrong, John, *Harvey and Lee: How The CIA Framed Oswald,* Berkeley, California, Quasar Books, 2003.

1264 De Mey, Flip, *The Lee Harvey Oswald Files: Why The CIA Killed Kennedy,* Belgium, Lannoo Publishing, 2016.

1265 Armstrong, *Harvey and Lee: How The CIA Framed Oswald.*

1266 Scott, Peter Dale, *Deep Politics and the Death of JFK,* Berkely, California, University of California Press, 1996.

1267 Russell, *The Man Who Knew Too Much.*

1268 Morley, Jefferson, *Our Man in Mexico: Winston Scott and the Hidden History of the CIA,* Lawrence, Kansas, University Press of Kansas, 2008.

1269 Newman, John, *Oswald and the CIA, New York,* New York, Carroll & Graf Publishers, Inc., 1995.

1270 De Mey, *The Lee Harvey Oswald Files: Why The CIA Killed Kennedy,* and Barron, John, *KGB: The Secret Work of Soviet Secret Agents, New York,* New York, Reader's Digest Association Publishers, 1974.

1271 Nechiporenko, Col. Oleg Maximovich, *Passport to Assassination: The Never-Before-Told Story Of Lee Harvey Oswald By The KGB Colonel Who Knew Him, New York,* New York, Carol Publishing Group, 1993.

1272 Ibid

1273 Newman, *Oswald and the CIA.*

1274 Summers, Anthony, *Conspiracy, New York,* New York, McGraw-Hill Book Company, 1980.

1275 Nechiporenko, *Passport to Assassination: The Never-Before-Told Story Of Lee Harvey Oswald By The KGB Colonel Who Knew Him.*

1276 Ibid

1277 Ibid

1278 Scott, Peter Dale, *Deep Politics and the Death of JFK,* Berkely, California, University of California Press, 1996.

1279 Summers, *Conspiracy.*

618

ENDNOTES

1280 Ibid

1281 Newman, *Oswald and the CIA.*

1282 Russo, Gus, *Live By the Sword, The Secret War Against Castro and the Death of JFK,* Baltimore, Maryland, Bancroft Press, 1998.

1283 Ibid

1284 Waldron, Lemar, and Hartmann, Thom, *Legacy of Secrecy: The Long Shadow of the JFK Assassination,* Berkeley, California, Counterpoint Press, 2008.

1285 Russo, *Live By the Sword, The Secret War Against Castro and the Death of JFK.*

1286 Albarelli, with Sharp and Kent, *Coup in Dallas: The Decisive Investigation into Who Killed JFK.*

1287 Newman, *Oswald and the CIA.*

1288 Albarelli, H.P. Jr., *A Secret Order, Investigating the High Strangeness and Synchronicity in the JFK Assassination,* Walterville, Oregon, Trine Day, 2013.

1289 Albarelli, with Sharp and Kent, *Coup in Dallas: The Decisive Investigation into Who Killed JFK.*

1290 Ibid

1291 Ibid

1292 Newman, *Oswald and the CIA.*

1293 Ibid

1294 Ibid and Russell, *The Man Who Knew Too Much.*

1295 Russell, *The Man Who Knew Too Much.*

1296 Albarelli, *A Secret Order, Investigating the High Strangeness and Synchronicity in the JFK Assassination.*

1297 Raab, Selwyn, *Five Families: The Rise, Decline, And Resurgence Of America's Most Powerful Mafia Empires, New York,* New York, Thomas Dunne Books, 2016.

1298 Albarelli, *A Secret Order, Investigating the High Strangeness and Synchronicity in the JFK Assassination.*

1299 Russell, *The Man Who Knew Too Much.*

1300 Newman, *Oswald and the CIA.*

1301 Ibid

1302 Russell, *The Man Who Knew Too Much.*

1303 Russell, Dick, *On the Trail of the JFK Assassins, A Groundbreaking Look at America's Most Infamous Conspiracy.*

1304 Ibid

1305 Armstrong, *Harvey and Lee: How The CIA Framed Oswald.*

1306 Newman, John M., *Countdown to Darkness: The Assassination Of President Kennedy, Volume II,* North Charleston, South Carolina, CreateSpace Independent Publishing Platform, 2017.

1307 Ibid

1308 Armstrong, *Harvey and Lee: How The CIA Framed Oswald.*

1309 Shenon, Philip, *A Cruel and Shocking Act: The Secret History of the Kennedy Assassination, New York,* New York, Henry Holt & Company, 2013.

1310 Armstrong, *Harvey and Lee: How The CIA Framed Oswald.*

1311 Ibid

1312 Russell, *The Man Who Knew Too Much.*

1313 Summers, *Conspiracy.*

1314 Ibid

1315 Newman, *Oswald and the CIA.*

1316 Russell, *The Man Who Knew Too Much.*

1317 Newman, *Oswald and the CIA.*

1318 Russell, Dick, *On the Trail of the JFK Assassins, A Groundbreaking Look at America's Most Infamous Conspiracy.*

1319 Albarelli, with Sharp and Kent, *Coup in Dallas: The Decisive Investigation into Who Killed JFK.*

619

Chapter Twenty-Four

1320 https://www.britannica.com/event/Profumo-affair

1321 Cohen, Andrew, *Two Days in June, John F. Kennedy and the 48 Hours That Made History,* Canada, McClelland & Stewart, 2014.

1322 Albarelli, H.P. Jr., with Sharp, Leslie and Kent, Alan, *Coup in Dallas: The Decisive Investigation into Who Killed JFK, New York,* New York, Skyhorse Publishing, 2021.

1323 Cohen, *Two Days in June, John F. Kennedy and the 48 Hours That Made History.*

1324 Ibid

1325 Ibid

1326 Ibid

1327 Dallek, Robert, *Camelot's Court: Inside The Kennedy White House, New York,* New York, Harper Collins, 2013.

1328 Dallek, Robert, *An Unfinished Life: John F. Kennedy, 1917-1963. New York,* New York, Little, Brown and Company, 2003.

1329 Janney, Peter, *Mary's Mosaic, The CIA Conspiracy to Murder John F. Kennedy, Mary Pinchot Meyer, and Their Vision for World Peace, New York,* New York, Skyhorse Publishing, 2012.

1330 Caufield, M.D., Jeffrey H., *General Walker and the Murder of President Kennedy, The Extensive New Evidence of a Radical-Right Conspiracy,* Moreland Press, 2015.

1331 Ibid

1332 Cohen, *Two Days in June, John F. Kennedy and the 48 Hours That Made History.*

1333 Waldron, Lamar, *The Hidden History of the JFK Assassination, The Definitive Account of the Most Controversial Crime of the Twentieth Century,* Berkeley, California, Counterpoint, 2013.

1334 Colby, Gerard, with Bennett, Charlotte, *Thy Will Be Done, The Conquest Of The Amazon: Nelson Rockefeller and Evangilism in the Age of Oil, New York,* New York, HarperCollins, 1995.

1335 Williams, Charles, *Adenauer: The Father of the New Germany, New York,* New York, John Wiley & Sons, Inc, 2000.

1336 Newman, John M., *JFK and Vietnam, New York,* New York, Warner Books, 1992.

1337 Douglas, James, W., *JFK and the Unspeakable, Why He Died & Why It Matters,* Maryknoll, New York, Orbis Books, 2008.

1338 Dallek, Robert, *Camelot's Court: Inside The Kennedy White House, New York,* New York, Harper Collins, 2013.

1339 Dallek, Robert, *An Unfinished Life: John F. Kennedy, 1917-1963. New York,* New York, Little, Brown and Company, 2003.

1340 Ibid

1341 Dallek, Robert, *An Unfinished Life: John F. Kennedy, 1917-1963. New York,* New York, Little, Brown and Company, 2003.

1342 Dallek, *An Unfinished Life: John F. Kennedy, 1917-1963.*

1343 Schlesinger, Arthur M. Jr., *Robert Kennedy and His Times,* Boston, Massachusetts, Houghton Mifflin Company, 1978.

1344 Ibid,

1345 Trento, Joseph J., *The Secret History of the CIA, New York,* New York, MJF Books, 2001.

1346 Woods, Randall B., *The Shadow Warrior: William Egan Colby and the CIA, New York,* New York, Basic Books, 2013.

1347 Halberstam, *David, Nun's Act A Surprise, New York Times article,* August 15, 1963.

1348 Bird, Kai, The Color of Truth, *McGeorge Bundy and William Bundy: Brothers In Arms, New York,* New York, Simon & Schuster, 1998, O'Leary, Brad, and Seymour, Lee, *Triangle of Death: The Shocking Truth About the Role of South Vietnam and the French Mafia in the Assassination of JFK,* Nashville, Tennessee, W Publishing Group, 2003, and Sheehan, Neil, *The Pentagon Papers: The Secret History of the Vietnam War, New York,* New York, Racehorse Publishing, 2017.

1349 O'Leary and Seymour, *Triangle of Death: The Shocking Trith About the Role of South Vietnam and the French Mafia in the Assassination of JFK.*

ENDNOTES

1350 McCoy, Alfred W., *The Politics of Heroin: CIA Complicity in the Global Drug Trade,* Chicago, Illinois, 2003, and O'Leary and Seymour, *Triangle of Death: The Shocking Truth About the Role of South Vietnam and the French Mafia in the Assassination of JFK.*

1351 Douglas, *JFK and the Unspeakable, Why He Died & Why It Matters.*

1352 Ibid

1353 Hersh, Seymour M., *The Dark Side of Camelot,* Boston, Massachusetts, Little Brown And Company, 1997, Clarke, Thurston, *JFK's Last Hundred Days, The Transformation of a Man and the Emergence of a Great President, New York,* New York, The Penguin Press, 2013, and O'Leary and Seymour, *Triangle of Death: The Shocking Trith About the Role of South Vietnam and the French Mafia in the Assassination of JFK.*

1354 Clarke, *JFK's Last Hundred Days, The Transformation of a Man and the Emergence of a Great President.*

1355 Trento, *The Secret History of the CIA.*

1356 Colby, Gerard, with Bennett, Charlotte, *Thy Will Be Done, The Conquest Of The Amazon: Nelson Rockefeller and Evangilism in the Age of Oil, New York,* New York, HarperCollins, 1995.

1357 Marrs, Jim, *Crossfire, The Plot That Killed Kennedy, New York,* New York, Carroll & Graf Publishers, Inc., 1989, and Summers, Anthony, *Conspiracy, New York,* New York, McGraw-Hill Book Company, 1980.

1358 Prouty, L. Fletcher, *JFK, The CIA, Vietnam And The Plot to Assassinate John F. Kennedy, New York,* New York, Carol Publishing Group, 1992.

1359 Halberstam, David, *The Best And the Brightest, New York,* New York, Ballentine Boks, 1993.

1360 Colby, William, and Forbath, Peter, *Honorable Men: My Life in the CIA, New York,* New York, Simon & Schuster, 1978, and Miller, Nathan, *Spying for America, the Hidden History of U.S. Intelligence, New York,* New York, Paragon House, 1989.

1361 Powers, Thomas, *The Man Who Kept the Secrets, Richard Helms and the CIA, New York,* New York, Alfred A. Knopf, 1979, and Albarelli, with Sharp and Kent, *Coup in Dallas: The Decisive Investigation into Who Killed JFK.*

1362 Marrs, *Crossfire, The Plot That Killed Kennedy,* and Russell, Dick, *The Man Who Knew Too Much, New York,* New York, Carroll & Graf Publishers/Richard Gallen, 1992.

1363 McCoy, *The Politics of Heroin: CIA Complicity in the Global Drug Trade.*

1364 Douglas, *JFK and the Unspeakable, Why He Died & Why It Matters.*

1365 O'Leary and Seymour, *Triangle of Death: The Shocking Trith About the Role of South Vietnam and the French Mafia in the Assassination of JFK.*

1366 Ibid

Chapter Twenty-Five

1367 Johnston, James, H., *Murder Inc.: The CIA Under John F. Kennedy,* Lincoln Nebraska, Potomac Books, an imprint of the University of Nebraska Press, 2019.

1368 Ibid

1369 Thomas, Evan, *The Very Best Men, Four Who Dared: The Early Years Of The CIA, New York,* New York, Simon & Schuster, 1995.

1370 Kaiser, David, *The Road to Dallas, The Assassination of John F. Kennedy,* Cambridge, Massachusetts, The Belknap Press of Harvard University Press, 2008.

1371 Johnston, *Murder Inc.: The CIA Under John F. Kennedy,* and Russo, Gus, *Live By the Sword, The Secret War Against Castro and the Death of JFK,* Baltimore, Maryland, Bancroft Press, 1998.

1372 Johnston, *Murder Inc.: The CIA Under John F. Kennedy,* and Schlesinger, Arthur M. Jr., *Robert Kennedy and His Times,* Boston, Massachusetts, Houghton Mifflin Company, 1978.

1373 Russo, *Live By the Sword, The Secret War Against Castro and the Death of JFK.*

1374 Scott, Peter Dale, *Deep Politics and the Death of JFK,* Berkely, California, University of California Press, 1996.

1375 Russell, Dick, *On the Trail of the JFK Assassins, A Groundbreaking Look at America's Most Infamous Conspiracy, New York,* New York, Skyhorse Publishing, 2008.

1376 Waldron, Lamar, and Hartmann, Thom, *Ultimate Sacrifice, John and Robert Kennedy, the Plan for a Coup in Cuba, and the Murder of JFK, New York,* New York, Carroll & Graf Publishers, 2005.

1377 Newman, John M., *Countdown to Darkness: The Assassination Of President Kennedy, Volume II,* North Charleston, South Carolina, CreateSpace Independent Publishing Platform, 2017.

1378 Waldron and Hartmann, *Ultimate Sacrifice,* John and Robert Kennedy, *the Plan for a Coup in Cuba, and the Murder of JFK.*

1379 Russell, *On the Trail of the JFK Assassins, A Groundbreaking Look at America's Most Infamous Conspiracy,* and Albarelli, H.P. Jr., with Sharp, Leslie and Kent, Alan, *Coup in Dallas: The Decisive Investigation into Who Killed JFK, New York,* New York, Skyhorse Publishing, 2021.

1380 Russell, *On the Trail of the JFK Assassins, A Groundbreaking Look at America's Most Infamous Conspiracy.*

1381 Ibid

1382 *Henry Hecksher info,* from https://spartacus-educational.com/

1383 Ibid

1384 Newman, John M., *Countdown to Darkness: The Assassination Of President Kennedy, Volume II.*

1385 Ibid

1386 Ibid

1387 Ibid

1388 Russo, *Live By the Sword, The Secret War Against Castro and the Death of JFK.*

1389 LaFontaine, Ray and Mary, Oswald Talked, *The New Evidence in the JFK Assassination,* Gretna, Louisiana, Pelican Publishing Company, 1996.

1390 Waldron and Hartmann, *Ultimate Sacrifice,* John and Robert Kennedy, *the Plan for a Coup in Cuba, and the Murder of JFK.*

1391 Johnston, *Murder Inc.: The CIA Under John F. Kennedy.*

1392 Russell, Dick, *The Man Who Knew Too Much, New York,* New York, Carroll & Graf Publishers/Richard Gallen, 1992.

1393 Bamford, James, *Body of Secrets, Anatomy of the Ultra-Secret National Security Agency, From the Cold War Through the Dawn of a New Century, New York,* New York, Doubleday, 2001.

1394 Talbot, David, Brothers, *The Hidden History of the Kennedy Years. New York,* New York, Free Press, 2007.

1395 Douglas, James, W., *JFK and the Unspeakable, Why He Died & Why It Matters,* Maryknoll, New York, Orbis Books, 2008.

1396 Clarke, Thurston, *JFK's Last Hundred Days, The Transformation of a Man and the Emergence of a Great President, New York,* New York, The Penguin Press, 2013.

1397 Johnston, *Murder Inc.: The CIA Under John F. Kennedy,* and Scott, *Deep Politics and the Death of JFK.*

1398 Thomas, *The Very Best Men, Four Who Dared: The Early Years Of The CIA.*

1399 Johnston, *Murder Inc.: The CIA Under John F. Kennedy.*

1400 Thomas, *The Very Best Men, Four Who Dared: The Early Years Of The CIA.*

1401 Riebling, Mark, *The Wedge: The Secret War Between The FBI and CIA, New York,* New York, Knopf, 1994.

1402 Russo, *Live By the Sword, The Secret War Against Castro and the Death of JFK.*

1403 Waldron, Lamar, *The Hidden History of the JFK Assassination, The Definitive Account of the Most Controversial Crime of the Twentieth Century,* Berkeley, California, Counterpoint, 2013.

1404 Scott, *Deep Politics and the Death of JFK.*

1405 Waldron, Lemar, and Hartmann, Thom, *Legacy of Secrecy: The Long Shadow of the JFK Assassination,* Berkeley, California, Counterpoint Press, 2008.

1406 Russo, *Live By the Sword, The Secret War Against Castro and the Death of JFK.*

1407 Trento, Joseph J., *The Secret History of the CIA, New York,* New York, MJF Books, 2001, and Thomas, *The Very Best Men, Four Who Dared: The Early Years Of The CIA.*

1408 Thomas, *The Very Best Men, Four Who Dared: The Early Years Of The CIA.*

1409 Russo, *Live By the Sword, The Secret War Against Castro and the Death of JFK.*

Endnotes

1410 Johnston, *Murder Inc.: The CIA Under John F. Kennedy.*

1411 Horne, Sir Alistaire, *A Savage War of Peace: Algeria 1954-1962, New York,* New York, Viking Press Publishing Company, 1978.

1412 Ibid

1413 Chung, Cynthia, *The Empire On Which The Black Sun Never Set: The Birth of International Fascism & Anglo-American Foreign Policy,* Canada, 2022.

1414 Ibid

1415 Orbach, Danny, *Fugitives: A History of Nazi Mercenaries During the Cold War, New York,* New York, Pegasus Books, 2022.

1416 Dorril, Stephen, *Blackshirt: Sir Oswald Mosley and British Fascism,* London, England, Viking Press, 2006.

1417 Smith Stuart, *Otto Skorzeny: The Devil's Disciple,* Oxford, England, Ospry Publishing, 2018.

1418 Dorril, *Blackshirt: Sir Oswald Mosley and British Fascism.*

1419 Orbach, *Fugitives: A History of Nazi Mercenaries During the Cold War, New York.*

1420 Horne, *A Savage War of Peace: Algeria 1954-1962.*

1421 Sully, Francois, *Age of the Guerilla, The New Warfare, New York,* New York, Parents' Magazine Press, 1968.

1422 https://en.wikipedia.org/wiki/Paris_massacre_of_1961

1423 Horne, *A Savage War of Peace: Algeria 1954-1962.*

1424 Mellen, Joan, *Our Man in Haiti, George de Mohrenschildt and the CIA in the Nightmare Republic,* Walterville, Oregon, Trine Day, 2012.

1425 Albarelli, H.P. Jr., with Sharp, Leslie and Kent, Alan, *Coup in Dallas: The Decisive Investigation into Who Killed JFK, New York,* New York, Skyhorse Publishing, 2021.

1426 Ganser, Daniele, *Nato's Secret Armies: Operation Gladio and Terrorism in Western Europe,* London, England, Frank Cass, 2005.

1427 Chung, *The Empire On Which The Black Sun Never Set: The Birth of International Fascism & Anglo-American Foreign Policy.*

1428 Ibid

1429 Russell, *The Man Who Knew Too Much.*

Chapter Twenty-Six

1430 North, Mark, Act of Treason. *The Role of J. Edgar Hoover in the Assassination of President Kennedy, New York,* New York, Carroll & Graf Publishers, Inc., 1991.

1431 McMillan, Priscilla Johnson, *Marina & Lee, New York,* New York, Harper & Row, 1977.

1432 Armstrong, John, *Harvey and Lee: How The CIA Framed Oswald,* Berkeley, California, Quasar Books, 2003.

1433 Summers, Anthony, *Conspiracy, New York,* New York, McGraw-Hill Book Company, 1980.

1434 Hurt, Henry, *Reasonable Doubt, New York,* New York, Rinehart and Winston, 1985.

1435 Armstrong, John, *Harvey and Lee: How The CIA Framed Oswald.*

1436 White, Ricky, J. Gary Shaw & Brian K. Edwards, *Admitted Assassin, Roscoe White and the Murder of President Kennedy,* Canyon Lake, Texas, Peniel Unlimited, LLC, 2023.

1437 Horne, Sir Alistaire, *A Savage War of Peace: Algeria 1954-1962, New York,* New York, Viking Press Publishing Company, 1978.

1438 Armstrong, *Harvey and Lee: How The CIA Framed Oswald,* and Albarelli, H.P. Jr., with Sharp, Leslie and Kent, Alan, *Coup in Dallas: The Decisive Investigation into Who Killed JFK, New York,* New York, Skyhorse Publishing, 2021.

1439 *Warren Commission document 205.646ff* from Russell, Dick, *The Man Who Knew Too Much,* Carroll & Graf Publishers/Richard Gallen, 1992, page 781.

1440 Jones, J. Harry Jr., *The Minutemen,* Garden City, New York, Doubleday & Company, 1968.

1441 North, Act of Treason. *The Role of J. Edgar Hoover in the Assassination of President Kennedy.*

1442 Scheim, David E., Contract On America, *The Mafia Murder of President John F. Kennedy, New York,* New York, Shapolsky Publishers, Inc., 1988.

Last Resort Beyond Last Resort

1443 LaFontaine, Ray and Mary, Oswald Talked, *The New Evidence in the JFK Assassination*, Gretna, Louisiana, Pelican Publishing Company, 1996.

1444 Benson, Michael, *Who's Who in the JFK Assassination, New York,* New York, Carol Publishing Group, 1993, and LaFontaine, Oswald Talked, *The New Evidence in the JFK Assassination.*

1445 Caufield, M.D., Jeffrey H., *General Walker and the Murder of President Kennedy, The Extensive New Evidence of a Radical-Right Conspiracy*, Moreland Press, 2015.

1446 McMillan, *Marina & Lee*, and Armstrong, *Harvey and Lee: How The CIA Framed Oswald.*

1447 De Mey, Flip, *The Lee Harvey Oswald Files: Why The CIA Killed Kennedy*, Belgium, Lannoo Publishing, 2016.

1448 Armstrong, *Harvey and Lee: How The CIA Framed Oswald.*

1449 Blakey, G. Robert, and Billings, Richard N., *The Plot To Kill The President, Organized Crime Assassinated J.F.K., New York,* New York, Times Books, 1981.

1450 Albarelli, with Sharp and Kent, *Coup in Dallas: The Decisive Investigation into Who Killed JFK.*

1451 Mellen, Joan, *Our Man in Haiti, George de Mohrenschildt and the CIA in the Nightmare Republic,* Walterville, Oregon, Trine Day, 2012.

1452 Armstrong, *Harvey and Lee: How The CIA Framed Oswald.*

1453 Russell, *The Man Who Knew Too Much.*

1454 New York Times article, *Stevenson Booed and Hit By Dallas Demonstrators,* October 25, 1963.

1455 Armstrong, *Harvey and Lee: How The CIA Framed Oswald.*

1456 Caufield, *General Walker and the Murder of President Kennedy, The Extensive New Evidence of a Radical-Right Conspiracy.*

1457 Ibid and Russell, *The Man Who Knew Too Much.*

1458 Waldron, Lamar, *The Hidden History of the JFK Assassination, The Definitive Account of the Most Controversial Crime of the Twentieth Century*, Berkeley, California, Counterpoint, 2013.

1459 Albarelli, with Sharp and Kent, *Coup in Dallas: The Decisive Investigation into Who Killed JFK*, and Lateer, J.W., *The Three Barons: The Organizational Chart of the Kennedy Assassination,* Walterville, Oregon, Trine Day, 2017.

1460 Russell, *The Man Who Knew Too Much*, and Caufield, *General Walker and the Murder of President Kennedy, The Extensive New Evidence of a Radical-Right Conspiracy.*

1461 FBI report, FBI file No. 100-16601, from *Oswald: The Secret Files,* Las Vegas, Nevada, Goldstein & Associates, Inc., 1992.

1462 Newman, John, *Oswald and the CIA, New York,* New York, Carroll & Graf Publishers, Inc., 1995.

1463 Armstrong, *Harvey and Lee: How The CIA Framed Oswald.*

1464 Albarelli, with Sharp and Kent, *Coup in Dallas: The Decisive Investigation into Who Killed JFK.*

1465 Summers, *Conspiracy.*

1466 Armstrong, *Harvey and Lee: How The CIA Framed Oswald.*

1467 LaFontaine, Oswald Talked, *The New Evidence in the JFK Assassination.*

1468 Albarelli, with Sharp and Kent, *Coup in Dallas: The Decisive Investigation into Who Killed JFK.*

1469 Weberman, Alan Jules, *The Oswald Code*, Createspace Independent Publishers, 2014, and *The San Francisco Sunday Examiner article,* June 22, 1975, and Albarelli, with Sharp and Kent, *Coup in Dallas: The Decisive Investigation into Who Killed JFK.*

1470 North, Act of Treason. *The Role of J. Edgar Hoover in the Assassination of President Kennedy.*

1471 Hosty, James P., *Assignment Oswald, New York,* New York, Arcade Publishing, 1996.

1472 Summers, *Conspiracy.*

1473 Albarelli, with Sharp and Kent, *Coup in Dallas: The Decisive Investigation into Who Killed JFK.*

1474 Russell, *The Man Who Knew Too Much.*

1475 *Warren Commission Report Vol. XVI,* p. 64, and Vol. V, p. 112.

1476 Epstein, Edward Jay, Legend, *The Secret World of Lee Harvey Oswald, New York,* New York, McGraw-Hill Book Company, 1978.

1477 Paine, Ruth, *Warren Commission Testimony,* Washington DC, *Warren Report Volume III,* 1964.

1478 Weberman, *The Oswald Code.*

624

Chapter Twenty-Seven

1479 Caufield, M.D., Jeffrey H., *General Walker and the Murder of President Kennedy, The Extensive New Evidence of a Radical-Right Conspiracy*, Moreland Press, 2015.

1480 Russell, Dick, *The Man Who Knew Too Much, New York,* New York, Carroll & Graf Publishers, 1992.

1481 LaFontaine, Ray and Mary, Oswald Talked, *The New Evidence in the JFK Assassination,* Gretna, Louisiana, Pelican Publishing Company, 1996.

1482 North, Mark, *Betrayal in Dallas: LBJ, The Pearl Street Mafia, And The Murder Of President Kennedy, New York,* New York, Skyhorse Publishing, 2011.

1483 Russell, Russell, *The Man Who Knew Too Much.*

1484 LaFontaine, Ray and Mary, Oswald Talked, *The New Evidence in the JFK Assassination*

1485 Popkin, Richard H., *The Second Oswald, New York,* New York, Avon Books, 1966.

1486 Summers, Anthony, *Conspiracy, New York,* New York, McGraw-Hill Book Company, 1980.

1487 Popkin, *The Second Oswald.*

1488 Ibid

1489 Ibid

1490 Russo, Gus, *Live By the Sword, The Secret War Against Castro and the Death of JFK*, Baltimore, Maryland, Bancroft Press, 1998.

1491 North, Mark, Act of Treason. *The Role of J. Edgar Hoover in the Assassination of President Kennedy, New York,* New York, Carroll & Graf Publishers, Inc., 1991.

1492 Waldron, Lamar, *The Hidden History of the JFK Assassination, The Definitive Account of the Most Controversial Crime of the Twentieth Century*, Berkeley, California, Counterpoint, 2013.

1493 Weberman, Alan J., and Canfield, Michael, *Coup D' Etat In America,* San Francisco, California, The Third Press, 1975.

1494 *Secret Service Report File* No. CO-2-34, 030, November 26-29, 1963.

1495 *Warren Commission Document* 1085U (FBI file May 26, 1964) from Russell, *The Man Who Knew Too Much.*

1496 Ibid

1497 Weberman and Canfield, *Coup D 'Etat In America.*

1498 Russell, *The Man Who Knew Too Much.*

1499 *FBI report,* March 27, 1964

1500 Caufield, *General Walker and the Murder of President Kennedy, The Extensive New Evidence of a Radical-Right Conspiracy.*

1501 Russell, *The Man Who Knew Too Much*, and Herbst, Walter, *It Did Not Start With JFK: The Decades Of Events That Led To The Assassination Of John F. Kennedy, Volume One,* Harrisburg, Pennsylvania, Sunbury Press, 2021.

1502 Riebling, Mark, *Church of Spies: The Pope's Secret War Against Hitler, New York,* New York, Basic Books, 2015.

1503 Williams, Paul L., Operation Gladio, *The Unholy Alliance Between The Vatican, The CIA, And The Mafia,* Amherst, New York, Prometheus Books, 2015, and Cooney, John, *The American Pope: The Life and Times of Francis Cardinal Spellman, New York,* New York, Times Books, 1984.

1504 Herbst, *It Did Not Start With JFK: The Decades Of Events That Led To The Assassination Of John F. Kennedy, Volume One.*

1505 Russell, *The Man Who Knew Too Much.*

Chapter Twenty-Eight

1506 Clarke, Thurston, *JFK's Last Hundred Days, The Transformation of a Man and the Emergence of a Great President, New York,* New York, The Penguin Press, 2013.

1507 Ibid

1508 Ibid

1509 Ibid

1510 Douglas, James, W., *JFK and the Unspeakable, Why He Died & Why It Matters*, Maryknoll, New York, Orbis Books, 2008.

1511 Johnston, James, H., *Murder Inc.: The CIA Under John F. Kennedy*, Lincoln Nebraska, Potomac Books, an imprint of the University of Nebraska Press, 2019.

1512 Kaiser, David, *The Road to Dallas, The Assassination of John F. Kennedy*, Cambridge, Massachusetts, The Belknap Press of Harvard University Press, 2008.

1513 Johnston, *Murder Inc.: The CIA Under John F. Kennedy*.

1514 Swanson, Michael, The War State, *The Cold War Origins of the Military-Industrial Complex and the Power Elite, 1945-1963,* North Charleston, South Carolina, CreateSpace Independent Publishing Platform, 2013.

1515 Johnston, *Murder Inc.: The CIA Under John F. Kennedy*.

1516 Clarke, *JFK's Last Hundred Days, The Transformation of a Man and the Emergence of a Great President*.

1517 Fursenko, Aleksandr, and Naftali, Timothy, *One Hell of a Gamble, The Secret History of the Cuban Missile Crisis, Khrushchev, Castro & Kennedy, 1958-1964, New York,* New York, W.W. Norton & Company, 1997.

Chapter Twenty-Nine

1518 Benson, Michael, *Who's Who in the JFK Assassination, New York,* New York, Carol Publishing Group, 1993

1519 LaFontaine, Ray and Mary, Oswald Talked, *The New Evidence in the JFK Assassination*, Gretna, Louisiana, Pelican Publishing Company, 1996.

1520 Scott, Peter Dale, *Deep Politics and the Death of JFK,* Berkely, California, University of California Press, 1996.

1521 LaFontaine, Ray and Mary, Oswald Talked, *The New Evidence in the JFK Assassination*.

1522 Summers, Anthony, *Conspiracy, New York,* New York, McGraw-Hill Book Company, 1980.

1523 Newman, John, *Oswald and the CIA, New York,* New York, Carroll & Graf Publishers, Inc., 1995.

1524 De Mey, Flip, *The Lee Harvey Oswald Files: Why The CIA Killed Kennedy,* Belgium, Lannoo Publishing, 2016.

1525 *Investigation of the Assassination of John F. Kennedy,* Appendix To Hearings, *Before The Select Committee On Assassinations of the U.S. House Of Representatives,* Sixty-Fifth Congress, Washington DC, Government Printing Office, 1979.

1526 Baker, Russ, *Family of Secrets: The Bush Dynasty, the Powerful Forces That Put It in the White House and What Their Influence Means for America,* London, UK, Bloomsbury Press, 2008, and Albarelli, H.P. Jr., with Sharp, Leslie and Kent, Alan, *Coup in Dallas: The Decisive Investigation into Who Killed JFK, New York,* New York, Skyhorse Publishing, 2021.

1527 Schlesinger, Arthur M. Jr., *Robert Kennedy and His Times,* Boston, Massachusetts, Houghton Mifflin Company, 1978.

1528 Manchester, William, *Death of a President: November 1963, New York,* New York, Harper & Row, 1967.

1529 Ibid

1530 Summers, *Conspiracy*.

1531 Ibid

1532 Manchester, *Death of a President: November 1963*, and Groden, Robert J., *The Killing of a President: The Complete Photographic Record of the JFK Assassination,* Studio Publishing, 1993.

1533 Groden, *The Killing of a President: The Complete Photographic Record of the JFK Assassination*.

1534 Manchester, *Death of a President: November 1963*.

1535 Ibid

1536 Epstein, Edward Jay, Legend, *The Secret World of Lee Harvey Oswald, New York*, New York, McGraw-Hill Book Company, 1978.

1537 Armstrong, John, *Harvey and Lee: How The CIA Framed Oswald,* Berkeley, California, Quasar Books, 2003.

ENDNOTES

1538 DiEugenio, James, *The JFK Assassination, New York,* New York, Skyhorse Publishing, 2016.

1539 Hurt, Henry, *Reasonable Doubt, New York,* New York, Rinehart and Winston, 1985.

1540 Benson, *Who's Who in the JFK Assassination.*

1541 Ibid

1542 Hurt, *Reasonable Doubt.*

1543 Rowland, Barbara, *Warren Commission Testimony,* Washington DC, *Warren Report Volume VI,* 1964, and Rowland, Arnold, *Warren Commission Testimony,* Washington DC, *Warren Report Volume II,* 1964.

1544 Benson, *Who's Who in the JFK Assassination.*

1545 Ibid

1546 Summers, *Conspiracy.*

1547 *FBI Report,* December 12, 1963, and Summers, *Conspiracy.*

1548 *Who's Who and Clay Shaw Trial Testimony.*

1549 Benson, *Who's Who in the JFK Assassination, and Worrell,* James, *Warren Commission Testimony,* Washington DC, Warren Report Volume II, 1964.

1550 Summers, *Conspiracy.*

1551 Ibid

1552 Ibid

1553 Ibid

1554 Ibid

1555 Ibid

1556 DiEugenio, *The JFK Assassination.*

1557 Armstrong, *Harvey and Lee: How The CIA Framed Oswald, and DiEugenio, The JFK Assassination.*

1558 Benson, *Who's Who in the JFK Assassination.*

1559 Russell, *The Man Who Knew Too Much.*

1560 *Report of the Warren Commission on the Assassination of President Kennedy: The Dramatic Official Answer to Who Killed Kennedy, New York,* New York, Bantam Books, 1964.

1561 Baker, Marion, *Warren Commission Testimony,* March 25, 1964, Washington DC, *Warren Report Volume III,* 1964.

1562 Ernest, Barry, *The Girl on the Stairs: The Search for a Missing Witness to the JFK Assassination,* New Orleans, Louisiana, Pelican Publishing, 2013.

1563 Armstrong, *Harvey and Lee: How The CIA Framed Oswald.*

1564 Ibid

1565 Ibid

1566 Benson, *Who's Who in the JFK Assassination.*

1567 Marrs, Jim, *Crossfire, The Plot That Killed Kennedy, New York,* New York, Carroll & Graf Publishers, Inc., 1989.

1568 Witt, Louis Steven, *House Select Committee on Assassinations Testimony,* September 25, 1978, Washington DC, HSCA Volume IV, 1979.

1569 Ibid

1570 Summers, *Conspiracy.*

1571 Ibid

1572 Caufield, M.D., Jeffrey H., *General Walker and the Murder of President Kennedy, The Extensive New Evidence of a Radical-Right Conspiracy,* Moreland Press, 2015.

1573 Albarelli, with Sharp and Kent, *Coup in Dallas: The Decisive Investigation into Who Killed JFK.*

1574 Hougan, Jim, *Spooks: The Haunting of America – The Private Use of Secret Agents, New York,* New York, William Morrow And Company, Inc., 1978.

1575 Albarelli, with Sharp and Kent, *Coup in Dallas: The Decisive Investigation into Who Killed JFK.*

1576 Smith Stuart, *Otto Skorzeny: The Devil's Disciple,* Oxford, England, Ospry Publishing, 2018.

1577 Jones, J. Harry Jr., *The Minutemen,* Garden City, New York, Doubleday & Company, 1968.

1578 Marrs, *Crossfire, The Plot That Killed Kennedy.*

627

1579 Ibid

1580 Summers, *Conspiracy*.

1581 Ibid

1582 Weberman, Alan J., and Canfield, Michael, *Coup D'Etat In America,* San Francisco, California, The Third Press, 1975

1583 Cameron, Steve, *The Deputy Interviews: The True Story Of JFK Assassination Witness And Former Dallas Deputy Sheriff Roger Dean Caig,* Steve Cameron Productions, 2019.

1584 Peterson, Sara, and Zachry, K.W., *The Lone Star Speaks: Untold Texas Stories about the JFK Assassination,* Baltimore Maryland, Bancroft Press, 2020.

1585 Peterson and Zachry, The Lone Star Speaks: *Untold Texas Stories about the JFK Assassination,* and Fannin, Gary, *The Innocence of Oswald: 50+ Years Of Lies, Deception & Deceit In The Murders Of President John F. Kennedy & Officer J.D. Tippit, 2015.*

1586 Armstrong, *Harvey and Lee: How The CIA Framed Oswald.*

1587 Summers, *Conspiracy.*

1588 Benson, *Who's Who in the JFK Assassination.*

Chapter Thirty

1589 Marrs, Jim, *Crossfire, The Plot That Killed Kennedy, New York,* New York, Carroll & Graf Publishers, Inc., 1989.

1590 *Report of the Warren Commission on the Assassination of President Kennedy: The Dramatic Official Answer to Who Killed Kennedy, New York,* New York, Bantam Books, 1964.

1591 Ibid

1592 Meek, Jeffrey L., *The JFK Files: Pieces of the Assassination Puzzle,* Judsonia, Arkansas, Raven's Inn Press, 2023.

1593 Armstrong, John, *Harvey and Lee: How The CIA Framed Oswald,* Berkeley, California, Quasar Books, 2003.

1594 Marrs, *Crossfire, The Plot That Killed Kennedy.*

1595 Ibid

1596 Waldron, Lemar, and Hartmann, Thom, *Legacy of Secrecy: The Long Shadow of the JFK Assassination,* Berkeley, California, Counterpoint Press, 2008.

1597 Jones, J. Harry Jr., *The Minutemen,* Garden City, New York, Doubleday & Company, 1968.

1598 Marrs, *Crossfire, The Plot That Killed Kennedy.*

1599 Armstrong, *Harvey and Lee: How The CIA Framed Oswald.*

1600 Marrs, *Crossfire, The Plot That Killed Kennedy.*

1601 Ibid

1602 Armstrong, *Harvey and Lee: How The CIA Framed Oswald.*

1603 https://www.youtube.com/watch?v=4n64fFUCSv0.

1604 Hosty, James P., *Assignment Oswald, New York,* New York, Arcade Publishing, 1996.

1605 https://www.dictionary.com/browse/clip-someone-s-wings.

1606 Albarelli, H.P. Jr., with Sharp, Leslie and Kent, Alan, *Coup in Dallas: The Decisive Investigation into Who Killed JFK, New York,* New York, Skyhorse Publishing, 2021.

1607 Armstrong, *Harvey and Lee: How The CIA Framed Oswald.*

1608 Marrs, *Crossfire, The Plot That Killed Kennedy.*

1609 Hosty, *Assignment Oswald.*

1610 Summers, Anthony, *Conspiracy, New York,* New York, McGraw-Hill Book Company, 1980.

1611 Ibid

1612 Scott, Peter Dale, *Oswald, Mexico, and Deep Politics, Revelations from CIA Records on the Assassination of JFK, New York,* New York, Skyhorse Publishing, 2013.

1613 Evans, Roland, and Novak, Robert, *Lyndon B. Johnson: The Exercise of Power, New York,* New York, Harper & Row, 1976.

ENDNOTES

1614 Summers, Anthony, Official and Confidential, *The Secret Life of J. Edgar Hoover, New York,* New York, G.P. Putnam and Sons, 1993.

1615 North, Mark, *Betrayal in Dallas: LBJ, The Pearl Street Mafia, And The Murder Of President Kennedy, New York,* New York, Skyhorse Publishing, 2011.

Chapter Thirty-One

1616 Dallek, Robert, *An Unfinished Life: John F. Kennedy, 1917-1963. New York,* New York, Little, Brown and Company, 2003.

1617 https://thehill.com/homenews/administration/312605-schumer-trump-being-really-dumb-by-going-after-intelligence-community/

1618 Bevins, Vincent, *The Jakarta Method: Washington's Anticommunist Crusade & the Mass Murder Program that Shaped Our World, New York,* New York, Public Affairs, 2020.

1619 Riebling, Mark, *The Wedge: The Secret War Between The FBI and CIA, New York,* New York, Knopf, 1994.

1620 Anderson, Scott, *The Quiet Americans: Four CIA Spies At The Dawn Of The Cold War – A Tragedy In Three Acts, New York,* New York, Doubleday Publishing, 2020.

1621 *FBI Memorandum,* September 27, FBI Record No. 1963, 124-10201-10416,

1622 *Frank Sturgis House Select Committee on Assassinations Testimony,* March 20, 1978, HSCA Record No. 180-10088-10086.

1623 Newman, John M., *Countdown to Darkness: The Assassination Of President Kennedy, Volume II,* North Charleston, South Carolina, CreateSpace Independent Publishing Platform, 2017.

1624 *FBI Memorandum,* September 27, 1963, 124-10201-10416, from Thomas, Ralph, *The Roscoe White Story: Grassy Knoll Assassin Or Hoax?,* Kindle Edition, 2018.

1625 *Secret Service Memorandum* dated November 26-29, 1963, Secret Service File No. CO-2- 34,030.

1626 Russell, Dick, *The Man Who Knew Too Much, New York,* New York, Carroll & Graf Publishers, 1992.

1627 Ibid

1628 Ibid

1629 Waldron, Lemar, and Hartmann, Thom, *Legacy of Secrecy: The Long Shadow of the JFK Assassination,* Berkeley, California, Counterpoint Press, 2008.

1630 Waldron, Lamar, *The Hidden History of the JFK Assassination, The Definitive Account of The Most Controversial Crime of the Twentieth Century,* Berkeley, California, Counterpoint, 2013.

1631 Talbot, David, Brothers, *The Hidden History of the Kennedy Years. New York,* New York, Free Press, 2007.

1632 Waldron and Hartmann, *Legacy of Secrecy: The Long Shadow of the JFK Assassination.*

1633 North, Mark, *Betrayal in Dallas: LBJ, The Pearl Street Mafia, And The Murder Of President Kennedy, New York,* New York, Skyhorse Publishing, 2011.

1634 Talbot, Brothers, *The Hidden History of the Kennedy Years.*

1635 *Warren Commission Report, Volume XVI,* Exhibit CE97.

1636 *State Department Report,* July 22, 1953.

1637 Horne, Sir Alistaire, *A Savage War of Peace: Algeria 1954-1962, New York,* New York, Viking Press Publishing Company, 1978.

1638 Bird, The Chairman, *John McCloy The Making of the American Establishment.*

1639 Ibid

1640 Talbot, David, *The Devil's Chessboard, Allen Dulles, the CIA, and the Rise of America's Secret Government, New York,* New York, Harper Collins Publishers, 2015.

1641 Kruger, Henrik, *The Great Heroin Coup: Drugs, Intelligence & International Fascism,* Walterville, Oregon, Trine Day Publishing, 2016.

1642 Talbot, The Devil's Chessboard, *Allen Dulles, the CIA, and the Rise of America's Secret Government.*

1643 Chung, Cynthia, *The Empire On Which The Black Sun Never Set: The Birth of International Fascism & Anglo_American Foreign Policy,* Canada, 2022.

1644 Albarelli, with Sharp and Kent, *Coup in Dallas: The Decisive Investigation into Who Killed JFK.*

1645 Kempe, *Berlin 1961: Kennedy, Khrushchev, And The Most Dangerous Place On Earth.*

1646 Ibid

1647 Smith Stuart, *Otto Skorzeny: The Devil's Disciple*, Oxford, England, Ospry Publishing, 2 2018.

1648 Russell, *The Man Who Knew Too Much*.

1649 Russo, *Live By the Sword, The Secret War Against Castro and the Death of JFK*.

1650 Waldron and Hartmann, *Legacy of Secrecy: The Long Shadow of the JFK Assassination*.

1651 Talbot, The Devil's Chessboard, *Allen Dulles, the CIA, and the Rise of America's Secret Government*.

1652 Bevins, *The Jakarta Method: Washington's Anticommunist Crusade & the Mass Murder Program that Shaped Our World*.

1653 Smith Stuart, *Otto Skorzeny: The Devil's Disciple*, Oxford, England, Ospry Publishing,   2018.

Index

A

Abelow, Martin Samuel, 338
Abernathy, Joe, 509
Acheson, Dean, 23, 54, 58, 60, 61, 70, 71, 157, 190, 288
Adamcik, John Paul, 472
Adams, Robert, 128, 473, 480
Adams, Don, 366, 488
Adams, Victoria, 524
Adenauer, Konrad, 70, 83, 295, 433, 565, 575
Adoula, Cyrille, 117, 119
Adzhubei, Aleksei, 22, 196
Aguilar, Manuel, 281
Aguilera, Leopoldo, Jr., 353
Ahern, James, 174
Alba, Adrian, 340, 341
Alberu, Luis, 417, 418
Alderman, Harold Gordon, 337
Alderson, Lawrence, 99, 100, 102
Aleman, Jose, Jr., 176, 455
Alentado Leon, Antonio, 392
Alexander, Bill, 549
Alexander, Vereen, 366
Allen, George, 159
Allen, Robert S., 46
Allison, Jim, 476
Almeida, Juan, 307-310, 452, 455-458, 554, 558, 560, 564
American Nazi Party, 54, 218, 233, 241, 242, 248
Amin, Idi, 10
Amini, Ali, 293
Amworld/Omega Plan, 1, 2, 5, 10, 18, 89, 156, 269, 275, 276, 307, 312, 314, 365, 370, 371, 392, 442-451, 461, 464, 465, 553-558, 560, 564, 570
  Warnings of, 495
Anderson, Admiral George, 189, 191, 194
Anderson, Clark, 353
Andreotti, Giulio, 294
Andrews, Dean, 351, 356, 362, 363, 401, 413
Andrews, James A., 546
Angel and Leopoldo, 350-352, 356, 367, 368, 378, 392, 393, 400, 402

Angers, Robert J., 387
Angleton, James, 8, 11, 17, 84, 89, 94, 98, 166, 215, 274, 309, 311, 313, 340, 409, 448, 462, 464, 474, 567, 557, 560, 561, 565-567, 570
  HT/Lingual and American defectors, 39, 51
  anti-Communist, 80, 81, 82, 206, 258, 501, 573, 574
  assassinations, 90, 97, 125
  part of Lafitte/Skorzeny JFK assassination team, 129, 183, 276, 296, 315, 316, 329, 347, 351, 353, 367, 447, 463, 473, 475, 545, 558, 569
Angleton, Hugh, 80, 81
Apple, Bob, 541
Arbenz, Jacobo, 96, 566
Arcacha Smith, Sergio, 29, 31, 150, 225, 319-321, 323-325, 332, 343-345, 363, 364, 376, 378
Argoud, Antoine, 459, 566
Arnold, Carolyn, 520, 522
Arnold, Gordon, 518, 530, 531
Arnold, James, 366
Aron, Raymond, 70, 71
Artime, Manuel, 10, 11, 30, 31, 206-208, 225, 226, 276, 280, 282, 298, 300, 301, 304, 305, 307, 310, 311, 370, 443-451, 455, 504, 555, 556-558
Arvad, Inga, 165
Askins, Charles "Boots," 447
Attwood, William, 453, 454, 456
Austin, Frank, 93
Austin, Horace, 357, 358
Ayers, Bradley, 282, 312, 401
Azcue, Eusebio, 410, 412

B

Badeaux, Hubert, 333
Bailey, Virgil, 562
Baker, Bobby, 150, 199, 254, 429, 430
Baker Marrion, 522-524, 536
Ball, George, 68, 73, 146, 437, 439
Ballen, Samuel, 141, 211
Bancroft, Mary, 216
Banister, Guy, 29-31, 39, 53, 150, 297, 316, 320, 321, 323-325, 333, 335, 344, 345, 353, 364, 374, 376, 377, 378, 383, 391, 544, 559, 560
  relationship with Lee Oswald, 29, 219, 315-319, 322, 323, 331, 332, 346, 359, 363, 367, 384, 570
  and Carlos Marcello, 30, 310, 328

631

racist and anti-Communist, 235, 391, 427
and Clay Shaw, 341-343
Banister, Ross, 317
Barham, Patte, 174
Barka, Ben, 101
Barker, Bernard, 30, 95, 149, 156, 273, 276, 279, 308, 310, 313
Barker, William W., Jr., 366
Barnes, Tracy, 8, 17, 30, 33, 84, 92, 93, 96, 97, 102, 124, 125, 140, 150, 185, 206, 253, 254, 273, 276, 291, 321, 352, 377, 380, 395, 440, 448, 463, 477, 485, 557, 560, 561, 565, 573
Barr, Candy, 349
Barrett, Bob, 482, 541, 543
Barron, John, 42
Bartes, Frank, 147, 355, 360, 361, 398
Bastien-Thiry, Jean Marie, 163
Batista, Fulgencio, 8, 26, 30-32, 35, 91, 92, 105, 114, 147, 149, 152, 155, 156, 204, 253, 278, 280, 307, 313, 344, 364, 377, 446, 553, 558
Batista, Laureano, 344
Batista, Victor, 354
Baumler, Tommy, 333
Bay of Pigs, 5, 7, 8, 17, 25-33, 35, 54, 58, 63, 64, 72-74, 90, 96, 103, 107, 138, 139, 144, 151, 180, 203, 204, 212, 252, 268, 273 274, 279, 280, 291, 298, 300, 302, 307, 308, 313, 319, 320, 322-324, 365, 393, 398, 401, 436, 456, 496, 523, 554, 561, 564, 572, 573, 577
Bayo, Eddie, 277
Beasley, Gerald L. Jr., 236
Becham, Thomas, 318, 335, 343
Becker, Edward, 176
Bell, Griffin, 244
Belmont, August, 150
Benson, Joseph G., 474
Bentley, Elizabeth, 80
Bentley, Paul, 541
Benton, Sam, 148, 311
Berle, Adolf A., Jr., 82
Bernhardt, Johannes, 75, 76, 78, 80, 87
Bertaux, Pierre, 81, 82
Betancourt, Romulo Ernesto, 106, 184
Bethel, Paul, 149, 321, 405
Bieck, Robert, 79
Bird, Kai, 22
Bishop, Maurice, 149, 155, 276, 399
Bishop, Willliam, 107, 148, 149, 275, 280, 281, 291, 345, 361, 512
Bissell, Richard, 10, 25, 26, 28, 31, 32, 73, 115, 144, 169, 296, 572

Blanco, Ana Maria, 413
Blankenbaker, Lloyd, W., 338
Bledsoe, Mary, 466, 467, 536, 540
Blough, Roger, 162, 163
Bochelman, Herman, 342
Bogard, Albert, 492, 493
Boggs, Hale, 514
Bogoiavlensky, Valentin, 211
Bolanos, Jose, 174
Bolden, Abraham, 515
Bolshakov, Georgi, 59, 71, 180, 182, 183, 185, 187
Bonsal, Philip, 7, 8
Bookbinder, George, 44
Bookhout, James W., 228
Boone, Eugene, 532
Borja, Isadro, 357
Bosch, Juan, 107, 377
Bosch, Orlando, 147, 204, 281, 345
Boucher, Colonel Jeff W., 152
Bouhe, George, 141
Bouvier, Janet, Lee, 133
Bowen, John Howard, 388, 403, 405-407, 426, 481
Bowers, Lee, 518
Bowles, Chester, 61, 64, 73, 112
Boyd, Harold, 200, 512
Braden, Jim (aka Eugene Hale Brading), 485, 528-530
Bradley, Ben, 429
Braga, George, 150, 151
Braga, Ronny, 150
Brandsetter, Frank, 155, 253, 272, 273, 291, 297, 463, 475, 512
Brantley, Ray, 347
Brengel, Mary, 320
Brennan, Howard, 521
Brentano, Heinrich, 70
Brewer, Johnny, 541, 542, 546
Brinegar, Johhny, 497
Bringuier, Carlos, 353-355, 357, 359-364, 366, 368, 369, 371, 372, 383, 388, 398, 402, 510
Brod, Mario, 166
Broglie, Warren, 88, 418, 421
Bronson, Charles, 521
Brooks, Jerry, 210, 324, 329
Broussard, Ernie, 387
Broutsas, Constantine, 448
Brown, Charles, T., 533
Brown, George, 139
Brown, Herman, 139

INDEX

Brown, J. Harlan, 396
Brown, Morgan, 529
Brown, Pat, 218
Bruce, David, 14, 69
Buckley, William F. Jr., 237
Buick, Robert, 420, 421
Buleni, Dickson, 119
Bundy, McGeorge, 22, 23, 73, 91, 144, 145, 182, 184, 189, 205, 268, 274, 282, 302, 303, 305, 441, 443, 453, 503
Bundy, Vernon, 343
Bundy, William, 23
Bunker, Ellsworth, 161, 162
Burbank, Thomas, 367
Burden, William Armistead Moale, Jr., 108, 109, 111
Burke, Admiral Arleigh, 24, 34, 64, 145, 271, 322
Burkley, George, 571
Burnham, James, 562, 563
Burris, Howard, 186
Burros, Dan, 242
Burroughs, "Butch", 538, 539, 541, 542, 545, 547
Bush, George H.W., 139, 291
Butler, Edward, 333, 371
Butler, Jasper Clayton, 542
Buttari, Edgardo, 365
Butterworth, Alfred T., 376
Byars, Billy, 549
Byrd, Harold, 290

C

Cabell, Charles, 33, 73, 144
Caire, Ronnie, 325, 344
Caldwell, William, 556
Califano, Joseph, 269, 302, 305, 504
Callahan, John, 541
Calomaris, Anthony, 175
Campbell, Allen, 317, 383, 384
Campbell (Exner), Judith, 166-169, 171, 172, 177, 198, 208
Capone, Al, 165
Caracci, Frank, 348
Carbajal, Ruben, 401
Cardona, Jose Miro, 91, 147, 270, 273
Carmen, Jeanne, 171
Carr, Richard, 519, 525, 526
Carr, Waggoner, 509, 548-550
Carroll, Bob, 541
Carter, Cliff, 548
Carter, Marshall S., 184

Carter, Tom, 38
Case, Archie, 174
Cash, Harvey, 407
Castro, Fidel, 7, 8, 15, 18, 25, 27, 32, 35, 106, 111, 145, 148, 150, 156, 179, 182, 203, 217, 248, 271, 273, 277, 278, 283, 287, 291, 298-300, 302, 303, 308, 322, 323, 333, 339, 350, 355, 365, 404, 449, 452, 474, 551-555
    threats against President Kennedy, 3
    spreading revolution, 4
    Bay of Pigs, 28-30, 33
    assassination attempts against, 31, 87-92, 95, 97, 98, 114, 151, 153, 157, 167-169, 190, 309-312, 361, 444
    normalize relations with U.S., 14, 267, 274, 282, 304, 305, 313, 453, 454
    Cuba Missile Crisis deal, 192, 194
Castro, Raul, 151
Castro Alba, Celio, 395, 396
Charles, Clemard, 474, 475
Chaves, Frank, 148
Childs, Marquis, 14, 56
Central Intelligence Agency (CIA), 21, 34, 38, 62, 73, 77, 78, 80, 83, 105, 145, 158, 169, 170, 217, 273, 288, 291, 320, 322, 341, 342, 440, 450, 544, 545, 556
    felt betrayed by JFK, 1, 16, 17, 65, 66
    and Berlin and Germany, 16, 18, 436
    sabotage JFK, 25, 26, 29, 33, 63
    tracking Oswald in Russia, 39, 43-47, 51, 52, 125, 139
    Lumumba Assassination, 109-116
    Castro assassination attempts, 3, 31, 88, 90, 91, 92, 95, 168, 177
    Trujillo assassination, 107
    Missile Crisis, 180-184, 188, 190
    second invasion of Cuba, 156, 206, 267, 270, 279-282, 298, 300, 301, 303-307, 309, 311-313, 370, 371, 443-446, 451, 452, 455-457
    war on Cuba, 27, 28, 30, 84, 147, 151-155, 157, 185, 186, 278, 302
    Oswald in Mexico, 415, 421-426, 478, 479, 567
    Slumberger break in, 323-325
    and Lafiite/Skorzeny group, 84, 296, 297, 455, 544, 545, 560, 564, 565, 567
Challe, Maurice, 296
Chambers, Whitaker, 82
Charles, Clemard, 155
Chase, Gordon, 453
Cheek, Bertha, 471, 472, 540

633

Cheever, Bruce, 305

Cherkasova, Lydia, 41, 42

Cienfuegos, Camilo, 405

Cisneros, Rogelio, 392

Claasen, Fred, 523

Clark, Burnell, 374

Clark (aka Sherbatoff), Gali, 208, 213, 477, 569

Clark, George, 343

Clark, Max, 208, 477

Claunch, Max, 243

Clay, Lucius, 7, 278, 556, 565

Clements, Manning, 38

Climes, Tom, 301

Cobb, June, 88, 95, 98, 149, 156, 213, 214, 223, 272, 273, 276, 321, 340, 361, 365, 379, 394, 463

  in Mexico City, 390, 415, 416, 418, 419

Cogswell, Jack, 475

Cohen, Mickey, 349

Colby, William, 16, 17, 188, 252, 258, 305, 401, 440

Coleman, Walter, 243

Collins, Corrie, 374

Concutelli, Pierluigi, 564

Conein, Lucien, 84, 86, 93, 101, 102, 293, 440

  Vietnam coup, 439, 441, 463, 506

Connally, John, 318, 513, 516

Connally, Nellie, 516

Connell, Lucille, 391, 393, 397

Conner, Hal, 175

Contreras, Oscar, 412, 417

Cooper, Roy, 525, 526

Cornwall, Gary, 490

Corso, Colonel Philip J., 37, 501

Corson, Lieutenant Colonel William R., 84, 158

Costello, Frank, 165, 419

Cottrell, Sterling, 268

Courson, Bill, 541

Courtney, Kent, 352

Coyle, Ed J., 508-510

Crafard, Larry, 479

Craig, Roger, 525, 526, 548

Cram, Cleveland, 409

Creel, Dana, 109

Crichton, Jack, 9, 84, 117, 126, 143, 228, 236, 290-292, 297, 403, 469, 512

Crommelin, Admiral John G., 488, 500

Cronkite, Walter, 433

Crosby, Bing, 170

Crouchet, Erick, 376

Croy, Kenneth H., 543

Crozier, William, 154

Cruz, Miguel, 361, 362

Cuban Missile Crisis, 11, 14

Cuban Revolutionary Council (CRC), 31, 91, 147, 153, 270, 280, 319, 321, 344, 345, 354

Cubela, Rolando, 3, 153, 444, 445, 452, 454-458, 474, 507, 554, 558, 570

Cuesta, Tony, 147, 149, 281

Cullins, John, 40, 41

Cunningham, E.L., 509, 541

Currington, John, 218, 529

Curry, Jesse, 244, 489, 509, 523, 534, 563

Cushman, Colonel Robert, 163

Czeschlak, Jose Moise (aka Jose Marie Andre Mankel), 113

D

D'Agostino, Antoine, 94

D'Amelio, Carlo, 342

Daniel, Jean, 504

Daniels, Hawk, 176

Dannelly, Lee, 387

D'Arco, John, 168

David, Christian, 101, 469

Davidson, Alexi, 126, 127

Davidson, Irving, 150, 254

Davidson, Mary, 233, 235

Davidson, Natasha, 126

Davis, Carolyn, 94, 183, 390, 396, 418, 463, 475

Davis, Edward Michael, 173

Davis, George, 176

Davis, Howard Kenneth, 147, 360

Davis, Jack, 539, 545, 547

Davis, Jimmy, 367

Davis, L.P., 382

Davis, Thomas Eli, 84, 88, 89, 94, 95, 213, 214, 281, 293, 295-297, 316, 319, 321, 347, 377, 389-391, 394, 396, 403, 427, 463, 475, 554

  in Mexico City, 415, 416, 418, 419

Day, J.C., 532, 533, 534

Dayal, Rajeshwar, 112

Deageano, Peter, 382

Dealey, Ted, 57

Dean, Harry, 357

De Brueys, Warren, 331, 332, 355, 356, 358, 362, 364, 490

Decker, Bill, 532, 533, 571

Decker, George Henry, 64

DeCourcy, John, 342

INDEX

Dedon, Bobby, 375

De Gaulle, Charles, 9, 59, 87, 99, 101, 102, 110, 163, 221, 287, 292, 294-296, 324, 342, 461, 462, 464, 562, 565, 568, 569, 577, 578

de Goicochea Sanchez, Fermin, 397, 398

de LA Beckwith, Byron, 432

de la Llama, 333

DeLaparra, Eugene, 327, 328, 490, 558

deLoach, C.D., 430

de los Reyes, Gustavo, 150, 279

del Valle, Eladio, 31, 150, 151, 225, 275, 321

del Valle, General Pedro, 233-236, 242, 463, 472, 488, 500-502, 530

De Menil, 139

De Mil, Jean, 342

de Mohrenschildt, George, 89.134, 155, 208, 210, 211, 216-218, 221, 226, 228, 252-254, 291, 292, 297, 342, 390, 477

  bio, 136-139

  with Oswald, 131, 139-143, 209, 210, 212, 215, 238, 247, 562

  in Haiti, 474, 475, 554

de Mohrenschildt (LeGon), Jeanne, 137-141, 211, 215, 297

Dempsey, Jack, 362

Dennison, Admiral Robert, 60, 145, 181, 187

de Pinillos.Joaquin Martinez, 499, 559

DePugh, Robert, 218, 219, 237, 241, 242, 395, 540, 561

Devlin, Larry, 111, 112, 116

de Vosjoli, Phillipe, 9, 129, 183, 296, 297, 462-464, 474, 475, 560, 561, 566

Dewey, Thomas, 288

de Young, Maurice, 474

Diem, Ngo Dinh, 66-69, 160, 265, 305, 437-441, 463, 507, 552

Diggs, Marshall, 93

Dillard, Thomas, 523

Dillon, C. Douglas, 108, 111, 190

DiMaggio, Joe, 173

Dinkin, Eugene B., 475, 476, 487, 488, 513, 558

Di Spadaforo, Prince Gutierrez, 342

Dobrynin, Anatoly, 186, 191, 294

Dodd, Thomas, 121

Dolan, James, 529

Domvile, Edward, 501

Donnelly, Walter, 163

Donovan, Edna, 166

Donovan, James, 274

Donovan, William, 78, 82, 85, 89, 288, 289, 291-293, 342, 440, 566

Dorfman, Allen, 477

Dorticos, Osvaldo, 186

Dougherty, Jack, 517

Doughty, George, 543

Douglas, Daniel, 499

Douglas, James, 103

Douglas, William, 33

Dowell, Doris, 383

Drain, Vincent, 532-534

Drane, Maxine Kemp, 375

Dryer, Joseph, 474, 475

Du Berrier, Hilaire, 469

Ducos, Leopoldo Ramos, 148

Dulles, Allen, 5, 7, 17, 21, 49, 55, 61, 63, 66, 72, 73, 91, 104, 106, 144, 149, 150, 162, 163, 181, 215, 216, 274, 278, 418, 436, 462, 469, 549, 553, 555, 557, 560, 561, 563, 565, 566, 570

  sabotaged Eisenhower, 7, 8 , 25, 281

  sabotaged Kennedy, 26

  Bay of Pigs, 27-29, 33, 34

  position on Berlin and Germany, 8, 507

  stay behind armies in Europe, 49, 78, 82, 85, 86, 89, 290-292, 342

  Indonesia, 72, 161, 162

  work with Nazis, 9, 85, 86, 286, 289, 293

  Lumumba assassination, 109-111, 113

  possible role in Hammarskjold death, 121, 122

Dulles, John Foster, 12, 13

Dunn, William, sr., 374

Duque, Evilio, 281

Duran, Ruben, 414, 416

Duran, Silvia, 413, 425

  with Oswald at Cuban Embassy, 407, 408, 410, 412, 413

  Oswald and Twist Party, 414-416

  allegations of sexual relations with Oswald, 415, 417, 418

Duvalier, Francois, 89, 252, 254, 554

E

Easterling, Robert, 384, 385

Echevarria, Homer, 495, 557milte

Edwards, Sheffield, 90-92, 101, 169, 440

Egerter, Ann, 422, 450

Egge, Bjorn, 118

Eichenbaum, Rudy, 349

Einspruch, Burton, 393, 397

Eisenhower, Dwight D., 4, 5, 12, 13, 17, 22, 24-27, 29, 33, 34, 37, 59, 62, 63, 73, 76, 106, 108, 111, 112, 163, 185, 196, 197, 250, 288, 404, 446, 453

635

Elder, Walter, 462
Elena, Martin, 91
Elkins, Charles, 236
Ellsberg, Daniel, 194
Ellsworth, Frank, 221, 397, 497-499, 508-510
Elrod, John, 499, 509, 510
Erdrich, Robert H., 337, 511
Eroshkin, Nikolai, G., 125, 450
Escalante, Fabian, 291
Espinosa, Victor, 452
Esterline, Jake, 163
Euins, Amos, 519
Evans, Courtney, 171
Evans, Evans, 316
Evans, Julian, 316
Evers, Medgar, 432, 433
Ewell, James, 489, 541

F

Fain, John W., 132, 134
Farmer, James, 374
Federal Bureau of Investigation (FBI) 21, 28, 32, 35, 43, 45, 46, 48, 51, 80, 81, 84, 91, 99, 100, 102, 217, 235, 241, 244, 310, 311, 315, 318-320, 322, 325-328, 335, 337, 344-346, 350, 351, 487, 488, 500, 521, 522

  possible connection to Lee Oswald, 132-136, 341, 470, 489

  tracking Oswald, 36, 37, 133, 136, 209, 222, 226, 229, 246, 247, 316, 317, 329-332, 337, 338, 341, 354, 355, 372, 373, 378, 385, 386, 389, 407, 411, 467, 470, 473, 475-478, 481, 482, 490, 504

  interviewed Oswald after return from Russia, 132, 134, 135

  interviewed Oswald in New Orleans, 38, 39
  crackdown on Cuban exiles, 354, 355, 455
  suppress evidence, 489
  concern over Oswald impostor, 38, 39, 47, 53

  tracking JFK, 165, 168, 169, 171, 198
  post-assassination interrogation, 228,
Feldman, Myer, 58
Fellers, General Bonner, 232, 234, 289, 501
Felt, Admiral Harry, 159
Fenner, Nanny, 483, 484
Fernandez, Fernando, 354
Fernandez Hechevarria, Alberto, 147, 150, 279
Fernandez Parajon, Enrique, 364
Fernandez Rocha, Luis, 205, 278
Ferrell, Mary, 99, 218

Ferrie, David, 30, 31, 150, 225, 275, 310, 316-324, 327, 331-333, 335, 341-343, 345, 346, 352, 363, 374-378, 381, 383, 384, 529, 559
Fischer, George, 127
Fisher, John, 271
Fitzgerald, Deborah, 396
FitzGerald, Desmond, 3, 74, 270, 277, 300, 302-306, 443-446, 450, 451, 474
  Cubela operation, 454-457, 507
Flannery, James, 365
Flinn, Dennis, 80
Floyd, Jake, 406
Fonzi, Gaeton, 96, 399-401, 412
Ford, Charles, 184
Ford, Declan, 143
Ford, Gerald, 563
Ford, Katya, 143
Formosa, Johnny, 170
Forrest, Helen, 525, 526
Forrestal, Michael, 158, 160, 439
Forster, Clifford, 116
Francia, Salvatore, 564
Franco, Francisco, 75, 79, 284, 288-290, 403, 500
Frank, Warren, 180
Frazier, Robert, 533
Frazier, Wesley, 473, 494, 502, 516, 517
Fredricksen, Norman, 215
Fritz, Will, 472, 532-534, 547, 548
Fruge,Francis, 374
Fuego, Manuel, 93
Fulbright, J. William, 56, 514

G

Galbraith, John Kenneth, 68, 69, 158
Gale, Colonel William P., 232, 235, 236, 242, 488, 500, 557
Gallagher, Major General, 440
Garner, Jesse, 363
Garner, Nina, 329, 355, 363, 385, 477, 478
Garrison, Jim, 295, 316, 318, 319, 323, 324, 333, 341, 343, 344, 352, 357, 358, 363, 364, 367, 374-376, 381, 383, 384, 395
Garro de Paz, Elena, 414, 416
Gatlin, Maurice, 29, 297, 324, 325, 342
Gaudet, William, 318, 319, 329, 333, 341, 357, 378, 387, 403, 413, 470
Gehlen, Reinhard, 77, 78, 83-87, 89, 124, 127, 215, 284, 297 ,501
Genzman, Robert, W., 490
Gerasimov, Vitaley, 43, 135
Gerdes, Vernon, 323, 324

German, Ella, 41, 45
Giancana, Sam, 30, 88, 90, 92, 98, 166-173, 198, 276, 311, 348
Gill, G. Wray, 320
Gillin, Edward, G, 381, 382
Gilpatric, Roswell, 23, 64, 69, 91, 160, 299, 504
Givens, Charles, 519, 520
Gleichauf, Justin, 156
Glover, Everett, 211, 213-217, 473, 477, 569
Goldsmith, Michael, 422, 490
Goldwater, Barry, 69, 432
Gonzales, Henry, 514
Gonzales, Pedro, 489, 490
Gonzalez, Henry B., 220
Gonzalez, Reinaldo, 391
Goodpasture, Anne, 450
Gordon, Patsy, 52
Gottlieb, Sidney, 113, 365, 376
Gracey, Lochart F. Jr., 234
Grandison, Lionel, 172, 174
Gravel, Mike, 442
Gravitas, Dorothy, 143
Gray, Brigadier General David W., 28, 32
Gray, Gordon, 103
Greenson, Ralph, 171-174
Greenstein, Art, 52
Gregory, Peter, 128
Griffin, Burt, 472
Griffin, Will Hayden, 39
Grinnan, Joseph, 481
Groden, Robert, 521
Groves, David U., 449
Gruenther, Alfred M., 13
Guerin-Serac, Yves, 463, 464, 564
Guevera, Che, 449, 474
Guillaume, Pierre, 197
Guitart, Agustin, 398
Gusev, N.I., 180
Guthman, Edwin O., 430
Gutierrez, Eloy Menoyo, 149-151, 188, 205, 279, 281, 307, 311, 449, 495, 557
Gutierrez, Pedro, 414

H

Hack, Jeanne, 382
Haig, Lieutenant Colonel Alexander, 5, 269, 302, 457
Halberstam, David, 68
Hale, I.B., 199, 208
Hale, Virginia, 208
Haley, J. Evetts, 472

Hall, Cliff, 382
Hall, James, 174
Hall, Loran, 89, 213, 214, 281, 297, 321, 390, 394-397, 404, 405, 415, 419, 463, 475, 554
Hall, Lyola, 141
Halpern, Sam, 103, 301, 302
Hamblen, C.A., 466
Hammarskjold, Dag, 116, 117, 121, 122
  Plane crash, 118-120
Hand, Frank, 157
Hanfstaengl, Ernst, 500
Harding, George Jr., 235
Hardway, Dan, 564
Hardy, A. Gordon, 476
Hargis, Billy James, 232, 235, 237, 238
Harker, Daniel, 3
Harkins, General Paul, 158, 159, 161, 435, 437
Harkness, D.V., 531
Harriman, Averell, 60, 61, 65, 73, 112, 158, 160, 252, 260, 263, 265, 432, 433, 437-439, 443
Harvey, William, 11, 30, 80, 81, 91, 96, 101, 103, 104, 113, 125, 131, 139, 213, 270, 309, 311, 409, 444, 553, 564
  head of assassinations, 6, 8, 87, 88, 90, 92, 95, 97, 98, 101, 102, 113, 115, 297, 311, 364, 439, 440, 464
  Berlin station chief, 83, 87, 124, 273, 320, 448, 565
  part of JFK assassination plot, 84, 89, 94, 141, 215, 276, 353, 365, 369, 370, 447, 557, 560, 561, 570
  war on Cuba, 92, 93, 95, 144, 146, 147, 152-154, 184, 190, 203
  with John Roselli 97, 157, 309, 311, 313
  with June Cobb, 212, 214, 340
  Rome station chief, 257, 258
Heath, Robert G., 375, 376
Hecksher, Henry, 8, 10, 17, 62, 84, 94-97, 102, 149, 156, 273, 310, 313, 321, 335, 352, 380, 445-447, 449-451, 463, 555-557, 560, 561, 565
  Bio, 448
Hedgeman, Victor, 113, 115
Heitman, Wallace Ren "Wally", 39
Helm, Harold L., 395
Helms, Richard, 38, 73, 85, 91, 92, 97, 100, 103, 113, 146, 153, 154, 157, 205, 206, 278, 296, 302, 305, 306, 309, 311, 312, 322, 349, 404, 417, 423, 427, 428, 438, 453, 454, 505
Hemming, Gerry Patrick, 147, 148, 156, 204, 234, 280, 318, 321, 345, 360, 361, 364, 365, 394, 397, 405

637

Hench, Thomas J., 352
Henderson, Ruby, 518, 519, 521
Herter, Christian, 108, 446
Hickey, Edward J., 37, 427
Hickey, Thomas Franics, 181
Hidell, Robert, 316
Higganbotham, George, 333
Hill, Gerald, 541
Hilsman, Roger, 160, 437-439, 441, 506
Hilton, Conrad, 272, 273, 418, 463
Himmler, Heirich, 286
Hiss, Alger, 80, 82
Ho Chi Minh, 440
Hochschild, Harold, 109
Hoffa, Jimmy, 148, 155, 166, 170, 171, 176, 177, 276, 281, 361, 476
Hoke, John, 216
Hoke, Silvia, 216, 487
Holbik, Mike K., 449
Hoover, Herbert, 273
Hoover, J. Edgar, 52, 177, 178, 242, 276, 320, 329, 355, 369, 380, 393, 426, 470, 488, 491, 549, 570
    offended by Kennedy brothers, 21, 165, 170-172, 175, 230, 231, 429, 430
    concerned with Oswald impostor, 36, 132, 424, 427
    CIA/Mafia assassination plots, 90, 91, 168, 169, 170
    Oswald lone gunman, 100, 534, 548
    Anti-Communist, 315
    Oswald in Mexico City, 389, 407, 424
Hosty, James, 242, 389, 393, 451, 467, 480, 482-484, 486-488, 500, 543, 548, 549, 559, 568
    tracking Oswald, 209, 210, 222, 241, 327, 330, 386, 475, 478, 479, 481
    investigating gunrunning in Dallas, 398, 507-510
Houston, Lawrence, 92
Howard, Lawrence, Jr., 394-396
Howard, Lisa, 267, 453, 506
Howard, Tom, 390
Hudkins, Lonnie, 354, 413
Hughes, Paul, 404, 405
Hughes, Sarah, 472
Humphrey, Hubert, 514
Hunt, H.L., 93, 131, 139, 200, 218, 221, 232, 233, 237, 245, 271, 290, 319, 320, 396, 485, 498, 512, 529, 568
Hunt, Howard, 30-32, 95-97, 153, 156, 206, 273, 298, 310, 313, 321, 356, 361, 365, 420,

446-448, 485, 557, 560, 561
Hunt, Lemar, 485, 515
Hunt, Nelson Bunker, 485, 529, 530
Hunt, St. John, 96
Hutchinson, Leonard, 492, 493
Hyde, Carl, 487
Hyde, Carol, 216
Hyde, Marie, 46, 47
Hyde, William Avery, 216

I

Insalmo, Ernest, 326
Insua, Marcella, 393
Isbell, Harris, 376
Issacs, Harold, 45, 127, 216
Ivanov, Eugene, 429

J

Jamison, John, 540
January, Wayne, 502
Jarman, "Junior," 520-522
Jeffries, Norman, 174
Jehan, Jean, 88
Jelisavcic, Mikailo, 51-53, 379
Jenkins, Walter, 104
Jimenez, Vico, 300
Joannides, George Efthyron, 154, 205, 369, 370, 446
Johns, Lem, 571
Johnson, Arnold, 372
Johnson, Hamilton, 323
Johnson, Haynes, 457, 572
Johnson, Lyndon B., 46, 60, 66, 67, 70, 104, 126, 139, 186, 199, 269, 276, 429, 436, 457, 506, 509, 513, 549, 570,
Johnson, Priscilla, 38, 127, 216
Johnson, Robert, 37
Johnson, U. Alexis, 73, 91
Jones, Robert E., 510
Julien, Harold, 118

K

Kaack, Milton, 355, 371, 385, 476
Kail, Samuel G., 155, 156, 253, 272, 273, 297, 475
Kalaris, George, 421
Kalonji, Albert, 109
Kankasa, Timothy Jiranda, 119
Kasa-Vubu, Joseph, 112
Kay, Kathy, 471
Kaysen, Carl, 69
Keating, Kenneth, 183, 185, 188
Keeler, Christine, 429

INDEX

Kellerman, June, 571
Kellerman, Roy, 570, 571
Kelley, Thomas J., 509
Kelly, J.J., 165
Kennan, George, 11, 12, 18, 86, 129, 250, 436, 453, 506, 573
Keenan, Laurence, 414,
Kennedy, Angelo, 300
Kennedy, Edward, 112
Kennedy, Jacqueline, 137, 515
Kennedy, John F., 1, 10, 11, 13, 17, 21-24, 26, 28, 29, 32-34, 55-57, 59, 61, 70, 73, 74, 112, 113, 117, 118, 120, 121, 144, 158, 170, 177, 179, 181, 196, 197, 200, 230, 231, 234, 237, 271, 282, 295, 297, 314, 315, 444, 513, 515, 552
  concerns over assassination, 13, 55, 56, 164, 514, 515,
  hatred for, 24, 25, 55-58, 194, 195, 206, 207, 272, 302, 303, 394, 401, 503, 507, 513, 514, 516, 554
  on Berlin and Germany, 1, 7, 14, 21, 27, 58, 60-62, 70-72, 146, 182, 187, 189, 204, 553, 566, 567
    with Khrushchev in Vienna, 58, 59
    Judith Campbell, 166-169
    on Laos, 62-65
    on Vietnam, 65-69, 159-161, 433-437
    Vietnam coup, 437-439, 441, 442
    on Indonesia, 72, 73, 161, 162
    on Cuba, 92, 144, 145, 154, 234, 235, 267, 443
    second Invasion of Cuba, 204-206, 269, 270, 298-300, 305-308, 310, 313, 452, 456
    steel crisis, 162, 163
    Marilyn, Monroe, 171-173, 175
    Missile Crisis, 182-194, 202, 268, 553
    TFX, 198, 199
    release of Bay of Pigs prisoners, 203
    curbs Cuban exile activity, 204, 274, 278
    Ellen Rometsch, 429, 430
    on civil rights, 430
    Test Ban Treaty, 433, 503
    America University speech, 431, 432
Kennedy, Joseph, 90, 167, 168, 527
Kennedy, Robert F. (Bobby), 1, 5, 6, 10, 15, 16, 18, 23, 27, 31, 34, 63, 90-92, 94, 102, 144, 161, 163, 196, 199, 231, 314, 321, 430, 439, 444, 505, 559, 570
    secret meetings with Russians, 21, 59, 71, 180, 182, 183, 186, 187, 191
    war on Cuba, 102-104, 146, 148, 152-154,

147, 207, 273, 274, 278
    and organized crime, 166-170, 176, 177, 199, 276
    Marilyn, Monroe, 171-175
    Missile Crisis, 180, 181, 183,-188, 190, 191, 203, 268, 294
    second Invasion of Cuba, 206, 269, 270, 274, 279-283, 298-300, 303, 305-310, 312, 313, 370, 445, 446, 454, 457, 500, 507, 552-554, 556, 557
    General Walker, 201, 202
    George Wallace, 430, 431, 432
Keough, Eugene, 165
Khrushchev, Nikita, 14, 16, 21, 22, 25, 33, 35, 41, 58-62, 69, 70, 71, 110, 159, 179, 191, 192, 251, 252, 255, 267, 268, 299, 395, 396, 432, 455, 503, 512, 551
    on Berlin: 33, 35, 69, 181, 185-187, 189, 199, 250, 554, 566
    Missile Crisis, 180-183, 186, 192-194, 553
Khrushchev, Sergei, 192
Kieffer, Colonel John F., 93
Kilgallen, Dorothy, 173
King, J.C., 163, 370, 416, 417
King, Martin Luther, 321
Kissinger, Henry, 563, 566
Kleberg, Robert, 150, 151, 153, 155, 279
Kline, William M., 386
Kloepfer, Henry, Warner, 383
Kloepfer, Ruth, 383
Knappstein, Karl-Hemrich, 76
Knight, John R., 366
Knights of Malta, 150, 418, 463, 501
Koch, Graham R. E., 346, 393
Kohly, Mario Garcia, 29-31, 35, 92, 93, 115, 116, 185, 275, 321, 360, 361
Koslov, Nikolai Vasilievich, 51
Koslova, Olympiada, 51
Kostikov, Valery, 3, 90, 409-411, 417, 421, 485, 570
Kramer, Monica, 46, 47
Krimmerman, Leonard, 366
Krock, Arthur, 68
Krulak, General Charles, 282, 434, 437, 439
Krystinic, Raymond, 476
Kuetemeyer, Wilhelm, 212

L

Labadie, Stephen J., 369
Laborde, Laurence Joseph, 147, 360
Lafitte, Jean Pierre, 9, 30, 77, 88, 89, 94, 95, 100, 129, 141, 156, 177, 183, 205, 206, 213,

639

272, 273, 289, 291, 293, 321, 331, 333, 340, 353, 376, 379, 381, 390, 400, 405, 419, 423, 430, 440, 449, 450, 463, 468, 474, 481, 511, 529, 555, 557, 560, 561, 564, 565, 566

  CIA drug experiments with George Hunter White, 88, 89, 94, 95

  datebook entries, 95, 100, 214, 295, 296, 316, 328-330, 347, 348, 351, 365, 367, 369, 403, 428, 469, 473, 479, 480, 484, 512, 530, 544, 545, 567, 569

  used Hidell alias, 335, 342, 378, 380

Lancelot, Jacqueline, 474, 475, 554

Langoscsh, Joseph, 454

Lansdale, General Edward, 66, 67, 73, 82, 104, 144, 151, 152, 155, 157, 188, 193, 195, 352, 506, 555

Lansky, Meyer, 30, 171

Lanusa, Jose, Antonion, 510

Lanz, Pedro Diaz, 95

LaSavia, Myrtle, 383

LaSavia, Tony, 383

Lauchi, Rich, 218, 281, 324, 345

Laurie, James McKenzie, 119

Lawford, Lady May, 174, 175

Lawford, Patricia, 166, 170, 172, 175

Lawford, Peter, 166, 170-175, 571

Lawrence, Jack, 528

Leake, Hunter, 322, 323

Leap, Harold, 356

Le Cavelier, Gilbert, 560

Lechuga Hevia, Carlos, 413

Lee, Vincent, 334, 336, 337, 361

LeGon, Robert, 211

Le, Kong, 63

LeMay, Curtis, 14, 16, 23, 64, 189, 191, 194, 198

Lemnitzer, Lyman, 13, 23, 24, 27, 28, 33, 35, 55, 64-66, 70, 73, 91, 103, 145, 151, 152, 159, 181, 564

Le Pen, Jean-Marie, 460

Lesser, Michael, 374

Levine, Isaac Don, 82, 126, 292

Lewallen, James, 341

Lewis, Aubrey, 466

Lewis, David, 319, 363

Lewis, Lummie, 528

Liebeler, Wesley, 393, 398

Lincoln, Evelyn, 169

Linner, Sture, 120

Litchfield, Wilburn Waldron, 471, 472

Lobo, Julio, 150-152

Lodge, Henry Cabot, 437-439, 441, 442,
  Vietnam coup, 506

Logue, Lester, 394-396

Lopez, Ed, 412

Lorenz, Marita, 361

Luce, Clare Boothe, 185, 188, 205, 271, 273, 322, 446, 555

Lumpkin, Colonel George, 273

Lumumba, Patrice, 109-113, 116, 121

Luns, Joseph, 161

Luther, Duane, 107

Lynden, Count Harold d'Aspremont, 111

Lyons, K.E., 541

M

MacArthur, Douglas, 25, 54, 107, 124, 195, 232-234, 236, 273, 275, 469, 501

Mackey, Father Konrad Simonsen, 79

MacMillan, Harold, 14, 60, 192, 193, 294, 429

Maheu, Robert, 90

Mahoney, William, 505

Mahoney, Richard, 96

Malik, Adam, 161

Malinovsky, Rodion, 179

Malone, Jack, 150, 153, 279

Mamantov, Ilya, 126, 143, 228, 292, 403, 512

Manion, Dean, 353

Mann, Thomas, 103, 353, 414

Mannix, Bill, 415

Mansfield, Mike, 160

Marachini, Dante, 341

Marcello, Anthony, 326, 328

Marcello, Carlos, 29-32, 150, 155, 166, 176, 177, 254, 276, 279, 310, 311, 315, 320, 325-328, 347-349, 360, 419, 490, 529, 558, 559, 570

Marcello, Peter, 346, 348

Marcello, Vincent, 327, 328

Marchetti, Victor, 31, 322

Marcus, Stanley, 395

Margain, John, 353

Marshall, George, 287

Martello, Francis, 39, 357-359, 362, 366, 369, 372, 373

Martin, Consuela, 318

Martin, Dean, 170

Martin, Edwin, 267

Martin, Jack, 318, 342, 343, 347

Martin, Johnny, 392

Martin, William A.R., 333

Martino, John, 88, 94, 95, 156, 277, 309, 310, 322, 395, 397, 398, 523, 542, 559

Marx. Karl, 318

Masen, John Thomas, 395, 398, 497, 498,

499, 508, 509, 558
Masferrer, Rolando, 31, 32, 148-151, 225, 272, 275, 280, 281, 360, 361, 365, 450, 474, 555, 562
Matlack, Dorothy, 155, 156, 272, 297, 475
Matsukata, Saburo, 137
May, Robert L., Jr., 348
Maynor, Harry, 358, 371
McAuliffe, Martin, 383
McCloy, John, 89, 117, 118, 343, 344, 533, 563, 567
McConaughy, Walter, 73
McCone, John, 5, 73, 74, 91, 92, 144, 146, 181-183, 190, 193, 274, 282, 300, 303, 304, 309, 312, 438, 443, 452, 453, 457, 462
McDonald, Betty, 215
McDonald, M.N., 542
McFarland, John, 388, 405, 407
McFarland, Meryl, 388, 405, 407
McGee, Frank, 7
McGehee, Edwin Lea, 374
McGrath, Angela, 119
McKeown, Robert, 377
McLaney, Mike, 90, 148
McLaney, William, 345
McNamara, Robert, 5, 23, 24, 28, 34, 55-57, 60, 61, 64, 69, 73, 144, 145, 152, 157-162, 184, 187, 188, 190, 191, 194, 195, 197, 249, 263, 264, 270, 274, 302, 303, 434, 435, 437, 439, 443, 455, 457, 505
McWillie,, Lewis, 95, 347-349
Meadows, Algur, 403
Meller, Anna, 133, 141, 143
Mendenhall, Joseph, 434
Mennen, George "Soapy," 121
Menshikov, Mikhail, 21, 22
Mercer, Julia Ann, 517, 518
Merchant, Livingston, 104
Meredith, James, 200-202
Merezhinsky, Yuri, 41
Mertz, Michael, 99, 100, 101, 102
Messerschmitt, Willi, 289
Meyer, Cord, 45, 96, 107, 127, 171, 216, 255, 256
Meyers, Lawrence, 381, 529
Mikoyan, Anastas, 180
Mikoyan, Serge, 180
Miler, Newton "Scotty," 462
Miller, Dusty, 293, 294
Miller, Lawrence Reginald, 498, 499, 509, 510, 518
Milteer, Joseph, 235, 472, 487, 488, 500, 515, 557

Minh, Duong Vasn, 441
Mirabal, Alfredo, 408, 412
Mirabal, Maria Teresa, 106
Mirabal, Minerva, 106
Mirabal, Patria, 106
Mintenbaugh, James, 42
Minutemen, 54
Mobutu, Joseph, 111, 112
Mohr, John P., 430
Molina, Enrique, 281
Mollenhoff, Clark, 430
Mondoloni, Paul, 89, 94, 95
Monroe, Marilyn, 171-175, 177, 198, 231
Montini, Cardinal, 79
Mooney, Luke, 533
Moore, J. Walton, 138, 140, 477
Monaghan, William I., 371
Morales David, 92, 95-97, 149, 156, 157, 273, 276, 310, 312, 313, 321, 400-402, 440, 448, 463, 557, 565
Morgan, Reeves, 374
Morgan, William, 8, 149, 150, 279, 307, 565
Morris, Robert, 201, 245, 395-397
Morrison, DeLesseps, 325
Moorman, Mary, 531
Morro, Aldo, 561
Morrow, Hubert, 493
Morrow, Robert, 29, 124, 150, 185, 275, 343, 352, 360, 361, 377
Mosby, Aline, 38
Mosk, Stanley, 219
Mosley, Oswald, 459, 460
Mosley, Thomas, 495
Moyers, Bill, 436
Moynihan, Daniel Patrick, 194
Muller, Alberto, 153
Muller, Josef, 563
Murchison, Clint, 139, 150, 200, 254, 290, 342, 463, 512
Murphy, Joe, 517
Murray, Eunice, 173, 174
Murray, Nora, 44
Murret, Charles (Dutz), 177
Murret, Lillian, 315, 366, 477
Murret, Marilyn Dorothea, 45, 46, 127
Murrow, Edward R., 54
Mussolini, Benito, 76, 81, 130, 288, 342

N

Nagell, Richard, Case, 15, 17, 52, 102, 124, 125, 177, 234, 243, 318, 321, 336, 350, 356, 362, 377, 380, 381, 401, 403, 445, 450, 467,

479, 486, 488, 544, 555, 567, 575
  investigates anti-Castro groups, 224, 225, 226, 234, 275, 276, 319, 352, 545, 561, 562, 565, 571
  in Mexico City, 353, 354, 400, 419-421, 423, 426, 511
  warning to Oswald, 378, 379, 387, 402, 428, 568
  shoots up El Paso bank, 52, 225, 247, 379, 380, 427
  investigates Lee and Marina, 225, 226, 228, 562
  uses Hidell alias, 226, 316, 335, 336, 342
Nagy, Ferenc, 342
Naman, Rita, 46, 47
National States Rights Party, 54
Naumann, Werner, 78
Nechiporenko, Oleg, 409-411, 426
Newcomb, Pat, 173, 175
Newman, Sam, 344
Ngulube, Margaret, 119
Nitschke, Ivan E., 317, 323, 324
Nitze, Paul, 69, 190, 268
Nixon, Richard M., 7, 21, 25, 27, 30, 31, 61, 87, 194, 514, 565
Nkrumah, Kwame, 112, 505
Nhu, Ngo Dinh, 434, 438, 441, 463
Noel, James, 151, 156, 273
Nolan, John, 274
Nolting, Frederick, 67, 159
Nonte, George Charles, Jr., 498, 499, 509, 558
Norman, Harold, 520-522
Norstad, Lauris, 60
Norwood, Hal, 560
Nosavan, Phoumi, 62, 63
Novel, Gordon, 323, 324, 345
Nunez, Orlando, 396

O

Oberlander, Theodor, 500
Ochsner, Alton, 371
O'Conner, James, J., 364
Odio, Amador, 391
Odio, Annie, 391-393, 396
Odio, Sarita, 391, 393, 397, 398
Odio, Silvia, 388, 393, 401, 470
  bio, 391
  involved in Cuban exile involvement, 392, 396, 398
  Oswald visit, 392-394, 397, 402, 427
  knew Oswald, 397, 470
O'Donnell, Kenneth, 571

Odum, Bardwell, 480, 483
O'Dwyer, Paul, 419
O'Dwyer, William, 419
Ofstein, Dennis, 142, 208
O'Hare, John, 360
Oliva, Erneido, 456
Oliver, Beverly, 227, 467
Olsen, Harry, 471, 472
Orbach, Danny, 87
Orlov, Lawrence, 140, 141, 183, 215, 475, 477, 570
Orta, Juan, 364
Osborn, Frederick, Jr., 216
Osborn, Frederick, Sr., 216
Osborn, Henry Fairfield, 216
Osborn, Nancy, 216
Osborne, Albert, 388, 403, 405-407, 426
Ostre, Joseph, 320
Oswald, Lee Harvey, 11, 14, 15, 29, 31, 88-90, 95, 100, 102, 133, 142, 143, 148, 154, 177, 183, 208, 216-218, 225, 227, 229, 234, 235, 247, 248, 285, 297, 309, 310, 313, 321, 322, 348-350, 352, 353, 363, 397, 399, 400, 405, 427, 450, 495, 498, 500, 502, 508, 516, 519, 520, 522-525, 535-537, 544-547, 551, 572
  false evidence of Cuban/Russian involvement in assassination, 2, 3
  in Russia, 36-42, 44-53
  patsy, 15, 468, 567
  CIA sleeper agent, 36-39, 47, 48, 53, 97, 98, 427, 428
  return from Russia, 123-128
  involvement with FBI, 132-135, 355, 356, 358, 359, 489, 490
  and White Russians, 133, 134, 136, 140-143, 211
  correspondence with left-wing organizations, 135, 136, 467, 479
  with George de Mohrenschildt, 139-141, 210, 212-215, 291
  CIA interest in, 139, 140
  in Dallas (pre-New Orleans), 131, 142, 143, 209, 211, 222, 238, 246
  with the Minutemen, 210, 219-223, 226, 228, 247, 285
  mind altering drug program, 213
  rifle purchase, 223, 224, 226
  backyard photos, 226-228
  Walker shooting, 238-241, 243-246, 561, 568
  Fair Play For Cuba Committee, 246, 247
  in Mexico City, 272, 312, 313, 317, 353,

354, 400, 407-423, 426

in New Orleans, 295, 296, 297, 310, 315-319, 323, 325-331, 334-336, 338-341, 343-345, 347, 350, 351, 369, 378, 381, 382, 391, 401, 402, 568

attempt to infiltrate leftist groups, 101, 333, 334, 336-340, 345, 346, 352, 354-357, 360-364, 366, 367, 372, 373

Hidell alias, 88, 222-224, 226, 316, 334-338, 340, 342, 367, 421, 477, 510, 511, 532, 543, 548

Jackson/Clinton Mississippi visit, 374-376

Stuckey radio debate, 371, 372

warning from Richard Nagell, 378, 379, 403, 568

leaves New Orleans and travels to Mexico, 272, 383-388, 389, 394, 402, 403, 405, 407

political philosophy, 229, 459

anxiety before assassination, 409-411, 568, 569

in Dallas (after Mexico City) 411, 412, 466, 470-479, 491

Oswald sightings in Dallas, 491-497

from Book Depository to boarding house, 535-538

at Texas Theater, 538-542, 544

interrogation of, 547-549

Oswald, Marguerite, 47, 141, 357

Oswald, Marina, 2, 39, 40, 43, 82, 128, 134, 208, 209, 211, 217, 222, 224, 227, 228, 239, 240, 244, 292, 315, 330, 334, 383, 403, 409, 450, 466, 478, 479, 483, 491, 492, 494, 512, 516

meets Lee, 41, 42

CIA's concerns with, 43, 44, 47, 125

travels to U.S., 48, 49, 53, 123, 125, 126, 216

and White Russian community, 136, 140-143

with Ruth Paine, 215, 226, 247, 316, 339, 373, 381, 467, 473, 477, 486, 487, 493, 502, 533

with Richard Case Nagell, 225, 319, 562

Oswald, Robert, 128, 141, 142, 222

Oswald, Vada, 128

Oswald, Victor, 84, 87-89, 95, 236, 284, 293, 297, 390, 419, 423, 451, 463

Otash, Fred, 174

Owens, Calvin "Bud", 543

Oxford, J.L. 472

P

Pacho, Felix Guillermo Othon, 398

Pageenhardt, Charles John, 39

Paine, Michael, 215-217, 228, 467, 476-478

Paine, Ruth, 3, 143, 215-217, 226, 228, 249, 316, 339, 366, 373, 381, 383, 466, 472, 473, 477-481, 483, 485-487, 491-493, 502, 508, 510, 516, 517, 533, 548, 568

Palmer, Henry Earl, 374, 375

Palmer, Tom, 471

Paneque, Victor, 281

Papich, Sam, 90, 311, 556

Papon, Maurice, 122

Pappelis, Theophanis E., 331

Parker, William, 174

Parrott, Tom, 104

Partin, Edward, 176

Pasternak, Boris, 51

Patchall, James, 269

Paula, Juan A., 365

Pawley, William, 30, 32-35, 84, 96, 106, 155, 163, 205, 236, 277, 287, 288, 290, 322, 360, 446, 463, 555, 556

Pecora, Nofio, 177

Pearce, T. Joe, 534

Pearson, Drew, 14, 56

Pecora, Nofio, 349

Pedromo Sanjenis, Joaquin, 365

Pena, Orestes, 331, 356, 357, 362, 401

Penkovsky, Oleg, 126, 127

Penn, Lovell, 467

Pennington, James, 525, 526

Peover, D.E., 119

Perez, Jean Claude, 560

Perrel, George, 398

Perroud, Edmond, 114

Petrov, Vladimir, 86

Peyrefitte, Alain, 572

Pfuntner, Jordan James, 152

Phillips, David Atlee, 11, 29, 95, 96, 149, 150, 153-156, 184, 253, 272, 276, 277, 279, 297, 310, 312, 313, 321, 340, 356, 365, 399, 400, 402, 413, 415, 420, 424, 426, 446-449, 463, 475, 485, 539, 540, 556, 557

Phouma, Souvanna, 62, 63

Pichel, Charles Thourot, 500, 501

Pico, Renaldo, 365

Piedra, Orlando, 364, 365

Pierre, Cleary F'N, 128

Pierson, Jane, 213, 214

Pifer, Alan, 109

Pipe, Eddie, 520

Pliyev, Issa, 186

Pompidou, George, 221

643

Poole, Walter S., 60
Poretto, Joseph, 326
Postal, Julia, 541, 542
Powell, James, 508, 523
Powell, John, 519
Power, General Thomas, 190
Powers, David, 571
Powers, Francis Gary, 40, 41
Price, C.J., 38, 428
Price, Howard, 493
Prio, Carlos, 31, 148, 150, 155, 205, 275, 278, 280, 281, 347, 377, 446, 451, 452, 556, 557
Prizentsev, Lev, 43
Proctor, Thomas G., 88, 89, 183, 236, 297, 418, 419, 463, 475
Profumo, John, 429
Prouty, Fletcher, 74, 139, 155, 197, 436, 437
Provenzano, Tony, 148
Pugh, Oran, 386
Punder, Herman, 500

Q

Quesada, Carlos Rodriguez, 360, 361
Quigley, John, 38, 358, 359, 369, 386, 396, 511
Quintero, Rafael "Chi Chi", 447
Quiroga, Carlos, 320, 362-364

R

Rabel, Luis, 147
Radford, Arthur, 13
Ragano, Frank, 177, 276
Raigorodsky, Paul, 342
Raikin, Spas T., 127, 128
Rainach, Willie, 333
Rainold, Robert R., 371
Rand, Henry, 44
Randle, Linnie Mae, 472, 516, 517
Rankin, Lee, 49, 210, 349, 393, 550
Ray, Girod, 337
Ray, Manuel, 31, 147, 206, 298, 307, 310, 311, 364, 392, 394, 447, 559
Rayburn, Sam, 199
Reagan, Ronald, 563
Reboso, Charles "Bebe," 365
Reeves, Rosser, 272
Reid, Barbara, 382
Reid, Elizabeth, 525
Reily, Eustis, 371
Reily, William, 316
Reissman, Dr. Leonard, 366
Remer, Otto-Ernst, 78, 83

Reston, James "Scooty," 71
Revill, Jack, 508, 509, 510
Reynolds, Don, 199
Reynolds, Harold, 489, 490
Reynolds, Steve, 90
Rhode, Michael, 396
Riordan, James R., 366
Rivard, Lucien, 94
Rivele, Steve J., 101
Rivero, Chito, 497
Roache, Wendall, 331
Roberts, Delphine, 317, 322, 324, 345, 350, 353
Roberts, Earlene, 470-472, 537-539, 545
Roberts, Major Archibald, 233, 235, 236
Robertson, William "Rip", 95-97
Robinson, Marvin, 525, 526
Rocha, Luis Fernandez, 153, 154
Rockefeller, David, 145, 343, 563
Rockefeller, Nelson, 299, 433, 563
Rockefeller, William III, 343
Rockwell, George Lincoln, 241, 242, 488, 500
Rodriguez, Alvareda, Jorge, 392
Rodriguez, Arnesto, 344, 346, 363
Rodriguez, Arnesto Sr., 363, 364
Rodriguez de Lopez, Maria, 344
Rodriguez, Manolito, 497
Rodriguez, Manuel, 495-498
Rogers, Walt, 495
Rolleston, Cedric, 387
Romack, James, 531
Roemer, William, 172, 173
Romero, Jessie, 387
Rometsch, Ellen, 199, 429, 430
Roosevelt, Eleanor, 54
Roque, Manuel Salvat, 153, 510
Rorke, Alexander, 147, 204
Rose, Earl, 38
Rose, Guy "Gus" F., 472, 547, 548
Roselli, Johnny, 30, 32, 88, 90-92, 94-98, 157, 166-169, 171, 172, 257, 273, 279, 280, 309-313, 322, 348, 555, 564
Rositzke, Harry, 86
Rostow, Walt, 23, 63, 67, 73
Rothermel, Paul, 319, 484, 530
Rothman, Norman, 310
Rousselot, John, 57
Roux, Michel, 99
Rowen, Henry, 69
Rowland, Arnold, 518, 519, 521
Rowland, Barbara, 518
Rowley, James, 571

INDEX

Ruby, Jack, 15, 227, 297, 310, 318, 319, 321, 339, 343, 348, 378, 381, 386, 387, 393, 395, 403, 405, 419, 421, 467, 471, 472, 476, 479, 481, 483, 485, 496, 498, 499, 517, 518, 523, 529, 537, 540, 542, 544, 559, 570, 572
  calls to gangsters, 346-349, 477
  gun running, 88, 89, 214, 295, 350, 371, 377, 390, 500, 509
    knowledge of second invasion of Cuba, 310
    organized crime connections, 95, 148, 177
Rudel, Hans-Ulrich, 83, 286-290, 343, 459, 460, 562, 563
Ruiz, Jose Solis, 500
Rusk, Dean, 5, 23, 27, 31, 32, 33, 37, 47, 55, 60, 61, 70, 73, 103, 112, 117, 145, 157, 184, 189, 270, 304, 427, 433, 457, 503, 504, 506
Russell, Bertrand, 285
Russell, Richard B., 37

S

Sagalyn, Arnold, 509
Salan, Raoul, 197, 461, 462, 468, 469, 476
Salinger, Pierre, 61, 184, 434
Salisbury, Harrison, 22
Sancar, Ilhami, 294
Sanchez, Nestor, 444, 445, 452, 454-457
Sanders, H. Barefoot, 514, 548, 550
San Roman, Pepe, 203, 204, 300
San Roman, Roberto, 300
Santelli, Jacques, 114
Santiago, Filipe Vidal, 244
Sapp, Charles, 234, 515
Sargen, Andres, 495
Schacht, Hjalmar, 77, 284, 289, 292-294, 342
Schellenberg, Walter, 114, 285, 286
Scherbatow, Alexis, 208
Schlesinger, Arthur, 24, 25, 61, 63, 194, 205, 270, 301, 429, 445, 503
Schmidt, Bob, 246
Schmidt, Larry, 245, 246, 396, 476
Schmidt, Volkmar, 211-215, 218, 228, 238, 319, 473, 477, 562, 569
Schroeder, Erich, 287
Schurman, Ted, 478
Schwarz, Fred c., 231
Schwegmann, John, Jr., 383
Sciambra, Andrew, 374
Scott, Paul, 46
Scott, Peter Dale, 62
Scott, Winston, 312, 313, 409, 413-418, 423
Scranton, Paul, 176
Sebert, General Edwin, 84

Senator, George, 479
Setyaev, Leo, 39, 359
Sevareid, Eric, 54
Seymour, William, 394-396
Shackley, Ted, 84, 86, 92, 157, 180, 271, 278, 301, 312, 448, 454, 457, 565
Shanklin, Gordon, 330, 483, 484, 489, 549
Shannon, Edith, 475
Sharp, Leslie, 9
Shaw, Clay, 296, 297, 318, 343, 371, 374, 375, 377, 378, 383, 384, 406
  part of Permindex, 295, 297, 324, 331, 462
  datebook entries, 295, 296, 316
  CIA connection, 341
  fascist connections, 342
Shelley, Bill, 520
Shepard, Lemuel, 501
Sherbatoff, Princess, 208
Sherman, Mary, 332
Shickshinny Knights, 500, 501
Shimon, Joe, 157, 170, 311
Shimon, Toni, 311
Shirkovsky, Eduard, 40
Shirokova, Rima, 35
Shoup, David M., 64, 189, 190
Sichel, Peter, 449
Sierra Martines, Paulino, 1, 5, 11, 17, 278-282, 301, 311, 313, 348-350, 371, 377, 399, 446, 451, 495, 496, 544, 555-557, 561, 562, 564, 565, 572
Silva, Frank, 375, 376
Silver, Arnold, 114
Silverthorne, Joseph, 369, 370
Simango, David, 119
Sinatra, Frank, 166-168, 170, 171, 173, 473
Siragusa, Charles, 88, 89, 95, 101, 156, 370, 390, 419, 440
Skelton, Byron, 514
Skorzeny, Ilse, 460
Skorzeny, Otto, 9, 81, 85, 87, 89, 126, 238, 273, 297, 342, 353, 400, 462, 463, 464, 468, 469, 500, 502, 544, 563, 567, 579
  ex-Nazi stay behind army, 79, 127, 459, 566
  CIA connections, 82, 86, 114, 215, 236, 289, 290, 292, 324, 331, 343, 448, 564
  in Madrid, 8, 76, 117, 127, 131, 289, 403
  Nazi background, 76, 77
  post-war Nazi alliances, 78, 80, 83, 84, 284-287, 290, 293, 294, 343, 460, 562
  involvement in Belgian Congo, 109, 110, 112, 115, 116
  plot to assassinate JFK, 129, 177, 276, 295,

645

404, 423, 451, 455, 475, 530, 557, 560, 561, 565, 572, 575
Slack, Garland, 494, 516
Slack, Lucille, 516
Slatzer, Robert, 172
Slawson, W. David, 38
Smathers, George, 106
Smith, Arthur L., 93
Smith, Charles, E., 201
Smith, David, 330, 331
Smith, Horace, 62
Smith, Howard, 112
Smith, Hudson, 77
Smith, Joe, 531
Smith, Walter Bedell, 81, 84
Smith, Wayne, 96
Smoot, Dan, 472
Snyder, Richard, 48, 50
Sobolev, Igor, 43
Soboleva, Ella, 43
Socarraz, Miguel L. 496
SOFINDUS, 75, 284, 293
Solie, Bruce, 487
Somersett, William, 233, 234, 487, 488
Sommer, Hans, 85
Somoza, Luis, 305, 404, 405, 444, 448, 556
Sorenson, Ted, 61, 184, 186, 189, 190
Sorrels, Forrest, 571
Souetre, Jean, 9, 99, 100, 102, 197, 293, 295, 297, 316, 419, 423, 462, 464, 476, 530, 560, 561, 566, 576
Soustelle, Jacques, 296
Speidel, Hans, 289
Spencer, John, 384
Spindel, Bernard, 174
Spofford, Charles, 272
Sprague, Richard, 424, 425
Stalin, Joseph, 12, 16, 41, 44, 133, 134
Steele, Richard, 366
Stein, Esther, 343
Stern, Edgar, 371
Stern, Edith, 371
Stevens, Marguerite D., 51, 487
Stevenson, Adlai, 61, 189, 205, 456, 472, 476, 514
Stevenson, M.W., 509
Stilwell, General Joseph, 271
Stinson, Julian, 432
Stockton, Bayard, 30
Stokes, Louis, 177
Stombaugh, Paul, 533
Stovall, Bob, 466

Stratemeyer, Lieutenant General George E., 234
Stuckey, William, 371
Studebaker, R.L., 533
Sturgis (aka Fiorini), Frank, 95, 116, 147-149, 156, 204, 272, 276, 311, 313, 321, 322, 345, 361, 365, 394, 404, 463, 502, 556
Styles, Sandra, 524
Sucharov, Bert, 404
Sukarno, President, 72, 161, 162, 552, 565
Sullivan, William, 37, 484, 490
Summers, Malcom, 531
Sumner, 325-327, 490, 558
Suner, Ramon Serrano, 290
Surrey, Robert, 237, 241-243, 246, 472, 476
Svensson, Arne, 119
Swenson, Harold, 454, 455
Swift, Wesley A., 235, 488, 500, 557

T

Taylor, Alexandra, 133, 141, 142
Taylor, E.E., 541
Taylor, Gary, 141, 142, 209
Taylor, General Maxwell, 34, 35, 65, 67-70, 73, 91, 144, 158, 188-190, 205, 249, 263, 303, 308, 431, 433-435, 437, 439, 504
Teller, Edward, 433
Tennyson, Bill, 395
Thiriart, Jean-Francois, 110
Thomas, Norman, 216
Thompson, A. Roswell, 343
Thompson, Llewellyn, 60, 181
Thornley, Kerry, 141, 215, 335, 336, 338, 343, 389
  with the Oswalds, 382-384
Thurmond, Strom, 56
Tilson, Tom, 526
Timmins, B.H., 509
Tippit, J.D., 14, 15, 244, 427, 537-539, 542, 543, 545-548, 569
Titovets, Ernst, 41, 42
Tobias, Mahlon, 222
Tollerton, Mary, 540
Tompkins, Brigadier General Rathvon M., 49
Toney, J.B., 541
Torres, Bernardo, 365
Trafficante, Santo, 30-32, 88, 90, 92-95, 98, 101, 148-150, 155, 156, 168, 175-177, 205, 214, 276, 279, 281, 309, 311, 321, 322, 348, 361, 365, 369, 370, 419, 455, 463, 523, 529, 555, 561
Trapnell, Garrett, 399-401, 488, 557

INDEX

Tregle, Ben, 327
Trosclair, P.J., 333, 334
Trotsky, Leon, 133, 134, 562
Trujillo, Rafael Leonidas, 105-107, 148, 275, 554
Trull, William, 278, 279
Truly, Roy, 473, 481, 522-524, 535
Truman, Harry, 11, 23, 54, 73, 122, 288
Tshombe, Moise, 109, 110, 115-117, 121
Tujague, Gerard F., 316
Turner, William, 310
Tutu, Desmond, 121
Twiford, Howard, 387
Tyler, Carole, 199
Tzitzichvili, David, 115

U

Udall Stewart, 185, 186
Urquhart, Brian, 116

V

Valdes, Juan, 332
Valentine, Douglas, 98
Vallee, Thomas, 515
Vallejo, Rene, 453, 454
Vance, Cyrus, 5, 269, 302, 303, 457
Van Don, Tran, 441
Van Roijen, Herman, 161
Varona, Tony, 30-32, 275, 280-282, 307, 311, 451, 456, 457
Veciana, Antonio, 149, 151-153, 155, 184, 188, 193, 195, 271, 272, 281, 352, 399, 540, Vernard, Wickliffe, 236
Vial, A.G., 359
Vlasov, Andrey, 85
Volkland, Al, 537
Volkland, Lou, 537
von Finckenstein, Ilse, 77
von Hohenlohe, Price Max, 286
von Kleist, Richard, 419
von Leers, Johann, 78
von Maydell, Kostantin, 137
von Stahl, 501

W

Wade, Henry, 321, 394, 496, 532, 548, 549, 550, 551
Waehauf, Franz, 419, 421
Waldron, Lemar, 29
Walker, General Edwin, 144, 210, 212, 218, 221, 234, 235, 238, 242, 246, 296, 320, 333, 339, 357, 380, 396, 463, 470, 472, 476, 478, 498, 509, 529, 555

right-wing indoctrination of troops, 54
fascist philosophy, 200, 226, 233, 236, 237
University of Mississippi insurrection, 200, 201, 202, 241
failed assassination attempt, 2, 239-241, 243-245, 561, 567, 575
datebook entries, 295, 328, 469, 530
Wallace, George, 430, 431
Walter, William, 356, 358, 490, 491, 558
Walther, Carolyn, 519
Walthers, Buddy, 472, 496, 541
Walton, Bob, 401
Ward, Hugh, 324, 325
Ward, Stephen, 429
Warren Commission, 38, 39, 49, 53, 82, 89, 126, 129, 140-142, 208, 210, 211, 215, 217, 221-224, 226, 236, 239, 243, 313, 325, 330, 332, 338, 349, 354, 359, 362, 363, 366, 372, 378, 384, 388, 392-394, 396, 398, 427, 457, 470, 472, 473, 476, 486, 492, 496, 508, 509, 512, 520-522, 524, 533, 534, 536-538, 542, 549, 571
Warren, Earl, 219, 230, 514, 570
Watts, General Clyde, 233
Weatherford, Harry, 472
Weber, Guy, 110
Webster, Robert E., 43-45
Wedemeyer, General A.C., 56, 234
Weiner, Sam, 467
Weinstock, Louis, 136
Weissman, Bernard, 481
Weitzman, Seymour, 531, 532
Welch, Robert, 233, 237
Welensky, Roy, 117
WerBell, Mitchell, 93, 94
West, Jean, 381, 384, 529
West, Louis, 214
Westbrook, W.R., 542, 543
Westrell, C.F., 118
Weyl, Nathaniel, 322
Whaley, William, 536, 537
Wheeler, General Earle, 189, 455
White, Ben, 94
White, General Robert M., 64
White, Geneva, 227, 467
White, George, Hunter, 88, 89, 94, 95, 156, 206, 370, 373, 390, 419, 440
White, Roscoe, 227, 467-469, 472
Whitten, John, 423
Whitter, Donald, 498-500, 509, 510, 518
Wiedemayer, Otto, 286
Wikler, Abraham, 376

647

Wiley, Alexander, 187

Williams, Bonny Ray, 521

Williams, Enrique (Harry), 206, 279, 280, 282, 298, 300, 308-310, 313, 365, 443, 455,-457, 554

Williams, J. Doyle, 533

Williams, Thomas, 374

Willoughby, Charles, 9, 84, 124, 125, 127, 177, 234, 236, 237, 245, 246, 272, 275, 284, 288, 289, 290, 296, 451, 463, 469, 476, 500-502, 529, 530, 555, 557, 560, 561

Wilmouth, Robert, 223

Wilson, Gary, 481

Wilson-Hudson, John, 214, 348, 351, 381, 403, 404, 405, 419, 481, 567

Wilson, Matt O., 357

Wilson, Vice Admiral Ralph, 24

Wisner, Frank, 8, 12, 16, 17, 82, 84-87, 129, 183, 215, 292, 342, 475, 502, 557, 560, 561, 563, 565, 570, 573, 574, 578, 579

Wisk, Ronnie A., 395

Witt, Louis Steven, 527, 528

Wood, Homer, 492

Wood, Ward, 174

Woodfield, William, 175

Woodside, Aline, 375

Worrell, James, 519, 524, 526

Wright, James, 513

Wright, Peter, 90

Wronski, Peter, 45

Wybot, Roger, 81, 82

Y

Yarborough, Ralph, 513

Yates, Ralph Leon, 494

Yatskov, Pavel, 410

Yeo-Thomas, Forest Frederick Edward, 76, 77

Young, Felix, 166

Young, Ruth Forbes Paine, 216

Z

Ziger, Alexander, 40

Zigiotti, Giuseppe, 342

Zonlick, James, 175

ZR/RIFLE, 8, 87-89, 93, 97, 98, 101, 113, 115, 157, 213, 297, 439, 464, 573, 574